OXFORD READINGS IN PHILOSOPHY

RACE AND RACISM

Published in this series

The Problem of Evil, edited by Marilyn McCord Adams and
Robert Merrihew Adams
The Philosophy of Artificial Intelligence, edited by Margaret A. Boden
The Philosophy of Artificial Life, edited by Margaret A. Boden
Self-Knowledge, edited by Quassim Cassam
Locke, edited by Vere Chappell
Descartes, edited by John Cottingham
Virtue Ethics, edited by Roger Crisp and Michael Slote
The Philosophy of Law, edited by R. M. Dworkin
Environmental Ethics, edited by Robert Elliot
Plato I and II, edited by Gail Fine
Theories of Ethics, edited by Philippa Foot
Scientific Revolutions, edited by Ian Hacking
The Philosophy of Mathematics, edited by W. D. Hart
The Philosophy of Biology, edited by David L. Hull and Michael Ruze
The Philosophy of Time, edited by Robin Le Poidevin and Murray MacBeth
The Philosophy of Action, edited by Alfred R. Mele
Properties, edited by D. H. Mellor and Alex Oliver
The Philosophy of Religion, edited by Basil Mitchell
Meaning and Reference, edited by A. W. Moore
The Philosophy of Science, edited by David Papineau
Ethical Theory, edited by James Rachels
Consequentialism and its Critics, edited by Samuel Scheffler
Applied Ethics, edited by Peter Singer
Causation, edited by Ernest Sosa and Michael Tooley
Theories of Rights, edited by Jeremy Waldron
Free Will, edited by Gary Watson
Demonstratives, edited by Palle Yourgrau

Other volumes are in preparation

RACE AND RACISM

Edited by
BERNARD BOXILL

OXFORD
UNIVERSITY PRESS

OXFORD

UNIVERSITY PRESS

Great Clarendon Street, Oxford OX2 6DP

Oxford University Press is a department of the University of Oxford.
It furthers the University's objective of excellence in research, scholarship,
and education by publishing worldwide in

Oxford New York

Athens Auckland Bangkok Bogotá Buenos Aires Calcutta
Cape Town Chennai Dar es Salaam Delhi Florence Hong Kong Istanbul
Karachi Kuala Lumpur Madrid Melbourne Mexico City Mumbai
Nairobi Paris São Paulo Shanghai Singapore Taipei Tokyo Toronto Warsaw

with associated companies in Berlin Ibadan

Oxford is a registered trade mark of Oxford University Press
in the UK and in certain other countries

Published in the United States
by Oxford University Press Inc., New York

British Library Cataloguing in Publication Data

Data available

Library of Congress Cataloging in Publication Data

Data available

ISBN 0–19–875267–9

1 3 5 7 9 10 8 6 4 2

Typeset in Times
by RefineCatch Limited, Bungay, Suffolk
Printed in Great Britain by
Biddles Ltd., Guildford and King's Lynn

CONTENTS

Introduction   1
Bernard Boxill

1. Race and Philosophic Meaning   43
Naomi Zack

2. Toward a Critical Theory of "Race"   58
Lucius Outlaw

3. White Woman Feminist 1983–1992   83
Marilyn Frye

4. Does Race Matter?   101
Pierre L. van den Berghe

5. How Heritability Misleads about Race   114
Ned Block

6. Responses to Race Differences in Crime   145
Michael Levin

7. Rights, Human Rights, and Racial Discrimination   180
Richard A. Wasserstrom

8. Two Kinds of Discrimination   193
Adrian M. S. Piper

9. 'Difference', Cultural Racism and Anti-Racism   238
Tariq Modood

10. The Heart of Racism   257
J. L. A. Garcia

11. Bakke's Case: Are Quotas Unfair?   297
Ronald Dworkin

12 Racism and Sexism   307
Richard A. Wasserstrom

13. Sexism and Racism: Some Conceptual Differences   344
Laurence Thomas

14. Group Autonomy and Narrative Identity: Blacks and Jews 357
    Laurence Thomas

15. African Identities 371
    Kwame Anthony Appiah

16. Social Movements and the Politics of Difference 383
    Iris Marion Young

17. Race, Multiculturalism and Democracy 422
    Robert Gooding-Williams

18. Kant and Race 448
    Thomas E. Hill Jr. and Bernard Boxill

    Notes on the Contributors 473
    Further Reading 475
    Index of Names 479

INTRODUCTION

BERNARD BOXILL

Racial classification today is commonplace; people routinely catalogue each other as members of this or that race, and seem to assume that everyone can be thus catalogued. They also seem to assume that human beings have always routinely classified each other as members of races. But on this issue there is scholarly disagreement. Some authorities, Thomas F. Gossett, for example, claim to find the idea of race 5,000 years ago, in India, and among the early Chinese, Egyptians, and Jews.[1] Others, however, and these now seem to be in the majority, contend that the idea of race is modern. According to Ivan Hannaford, for example, the idea of race was 'invented' or 'fabricated' only in the eighteenth and nineteenth centuries, after the 'French and American revolutions and the social upheavals which followed'.[2] If he is right, the practice of racial classification that people take for granted today might have begun only 200 years ago.

Many scholars also maintain that the races are modern inventions. 'Historians', David Brion Davis observes, have increasingly recognized that the 'races' are the 'inventions' of Europe's 'imperial expansion'.[3] Davis's claim should not be confused with Hannaford's. Davis's claim is that the races did not exist until Europe's imperial expansion. Hannaford's claim is that people did not think of each other in racial terms until the French and American revolutions. While Hannaford's claim is controversial, Davis's seems plainly false. It implies that the races came into existence only two or three centuries ago, but the common-sense and plausible view is that the races are ancient, even if the idea of race is modern. The common-sense view seems plausible because it assumes that the various groups of white-skinned, black-skinned and yellow- and brown-skinned peoples that we call the races

---

[1] Thomas Gossett, *Race: The History of an Idea in America* (New York: Oxford University Press, 1997), 3.

[2] Ivan Hannaford, *Race: The History of an Idea in the West* (Baltimore: Johns Hopkins University Press, 1996), 4, 5.

[3] David Brion Davis, 'Contesting Race: A Reflection', *William and Mary Quarterly*, 54/1 (Jan. 1997), 7.

are biological races. If these groups are biological races they are probably ancient, for the biological races are natural kinds and natural kinds are usually ancient. But Davis denies that the groups we call the races are biological races. His comment begins with the remark that 'responsible scientists have long discredited any biological or genetic definition of racial groups'.[4] On his account the groups we call the races are 'social constructions'. Briefly and roughly social constructions are classes of individuals that exist only because of our ideas, beliefs, and practices. If Davis is right that the races are such classes of individuals, then he may also be right that they came into existence only after Europe's imperial expansion, if the ideas, beliefs, and practices necessary for their existence appeared only after or during that period.

I develop these topics in the ensuing sections. In the first section I discuss the invention of the idea of the biological races. My approach is Rousseauian. That is, I begin with the assumption that human nature is originally good, and try to explain how and why racial prejudice and discrimination are nevertheless customary. Specifically, I argue that Europeans invented the idea of race for what appeared to them to be sound scientific reasons, and that the idea then helped to further corrupt them. In the next section I give a brief review of the uses made of the idea of the biological races. The following section takes up the claim that the races, as we know them, are not biological races, but social constructions. I argue that even in that case, and indeed even if there are no such things as biological races, the races as we know them would not exist were there no such thing as the *idea* of the biological races. That idea may be fatally flawed, it may refer to nothing, but it is among the ideas necessary for the existence of the social constructions that nowadays many philosophers, historians, and social scientists say the races are. Finally I consider the case for saying that the biological races do not exist. I believe that philosophers tend to overstate the case. The races as we know them may be social constructions rather than biological races, but it does not follow that the biological races do not exist.

THE INVENTION OF THE IDEA OF RACE AS A BIOLOGICAL KIND

If the idea of the biological races was invented in the modern period, then the Europeans made the invention. Everyone is agreed on this point. Everyone is not, agreed, however, on why the Europeans made the invention.

---

[4] Davis, 'Contesting Race', 7.

According to Naomi Zack, for example, 'modern concepts of race derive from eighteenth- and nineteenth-century pseudoscience that rationalized European colonialism and chattel slavery'.[5] On this view Europeans invented the idea of biological race after they had enslaved Africans as part of a strategy to rationalize a crime that was already well under way. But on another view, Europeans had the idea of race before they enslaved Africans and the idea paved the way to that crime. In 'The Iberian Roots of American Racist Thought', for example, James Sweet argues that 'Iberian racism was a necessary pre-condition for the system of human bondage that would develop in the Americas during the sixteenth century and beyond'.[6] The historian Betty Wood sets out the debate as follows:

Some see it [the enslavement of West African peoples] as a process emerging out of a racial ideology that, even before the English began to colonize the New World, had identified West Africans as potential candidates for enslavement. Others downplay the initial significance of ethnicity and claim that economic and demographic consider-ations largely explain the substitution of involuntary African workers for indentured European servants in the English plantation colonies ... The racist theory that underpinned the slave laws that began to be drawn up during the second half of the seventeenth century was a post hoc phenomenon.[7]

The first position that she lists suggests that Europeans had the idea of race before they enslaved Africans and that the idea helped to identify Afri-cans as candidates for enslavement. But it does not make clear why Euro-peans came to have the idea of race in the first place. Winthrop Jordan's famous book *White over Black* suggests that they came to have the idea because they invented it to explain the physical differences between them-selves and the people they were meeting on the other continents. As Jordan put it, the Europeans' 'discovery' that various groups of men looked very different from each other 'demanded explanation', Africans' black skin exciting particular wonder, and became, he says, a 'standing problem for natural philosophers'. Of course, Europeans offered many explanations of the physical differences between themselves and non-Europeans that made no appeal to the idea of race, for example that the differences were due to climatic contrasts between Europe and Africa, and on one account that Africans were black because they suffered from leprosy. But some of the explanations they offered for the physical differences between Europeans and non-Europeans, for example Sir Thomas Browne's 'quasi-genetic' argument that the blackness of Africans was carried in the sperm, appeal

---

[5] Naomi Zack, *Bachelors of Science: Seventeenth Century Identity Then and Now* (Philadelphia: Temple University Press, 1996), p. x.

[6] James Sweet, 'The Iberian Roots of American Racist Thought', *William and Mary Quarterly*, 54/1 (Jan. 1997), 166.

[7] Betty Wood, *The Origins of American Slavery* (New York: Hill & Wang, 1997), 7.

unmistakably to the idea of race. Naturally the idea is not as fully elaborated as it became in the eighteenth and nineteenth centuries, but its key ingredient is clearly there: namely that the members of a race carry within themselves a minute but potent and practically unalterable structure that accounts for their observable similarities to each other and their observable differences from the members of other races; and that this structure, later called a racial essence, is unfailingly passed on from parents to offspring. Sweet makes the similar point that the idea of race in eighteenth- and nineteenth-century Spain was an elaboration of ideas that were invented much earlier. As he observes, although 'a fully developed ideology of race was not articulated in fifteenth century Iberia', the 'pseudo scientific claims' of race science developed during the eighteenth and nineteenth centuries 'merely reinforced notions of biology that had been evolving for centuries'.[8]

The second position Wood outlines, that the idea of the biological races was invented as part of a rationalization of slavery, is implicit in Eric Williams's equally famous book *Capitalism and Slavery*. According to Williams, 'Slavery in the Caribbean has been too narrowly identified with the Negro. A racial twist has thereby been given to what is basically an economic phenomenon. Slavery was not born of racism; rather, racism was the consequence of slavery. Unfree labor in the New World was brown, white, black, and yellow; Catholic, Protestant and pagan.'[9] This passage suggests that the enslavers did not care what colour their slaves were; that they enslaved Africans simply to get rich, and then invented the idea that they were an inferior biological race to explain, justify, and normalize what they were doing.

Nowadays it seems to be taken for granted in many academic circles that Europeans invented the idea of the biological races in order to rationalize their enslavement of Africans, and more generally their dispossession, subjugation, and genocide of non-Europeans. The frequent use of the word 'fabricate' to describe the invention of the idea of race, and claims that the idea was mere pseudo-science, attest to this. Few seem to consider seriously the possibility that Europeans invented the idea of race for a serious and legitimate scientific reason, namely, to explain why they differed so strikingly from non-Europeans. This attitude is simplistic. It supposes that human beings are disposed to justify their crimes, and often do so by inventing and persuading themselves to believe stories that they know on some level to be false. But it does not adequately describe the conditions that enable them to believe such stories, nor does it draw out the implications of the insight it appeals to. For example, if human beings invent stories to justify crimes they

---

[8] Sweet, 'The Iberian Roots of American Racist Thought', 165.
[9] (Chapel Hill: University of North Carolina Press, 1995), 7.

have already committed, it seems reasonable that they also need stories to justify crimes that they are going to commit. Some of these stories may be rationalizations before the fact, so to speak. But the possibility I want to develop is that ideas invented for morally neutral reasons often pave the way to crime and facilitate its rationalization.

Rousseau has emphasized this point more than any other philosopher. As he argued, the inventions of the ideas of comparative personal worth, of the division of labour, and of private property, probably for morally innocent reasons, were the first steps to slavery and oppression. I will suggest that the motives for inventing the idea of race were similarly innocent, and its consequences similarly deadly. It was invented for morally neutral reasons, probably to explain human physical variety; but it paved and eased the way to the European enslavement of Africans, and was among the background assumptions that enabled Europeans to rationalize their enslavement of Africans. Since that rationalization rests on the claim that Africans are a race of natural slaves, I agree that our present understanding of race is partly the result of the Europeans' rationalization of African slavery. My point is that it rests on an earlier or conceptually prior idea of race invented for legitimate scientific reasons.

The view that Europeans invented the idea of race to rationalize their enslavement of Africans faces the following preliminary problem. By the time Europeans started enslaving Africans, slavery was already an ancient human institution, and there were already many rationalizations for it. For example, it was widely held that infidels and prisoners of war are justifiably enslaved, and Aristotle had argued that some human beings are 'natural slaves'. With such well-tried rationalizations of slavery already available, why did Europeans go to the trouble of inventing the entirely new idea of race to rationalize their enslavement of Africans?

One likely answer to this question appeals to the philosophy of natural rights in ascendancy at the time of Europe's expansion. At the same time that Europeans were conquering America and enslaving Africans and Native Americans to work in the sugar, tobacco, and cotton plantations they established there, their philosophers were arguing persuasively that all human beings have natural rights to life, liberty, and property. These arguments created a dilemma for the Europeans. On the one hand, the slave plantations in the New World were engendering a triangular trade in slaves, raw materials and manufactured goods between Africa, America, and Europe that was on some accounts financing the Industrial Revolution and transforming European societies from stagnating medieval fortresses into thriving modern states. On the other hand, the philosophy of natural rights, especially its claim that all human beings have inherent rights to liberty, seemed to undermine many of the tradition justifications for slavery. For example, the traditional argument that infidels and prisoners of war can be justly enslaved is unsound, if the philosophy of natural rights is correct. Infidels and prisoners of war are human beings and consequently have inherent rights to liberty.

Europeans could have avoided this dilemma by arguing that Africans were not human beings, and consequently that the philosophy of natural rights did not imply that they had rights to liberty. But few took this option; presumably, arguing that Africans were not human beings strained credulity, and rationalizations must be believed to be successful. Most adapted one of the traditional rationalizations of slavery. For example, John Locke, who had his reasons for rationalizing black slavery, tried to reinstate, with a qualification, the old argument that prisoners of war can be justly enslaved.[10] The qualification was based on the idea that a person can forfeit his natural rights to life and liberty by a suitably serious violation of natural law. Locke argued that waging an unjust war was such a violation of natural law, and consequently that prisoners taken while waging an unjust war could be justifiably enslaved.[11] According to Peter Laslett, Locke believed that this argument could be used to justify black slavery. Locke, he says, regarded 'negro slaves as justifiably enslaved because they were captives taken in a just war, who had forfeited their lives "by some Act that deserves Death"'.[12] But Locke's argument does not come down to us as the way Europeans rationalized enslaving Africans probably because it is simply not credible. Its main premiss, that negro slaves were captives taken in just wars, is somewhat implausible. But the real scandal is that Locke seemed to allow that their children were justifiably enslaved. Since these children could not possibly have engaged in unjust wars, Locke's view is utterly preposterous, given his own contention that all human beings are born with inherent rights to life and liberty.

This left Aristotle's argument that certain human beings are natural slaves and consequently are permissibly enslaved as the only possibly viable traditional ground available to Europeans for rationalizing black slavery. To use this argument to rationalize enslaving Africans Europeans had to persuade themselves that Africans were natural slaves, and according to the view under consideration, they invented the idea of race to do so.

The view that the idea of race was invented to help rationalize slavery would perhaps not need elaborate defence if the only conceivable reason

---

[10] Locke had investments in the African slave trade.

[11] John Locke, *The Second Treatise of Government*, ed. Peter Laslett (Cambridge: Cambridge University Press, 1967), 302.

[12] Ibid. 302, 303.

Europeans could have had for inventing the idea was to use it for that purpose. But Europeans may have invented the idea of race to explain some of the physical differences between themselves and non-Europeans. I agree, of course, that the idea of race provided a suitable ground for attempting a justification of the claim that Africans were natural slaves. Since races have distinctive intellectual and emotional qualities, if Africans were a race, an argument could be mounted that they had the distinctive intellectual and emotional qualities of natural slaves. But although the idea of race was used it this way, it does not follow that it was invented to be so used. It could have been invented for some other purpose, and then commandeered by the rationalizers of slavery. Further, the popular and possibly true contention that the idea of race is invalid does not entail that the idea was a fabrication. Not every unsound justification is a rationalization. Rationalizations involve more than falsehoods or logical errors. They involve deception, in many cases deliberate deception, and the inventors of the idea of race need not have invented it to try to deceive anyone, deliberately or otherwise, even if the idea they invented was invalid. Finally, even if the inventors of the idea of race invented it to deceive, those who insist that it was invented to rationalize slavery must give an account of how the deception was effected, for, as I have indicated, rationalizations must be believed if they are to be successful.

Perhaps we can explain how people were deceived into believing in the idea of race by appealing to the fact that people often manage to persuade themselves to believe even obvious falsehoods, if they want to believe these falsehoods badly enough. Of course, people do not persuade themselves to believe falsehoods while being clear that what they are persuading themselves to believe is false. This is especially the case when they have reason to suspect that the falsehood they are trying to believe is part of a rationalization. They may want to believe it, but they also want to feel justified in believing it, for they want to keep at least the illusion of being reasonable. So they try to persuade themselves that it is true, usually by gathering and concentrating their attentions on anything that seems to support it, and ignoring or explaining away anything that confounds it. We can suppose that Europeans must have wanted badly to believe that Africans were a race of natural slaves, for if they could believe this, they would feel better about themselves for enslaving Africans. Consequently, they could perhaps have persuaded themselves that Africans were natural slaves, if they could find plausible allegations to support this view and ignore the evidence against it. In eighteenth-century Europe this might not have been too difficult. Few Europeans had first-hand evidence of Africans. Most got their 'evidence' about Africans and non-Europeans second- and third-hand from the actual conquerors and enslavers. These men were not much bothered by the fact that their behaviour violated rights the philosophers championed. But they knew that the natural rights philosophy had gained wide acceptance, and they were concerned with their reputations, even if they are not concerned with justice. They also knew that they would have to justify their behaviour to people who might be more critical of it, if only because it did not profit them directly, and that some of these people could perhaps curtail their murderous adventures. So they brought or sent home false and derogatory accounts of the people they were conquering and enslaving. These accounts told of such degradation, stupidity, and savagery that it is not surprising that Europeans believed not only that Africans were a race apart, but also that they were a race of natural slaves.

Jordan stresses that Englishmen at first took the tall tales about African savagery seriously. As he put it, 'an appetite for wonder seems to have been built into Western culture'.[13] By Kant's day, however, a healthier scepticism must have set in. In a remarkable passage Kant wrote:

one may prove that Americans and Negroes are races which have sunk below the level of other members of the species in terms of intellectual abilities—or alternatively, on the evidence of no less plausible accounts, that they should be regarded as equal in natural ability to all the other inhabitants of the world. Thus the philosopher is at liberty to choose whether he wishes to assume natural differences or to judge everything by the principle *tout comme chez nous*, with the result that all the systems he constructs on such unstable foundations must take on the appearance of ramshackle hypotheses.[14]

In other words, by the early nineteenth century at least the evidence available to most Europeans about Africans was mixed. Some of it might have supported the view that Africans were natural slaves, but some of it supported the view that Africans were just as intelligent and just as entitled to their freedom as other peoples.

The evidence of African equality available to Europeans would have made it difficult for them to believe that Africans were a race of natural slaves, but not impossible. Their desire to believe that Africans were natural slaves would have inclined them to ignore that evidence and to channel their attention on whatever stories they could find of African degradation. This strategy could also have been seconded by their reliance on the Bible. Thus it is sometimes suggested that the Bible's story of Ham's curse told Christians that God had ordained Africans to be the slaves of Europeans. According to that story, Ham had looked at Noah, his father, as Noah lay drunk and naked, and when Noah awoke and discovered Ham's indiscretion, he cursed

---

    [13] Jordan, *White over Black*, 25.
    [14] Immanuel Kant, *Political Writings*, ed. Hans Reiss (Cambridge: Cambridge University Press, 1991), 217.

Canaan, Ham's son, saying he would be 'the servants of the servants' of his brothers. One problem with using this story to help explain why Europeans believed that they were permitted to enslave Africans is that it was used in the seventeenth century, as Jordan notes, 'almost entirely as an explanation of color rather than as justification for Negro slavery'.[15] Only later, in the nineteenth century, after slavery was well established, was it used to argue that the Negro was fittingly enslaved. A deeper problem is that even if the story says that God ordained that Ham's children were to be slaves, it does not say that Africans were to be the slaves of Europeans. Biblical scholars put that more specific charge into it. If Ham's story accounts for the European belief that enslaving Africans was permissible, we must explain why the scholars interpreted the story as they did, and why people believed them.

Perhaps we can do this by appealing to Europeans' attitudes to the colour black. Jordan tells us that in Elizabethan England it had long connoted filthiness, sin, baseness, ugliness, and evil.[16] Arguably these connotations may have generated negative attitudes towards black-skinned Africans that disposed the scholars to interpret Ham's story as they did, and inclined the people to believe the scholars. But Davis is right that it is 'simplistic' to assume that the admittedly widespread 'association of blackness with death, danger, evil, and grief', can account for the 'conviction that Africans were in some way "made" to be slaves'.[17] Even if Europeans' negative connotations about the colour black inclined them to believe negative things about Africans, it does not follow that these negative attitudes inclined them to believe specifically that Africans were made to be their slaves. Further, if at first Europeans were repelled by the colour of Africans' skins, we need to explain why they continued to be so repelled. There is nothing inherently threatening or evil about the colour black. Some black things are threatening and evil, but some are not. Indeed Europeans did not invariably associate blackness with evil. So even if Europeans were at first repelled by Africans' black skin, there is every reason to expect that this attitude would change as their contacts with Africans grew, and they began to notice their good qualities. As Davis notes, 'color symbolism is usually abstract, ambiguous, and reversible'.[18]

Perhaps we can explain why European attitudes to Africans did not change by reflecting on how much our willingness or ability to judge others fairly depends on our sympathy for them. If we sympathize with them, we

[15] Jordan, *White over Black*, 18, 19.
[16] Ibid. 7.
[17] David Brion Davis, *Slavery and Human Progress* (New York: Oxford University Press, 1984), 38.
[18] Ibid. 38.

are willing and perhaps disposed to seek and to consider evidence that puts them in a favourable light. If we have less sympathy for them, we are less willing, and perhaps less able, to do so. Indeed, if we have little sympathy for them, we may become disposed to seek evidence that puts them in an unfavourable light. But we are inclined to sympathize with those we believe are like us, that is, those we see ourselves in, and tend to feel less or little sympathy for those who seem strange and alien, and whose appearance and customs do not reflect our image of ourselves. Consequently, given that Europeans found Africans to be strange and alien, and not at all like themselves, it is likely that they felt little sympathy for them, and this might have hardened their negative attitudes to Africans, and disposed them to believe that Africans were ordained to be their slaves.

It is very likely true that Europeans had relatively little sympathy for Africans. Their lack of sympathy for Africans is confirmed by their clear preference for enslaving Africans rather than Europeans, for enslaving others debases and demeans them, and, other things equal, we prefer to debase and demean those we do not sympathize with rather than those we do sympathize with. It may be objected that this argument begs the question. If Europeans lacked sympathy for Africans, then, other things equal, probably they would prefer enslaving Africans to enslaving Europeans. But Europeans may have preferred enslaving Africans to enslaving Europeans for reasons other than a lack of sympathy for them. In *Capitalism and Slavery*, for example, Williams suggests that Europeans preferred African slaves to European slaves, because they believed that African slaves could be worked harder than European slaves, and consequently were more profitable. Thus he maintains that at first, 'unfree labor in the New World was brown, white, black and yellow', and underscores this claim with the argument that Europeans first tried enslaving the Indians, and that when this failed that they first turned to poor whites. But the implication that Europeans were indifferent to the colour of their slaves rests on an equivocation between *unfree* labour and *slave* labour. As Williams describes the unfree labor of the 'poor whites', it seems that they were not strictly slaves, but 'indentured servants', 'redemptioners', and 'convicts', who had either made agreements or committed crimes that bound them to service for a stipulated time. If so, then either only Negroes were enslaved, or only Negroes were enslaved without any appeal to the traditional grounds for enslaving others.[19] This strongly suggests that, other things equal, Europeans preferred to enslave Africans than to enslave each other, and that this preference followed from their having less sympathy for Africans than for Europeans.

[19] Williams, *Capitalism and Slavery*, 9.

I do not mean that Europeans never enslaved each other. Perhaps they sometimes did. Zack claims that after Cromwell's war against Ireland 'Irish prisoners were remanded to three Bristol merchants for sale as slaves in the West Indies'.[20] But it is worth noting that some historians reject the notion that the English literally enslaved the Irish in the West Indies. Thus while Betty Wood concedes that the Irish in Barbados were 'worked so long and hard that the English sometimes referred to them as "white slaves"', she denies that 'the Irish in Barbados' were ever 'legally enslaved by the English'. Further, her suggestion that the 'white skin' of the Irish might have saved them from enslavement by the English suggests that even the bare physical similarities between Europeans might have inclined them to feel enough sympathy for each other to make them reluctant to enslave each other.[21] Even if such sympathy saved the white-skinned Irish from the horrible fate the black-skinned Africans were consigned to routinely, it was often attenuated or outweighed by special reasons, or by contrary sentiments like greed, pride, and avarice. I concede, therefore, that Cromwell might have enslaved the Irish prisoners of war. But this concession is consistent with my thesis that sympathy for these prisoners based on their white skins inclined him not to do so, if he appealed to a special reason that could overcome that inclination. Almost certainly he appealed to such a reason. Since the self-righteous Cromwell unquestionably believed that his Irish prisoners were taken in a just war, he almost certainly justified their enslavement on the traditional ground that prisoners taken in a just war were permissibly enslaved.

In sum it seems likely that Europeans felt little sympathy for Africans, and consequently easily persuaded themselves that they were natural slaves. This can be explained by the fact that Europeans found Africans to be alien and strange. But why did Europeans continue to find Africans strange and alien after years of increasing contact and association with them? As people associate with each other they tend to find their differences less distracting and alarming, and become disposed to notice and to be moved by their common humanity. That at least is the hope of the advocates of racial integration, and that hope is not unreasonable. Given the salience and consequence of our common humanity, we are inclined to see ourselves in each other, and normally succeed in doing so unless we are hindered. Consequently, barring such hindrances, Europeans' increasing contacts with Africans should have changed their alienation from Africans to sympathy and appreciation, and led them to reject the lie that Africans were a race of natural slaves.

---

[20] Zack, *Bachelors of Science*, 171.
[21] Betty Wood, *The Origins of American Slavery*, 47.

Obviously this is not the way things turned out. Speaking of the relations between the black and white people, for example, Du Bois commented that 'despite much physical contact and daily intermingling' their 'thoughts and feelings' do not 'come into direct contact and sympathy' with each other.[22] Strangely, given their 'daily intermingling', Du Bois seemed to believe that ignorance of each other caused their lack of sympathy for each other. The 'tragedy' of the age, he noted, is that 'men know so little of men'.[23] If I was right that the salience of our humanity inclines us to see ourselves in each other, and consequently to know each other, then given the 'daily intermingling' of black and white people, something must hinder them from seeing and knowing each other. Du Bois claimed famously and metaphorically that it was as if a vast 'veil' separated black and white people. My interpretation of Du Bois's metaphor is that the veil he spoke of is the idea of race.

Let us review the argument up to this point. We began with the assumption that the idea of race was an obvious fabrication invented to rationalize the enslavement of Africans. Given that rationalizations must be believed to be successful, and that people cannot simply will themselves to believe in obvious fabrications just because they want to believe in them, the problem was to explain how Europeans came to believe in the idea of race. The most credible solution to this problem is that Europeans' interests, attitudes, and prejudices 'blinded' them to the fact that the idea of race was a fabrication. But it ran into the difficulty that the attitudes and prejudices in question should have changed to sympathy and understanding as contacts between Europeans and Africans grew. Its failure suggests that we should critically examine the merits of the assumption that the idea of race is an obvious fabrication.

This assumption seems highly suspicious if we consider certain implications of the current contention that the idea of race is modern, and that Europeans invented it in the eighteenth and nineteenth centuries, when they were engaged in enslaving Africans. The implication that Europeans' invention of the idea of race was a consequence of their enslavement of Africans raises obvious difficulties. As Davis notes, the fact that 'antiblack racism can erupt in modern Japan, China, and Russia, countries far removed from the historical effects of black slavery', raises the question whether 'this kind of racism is universal, immutable, perhaps inevitable'.[24] A more radical difficulty is even more conspicuous. If the Europeans' invention of the idea of

---

[22] W. E. B. Du Bois, *Souls of Black Folk*, ed. Robert Gooding Williams and David Blight (Bedford: St Martin's Press, 1996), 134.

[23] Ibid. 164.

[24] Davis, 'Contesting Race', 8.

race was a consequence of their enslavement of Africans, then arguably the people of ancient imperial powers invented the idea of race when they were enslaving the people they conquered, and consequently the idea of race may *not* be modern.

This speculation is usually squashed with the comment that the ancients could not have invented the idea of race, for, although it is pseudo-science, its invention depended on a background of modern science. But the comment is specious. When science became the greatest intellectual force in society, some people began using or misusing its most sophisticated discoveries to support the idea of race. But these rationalizations need not be part of the idea of race. For example, genetic science is sometimes used to defend the idea of race, but its findings cannot be part of the idea of race because it was developed after the early eighteenth century, when the idea of race was allegedly invented.

The notion that the race idea depends on a background of modern science becomes even less plausible when we notice that Kant is supposed to have played a major part in inventing it. As we shall see, Kant's contribution to the invention of the idea of race drew on the Aristotelian theory of essences and natural kinds, which implies that the ancients must have had some of the tools to invent the race idea. Zack concedes that the modern idea of race depends on the theory of essences and that the ancients had the theory, but adds a twist that makes it even more mysterious that they did not use it to invent an idea of race. According to Zack, 'The present folk concept of race did not exist when essentialist theories of ontology and meaning were widely accepted in the ancient and medieval periods. And essentialist theories of ontology and meaning were philosophically dethroned by the later half of the nineteenth century, when American scientists constructed speculative theories of the hierarchy of human races, based on the philosophical essentialism.'[25] But if the moderns invented the idea of race using 'dethroned', essentialist theories, why did not the ancients invent the idea given that the essentialist theories necessary to do this were 'widely accepted' when they lived?

The view that modern Europeans invented the idea of race to rationalize slavery suggests that the answer to this question is that the ancients saw no need to rationalize slavery, presumably because they did not regard it as morally problematic. But the popular notion that the ancients did not regard slavery as morally problematic is unpersuasive. In the first place, as we have seen, they had many rationalizations for it. Further, even when they did not literally rationalize slavery, they seem to have been discomforted by it, and to have employed strategies to ease that discomfort. Davis's comment that

---

[25] 'Race and Philosophic Meaning', in Zack, *Race/Sex*, 30.

many societies in the ancient world thought of slavery as a 'degrading and contemptible condition suitable only for aliens and enemies who were ethnically distinct' illustrates the point.[26] It suggests that many of the ancients felt uncomfortable about enslaving other human beings, and that they made only 'aliens', 'enemies', and the 'ethnically distinct' their slaves in order to distance them from their sympathy, and consequently to lessen their discomfort at enslaving them. But the invention of the idea of race would have enabled the ancients to think of their slaves as racially different from themselves, and this would have been a most effective way to distance their slaves from their sympathy. If people invent ideas to rationalize their crimes and more generally to ease the moral discomfort their crimes arouse, and if the ancients had the tools to invent the idea of race, why then did they not anticipate the moderns?

Aristotle's position that 'barbarians' were 'natural' slaves raises the question more sharply. The Greeks' use of the word 'barbarian' to refer to the aliens they enslaved is, of course, an example of the strategy of distancing slaves from the sympathy of their enslavers. But Aristotle's further contention that barbarians were 'natural' slaves indicates that he also wanted to find an intellectually satisfying justification for enslaving them; that is, that he wanted to rationalize the practice. Clearly, then, if the moderns' desire to rationalize slavery led them to invent the idea of race, we are entitled to ask why Aristotle's desire to rationalize slavery did not similarly lead him to invent the idea of race.

One way to deal with the puzzle is to suppose that Aristotle did invent or at least have the idea of race. This possibility is worthy of serious attention. The contemporary consensus that the idea of race is modern may rest on the optimistic assumption that the idea is an aberration peculiar to the modern period, a part of the European folly as it expanded globally, and is likely to disappear almost of its own accord. As Zack put it, 'There was a time before the racial paradigm had been constructed, just as there will be a time when it will disappear or shift.'[27] But the race idea may be ancient. In his important book on race *The Mismeasure of Man* Stephen Jay Gould observes that Plato speculated in the *Republic* that some people are 'constructed of intrinsically inferior material'.[28] Plato's speculation seems to capture some of the key assumptions of the race idea, and if this is indeed the case, the sources of the idea of race may be deeper and less tractable than the

---

[26] Davis, *Slavery and Human Progress*, 86.

[27] Naomi Zack, 'Philosophy and Racial Paradigms', *Journal of Value Inquiry*, 33 3 (Sept. 1999).

[28] (New York: W. W. Norton, 1981), 31. Gould says that Plato eventually branded the idea a lie. I disagree.

contemporary consensus seems to suppose. In that case, the strategies it suggests for dealing with the problems of race may be inadequate.

I am persuaded, however, that Aristotle did not have the idea of race. Admittedly his views about 'barbarians' came close. He seems to have conceived of them very much as those who rationalized slavery 2,000 years later thought of the people they enslaved. They argued that Africans were natural slaves; Aristotle thought that barbarians were natural slaves. They thought that Africans passed on their slavish natures to their children; he must have supposed that 'barbarians' too passed on their slavish nature to their children, for in Greek slavery the children of slaves were also slaves. Indeed the Greeks seem to have been well acquainted with the idea that parents pass on their superior and inferior traits to their children, for it is clearly taken for granted in Plato's discussion of breeding arrangements in the *Republic*. But Aristotle evidently did not take the crucial step of using the theory of natural kinds and essences to argue that there were such things as races.

Since Aristotle failed to invent the idea of race, although he had the tools and opportunity to do so, we can only suppose that he saw no reason to. Further, if he saw no reason to invent the idea of race, but desired to rationalize slavery, it follows that this desire gave him no reason to invent the idea of race. Why then are we entitled to suppose that modern Europeans' desire to rationalize slavery gave them any reason to invent the idea of race? Aristotle rationalized Greek slavery by arguing that barbarians were natural slaves. Why then could not modern Europeans rationalize their slavery by arguing that Africans were natural slaves? Why did they have to add that Africans were a *race* of natural slaves? Perhaps some difference in the intellectual or moral contexts of ancient Greece and eighteenth-century Europe answers this question. But what difference? We have eliminated the possibility that the ancients lacked the theory necessary to invent the idea of race; they invented that theory. Nor can we plausibly argue that modern Europeans invented the idea of race to justify enslaving only Africans; the Greeks enslaved only 'barbarians'. I suggested earlier that the popular modern view that all human beings have natural rights to life and liberty forced eighteenth-century Europeans to abandon the ancient rationalizations of slavery and to invent the idea of race to do the job. But this suggestion seems unsatisfactory on closer examination. The idea that Africans are a race of natural slaves requires as radical a qualification of the view that all human beings have natural rights to life and liberty as the notion that Africans are natural slaves.

The intellectual and moral contexts of ancient Greece and eighteenth-century Europe differed in ways relevant to the present issue, but not because the idea of race had to be invented to rationalize slavery in one context but not in the other. If human ingenuity discovered ways to rationalize slavery without the idea of race in one of the contexts, it would have found ways to do so in the other. The relevant difference between the contexts is that the ancient Greek context contained no idea of race and the modern European context did. Having the idea of race, modern Europeans noticed that it could be used it to rationalize slavery, and they commandeered it for this purpose. But they invented it for some other reason.

Sound historical considerations suggest that modern Europeans had reasons to invent the idea of race—other than to use it to rationalize slavery—and that the ancient Greeks did not have such reasons. The historians tell us that the idea of race was invented in the eighteenth century, that is, during the Enlightenment, when Europeans became increasingly confident that experience and reason enabled them to explain all natural phenomena, and increasingly inclined to use these resources to account for any natural phenomena that struck them as demanding explanation. We know that eighteenth-century Europeans were struck by the physical differences between themselves and Africans and believed that these differences demanded explanation; and the apparent casualness of ancient Greeks about their physical differences from the Nubians suggests that they could hardly have believed that these differences demanded explanation. Consequently, if the idea of race could conceivably be useful in explaining the physical differences between Europeans and Africans, eighteenth-century Europeans might well have had reasons to invent the idea of race that Aristotle and the ancients might not have had.

To confirm this conclusion we need to show that the idea of race would have seemed useful in explaining the physical differences between Europeans and Africans and consequently that eighteenth-century Europeans might well have invented it for that purpose. As I have already allowed, they did not resort immediately to the idea of race to explain those differences. At first they tended to explain the differences by appealing to environmental causes; for example, that Africans had black skins because the tropical sun of their continent burned them black. But further observation taught them that this was not the case. The environment caused some changes; for example, the sun bronzed Europeans when they went to the tropics. But such environmental factors did not seem able to account for the characteristic differences in skin colour between Europeans and Africans, because Europeans became white again when they returned to Europe, and Africans remained black even if they remained in the temperate zones for generations.

The Aristotelian theory of natural kinds already at hand seemed to provide the tools to solve this puzzle. According to this theory the fundamental objects of science can be divided into classes of things that share a similar internal structure or essence. The essence of each such class of things is unobservable to the naked eye, but it causes the things in the class to have the characteristic properties and appearances in virtue of which they are classed together. Further, because essences are practically unalterable, the classes of things they distinguish do not change into each other. This theory probably suggested to the scholars that Europeans and Africans retained their characteristic appearances in different environments because they had different racial essences. That is, Africans remained black wherever they were because certain unobservable factors in their internal structures caused them to be black; and, despite tanning, the Europeans retained the tendency to be white because certain unobservable factors in their internal constitutions caused them to retain that tendency. The theory that eventually emerged can be summarized in four main claims: (1) Human beings can be divided into classes called races. (2) Each race has distinctive and readily observable physical properties that make it easy to tell what race a human being belongs to. (3) The members of each race share a certain practically unalterable biological structure or essence that they do not share with the members of the other races. (4) These essences are unobservable to the naked eye, but they are potent and important, for they are invariably passed on biologically from parents to children, and cause the races to have their distinctive physical properties.

I want to emphasize the naturalness of the European invention of the idea of race at this point in their history. They fancied that reason and experience could be used to solve all puzzles. The Aristotelian theory of natural kinds and essences was available to them and leads naturally to the idea of race when it is used to solve the puzzle of the physical differences between Europeans and Africans. Naturally Europeans used the theory to solve the puzzle and invented the idea of race.

Admittedly there were problems with the idea of essences. Most generally, Locke had argued famously that real essences are unknowable. This implies that racial essences are unknowable, and consequently that the races cannot be distinguished even if they exist. Perhaps this was why he resorted to the implausible argument that African slaves were prisoners in an unjust war to try to rationalize black slavery. A more particular problem arose in the context of the debate between the monogenesists and the polygenesists. The monogenesists argued that all human beings are descended from a common stock, and consequently that we are all related, at least distantly. The polygenesists argued that the races are not related, but arose separately and perhaps at different times and in different parts of the world, so that Africa, Asia, Europe, and America might each have its own race of human beings.

The monogenesists had the advantage of having the Bible on their side. But their position faced this difficulty: if human beings are all descended from a common stock, the members of which presumably all shared the same essence, and essences are practically unalterable, it seems impossible that they are now divided into races each with a different essence.

The polygenesists solved the problem by denying that it arose; that is, as we have seen, they abandoned the idea that the different races were descended from a common stock. But their theory ran afoul of the Buffonian rule that organisms capable of producing fertile offspring were descended from common ancestors, for it was known by then that the different races were capable of interbreeding, and that the offspring of such interbreedings were fertile. The monogenesists' theory, on the other hand, was consistent with the Buffonian rule, and also had the advantage of parsimony over polygenesism, for it postulated one rather than several separate creations of humans. Their problem, as I have indicated, was to explain how the races could have different essences if they were descended from a common stock the members of which had the same essence. According to the monogenesists the different races exist because different members of the original stock migrated to different parts of the world where climatic and other environmental pressures gradually caused their descendants to develop into the races. But this seemed to imply that environmental pressures could change the essence of the original human stock into the different racial essences of the different races, which seemed inconsistent with the fundamental assumption that essences are unalterable.

Kant tried to solve this problem, and consequently to support the monogenesists' idea that all human beings are descended from a common stock, by a clever adaptation of the theory of essences. Specifically he substituted a set of what he called 'germs' for a human essence. The original human stock possessed these 'germs' and passed them on to all the present human races.[29] To explain how the races appeared to be so different from one another he started with the assumption that the capacities to cause the characteristics of all the human races were already present though latent in the germs of the original human stock.[30] Then he argued that when different sections of that stock migrated to different parts of the world, the different environments they encountered activated different sets of capacities in their germs, and in this way caused the different races to appear. This implied that, despite their physical and other differences, the races still equally possessed the same

[29] e.g. Immanuel Kant, 'On the Different Races of Man', in Earl Count (ed.), *This is Race* (New York: Henry Shuman, 1950), 16–24.

[30] Ibid. 19.

human essence and consequently were still equally human. To explain why the races did not change into each other when their environments were switched, for example when Africans moved to Europe or when Europeans moved to Africa, Kant argued that once the capacities in the germs were activated they could not be made latent again. This in effect postulated an unchangeable racial essence, and enabled Kant to claim both that there was an unchangeable human essence and that there was an unchangeable racial essence.[31]

My position is not that Kant's reasoning is objectively sound, and that the idea of race he develops is valid in some eternal and absolute sense. Certainly it is not. My position is that the idea of race he develops is not an obvious fabrication. Hindsight and 200 years of science tell us that he was badly mistaken, but the crucial point is that his contemporaries seem to have found his reasoning persuasive enough to take the race idea seriously. It will be objected that fabrications are usually supported by ostensibly good reasons because they are designed to deceive. That is, although Kant and the other inventors of the idea of race pretended to have invented it to explain human differences, their real motive was to justify or excuse enslaving Africans. But how do we know that Kant's motives were other than the one that seems patent in his discussion, namely, the desire to explain a certain kind of human difference? The idea of race he helped to invent was used to rationalize enslaving Africans, but he need not have invented it to be used for that purpose. Neither are his mistakes inexplicable except on the assumption that they were caused by ulterior motives. They are of the sort that human beings make when they are trying to solve a difficult problem, and appeal to a flawed theory to help them solve it.

But let us suppose for the sake of argument that Kant had evil motives for inventing the idea of race. Nothing about his reasons for the validity of the idea follows from this. The motives someone may have for making an invention have no logical bearing on the reasons he gives for its validity. He may have bad motives for inventing it, but good reasons for its validity. In particular, Kant may have had evil motives for inventing the idea of race, but given persuasive reasons for its validity. More generally, even if the idea of race was invented to rationalize the enslavement of Africans, it does not follow that it was an obvious fabrication, or even that it was a fabrication. This is the current dogma, but it is a mistake. A fabrication, at least in the sense it is used in the present context, is a forgery; that is, it is something

---

[31] The difficulty is analysed in Arthur Lovejoy, 'Kant and Evolution', in Bentley Glass, Owen Temkin, and William L. Straus Jr. (eds.), *Forerunners of Darwin 1795–1859* (Baltimore: Johns Hopkins University Press, 1959), 173–206.

designed to look genuine though it is a fake. But, as I have shown, the idea of race may have been invented for evil purposes and still be valid. Indeed the idea of race may be invalid, it may have been invented for evil purposes, and yet the reasons given for its validity may be persuasive.

The supposition that the inventors of the idea of race gave persuasive reasons for the validity of the idea of race immediately eliminates the problem that Europeans could hardly have accepted the race idea as valid while maintaining the illusion of being reasonable. They accepted the validity of the race idea while maintaining the illusion of being reasonable because they had persuasive reasons to accept the race idea as valid. The supposition also avoids the problem of explaining why Europeans did not dismiss out of hand the claim that Africans were a race of natural slaves. This is a problem on the supposition that the idea of race was an obvious fabrication, for in that case the claim that Africans are a race of natural slaves is necessarily and obviously false. But if there were persuasive reasons for the validity of the idea of race, the claim that Africans are a race of natural slaves is not necessarily false. Neither would it have been obviously false to eighteenth-century Europeans. Given the misinformation about Africans available to them, they were entitled and perhaps even obligated to entertain the claim seriously, although they should in the end have seen that it was absolutely false.

If this is correct, we still have to give an account of how Europeans managed to believe that Africans were a race of natural slaves. The idea of race features prominently in that account. First it led to a theory of racial inferiority and superiority. Although the theory is false, there need not have been anything extravagantly strained about it when it was first proposed. The physical differences between people were not the only things European scholars had to explain. They also had to explain why Europeans expanded into the other continents rather than the other way around. How was it possible for such a relatively small number of people to conquer the world? This question must have seemed as pressing as the question of the physical differences between Europeans and non-Europeans. Its straightforward answer is that Europeans were superior in the arts of war to the peoples they conquered. But whence came this superiority? Given that we are supposing that the Europeans had already devised a theory of racial essences to explain the observable physical differences between themselves and non-Europeans, I suggest that many of them would have found it natural to infer that their superiority in the arts of war over the peoples they conquered stemmed from the same general causes that explained their physical differences from these peoples. That is, they would have found it natural to infer that their superiority in the arts of war stemmed from their racial essences, and consequently that they were inherently more intelligent, creative, and disciplined than other peoples.

This inference was not valid. Many contemporary natural and social scientists argue that geographical and historical accidents explain Europe's superiority in the arts of war better than race.[32] But these explanations were presented in the late twentieth century, and it is unclear that persuasive versions of these explanations were available in the seventeenth and eighteenth centuries. We must also remember that Europeans had at first appealed to environmental factors to explain the physical differences between themselves and Africans, and that these explanations had proved hopelessly inadequate. This would naturally make the appeal to quasi-genetic explanations to explain the other differences seem more attractive.

A theory of racial inferiority may have seemed to explain the European domination of the other continents, and it moved Europeans a step closer to believing that Africans were a race of natural slaves. But there is still a conceptual and moral chasm between claiming that Africans are intellectually inferior to Europeans and claiming that they are a race of natural slaves. People can be less intelligent than others and not be natural slaves. As I now argue, certain consequences of the wide acceptance of the idea of race helped Europeans cross that chasm.

Davis asks, 'When we categorize people by such criteria [physiognomy, phenotype, language, religion, social status, and even gender], temporarily repressing what we share and accentuating our differences, does the resulting Otherness inevitably debase and demean . . . ?'[33] This question is somewhat misleading. Of course, we do not inevitably debase and demean others if we *temporarily* repress what we share with them and accentuate how we differ. The danger to others comes when we develop a habit of repressing what we share with them and of accentuating how we differ. Such a habit develops easily into a habit of not seeing what we share with others, and if we do not see what we share with others, we will not see ourselves in them, and we must see ourselves in them to have sympathy for them. This is basically the secret of the race idea's terrible power to corrupt. It classifies people into different races on the basis of the obvious physical differences between them that it calls racial differences, and then insists that these differences are signs of built-in, important, and intractable intellectual, temperamental, and moral differences. But people tend to concentrate their attentions on features of themselves and others that they take to be important, and to ignore or repress what they take to be less important. Naturally, then, believers of the

[32] See e.g. David Landes, *The Wealth and Poverty of Nations* (New York: W. W. Norton, 1998).
[33] 'Contesting Race', 7.

race idea—and they are mostly all of us—develop a habit of concentrating their attentions on their racial differences when they think of or associate with people of other races, and of ignoring or repressing what they share with such people. If what I said earlier is sound, this develops easily into a habit of not seeing what they share with people of the other races, of not seeing themselves in such people, and consequently of not sympathizing with them. These vicious consequences of the wide acceptance of the race idea helps explain why Europeans continued to find Africans strange and alien in spite of growing contacts with them. They also vindicate my earlier claim that the Du Boisian veil that separates the races and obscures their understanding of each other is nothing other than the idea of race.

Another consequence of the wide acceptance of the race idea is that it seemed to provide Europeans with evidence that Africans were natural slaves. People born and raised in slavery tend to behave slavishly. Observers ignorant or unimpressed by the race idea usually put this down to the way slaves are treated. But because the race idea supposes that a racial essence accounts for the behaviour of the members of a race, it gives those who are impressed by it an excuse to take the slavish behaviour of slaves to be evidence of an essence that determines how they behave. In short, their slavish behaviour is taken to be evidence that they are natural slaves. The case of Jefferson and his contemporaries illustrates the point. One of Jefferson's excuses for not freeing his slaves was that they were as 'incapable as children of taking care of themselves'.[34] He did not allow this 'slavish' behaviour of his slaves to persuade him that they were natural slaves, because he added that men of any colour would behave in a similar way if they too were raised as slaves. But apparently many of his contemporaries did allow themselves to be so persuaded. As Jefferson noted, 'not reflecting' that the 'degraded' condition of their slaves was 'the work of themselves and their fathers', they 'never doubted' that their slaves were 'as legitimate subjects of property as their horses and cattle'.[35] In drawing them to this conviction, the race idea did not only appeal to their interest in believing that Africans were natural slaves. It also exploited their intellectual laziness. Environmental explanations for the 'degraded' condition of their slaves were available—Jefferson, for example, appealed to them—but they required a greater imaginative effort than the explanations that flowed so easily from the idea of race.

I do not mean that it was impossible for Europeans to resist the seductions

<hr/>

[34] *Jefferson: Political Writings*, ed. Joyce Appleby (Cambridge: Cambridge University Press, 1999), 494.
[35] Ibid. 494.

of the race idea. Many did to different degrees. Thomas Jefferson is a particularly interesting example of someone who partially resisted its seductions. He believed that blacks were inherently inferior intellectually to whites; 'nature', he said, had been 'less bountiful to them in "endowments of the head"'.[36] And he was a slave-holder, who must have desperately wanted to find a satisfying rationalization of slavery. But, as we have just seen, he spotted the error in the inference that the slavish behaviour of his slaves was evidence that they were natural slaves. More generally his lifelong insistence that the enslavement of blacks was a crime implies that he could never bring himself to cross the moral chasm between claiming that blacks were intellectually inferior to whites and claiming that they were natural slaves. But Jefferson did not altogether resist the lure of the race idea. It is, I think, the best explanation of the shocking lapse of his usual acuity when he argued for black intellectual inferiority, and for his casual dismissal of any evidence that could show that he was mistaken.

I have argued that, as the idea of race became widely accepted, it drew a veil between the races that clouded their understanding of each other and hardened their mutual alienation. I have also argued that these consequences of the wide acceptance of the race idea helped to perpetuate and to rationalize the practice of slavery. If I am right, the invention of the idea of race probably made it easier for Europeans to commit the crime of slavery, and to be self-righteous, arrogant, and cruel. But my purpose has not been to justify or excuse European behaviour. They were at fault for what they did. Rationalizations make crimes easier to commit, and make it possible to understand how certain crimes could have been committed, but they never justify or excuse crime. My purpose has been first to test and defend the Rousseauian insight that intellectual and moral progress do not always go hand in hand, and that in our efforts to understand we sometimes invent concepts and ideas that may darken and corrupt even as they illuminate.

More practically my purpose has been to counter what I take to be a dangerous oversimplification of the race issue and to help improve our ability to deal with the problems the idea of race generates. Too many philosophers are declaiming that the idea of race is a complete 'fabrication' and a 'fiction', thereby implying that it was from the first a sham that evil men invented expressly to rationalize the outrageous crimes of slavery and genocide. This is implausible, because if Europeans were so irrational that they could invent and swallow an obvious fabrication in order to rationalize the crime of slavery, they would not have felt the need to rationalize slavery in the first place. As I have argued, the race idea was probably invented by

---

[36] Thomas Jefferson, 'Notes on the State of Virginia', in *Jefferson: Political Writings*, 476.

sincere men intent on solving what they took to be a conspicuous and pressing scientific problem: how can human beings look so different when they
are all descended from the same stock? Their arguments were certainly
flawed; with hindsight we see this with painful clarity. But it is illogical to
infer that the flaws in these arguments must have been equally obvious when
the arguments were first introduced.

The inference is also dangerous because it misrepresents the attitudes that
led to and sustained the momentous crime of slavery, and consequently may
blind us to equally momentous crimes that may very well be in the offing, or
may even now be routinely committed. If we think that the ideas that lead
people into committing horrible crimes are always obviously flawed and evil,
we ill equip ourselves to deal with future dangers. The idea of race is without
any doubt a very dangerous idea, for it helped to corrupt its inventors, but it
does not follow that they invented it for corrupt reasons. Ideas innocently
conceived often have bad consequences. The conception of human nature
that emerges from this consideration is far more menacing that a conception
that conceives of us as obvious rogues. This is a truth that forces itself on us
at every turn, but we are reluctant to face up to it and to explore and accept
its implications.

It may be objected that, if the race idea is as dangerous as I have argued it
is, then I should agree with philosophers who want to ban it as pseudo-
science and inherently racist. But they are mistaken. Ideas may be dangerous, and may have had bad consequences, but it does not follow that they
cannot have good uses. We do not inevitably debase and demean others just
because we categorize ourselves racially. The practice has its dangers, for it
distances others from our sympathy. But these dangers can be avoided if we
design institutions that remind us of our deep similarities. As Albert Mosley
persuasively argues, although the use of ordinary concepts of race merits
close scrutiny, and great care, such concepts may be necessary in the defence
of affirmative action, and some black people have used them to develop a
positive sense of self-identity and self-pride.[37]

APPLICATIONS OF THE IDEA OF RACE

Europeans may have invented the idea of race to explain their differences
from black Africans or to justify enslaving black Africans. Inevitably, however, it generated claims that there were racial differences among Europeans,

[37] Albert Mosley, 'Are Racial Categories Racist?', *Research in African Literatures*, 284 (Winter
1997), 101–11.

and that some white races were superior to others. In nineteenth-century Europe, for example, Joseph Arthur, the comte de Gobineau, Houston Stewart Chamberlain, and their disciples, proposed the superiority of the Aryan, Nordic, or Teutonic races among the white races. These ideas became politically important in the United States when massive immigration from Europe in the mid-nineteenth century, especially from Ireland, raised nativist resentments. At that point there occurred what one historian has described as a 'fragmentation within the white race'.[38] That is, although the Irish were acknowledged to be white, their critics maintained that they were also Celtic, and racially different from and inferior to Anglo-Saxons and Teutons.

A different fragmentation occurred at the end of the nineteenth century, when most of the immigrants began coming from eastern and southern Europe, and nativist resentment shifted to them. At that point, the salient racial differences among whites became the differences between the north and west Europeans, who were already in the United States in great numbers, and the newcomers from eastern and southern Europe. Further, psychologists began providing evidence that seemed to justify nativist fears. Using the results of mental tests administered to 1.75 million recruits during the First World War, these psychologists argued that the Nordics, Europeans from northern and western Europe, were inherently more intelligent than the Alpines and Mediterraneans from eastern and southern Europe, and indeed that a considerable number of the latter were mentally defective. These arguments helped in the passage of the Immigration Restriction Act of 1924 which severely restricted immigration from southern and eastern Europe.

Intriguingly, however, the fragmentation of the white race did not last. Historians of the period tell us that by 1920 the white race was 'reconsolidated', and the salient racial division in the nation became again what it had been traditionally, a division between whites, now consisting of a variety of European groups, and blacks. The theorists of racial inferiority then returned to their favourite theme that blacks were inferior to whites of all types. Its most recent appearance in the United States is Richard Herrenstein and Charles Murray's hotly debated *The Bell Curve*.[39] But Arthur Jensen's article, 'How Much can we Boost I.Q. and Scholastic Achievement?' in the *Harvard Education Review* of 1967 initiated the contemporary discussion.[40] Using the fact that black youngsters have an average IQ about 15 points below those of their white peers, Jensen argued that on

---

[38] Matthew Frye Jackson, *Whiteness of a Different Color* (Cambridge, Mass.: Harvard University Press, 1992), 38
[39] (New York: Free Press, 1994).
[40] *Harvard Education Review*, 39 (1967), 1–123.

average blacks have less of the intellectual ability necessary for scholastic achievement than whites. Although the consensus among those indulging in these issues is that blacks are intellectually inferior to whites, some theorists claim to detect racial differences in intelligence among whites, suggesting the possibility that a 'refragmentation' of the white race may be in the offing. Thus, the British psychologist H. J. Eysenck has argued that the average Irish IQ is about 15 points lower than the average English IQ, and that environmental causes cannot explain this difference.[41] Interestingly, however, some of the theorists of race and intelligence now argue that whites are not the most intelligent race. For example, using IQ test results, Richard Lynn and others argue that Asians, especially Hong Kong Chinese, are on average more intelligent than whites.[42] Ashkenazi Jews have the highest IQ of all, but most of the people making these comparisons do not call them the most intelligent race, presumably on the ground that the Jews are a white ethnic group rather than a race.

Finally, although most attention has focused on the alleged innate intellectual differences between the races, some scholars argue that important temperamental differences between the races also flow from their racial essences or genetic make-up. A typical claim is that blacks are congenitally more impulsive and less able to delay gratification than whites and Asians.

Jensen's argument relied heavily on the assumption that intelligence is a highly heritable trait, and in his article he naturally appealed to the work of the British psychologist Sir Cyril Burt, whose work was thought to provide the main grounds for that assumption. Burt claimed to have studied fifty-three pairs of identical twins separated at birth and reared in different environments, and to have found that their IQs were very similar. Since identical twins have the same genotype, this claim strongly supported the view that intelligence is a highly heritable trait, supposing that IQ measures intelligence. Unfortunately for Jensen, various scholars have shown that Burt's studies were at least partly fabricated, but he has continued to maintain that blacks are congenitally less intelligent that whites.

Burt did not use his theories about the high IQ of inheritance to argue that some races are intellectually superior to others, possibly because race had not yet become politically controversial in Britain when he was formulating his theories. But this situation had changed in Britain by the time Jensen published his article. After the Second World War blacks, Indians, and Pakistanis from the British Commonwealth began to settle in Britain in considerable numbers, and the friction between them and the native

---

[41] H. J. Eysenck, *Race, Intelligence and Education* (London: Temple Smith, 1971), 127.

[42] Barry Santman, 'Theories of East Asian Superiority', in Russell Jacoby and Naomi Glauberman (eds.), *The Bell Curve Debate* (New York: Random House, 1995), 201–21.

population erupted in the Notting Hill race riots of 1958. In that heated atmosphere it is no wonder that Eysenck undertook to popularize Jensen's views in Britain. Probably these views helped the passage of legislation limiting immigration into England from some of the Commonwealth countries.

Many countries have used theories of racial inferiority to support restrictive immigration and naturalization policies. Besides the two examples already noted, the US naturalization law of 1790 restricting naturalization to 'free white persons' seems to have been based on the view that the demands of citizenship, especially the demands of effective and responsible political participation, exceeded the abilities of non-whites. On the other hand, the United States does not seem to have the same determination to limit citizenship to those of 'common blood' as Germany or Japan, because at least after the 14th Amendment of 1868 all persons born in the United States are citizens. In the United States there was also at first no restriction on immigration, at least until non-white persons began immigrating in large numbers. Thus the Chinese immigration into California in the 1850s was tolerated until about 1870, when organized labour groups began protesting their presence. At this point the view that the yellow race is inferior to the white race, long maintained by European race theorists, became politically important in America. Legislation in 1882 and in 1888 and 1892 excluding Chinese from immigrating to the United States seemed clearly based on the idea of the congenital inferiority of the yellow race.

It is arguable, however, that racially restrictive naturalization and immigration policies do not always rest on ideas of racial inferiority and superiority. German policy, for example, makes it very difficult for immigrants not of German descent to become citizens; even people born and educated in Germany and who speak nothing but German are not automatically German citizens if they are not of German descent. On the other hand, anyone of German descent can claim German citizenship even if he or she was not born in Germany, does not speak German, and has never visited the country. Very similar policies are in force in Japan. Although Germany's record in the Holocaust may raise the suspicion that such policies are based on ideas of the racial superiority of Germans, they may rely instead on claims that citizens are more likely to act cooperatively if they perceive themselves to be of 'common blood'. Such claims may, of course, be false; or they may presuppose a more intense cooperation among citizens than any state can justifiably require of its citizens. But they need not assume that some races are superior to others.

Of course, countries have used theories of racial inferiority to rationalize policies other than restrictive immigration and naturalization policies. As we have seen, slavery was rationalized by the idea that blacks were natural slaves, unfit and unable to govern themselves. More recent policies may rely on a similar rationalization. Consider, for example, the practice of excluding blacks from voting and from political participation in general, and the various policies of *de jure* segregation in education and residence common in the United States for much of the twentieth century. Whites may have designed and implemented these practices believing that they served their economic interests. I suspect, however, that the argument they found most appealing was that blacks were so intellectually incompetent or so impulsive and unable to delay gratification as to be incapable of rational self-control that it was unwise to live next door to them, or to allow one's children to go to school with them, or to let them affect the political process. The vehement criticisms of Lani Guinier's recent proposals to increase effective black political participation, especially the transparently bogus objection that her proposals are anti-democratic, suggest that doubts about the political competency of blacks may linger.

Consider also Great Britain's practice in the nineteenth century of allowing fully representative governments only to those of her colonies populated mainly by Europeans or their descendants. Uday Singh Mehta charges that in *Considerations on Representative Government* J. S. Mill rationalized the practice based on what he took to be 'the crucial distinction in terms of readiness for representative institutions by reference to 'those of our blood' and those not of our blood'.[43] Although I cannot agree with Mehta—I think Mill was reporting the rationalization, not endorsing it—it is quite clear that the politicians and bureaucrats who devised and implemented the practice justified it on precisely these grounds.

But not all racially offensive policies are based on the idea that the non-white races are unfit for self-government. Some are based on the idea that certain races are intellectually inferior, though perhaps not unfit for self-government. An early example is Jefferson's proposed policy to emancipate the slaves and then send them to some other part of the world. Jefferson seems to have believed that the slaves were capable of self-government, for he proposed to send them where they could become a 'free and independent people'. But his arguments for deporting them assumed that they were inferior and that the racial amalgamation that would follow if they were allowed to remain in the country would 'stain' the blood of the master.

In the contemporary period most legal policies based openly on black inferiority have been withdrawn, though many remain that may be based

---

[43] Uday Singh Mehta, *Liberalism and Empire* (Chicago: University of Chicago Press, 1996), 15 n. 22.

covertly on ideas of black inferiority. One possibility is the practice of 'racial profiling', allegedly common in the United States. In racial profiling the police use the fact that an individual is black to help them decide whether they should detain or arrest him for certain, usually violent crimes. Further, pundits are always pressing either for the introduction of policies based on the idea of black inferiority, or for the curtailment of policies that they believe are based on the false assumption that blacks are by nature equal to whites. Nowadays the favourite target is affirmative action. Some critics charge that it assumes that black underachievement is caused by unjust discrimination when in fact it is caused by black impulsiveness and a con-genital lack of intellectual talent.

RACE AS SOCIAL CONSTRUCT

Earlier I contrasted social constructions with natural kinds. If the races are natural kinds, their members share essences because the members of natural kinds share essences. If races are social constructions, their members do not share essences though they share important properties or conditions that justify their being classed together. We may suppose that nature or God makes natural kinds, but human beings make social constructions because of their choices, the beliefs they hold, and the practices they devise and implement. Examples of classes that are social constructions are teams, clubs, juries, representative democracies, and nations. Teams and clubs exist only because people choose to join them, and their members need not share an essence that would justify classifying them together if they did not choose to join the team or club. Juries exist only because some people settle their legal disputes by presenting them before bodies of individuals sworn to give verdicts according to the law. Representative democracies exist only because the citizens of certain states elect their rulers. And nations exist only because their members have certain beliefs about themselves, including apparently certain false beliefs.

Some social constructions are made intentionally and some unintention-ally. For example, teams are usually made intentionally, but nations can be made intentionally or unintentionally. Nations are made intentionally when powerful and persuasive 'nation-builders' deliberately and with foresight devise and implement the practices that give the individuals that comprise the nation the various common qualities and loyalties that characterize the members of a nation. But nations can also be made unintentionally, when, by chance, people adopt or inherit practices that give them those common qualities and loyalties. The view that the races are social constructions is often associated with the claim that Europeans invented the races. This may be true, but it does not follow from the view that the races are social constructions. Inventions are always made intentionally, but, as we have just seen, social constructions are sometimes made unintentionally, as the by-products of individuals pursuing ends other than the creation of the social construction their actions bring into existence.

Different authors may have different accounts of how the races are socially constructed. We should expect this, since different authors may have different views about the properties or conditions individuals must share to be a race. The same author may also have different accounts of how the races are socially constructed if he has different views about what these properties or conditions are. W. E. B. Du Bois had two accounts.

The first is in his essay of 1897 'The Conservation of Races'. According to Du Bois in that essay, a race is a family of human beings, only 'generally' of 'common blood', but 'always' of 'common history traditions and impulses who are both voluntarily and involuntarily striving together for certain more or less vividly conceived ideals of life'.[44] This definition presents race as a social construction because it suggests that individuals are members of a race because they share impulses and ideals that result from their common history. But it is misleading. The problem is that the classes of individuals it identifies as the races are not the races as these are commonly understood. For example, black people are commonly identified as a race, but they often do not share either impulses or ideals. The resulting confusion led Du Bois to make the unfortunate pronouncement that black people who did not strive together for the ideals he thought emerged from their common history were servile imitators of other cultures. Apart from the paradox that his account implies that such people are not black people, pronouncing them servile imitators is likely to lose their cooperation in the fight against racism.

Du Bois's second and, I think, more successful account of how race is socially constructed is in his essay 'The White World'. Here Du Bois observes that a certain class of people will be compelled to ride 'Jim Crow' if they go to Georgia, and claims that it is that class of people that are black people.[45] This account is easy to misunderstand. For example, it may be supposed that it defines black people as people with black skins, since the conductors on the trains in Georgia who compelled blacks to ride Jim Crow identified them by their black skins. But some of the people the conductors compelled to

---

[44] W. E. B. Du Bois, 'The Conservation of Races', in *The Souls of Black Folk*, 230.
[45] W. E. B. Du Bois, 'The White World', in Julius Lester (ed.), *The Seventh Son*, 2 vols., ii (New York: Vintage, 1971), 512. 'Jim Crow' is the systematic practice of discrimination against and segregation of black people. The term is often used to describe accommodations or employment reserved for black people

ride Jim Crow did not have black skins: the conductors simply knew or believed that they had ancestors who had black skins. And Du Bois was not defining black people as people with black skins or as people with ancestors with black skins. On his account this would confuse the marks by which people are identified as black with the condition that makes them black. Although the conductors on trains in Georgia may have identified black people by their black skins or by their ancestry, Du Bois's claim was that such people are black because they are compelled to ride Jim Crow.

But why did conductors on trains in Georgia compel people with black skins or with ancestors with black skins to ride Jim Crow? Let us put the question more generally: why, in Georgia, did white-skinned people insult and mistreat black-skinned people? (I use 'white-skinned people' and 'black-skinned people' as abbreviations for 'people with white skins and no black-skinned ancestors' and 'people with black skins or with ancestors with black skins'.) The answer to this question is as follows: white-skinned people believed that black-skinned people were a different and inferior biological race; and they were able to devise and implement institutions and practices that expressed that belief and the attitudes that tended to accompany it. Naturally the institutions and practices that express the belief that black-skinned people are an inferior biological race to white-skinned people tend to impose burdens on black-skinned people that are to the advantage of white-skinned people, or subject black-skinned people to peculiar indignities. For example, in Georgia white-skinned people compelled black-skinned people to ride Jim Crow.

It may be objected that the social construction of the black race does not require that white-skinned people believe that black-skinned people are a different and inferior race. Suppose that white-skinned people did not believe that black-skinned people were a biological race. (Note that the bare belief that a black person must have a black-skinned ancestor does not necessarily include the belief that blacks are a biological race.) But suppose that they mistreated and insulted black-skinned people because they believed that black-skinned people were a different and inferior ethnic, cultural, or national group, or that they were unintelligent, or poor, or dirty, or criminally inclined, or non-citizens. If white-skinned people were able to implement institutions and practices that expressed these beliefs and the attitudes that tend to accompany such beliefs, they would probably impose burdens and indignities on black-skinned people, and it may seem that such people could be fairly described as a socially constructed race.

The trouble with this objection is that it fails to remember that not every social construction of a class of people is a race; not even when the people in the class are identified by their skin colour. The precise beliefs and attitudes that lead to their differential treatment make a difference. They must be the beliefs and attitudes that are generally held about allegedly inferior races. If they are not, they may define a certain class of individuals, but that class of individuals will not be a socially constructed race. This may seem odd, because white-skinned people mistreat and insult black-skinned people because they believe that black-skinned people are dirty, or poor, or unintelligent, or criminally inclined, or culturally different, and so on. But believing that someone is dirty, or poor, or unintelligent, or criminally inclined, or culturally different, is not the same as believing that she is these things just because she is a member of a biological race. The belief that she is these things just because she is a member of a biological race, and consequently that they are racial traits, puts a peculiar stamp on the way she will be mistreated and insulted. White-skinned people who are poor or stupid, or culturally different, or criminally inclined, may be mistreated and insulted, but they are not mistreated and insulted in exactly the same way black-skinned people are mistreated and insulted. The difference can be traced to the fact that black-skinned people are believed to be members of an inferior race, and that their poverty or stupidity or criminality are racial traits. Racial traits are held to be inborn, permanent, and inevitably inherited. In particular, the racial traits of an inferior race are held to contaminate for ever the offspring of a member of a superior race who is so reckless and irresponsible as to mix his or her seed with the seed of a member of an inferior race. Naturally, then, the members of the superior race see the inferior race as not only dangerous and contaminating to them, but as dangerous and contaminating to their posterity as well. This infuses a fierce, self-righteous, and desperate venom into the way the members of an allegedly inferior race are mistreated and insulted, hardening it with the resolve that it must continue for ever. If this is correct, the belief that people are members of a biological race, with all that this implies, is essential to the social construction of the races. Without such a belief, cultural, ethnic, or class prejudice may result in the social construction of certain classes of individuals, but these classes will not be races.

Du Bois's second account of how race is socially constructed is therefore that the belief that black-skinned people are an inferior biological race, and the practices expressing that belief, make them a race. Unlike his first account, the class of individuals this second account identifies as black largely coincides with the class of individuals commonly thought of as black. Black people may not share ideals and impulses, but they are threatened by the same indignities. Further, although there are usually class differences within a race, and these differences make a difference, all people commonly thought of as black have to deal, in one way or another, with these indignities. The rich black man in Georgia had to ride Jim Crow with the poor black man, or find some other means of transportation. Even the black man who looks white and can 'pass' has to deal with the indignities, though in a different way. There is one class of individuals this account fails to pick out as black that the ordinary account picks out as black. This is the class of individuals who are believed to have no black ancestry, and who themselves suppose that they have no black ancestry, though they do in fact have black ancestry. On the ordinary account such people are black, though they do not know it, but they do not have to deal with the indignities that construct blacks as a class, even in the way that a person who 'passes' must deal with these indignities.[46] The discrepancy can be handled by amending Du Bois's account so that it reads: a person is black if he would have to ride Jim Crow in Georgia were his ancestry known to the conductors.

Tommy Lott has defended Du Bois's definition of race in 'The Conservation of Races'. According to Lott, Du Bois wanted to get African Americans to invent themselves as a cultural group because he wanted blacks to be strong, and believed that the 'strength of a group lies in its cultural integrity'.[47] Lott may well be right. Du Bois certainly urged blacks to adopt practices and institutions that would have made them into a cultural group had they followed his advice. He was in intention like those 'nation-builders' I mentioned earlier, except that he did not succeed in building a nation. He was also right that a common culture can make a group strong. For example, it can make a group strong by facilitating cooperation among its members. It can do this by helping them to communicate with each other easily, and to trust each other. It can help them to communicate with each other easily by giving them a common language and the same symbols. It can help them to trust each other by strengthening the bonds of sympathy among them. Sympathy tends to be stronger between people who feel that they resemble each other in significant ways, and culturally similar people are likely to feel that they resemble each other in significant ways. Since we avoid harming or offending those we sympathize with, and trust those who avoid harming or offending us, it follows, other things equal, that we are more likely to trust those culturally like us than we are to trust those culturally unlike us.

But the question is whether a common culture is necessary for cooperation. If it is not, the benefits of a common culture may not justify incurring the costs of trying to create it, for, as we have seen, these costs can be high. And a common culture is not a necessary condition for cooperation. It may

---

[46] See Charles W. Mill's elegant discussion in 'But What Are You Really?' in *Blackness Visible* (Ithaca: Cornell University Press, 1998), 41–66.

[47] Tommy Lott, 'Du Bois and the Invention of Race', in Lott, *The Invention of Race* (Oxford: Blackwell, 1998), 66.

be a ground of sympathy, and sympathy may be necessary for cooperation, but a common culture is not the only ground of sympathy. Being the victim or potential victim of the same indignities is another. It is certainly capable of persuading people to feel that they are like each other in very important ways. If blacks are victims or potential victims of the same indignities, and perceived similarities are the basis of sympathy, they may feel considerable sympathy for each other even if they do not share a culture. Similarly, a common culture is not the only thing that can facilitate communication. For example, being fearful or at least apprehensive of the same affronts and violations is likely to make blacks particularly alert to signs or evidence of impending affronts and violations. Although these cues are there for anyone to see if she knows what to look for, and is willing to try to see them, it may be difficult for those not similarly sensitized to notice them, or even to be persuaded that they exist. If this is correct, most black people have ready access to a body of facts that are important to all of them, and this will enable them to understand each other quickly and easily.

It may be objected that Du Bois was trying to give black people an 'identity' that would make them confident and able to act decisively, but that thinking of themselves as the victims or potential victims of Jim Crow practices is unlikely to have this result.[48] But I am not saying that blacks should think of themselves only or mainly as the victims or potential victims of Jim Crow practices. This would be unfortunate. They can and should think of themselves in other ways. The point is that they need not think of themselves as members of the same cultural group to be able to act cooperatively. It may be enough that they think of themselves as members of an alliance of possibly very different peoples, formed to achieve a goal they all share—the overcoming of anti-black racism.

Du Bois's second account of how race is socially constructed can be generalized to cover the social construction of the various races. Generally the view is that Europeans invented the non-white races by inventing the idea of biological race, designating certain peoples as inferior biological races, and using their power to implement practices that express that belief. They also invented the white race by designating themselves the superior race and using their power to implement practices that express that belief. In this case naturally these practices tend to accord them special benefits, respect, and esteem, usually at the expense of the non-white races. But the view that Europeans invented the races is no longer tenable. Perhaps they started the practice, but it is likely that they no longer hold the monopoly.

If the preceding discussion is sound, the social construction of the races

---

[48] Ibid. 49.

depends on certain beliefs and practices. The practices may change if the interests they serve change, and when this happens the boundaries of races may also change. For example, in the United States anyone with the slightest African ancestry is classified as black, though she may not be classified as black in some parts of Latin America. The view that the races are social constructions supposes that the interests of powerful whites in the United States and Latin America explain this difference in racial classification. This is not implausible. In the United States classifying as many people as possible as blacks served the interests of slave owners for they were legally permitted to enslave only blacks, and the ban on importing African slaves severely limited their slave supply. In Latin America, however, although only blacks could be legally enslaved, the supply of African slaves was practically unlimited, and consequently there was not the same urgency to classify as many people as possible as blacks. A similar analysis suggests why the classification 'coloured' existed in the Union of South Africa. The whites were a small minority and understood that it would be difficult to maintain their rule if they had to deal with a unified 'black' race. So they divided the 'black' race into two, a 'coloured' race and an 'African' race, and ruled for longer than they would otherwise have. The same strategy—to divide and rule—may explain the favourable attitude to the current movement to create a mixed-race category in the United States. Perhaps, as the non-white population grows relatively to the white population, whites are beginning to see that in order to maintain their rule they must divide those they rule.

Given that the boundaries of a race are liable to change if it is a social construction, and the white race is a social construction, it follows that the boundaries of the white race are liable to change. Recently this issue has received enormous attention. The object of that attention seems to be to prove that racial prejudice has affected far more people than we have supposed; that in particular it has been directly not only at Jews, blacks, Asians, and other non-whites, but at whites as well. But the point is not that non-whites have had racially prejudiced views about whites; it is that some whites have had racially prejudiced views about other whites. The argument comes in two versions. One is that there are racial divisions among white Europeans, and that in America some of the better-placed white races have practised racial discrimination against some of the less well-placed white races. The other is that in America some European races were not always white, though they have recently become white. Both versions of the argument allow that by the middle of the twentieth century hardly anyone drew racial divisions among Europeans. And both suggest that this disappearance of racial divisions among Europeans reveals that racial boundaries are liable to change readily. The first does so on the ground that the boundaries between the white races have changed readily; the second on the ground that the boundaries of the white race have changed readily. Unfortunately both versions of the argument trivialize racial prejudice and give comfort and ammunition to racial bigots.

American attitudes to European immigrants have varied. Early Americans seem to have assumed that all whites were at least potentially capable of self-government. Jefferson, for example, proposed to send ships to get 'white' immigrants to replace the deported slaves; and the first naturalization law of 1790 limited naturalized citizens to 'free white persons'. But according to some authors, Americans began to question that assumption when massive immigration from Ireland, Italy, and southern and eastern Europe began after 1840. Allegedly the feeling grew that these immigrants were racially different from the native, mostly Anglo-Saxon stock and that some of them were not capable of participating in the life of a republic. On one account the immigrants were white, though racially different from the Anglo-Saxons. This is the first version of the argument that racial boundaries vary readily. On another account some of the immigrants were not even white, though they readily became white. This is the second version of the argument that racial boundaries vary readily.

Let us begin with the first version of the argument. I have allowed that de Gobineau, Chamberlain, and others argued that the Aryan, Nordic, and Teutonic races were superior to the other white races. And I allowed too that many native-born white Americans discriminated against the newer immigrants, sometimes using language that suggests that they did so on racial grounds. But the discrimination disappeared too quickly to have been genuine racial discrimination. As I have argued racial discrimination is hardened by the resolve that it should continue for ever, and the scholars tell us that by the middle of the twentieth century hardly anyone in America drew racial divisions among Europeans. I grant, of course, that the firmest resolution can change, but when it changes quickly one is entitled to wonder whether it was a firm resolution.

Let us now consider the argument that some of the European immigrants of the nineteenth and early twentieth century were not at first considered to be white, though they eventually became white. A particular version of the above argument focuses on the Irish.[49] Some people seem to think that Americans perceived the Irish as non-white because they were often depicted disparagingly in racial terms, and sometimes as dark-skinned. But since the Irish are not dark-skinned, the obvious implication is that the depictions were used pejoratively to express contempt for the Irish rather than to say

[49] See, for example, Noel Ignatiev, *How the Irish Became White* (New York and London: Routledge, 1995).

that they were non-white. The fact that there were signs saying 'No blacks or Irish allowed' is sometimes cited as evidence that the Irish were not considered white, or even that they were considered black. But these signs only show that the Irish were discriminated against. They do not show that they were discriminated against because they were considered black or even non-white. Race prejudice is not the only kind of prejudice. Nor is racial oppression the only kind of oppression. With characteristic confidence Orlando Patterson claims, 'As is well known, no "white" person in his right mind considered the Irish 'white' up to as late as the 1920's.'[50] This should come as a surprise to Andrew Jackson, the immensely popular sixth president of the United States, who was, of course, Irish. It may be objected that Jackson was elected before the massive Catholic immigration from Ireland aroused anti-Irish prejudice, but this raises the possibility that anti-Irish prejudice was religious and ethnic rather than racial. Patterson's claim would also come as a surprise to Frederick Douglass, who records that the Irish immigrants of the nineteenth century clearly and firmly considered themselves white, and, though generally despised, were considered to be white by the general population. Patterson notes, as if it clinches his argument, that 'as late as the last quarter of the nineteenth century, being called an Irishman was as great an insult as being called a nigger'. But this argument assumes, falsely, of course, that if an epithet is as great an insult as a racial epithet then it too must be a racial epithet. And Patterson's final comment 'The Irish "Catholic race" was stereotyped here, as in Victorian England as simian, bestial, lazy and riotous . . .' all but admits that the Irish were treated contemptuously because they were Catholic rather than because they were believed to be non-white.

A possibly more persuasive argument that the boundaries of the white race vary is that the Jews and Arabs are now classified as white in the United States though some relatively short time ago they were classified as non-white. According to this argument, certain key conventions and institutions changed enabling Jews and Arabs to become white. But why did these conventions and institutions change in this way? For the case of the Arabs it may be argued that the oil-richness of the Arab countries made the difference. Americans and Europeans could not afford to treat the people they depended on for oil as racial inferiors. This argument is not altogether compelling because early theorists of race such as Kant classified Arabs as white. If they were expressing widespread racial prejudices, the claim that Arabs were classified as non-white may be false or exaggerated. And why did the Jews become white? The usual answer is that they worked their way into the upper and middle classes. This response is smug and offensive because it

---

[50] Orlando Patterson, *The Ordeal of Integration* (Washington: Civitas, 1997), 75.

insinuates that blacks have failed to 'become' white because they lack the talent and determination to work themselves into the upper and middle classes. In fact blacks have not worked themselves up into the upper and middle classes because they are not white. One of the most important reasons why a group of people is able to work themselves into the upper and middle classes is that its members are already considered to be white.

Critics are liable to object that I am 'reifying' the idea of a white race. It is unclear what they can mean. To reify is to make concrete what is abstract. But the white race is not an abstraction because it is a social construction! Neither is it part of the very idea of a social construction that the boundaries of every class that is a social construction must fluctuate. Consequently, my criticisms of the arguments that the boundaries of the white race have fluctuated do not mean that I deny that the white race is a social construction. I am suggesting that the white race is a social construction whose boundaries have not fluctuated much. To overlook this is to overlook the intransigence of racial prejudice. The optimistic stories of non-white races becoming white in a generation trivializes the problem of racial prejudice. Inevitably they insinuate that blacks have not become white because they lack talent and drive, and in this way they contribute to racial prejudice.

DOES RACE EXIST?

There are two important versions of the claim that there are no races: there are no races as these are commonly understood, and there are no biological races. These two claims are distinct, though related. The first follows from the second. If there are no biological races, the races as commonly understood do not exist because as commonly understood the races are biological races. But the second does not follow from the first. If the races as commonly understood do not exist, it follows that the races as commonly understood are not biological races, but it does not follow that there are no biological races. There may be biological races though these fail to coincide with the races as commonly understood. Let us begin with the claim that there are no races as these are commonly understood.

The argument for this claim begins with the observation that telling an individual's race is not always easy. The average person assigns people to this or that race according to their easily observable features, usually their skin colour, facial features, and hair texture. For example, he generally classifies dark-skinned people with tightly curled hair as black, and white-skinned people with wavy hair as white, and usually he does so easily and correctly. Sometimes, however, he misclassifies or cannot classify a passer-by. Suppose, for example, that someone has white skin and thin lips, but tightly curled hair and a broad nose. The average person may classify her as white or as black, depending on how white her skin, how thin her lips, how tightly curled her hair, and how broad her nose, and in either case he may be mistaken. Or he may admit that he cannot tell whether she is white or black, or something else altogether. More generally the physical signs that supposedly label the races are often hard to detect, or perhaps sometimes even non-existent. Some black people pass as white, or do not even know they are black. Reportedly the Nazis who believed that the Jews were a race sometimes had trouble telling Jews from Gentiles.

Some commentators think that this shows that terms like 'white' and 'black' are meaningless, possibly because they assume that general terms are meaningful only if a conjunction of properties supply necessary and sufficient conditions for their correct use. But many meaningful general terms fail this test. A famous example is 'game'. Something is a game if it has enough of a 'cluster' of properties, like being entertaining, having a winner and a loser, and involving the gaining and losing of points, but not every game has all of these properties. If 'race' terms like 'white' and 'black' are meaningful because they are like the term 'game', in this respect someone would be white if she has enough of a cluster of properties like white skin, wavy hair, thin lips, and a narrow nose. Similarly, someone would be black if she has enough of a cluster of properties like black skin, tightly curled hair, thick lips, and a broad nose. This might explain why the average person might be uncertain whether someone with white skin, thin lips, but tightly curled hair and a broad nose was white or black. He may be uncertain whether she has enough of the relevant cluster of properties to be white, or enough of the relevant cluster of properties to be black.

In the racial conventions in most of the world, especially in the United States, Great Britain and the English- and French-speaking Caribbean, a person may be black even if she has none of the cluster of properties in question. Similarly, she may fail to be black even if she has most or perhaps even all of them. So perhaps there are necessary and sufficient conditions for using 'black' correctly, although black skin, tightly curled hair, thick lips, and a broad nose are evidently not among them. In fact, one condition is both necessary and sufficient for being black—having a black ancestor. That is, one is black only if one has a black ancestor, and if one has a black ancestor, then one is black.

It may be conceded that having a black ancestor is a *sufficient* condition for being black, and consequently that one need not look black to be black. But is having a black ancestor *necessary* for being black? Isn't *looking* black a sufficient condition for being black, and having a black ancestor only a test for identifying black people who fail to look black? Suppose, for example, that a person has a black skin, tightly curled hair, thick lips, and a broad nose. Wouldn't everyone straight away take him to be black, without bothering to check his ancestry? The answer to this question is 'yes', for the most part, but it fails to show that having a black ancestor is not a necessary condition for being black. In *Black Like Me*, Charles Griffin, a white man, described how he stained his white skin and disguised his blue eyes so that he looked black. Although most people took him to be black, he himself knew that he was not black. The reason he knew, or at least believed, that he was not black was that he knew or believed that he had no black ancestry. If those who took him to be black knew what he knew, they too would have known that he was not black.

The racial conventions therefore suppose that the racial signs are strictly speaking only signs that enable people to classify themselves and others, quickly and fairly reliably, as black. Although most white people look white and most black people look black, there are black-looking white people and white-looking black people. An octoroon, for example, will probably look white because he has seven white great-grandparents and only one black great-grand-parent, but the racial conventions unequivocally classify him as black, and there is nothing logically or conceptually odd about them for doing so. Indeed, skin colour, hair texture, and facial features are not the only racial signs; accent, mannerism, habits and tastes, and even clothes can be racial signs. For example a person can be identified as Jewish by his *yarmulke*. Of course, a person's clothes can mislead us about his race; but, as I have noted, so also can his skin colour, his hair texture, and his facial features. Skin colour, hair texture, and facial features are the favourite racial signs because they are usually inherited and harder to change than accents and clothes, and for this reason are usually more reliable. But when they can be changed, they follow the same logic as racial signs as clothes that are easily changed. Charles Griffin remained a white man despite the changes in his skin colour, and Michael Jackson remains a black man despite the changes in his skin colour and facial features.

If the foregoing is correct, a person who does not have a black ancestor is not black; and if he has a black ancestor, then he is black. As a definition of 'black' this is obviously flawed because the definition of a term cannot include the term itself. Some authors therefore prefer to name the races by reference to their continent of origin, rather than by their skin colours, and therefore as Europeans, Africans, Asians, Australasians, and Native Americans, rather than as white, black, brown, and yellow. According to Michael Levin, for example, 'a Negroid is anyone (75% or more of) whose ancestors 40 or more generations removed, with no upper bound, were born in Africa,

and likewise for Mongoloids and Caucasoids'; and he claims that this definition 'captures ordinary usage'.[51]

He is mistaken, however. Ordinary usage tells us that a person with any
African ancestry is black, not that he is black if 75 per cent of his ancestry is
African. But suppose that Levin has given us a way to define the races that
does not beg any questions. It does not follow that the definition is useful or
significant. It would be significant and perhaps useful if it enabled us to
distinguish and identify races that were interestingly, significantly, and
importantly different. But many philosophers insist that biological science
has found no interesting, significant, and important differences between the
races as Levin defines them. In particular they insist that it has found nothing vaguely comparable to a racial essence that would enable us to predict
and explain interesting, significant, and important differences between the
races. A contrast is often drawn between sex and race. For sex, the chromosomal markers XX and XY can be used to predict and explain the presence
of less general sexual traits like ovaries and testicles. But biological science
has found nothing that can be used to predict and explain important differences between the races like differences in intelligence. A brief essay by Paul
Hoffman is often cited. Hoffman claims that 'race accounts for only a minuscule .012 per cent difference in our genetic material'.[52] The implication,
though he does not say it explicitly, is that there cannot be important innate
differences between the races. Levin has responded that 'subtle genetic differences can have large "non-linear" effects',[53] and as a counter-example to
Hoffman's argument cites the fact that chimpanzees and humans share 98.5
per cent of their genetic material, though of course they differ from each
other in important ways. On this ground he maintains that Hoffman's claim
about the minuscule genetic differences between the races fails to show that
races do not differ from each other in important ways.

I see no ground that would justify rejecting Levin's argument definitively.
But perhaps it can be weakened depending on whether Hoffman's 0.012 per
cent figure refers only to genetic differences between people 100 per cent of
whose ancestors come from different continents, or if it includes people 75
per cent of whose ancestors come from different continents or 1 per cent of
whose ancestors come from different continents. If we say that blacks are
people all of whose ancestors come from Africa, and whites are people all of
whose ancestors come from Europe, and that blacks and whites differ in
genetic material by only 0.012 per cent, there is a slight if definite possibility

[51] Michael Levin, *Why Race Matters* (Westport, Conn.: Praeger, 1997), 21.
[52] Paul Hoffman, 'The Science of Race', *Discover*, 4 (Nov. 1994), 4.
[53] Levin, *Why Race Matters*, 21.

that this small difference may still have large non-linear effects. But presumably the genetic difference between the two races will be a lot smaller if we include among black people those whose ancestry is almost but not quite 100 per cent European. In that case it seems incredible to suppose that the genetic difference could still have large non-linear effects. But on the ordinary conception of race black people include people whose ancestry is almost 100 per cent European. One could still argue, I imagine, that however small the genetic difference, it could still have large non-linear effects. My point is that insisting on this possibility becomes less and less plausible as the genetic differences become smaller and smaller.

The conclusion to be drawn from this discussion is that we cannot altogether rule out the possibility that there are biological races and that there may be important differences between them, even if it is almost certain that the races as commonly understood are not biological races. The race idea has caused us a lot of trouble, and I have suggested that this is no accident because the idea is inherently dangerous. It would be much more comforting to be able to claim confidently that there is no such thing as race. But I do not see that philosophers have established this strong claim, and it is certain to backfire if persuasive counter-arguments are urged.[54] What is important to stress is that the possible existence of race raises no fundamental difficulties for any morality that rejects bigotry, favouritism, injustice, and disrespect. If, conceivably, there are biological races, and there are important intellectual differences between them on average, it still remains that what the races have in common, their capacity for rationality and morality, remains a solid basis for maintaining that every human being has equal moral rights to life, liberty, and respect. But if the possible existence of biological race raises no fundamental difficulties for morality, it does raise practical problems. As I have argued, even if the race idea is devised from the commendable motive to help us understand ourselves, it is also peculiarly dangerous and seductive, undermining our sympathy for others and making it possible to generate false evidence for false conclusions. Our task is to devise institutions to prevent it from having these effects, and to suppress those conditions from arising that have in the past made its evil potentialities almost irresistible.

---

[54] Albert G. Mosley has emphasized this point. See his 'Negritude, Nationalism, and Nativism: Racists or Racialists?' in Leonard Harris (ed.), *Racism* (Amherst, NY: Humanities Books, 1999), 74–86.

1

RACE AND PHILOSOPHIC MEANING

NAOMI ZACK

It is not always clear if a philosophic theory of meaning is meant to be descriptive or prescriptive of ordinary, scientific, or perhaps only philosophic usage. Still, theories of meaning can be applied as tests for the meaningfulness of non-philosophic terms. Something would be wrong with a term that "failed" all or most philosophic theories of meaning tests, especially those which many other terms pass—although the failed term might not be meaningless in non-philosophic usage.

I will minimally argue here that the ordinary or folk term 'race', particularly in the cases of 'black' and 'white' as used in the United States, fails important philosophic meaning tests, according to essentialism, nominalism, and the new theory of reference. As a result, it should be clear that only pragmatic theories of meaning could render 'race' philosophically meaningful, although at the cost of the biological foundationism upon which the folk concept of race purports to rest.

Let me begin with a neutral version of the present folk meaning of "race." Roughly, there is an assumption that there are three main human racial groups (although the federal census has admitted more at different times): white, black, and Asian. These races are not as distinct as species, because interbreeding is possible, and they are something like breeds, i.e., natural biological groupings of human beings into which all individuals can be sorted, based on traits like skin color, hair texture, and body structure. Although different races have different histories and cultures, their histories and cultures are not part of the biological foundation of racial differences.

From Naomi Zack, 'Race and Philosophic Meaning', in Naomi Zack (ed.), *Race/Sex: Their Sameness, Difference, and Interplay* (New York: Routledge, 1997).

For criticism of previous versions of these ideas, I am grateful to my colleagues in the Philosophy Department at the University at Albany: Ron McClamrock, Robert G. Meyers, John Kekes, and Berel Lang. Thanks also to Thomas Magnell for comments on a paper I read at the 1993 International Society for Value Inquiry Conference at the University of Helsinki, and to Leonard Harris and an anonymous reviewer of the American Philosophical Association *Newsletter on Philosophy and the Black Experience*, where this article first appeared (94/1 (Fall 1994), 14–20).

This biological foundation has value-neutral or factual support from science, and if a racial term is attributed to an individual, then something factual has been said about her. In other words, the term 'race' refers to something real.

I. ESSENTIALISM AND RACE

According to Aristotelian and Thomist doctrines of essence and substance, things are what they are because they contain the essences of the kinds to which they belong: essences (somehow) inhere in individual things that are substances; and the essences of substances support their accidental attributes. Words that refer to kinds of things have definitions that describe the essences of those kinds.

The present folk concept of race did not exist when essentialist theories of ontology and meaning were widely accepted in the ancient and medieval periods.[1] And, essentialist theories of ontology and meaning were philosophically dethroned by the later half of the nineteenth century, when American scientists constructed speculative theories of the hierarchy of human races, based on philosophical essentialism. These scientists posited a unique essence or "genius" for each race that was present in all its members: in cultural and biological rank, the white race was highest, the black race lowest; the essence of the black race was infinitely transmittable from one generation of direct genealogical descent to the next, but the essence of the white race could only be preserved if the essence of the black race were not present with it in the same individual.[2]

We expect folk world views to lag behind scientific ones, but these nineteenth-century racial theories are a case study of science turning away from empiricist philosophy and its methodological implications. For example, nineteenth-century scientists of race did not attempt to isolate "racial essences" for study but merely spoke vaguely of those essences as "in the blood."[3] Insofar as a universal negation can be affirmed, it is now

---

[1] For discussions of whether the modern concept of race was in use in the ancient world, see: M. I. Finley, *Ancient Slavery and Modern Ideology* (New York: Pelican, 1983), 97, 117–19; Martin Bernal, *Black Athena* (New Brunswick, NJ: Rutgers University Press, 1987), 339–445.

[2] See e.g., John C. Mencke, *Mulattoes and Race Mixture* (Ann Arbor: University of Michigan Research Press, 1979), 39–46.

[3] Almost any nineteeth-century reference to race makes heavy use of the blood metaphor, and even physicians believed that the blood of different races was different in "essential" ways. See e.g., Robert J. Sickles, *Race, Marriage, and the Law* (Albuquerque: University of New Mexico Press, 1979), 53–4. The only empirical difference in blood types among groups of people that is credited by scientists is a somewhat geographical distribution of the four major blood types over the surface of the planet. See N. P. Dubinin, "Race and Contemporary Genetics," in Leo Kuper (ed.), *Race, Science, and Society* (New York: Columbia University Press, 1975), 71–4.

accepted by scientists that there are no racial essences which inhere in individuals and determine their racial membership. Nevertheless, varied combinations of ancient philosophical essentialism and nineteenth-century scientific racialism linger to this day in American folk concepts of race.

When ordinary folk would not expect to find scientific support for the existence of essences of other human traits or kinds of objects, but still speak of racial essences, they are mistaken to do so. If attributing a race to an individual means attributing the essence of that race to him, then, on those grounds, the ordinary term 'race' is meaningless. But, of course, many terms which were in the past believed to refer to essences have remained meaningful in terms of non-essentialist theories of meaning, such as nominalism. So the next step, here, is to test the ordinary meaning of race against nominalist theories of meaning.

II. LOCKE'S NOMINALISM

John Locke shaped the modern form of nominalism.[4] Locke was reluctant to talk about substance because it could not be known either from sense experience or by reflection upon the ideas of the mind.[5] In keeping with this agnosticism, Locke addressed *essence* through analyses of the meanings of terms, as opposed to something *in re*. For Locke, the essence of a (particular) thing was the idea of the kind of thing it was, which idea was "in the mind," and "made by" the mind.[6] Locke also held that those things which were to correspond to an idea could be decided without restrictions imposed by the things themselves. This meant that sorting things into kinds, including sorting beings into species, was an arbitrary process. For example, he suggested that it was a matter of stipulation whether infants with what today would be considered severe birth defects should be classed as human beings.[7] Furthermore, what counted as a species for Locke seemed to have been the result of decisions about the meanings of words. For example, he speculated that a

---

[4] See Stephen P. Schwartz, "Introduction," in Stephen P. Schwartz (ed.), *Meaning, Necessity, and Natural Kinds* (Ithaca, NY: Conrnell University Press, 1977), 16–17; Michael Ayers, *Locke*, ii, *Ontology* (New York: Routledge, 1991), 65–7.

[5] See Peter H. Nidditch (ed.), John Locke, *Essay concerning Human Understanding*, IV. iii. 5 (1–6) (Oxford: Oxford University Press, 1990), 338–40. All quotes from Locke and *Essay* citations in this paper refer to this edition.

[6] As Stephen Schwartz interprets Locke, the nominalism of the old theory of meaning is that essences are ideas, i.e., things in the mind. See Schwartz, "Introduction," 16–17; and Locke, *Essay*, III. iii. 12, pp. 414–15.

[7] For Locke's stipulative view of species, see *Essay*, III. vi. 27, p. 454.

rational parrot could not be called a man because human shape is part of the
definition of 'man.'[8]

Thus, Locke did not seem to think that which beings were to count as
human was determined by natural structures outside of ideas and words.
Indeed, throughout his discussion of "monsters" and his account of a story
about an intelligent parrot, in the *Essay* chapter "On Personal Identity," he
seems to regret that human morphology is ordinarily a necessary part of
what it means to be a 'man.'[9] From this, one could read Locke as denying
the existence of natural kinds, or species, in any objective sense, since if there
are natural kinds or species, surely the group of human beings, in their
customary human form, would qualify.[10]

Even if one follows Locke in denying the objectivity of natural kind taxonomy, such extreme nominalism requires empirical and logical criteria for
defining terms that are used to classify objects that are in common sense
believed to exist independently of thought and language. The traditional
distinction between *intension* and *extension* does some of this work: the
definition of a term is its intention; the class of objects, each one of which
can be picked out by the definition, is the term's extension; and intension
determines extension.[11] Typically, the intension states necessary and sufficient conditions, or conjunctions of properties, that must be present for an
object to belong to the extension.[12] When terms with accepted extensions
cannot be defined by such conditions or conjunctions, because the members
of their extensions share clusters of properties or bear only "family resemblances" to one another, then the terms can be defined by disjunctions of
properties. Overall, the definition of a term ought to pick out only its extension and not the extension of a term with a different intension; though, in
borderline cases, precising definitions can be developed.[13] These criteria for
definitions suggest that the determination of extension by intension does not
preclude investigating extension in order to get intension "right." Finally,
even though a definiens is analytically connected to its definiendum, the

[8] That is, for Locke, there is no deep connection between morphology and natural kinds, or
species, viz.:

Since I think I may be confident, that whoever should see a Creature of his own Shape and Make, though it had no
more reason all its Life, than a *Cat* or a *Parrot*, would call him still a *Man*; or whoever should hear a *Cat* or *Parrot*
discourse, reason, and philosophize, would call or think it nothing but a *Cat* or a *Parrot*, and say, the one was a dull
irrational *Man*, and the other a very intelligent rational *Parrot*. (*Essay*, II. xxvii. 8, p. 333)

For a more complete discussion of the absence of the modern concept of race in Locke's writing,
see Naomi Zack, *Bachelors of Science: Seventeenth Century Identity Then and Now* (Philadelphia:
Temple University Press, 1996), ch. 12.

[9] Ibid. 335. See also mention of monsters in *Essay* III. vi. 17, pp. 448–9, and III. vi. 27, pp. 454–5.

[10] See Ayers, *Locke*, ii. 85–7.

[11] See Irving M. Copi, *Introduction to Logic* (New York: Macmillan, 1961), 107–12.

[12] Schwartz, "Introduction," 14–18.

[13] Copi, *Introduction to Logic*, 104 ff.

definiens cannot be vacuous: For example, it would be vacuous to define a cat as an animal with cats for parents, or to define wood as a stuff similar to other stuff called "wood."[14]

III. THE PROBLEMS WITH 'RACE' ACCORDING TO NOMINALISM

As noted earlier, races are ordinarily held to be real and racial differences are assumed to be physical differences. However, contemporary biologists and anthropologists define a 'race'—when they infrequently use the term—as a group of people who have more of some genetic or heritable traits than other groups. In scientific practice, there are no racial genes *per se*, but merely genes for traits that have been identified as racial traits in folk culture. Such racially significant genes are no different in principle from other phys-ical genes, i.e., they may be dominant or recessive, combine with other genes, "blend," mutate, or result in differing phenotypes due to the overall geno-typical environment. There is no defining collection of racially significant genes, for any presumptive race, that always gets inherited together, and no defining collection of phenotypical traits that all members of any race have.[15]

Thus, the failure of 'race' against nominalist meaning criteria is that there are no necessary, sufficient, or necessary and sufficient conditions of indi-vidual human biological traits, which need be present for black or white racial designation. Consider black designation, first. The group of American blacks has been estimated to have 30 percent of the genes for characteristics considered racial that the group of American whites has.[16] This overlap

[14] See ibid.; also Merilee H. Salmon, *Introduction to Logic and Critical Thinking* (New York: Harcourt, Brace, Jovanovich, 1984), 330. Technically, these are circular definitions, but it is their almost comical, explicit surface circularity that I am calling vacuous.

[15] For these facts about race and racial inheritance, see e.g., L. C. Dunn, "Race and Biology," in Kuper (ed.), *Race, Science, and Society*, 61–7; L. C. Dunn and Theodosius Dobzhansky, *Heredity, Race, and Society* (New York: Mentor, 1960), 114 ff. For a recent discussion of the conceptual issues involved in genetic atomism versus contemporary theories that genes interact with each other as well as with the overall genotypical environment, see Ernst Mayr, "The Unity of the Genotype," in Robert N. Brandon and Richard M. Burran (eds.), *Genes, Organisms, Populations* (Cambridge, Mass.: MIT Press, 1984), 69–86. However, it should be noted that even though genes underlying traits perceived to be racial may interact in these ways, so that an atomistic model does not apply, the interactive model does not reliably clarify racial inheritance because there is no phenotypical group of traits which can be identified in order to resort to this model for the inheritance of the gene underlying the phenotype. For example, if parents with known ancestry have a child who is phenotypically white, one would resort to the interactive genetic model only on the assumption that the child would have to be black because he or she has black ancestry.

[16] For a discussion of antebellum racial mixing among the black population, see Joel Williamson, *New People* (New York: Free Press, 1980), 9–26, 125.

between the classes of designated blacks and whites is related to other problems with genetic definitions of blackness: over 80 percent of the class
of blacks has some racially significant genes in common with the class of
whites; there are greater racially significant genetic differences among black
people than among white people; and some black people have no black
racial genes (but merely at least one known designated black ancestor).[17]
Also, there probably never has been a pure black or white race, and neither the Europeans who settled this continent nor the Africans brought
here as chattel slaves were "racially pure." Therefore, the above descriptions of the problems with American black racial classification that presupposes pure black and white races before known mixtures are even
oversimplified.[18]

There are matching problems with a nominalist account of the folk concept of white race. The absence of black genes, or of a black phenotype, is
not sufficient for folk white racial designation: Rather, to be white, regardless
of phenotype, an individual must have no black (or any other nonwhite)
forebears. This is another way of saying that there are no positive individual
biological traits for whiteness that are present in all white individuals.

If folk concepts of black and white race cannot be defined by scientific
terms for non-overlapping classes of racial genes neither can they be defined
by reference to phenotype or appearance: perceptions of racial appearance
are unstable and too variable to be translated into necessary and sufficient
conditions; many physical characteristics that people interpret as racial
characteristics in others are interpreted that way only after the persons in
question have been assigned to races, based on what is known about their
ancestors. To put it crudely, some black people look white, some white
people look black, and some white or black people look racially
indeterminate—and how anyone looks racially varies among observers.[19]

In American life, ever since slavery, black and white racial designations
have ultimately rested on the so-called "one-drop rule," which can be
expressed by this schema, S:

An individual, X, is black if X has one black forebear any number of generations
back; An individual, Y, is white if Y has no black forebears any number of generations
back (and no other nonwhite forebears).[20]

The problem with S is that blackness is indefinitely anchored because any
black forebear need be black only on account of a black forebear; and since

---

[17] See Debunin, "Race and Contemporary Genetics," 84 ff.
[18] Thanks to Thomas Reynolds for pointing out the oversimplification.
[19] See e.g., Adrian Piper, "Passing for White, Passing for Black," *Transitions*, 58 (1992), 4–58.
[20] For a more comprehensive discussion of this schema, see Naomi Zack, *Race and Mixed Race*
(Philadelphia: Temple University Press, 1993), chs. 2 and 3.

whiteness is defined as the absence of a black forebear, whiteness is a negation which rests on indefinite blackness.

If races were human breeds, there would be no reason to prevent the designation "mixed race" for individuals who have both black and white forebears.[21] But the one-drop rule prevents exactly that—mixed race people are always designated black. Regardless of how individuals may identify themselves privately, for all cases of mixed black and white race the one-drop rule is implemented officially, in law as well as public policy: Since 1915, the federal government has not recognized a category of mixed black and white race in the U.S. Census or in any federal system of racial classification;[22] in state and local record-taking anyone with a known black ancestor must be classified as black, and (except for two states) school children with recorded black and white parentage are classified as black.[23]

In the language of nominalism, the terms 'black' and 'white' purport to have mutually exclusive intensions and should therefore have mutually exclusive extensions, which they do not. But when the extensions of 'black' and 'white' overlap, that overlapping extension takes on the intension of 'black.' Either extension is determining intension, here, which should not happen, or the extension of 'black' is simply ambiguous because there is no way to exclude the intension of 'white' from it.

A cluster theorist or family-resemblance nominalist might propose that even though race cannot be defined by necessary and sufficient conditions, the concept has a (real) extension of individuals who share different amounts of those physical traits considered to be racial, family relations with other people in the same racial group, and self-identification as members of that group—not to mention identification by members of other racial groups.[24] While this proposal might seem to protect the folk ideas of black and white race by loosening up the classical nominalist meaning requirement of necessary and sufficient conditions, it does not preserve the *intention* behind American racial designations. It is usually intended that a racial designation of an individual say something pertaining to the biology of that individual and not about someone to whom the individual may be

[21] Many dictionaries define "race" as "breed." For a discussion of human–human breeding and black and white race in the United States, see Zack, *Bachelors of Science*, ch. 4.

[22] For details on the history of black and white official racial classification in America, see F. James Davis, *Who is Black?* (University Park: Penn State Press, 1991), chs. 1 and 4; Zack, *Bachelors of Sciences*, ch. 8.

[23] The two states are Ohio and Georgia (legislation pending). See *Project Race Newsletter* (Roswell, Ga.; Apr. 1993).

[24] This is the basis on which Anthony Appiah accepts folk ideas of race. See Anthony Appiah, "But would that Still be Me? Notes on Gender, 'Race', Ethnicity as Sources of Identity," *Journal of Philosophy*, 10 (Oct. 1990), 493–8.

related. If the cluster-theory meaning were intended when an American is
designated black, that is, if such a designation were analogous to calling
something a game, then it would be appropriate to qualify the designation
by indicating what kind of black the individual in question was. But this
never happens officially and is rare socially.[25] The "life form" or game of
black and white race is exclusively disjunctive, and morphological variations
within blackness are not enough to give rise to subcategories that stand up
on their own in racial terms, i.e., in the game of black race there are no
analogues to divisions such as games of chance, games of skill, games with
balls, etc. When Americans are designated white, they may qualify their
racial categories with reference to national origin of forebears who are also
assumed to have been white. Still, it is not clear if this practice among whites
points to purely cultural distinctions or racial distinctions within the white
race. (Until the 1920s, social scientists maintained that Irish, Germans, Italians, and Poles were all separate races, and until after World War II, Jews
were considered a race.[26] At present, all these groups are considered white
ethnic groups.)

A black person is someone with a black forebear; a white person is someone with no black forebears; some black people have white forebears: these
definitions of 'black' and 'white' are more vacuous than defining a cat as an
animal with two cat parents or wood as a stuff resembling other wood
stuffs—a black person need not have two black parents or be similar in racial
respects to other black people.

To return to Locke, before leaving nominalism, it should be noted that
folk ideas of black and white are ideas of kinds, in the mind, created by the
mind, and, indeed, without correspondence in their boundaries to any
boundaries fixed by nature. There is no reason to believe that there are any
kinds in the world which correspond to the ideas that the words "black race"
and "white race" name. Up to this point, according to extreme nominalist
standards, concepts of black and white race fare no worse than any other
concepts of kinds. However, the problem with these racial concepts is that
they do not meet the empiricist qualifications to nominalism that are met by
other kind terms accepted by science and common sense, e.g., 'cat' and
'wood.' So, the ordinary term 'race' fails the meaning test of nominalism yet
nominalism holds up for terms similar to 'race.' Therefore, unlike the previous case of race and essentialism, where the philosophic theory was itself

[25] See, by contrast, the situation of classification for Native Americans: Terry P. Wilson, "Blood
Quantum: Native-American Mixed Bloods," in Maria P. P. Root (ed.), *Racially Mixed People in
America* (New Brunswick Park: Sage, 1992), 108–26.

[26] For an analysis of the history of concepts of race in the field of sociology, see R. Fred
Wacker, *Ethnicity, Pluralism, and Race* (Westport, Conn.: Greenwood, 1983).

defective on scientific grounds, the problem here is with the term 'race' and not with nominalism.

IV. THE NEW THEORY OF REFERENCE APPLIED TO 'RACE'

If races were natural kinds, then the new theory of reference would appear to preserve the meaningfulness of the ordinary term 'race.' I will therefore begin with an application of the new theory of reference to folk ideas of race. After it becomes clear that races do not qualify as natural kinds, according to the new theory of reference, it should be obvious that this application is bogus.

According to the new theory of reference, natural kind words are *rigid designators* that are more like proper names than terms that can be defined by the necessary and sufficient conditions which objects must meet to be part of their extensions. On this theory, 'black race' would mean, because it would refer to, as a proper name, all of the human beings who in folk terms are called "black." Thus, the failure of ordinary folk to come up with necessary and sufficient conditions for blackness, which apply to all who are, have been, or will be named by the word "black," is no longer the semantic problem it was according to the old nominalist theory of meaning. The meaning of the word "black" is simply its real world extension, and not any verbal or mental definition "in the head" (or on paper). Similarly, "white" is a name for a group of people, which does not overlap with the group that is named by "black" (or by names for other nonwhite groups). While the rules for racial sorting may not make sense according to nominalist criteria, these racial names have always been intelligently used in the American linguistic community.

Continuing with this new theory of reference interpretation of folk racial words, while it may be a matter of culture that some physical traits have been picked out as racial traits, the genes which underlie those traits, and which are clustered in different ways within each racial group, can be studied within the legitimate sciences. Those genes are scientific entities which, as in the relation of XY and XX to male and female, or H_2O to water, are necessarily related to their phenotypes. The genes for racial skin colors, for example, would be the genes for those skin colors in all possible worlds.[27] Furthermore, like the case of XX and femaleness, the technical scientific meanings of physical racial traits need not be part of the folk meaning of concepts of race. The scientific meanings may refer to underlying traits

[27] That is, like the case of water on twin-earth, which is not H_2O, and therefore not water, brown skin due to a sun tan or makeup rather than to a gene is not racial brown skin.

which are objects of biological or chemical study, and folk speakers may be totally unaware of them. The folk meanings of race names may thus be neutrally *stereotypical* (like part of the folk meaning of 'lemon' as "yellow and sour"), because they refer to phenotypical properties as opposed to genes. (This is in addition to how they are stereotypical in that ordinary sense of 'stereotype' which devalues.)

Finally, on this reference account of folk race words, although both the black and white racial groups have changed throughout American history, and the black group contains people who have white as well as black ancestry, folk usage of racial words as proper names is supported by the perceived correctness of this usage in the past, and the shared belief that others in the culture have the same understanding of the correctness of the usage. The change over time in the amount and distribution of racially significant genetic traits in the black race (i.e., the effects of "racial mixing"), is no different than the change in the amount and distribution of genetic traits to which varying significance is attached in the case of animal breeds, over time: Cows, for example, produce more milk than in the past and are still properly called "cows"; non-domesticated breeds of animals are subject to evolutionary-type changes. The one-drop rule whereby a person is black if she has one black ancestor, could be viewed as a *living mnemonic* in the (real world) causal process whereby racial words come to be applied correctly and confidently. This living mnemonic assures that a person who is of black descent will be labeled in a way that refers to past labeling, not unlike other forms of hereditary labels, such as "baron" or (unfortunately) "untouchable." The mnemonic also has the utility of providing an automatic rule for the racial sorting of infants, and it allows American society the stability of automatically perpetuating, over generations, its group differences based on race. This situation is similar to the mistaken common sense that tomatoes are vegetables and spiders are insects, or to older beliefs in the existence of witches. In these examples, folk names or assumptions which are not in accord with scientific reality are nonetheless meaningful, due to folk experience. And here the case rests for a new theory of reference reconstruction of American concepts of black and white race.

V. PROBLEMS WITH THE NEW THEORY OF REFERENCE MEANING OF RACE

If the scientific realism of the new theory of reference is important, and according to Saul Kripke, W. V. O. Quine, Hilary Putnam, and others of its architects it is very important, then the above reconstruction of folk ideas of race within the purview of that theory is misleading. The core problem is that races do not qualify as natural kinds, and once this is clearly understood it follows that any historical account of the causal process whereby race words function as proper names, while it might be an interesting cultural study, does not contribute to semantic knowledge that can be directly used; instead, the result is that race words can only be mentioned by informed speakers and writers.

How is it that races are not natural kinds? In this context, there is not merely the empirical point that there are no racial essences, or the empirical-nominalist point that there are no uniform necessary and sufficient conditions for the application of race concepts. The problem is the lack of evidence that there is anything specifically racial on a genetic level: Not only are there no genetic racial essences, or nominalist analogues to such essences, but there are not even any racial *accidents*, genetically. It is not merely that a person designated black or white at a certain time and place might with the same physical traits be otherwise racially designated in a different time and place, i.e., not merely that the bearer of a racial label does not bear it in all real worlds, or, a fortiori, in all possible worlds. Rather, there is no purely racial sub-structure *per se*, to which morphology that is perceived or judged to be racial on a folk level, can be necessarily or (even contingently) connected. This last failure needs to be spelled out in some detail.

Suppose one compares racial designations with sexual ones. Despite many borderline cases in sexual dimorphism, for both phenotypes and genotypes, there are large numbers of human beings who genotypically, on a chromosomal level, fit the exclusive disjunction of XY or XX. To say that an individual is XY has explanatory force in predicting both primary and secondary physical sexual traits, and this explanatory force is on a more general nomological level than statements about the genotypes or phenotypes of primary or secondary physical sexual traits. Thus, in addition to XY and XX, there are genes for testicles, ovaries, and male and female body hair patterns.[28] But, by contrast, with race, while there are genes for morphology perceived or judged to be racial, such as hair texture and skin color, there are no chromosomal markers for black race or white race (or any other race), no genes for race *per se*, and, indeed, nothing which is analogous to XY, XX, or to any of the borderline sexual-type combinations of X and Y, for instances of mixed race.

---

[28] This is an oversimplification of the genetics of sex because the study of genotypically sex-linked, non-sexual abnormalities as well as the genetics of sexually indeterminate individuals is such an important part of the epistemology of selecting XX and XX as the paradigm of human sexual dimorphism. See e.g., Daniel J. Kevles, *In the Name of Eugenics* (Berkeley: University of California Press), 238–50.

Although the genes for specific hair textures, skin colors, body structures, and facial features, judged or perceived to be racial, may be necessarily associated with those traits, the lack of a genetic racial substructure means that *race* is not necessarily associated with those traits. Although it may be argued that the folk meaning of 'race' is a cluster or family-resemblance-type of meaning, and that these kinds of meanings refer to varying accidents, as opposed to essences, the lack of any specifically racial genetic substructures means that there are no racial accidents. It is not merely the case, as Anthony Appiah has asserted, for instance, that sexual identity is an ethical matter more central to who a person is than racial identity.[29] Instead, more strongly, the sexual identification paradigm is objective or real in a scientific way, while the racial part of clusters of racial traits are solely "in the head." Race is a social construction imposed on human biological differences which are not in themselves racial—because nothing is racial which is not "in the head."[30] Again, the genes for traits deemed racial are scientifically real but there is no racial aspect of these genes which is scientifically real. And yet, on a folk level, the prevailing assumption is that race itself is physically real.

These days no one claims that human races are distinct species. But might they not be breeds—a result of human–human breeding—and in that sense natural kinds? All of the major races seem to be associated with places, which are natural (i.e., Africa, Northern Europe, Asia), and groups called races are composed of biological human beings, which are also natural. Why, then, aren't races-as-breeds natural kinds, in the new theory-of-reference sense, since they clearly are natural kinds according to folk taxonomy? The answer is that, as Quine points out, in scientific taxonomy, underlying trait terms are the only analogue for the folk meaning of 'kind.'[31] It is also important to realize, at this juncture, that the term 'natural kind' does not derive from folk usage but from new theory of reference claims that meaning relies on scientific usage. In scientific usage, underlying trait terms have explanatory power—they explain structures and events described or named by "overlying" trait terms.[32] While groups from different geographical areas can be called natural kinds in a sense that accounts for their common history, culture, and in-group recognition, no explanatory power is added by adding the term 'race' to such group terms, and that zero

[29] Appiah, "But would that still be Me?," 495–7.

[30] This is, of course, in contrast to Hilary Putnam's arguments that meanings "just ain't in the head." See Hilary Putnam, "Meaning and Reference," in Schwartz (ed.), *Meaning, Necessity, and Natural Kinds*, 120–4.

[31] W. V. Quine, "Natural Kinds," in Schwartz (ed.), *Meaning, Necessity, and Natural Kinds*, 174–5.

[32] See William K. Goosens, "Underlying Trait Terms," in Schwartz (ed.), *Meaning, Necessity, and Natural Kinds*, 133–54.

increment may drop into minus territory when, as with black Americans, the term 'race' is applied on the basis of geographical origin of some of the ancestors of some members of the kind.

Michael Ayers indicates that without a previous definition of 'similarity,' biological beings cannot be sorted into kinds based on their similarity to beings that have already been so sorted.[33] At some point in the epistemology of taxonomy, reference to either underlying structures or history is required. The latter historical requirement brings us back to the foregoing interpretation of the one-drop rule as a living mnemonic which sorts people into the black group based on black descent. This appears to mean that the history of racial words rides on the history of individuals' families. But not all biological family members need be, or ever have been, of the same race. Indeed, American racial history is replete with stories of white and black branches of the same biological families and this means that something other than biology has divided the branches;[34] in fact, it is only black Americans for whom racial membership is positively determined by biological descent. And, as already noted, there is no way in which all black Americans are similar so that the relevant and necessary degree or kind of similarity can be specified. That is, there is no scientific way to pick out the black family members who "make" an individual black.

Therefore, no non-circular causal account of folk racial words is possible. Such words cannot be proper names because the proper name of an individual's forebear is not, in this sense of reference, the proper name of that individual, and we may not even know what—or, if anything—it was about the relevant forebear that made the proper name in question the correct proper name for him.

To be sure, there are strong American traditions about how people get sorted racially, but the only uniform empirical content to trait terms for the beings named by racial words is that they have been so named. All we can definitely say is that racial groups are groups that have had racial traits attributed to them, and that the individual members of such groups get sorted into them if their ancestors have had the relevant racial words attributed to them, or not (since a person is white if she has no nonwhite forebears).

A more (philosophically) technical way to state these problems with a causal-historical explanation of racial words is to construe racial proper name words as *attributive*, in Keith Donnellan's sense, as opposed to

[33] Ayers, *Locke*, ii. 81.
[34] See e.g., Patricia J. Williams, *The Alchemy of Race and Rights* (Cambridge, Mass.: Harvard University Press, 1991), 154–5.

descriptive or referential.[35] In this way, racial words pick out individuals who exist, regardless of whether or not they fit the descriptions attached to the racial words. The descriptions attached to the racial words (names) are stereotypes. Racial names have stereotypical connotations in terms of both physical morphology as well as value judgments.

While this new theory of reference's attributive account of racial concepts does preserve some of the folk meaning in racial concepts, like the interpretation of the one-drop rule as a premising definition on a family-resemblance nominalist account of meaning, it fails to preserve folk intentions in the use of racial words. People do not think that all they mean by race words are stereotypical names that some call others, in order to pick them out. To conclude, the new theory of reference does not preserve the meaningfulness of folk terms of race, and the fault is with those terms because the new theory works satisfactorily with the meanings of other apparent natural kind terms that have scientific analogues.

VI. PRAGMATISM AND RACE

There are two kinds of pragmatic meaning theories that could be relevant to 'race' but only the second is. The first is scientific pragmatism, which shows the purposiveness and intentionality behind all concepts, even the most exact scientific ones; the specialized philosophy-of-science form of this kind of pragmatism is an instrumentalist view of scientific theories and theoretical terms. This kind of pragmatic meaning is not relevant to race because race is insufficiently empirical: there are no confirmed scientific theories about race as it is understood on a folk level, and race is not a theoretical term in science.

The second kind of pragmatic meaning is axiological and it has some of the connotations of the folk word "pragmatic": efficient, useful, and morally compromised. The folk concept (i.e., the meaning of the word) of race is morally compromised in two ways. Its pragmatic meaning is not the kind of meaning that most folks in the linguistic community are prepared to admit is its only meaning, because they want to believe that race has a neutral, factual basis, supported by science. And, some of the purposes served by the imposition of racial categories on human beings have been evil. This is not surprising, because people lie and create illusions in order to mask wrongful motives and actions, and 'race' as it is vulgarly understood qualifies as such

---

[35] See Keith S. Donnellan, "Reference and Definite Descriptions," in Schwartz (ed.), *Meaning, Necessity, and Natural Kinds*, 42–66.

a lie and illusion. For example, after it became illegal to import slaves into the United States and the cotton gin intensified the demand for slave labor in the Southern economy, there was widespread "breeding" of slaves and widespread miscegenation among the slave population. By that time, only blacks could legally be enslaved, so it was pragmatic to designate the mixed-race and white offspring of slave mothers as black.[36] A second example of the axiologically pragmatic meanings of race can be found in constructions of race by nineteenth-century scientists, in which blacks always fared worse than whites in measurements of cranial size. The relevant data was manipulated to confirm the dominant ideology that blacks were "inferior" to whites.[37]

Of course, not all of the pragmatic meanings of 'race' are morally bad or compromised. While the evidence for changing the belief that culture was racially hereditary was available since the 1920s, it wasn't until the racist horrors of World War II registered in civilized global consciousness that the United Nations issued a series of position papers on the historical, rather than racial origins, of cultural difference.[38] Also, contemporary white liberal society engages in affirmative constructions of blackness that attempt to be helpful and benevolent towards blacks. Finally, it is no less pragmatic in this axiological sense that the American black emancipatory tradition has always responded to pragmatic white racist constructions of blackness with its own pragmatic constructions of blackness. Consider, for instance, the following excerpt from Leonard Harris' introduction to the pragmatic philosophy of Alain Locke:

A social identity entails for Locke the positive valuation of an interest, an affective feeling, a method of representation, and a system or process of continual transvaluation of symbols.
. . . The Negro race and the Negro culture were for Locke two distinct phenomena that by dint of history were identified as synonymous. Loyalty to the uplift of the race for Locke was thus, *mutatis mutandis*, loyalty to the uplift of the culture.[39]

One final point given limitations of space: If Alain Locke's equation of race to culture is related to current discussion, then race will be reduced to ethnicity.

---

[36] Indeed, the universal human rights affirmed in the United Nations Charter do seem to support such a right to self-identification. See Naomi Zack, "Mixed Race and Public Policy," Paper read at Feminism and Social Policy Conference at University of Pittsburgh, 1993; *Hypatia*, 10/1 (Winter 1995), 120–32.

[37] See Stephen J. Gould, *The Mismeasure of Man* (New York: W. W. Norton, 1981), 73–108.

[38] See the United Nations' "Four Statements on the Race Question," repr. in Leo Kuper (ed.), *Race, Science, and Culture* (New York: Columbia Press, 1975), app.

[39] Leonard Harris (ed.), *The Philosophy of Alain Locke* (New York: Temple University Press, 1989), introd., p. 20.

2

TOWARD A CRITICAL THEORY OF "RACE"

LUCIUS OUTLAW

A NEED FOR RETHINKING

For most of us that there are different races of people is one of the most obvious features of our social worlds. The term "race" is a vehicle for notions deployed in the organization of these worlds in our encounters with persons who are significantly different from us particularly in terms of physical features (skin color and other anatomical features), but also, often combined with these, when they are different with respect to language, behavior, ideas, and other "cultural" matters.

In the United States in particular, "race" is a constitutive element of our common sense and thus is a key component of our "taken-for-granted valid reference schema" through which we get on in the world.[1] And, as we are constantly burdened by the need to resolve difficulties, posing varying degrees of danger to the social whole, in which "race" is the focal point of contention (or serves as a shorthand explanation for the source of contentious differences), we are likewise constantly reinforced in our assumption that "race" is self-evident.

Here has entered "critical" thought: as self-appointed mediator for the resolution of such difficulties by the promotion (and practical effort to realize) a given society's "progressive" evolution, that is, its development of new forms of shared self-understanding—and corresponding forms of social practice—void of the conflicts thought to rest on inappropriate valorizations and rationalizations of "race." Such efforts notwithstanding, however, the "emancipatory project"[2] has foundered on the crucible of "race." True

From Lucius Outlaw, 'Toward a Critical Theory of "Race"', in David Theo Goldberg (ed.), *The Anatomy of Racism* (Minneapolis: University of Minnesota Press, 1990).

[1] Alfred Schutz and Thomas Luckmann, *The Structures of the Life-World*, trans. Richard M. Zaner and H. Tristram Engelhardt Jr. (Evanston, Ill.: Northwestern University Press, 1973), 8.

[2] The anticipation of "a release of emancipatory reflection and a transformed social praxis" that emerges as a result of the restoration, via critical reflection, of "missing parts of the historical self-formation process to man and, in this way, to release a self-positing comprehension which

to the prediction of W. E. B. Du Bois, the twentieth century has indeed been dominated by "the problem of the color line." It will clearly be so for the remainder of the century, and well into the twenty-first. For on one insightful reading, we are now in a period in which a major political struggle is being waged, led by the administrations of Ronald Reagan and George Bush, to "rearticulate"[3] racial meanings as part of a larger project to consolidate the victory of control of the state by those on the Right, control that allows them to set the historical agenda for America, thus for the Western "free" world.

Of course, it *must* be said that the persistence of social struggles—in the United States and elsewhere—in which "race" is a key factor is not due simply to a failure to realize emancipatory projects on the part of those who championed them. While there is some truth to such an analysis, the fuller story is much more complex. Nor has the failure been total. It is possible to identify numerous points in history, and various concrete developments, that were significantly influenced—if not inspired entirely—by emancipatory projects informed by traditions of critical theoretical thought: from the New Deal to the modern freedom (i.e., civil rights), Black Power, and antiwar movements; to the modern women's and environmental movements in the United States and elsewhere; to anticolonial, anticapitalist, antidictatorial, antiracist struggles throughout the so-called Third World and Europe.

Still, the persistence of struggles around matters involving "race" requires that those of us who continue to be informed by leftist traditions of critical thought and practice confront, on the one hand, unresolved problems. On the other, by way of a critical review of our own traditions, we must determine the extent to which those traditions have failed to account appropriately for "race" (i.e., provide an understanding that is sufficiently compelling for self-understanding and enlightening of social reality) in a way that makes practically possible mobilization sufficient to effect social reconstructions that realize emancipatory promises. It may well be that we will need to review what we think will constitute "emancipation" and whether our notions coincide with those of liberation and self-realization indigenous to persons and traditions of various "racial" groups

---

enables him to see through socially unnecessary authority and control systems." Trent Schroyer, *The Critique of Domination: The Origins and Development of Critical Theory* (Boston: Beacon Press, 1973), 31.

[3] "Rearticulation is the process of redefinition of political interests and identities, through a process of recombination of familiar ideas and values in hitherto unrecognized ways." Michael Omi and Howard Winant, *Racial Formation in the United States: From the 1960s to the 1980s* (London: Routledge & Kegan Paul, 1986), 146 n. 8.

that would be assisted by us, or who wage their own struggles with assistance from leftist traditions.

No more compelling need is required for our undertaking such reviews than that of getting beyond the interminable debate whether "race" *or* "class" is the proper vehicle for understanding (and mobilizing against) social problems with invidiously racial components. The present essay is another installment in this ongoing rethinking.[4] Here the focus will be less on the limitations of traditions of critical theory and practice with respect to the privileging of "class" over "race" and more on rethinking "race." A primary concern will be to question "race" as an obvious, biologically or metaphysically given, thereby self-evident reality—to challenge the presumptions sedimented in the "reference schemata" that, when socially shared, become common sense, whether through a group's construction of its life world and/or through hegemonic imposition.[5]

This rethinking will involve, first, a review of the career of "race" as a concept: the context of its emergence and reworking, and the changing agendas of its deployment. Second, a brief recounting of approaches to "race" within traditions of critical theory will facilitate responding to the central question of the essay: "Why a critical theory of "race" today?" This question is generated by the need to face a persistent problem within Western societies but, in the United States and European societies in particular, one that today presents a new historical conjuncture of crisis proportions: the prospects—and the concrete configurations—of democracy in the context of historic shifts in the demographics of "racial" pluralism. The centripetal, possibly balkanizing forces of racial pluralism have been intensified during the past quarter-century by heightened group (and individual) "racial" self-consciousness as the basis for political mobilization and organization without the constraining effects of the once dominant paradigm of

[4] For previous installments in this discussion, see my "Race and Class in the Theory and Practice of Emancipatory Social Transformation," in Leonard Harris (ed.), *Philosophy Born of Struggle: Anthology of Afro-American Philosophy from 1917* (Dubuque: Kendal/Hunt, 1983), 117–29; "Critical Theory in a Period of Radical Transformation," *Praxis International*, 3 (July 1983), 138–46; and "On Race and Class; or, On the Prospects of 'Rainbow Socialism,'" in Mike Davis, Manning Marable, Fred Pfeil, and Michael Sprinker (eds.), *The Year Left 2: An American Socialist Yearbook* (London: Verso, 1987), 106–21.

[5] On life-world construction see Schutz and Luckmann, *The Structures of the Life-World*, and Peter L. Berger and Thomas Luckmann, *The Social Construction of Reality* (Garden City, NY: Doubleday, 1966). "Hegemonic imposition" is a notion much influenced by the ideas of Antonio Gramsci (e.g., *Selections from the Prison Notebooks*, end. and trans. Quintin Hoare and Geoffrey Nowell Smith [New York: International, 1971]), although a now classic formulation of the basic insight was provided by Marx (and Engels?) in *The German Ideology*: "The ideas of the ruling class are in every epoch the ruling ideas; i.e., the class which is the ruling *material* force of society, is at the same time its ruling *intellectual* force" (in *The Marx–Engels Reader*, 2nd edn., ed. Robert C. Tucker [New York: Norton, 1978], 172; emphasis in original).

"ethnicity," in which differences are seen as a function of sociology and culture rather than biology.[6]

According to the logic of "ethnicity" as the paradigm for conceptualizing group differences and fashioning social policy to deal with them, the socially devisive effects of "ethnic" differences were to disappear in the social-cultural "melting pot" through assimilation, or, according to the pluralists, ethnic identity would be maintained across time but would be mediated by principles of the body politic: all *individuals*, "without regard to race, creed, color, or national origin," were to win their places in society on the basis of demonstrated achievement (i.e., merit). For both assimilationists and pluralists, *group* characteristics (ethnicity) were to have no play in the determination of merit; their legitimacy was restricted to the private sphere of "culture." This has been the officially sanctioned, and widely socially shared, interpretation of the basic principles of the body politic in the United States in the modern period, even though it was, in significant measure, a cover for the otherwise sometimes explicit, but always programmatic, domination of Africans and of other peoples.

For the past twenty years, however, "race" has been the primary vehicle for conceptualizing and organizing precisely around group differences with the demand that social justice be applied to *groups* and that "justice" be measured by *results*, not just by opportunities. With the assimilation project of the ethnic paradigm no longer hegemonic, combined with the rising demographics of the "unmeltable ethnics" in the American population (and the populations of other Western countries, including Great Britain, France, and West Germany) and the preponderance of "race thinking" infecting political life, we have the battleground on which many of the key issues of social development into the twenty-first century will continue to be waged. Will "critical theory" provide assistance in this area in keeping with its traditions—that is, enlightenment leading to emancipation—or will it become more and more marginalized and irrelevant?

ON "RACE"

There is, of course, nothing more fascinating than the question of the various types of mankind and their intermixture. The whole question of heredity and human gift depends upon such knowledge; but ever since the African slave trade and before the

---

[6] "In contrast to biologically oriented approaches, the ethnicity-based paradigm was an insurgent theory which suggested that race was a *social* category. Race was but one of a number of determinants of ethnic group identity or ethnicity. Ethnicity itself was understood as the result of a group formation process based on culture and descent." Omi and Winant, "The Dominant Paradigm: Ethnicity-Based Theory," in *Racial Formation in the United States*, 14–24: 15.

rise of modern biology and sociology, we have been afraid in America that scientific study in this direction might lead to confusions with which we were loath to agree; and this fear was in reality because the economic foundation of the modern world was based on the recognition and preservation of so-called racial distinctions. In accordance with this, not only Negro slavery could be justified, but the Asiatic coolie profitably used and the labor classes in white countries kept in their places by low wage.[7]

Race theory . . . had up until fairly modern times no firm hold on European thought. On the other hand, race theory and race prejudice were by no means unknown at the time when the English colonists came to North America. Undoubtedly, the age of exploration led many to speculate on race difference at a period when neither Europeans nor Englishmen were prepared to make allowances for vast cultural diversities. Even though race theories had not then secured wide acceptance or even sophisticated formulation, the first contacts of the Spanish with the Indians in the Americas can now be recognized as the beginning of a struggle between conceptions of the nature of primitive peoples which has not yet been wholly settled. . . . Although in the seventeenth century race theories had not as yet developed any strong scientific or theological rationale, the contact of the English with Indians, and soon afterward with Negroes, in the New World led to the formation of institutions and relationships which were later justified by appeals to race theories.[8]

The notion of "race" as a fundamental component of "race thinking"—that is, a way of conceptualizing and organizing social worlds composed of persons whose differences allow for arranging them into groups that come to be called "race"—has had a powerful career in Western history (though such thinking has not been limited to the "West") and continues to be a matter of significant social weight. Even a cursory review of this history should do much to dislodge the concept from its place as provider of access to a self-evident, obvious, even ontologically *given* characteristic of humankind. For what comes out of such a review is the recognition that although "race" is continually with us as an organizing, explanatory concept, what the term refers to—that is, the origin and basis of "racial" differences—has not remained constant. When this insight is added to the abundant knowledge that the deployment of "race" has virtually always been in service to political agendas, beyond more "disinterested" endeavors simply to "understand" the basis of perceptually obvious (and otherwise not obvious, but real nonetheless) differences among human groups, we will have firm grounds for a rethinking of "race." Such a rethinking might profitably be situated in a more sociohistorically "constructivist" framework, namely, one in which "race" is viewed, in the words of Michael Omi and Howard

---

[7] W. E. B. Du Bois, "The Concept of Race," in *Dusk of Dawn: An Essay toward an Autobiography of a Race Concept* (New York: Schocken Books, 1968 [1940]), 103.

[8] Thomas F. Gossett, *Race: The History of an Idea in America* (Dallas: Southern Methodist University Press, 1963), 16–17.

Winant, as a social "formation."[9] But first, something of the career of the concept.

"RACE" AND SCIENCE

The career of "race" does not begin in science but predates it and emerges from a general need to account for the unfamiliar or, simply, to classify objects of experience, thus to organize the life world. How—or why—it was that "race" came to play important classifying, organizing roles is not clear:

The career of the race concept begins in obscurity, for experts dispute whether the word derives from an Arabic, a Latin, or a German source. The first recorded use in English of the word "race" was in a poem by William Dunbar of 1508. . . . During the next three centuries the word was used with growing frequency in a literary sense as denoting simply a class of persons or even things. . . . In the nineteenth, and increasingly in the twentieth century, this loose usage began to give way and the word came to signify groups that were distinguished biologically.[10]

This nineteenth-century development was preceded by others in earlier centuries that apparently generated a more compelling need for classificatory ordering in the social world and, subsequently, the use of "race" as such a device. First, there were the tensions within Europe arising from encounters between different groups of peoples, particularly "barbarians"— whether defined culturally or, more narrowly, religiously. (And it should be noted that within European thought, and elsewhere, the color black was associated with evil and death, with "sin" in the Christian context. The valorizing power inherent in this was ready-to-hand with Europe's encounter with Africa.) A more basic impetus, intensified by these tensions, came from the need to account for human origins in general, for human diversity in particular. Finally, there were the quite decisive European voyages to America and Africa, and the development of capitalism and the slave trade.[11]

The function of "race" as an ongoing, classificatory device gained new authority and a new stage in the concept's career developed when, in the eighteenth century, "evidence from geology, zoology, anatomy and other fields of scientific enquiry was assembled to support a claim that racial classification would help explain many human differences."[12] The concept

---

[9] "Our theory of racial formation emphasizes the social nature of race, the absence of any essential racial characteristics, the historical flexibility of racial meanings and categories, the conflictual character of race at both the 'micro-' and 'macro-social' levels, and the irreducible political aspect of racial dynamics." Omi and Winant, *Racial Formation in the United States*, 4.

[10] Michael Banton and Jonathan Harwood, *The Race Concept* (New York: Praeger, 1975), 13.

[11] Ibid. 14.

[12] Ibid. 13.

provided a form of "typological thinking," a mode of conceptualization that was at the center of the agenda of emerging scientific praxis at the time, that served well in the classification of human groups. Plato and Aristotle, of course, were precursors of such thinking: the former with his theory of Forms; the latter through his classification of things in terms of their "nature." In the modern period the science of "race" began in comparative morphology with stress on pure "types" as classificatory vehicles. A key figure contributing to this unfolding agenda was the botanist Linnaeus.[13]

A number of persons were key contributors to the development of theories of racial types. According to Banton and Harwood, Johann Friedrich Blumenbach provided the first systematic racial classification in his *Generis humani varietate nativa liber* ("On the Natural Variety of Mankind," 1776). This was followed by the work of James Cowles Prichard (*Generis humani varietate*, 1808).[14] Georges Cuvier, a French anatomist, put forth a physical-cause theory of races in 1800 in arguing that physical nature determined culture. He classified humans into three major groups along an implied descending scale: whites, yellows, and blacks. As Banton and Harwood interpreted his work, central to his thinking was the notion of "type" more than that of "race": "Underlying the variety of the natural world was a limited number of pure types and if their nature could be grasped it was possible to interpret the diverse forms which could temporarily appear as a result of hybrid mating."[15]

Other important contributions to the developing science of "race" include S. G. Morton's publication of a volume on the skulls of American Indians (1839) and one on Egyptian skulls (1845). His work was extended and made popular by J. C. Nott and G. R. Gliddon in their *Types of Mankind* (1854). Charles Hamilton Smith (*The Natural History of the Human Species*, 1848) developed Cuvier's line of argument in Britain. By Smith's reckoning, according to Banton and Harwood, "The Negro's lowly place in the human order was a consequence of the small volume of his brain."[16] Smith's former student, Robert Knox (*The Races of Man*, 1850), argued likewise. Finally, there was Count Joseph Arthur de Gobineau's four-volume *Essay on the Inequality of Human Races* (1854) in which he argued that, in the words of Banton and Harwood, "the major world civilizations . . . were the creations

---

[13] "The eighteenth-century Swedish botanist Linneaus achieved fame by producing a classification of all known plants which extracted order from natural diversity. Scientists of his generation believed that by finding the categories to which animals, plants and objects belonged they were uncovering new sections of God's plan for the universe. Nineteenth-century race theorists inherited much of this way of looking at things." Banton and Harwood, *The Race Concept*, 46.

[14] Ibid. 24–5. Both works were closely studied in Europe and the United States.

[15] Ibid. 27.

[16] Ibid. 28.

of different races and that race-mixing was leading to the inevitable deterioration of humanity."[17]

Two significant achievements resulted from these efforts. First, drawing on the rising authority of "science" as the realization and guardian of systematic, certain knowledge, there was the legitimation of "race" as a gathering concept for morphological features that were thought to distinguish varieties of *Homo sapiens* supposedly related to one another through the logic of a *natural* hierarchy of groups. Second, there was the legitimation of the view that the behavior of a group and its members was determined by their place in this hierarchy. "*Homo sapiens* was presented as a species divided into a number of races of different capacity and temperament. Human affairs could be understood only if individuals were seen as representatives of races for it was there that the driving forces of human history resided."[18] These science-authorized and -legitimated notions about "race," when combined with social projects involving the distinguishing and, ultimately, the control of "racially different" persons and groups (as in the case of the enslavement of Africans) took root and grew to become part of common sense. "Race" was now "obvious."

For Banton and Harwood, this science of "race" peaked during the middle of the nineteenth century. By the century's end, however, a variety of racial classifications had brought confusion, in part because "no one was quite sure what races were to be classified *for*. A classification is a tool. The same object may be classified differently for different purposes. No one can tell what is the best classification without knowing what it has to do."[19] The situation was both assisted and complicated by the work of Darwin and Mendel. Social Darwinism emerged as an effort by some (notably Herbert Spencer and Ludwig Gumplowicz) to apply Darwin's principles regarding heredity and natural selection to human groups and endeavors and thereby provide firmer grounding for the science of "race" (something Darwin was reluctant to do). Such moves were particularly useful in justifying the dominance of certain groups over others (British over Irish; Europeans over Africans . . .). On the other hand, however, Darwin's *Origins* shifted the terrain of scientific discourse from morphology and the stability of "pure types" to a subsequent genetics-based approach to individual characteristics and the effects on them of processes of change, thus to a focus on the

---

[17] Ibid. 29–30. These authors observe that while Gobineau's volumes were not very influential at the time of their publication, they were later to become so when used by Hitler in support of his claims regarding the supposed superiority of the "Aryan race."

[18] Ibid. 30.

[19] Ibid. 38.

analysis of variety. In the additional work of Mendel, this development proved revolutionary:

> A racial type was defined by a number of features which are supposed to go together. . . . The racial theorists of the nineteenth century assumed there was a natural law which said that such traits were invariably associated and were transmitted to the next generation as part of a package deal. Gregor Mendel's research showed that this was not necessarily the case. . . . [It] also showed that trait variation *within* a population was just as significant as trait variations *between* populations . . . traits do not form part of a package but can be shuffled like a pack of playing cards.[20]

And, since environmental impacts that condition natural selection, in addition to heredity and the interplay between dominant and recessive traits, are important factors in the "shuffling" of traits, the notion of "pure" racial types with fixed essential characteristics was displaced: biologically (i.e., genetically) one can only speak of "clines."[21]

The biology of "races" thus became more a matter of studying diversities within—as well as among—groups, and, of particular interest, the study of how groups "evolve" across both time and space. To these efforts were joined others from the *social* science of "race": that is, understanding groups as sharing some distinctive biological features—though not constituting pure types—but with respect to which sociocultural factors are of particular importance (but in ways significantly different from the thinking of the nineteenth-century theorists of racial types).

For many scientists the old (nineteenth-century) notion of "race" had become useless as a classificatory concept, hence certainly did not support in any truly scientific way the political agendas of racists. As noted by Livingstone, "Yesterday's science is today's common sense and tomorrow's nonsense."[22] Revolutions within science (natural and social) conditioned transformed approaches to "race" (although the consequences have still not completely supplanted the popular, commonsensical notions of "races" as pure types as the Ku Klux Klan, among others, indicates).

The conceptual terrain for this later, primarily twentieth-century approach to "race" continues to be, in large part, the notion of "evolution" and was significantly conditioned by the precursive work of Mendel and Darwin, social Darwinists notwithstanding. In the space opened by this

---

[20] Banton and Harwood, *The Race Concept*, 47–9; emphasis in original.

[21] "An article by an anthropologist published in 1962 declared in the sharpest terms that the old racial classifications were worse than useless and that a new approach had established its superiroity. This article, entitled 'On the Non-existence of Human Races', by Frank B. Livingstone, did not advance any new findings or concepts, but it brought out more dramatically than previous writers the sort of change that had occurred in scientific thinking . . . The kernel of Livingstone's argument is contained in his phrase 'there are no races, there are only clines'. A cline is a gradient of change in a measurable genetic character. Skin colour provides an easily noticed example." Ibid. 56–7.

[22] Ibid. 58, quoted by Banton and Harwood.

concept it became possible at least to work at synthesizing insights drawn from both natural science (genetics, biochemistry) and social science (anthropology, sociology, psychology, ethnology) for a fuller understanding of "geographical races":[23] studies of *organic* evolution focus on changes in the gene pool of a group or groups; studies of *superorganic* evolution are concerned with changes in the "behavior repertoire" of a group or groups—that is, with the sociocultural development.[24] And it is a legitimate question—though one difficult to answer—to what extent, if at all, superorganic evolution is a function of organic evolution or, to add even more complexity, to what extent, if at all, the two forms of evolution are mutually influential. The question of the relations between both forms of development continues to be a major challenge.

But what is a "race" in the framework of organic evolution and the global social context of the late twentieth century? Certainly not a group of persons who share genetic homogeneity. That is likely only in the few places where one might find groups that have remained completely isolated from other groups, with no intergroup sexual reproductions. Among other things, the logics of the capitalist world system have drawn virtually all peoples into the "global village" and facilitated much "interbreeding." But capitalism notwithstanding, "raciation" (i.e., the development of the distinctive gene pools of various groups that determine the relative frequencies of characteristics shared by their members, but certainly not by them alone) has also been a function, in part, of chance. Consequently:

Since populations' genetic compositions vary over time, race classifications can never be permanent; today's classification may be obsolete in 100 generations. More importantly, modern race classifications attempt to avoid being arbitrary by putting populations *of presumed common evolutionary descent* into the same racial group. Common descent, however, is inferred from similarity in gene frequencies, and here the problem lies. For . . . a population's gene frequencies are determined not only by its ancestry but also by the processes of natural selection and genetic drift. This means that two populations could, in principle, be historically unrelated but genetically quite similar if they had been independently subject to similar evolutionary forces. To place them in the same racial group would, as a step in the study of evolution, be quite misleading. In the absence of historical evidence of descent, therefore, it is difficult to avoid the conclusion that classifying races is merely a convenient but biologically arbitrary way of breaking down the variety of gene frequency data into a manageable number of categories.[25]

---

[23] "When we refer to races we have in mind their geographically defined categories which are sometimes called 'geographical races', to indicate that while they have some distinctive biological characteristics they are not pure types." Ibid. 62.
[24] Ibid. 63. "The main mistake of the early racial theorists was their failure to appreciate the difference between organic and superorganic evolution. They wished to explain all changes in biological terms." Ibid. 66.
[25] Ibid. 72–3; emphasis in original.

When we classify a group as a "race," then, at best we refer to generally shared characteristics derived from a "pool" of genes. Social, cultural, and geographical factors, in addition to those of natural selection, all impact on this pool, thus on raciation: sometimes to sustain the pool's relative configuration (for example, by isolating the group—culturally or physically—from outbreeding); sometimes to modify it (as when "mulat-toes" were produced in the United States in significant part through slave masters of European descent appropriating African women for their—the "masters'"—sexual pleasure). It is possible to study, with some success, the evolution of a particular group over time (a case of *specific* evolution). The prospects for success are more limited, however, when the context of concern is *general* evolution—that is, the grouping of all of the world's peoples in ordered categories "with the largest and most heterogeneous societies in the top category and the smallest and most homogeneous in the bottom."[26] In either case—general or specific evolution—the concern is with superorganic evolution: changes in behavior repertoires. And such changes are not tied to the genetic specificities of "races."

But not all persons (or groups) think so. Although evolutionary—as opposed to typological—thinking, in some form, is at present the dominant intellectual framework for systematic reconstructions and explanations of human natural and social history, it, too, has been enlisted in the service of those who would have "science" pass absolution on their political agendas: that is, to legitimate the empowerment of certain groups, certain "races," over others. Even shorn of the more crude outfittings of social Darwinism's "survival of the fittest" (those in power, or seeking power, over others being the "fittest," of course), the field of the science of "race" is still occupied by those offering orderings of human groups along an *ascending* scale with a particular group's placement on the scale being a function of the level of their supposed development (or lack thereof) toward human perfectibility: from "primitive" to "civilized" (circa the nineteenth century); from "undeveloped" or "underdeveloped" to "developed" or "advanced" (circa the twentieth century).

Such arguments find fertile soil for nourishment and growth now that "evolution" (organic and superorganic, often without distinction), fre-quently conceived as linear development along a single path which *all* "races" have to traverse, is now a basic feature of our "common sense," Creationists excepted, and as we still face political problems emerging from conflicts among "racial" groups. "Race" continues to function as a critical yardstick for the rank-ordering of racial groups both "scientifically" and

---

[26] Banton and Harwood, *The Race Concept*, 77.

sociopolitically, the latter with support from the former. At bottom, then, "race"—sometimes explicitly, quite often implicitly—continues to be a major fulcrum of struggles over the distribution and exercise of power.

Certainly one of the more prominent contemporary struggles has centered on the validity of measurements of the "intelligence" of persons from different "racial" groups that purport to demonstrate the comparative "intelligence" of the groups. This struggle is propelled by the social weight given to "intelligence" as an important basis for achievement and rewards in a meritocratic social order. At its center is the question of the dominant roles played by either the genes or the environment in determining "intelligence" (and, by extension, in determining raciation).

Whichever way the question is answered is not insignificant for social policy. If the genes predominate, some argue, then social efforts in behalf of particular groups (e.g., blacks, women, Hispanics, etc.) intending to ameliorate the effects of disadvantageous sociohistorical conditions and practices are misguided and should be discontinued. It would be more "rational" to rechannel the resources poured into such efforts into "more socially productive" pursuits. On the other hand, if environmental factors dominate, then in a liberal democracy, for example, where justice prevails disparities of opportunities (and results?) among "racial" groups must be corrected, especially when the disparities are the result of years, even centuries, of invidious discrimination and oppression.

The politics of "race" are played out on other fields besides that of "intelligence." Modern science has also been concerned with whether the genes of a "race" determine its cultural practices and/or social characteristics. The findings?

All the known differences between geographical races in the frequency of genes which affect behavior are . . . quite trivial. Yet in principle it is possible that there may be genetic differences affecting socially, politically or economically significant behaviours and it seems reasonable to expect that the more population geneticists and physical anthropologists look for such genetic differences, the more will they discover. Because, however, of (1) the relative plasticity of human behaviour, (2) the genetic heterogeneity of all human populations, and (3) the mass of data suggesting the importance of situational determinants (e.g., economic and political factors) in explaining race relations, there is at present little reason to expect that a substantial part of intergroup relations will ever be explicable in genetic terms.[27]

But if not the genes, what about "evolution"? Has it produced differences in behavior and biological mechanisms for survival in different "races"? Is it possible to extrapolate from studies of the evolution of animal behavior to the evolution of human behavior? According to Banton and Harwood, such

---

[27] Ibid. 127–8.

efforts are inconclusive, the conclusions being at best hypothetical and difficult to test on humans. Moreover:

... the difficulty with generalising about evolution is that it is a process that has happened just once. With relatively few exceptions it is impossible to compare evolutionary change with anything else, or to say what would have happened had one of the components been absent. Therefore everything has its place in evolution ... If everything has its place then, by implication, everything is justified.[28]

What, then, after this extended review of the science of "race," are we left with by way of understanding? With the decisive conclusion, certainly, that "race" is *not* wholly and completely determined by biology, but is only partially so. Even then biology does not *determine* "race," but in complex interplay with environmental, cultural, and social factors provides certain boundary conditions and possibilities that affect raciation and the development of "geographical" races. In addition, the definition of "race" is partly political, partly cultural. Nor does the modern conceptual terrain of "evolution" provide scientifically secure access to race-determining biological, cultural, social developmental complexes distributed among various groups that fix a group's rank-ordered place on an ascending "great chain of being." Racial categories are fundamentally *social* in nature and rest on shifting sands of biological heterogeneity.[29] The biological aspects of "race" are conscripted into projects of cultural, political, and social construction. "Race" is a *social* formation.

This being the case, the notion of "evolution" is particularly fruitful for critical-theoretical rethinking of "race." As has been indicated, in the biological sciences it dislodged the nineteenth-century notion of races as being determined by specific, fixed, natural characteristics and made possible better understandings of racial diversities *and* similarities. In addition, as a concept for organizing our thinking about change, "evolution" continues to provide a powerful vehicle for studying human sociohistorical development. It is a notion that is part and parcel of the terrain of critical social thought of the nineteenth and twentieth centuries.

ON "CRITICAL THEORY" AND "RACE"

There is some ambiguity surrounding the notion of "critical theory" within traditions of *social* theory—beyond the fact that it is a phrase now used in reference to certain contemporary efforts in literary studies. On the one hand, the phrase is used to refer to a tradition of significantly revised and

---

[28] Banton and Harwood, *The Race Concept*, 137.   [29] Ibid. 147.

extended Marxism initiated by a group of theorists often referred to as "the Frankfurt School."[30] In this case "critical theory" is the name Max Horkheimer, an early director of the Institute for Social Research (established in Frankfurt, Germany in the late 1920s, hence the name "Frankfurt School"), gave to what he projected as the appropriate character and agenda for theoretical work directed at understanding—and contributing to the transformation of—social formations that, in various ways, blocked concrete realizations of increased human freedom.[31] This characterization of the nature of social theorizing and its agenda was shared by other members of the Institute (Herbert Marcuse, Theodor Adorno) even though still other members (Erich Fromm, Henryk Grossman) approached matters differently and used different methods in doing so. Further, there were theoretical differences between Horkheimer, Adorno, and Marcuse (and in Horkheimer's own thinking) over time that are masked by the label "critical theory."[32] Still, the label stuck and even today is used to identify a mode of social thought in the Frankfurt School tradition that continues in the work of a number of persons, Jürgen Habermas no doubt being one of the most widely known. Particularly through the influences of Marcuse on many in the generation coming of age in the 1960s during the socially transforming of the great social mobilizations of the civil rights, black power, and antiwar movements, it is a tradition that has been especially influential in the United States, in part because it brought many of us of that generation to Marx, without question the major intellectual precursor to Frankfurt School critical theory (along with Kant, Hegel, Freud, Lukács, and others). And here lies the ambiguity, for, on the other hand, the phrase is often expanded to include Marx's work, and that in the various currents of Marxism as well, the Frankfurt School included. In the words of Erich Fromm: "There is no 'critical theory'; there is only Marxism."[33] Thus, while the various schools of Marxism, of whatever pedigree, all share important "family resemblances," there are, as well, significant differences among them sufficient to demand

---

[30] For discussions of Frankfurt School critical theory see, for example, Martin Jay, *The Dialectical Imagination: A History of the Frankfurt School and the Institute of Social Research, 1923–1950* (Boston: Little, Brown, 1973); Zoltán Tar, *The Frankfurt School: The Critical Theories of Max Horkheimer and Theodor W. Adorno* (New York: Wiley, 1977); David Held, *Introduction to Critical Theory: Horkheimer to Habermas* (Berkeley: University of California Press, 1980); and Schroyer, *The Critique of Domination.*

[31] Among Horkheimer's characterizations of critical theory is his now classic essay "Traditional and Critical Theory," repr. in Max Horkheimer, *Critical Theory*, trans. Matthew J. O'Connell *et al.* (New York: Herder & Herder, 1972), 188–243.

[32] Tar, *The Frankfurt School*, 34.

[33] From a personal telephone conversation with Fromm during one of his last visits to the United States in 1976.

that each be viewed in its own right.[34] This is particularly the case when we come to the issue of "race" in "critical theory."

For a number of complex reasons, the Frankfurt School, for all of its influence on a generation of "new" leftists of various racial/ethnic groups many of whom were being radicalized in struggles in which "race" was a key factor, was not known initially so much for its theorizing about "racial" problems and their resolution as for its insightful critique of social domination generally. Although members of the Institute, according to Martin Jay, were overwhelmingly of Jewish origins, and the Institute itself was made possible by funds provided by a member of a wealthy Jewish family expressly, in part, to study anti-Semitism, all in the context of Germany of the 1920s and early 1930s, "the Jewish question" was not at the center of the Institute's work.[35]

This changed in the late 1930s and early 1940s. With the rise of Hitler and the Nazis, the Institute was eventually moved to New York in 1935 (and California in 1941) where its work continued until after the war (when it was reestablished in West Germany in the 1950s). The focus of the Institute's work during this time was the battle against fascism with debates centering on the character of the changed nature of the economy in twentieth-century capitalism; that is, the expression of group sentiments were to be understood in the historical context of the society.[36]

In this, notes Jay, the Institute broke significant new ground. No less so in another major contribution they made to the Marxian legacy, through the work of Fromm especially, that made their studies of anti-Semitism so informative: the articulation, later supported by extensive empirical studies, of a social psychology—and of individual psychology and character structure in the context of the social—drawing off the work of Freud (among others), in the context of Marxian social theory. This made possible analyses that linked cultural, political, *and* economic structural and dynamic features of the social world, and the character structure of the person, which helped to illuminate the de facto conditions of possibility for the emergence and social maintenance of Nazi fascism and anti-Semitism. Here, particularly, is

[34] For a particularly conversant overview of the various currents of Marxism and their philosophical and historical backgrounds, see Leszek Kolakowski, *Main Currents of Marxism*, 3 vols. (Oxford: Oxford University Press, 1978).

[35] "If one seeks a common thread running through individual biographies of the inner circle [of the Institute], the one that immediately comes to mind is their birth into families of middle or upper-middle class Jews. . . . If one were to characterize the Institute's general attitude towards the 'Jewish question', it would have to be seen as similar to that expressed by another radical Jew almost a century before, Karl Marx. In both cases the religious or ethnic issue was clearly subordinated to the social. . . . In fact, the members of the Institute were anxious to deny any significance at all to their ethnic roots." Jay, *The Dialectical Imagination*, 31–2.

[36] Ibid. 143, 152.

to be found the significance of Frankfurt School critical theory for our discussion of "race."

In the course of the Institute's work during its stay in the United States, the concern with anti-Semitism became less and less the focus as members of the Institute concentrated increasingly on "prejudice" more generally, although still fundamentally as related to authority and authoritarianism. Initiated by the American Jewish Committee in 1944 and conducted through its Department of Scientific Research established for that purpose, with the collaboration of the Berkeley Public Opinion Study, the Institute conducted major empirical studies, with critical philosophical analyses of the findings, of "one or another facet of the phenomenon we call prejudice." The object of the studies, it was noted, was "not merely to describe prejudice but to explain it in order to help in its eradication." The sweep of the project involved studies of the bases and dynamics of prejudice on individual, group, institutional, and community levels all in the context of the social whole.[37]

The Authoritarian Personality, the result of an integrated set of studies and analyses, was one among a number of volumes that grew out of this project. As Horkheimer notes in its preface, it is a book that deals with "social discrimination," and its authors, in the terms of the *credo* of critical theory, were "imbued with the conviction that the sincere and systematic scientific elucidation of a phenomenon of such great historical meaning can contribute directly to an amelioration of the cultural atmosphere in which hatred breeds."[38] It is especially pertinent to this discussion of "race," Daniel Levinson's chapter on ethnocentric ideology in particular.[39]

Here two conceptual moves are to be noted. First, Levinson substitutes "ethnocentrism" for "prejudice":

Prejudice is commonly regarded as a feeling of dislike against a specific group; ethno-centrism, on the other hand, refers to a relatively consistent frame of mind concerning "aliens" generally. . . . Ethnocentrism refers to group relations generally; it has to do not only with numerous groups toward which the individual has hostile opinions and attitudes but, equally important, with groups toward which he is positively disposed.

A theory of ethnocentrism offers a starting point for the understanding of the psychological aspect of *group* relations. (p. 102, my emphasis)

Equipped with a wider gathering concept, Levinson is able to make yet another move, one he thinks crucial to gaining the understanding being

---

[37] Max Horkheimer and Samuel H. Flowerman, "Foreword to Studies in Prejudice," in Theodor W. Adorno *et al.*, *The Authoritarian Personality* (New York: Norton, 1950), pp. vi, vii.

[38] Ibid., p. ix.

[39] The following discussion centers on the fourth chapter in *The Authoritarian Personality*, "The Study of Ethnocentric Ideology," by Daniel J. Levinson. Page references will be included in the text.

sought: "The term 'ethnocentrism' shifts the emphasis from 'race' to 'ethnic group'" (p. 103). What was gained by this?

... apart from the arbitrariness of the organic basis of classification, the greatest dangers of the race concept lie in its hereditarian psychological implications and in its misapplication to cultures. Psychologically, the race theory implies, whether or not this is always made explicit, that people of a given race (e.g., skin color) are also very similar psychologically because they have a common hereditary family tree ... Furthermore, the term "race" is often applied to groups which are not races at all in the technical sense ... There is no adequate term, other than "ethnic," by which to describe cultures (that is, systems of social ways, institutions, traditions, language, and so forth) which are not nations ... From the point of view of sociology, cultural anthropology, and social psychology, the important concepts are not race and heredity but social organization (national, regional, subcultural, communal) and the interaction of social forms and individual personalities. To the extent that relative uniformities in psychological characteristics are found within any cultural grouping, these uniformities must be explained primarily in terms of social organization rather than "racial heredity." (p. 103)

As noted in the previous section, the conclusion had been reached in contemporary natural and social science that, at the very least, "something other than racial heredity", understood as biological homogeneity, had to serve as a basis for understanding group characteristics and intergroup dynamics. Frankfurt School critical theory was distinctive as critical philosophical theory and material, social, analysis (a la Marx), fortified by Freudian psychology, deployed in cultural analyses of authority and mass culture. In the Institute's American sojourn particularly, there developed an explicit concern to bring critical thought to bear on the problems of invidious group-based and group-directed discrimination and oppression. "Race" was viewed as an adequate vehicle for such a task. Conditioned by a commitment to engage in critical praxis as an interdisciplinary venture that drew on the best science available (including that on "race"), these social theorists, through an approach to prejudice cum ethnocentrism fashioned from Hegelian, Marxian, Freudian elements, provided a means for getting at the problems of "race"—more precisely of race-*ism*—that was both critical and radical: within the context of an emancipatory project, it cut through social thought based on a reified, erroneous, even fraudulent philosophical anthropology that derived the culture, psychology, and social position of various groups from the biologizing of their "racial types."

Herbert Marcuse, among all members of the Frankfurt School, is most responsible for conveying this legacy to the "New Left" generation of the United States and Western Europe. In contrast to other members of the Institute, he became the most integrated into the American scene and chose to remain in the country when other members returned to Germany in the

1950s.[40] Influential as a teacher and colleague in a number of institutions, his *One Dimensional Man* inducted many of us into critical theory.[41] Here was an understanding of the social order in a way the necessity of which had been driven home to many of us as, in the context of concrete struggles, we came up against the limits of the idealism fueled by the thought of liberal democracy. For a significant group of persons involved in struggles over the "color line," the limits—and their attempted transcendence—were indicated in the evolution of the struggle for "civil rights" to one seeking "Black Power."[42]

But the Frankfurt School did *not* introduce Marxism to the United States. Nor, consequently, was it the first group of Marxian radical theorists to confront the problems of "race." There were other, much older legacies, in fact.[43] It is this history of multiple legacies that makes for the ambiguity of "a critical theory of race" when "critical theory" covers both the Frankfurt School *and* Marxian traditions in general. For an obvious, critically important question is, "Why, given other Marxian legacies, did the New Left seek guidance in the work of the Frankfurt School which might be applied to the problems of 'race,' among others"?

[40] The significance of the Studies in Prejudice notwithstanding, Martin Jay, for example, has noted the strategic moves adopted by Institute members on their movement to New York (e.g., continuing to publish their works in German, rather than English) that limited their integration into the mainstream of American social science. See *The Dialectical Imagination*, 113–14; and Held, *Introduction to Critical Theory*, 36.

[41] Subtitled *Studies in the Ideology of Advanced Industrial Society*, the book was published by Beacon Press (Boston) in 1964. His *An Essay on Liberation* (Beacon Press, 1969) was an important—though problematic—sequel that attempted to come to terms with the massive mobilizations of the late 1960s in the United States and Western Europe, Paris (1968) in particular. In the latter case (Paris), during a student-initiated national strike, Marcuse was celebrated as one of the "three 'M's" of revolutionary heroes: "Marx, Mao, Marcuse." For pertinent writings in regard to Marcuse, see, for example: *The Critical Spirit: Essays in Honor of Herbert Marcuse*, ed. Kurt H. Wolff and Barrington Moore Jr. (Boston: Beacon Press, 1967); Paul Breines (ed.), *Critical Interruptions: New Left Perspectives on Herbert Marcuse* (New York: Herder & Herder, 1970). *The Critical Spirit* includes a helpful Marcuse bibiliography.

[42] See Clayborne Carson, *In Struggle: SNCC and the Black Awakening of the 1960s* (Cambridge, Mass.: Harvard University Press, 1981); and Robert Allen, *Black Awakening in Capitalist America* (Garden City, NY: Doubleday, 1969).

[43] For important discussions, see T. H. Kennedy and T. F. Leary, "Communist Thought on the Negro," *Phylon*, 8 (1947), 116–23; Wilson Record, "The Development of the Communist Position on the Negro Question in the United States," *Phylon*, 19 (Fall 1958), 306–26; and Philip Foner, *American Socialism and Black Americans* (Westport, Conn.: Greenwood Press, 1977). For discussions by black thinkers, see, among others, Cedric J. Robinson, *Black Marxism: The Making of the Black Radical Tradition* (London: Zed Press, 1983); Henry Winston, *Class, Race and Black Liberation* (New York: International Publishers, 1977); Harry Haywood, *Black Bolshevik: Autobiography of an Afro-American Communist* (Chicago: Liberator Press, 1978); James Boggs, *Racism and the Class Struggle: Further Pages from a Black Worker's Notebook* (New York: Monthly Review Press, 1970); Manning Marable, *Blackwater: Historical Studies in Race, Class Consciousness and Revolution* (Dayton: Black Praxis Press, 1981); Oliver Cox, *Caste, Class and Race* (New York: Modern Reader, 1970); and Harold Cruse, *The Crisis of the Negro Intellectual* (New York: Morrow, 1967).

With respect to what we might call the black New Left, but with regard to many nonblack New Leftists as well, this question has been insightfully probed by Harold Cruse. For him, a crucial reason had to do with what he termed the "serious disease of 'historical discontinuity'":

> ... since World War I a series of world-shaking events, social upheavals and aborted movements have intruded and sharply set succeeding generations of Negroes apart in terms of social experiences. The youngest elements in the Negro movement today are activists, of one quality or another, who enter the arena unfortified with the knowledge or meaning of many of the vital experiences of Negro radicals born in 1900, 1910, 1920, or even 1930. The problem is that too many of the earlier-twentieth-century-vintage Negro radicals have become too conservative for the 1940ers. Worse than that, the oldsters have nothing to hand down to the 1940ers in the way of refined principles of struggle, original social theory, historical analysis of previous Negro social trends or radical philosophy suitable for black people.... All the evidence indicates that the roots of the current crisis of the Negro movement are to be found in the period between the end of World War I and the years of the Great Depression.... most of the social issues that absorb the attention of all the Negro radical elements today were prominently foreshadowed in these years. Yet the strands between the period called by some the "Fabulous Twenties" and the current Negro movement have been broken.[44]

The disease of discontinuity affected more than black youth. It was further facilitated by the anti-Communist repression led by Senator Joseph McCarthy, which had "a distinctly deleterious effect" not only on the leadership of black movements at the time, as Cruse notes, but on "radical" leadership in general.[45]

This discontinuity, bolstered by McCarthyism, was institutionalized in the curricula of most American colleges and universities, both black and white: virtually none provided systematically mediated learning regarding the history of previous struggles in which "radicals" had played important roles. Thus, when we remember that the U.S. New Left generation emerged principally on campuses and was forged in the crucibles of the modern civil rights and antiwar movements whose troops and general staff included thousands of students, the availability and attractiveness of Frankfurt School critical theory was *in part* a function of happy historical conjuncture: it was available when members of a generation were in need—and actively in search—of understandings to guide them in the transformation of a society that, when measured by its own best principles, was found seriously deficient.

---

[44] Harold Cruse, *Rebellion or Revolution?* (New York: William Morrow, 1968), 127, 130.

[45] "The hysteria of the time (which was labeled as McCarthyism, but which ranged far beyond the man) had shaken many persons, cowed others, silenced large numbers, and broken the radical impetus that might have been expected to follow the ferment and agitation of the 1930s and 1940s." Vincent Harding, *The Other American Revolution*, Center for Afro-American Studies Monograph Series, iv, Center for Afro-American Studies (Los Angeles, Calif.) and Institute of the Black World (Atlanta, Ga., 1980), 148.

Those who suffered the deficits were no longer willing to do so, and were moving to secure their "freedom." Many others were moved to share in the struggles committed to the realization of what the principles called for. Marcuse, himself a teacher and scholar, was among others a major contributor to the recovery from discontinuity by providing an important linkage with Marxian (and Freudian) critical social thought that aided the conceptualization and understanding of the social order as a whole, within a global, historical context, in which it was possible to situate particular problems that were the focus of struggle, including, to some extent, those of the color line.

But only in part was this a matter of happy coincidence. The linkages between the old and new Lefts were never *completely* broken. Many young whites, in particular, were supported in their efforts by parents and others who themselves had been—and still were—radical activists of previous generations. There was another crucial factor, particularly as experienced by blacks "on the Left," an experience that has been formed into its own legacy: the felt *inadequacy* of Marxian Communist and Socialist projects with respect to "the Negro question," the ultimate test case of the problem of "race." At the core of this legacy is the *other side* of the science of "race": not its scientific, critical conceptualization, but the lived experiences of *real* persons whose experiences are forged in life worlds in part constituted by self-understandings that are in large measure "racial," no matter how "scientifically" inadequate.[46] Other Left theoretical and practical activities, advanced by various groups and parties, ran aground on this reality. Frankfurt School critical theory, unconstrained by dogmatic adherence to "the party line," offered a conceptualization of revolutionary social transformation while, at the same time, it took democratic freedom seriously. Since, at the time, on the black side of struggles involving "race," Black Nationalism was an increasingly ascendant force that even those on the white side had to contend with, and since participants from both "sides" had been forged in large part by liberal democracy, the vision of a new society that decidedly antidogmatic Frankfurt School critical theory helped to shape (particularly by not centering on *class* theory) was potentially more promising as a resolution of racism while preserving black integrity. In this regard there was the promise that the legacy of inadequacy of other traditions of Marxist thought might be overcome.

Oversimplified, the inadequacy had to do with the reductionism in the theorizing about "race" in those Marxian traditions that attempted to

---

[46] A full exploration of "race" in the context of critical theory from the *black* side, if you will, requires a separate writing. For some of my thinking, see the previous installments cited in n. 4, as well as in the writings of persons listed in n. 43.

confront problems of the color line through approaches that rested on
close adherence to a particular reading of the *classic* texts of the "mature"
Marx and Engels, a reading sanctified after the Russian Revolution of
1917 by the subsequent Communist Internationals: *class* was the central—
indeed, the only—vehicle for fully and properly understanding social
organization and struggle. Problems of "race" are to be understood, then,
as secondary to the "primary contradiction" of class conflict that is
indigenous to social relations in capitalist social formations given the relations of the various classes to the means of production, relations that, at
the very least, determine classes "in the last instance." The prospects for
progressive social transformation and development, within and beyond
capitalism, on this view, are dependent on successful organization and
struggle by the international working class, racial differences notwithstanding. Such differences were to be transcended in the brotherhood of class
solidarity beyond their opportunistic manipulation by the class of owners
and managers, who used them as devices to foster divisions among workers, and by supposedly misguided, chauvinistic blacks (e.g., Marcus
Garvey).

The history of Marxian Communist and Socialist organizations in the
United States and elsewhere, populated, on the whole, by persons of European descent, is littered with errors, tragedies, and faces resulting from the
dogmatic application of this approach.[47] A key source of the difficulty is the
inadequate philosophical anthropology presumed by the privileging of
"relations to the means of production" as the definitive determinant of
groups defined by these relations, thus of the persons in those groups.[48]
Aside from problems involving the racism of white workers in the class
struggle, and, frequently, the paternalism of the white leadership, for many
African-Americans "proletarianism internationalism" was not enough of a
basis for forging a new Communist or Socialist world; it disregards—or
explicitly treats as unimportant—much that they take to be definitive
of African-Americans as a *people*. Identifying and nurturing these

[47] In the African context, for example, note Aimé Césaire's protest in his resignation from the
Communist Party in 1956: "What I demand of Marxism and Communism. Philosophies and
movements must serve the people, not the people the doctrine and the movement. . . . A doctrine is
of value only if it is conceived by us and for us, and revised through us. . . . We consider it our duty
to make common cause with all who cherish truth and justice, in order to form organizations able
to support effectively the black peoples in their present and future struggle—their struggle for
justice, for culture, for dignity, for liberty." Cedric Robinson, *Black Marxism*, 260, as cited by
David Caute, *Communism and the French Intellectuals, 1914–1960* (New York: Macmillan, 1964),
211.
[48] For a characterization and critique of this philosophical anthropology and its relation to
class theory in Marx *et al.*, see my "Race and Class in the Theory and Practice of Emancipatory
Social Transformation."

characteristics, and the institutions and practices that generate, shape, sustain, and mediate them, constitutes a complex tradition of its own, that of "Black Nationalism."[49] It is a tradition that continues to inform approaches to "race" from the black side, within Marxian critical theory as well (though not that of the Frankfurt School). In 1928–29, for example, with impetus from black Communists (Cyril Briggs, Richard B. Moore, and Harry Haywood), who also had roots in the decidedly nationalist African Black Brotherhood, the Communist International took the position that blacks in the "black belt" of the southern United States were an oppressed "nation." The program for their liberation thus called for "self-determination" and "national independence." This was the official position, on and off, for nearly thirty years (1928–57) and was carried out in this country by the Communist Party of the United States of America (CPUSA).[50]

The house of "critical theory" has thus been divided on the issue of "race," sometimes against itself: the approach of the tradition of the Frankfurt School on one side; those of other Socialist and Communist organizations, of many persuasions, on the other, with numerous schools of thought and practice in between: "race" is without scientific basis as an explanatory notion (Frankfurt School); "race," while real, is a factor of conflict secondary to the primary contradiction of class struggle ("classical," "official" Marxism); "race" is the basis of a nation—a group whose members share common history and culture ("official" Marxism of 1928–57). Certainly the divergences have as much to do with social matters as with matters theoretical: the concrete histories of different groups, their agendas, their locations, the personal histories of their members, and so forth. Still, those of us who continue to be informed by legacies and agendas of "critical social theory" must move past this "Tower of Babel" in our own midst if we are to meet the challenges of the present and near future.[51]

---

[49] Literature on this tradition is abundant. See, for example, John Bracey Jr. *et al.* (eds.), *Black Nationalism in American* (New York: Bobbs-Merrill, 1970); Sterling Stuckey, *The Ideological Origins of Black Nationalism* (Boston: Beacon Press, 1970); Alphonso Pinkney, *Red, Black and Green: Black Nationalism in the United States* (New York: Cambridge University Press, 1976); and M. Ron Karenga, "Afro-American Nationalism: Beyond Mystification and Misconception," in *Black Books Bulletin* (Spring 1978). 7–12. In addition, each of these includes a substantial bibliography.

[50] See Cedric J. Robinson, *Black Marxism: The Making of the Black Radical Tradition*, 300, and Kennedy and Leary, "Communist Thought on the Negro."

[51] "There is a kind of progressive Tower of Babel, where we are engaged in building an edifice for social transformation, but none of us are speaking the same language. None understands where the rest are going." Manning Marable, "Common Program: Transitional Strategies for Black and Progressive Politics in America," in *Blackwater: Historical Studies in Race, Class Consciousness and Revolution*, 177.

WHY A CRITICAL THEORY OF "RACE" TODAY?

Since the Black Nationalist tradition has continued to stress "race" over class, and classical Marxism class over "race," the "class or race" debates have persisted, at great expenditures of paper and ink, not to mention years of interminable struggle, confusion, and failure to conceive and secure the realization of promised emancipation. As we continue to struggle over matters of "race" in the United States and other societies, with very real possibilities for increased conflict, it is not enough to view today's problems as being brought on by the "heightened contradictions" of late capitalism attendant to the policies of neoconservative administrations conflicting with struggles for national liberation and socialism/communism in the "Third World." More is needed, both theoretically and practically.

"Both race *and* class" has been the response of some participants in the debate; "Left Nationalists" such as Manning Marable, on the one hand; theorists of the role of race in market relations and in social stratification (i.e., the social distribution of resources) such as William J. Wilson and Edna Bonacich, on the other.[52] Still others have proposed notions of "people-class," "eth-class," and "nation-class."[53] Yet all of these approaches, mindful of nationalist traditions from the black side, as well as of previous running-agrounds on "race," still presuppose the reality of "race."

But what is that reality? And "real" for whom? Would it be helpful for contemporary critical theory to recover the insights of twentieth-century science of "race" and those of the Frankfurt School regarding "race," "prejudice," and "ethnocentrism" and join them to recently developed critical-theoretic notions of social evolution to assist us in understanding and contributing to the emancipatory transformation of the "racial state" in its present configuration?[54] For, if Omi and Winant are correct: in the United States, the state is *inherently* racial, every state institution is a *racial* institution, and the entire social order is equilibrated (unstably) by the state to preserve the prevailing racial order (i.e., the dominance of "whites" over

---

[52] See Marable's *Blackwater: Historical Studies in Race, Class Consciousness and Revolution* and "Through the Prism of Race and Class: Modern Black Nationalism in the U.S.," *Socialist Review* (May–June 1980); William J. Wilson's *The Declining Significance of Race: Blacks and Changing American Institutions* (Chicago: University of Chicago Press, 1978); and Edna Bonacich's "Class Approaches to Ethnicity and Race," *Insurgent Sociologist*, 10 (Fall 1980), 9–23. For a fuller discussion of approaches to "race" through the prism of the paradigm of class theory, see Omi and Winant, *Racial Formation in the United States*, 25–37.

[53] On "nation-class," see James A. Geschwender, *Racial Stratification in America* (Dubuque, Ia: Brown, 1978).

[54] The recent notions of social evolution I have in mind are those of Jürgen Habermas. See, in particular, his "Historical Materialism and the Development of Normative Structures" and "Toward a Reconstruction of Historical Materialism," in Jürgen Habermas, *Communication and the Evolution of Society*, trans. Thomas McCarthy (Boston: Beacon Press, 1979), 95–177.

blacks and other "racial" groups);[55] during the decades of the 1950s through the 1970s, the civil rights, Black Power, Chicano, and other movements assaulted and attempted the "great transformation" of this racial state; however, the assaults were partial, and thus were not successful (as evidenced by the powerful rearticulation of "race" and reforming of the racial state consolidating power and dominance in the hands of a few "whites" in service to "whites" presently under way), because "all failed to grasp the comprehensive manner by which race is structured into the U.S. social fabric. All *reduced* race: to interest group, class faction, nationality, or cultural identity. Perhaps most importantly, all these approaches lacked adequate conceptions of the racial state"[56]—if they are correct, might this not be case enough (if more is needed) for a new critical theory of "race" cognizant of these realities?

Omi and Winant think so, and propose their notion of "racial formation." It is a notion intended to displace that of "race" as an "essence" ("as something fixed, concrete and objective . . . "), or, alternatively, as a "mere illusion, which an ideal social order would eliminate." Thus, race should be understood as

> . . . *an unstable and "decentered" complex of social meanings constantly being transformed by political struggle* . . . The crucial task . . . is to suggest how the widely disparate circumstances of individual and group racial identities, and of the racial institutions and social practices with which these identities are intertwined, are formed and transformed over time. This takes place . . . through *political contestation over racial meanings.*[57]

Central to their argument is the idea that "race" is socially and historically constructed and changes as a consequence of social struggle. "Race," in a racial state, is thereby irreducibly political.

The discussions and analyses of Omi and Winant, facilitated by their notion of "racial formation," are insightful and informative, particularly for their reading of the "rearticulation" of "race" by the Reagan administration. What these theorists offer is an important contribution to a revised and much needed critical theory of race for the present and near future. And part of the strength of their theorizing lies in the advance it makes beyond the reductionist thinking of other leftist theorists while preserving the sociohistorical constructivist (socially formed) dimensions of "race."

Part of the strength lies, as well, in the resituating of "race" as a "formation." For what this allows is an appreciation of the historical and socially constructive aspects of "race" within the context of a theory of social

[55] Omi and Winant, *Racial Formation in the United States*, 76–9.
[56] Ibid. 107.
[57] Ibid. 68–9; emphasis in original.

evolution where *learning* is a central feature.[58] Then we would have at our
disposal the prospects of an understanding of "race" in keeping with the
original promises of critical theory: enlightenment leading to emancipation.
Social learning regarding "race," steered by critical social thought, might
help us to move beyond racism, without reductionism, to pluralist socialist
democracy.

Lest we move too fast on this, however, there is still to be explored the
"other side" of "race": namely, the lived experiences of those within racial
groups (e.g., blacks for whom Black Nationalism, in many ways, is fundamental). That "race" is without a scientific basis in biological terms does *not*
mean, thereby, that it is without any social value, racism notwithstanding.
The exploration of "race" from this "other side" is required before we will
have an adequate critical theory, one that truly contributes to enlightenment
and emancipation, in part by appreciating the integrity of those who
see themselves through the prism of "race." We must not err yet again in
thinking that "race thinking" must be completely eliminated on the way to
emancipated society.

That elimination I think unlikely—and unnecessary. Certainly, however,
the social divisive forms and consequences of "race thinking" ought to be
eliminated, to whatever extent possible. For, in the United States in particular, a new historical conjuncture has been reached: the effort to achieve
democracy in a multi-"ethnic," multi-"racial" society where "group thinking" is a decisive feature of social and political life. A critical theory of
"race" that contributes to the learning and social evolution that secures
socialist, democratic emancipation in the context of this diversity would,
then, be of no small consequence.

---

[58] See Habermas, *Communication and the Evolution of Society*.

3

WHITE WOMAN FEMINIST 1983–1992

MARILYN FRYE

INTRODUCTION

This essay is the latest version of something I have been rewriting ever since my essay "On Being White" was published in *The Politics of Reality*. In a way, this *is* that first essay, emerging after several metamorphoses.

"On Being White" grew out of experiences I had in my home lesbian community in which I was discovering some of what it means for a woman, a feminist, to be white. These were very frustrating experiences: they played out and revealed the ways in which the fact that I am white gave unbidden and unwanted meanings to my thought and my actions and poisoned them all with privilege.

An intermediate version of this work, delivered at various colleges and universities around 1984–86, began with the following account of my attempts to come to grips with the fact of being white in a white-supremacist racist state, and with some of the criticism my first effort had drawn.[1]

Many white feminists, myself included, have tried to identify and change the attitudes and behaviors which blocked our friendly and effective comradeship with women of color and limited our ability to act against institutional racism. I assumed at first that these revisions would begin with analysis and decision: I had to understand the problems and then do whatever would effect the changes dictated by this understanding. But as I entered this work, I almost immediately learned that my competence to do it was questionable.

The idea was put to me by several women of color (and was stated in writings by

From Marilyn Frye, 'White Woman Feminist 1983–1992', in Marilyn Frye, *Willful Virgin: Essays in Feminism 1976–1992* (Freedom, Calif.: Crossing Press, 1992).

[1] The working title during that period was "Ritual Libations and Points of Explosion," which referred to a remark made by Helene Wenzel in a review of my *Politics of Reality* which appeared in *The Women's Review of Books*, 1/1 (Oct. 1983). Wenzel said: "Even when white women call third world women our friends, and they us, we still agonize over "the issue." The result is that when we write or teach about race, racism and feminism we tend either to condense everything we have to say to the point of explosion, or, fearing just that explosion, we sprinkle our material with ritual libations which evaporate without altering our own, or anyone else's consciousness." And, coming down to cases, she continued: "Frye has fallen into both of these traps."

women of color) that a white woman is not in a good position to analyze institutional or personal racism and a white woman's decisions about what to do about racism cannot be authentic. About conscious-raising groups for white women, Sharon Keller said to me in a letter, "I think that there are things which white women working together can accomplish but I do not think that white women are in the best positions usually to know what those things are or when it is the right time to do them. It would go a long way . . . for white women to take seriously their [relative] helplessness in this matter." White women's analysis of their own racism has also often been heard by women of color as "mere psychologizing." . . . To be rid of racism, a white woman may indeed have to do some introspecting, remembering and verbalizing of feelings, but the self-knowledge which she might achieve by this work would necessarily produce profound change, and there are many reasons why many white women may not want to change. White women's efforts to gain self-knowledge are easily undermined by the desire not to live out the consequences of getting it; their/our projects of consciousness-raising and self-analysis are very susceptible to the slide from "working on yourself" to "playing with yourself." . . . Apparently the white woman herself is ill-situated for telling which is which . . .

All of my ways of knowing seemed to have failed me—my perception, my common sense, my good will, my anger, honor and affection, my intelligence and insight. Just as walking requires something fairly sturdy and firm underfoot, so being an actor in the world requires a foundation of ordinary moral and intellectual confidence. Without that, we don't know how to be or how to act; we become strangely stupid; the commitment against racism becomes itself immobilizing. Even obvious and easy acts either do not occur to us or threaten to be racist by presumptuous assumptions or misjudged timing, wording, or circumstances. Simple things like courtesy or giving money, attending a trial, working on a project initiated by women of color, or dissenting from racist views expressed in white company become fraught with possibilities of error and offense. If you want to do good, and you don't know good from bad, you can't move.[2] Thus stranded, we also learned that it was exploitive and oppressive to ask for the help of women of color in extricating ourselves from this ignorance, confusion, incompetence and moral failure. Our racism is our problem, not theirs.[3]

Some white women report that the great enemy of their efforts to combat their own racism is their feelings of guilt. That is not my own experience, or that is not my word for it. The great enemies in my heart have been the despair and the resentment which come with being required (by others and by my own integrity) to repair something apparently irreparable, required to take responsibility for something apparently beyond my powers to effect. Both confounded and angry, my own temptation is to collapse—to admit defeat and retire from the field. What counteracts that temptation, for me, seems to be little more than willfulness and lust: I *will* not be broken, and my appetite for woman's touch is not, thank goodness, thoroughly civilized to the established categories. But if I cannot give up and I cannot act, what do Will and Lust recommend? The obvious way out of the relentless logic of my situation is to cease being white.

---

[2] For some critical reflection on "wanting to do good," and on "not knowing how to act," see "A Response to *Lesbian Ethics*: Why Ethics?" in Frye, *Willful Virgin*.

[3] Actually, what I think women of color have communicated in this matter is not so harsh as that. The point is that no one can do someone else's growing for her, that white women must not expect women of color to be *on call* to help, and that there is a great deal of knowledge to be gained by reading, interacting, paying attention, which white women need not ask women of color to supply. Some women of color have helped me a great deal (sometimes in spite of me).

THE CONTINGENCY OF RACEDNESS

I was brought up with a concept of race according to which you cannot stop being the race you are: your race is an irreversible physical, indeed, onto-logical fact about you. But when the criteria for membership in a race came up as an issue among white people I knew, considerations of skin color and biological lineage were not definitive or decisive, or rather, they were so precisely when white people decided they should be, and were not when white people wanted them not to be. As I argued in "On Being White",[4] white people actively legislate matters of race membership, and if asserting their right to do so requires making decisions that override physical criteria, they ignore physical criteria (without, of course, ever abandoning the ideo-logical strategy of insisting the categories are given in nature). This sort of behavior clearly demonstrates that people construct race, actively, and that people who think they are unquestionably white generally think the criteria of what it is to be of this race or that are theirs to manipulate.[5]

Being white is not a biological condition. It is being a member of a certain social/political category, a category that is persistently maintained by those people who are, in their own and each others' perception, most unquestion-ably in it. It is like being a member of a political party, or a club, or a fraternity—or being a Methodist or a Mormon. If one is white one is a member of a continuously and politically constituted group which holds itself together by rituals of unity and exclusion, which develops in its mem-bers certain styles and attitudes useful in the exploitation of others, which demands and rewards fraternal loyalty, which defines itself as the paradigm of humanity, and which rationalizes (and naturalizes) its existence and its practices of exclusion, colonization, slavery and genocide (when it bothers to) in terms of a mythology of blood and skin. If you were born to people who are members of that club, you are socialized and inducted into that club. Your membership in it is in a way, or to a degree, compulsory—nobody gave you any choice in the matter—but it is contingent and, in the Aristotel-ian sense, accidental. Well then, if you don't like being a member of that

---

[4] Frye, *The Politics of Reality* (Freedom, Calif.: Crossing Press, 1983), 115–16.

[5] It is easy for a white person who is trying to understand white privilege and white power in white supremacist states to make the mistake of (self-servingly) exaggerating that power and privilege, assuming it is total. In this case, I was earlier making the mistake of thinking that white domination means that white people totally control the definition of race and the races. Reading bell hook's *Yearning* (Boston: South End Press, 1990), I awoke to the fact that afro-americans (and other racialized people) are engaged also in the definition of Black (and other "race" categories); white people have the power to enforce their own definitions in many (but not all) situations, but they are not the only people determining the meanings of race categories and race words, and what they determine for themselves (and enforce) is not necessarily congruent with what others are determining for *themselves*.

club, you might think of resigning your membership, or of figuring out how to get yourself kicked out of the club, how to get yourself excommunicated.

But this strategy of "separation" is vulnerable to a variety of criticisms. A white woman cannot cease having the history she has by some sort of divorce ritual. Furthermore, the renunciation of whiteness may be an act of self-loathing rather than an act of liberation.[6] And disassociation from the race-group one was born into might seem to be an option for white folks, but seems either not possible or not politically desirable to most members of the other groups from which the whites set themselves off.[7] This criticism suggests that my thinking of disassociating from membership in the white fraternity is just another exercise (hence, another reinforcement) of that white privilege which I was finding so onerous and attempting to escape. All these criticisms sound right (and I will circle back to them at the end of the essay), but there is something very wrong here. This closure has the distinctive finality of a trap.

In academic circles where I now circulate, it has become a commonplace that race is a "social construction" and not a naturally given and naturally maintained grouping of human individuals with naturally determined sets of traits. And the recognition of race as non-natural is presumed, in those circles, to be liberatory. Pursuing the idea of disassociating from the race-category in which I am placed and from the perquisites attached to it is a way of pursuing the question of what freedom can be made of this, and for whom. But it is seeming to me that race (together with racism and race privilege) is apparently *constructed as* something inescapable. And it makes sense that it would be, since such a construction would best serve those served by race and racism. *Of course* race and racism are impossible to escape; of course a white person is always in a sticky web of privilege that permits only acts which reinforce ("reinscribe") racism. This just means that some exit must be forced. That will require conceptual creativity, and perhaps conceptual violence.

The "being white" that has presented itself to me as a burden and an insuperable block to my growth out of racism is not essentially about the color of my skin or any other inherited bodily trait, even though doctrines of color are bound up with this status in some ways. The problem then, is to find a way to think clearly about some kind of whiteness that is *not essentially* tied to color and yet has some significant relation to color. The

---

[6] I want to thank María Lugones, whose palpably loving anger on this point made me take it seriously. See "Hablando Cara a Cara/Speaking Face to Face: An Exploration of Ethnocentric Racism," in Gloria Anzaldúa (ed.), *Making Face, Making Soul: Haciendo Caras: Critical and Creative Perspectives by Women of Color* (San Francisco: aunt lute foundation press, 1990).

[7] Carrie Jane Singleton, "Race and Gender in Feminist Theory," *SAGE*, 6/1 (Summer 1989), 15.

distinction feminists have made between maleness and masculinity provides a clue and an analogy. Maleness we have construed as something a human animal can be born with; masculinity we have construed as something a human animal can be trained to—and it is an empirical fact that most male human animals are trained to it in one or another of its cultural varieties.[8] Masculinity is not a blossoming consequence of genetic constitution as lush growths of facial hair seem to be in the males of many human groups. But the masculinity of an adult male is far from superficial or incidental and we know it is not something an individual could shrug off like a coat or snap out of like an actor stepping out of his character. The masculinity of an adult male human in any particular culture is also profoundly connected with the local perceptions and conceptions of maleness (as "biological"), its causes and its consequences. So it may be with being white, but we need some revision of our vocabulary to say it rightly. We need a term in the realm of race and racism whose grammar is analogous to the grammar of the term 'masculinity'. I am tempted to recommend the neologism 'albosity' for this honor, but I'm afraid it is too strange to catch on. So I will introduce 'whitely' and 'whiteliness' as terms whose grammar is analogous to that of 'masculine' and 'masculinity'. Being white-skinned (like being male) is a matter of physical traits presumed to be physically determined; being whitely (like being masculine) I conceive as a deeply ingrained way of being in the world. Following the analogy with masculinity, I assume that the connection between whiteliness and light-colored skin is a *contingent* connection: this character could be manifested by persons who are *not* "white;" it can be absent in persons who *are*.

In the next section, I will talk about whiteliness in a free and speculative way, exploring what it may be. This work is raw preliminary sketching; it moves against no such background of research and attentive observation as there is to guide accounts of masculinity. There is of course a large literature on racism, but I think that what I am after here is not one and the same thing as racism, either institutional or personal. Whiteliness is connected to institutional racism (as will emerge further on in the discussion) by the fact that individuals with this sort of character are well-suited to the social roles of agents of institutional racism, but it is a character of persons, not of

---

[8] I am not unmindful here of the anxiety some readers may have about my reliance on a distinction between that which is physically given and that which is socially acquired. I could immensely complicate this passage by shifting from the material mode of talking about maleness and skin colors to the formal mode of talking about conceptions or constructions of maleness and skin colors. But it would not make anything clearer. It is perfectly meaningful to use the terms 'male' and 'white' (as a pigment word), while understanding that sex categories and color categories are "constructed" as the kinds of categories they are, i.e., physical categories, as opposed to social categories like *lawyer* or arithmetic categories like *ordinals*.

institutions. Whiteliness is also related to individual or personal racism, but I think it is not one and the same thing as racism, at least in the sense where 'racism' means bigotry/hate/ignorance/indifference. As I understand masculinity it is not the same thing as misogyny; similarly, whiteliness is not the same thing as race-hatred. One can be whitely even if one's beliefs and feelings are relatively well-informed, humane and good-willed. So I approach whiteliness freshly, as itself, as something which is both familiar and unknown.

WHITELINESS

To begin to get a picture of what whiteliness is, we need to invoke a certain candid and thoughtful reflection on the part of white people, who of course in some ways know themselves best; we also need to listen to what people of color perceive of white people, since in some ways they know white people best. For purposes of this brief and preliminary exploration, I will draw on material from three books for documentation of how white people are as presented in the experience of people of color. The three are *This Bridge Called my Back*,[9] which is a collection of writings by radical women of color, *Feminist Theory: From Margin to Center*,[10] by Black theorist bell hooks, and *Drylongso*,[11] which is a collection of narratives of members of what its editor calls the "core black community."[12] For white voices, I draw on my own and on those I have heard as a participant/observer of white culture, and on Minnie Bruce Pratt.

Minnie Bruce Pratt, a feminist and a white southerner, has spelled out some of what I would call the whitely way of dealing with issues of morality and change.[13] She said she had been taught to be a *judge*—a judge of responsibility and of punishment, according to an ethical system which

---

[9] Cherríe Moraga and Gloria Anzaldúa (eds.), *This Bridge Called My Back: Writing By Radical Women of Color* (Brooklyn, NY: Kitchen Table, Women of Color Press, 1981). I quote from writings by Barbara Cameron, Chrystos, doris davenport, and Mitsuye Yamada.

[10] bell hooks, *Feminist Theory: From Margin to Center* (Boston: South End Press, 1985).

[11] John Langston Gewaltney, *Drylongso: A Self-Portrait of Black America* (NY: Random House, 1983). I quote from statements by Jackson Jordan Jr., Hannah Nelson, John Oliver, Howard Roundtree, Rosa Wakefield, and Mabel Lincoln.

[12] The people speaking in *Drylongso* were responding to questions put by an interviewer. The narratives as published do not include the questions, but the people clearly were asked in some manner to say something about how they see white people or what they think white people generally are like. Most of them but not every one, prefaced or appended their comments with remarks to the effect that they did not think white people were "like that" by birth or blood, but by being brought up a certain way in certain circumstances.

[13] "Identity: Skin Blood Heart," in Elly Bulkin, Minnie Bruce Pratt, and Barbara Smith (eds.), *Yours in Struggle* (Brooklyn, NY: Long Haul Press, 1984).

countenances no rival; she had been taught to be a *preacher*—to point out wrongs and tell others what to do; she had been taught to be a *martyr*—to take all responsibility and all glory; she had been taught to be a *peacemaker*—because she could see all sides and see how it all ought to be. I too was taught something like this, growing up in a small town south of the Mason–Dixon line, in a self-consciously Christian and white family. I learned that I, and "we," knew right from wrong and had the responsibility to see to it right was done; that there were others who did not know what is right and wrong and should be advised, instructed, helped and directed by us. I was taught that *because* one knows what is right, it is morally appropriate to have and exercise what I now would call race privilege and class privilege. Not "might is right," but "right is might," as Carolyn Shafer put the point.[14] In any matter in which we did not know what is right, through youth or inexpertise of some sort, we would await the judgment or instruction of another (white) person who does.

DRYLONGSO.   White people are bolder because they think they are supposed to know everything anyhow. (p. 97)

White men look up to their leaders more than we do and they are not much good without their leaders. (p. 99)

White people don't really know how they feel about anything until they consult their leaders or a book or other things outside themselves. (p. 99)

White people are not supposed to be stupid, so they tend to think they are intelligent, no matter how stupidly they are behaving. (p. 96)

MARGIN.   The possibility [they] were not the best spokespeople for all women made [them] fear for [their] self-worth. (p. 13)

Whitely people generally consider themselves to be benevolent and good-willed, fair, honest and ethical. The judge, preacher, peacemaker, martyr, socialist, professional, moral majority, liberal, radical, conservative, working men and women—nobody admits to being prejudiced, everybody has earned every cent they ever had, doesn't take sides, doesn't hate anybody, and always votes for the person they think best qualified for the job, regardless of the candidates' race, sex, religion or national origin, maybe even regardless of their sexual preferences. The professional version of this person is always profoundly insulted by the suggestion that s/he might have permitted some personal feeling about a client to affect the quality of services rendered. S/he believes with perfect confidence that s/he is not prejudiced, not a bigot, not spiteful, jealous or rude, does not engage in favoritism or discrimination. When there is a serious and legitimate

---

[14] For more exploration of some of the meanings of this, see "Response to *Lesbian Ethics*: Why Ethics?" in Frye, *Willful Virgin*.

challenge, a negotiator has to find a resolution which enables the professional person to save face, to avoid simply agreeing that s/he made an unfair or unjust judgment, discriminated against someone or otherwise behaved badly. Whitely people have a staggering faith in their own rightness and goodness, and that of other whitely people. We are not crooks.

DRYLONGSO.   Every reasonable black person thinks that most white people do not mean him well. (p. 7)

Every reasonable black person thinks that most white people do not mean him well. (p. 7)

They figure, if nobody blows the whistle, then nothing wrong has gone down. (p. 21)

White people are very interested in seeming to be of service . . . (p. 4)

Whitefolks *can't* do right, even if there was one who wanted to . . . They are so damn greedy and cheap that it even hurts them to *try* to do right. (p. 59)

BRIDGE.   A child is trick-or-treating with her friends. At one house the woman, after realizing the child was an Indian, "quite crudely told me so, refusing to give me treats my friends had received." (p. 47)

DRYLONGSO.   I used to be a waitress, and I can still remember how white people would leave a tip and then someone at the table, generally some white woman, would take some of the money. (p. 8)

BRIDGE.   The lies, pretensions, the snobbery and cliquishness. (p. 69)

We experience white feminists and their organizations as elitist, crudely insensitive, and condescending. (p. 86)

White people are so rarely loyal. (p. 59)

Whitely people do have a sense of right and wrong, and are ethical. Their ethics is in great part an ethics of forms, procedures and due process. As Minnie Bruce Pratt said, their morality is a matter of "ought-to," not "want to" or "passionately desire to." And the "oughts" tend to factor out into propriety or good manners and abiding by the rules. Change cannot be initiated unless the moves are made in appropriate ways. The rules are often-rehearsed. I have participated in whitely women's affirming to each other that some uncomfortable disruption caused by someone objecting to some injustice or offense could have been avoided: had she brought "her" problem forth in the correct way, it could have been correctly processed. We say:

She should have brought it up in the business meeting.

She should have just taken the other woman aside and explained that the remark had offended her.

She should not have personally attacked me; she should have just told me that my behavior made her uncomfortable, and I would have stopped doing it.

She should take this through the grievance procedure.

By believing in rules, by being arbiters of rules, by understanding agency in terms of the applications of principles to particular situations, whitely people think they preserve their detachment from prejudice, bias, meanness and so on. Whitely people tend to believe that one preserves one's goodness by being principled, by acting according to rules instead of according to feeling.

DRYLONGSO. We think white people are the most unprincipled folks in the world . . . (p. 8)

White people are some writing folks! They will write! They write everything. Now they do that because they don't trust each other. Also, they are the kind of people who think that you can think about everything, about whether you are going to do, before you do that thing. Now, that's bad for them because you can't do that without wings . . . All you can do is do what you know has got to be done as right as you know how to do that thing. White people don't seem to know that. (p. 88)

. . . he keeps changing the rules . . . Now, Chahlie will rule you to death. (p. 16)

Authority seems to be central to whiteliness, as you might expect from a people who are raised to run things, or to aspire to that: belief in one's authority in matters practical, moral and intellectual exists in tension with the insecurity and hypocrisy that are essentially connected with the pretense of infallibility. This pretentiousness makes the whitely person simultaneously rude, condescending, overbearing and patronizing on the one hand, and on the other, weak, helpless, insecure and seeking validation of her or his goodness.

DRYLONGSO. White people have got to bluff it out as rulers . . . [they] are always unsure of themselves. (p. 99)

No matter what Chahlie do, he want his mama to pat him on the head and tell him how cute he is. (p. 19)

. . . [I]n a very real sense white men never grow up. (p. 100)

Hard on the outside, soft on the inside. (p. 99)

BRIDGE. Socially . . . juvenile and tasteless. (p. 99)

No responsibility to others. (p. 70)

The dogmatic belief in whitely authority and rightness is also at odds with any commitment to truth.

DRYLONGSO. They won't tell each other the truth, and the lies they tell each other sound better to them than the truth from our mouths. (p. 29)

As long as they can make someone say rough is smooth, they are happy . . . Like I told you, whitefolks don't care about what the truth is . . . It's like when you lie but so much, you don't know what the truth is. (p. 21)

You simply cannot be honest with white people. (p. 45)

BRIDGE.   White feminists have a serious problem with truth and "accountability."
            (p. 85)

And finally, whitely people make it clear to people of other races that the
last thing the latter are supposed to do is to challenge whitely people's
authority.

BRIDGE.   [W]e are expected [by white women] to move, charm or entertain, but
            not to educate in ways that are threatening to our audiences. (p. 71)

MARGIN.   Though they expected us to provide first hand accounts of black experi-
            ence, they felt it was their role to decide if these experiences were authen-
            tic. (p. 11)

Often in situations where white feminists aggressively attacked individual
black women, they saw themselves as the ones who were under attack, who
were the victims (p. 13).

DRYLONGSO. Most white people—anyways all the white people I know—are people
            you wouldn't want to explain anything to. (p. 67)

No wonder whitely people have so much trouble learning, so much trouble
receiving, understanding and acting on moral or political criticism and
demands for change. How can you be a preacher who does not know right
from wrong, a judge who is an incompetent observer, a martyr who victim-
izes others, a peace-maker who is the problem, an authority without authority, a grownup who is a child? How can someone who is supposed to be
running the world acknowledge their relative powerlessness in some matters
in any politically constructive way? Any serious moral or political challenge
to a whitely person must be a direct threat to her or his very being.

WHITELINESS AND CLASS

What I have been exploring here, and calling "whiteliness," may sound to
some like it is a character of middle class white people, or perhaps of middle
class people whatever their race; it may sound like a class phenomenon, not
a race phenomenon. Before addressing this question more deeply, I should
just register that it is my impression, just looking around at the world, that
white self-righteousness is not exclusive to the middle class. Many poor and
working class white people are perfectly confident that they are more intelligent, know more, have better judgment and are more moral than Black
people or Chicanos or Puerto Ricans, or Indians, or anyone else they view as
not-white, and believe that they would be perfectly competent to run the
country and to rule others justly and righteously if given the opportunity.

But this issue of the relation of whiteliness to class deserves further attention.

Though I think that what I am talking about *is* a phenomenon of race, I want to acknowledge a close interweaving and double-determination of manifestations and outcomes of race and of class, and to consider some of the things that give rise to the impression that what I'm calling whiteliness may really be just "middle-class-ness." One thing that has happened here is that the individual who contributed to the observations assembled in the preceding section as a "participant observer" among white people (viz., the author of this analysis) is herself a lifelong member of the middle class. The whiteliness in which she has participated and about which she can write most vividly and authentically is that of her own kin, associates, and larger social group. This might, to a certain extent, bias that section's description of whiteliness toward a middle-class version of it.

Another reason that what I am calling whiteliness might appear to be a class character rather than a race one is that even if it is not peculiar to whites of the middle classes, it is nonetheless peculiarly suitable to them: it suits them to their jobs and social roles of managing, policing, training and disciplining, legislating and administering, in a capitalist bureaucratic social order.

Another interesting point in this connection is that the definition of a dominant race tends to fasten on and project an image of a dominant group within that race as *paradigmatic* of the race.[15] The ways in which individual members of that elite group enact and manifest their racedness and dominance would constitute a sort of norm of enacting and manifesting this racedness which non-elite members of the race would generally tend to assimilate themselves to. Those ways of enacting and manifesting racedness would also carry marks of the class position of the paradigmatic elite within the race, and these marks too would appear in the enactments of race by the non-elite. In short, the ways members of the race generally enact and stylistically manifest membership in the race would tend to bear marks of the class status of the elite paradigmatic members of the race.

I do not think whiteliness is just middle-class-ness misnamed. I think of whiteliness as a way of being which extends across ethnic, cultural, and class categories and occurs in ethnic, cultural, and class varieties—varieties which may tend to blend toward a norm set by the elite groups within the race. Whatever class and ethnic variety there is among white people, though, such

---

[15] Cf. Étienne Balibar, "Paradoxes of Universality," trans. Michael Edwards, in David Theo Goldberg (ed.), *Anatomy of Racism* (Minneapolis: University of Minnesota Press, 1990), 284–5, extracted from "Racisme et nationalism," in Étienne Balibar and Immanuel Wallerstein, *Race, Nation, Classe* (Paris: Éditions La Decouverte, 1988).

niceties seem often to have no particular salience in the experience people of other races have with white people. It is very significant that the people of color from whose writings and narratives I have quoted in the preceding section often characterize the white people they talk about in part by class status, but they do not make anything of it. They do not generally indicate that class differences among white people make much difference to how people of color experience them.

Speaking of the oppression of women, Gayle Rubin noted its "endless variety and monotonous similarity."[16] There is great variety among the men of all the nationalities, races, religions and positions in various economies and polities, and women do take into account the particulars of the men they must deal with. But when our understanding of the world is conditioned by consciousness of sexism and misogyny, we see *also*, very clearly, the impressive and monotonous *lack* of variety among "masculinities." With my notion of whiteliness, I am reaching for the monotonous similarity, not the endless variety, in white folks' ways of being in the world. For various reasons, that monotonous similarity may have a middle-class cast to it, or my own perception of it may give it a middle-class cast, but I think that what I am calling "whiteliness" is a phenomenon of race. It is integral to what constructs and what is constructed by race, and only more indirectly related to class.

FEMINISM AND WHITELINESS

Being whitely, like being anything else in a sexist culture, is not the same thing in the lives of white women as it is in the lives of white men. The political significance of one's whiteliness interacts with the political significance of one's status as female or male in a male-supremacist culture. For the white men, a whitely way of being in the world is very harmonious with masculinity and their social and political situation. For white women it is, of course, all very much more complicated.

Femininity in white women is praised and encouraged but is nonetheless contemptible as weakness, dependence, feather-brainedness, vulnerability, and so on, but whiteliness in white women is unambivalently taken among white people as an appropriate enactment of a positive status. Because of this, for white women, whiteliness works more consistently than femininity does to disguise and conceal their negative value and low status as women, and at the same time to appear to compensate for it or to offset it.

Those of us who are born female and white are born into the status created

[16] "The Traffic in Women," in Rayna R. Reiter (ed.), *Toward an Anthropology of Woman* (New York: Monthly Review Press, 1975), 160.

by white men's hatred and contempt for women, but white girls aspire to Being and integrity, like anyone else. Racism translates this into an aspiration to whiteliness. The white girl learns that whiteliness is dignity and respectability; she learns that whiteliness is her aptitude for partnership with white men; she learns that partnership with white men is her salvation from the original position of Woman in patriarchy. Adopting and cultivating whiteliness as an individual character seems to put it in the woman's own power to lever herself up out of a kind of nonbeing (the status of woman in a male supremacist social order) over into a kind of Being (the status of white in white supremacist social order). But whiteliness does not save white women from the condition of *woman*. Quite the contrary. A white woman's whiteliness is deeply involved in her oppression as a woman and works against her liberation.

White women are deceived, deceive ourselves and will deceive others about ourselves, if we believe that by being whitely we can escape the fate of being the women of the white men. Being rational, righteous, and ruly (rule-abiding, and rule-enforcing) do for some of us some of the time buy a ticket to a higher level of material well-being than we might otherwise be permitted (though it is not dependable). But the reason, right, and rules are not of our own making; the white men may welcome our whiteliness as endorsement of their own values and as an expression of our loyalty to them (that is, as proof of their power over us), and because it makes us good helpmates to them. But if our whiteliness commands any respect, it is only in the sense that a woman who is chaste and obedient is called (by classic patriarchal reversal) "respectable."

It is commonly claimed that the Women's Movement in the United States, this past couple of decades, is a white women's movement. This claim is grossly disrespectful to the many feminists whom the label 'white' does not fit. But it is indeed the case that millions of white women have been drawn to and engaged in feminist action and theorizing, and this creative engagement did *not* arise from those women's being respected for their nice whitely ways by white men: it arose from the rape, battery, powerlessness, poverty or material dependence, spiritual depletion, degradation, harassment, servitude, insanity, drug addiction, botched abortions and murder of those very women, those women who are white.[17]

---

[17] Carolyn Shafer is the one who brought to my attention the fact that there is a certain contradiction in claiming *both* that this stage of the women's movement was created by and belongs to white women *and* (on the grounds of the generally better material welfare of white women, compared to women of other races in the U.S.) that white women are not all that badly off and don't really know what suffering is about. If white women were as generally comfortable, secure and healthy as they might appear to some observers, they would not have participated as they have in an enormous movement whose first and most enduring issues are bodily integrity and economic self-sufficiency.

As doris davenport put it in her analysis of white feminists' racism:

A few of us [third world women] . . . see beyond the so-called privilege of being white, and perceive white wimmin as very oppressed, and ironically, invisible . . . [I]t would seem that some white feminist could [see this] too. Instead, they cling to their myth of being privileged, powerful, and less oppressed . . . than black wimmin . . . Somewhere deep down (denied and almost killed) in the psyche of racist white feminists there is some perception of their real position: powerless, spineless, and invisible. Rather than examine it, they run from it. Rather than seek solidarity with wimmin of color, they pull rank within themselves.[18]

For many reasons it is difficult for women (of any intersection of demographic groups) to grasp the enormity, the full depth and breadth, of their oppression and of men's hatred and contempt for them. One reason is simply that the facts are so ugly and the image of that oppressed, despised and degraded woman so horrible that recognizing her as oneself seems to be accepting utter defeat. Some women, at some times, I am sure, must deny it to survive. But in the larger picture, denial (at least deep and sustained denial) of one's own oppression cuts one off from the appreciation of the oppression of others which is necessary for the connections one needs. This is what I think Cherríe Moraga is pointing out when she says:

Without an emotional, heartfelt grappling with the source of our own oppression, without naming the enemy within ourselves and outside of us, no authentic, non-hierarchical connection among oppressed groups can take place.[19]

If white women are not able to ally with women of other races in the construction of another world, we will indeed remain, defeated, in this one.

White women's whiteliness does not deliver the deliverance we were taught it would; our whiteliness interferes with our ability to form necessary connections both by inhibiting and muddling our understanding of our own oppression as women, and by making us personally obnoxious and insufferable to many other women much of the time; it also is directly opposed to our liberation because it joins and binds us to our oppressors. By our whitely ways of being we enact partnership and racial solidarity with white men, we animate a social (if not also sexual) heterosexual union with white men, we embody and express our possession by white men.

A feminism that boldly names the oppression and degraded condition of white women and recognizes white men as its primary agents and primary beneficiaries—such a feminism can make it obvious to white women that the various forms of mating and racial bonding with white men do not and will never save us from that condition. Such a feminist understanding might free

---

[18] "The Pathology of Racism: A Conversation with Third World Wimmin," in Moraga and Anzaldúa (eds.), *This Bridge Called My Back*, 89–90.
[19] *This Bridge Called My Back*, 21.

us from the awful confusion of thinking our whiteliness is dignity, and might make it possible for us to know that it is a dreadful mistake to think that our whiteliness earns us our personhood. Such knowledge can open up the possibility of practical understanding of whiteliness as a learned character (as we have already understood masculinity and femininity), a character by which we facilitate our own containment under the "protection" of white men, a character which interferes constantly and (often) conclusively with our ability to be friends with women of other races, a character by which we station ourselves as lieutenants and stenographers of white male power, a character which is not desirable in itself and neither manifests nor merits the full Being to which we aspire. A character by which, in fact, we both participate in and cover up our own defeat. We might then include among our strategies for change a practice of unlearning whiteliness, and as we proceed in this, we can only become less and less well-assimilated members of that racial group called "white." (I must state as clearly as possible that I do not claim that unbecoming whitely is the only thing white women need to do to combat racism. I have said that whiteliness is not the same thing as racism. I have no thought whatever that I am offering a panacea for the eradication of racism. I *do* think that *being* whitely interferes enormously with white women's attempts in general to be anti-racist.)

DISAFFILIATION, DECONSTRUCTION, DEMOLITION

To deconstruct a concept is to analyze it in a way which reveals its construction—both in the temporal sense of its birth and development over time and in a certain cultural and political matrix, and in the sense of its own present structure, its meaning, and its relation to other concepts. One of the most impressive aspects of such an analysis is the revelation of the "contingency" of the concept, i.e. the fact that it is only the accidental collaboration of various historical events and circumstances that brought that concept into being, and the fact that there could be a world of sense without that concept in it. The other very impressive thing about such analyses is what they reveal of the complex and intense interplay of construction of concepts and construction of concrete realities. This interplay is what I take to be that phenomenon called the "social construction of reality."

In combination, the revelation of the historical contingency of a concept and the revelation of the intricacy of interplay between concept and the concrete lived reality give rise to a strong sense that "deconstruction" of a concept simultaneously dismantles the reality in whose social construction the evolution of the concept is so closely involved. But things do not work that way. In the first place, analyzing a concept and circulating the analysis among a few interested colleagues does not make the concept go away, does not dislodge it from the matrix of concepts in the active conceptual repertoire even of those few people, much less of people in general. In the second place, even if the deconstructive analysis so drains the concept of power for those few individuals that they can no longer use it, and perhaps their participation in the social constructions of which that concept is a part becomes awkward and halting (like tying your shoelaces while thinking directly about what you are doing), it still leaves those social constructions fully intact. Once constructed and assimilated, a social construct may be a pretty sturdy thing, not very vulnerable to erosion, decay, or demolition.[20] It is one thing to "deconstruct" a concept, another to dismantle a well-established, well-entrenched social construct. For example, Foucault's revelations about the arbitrariness and coerciveness of classifications of sexualities did not put an end to queer-bashing or to the fears lesbians and gay men have of being victims of a witch-hunt.

I am interested, as I suggested earlier in this essay, in the matter of how to translate the recognition of the social-constructedness of races into some practice of the freedom these contingencies seem to promise, some way to proceed by which people can be liberated from the concrete reality of races as they are determined by racism. But the social-constructedness of race and races in the racist state has very different meanings for groups differently placed with respect to these categories. The ontological freedom of categorical reconstruction may be generic, but what is politically possible differs for those differently positioned, and not all the politically possibilities for every group are desirable. Attempts by any group to act in this ontological freedom need to be informed by understanding of how the action is related to the possibilities and needs of the others.

I have some hope that if I can manage to refuse to enact, embody, animate this category—the white race—as I am supposed to, I can free up my energies and actions from a range of disabling confinements and burdens, and align my will with the forces which eventually will dissolve or dismantle that race as such. If it is objected that it is an exercise of white privilege to dissociate myself from the white race this way, I would say that in fact this project is strictly forbidden by the rules of white solidarity and white supremacy, and is *not* one of the privileges of white power. It may also be

---

[20] My lover Carolyn was explaining what I do for a living to our coheart Keyosha, and included an account of "deconstruction." Keyosha, a welder and pipefitter in the construction trades, said that wasn't a real word and offered "demolition" as the real word for this. Carolyn then had to admit (on my behalf) that all this deconstructing did not add up to any demolition, and a made-up abstract word was probably suitable to this abstract activity.

objected that my adoption or recommendation of this strategy implies that the right thing to do, in general, for everyone, is to dissolve, dismantle, bring an end to, races; and if this indeed is the implication, it can sound very threatening to some of the people whose races are thus to be erased. This point is well-made by Franz Fanon in a response to Jean-Paul Sartre, described by Henry Louis Gates, Jr.

Reading Sartre's account of Négritude (as an antithesis preparatory to a "society without races," hence "a transition and not a conclusion"), Fanon reports "I felt I had been robbed of my last chance" . . . "Sartre, in this work, has destroyed black zeal . . ."[21]

The dynamic creative claiming of racial identities (and gender identity) that arose as devices of people's oppression has been a politically powerful and life-enhancing response of oppressed people in modern and contemporary times. For members of oppressor groups to suddenly turn around and decide to abolish races would be, it seems, genocide, not liberation. (I have a parallel unease about the project of dismantling the category of women, which some feminists seem to favor.)

But I am not suggesting that if white women should try to abandon the white race and contribute to its demolition, then women of other races should take the same approach to their racial categorization and their races. Quite the contrary. Approaches to the matter of dismantling a dominance-subordinance structure surely should be asymmetrical—they should differ according to whether one has been molded into its category of dominance or its category of subordination. My hope is that it may contribute to the demise of racism, if we upset the logical symmetry of race—if Black women, for instance, cultivate a racial identity and a distinctive (sexually egalitarian) Black community (and other women of racialized groups, likewise), while white women are undermining white racial identity and cultivating communities and agency among women along lines of affinity not defined by race. Such an approach would work toward a genuine redistribution of power.

GROWING ROOM

The experience of feminists' unlearning femininity, and our readiness to require men to unlearn masculinity shows that it is thinkable to unlearn whiteliness. If I am right about all this, then, indeed, we even know a good deal about how to do it.

---

[21] "Critical Remarks," in David Theo Goldberg (ed.), *Anatomy of Racism* (Minneapolis: University of Minnesota Press, 1990), 325.

We know that white feminists have to inform ourselves exhaustively of its politics. We know we have to avoid, or be extremely alert in, environments in which whiteliness is particularly required or rewarded (e.g., academia). We know we have to *practice* new ways of being in environments which nurture different habits of feeling, perception, and thought, and that we will have to make these environments for ourselves since the world will not offer them to us. We know that the process will be collective and that this collectivity does not mean we will blend seamlessly with the others into a colorless mass; women unlearning femininity together have not become clones of each other or of those who have been valuable models. As feminists we have learned that we have to resist the temptation to encourage femininity in other women when, in moments of exhaustion and need we longed for another's sacrificial mothering or wifing. Similarly, white women have to resist the temptation to encourage whiteliness in each other when, in moments of cowardice or insecurity, we long for the comfort of "solidarity in superiority," or when we wish someone would relieve our painful uncertainty with a timely application of judgments and rules.

Seasoned feminists (white feminists along with feminists of other races) know how to transform consciousness. The first break through is in the moment of knowing another way of being is possible. In this matter of a white woman's racedness, the possibility in question is the possibility of disengaging (on some levels, at least) one's own energies and wits from the continuing project of the social creation and maintenance of the white race, the possibility of being disloyal to that project by stopping constantly making oneself whitely. And this project should be a very attractive one to white women once we get it that it is the possibility of *not being whitely*, rather than the possibility of *being whitely*, that holds some promise of our rescuing ourselves from the degraded condition of women in white men's world.

4

DOES RACE MATTER?

PIERRE L. VAN DEN BERGHE

The facile, accepted, politically correct answer to the question in my title for the last half century of social science has been: 'only if you think it does'. A clear distinction was drawn between the discredited notion of biological race in the sense of subspecies, and the concept of social race, in the sense of the time-, place- and culture-specific association of certain behavioural, moral and intellectual traits with physical phenotypes. Biological race was asserted to be of dubious objective validity since the human species was not clearly subspeciated, and of no relevance to social scientists since there was no clear relationship between biological and social definitions of race. This simple formulation long seemed to close the book on the subject.

Having ruled out biology as a possible explanation for any behavioural variation in humans, the etiology of race and racism thus relied almost exclusively on psychological, social-structural or cultural explanations. This is not the place for a review of the literature, but racism was variously attributed to personality traits aggravated by frustrating experiences, or to rationalisations for exploitation, slavery, colonialism and so on, or to peculiarities of certain cultural traditions.[1] Those 'explanations' were not so much wrong as incomplete, *ad hoc* and situation- or culture-specific. They were, in short, proximate descriptions of specific sequences of events in particular places and times, and they had little standing as general scientific

From Pierre L. van den Berghe, 'Does Race Matter?', *Nations and Nationalism*, 1/3 (1995).

An earlier version of this article was delivered at the conference on 'Race and Nation' sponsored by the Association for the Study of Ethnicity and Nationalism at the London School of Economics and Political Science on 14 May 1993. I am thankful to the Graduate School and the Jackson School of International Studies of the University of Washington for a travel grant, and to the LSE for its hospitality in London.

[1] The literature is immense, and the following represent but a fraction of representative books from a wide range of perspectives: Allport (1954); Banton (1967, 1977, 1987, 1994); Barth (1969); Blalock (1967); Francis (1976); Fredrickson (1981); Gurr and Harff (1994); Myrdal (1994); Park (1950); Patterson (1982); Rex (1970, 1986); Rex and Mason (1986); Schermerhorn (1970); Smith (1981, 1986, 1993); Shibutani and Kwan (1965); Sowell (1981, 1983, 1994); Wagley and Harris (1958); Wilson (1973, 1978, 1987). My own *Race and Racism* (1967) is also squarely in the social science mainstream of the 1960s and 1970s.

explanations. The issue was further befuddled by the almost inevitable intrusion of a dense ideological and political fog into the arguments. Invective, self-censorship, moralism, indignation, bias and plain intellectual dishonesty frequently contaminated scholarly discourse, and indeed continue to do so. The ideological opprobrium which attaches to any serious consideration of the biological bases of human behaviour becomes especially virulent when the subject is race. The general revulsion of social scientists against racism leads them to avoid any consideration of human behavioural ecology for fear of political misuse of any knowledge gain. In short, when the subject is race, many social scientists are quite ready to espouse an obscurantist stance, and to be, in effect, social creationists about human behaviour.

In the last twenty years or so, an increasing body of findings makes it more and more difficult to accept the facile disassociation between the biological and the social.[2] Our behaviour, just as much as our anatomy, evolved by natural selection, and, therefore, can only be explained as the interaction of genotypes and environments to produce phenotypes. There *must* be a biological basis to behaviour as well as an environmental one, and the crux to understanding behaviour—human or non-human—lies in the unravelling of the complex interplay of genes and environment. This is no prescription for rigid 'biological determinism', a favourite red herring of social scientists, but it is an injunction to investigate linkages between biology and behaviour instead of dismissing the possibility of such linkages. Let me sequentially raise three questions: (1) Are there biological races in *Homo sapiens*? (2) Does the formation of *social* race have any *biological* underpinning? (3) If so, does this biological basis of social race formation explain the etiology of social race and racism in contemporary societies? To anticipate, my answer to these three questions will be respectively: no, yes and yes.

ARE THERE BIOLOGICAL RACES IN *HOMO SAPIENS*?

All taxonomies of subspecies of *Homo sapiens* have failed to establish exhaustive and mutually exclusive genetic populations in our species. In that conventional sense, there are no biological races in *Homo sapiens*. What we

---

[2] Any attempt to present this evidence would take us well beyond the subject of this article, but a sketchy beginner's bibliography would minimally include the following books: Alexander (1979, 1987); Barash (1979, 1986); Betzig (1986); Boyd and Richerson (1985); Chagnon and Irons (1979); Daly and Wilson (1983, 1988); Dawkins (1976, 1982); Lopreato (1984); Lumsden and Wilson (1981); Shepher (1983); Symons (1979); Trivers (1985); van den Berghe (1979, 1981). The bibliography in Daly and Wilson (1983) while already a decade old, contains over 700 titles.

do have, however, are large differences in the frequencies of certain alleles[3] in a great multiplicity of overlapping human groups yielding a wide range of genotypic as well as phenotypic variation on a number of traits, some behaviourally trivial, others not so.[4]

At least six important conclusions can be drawn from genetic heterozygosity[5] in humans:

1. Genes that are polymorphic (i.e., which can have one of several alternative alleles on a given locus on a chromosome) often are present in different proportions in different population groups, but they are independent of one another, and, therefore, different genes divide human populations along different lines. A frequency distribution map for the ABO blood types, for example, will not be consistent with one for genes that control skin pigmentation. Different gene clines[6] cut up populations along different lines.

2. Polymorphic genes almost always define *relative*, not absolute differences between populations. The differences in proportions are often small, and, furthermore they often follow gradual geographical clines rather than abrupt changes. For example, as one goes from the Mediterranean to the Arctic Circle in Europe, the proportion of blue eyes tends to increase, but there is no geographical line at which brown eyes stop and blue eyes begin.

3. Both phenotypic and genotypic[7] differences are almost invariably greater *within* subpopulations than *between* them. Distributions of individual measures tend to be wider than distributions of means of subgroups within the same population.

4. Genetic differences between human populations are sufficiently small that there is no evidence that interbreeding reduces fitness.[8] In fact, interbreeding is more likely to increase fitness that reduce it, especially in new environments. The bulk of the genetic evidence for humans favours the

---

[3] An allele is a specific form of a gene on a given locus (position) on a chromosome. A gene found on a given locus may have more than one variant (e.g. the gene that determines eye colour in humans), and each variant is called an allele.

[4] The field of human genetics is currently exploding, partly as a consequence of the monumental Human Genome Project, by far the largest, most concerted, best organised attempt at self-understanding in human history. A standard short introduction to human genetics is Cavalli-Sforza (1977).

[5] Heterozygosity refers to the presence of multi-allelic genes on any number of loci in the genome of individuals or populations.

[6] A cline is a gradual change in gene frequencies across the geographical range occupied by an organism.

[7] A phenotype is an observable property of an organism and can be either behavioural or anatomical. A genotype is the genetic constitution linked to an inheritable trait. Phenotype and genotype may be congruent with one another, but often are not.

[8] Fitness, in the genetic sense, refers to the contribution of a given genotype to the next generation of a population in relation to the contribution of other genotypes. The fitness of an organism is measured by its reproductive success relative to other organisms in the population.

hybrid-vigour hypothesis. Heterozygosity is the best hedge against extinction.

5. A large amount of migration and interbreeding in recent centuries between hitherto isolated populations has further reduced genetic differences between human groups and blurred geographical clines.

6. Having said all this, some of the genetic differences between both individuals and groups affect behaviour, directly or indirectly. For example, colour vision, handedness, lactose intolerance and other traits known to be under partial genetic control, differentially affect the ability of groups and individuals to use certain tools, perform certain tasks or eat certain foods. In some cases, the behavioural variation is mostly individual (handedness): in others, it is mostly sex-linked (colour vision); in others, it is partly group-linked (lactose intolerance, sickle cell anemia).

In short, no, there are no human races in the sense of well-defined subspecies, but partly genetically based behavioural differences between individuals, sexes, age groups and breeding populations have been established, and many more are likely to be discovered in the future. It is unscientific to pretend otherwise.

DO SOCIAL RACES HAVE ANY BIOLOGICAL UNDERPINNING?

At a trivial level, the answer to that question is an obvious 'yes'. A social race is *defined* as a group sharing physical (as distinguished from cultural) attributes.[9] But *must* there be such a linkage? Do physical difference between groups always lead to social differences? More generally, do physical phenotypes always matter socially? And, if so, why?

My theory, first stated a decade-and-a-half ago, is very simple.[10] All social organisms are biologically programmed to be nepotistic, i.e. to behave favourable (or 'altruistically') to others in proportion to their real or perceived degree of common ancestry.[11] Social organisms evolved to be

[9] Nearly thirty years ago, I distinguished race as 'a group that is socially defined but on the basis of physical criteria', from ethnicity which is 'socially defined but on the basis of cultural criteria' (van den Berghe 1967: 9–10). That definition is widely shared in the social science literature, e.g. Cashmore (1988), Farley (1995), Rex (1970), Sowell (1994), Wilson (1973).

[10] My main statement is contained in *The Ethnic Phenomenon* (1981), but the book was preceded by my 1978 article in *Ethnic and Racial Studies*. See also my 1986 piece in the Rex and Mason collection, *Theories of Race and Ethnic Relations*.

[11] The biological basis of nepotism has now been firmly established in hundreds of social species of both vertebrates and invertebrates. Indeed, nepotism is one of the main mechanisms of sociality in all known social organisms. See Daly and Wilson (1983); Dawkins (1976); Trivers (1985); and Wilson (1975), for a few book-length overviews of both the theoretical basis of, and the empirical evidence for, nepotism.

nepotistic because altruistic investment in unrelated organisms is biologically wasted and therefore *could* not evolve, as Darwin clearly saw well over a
century ago. The evidence, both human and non-human, for rampant nepotism is overwhelming. The bibliography on humans alone now runs into
several hundred titles. Favouring kin among humans is sometimes conscious,
sometimes unconscious, and biologically, it does not matter which. But, consciously or unconsciously, we must be able to discriminate according to
degree of biological relationship to ourselves, if our beneficence to others is
to increase our inclusive fitness.

For the most fundamental mammalian social tie, the mother-infant one, a
simple mechanism is typically present: identification and imprinting shortly
after birth by sight, sound, olfaction or a combination of these. Experimental switching of neonates has demonstrated these simple recognition
mechanisms in many mammalian species. But often, and certainly for
humans, the situation is much more complex. More than most (perhaps all)
other organisms, humans recognise and make fine gradations of kinship,
and dispense their largesse or their nastiness accordingly.[12]

Being intelligent and opportunistic animals, humans use all possible clues
of relatedness, with a preference for the ones that are reliable, quick and
cheap. Since it pays, in fitness maximisation terms, to be a fine-tuned discriminator of kinship in a wide range of situations involving hundreds or
even thousands of relationships, any readily identifiable, unfalsifiable marker
of probable common ancestry will be used. Specification of a few simple
properties of the marker itself, of the social circumstances of the individual,
and of the ecological conditions of the social encounter can lead one to
good behavioural predictions. For example, it can be predicted that, among
social mammals with heavy biparental investment in offspring, parenthood
will be 'tested' by males more than by females, because paternity is exposed
to much more uncertainty than maternity. Mothers *know* their babies are
theirs; fathers cannot be so sure, and therefore will look much more for
physical resemblance, especially for signature-like rare characteristics such
as a mole on the nose. Women concerned with paternal investment in their
offspring, on the other hand, can be expected to stress the physical resemblance of their babies to their mates more than to themselves. 'Isn't he his
father's spitting image?'

Let us now widen the focus from kinship in the narrow sense, to that form
of extended kinship we call race or ethnicity. Both racial and ethnic groups

---

[12] My 1979 book *Human Family Systems* was an attempt to reinterpret the conventional
anthropology of marriage and kinship in terms of the evolutionary biology of mating and reproduction. More extensive biological accounts of human mating and reproductive systems can be
found in Daly and Wilson (1983), and Symons (1979).

are socially defined by real or putative common descent, and the distinction between the two types of groups is merely in the relative salience of biological or cultural *markers* of membership. My contention is that, in both cases, the social concern is with common biological descent, *even when the markers are primarily cultural.*

There are three main objections to my formulation of ethnocentrism and racism as extended forms of biologically rooted nepotism.

1. The common descent of ethnic groups is often a myth, not a biological reality. Therefore, my argument is invalid. To which I reply: A myth, to be effective, has to be believed, and a myth of ethnicity will only be believed if members of an ethnic group are sufficiently alike in physical appearance and culture, and have lived together and intermarried for a sufficient period (at a minimum three or four generations) for the myth to have developed a substantial measure of biological truth. The Emperor of Japan can effectively claim to be the father of the Japanese nation in a way that Queen Victoria could never validate her claim as mother of India. Ethnicity or race cannot be invented or imagined out of nothing. It can be manipulated, used, exploited, stressed, fused or subdivided, but it must correlate with a pre-existing population bound by preferential endogamy and a common historical experience. Ethnicity is *both* primordial *and* instrumental.

2. If ethnicity and race are both rooted in the biology of nepotism, why is it that most ethnic groups stress cultural markers of membership rather than heritable physical ones? The answer here is quite simple: because most ethnic groups seek to differentiate themselves from their immediate neighbours in situations where some short-distance migration and intermarriage take place. Therefore, most ethnic groups *look* so much like their neighbours that they *must* rely on cultural markers of distinction. The proof of the biological pudding is that, where physical, genetic markers do a reliable job of differentiating between groups, they *are* used. In fact, the conditions under which racial groups do emerge are quite predictable: they appear after long-distance migration of sizeable groups across visible genetic clines: slavery, colonialism, indenture, voluntary migration, military conquest are so many examples, especially across large geographical barriers such as oceans or deserts. And racial groups can only survive as long as interbreeding remains relatively infrequent. Three or four generations of 25 per cent or more exogamy typically erode both racial and ethnic boundaries, and lead to the formation of new ethnic groups. Both race and ethnicity are *not* immutable, but their mutability is a function of exogamy over several generations.

3. If biological nepotism is extended to large groups, which, under modern conditions, often comprise millions of individuals, has not the concept been diluted to the point of meaninglessness, and reduced to a mere analogy?

Of course, the more distant the biological relationship between two individuals, the more diluted the benefits of nepotism become. Indeed, the biological model predicts that the preference is proportional to the degree of relationship. Relatedness is relative. Ego is at the core of a set of concentric circles defining declining degrees of relationship: nuclear family, extended family, lineage, clan, dialect group, subethnicity, nation. These levels of relatedness are imbedded into one another. Circumstances and interests will determine the level of solidarity which is activated at any given place and time, in a classical fission-and-fusion scheme such as British anthropologists have described for African segmentary lineage societies. But the principle of nepotism, however diluted, suffuses all levels, and there is no *a priori* reason why nepotistic discrimination should stop at any particular point, unless it can be displaced by a superior strategy of fitness maximisation. Brothers *do* murder each other, but not gratuitously and not as easily as strangers. When they do, there is usually a big payoff, such as a throne, an inheritance or a harem. To affirm the operation of nepotism, even in large groups, is not to deny the operation of other principles of cooperative behaviour (such as class solidarity), or fitness maximisation (such as deceit and treachery). The size of the group dilutes the effectiveness of solidary behaviour whatever the base of solidarity, but not more so for ethnic groups than for other social groups such as classes, corporations, clubs or army units, and perhaps even *less*. Ethnic and racial groups can be politically mobilised, even on a huge scale, with greater ease and rapidity, than other social groups, especially under external threat from an enemy who is himself defined in ethnic or racial terms.[13]

DOES THE BIOLOGY OF SOCIAL RACE EXPLAIN THE ETIOLOGY OF RACISM IN CONTEMPORARY SOCIETIES?

Better put, does my theory of the biological genesis of social race predict and explain contemporary racism better than competing theories? The answer, I think, is yes, not because it supplants other theories, but because it complements them at a higher level of theoretical generality. It provides a predictive scheme of when, where and why racism can be expected to wax and wane, on a world-wide basis, without having to invoke any special cultural, psychological or historical causes.

Racism, defined as discriminatory behaviour based on inherited physical appearance, can be expected to arise whenever variance in inherited physical

---

[13] I engage my critics at greater length in van den Berghe (1987).

appearance is greater *between* groups than *within* groups. This is a relatively rare event, except when two or more hitherto isolated populations migrate across large geographical obstacles. It is even rarer for intergroup variance to *remain* greater than intragroup variance for long, because contact generally brings about interbreeding. So, racism will appear after long-distance migration, but will only persist as long as social barriers to exogamy prevent intermixture, and thus the recreation of a more typical situation where intragroup genetic diversity exceeds intergroup differences. Racism cannot be sustained long if racial membership cuts across the microkinship of the family. Precisely *because* social race is an extension of the principle of nepotism, it cannot long survive interbreeding. Even the rare exceptions, such as relations between white and brown Afrikaners in South Africa, confirm the rule: the 'races' only survived the interbreeding of slavery because of the reimposition of an endogamous caste system after slavery.

Having specified the objective conditions which lead to the rise and the decline of racism, does it follow that racism will inevitably accompany these conditions? Unfortunately, I think the answer is, again, affirmative. Why? Because we are not only selfish maximisers, but intelligently opportunistic ones. Sociality is synonymous with discrimination. Only a fool behaves indiscriminately towards all. We must constantly decide when to be nice or nasty, trusting or suspicious. In the last analysis, we have only two bases for doing so: reciprocity and nepotism. Reciprocity is tricky, unstable, open to cheating, and often dependent on costly information or past experience. It only works between *individuals* who *know* one another well and who expect to *continue* interacting in a mutually beneficial way without deceit or coercion. For nepotism to yield its genetic reward, the only requirement is correct assessment of relatedness. It works best if the cost of that assessment is minimised, that is, if the assessment is reliable, easy and fast.

These simple principles enable us to predict which markers of group membership will be used under what conditions. Where neighbouring groups look alike physically, cultural markers do a better job of assessing group membership than genetic traits. Not all cultural markers are equally good. The *beret* may be a symbol of Basque ethnicity, but it is not reliable. Indeed, it has been usurped by millions of Frenchmen, Spaniards and others. Military uniforms are used for ready recognition of friend and foe from a distance, but they too are open to cheating. That is why costume is frequently a *symbol* of ethnicity, but never a *test* of it. Facial scarification is much more reliable than dress because it cannot easily be undone. Cultural markers of ethnicity which permanently change physical appearance are common: circumcision, tooth filing, tattoos and so on. Language is also a common marker. Even though it is strictly cultural, it is learned early in life and difficult to 'fake' in adulthood, because few people retain the ability to mimic the phonetics of a language learned after puberty. Until recent migrations, someone who spoke your dialect without a foreign accent was most likely to be a native fellow ethnic. But the drawback of language as a marker is that, though reliable, it is fairly slow. You have to ask questions before you shoot, and sometimes you cannot afford the delay.

Let us turn to biological markers. They only work between groups that look quite different. Between Zulus and Boers in South Africa, they worked with complete efficacy: you could shoot at 500 meters and never make a mistake. Norwegians and Swedes, on the other hand, could never be racists towards one another, even if they wanted to. They have to listen to one another before they can tell who is who. The Nazis tried to be racists with Jews but their biological markers worked with perhaps 10 to 15 per cent reliability. In practice, they used mostly cultural markers: circumcision, synagogue attendance, the Star of David, denunciations, surnames, etc. Nazi racial theory ludicrously outstripped the reality of genetic differences. They actually had a very difficult time picking out Jews from their Gentile neighbours, especially in the assimilated Jewry of Western Europe.

Physical markers, in short, only 'work' under the limiting and rare condition of genetic heterozygosity being greater between groups than within. If such a condition is present, however, does it follow that racism is inevitable? Not by a long shot, because most genotypic differences are phenotypically hidden by recessivity or are so cryptic as to be useless for purposes of quick and easy group membership ascription. Blood types, for instance, must be tested by antigens from a blood sample, and the test is slow and costly enough that soldiers in combat are *culturally* tagged (or, in the case of the SS in Nazi Germany, even tattooed) for their genotype.

In practice, then, only a few inherited phenotypes are culturally utilised to form social races, and they are chosen, not for their behavioural significance, but simply for their *visibility*. Skin pigmentation is the most widespread because it is the most visible from the greatest distance and subject to only a limited range of environmental variation. (The genetics of skin colour are still poorly understood and are probably under the control of four to six different loci.) Facial features (notably eye, lip and nose shape), hair texture and physical stature are also used where they are diacritic. For example, in Rwanda and Burndi where the Hutu-Tutsi-Twa distinction is marked by large group differences in height, stature is widely used as a criterion. It works better in Rwanda where a rigid caste system hindered interbreeding, than in the more fluid social structure of Burundi, but, in both cases, the physical distinction was used as a quick and dirty basis for sweeping genocidal action (against the Tutsi in Rwanda, against the Hutu in Burundi). A particularly gruesome atrocity against the Tutsi in Rwanda was to amputate them at the knee to cut them down to size.

This double condition of greater inter- than intragroup heterozygosity *and* high phenotypic visibility predicts when, where and why physical phenotypes get transmuted into social races. The reason why racism became the great pandemic of the nineteenth and twentieth centuries was simply the sudden acceleration of large-scale, long-distance migration across wide genetic clines. The social consequences were enormous and noxious because racial distinctions are peculiarly invidious and immutable, well beyond cultural distinctions. All group distinctions between in-group and out-group are designed to exclude potential competitors from competition for scarce resources, but racial distinctions are especially nasty because they are almost totally beyond individual control. You can learn a language, convert to a religion, get circumcised or scarified, adopt a dress style, but you cannot become tall or white.

In practice, social race is always a social stigma for the subordinate group, and all attempts to pretend otherwise have been singularly unsuccessful. Pragmatically, in terms of policy, it means that institutionalisation of racial categories, however innocuous or even benevolent it may appear, is frequently noxious in its consequences. I am thinking of such measures as racial questions on censuses, race-based affirmative action and similar measures, which have generally had the effect of reinforcing stigmatised racial distinctions.[14]

CONCLUSION

Let us now close the circle on the relationship between genes and behaviour. I have repeatedly stressed that behaviour, human and non-human alike, can only be understood within an evolutionary framework that gives equal weight to genes and environment acting in concert. For humans, culture is, of course, a large part of the social environment of our species. A genetic effect on behaviour can be direct and result from natural selection, even when it leads to a reduction in fitness (e.g. overeating when food is available, leading to obesity in affluent societies, but providing valuable caloric storage in unstable hunting and gathering economies characterised by cycles of feast

---

[14] Among the many critics of race-based measures to redress past racial inequities, see D'Souza (1992); Glaser (1975); Herrnstein and Murray (1994); and Sowell (1983). Most of these critics have come from the political right, but I have argued for more radical 'affirmative action' based on socio-economic criteria, not race or ethnicity.

and famine; or the craving for drugs which mimic the pleasurable sensations of natural enzymes).

The case of racism, however, is different. The linkage between genes and behaviour is clear, but it did not evolve by natural selection. Racism is conceivably a case of culture 'hijacking' genes which were selected for different ends (e.g. skin pigmentation regulating exposure to sun radiation in different latitudes), and making them serve a totally different social agenda. Yet, that social agenda itself had an underlying biological programme: fitness maximisation through nepotism. Finally, but not less importantly, that social agenda itself had an enormous feedback effect on the life chances of different groups, on their reproductive success, and therefore, in the final analysis, on the course of human evolution itself.

We are only in the infancy of understanding the co-evolution of genes and culture, but understand it we must if we are to make sense of our behaviour, especially behaviour, such as racism, which does not *seem* to make sense.

REFERENCES

Alexander, Richard D. (1979), *Darwinism and Human Affairs* (Seattle: University of Washington Press).
—— (1987), *The Biology of Moral Systems* (New York: Aldine de Gruyter).
Allport, Gordon W. (1954), *The Nature of Prejudice* (Cambridge, Mass.: Addison-Wesley).
Banton, Michael (1967), *Race Relations* (London: Tavistock)
—— (1977), *The Ides of Race* (London: Tavistock).
—— (1987), *Racial Theories* (Cambridge: Cambridge University Press).
—— (1994), *Discrimination* (Philadelphia: Open University Press).
Barash, David (1979), *The Whisperings Within* (New York: Harper & Row).
—— (1986), *The Hare and the Tortoise* (New York: Viking Penguin).
Barth, Fredrick (ed.) (1969), *Ethnic Groups and Boundaries* (Boston: Little, Brown).
Betzig, L. L. (1986), *Despotism and Differential Reproduction* (Hawthorne, NY: Aldine).
Blalock, Hubert M. (1967), *Toward a Theory of Minority Group Relations* (New York: Wiley).
Boyd, Robert, and Richerson, Peter J. (1985), *Culture and the Evolutionary Process* (Chicago: University of Chicago Press).
Cashmore, E. Ellis (1988), *Dictionary of Race and Ethnic Relations* (London: Routledge).
Cavalli-Sforza, L. L. (1977), *Elements of Human Genetics* (Menlo Park, Calif.: W. A. Benjamin).
Chagnon, Napoleon, and Irons, William (eds.) (1979), *Evolutionary Biology and Human Social Behaviour* (North Scituate, Mass.: Duxbury).
Daly, Martin, and Wilson, Margo (1983), *Sex, Evolution and Behavior* (Belmont, Calif.: Wadsworth).
—— (1988), *Homicide* (New York: Aldine de Gruyte).

Dawkins, Richard (1976), *The Selfish Gene* (Oxford: Oxford University Press).
—— (1982), *The Extended Phenotype* (San Francisco: W. H. Freeman).
D'Souza, Dinesh (1992), *Illiberal Education* (New York: Vintage Books).
Farley, John E. (1995), *Majority–Minority Relations* (Englewood Cliffs, NJ: Prentice Hall).
Francis, E. K. (1976), *Interethnic Relations* (New York: Elsevier).
Fredrickson, George M. (1981), *White Supremacy* (Oxford: Oxford University Press).
Glazer, Nathan (1975), *Affirmative Discrimination* (New York: Basic Books).
Gurr, Ted R., and Harff, Barbara (1994), *Ethnic Conflicts in World Politics* (Boulder, Colo.: Westview Press).
Herrnstein, Richard J., and Murray, Charles (1994), *The Bell Curve* (New York: Free Press).
Horowitz, Donald L. (1985), *Ethnic Groups in Conflict* (Berkeley: University of California Press).
Keyes, Charles F. (ed.) (1981), *Ethnic Change* (Seattle: University of Washington Press).
Kuper, Leo, and Smith, M. G. (1965), *Pluralism in Africa* (Berkeley: University of California Press).
Lieberson, Stanley (1980), *A Piece of the Pie* (Berkeley: University of California Press).
Lopreato, Joseph (1984), *Human Nature and Biocultural Evolution* (Boston: Allen & Unwin).
Lumsden, Charles J., and Wilson, E. O. (1981), *Genes, Mind and Culture* (Cambridge, Mass.: Harvard University Press).
Mason, Philip (1971), *Patterns of Dominance* (London: Oxford University Press).
Miles, Robert (1989), *Racism* (London: Routledge).
Myrdal, Gunnar (1944), *An American Dilemma* (New York: Harper).
Park, Robert Ezra (1950), *Race and Culture* (New York: Free Press).
Patterson, Orlando (1982), *Slavery and Social Death* (Cambridge, Mass.: Harvard University Press).
Rex, John (1970), *Race Relations in Sociological Theory* (New York: Schocken Books).
—— (1986), *Race and Ethnicity* (Philadelphia: Open University Press).
Rex, John, and Mason, David (eds.) (1986), *Theories of Race and Ethnic Relations* (Cambridge: Cambridge University Press).
Schermerhorn, Richard A. (1970), *Comparative Ethnic Relations* (New York: Random House).
Shepher, Joseph (1983), *Incest: A Biosocial View* (New York: Academic Press).
Shibutani, R., and Kwan, K. M. (1965), *Ethnic Stratification* (New York: Macmillan).
Smith, Anthony D. (1981), *The Ethnic Revival* (Cambridge: Cambridge University Press).
—— (1986), *The Ethnic Origin of Nations* (Oxford: Blackwell).
—— (1993), *National Identity* (Reno: University of Nevada Press).
Sowell, Thomas (1981), *Ethnic America, A History* (New York: Basic Books).
—— (1983), *The Economics and Politics of Race* (New York: William Morrow).
—— (1994), *Race and Culture: A World View* (New York: Basic Books).
Symons, Donald (1979), *The Evolution of Human Sexuality* (Oxford: Oxford University Press).
Trivers, R. L. (1985), *Social Evolution* (Menlo Park, CA: Benjamin Cummings).
van den Berghe, Pierre L. (1967), *Race and Racism* (New York: Wiley).

—— (1978), 'Race and ethnicity: a sociobiological debate', *Ethnic and Racial Studies* 1, 4: 401–11.

—— (1979), *Human Family Systems* (New York: Elsevier).

—— (1981), *The Ethnic Phenomenon* (New York: Elsevier).

—— (1986), 'Ethnicity and the sociobiology debate' in John Rex and David Mason (eds.), *Theories of Race and Ethnic Relations* (Cambridge: Cambridge University Press).

Wagley, Charles and Harris, Marvin (1958), *Minorities in the New World* (New York: Columbia University Press).

Wilson, E. O. (1975), *Sociobiology: The New Synthesis* (Cambridge, MA: Harvard University Press).

Wilson, William J. (1973), *Power, Racism and Privilege* (New York Macmillan).

—— (1978), *The Declinging significance of Race* (Chicago: University of Chicago Press).

—— (1987), *The Truly Disadvantaged* (Chicago: University of Chicago Press).

5

HOW HERITABILITY MISLEADS ABOUT RACE

NED BLOCK

1. INTRODUCTION

The Bell Curve's main argument for black genetic inferiority in IQ (Herrnstein and Murray 1994) depends for its persuasive force on conceptual confusions that have been tacitly accepted to some degree even by many of the book's sharpest critics. The book contains two lines of thought. One, which I will accept for present purposes, is: that IQ tests substantially measure "general intelligence", that IQ is socially important and that IQ is 60% heritable within whites. (I'll explain heritability below.) The second main line of thought—which I will be contesting—is the argument for genetic inferiority of American blacks. Before I get to their argument for this conclusion, I want to be clear about the conclusion itself. Murray has recently complained about misinterpretation in an article entitled "The real bell curve" (Murray 1994). He grumbles about critics, such as Stephen Jay Gould, who read the book as saying that racial differences in IQ are mostly genetic. He quotes from the book:

> If the reader is now convinced that either the genetic or environmental explanations have won out to the exclusion of the other, we have not done a sufficiently good job of presenting one side or the other. It seems highly likely to us that both genes and environment have something to do with racial differences. What might the mix be? We are resolutely agnostic on that issue; as far as we can determine, the evidence does not yet justify an estimate. (*Bell*, 311)

But the *resolute agnosticism* we see here is on the issue of which is *more* responsible for the low IQs of blacks, bad environment or genetic inferiority. What they are very much *not* agnostic about is that *part* of the IQ difference between blacks and whites is genetic, and (given their way of thinking about the matter) to the extent that *any* of this difference is genetic, blacks are genetically inferior.[1]

From Ned Block, 'How Heritability Misleads about Race', *Cognition*, 56 (1995).

[1] I am going along with a dangerous way of thinking here. As I will point out in the last section of this paper, this talk of part of an IQ difference is deeply problematic.

What is their argument? It proceeds from two facts: the first is the 60% heritability of IQ within whites and the second is the average 15-point IQ difference between whites and blacks.[2] A crude version of their argument goes like this. If IQ were completely genetic in whites and completely genetic in blacks, the IQ difference between whites and blacks would have to be completely genetic; but given that IQ is *largely* genetic (at least in whites), surely it is very probable that the IQ difference is partly genetic in origin. There is more to their argument than that; they raise issues about the pattern and the magnitude of the differences that I will get to later.

Herrnstein's and Murray's argument depends on thinking of the 15-point IQ difference as divisible into a genetic chunk and an environmental chunk. This way of thinking dictates the following three alternatives:

(1) Extreme environmentalism: Blacks are genetically on a par with whites, so all of the IQ gap is environmental.
(2) Extreme geneticism: Blacks are environmentally on a par with whites, so all of the IQ gap is genetic.
(3) The reasonable view: Blacks are worse off *both* genetically and environmentally: some of the gap is genetic, some environmental.

Option 1, extreme environmentalism, is thought to be excluded by the 60% heritability of IQ. Option 2, an equally extreme geneticism, is excluded by well-known environmental effects on IQ together with differences between black and white environments that are acknowledged by Herrnstein and Murray. So we are left with option 3, which on this way of putting the matter is the reasonable view—and it postulates *some black genetic inferiority*. But their way of putting the alternatives blots out a *crucial possibility*, namely that blacks are *much* worse off than whites environmentally and actually *better* off genetically. Allowing this option, we get a different set of alternatives: *genetically, blacks are worse off—or better off—or equal to whites.*

The idea of the missing alternative arises from the possibility that genetic IQ differences and actual measured IQ differences go in *opposite directions.* Even if you think that races are likely to differ genetically in IQ, the question remains of the *direction* of the genetic difference. In this scenario, black environments for the development of IQ are on the average sufficiently worse than white environments as to lower average black IQ *more* than 15 points. I don't say that this is *likely*, but I do say it is *possible* and its possibility is important. What you consider as *possible* affects what you think is an

---

[2] This is a widely accepted figure, but Nisbett (1995) gives some plausible arguments that the gap has narrowed. As he says, no study in the last two decades indicates a narrowing of the gap by less than 4.2 points. I am using Herrnstein's and Murray's figure, putting aside disagreements about the data so as to concentrate on the conceptual issues.

extremist position. The critics of Herrnstein and Murray have tended to trip over this possibility.

For example, in a *New York Times* op. ed. critique that describes *The Bell Curve* as "bogus" and "nothing but a racial epithet" (Herbert 1994), Bob Herbert insists that "the overwhelming consensus of experts in the field is that environmental conditions account for most of the disparity when the test results of large groups are compared". In effect, he uses known environmental effects on IQ to argue for a *low degree of genetic inferiority* in blacks. Even Stephen Jay Gould (in an otherwise excellent article in *The New Yorker*: Gould 1994) missteps here. Apparently accepting *The Bell Curve*'s way of conceiving of the issue, he complains that Herrnstein and Murray wrongly minimize the large environmental malleability of IQ. He says that they turn "every straw on their side into an oak, while mentioning but downplaying the strong circumstantial case for substantial malleability and little average genetic difference". Gould does little to guard against the natural interpretation of "little average genetic difference" in the context of discussion of *The Bell Curve* as *little average genetic inferiority of blacks*. Jim Holt's critique in the *New York Times* (Holt 1994) asks "How then do we account for the sizable gap in measured IQ?" and then goes on to emphasize prenatal explanations of most of "the racial gap". (Low birth weight is almost three times as common in black babies as in white babies—see Lieberman 1995.) But if one accepts the Herrnstein and Murray framework, it is a *stretch* to appeal to prenatal differences to reduce the size of the genetic inferiority all the way to zero. A somewhat different version of the same fallacy is a misplaced agnosticism. *US News and World Report* (Leo 1994), attempting to be neutral and unbiased, says of the IQ gap that "we don't know . . . how much is genetic, or how much environmental factors are responsible". That is, we don't know *how genetically inferior* blacks are. The *expectation*, that is, is that blacks are genetically inferior to *some* extent, but lacking information, we don't know *how much*. A number of the critics in the *New Republic* (31 October 1994) in turn, wonder about the size of the "genetic component of the black–white difference" (p. 10), thereby buying into the same way of thinking. Again, we can see that what you take as possible affects what you take as actual. As with the passage from Herrnstein and Murray that I quoted earlier, agnosticism ends up as agnosticism about just how genetically inferior blacks are.

If you accept *The Bell Curve*'s way of putting the options, evidence for environmental effects at best shows that the amount of genetic inferiority is little or nothing, and so the critics find themselves up against the wall of zero genetic difference. Given the set of alternatives provided by Herrnstein and Murray, the idea that the environmental difference between blacks and whites is big enough to account for 15 IQ points looks like an *extremist* hypothesis. But given the *actual* alternatives, that blacks are genetically on a par with whites, or worse off, or better off, zero genetic difference doesn't seem extremist at all.

But isn't the idea of black genetic superiority in IQ desperate and pathetic, merely a logical possibility? Roses are red, violets are blue. Color is genetic, so the color difference is genetic. Is there any real possibility that the genetic color difference is the opposite of the observed one? Toe number is genetic in sloths and in humans, and humans are observed to have five toes whereas sloths (that is, diurnal sloths) are observed to have three toes. Is there any real possiblity that the genetic toe difference between humans and sloths goes in the *opposite direction* from the observed toe number gap? Well, there is a very remote possibility that the three-toed sloth evolved six toes, but the three toes we observe are a result of a thalidomide-like chemical which has polluted their food during the years in which we have observed them.[3] But this possibility is only worth mentioning as an example of something *extremely unlikely*. And that leads to a principle that underlies all of Herrnstein's and Murray's thinking on race even though it is never articulated. Recall that the crude form of their argument is that if IQ were completely genetic in blacks and whites, then the black–white difference would have to be completely genetic as well; so given that IQ is 60% heritable within whites, very likely the black–white difference is partly genetic. The underlying principle is: *if a characteristic is largely genetic and there is an observed difference between two groups, then there is "highly likely"* (I allude to their term from the passage quoted in the first paragraph of this article) *to be a genetic difference between the two groups that goes in the same direction as the observed difference.* So given the substantial heritability of IQ, if East Asians are superior in measured IQ, then they are highly likely to be *genetically* superior; and if blacks are inferior in measured IQ, then they are highly likely to be *genetically* inferior in IQ.

Here is a roadmap to the rest of this article. The principle just mentioned is right on one sense of "genetic" and wrong on another. However, the sense in which it is *wrong* is the one that employs the figure of 60% heritability. In the sense in which the principle is right, IQ is not genetic. In the next section, I will explain the ambiguity in "genetic". Then I will explain why the

---

[3] Roses are red, violets are blue, color is genetic, so the color difference is genetic. This sounds like a tautology, but it isn't. Perhaps the easiest way to see that is to think of what it is for color to be genetic to implicitly involve appeal to the idea of a normal environment. If the environment is not normal (as in the thalidomide example) the conclusion may be false even when the premises are true.

principle just mentioned is wrong in the sense of "genetic" that really counts for their argument: *heritability*.

2. HERITABILITY VERSUS GENETIC DETERMINATION

The key to part of the fallacy of *The Bell Curve* is the distinction between two concepts: *genetic determination* and *heritability*. The concept of inheritance which allows us to speak of number of toes as genetic is the ordinary commonsensical idea of *genetic determination*. But the *scientific concept*, on which all Herrnstein's and Murray's data rely, is *heritability* and not *genetic determination*. Heritability has to do with what causes *differences* in the value of a characteristic, whereas genetic determination is a matter of what causes a particular value of the characteristic *itself*. Heritability is *defined* as a fraction: the ratio of *genetically caused* variation to *total* variation (environmental and genetic). *Genetic determination*, by contrast, is an informal and intuitive notion that has no quantitative definition (for reasons that I will explain later). It depends on the idea of a normal environment. A characteristic could be said to be genetically determined if it is coded in and caused by the genes and bound to develop in a normal environment. Genetic determination in a single person makes sense: my brown hair color is genetically determined. By contrast, heritability makes sense only relative to a population in which individuals differ from one another. You can't ask "What's the heritability of *my* IQ?"

We can get a handle on the difference by noticing that the number of fingers on a human hand or toes on a human foot is genetically determined: the genes code for five fingers and toes in almost everyone, and five fingers and toes develop in any normal environment. However, interestingly, the *heritability* of number of fingers and toes in humans is almost certainly very *low*. What's going on? If you look at cases of unusual numbers of fingers and toes, you find that most of the variation is environmentally caused, often by problems in fetal development. For example, when pregnant women took thalidomide some years ago, many babies had fewer than five fingers and toes. And if we look at numbers of fingers and toes in adults, we find many missing digits as a result of accidents. Genetic coding for six toes is rare in humans, though apparently not in cats. Heritability, you will recall, is a fraction: the ratio of genetically produced variation to total variation (total variation = variation due to all causes, genetic and environmental). If the genetically caused variation is small compared to the environmentally caused variation, then the heritability is low, even when the characteristic in question is genetically determined. So toe number is genetically determined but nonetheless low in heritability.[4]

Conversely, a characteristic can be *highly heritable* even if it is *not genetically determined*. Some years ago when only women wore earrings, the heritability of having an earring was high because differences in whether a person had an earring were "due" to a chromosomal difference, XX versus XY. Now that earrings are less gender-specific, the heritability of having an earring has no doubt decreased. But neither then nor now was having earrings genetically determined in anything like the manner of having five fingers. The heritability literature is full of high measured heritabilities for characteristics whose genetic determination is doubtful. For example, the same methodology that yields 60% heritability for IQ also yields 50% heritability of academic performance and 40% heritability of occupational status (Plomin *et al.* 1990: 393). More significantly, a child's *environment* is often a heritable characteristic *of the child*. If degree of musical talent is highly heritable and if variation in the number of music lessons a child gets depends on variation in musical talent, then the number of music lessons that a child gets may be heritable too, despite not being genetically determined. This is not an idle speculation. Recent studies of heritabilities of various features of children's environments show substantial heritabilities for many environmental features, for example, the "warmth" of the parents' behavior toward the child. Even number of hours of TV watched and number and variety of a child's toys show some heritability (Plomin and Bergeman 1991; see also Scarr and McCartney 1983). If this seems unintelligible, think of it this way: variation in these environmental properties is in part due to variation in heritable characteristics of the child, and so the environmental characteristics themselves are heritable. People who read *The Bell Curve* often suppose that a heritable characteristic is one that is passed down in the genes, but this identification is importantly flawed. The number and variety of a child's toys is not passed down in the genes. Heritability is a matter of the causation of differences, not what is "passed down".

By contrast, a characteristic is genetically determined if the characteristic itself—not differences in it—is caused by the genes. A characteristic can be genetically determined even if there is no genetically caused variation. Number of heads in humans is genetically determined even if there is no genetic variation in number of heads at all. I've mentioned physical characteristics, but there are many mental features that are genetically determined too. For example, if you put a pacifier of one of a number of shapes (e.g.,

---

[4] I am using a very liberal notion of genetic determination. On a finer grained notion, one might want to distinguish between "the genes code for X" and "the genes code for Y, but the result, given normal development, is X".

spherical or cubical or knobbly) in a newborn baby's mouth, the baby will look preferentially at a picture of the same shape. So something about the coordination between vision and feel is very likely genetically determined. But there may be little or no genetic variation in such mental characteristics, so they are genetically determined without, perhaps, being heritable.[5]

What "genetic determination" comes to depends heavily on what we count as a "normal" environment, as Kitcher (1996) notes. For example, we could think of a normal environment as one that is usual, or, rather differently, as one that allows people to thrive, even if it is uncommon. On the former notion, phenylketonuria (PKU) was once a genetically determined form of mental retardation. But on the latter, given that retardation can be avoided by a diet that is low in phenylalanine, it is not genetically determined. This example illustrates something that we will return to in the last section of the paper, namely that (as Kitcher notes), increasing knowledge often leads us to move from thinking of the genes determining X to the genes determining the tendency to develop X in certain environments. We now tend to think of what is genetically determined in the case of PKU not as retardation but rather as an inability to metabolize phenylalanine that can cause retardation if there is phenylalanine in the diet.

So what is genetically determined depends on what we count as a normal environment. But not so for heritability. It depends *not at all* on what environments are normal, but only on the balance of genetic and environmental differences in the causation of differences in the characteristic. We will return to this point later.

I have given examples of traits that are genetically determined but not heritable and, conversely, of traits that are heritable but not genetically determined. But the reader may be suspicious: what relevance do these weird examples have to the case of IQ? Maybe there is a range of normal cases, of which IQ is an example, for which the oddities that I've pointed to are just irrelevant?

Not so! In fact IQ is a great example of a trait that is highly heritable but not genetically determined. Recall that what makes toe number genetically determined is that having five toes is coded in and caused by the genes so as to develop in any normal environment. By contrast, IQ is enormously affected by *normal environmental variation* (and in ways that are not well understood). As Herrnstein and Murray concede, children from very low socio-economic status (SES) backgrounds who are adopted into high-SES

---

[5] What psychologists usually have in mind when they say that aspects of syntax are genetically determined (Chomsky 1975; Fodor *et al.* 1974) or that aspects of the concept of an object are genetically determined is that the source of the *information* that people end up with is the genes. This model does not apply to IQ.

backgrounds have IQs that are dramatically higher than their parents. The point is underscored by what Herrnstein and Murray call the Flynn effect: IQ has been rising about 3 points every 10 years worldwide. Since World War II, IQ in many countries has gone up 15 points, about the same as the gap separating blacks and whites in the USA. As Herrnstein and Murray note, no one knows why IQ has been rising. In some countries, the rise has been especially dramatic. For example, average IQ in Holland rose 21 points between 1952 and 1982 (Flynn, 1987a). In a species in which toe number reacted in this way with environment (e.g. a centipede-like creature which grows legs depending on how much it eats) I doubt that we would think of number of toes as genetically determined. The dramatic rises in IQ in Holland (and other countries) is a very significant fact which I will return to.

I said that these dramatic increases in IQ show that IQ is enormously affected by normal environmental variation. But this claim may appear to be in conflict with the following fact: that the correlations among adopted children in the same family are very small, near zero, by late adolescence (see Plomin and Daniels 1987; Plomin and Bergeman 1991). Doesn't that show that normal environmental variation has no effect? This is the opposite of the correct conclusion from these data. The low correlations among adopted children show that normal variation of the sort that exists even *within* families has a large effect. It should also be noted that the bottom of the socio-economic distribution is scanted in these data because this segment of the population is not favored by adoption agencies. Unfortunately, this segment of the population is all too normal. So what does not appear to have much of an effect on IQ (after adolescence) is variation in SES within the middle range and, in addition, number of books in the home, cultural activities of the parents and the like—in short, the sort of thing that psychologists measure about shared family environment.

One very important conclusion from both the Flynn data and the low correlation data just mentioned is that no one understands very much about how environmental variation differentially affects IQ. The cause of the large increases in Holland is simply unknown. Even Herrnstein and Murray concede that of the environmental variation in IQ "relatively little can be traced to the shared environments created by families. It is, rather, a set of environmental influences *mostly unknown at present*, that are experienced by individuals as individuals" (*Bell*, 108; emphasis added).

The crucial factor that has enabled the research that Herrnstein and Murray report to exist at all is the fact that one can measure the heritability of a characteristic without even having much of an idea of what the characteristic is. We needn't know what IQ tests measure in order to calculate the heritability of IQ—we need only be able to measure IQ, whatever it is, in various circumstances. Suppose you could place two pairs of genetically identical (one-egg) twin human fetuses in randomly chosen wombs, and then give them IQ tests after they had grown up in different environments (including different prenatal environments). Suppose twins Sally and Sarah were reared in very different environments—one impoverished, the other rich in intellectual stimulation—yet both ended up with the same high IQ; and twins Fred and Ted, also reared in very different environments, both had the same low IQ. That would indicate that the genetic differences in the population were contributing more to IQ variation than the environmental differences. So heritability of IQ would be high. The opposite procedure would be rearing genetically unrelated individuals in the same environment (note: same environment, not similar family, since that appears not to provide the same environment). To the extent that heritability is high, unrelated children reared in the same environment should not resemble one another any more than people chosen at random from the population. To the extent that heritability is low, their IQs should be highly correlated.

A common method for measuring heritability relies on comparisons of the correlations of IQ among one-egg twins raised by their biological parents compared with two-egg twins raised by their biological parents. Suppose you give IQ tests to two children and they get the same score. One has a one-egg (identical) twin, the other has a two-egg (fraternal) twin. Suppose that you can predict the score of the one-egg twin reliably, but that your prediction of the score of the two-egg twin is much less reliable. This would be an indication of high heritability of IQ because one-egg twins share all their genes whereas two-egg twins normally share half their genes.

Heritability studies of IQ *within white* populations in the USA and northern Europe have tended to yield moderately high heritabilities. Herrnstein and Murray's 60% is a reasonable figure. But it is important to note that no one would do one of these heritability studies in a mixed black/white population. Why not? If you place a pair of black one-egg twins in different environments "at random", you automatically fail to randomize environments, because the black twins will bring part of their environment with them; they are both black and will be treated as black.

I mentioned that heritability, unlike genetic determination can be very different in different populations. For example, the heritability of IQ could be decreased if half the population were chosen at random to receive IQ lowering brain damage. The quantity a/b gets smaller if b *gets larger*. By damaging the brains of some people, you make the environmentally caused variation larger. Another example that illustrates the same point: suppose we could make a million clones of Newt Gingrich, raising them in very different environments so there would be some variation in IQ, all environmentally caused. The quantity a/b is zero if a is zero. So heritability in that population would be zero because the ratio of genetic variation to total variation is zero if the genetic variation is zero. To take a real example, the heritability of IQ increases throughout childhood into adulthood. Plomin (1990a) gives heritability figures of under 20% in infancy, about 30% in childhood, 50% in adolescence and a bit higher in adult life. (Plomin notes that the results are not a consequence of increasing reliability of IQ tests.) Studies of older twins in Sweden (Pedersen et al. 1992) report an 80% heritability figure for adults by age 50 as compared to a 50% heritability for children. One possible reason for the rise in heritability is that although the genetic variation remains the same, environmental variation decreases with age. Children have very different environments; some parents don't speak to their children, others are ever verbally probing and jousting. Adults in industrialized countries, by contrast, are to a greater degree immersed in the same culture (e.g., the same TV programs). With more uniform environments, the heritability goes up.[6] Heritability can even be different in men and women. Suppose, for example, that variation in hair length in women depends on heritable variation in the hair itself, whereas hair length in men depends on non-heritable variation in conventions in peer groups. Then hair length would have higher heritability in women than in men. (I'll give an example later on which there are actual data.) I hope these points remove the temptation (exhibited in *The Bell Curve*) to think of the heritability of IQ as a constant (like the speed of light). Heritability is a population statistic just like birth rate or number of TVs and can be expected to change with changing circumstances. There is no reason to expect the heritability of IQ in India to be close to the heritability of IQ in Korea.

These issues are pathetically misunderstood by Murray, as shown by a recent CNN interview reported in *The New Republic* (Wright 1995). Murray declared "When I—when we—say 60 percent heritability, it's not 60 percent of the variation. It is 60 percent of the IQ in any given person." Later, he repeated that for the average person "60 percent of the intelligence comes from heredity" and added that this was true of the "human species", missing the points made above that heritability makes no sense for an individual and that heritability statistics are population-relative. In a letter to the editor that complains about being quoted out of context (Murray 1995), Murray quotes more of what he had said, namely: " . . . your IQ may have been determined overwhelmingly by genes or it may have been—yours personally—or overwhelmingly by environment. That can vary a lot from individual to

---

[6] Another possibility mentioned by Scarr and McCartney (1983) is that older children and adults make their own environments to a larger extent than younger children do.

individual. In the human species as a whole, you have a large genetic component." Though Murray embarrasses himself, *The Bell Curve* itself does not make these crude mistakes. Herrnstein, the late co-author, was a professional on these topics. But part of the upshot of this essay is that the book's main argument depends for some of its persuasive force on a more subtle conflation of heritability and genetic determination. And Murray's confusion serves to underscore just how difficult these concepts can be even for someone so numerate as Murray.

Again, the critics of the book are often confused on this topic. A recent op. ed. critique of Herrnstein and Murray in the *New York Times* (Hofer 1994) describes the basic thesis of the book as the claim that "genes, rather than experience, primarily determine the development of the complex sets of behaviors that underlie general intelligence". The article goes on to describe the book as linking "inherited intelligence" with race, and as drawing unwarranted conclusions about "genetic influences on general intelligence". Throughout the article, the language of genetic determination is substituted for the language of heritability. No wonder the article ends up conceding "the small differences in IQ between races and other genetically distinct groups that Mr. Murray and Professor Herrnstein set forth in endless detail".

What's the upshot of the distinction between genetic determination and heritability[7] for the argument of *The Bell Curve*? Let's go back to the sloth example: toe number is genetic in sloths and in humans; there is a difference in toe number (three versus five); so the toe number difference is genetic. This is a good argument: it strains the imagination to suppose that the genetic toe difference between sloths and humans goes in the opposite direction from the actual observed toe difference. The idea that our genes code for two toes despite the five toes we see at the beach is ludicrous. So in this sense the Herrnstein and Murray argument works for the concept of *genetic determination*. But the data on genes and IQ *do not* concern genetic determination, but rather *heritability*.

Is IQ genetically determined as well as heritable? No! As I already pointed out, IQ is very reactive to changes in environments in the *normal* range.

---

[7] The distinction between genetic determination and heritability might be challenged as follows: whenever a characteristic is genetically determined but not highly heritable, we can always increase its heritability by expanding the relevant population. Thus, number of digits has low heritability in people, but high heritability in the population that includes both people and animals that have different numbers of digits. (This line of thought appears in Sober 1993: 190.) Briefly, there are two problems with this reasoning. First, there is no guarantee that there will be other species that differ in the required way. To appeal to merely *possible* species would be a mistake, since *everything* is heritable relative to *some* range of possible species. Second, this reply does nothing to counter the cases of characteristics that are heritable but not genetically determined.

Recall the example of the large rise in Holland. Surely both 1952 and 1982 count as *normal*! (Of course it is one thing for IQ to be plastic to environmental changes and quite another thing for the changes to be ones that we know how to *manipulate*; in fact, as Herrnstein and Murray note, no known environmental intervention short of adoption changes IQ very much.) Further, the claim that IQ is genetically determined, is not the kind of quantitative claim on which Herrnstein and Murray would want to base their claims about genes and race.

Where are we? Here is an outline of the argument so far:

(1) The basic Herrnstein and Murray argument says: IQ is largely genetic in whites; there is a 15 point black/white difference; so part of the difference is probably genetic.
(2) "Genetic" is ambiguous.
(3) In the sense of *genetic determination*, IQ is not genetic in whites or anyone else, and in any case the issue is not quantitative.
(4) In the sense of *heritable*, IQ is largely genetic (among whites in the USA at least). But, I will argue below, in this sense of "genetic", the argument does not work.

I said at the outset that the confusion between genetic determination and heritability is partially responsible for the persuasive force of Herrnstein and Murray's argument. But even when this confusion is cleared up, their argument can appear very persuasive. In what follows, I will be leaving behind the issues just discussed about the distinction between genetic determination and heritability. I will be focusing on the logic of the argument from heritability to racial genetic differences. The upshot will be that the logic of the argument is flawed and that heritability is an uninteresting and misleading statistic.

3. HERITABILITY AND RACE DIFFERENCES

Arthur Jensen's 1969 article in the *Harvard Educational Review* started off the current controversy by arguing from heritability within whites to genetic differences between whites and blacks. In 1970, Richard Lewontin gave a graphic example that illustrates why this is a mistake (Fig. 1). Suppose you buy a bag of ordinary seed corn from a hardware store. This is ordinary genetically variegated (not cloned) corn. You grow one handful of it in a carefully controlled environment in which the seeds get uniform illumination and uniform nutrient solution. The corn plants will vary in height and since the environment is uniform, the heritability of height will be 100%. Now

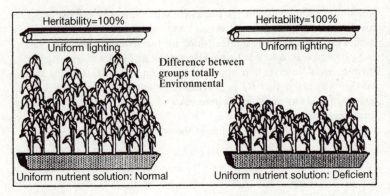

Fig. 1. Heritability can be high within each of two groups even though the difference between the groups is entirely environmental

take another handful of corn from the same bag which you grow in a similarly uniform environment but with a uniformly poor nutrient solution. The plants will vary in height again but all will be stunted. The heritability of height in both groups is 100%, but the difference in height between the groups is entirely environmentally caused. So heritability can be *total* within groups even if there is no genetic difference between groups.

The application to race is obvious: heritability is high within whites. But high heritability within groups licenses no conclusion about differences between groups.[8]

So we see that high heritability within groups does not dictate any genetic difference between groups. Nor does high heritability within groups dictate the *direction* of any genetic difference between groups. The stunted corn could have been genetically taller, with the genetic advantage outweighed by the environmental deprivation.

In reply to Lewontin's critique, Jensen focused on a principle very much like the one that underlies Herrnstein and Murray's reasoning. He said:

---

[8] Herrnstein and Murray mention Lewontin's point, but they do so in a way that distorts its crucial features. They leave out the 100% heritability within groups. In their version of the example, two handfuls of "genetically identical seed corn" are planted, one in Iowa and the other in the Mojave Desert (*Bell*, 298). So the heritabilities within the groups are zero (or undefined if all the corn in the Mojave dies). Also, their statement of the point conflates genetic determination with heritability. They say "That a trait is *genetically transmitted in individuals* [emphasis added] does not mean that group differences in that trait are also genetic in origin" (p. 298). However, the effect of Herrnstein and Murray having mentioned Lewontin's point, even in a distorted way, is that the critics have ignored it. And the effect of that is that the audience doesn't know about it.

The real question is not whether a heritability estimate, by its mathematical logic, can prove the existence of a genetic difference between the two groups, but whether there is any probabilistic connection between the magnitude of the heritability and the magnitude of group differences. Given two populations (A and B) whose means on a particular characteristic differ by x amount, and given the heritability (h_A^2 and h_B^2) of the characteristic in each of the two populations, the probability that the two populations differ from one another genotypically as well as phenotypically is some monotonically increasing function of the magnitudes of h_A^2 and h_B^2, (Jensen 1970: 104)

This argument has been repeated many times, by Jensen and others.[9]

Now if we knew nothing at all about two groups, *except* that they differed by 15 points in IQ and that IQ has some heritability in both, and we had to *guess* the causes, for all I've said so far, it would make sense to guess that the lower scoring group was disadvantaged *both* genetically and environmentally. (In the last section of the paper I'll show that even this weak principle is wrong.) However, the principle has no application to the *actual* racial question because we know *more* than nothing: we know that the environment can have huge effect on IQ (e.g., the Flynn effect of 3 points per decade and the 21-point increase in Holland) and that blacks are environmentally disadvantaged in a way that has been shown to count. But without being able to *measure* the effect of being treated as subnormal and the effect of a legacy of slavery and discrimination from the past, how do we know whether its average effect is sufficient to lower black IQ 15 points, or less than that—or *more* than that? Given the social importance of this issue, *guessing* is not appropriate.

I said that if we knew nothing except that there is a difference between two groups in a characteristic and that the characteristic has some heritability in both groups, we could guess that the lower group was disadvantaged both genetically and environmentally. Of course the reasoning is equally good for what Plomin, DeFries and McClearn call "environmentality", the "converse" of heritability (i.e., the proportion of variation due to environmental differences in the population). The danger of such guess-work in the absence of an evaluation of the relative environments is illustrated by gender and height. Women are shorter than men and height has some heritability and some "environmentality" in both groups. But the guess that women are deprived in environmental variables that affect height would be wrong. And

---

[9] The latest incarnation is an article in the *Wall Street Journal* (Arvey *et al.* 1994) by 52 behavior geneticists and psychometricians which is intended to correct misinformation in the debate about *The Bell Curve*. They mention the high heritability of IQ within whites and they add: "The reasons that blacks differ among themselves in intelligence appear to be basically the same as those for why whites (or Asians or Hispanics) differ among themselves. Both environment and genetic heredity are involved." And they hint at a conclusion much like that of Jensen and of Herrnstein and Murray about a probable black genetic deficiency. Herrnstein and Murray, however, are more cautious in not making claims about heritability within blacks.

an evaluation of these environmental variables would save us from a wrong guess here.

It is worth emphasizing the solidity of the data about the large increases in IQ in Holland. The 21-point increase reported by Flynn is based on comprehensive testing of all Dutch 18-year-olds who pass a medical exam (and there has been no change in the pass rate). The test used is Raven's Progressive Matrices, a widely respected "nonverbal test that is an especially good measure of *g*" (*Bell*, 273). Even Richard Lynn, the arch-Jensenist who is the source of much of *The Bell Curve*'s data on race, concedes this point. He says "The magnitude of the increase has generally been found to be about three IQ points per decade, making fifteen points over a fifty year period. There have, however, been some larger gains among 18-year-old conscripts in The Netherlands and Belgium amounting to seven IQ points per decade." Lynn also mentions that similar results have been found in France (Lynn 1992: 382). Herrnstein and Murray concede that "In some countries, the upward drift since World War II has been as much as a point a year for some spans of years" (p. 308). In an area where the facts are often contested, it is notable that this set of facts seems to be accepted by both sides.

Another fact that is widely accepted by all sides is that when it comes to specific identified genes and their products (e.g., genes for blood types) only about 7% of all human genetic variation lies between the major races of Africa, Asia, Europe and Oceania (Lewontin 1982). About 85% of this genetic variation is within ethnic groups, and about 8% is between ethnic groups within a single race (e.g., between Spaniards and Italians).

Herrnstein and Murray have heard appeals to the legacy of slavery and discrimination. They have a response, and their response forms part of their argument that I have not yet mentioned. They appeal to the pattern and the magnitude of racial differences. First, the pattern. They remind us that the black/white IQ difference is smallest at the lowest socio-economic levels (see Fig. 2), and this leads them to ask:

Why, if the B/W difference is entirely environmental, should the advantage of the "white" environment compared to the "black" be greater among the better-off and better-educated blacks and whites? We have not been able to think of a plausible reason. An appeal to the effects of racism to explain ethnic differences also requires explaining why environments poisoned by discrimination and racism for some other groups—against the Chinese or the Jews in some regions of America, for example—have left them with higher scores than the national average (*Bell*, p. 299).

But these facts are actually not hard to understand. Blacks and whites are to some extent separate cultural groups, and there is no reason to think that a measure like SES means the same thing for every culture. Herrnstein and Murray mention the work of John Ogbu, an anthropologist who has

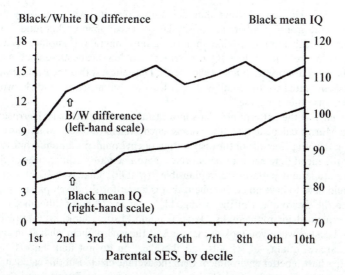

Fig. 2. The difference between average black and white IQ is smallest for the lowest 30% of SES. (Adapted from *Bell*, 288.)

distinguished a number of types of oppressed minorities (Ogbu, 1986). A key category is that of "caste-like" minorities who are regarded by themselves and others as inferior, and who, if they are immigrants, are not voluntary immigrants. This category includes the Harijans in India, the Buraku and Koreans in Japan and the Maori in New Zealand. He distinguishes them from groups like Chinese and Jews who are voluntary immigrants and have a culture of self respect. If higher-SES blacks still are to some extent part of a caste-like minority then they will be at an environmental disadvantage relative to higher-SES whites. But low-status blacks and whites are more likely to share a caste background. Note in Fig. 2 that for the bottom 30% in SES, blacks and whites are more similar in IQ than for the top 70%. As Henry Louis Gates points out (Gates 1994), affirmative action has had the effect of quadrupling the size of the black middle class since 1967. Most middle class blacks have arrived in the middle classes relatively recently, many of them under less than ideal conditions for the development of self respect. It would be surprising if children of these newly middle-class blacks were to have fully escaped their caste background in so short a time.

Ogbu notes that where IQ tests have been given "the children of these castelike minorities score about 10–15 points . . . lower than dominant group children". He notes further that differences remain "when minority and dominant group members are of similar socioeconomic background". But when "members of a castelike minority group emigrate to another society, the twin problem of low IQ test scores and low academic achievement appears to disappear" (Ogbu 1986: 32–3). Data suggest that the Buraku who have emigrated to this country do "at least as well at school and the work place" as other Japanese.[10]

That was the pattern: now let's move to the magnitude issue. Herrnstein and Murray calculate that "the *average* environment of blacks would have to be at the 6th percentile of the distribution of environments among whites . . . for the racial differences to be entirely environmental . . . differences of this magnitude and pattern are implausible" (p. 299). That is, 94% of whites would have to have an environment that is better for the development of IQ than the environment of the average black—if the 15-point difference is to be explained environmentally. Herrnstein and Murray think this is implausible because when you look at measures of the environment such as income of parents, quality of schools and the like, you do not find that 94% of whites have a better environment than the average black. But this calculation ignores the effect of being in Ogbu's category of a caste-like minority. Compare the Dutch 18-year-olds of 1982 with their fathers' cohort, the 18-year-olds of 1952. The difference is entirely environmental despite the probable substantial heritability within each group. Using the same procedures as Herrnstein and Murray, Flynn calculates that 99% of the 1982 group had to have a better environment for the development of IQ than the average member of the 1952 group (Flynn 1987b). Given differences of this magnitude among people of a uniform culture who are separated by only a single generation, is it really so implausible that 94% of whites have an environment better than a black at the 50th percentile?[11]

Let me sum up the argument of this section:

(1) If we knew nothing at all about two groups *except* that they differed by 15 points in IQ and that IQ is moderately heritable in both, then, for all I've said so far, we could guess that the lower scoring group was disadvantaged both genetically and environmentally.

---

[10] In a personal communication, Ogbu tells me that it is difficult to get data on Buraku immigrants to the USA partly because there are not very many of them and partly because no one wants to be identified as a Buraku. One of the studies he cites in Ogbu (1986) was actually published under a pseudonym.

[11] Herrnstein and Murray have a number of other independent arguments for black genetic inferiority, some of which are directly relevant to the point about caste-like minorities. In particular, they claim that the IQ of blacks in African countries in which they are not an oppressed caste is lower than that of American blacks. I am not impressed with the data that they provide. See Kamin (1995) on this topic.

(2) We know that IQ has risen 3 points per decade in very many industrialized countries since World War II (the Flynn effect) and that in some countries IQ has risen 7 points per decade for three decades or more. These large changes in IQ (equal to or larger than the black/white IQ gap) cannot be due to any genetic change.

(3) We know that only 7% of identified human genetic variation is within races.

(4) It appears that when members of caste-like minorities emigrate, the IQ gap narrows or disappears.

Conclusion: environmental differences, including the sort that affect blacks in the USA, are known to have large effects on IQ. We have no way at present of quantifying this effect. So we should draw no conclusion about the probability of any black genetic IQ advantage or disadvantage.

4. INDIRECT HERITABILITY

Earlier I said that genetic determination is not quantitative. Now I will explain why. Genetic determination is a species of causation. And causation is context-relative, as John Stuart Mill taught us.

To see this, imagine that a man is shot in the chest and dies. What caused his death? Of course he was shot, but, in addition, many other parts of the causal net—both conditions and events—were part of the mechanism by which the death was produced, e.g. bullet-permeable clothes, the intentions of the assassin, or (going further back in time) the invention of gunpowder. We do not usually think of such factors as causes, but in some contexts we do. You can cause someone's death by replacing some of the kevlar in his bullet-proof vest with cotton when you know he will be targeted by a sharp-shooter who aims for the heart.

The *entire* causal net—the totality of factors that influence an event—is an objective matter, but which *parts* of the net count as "the cause" or even "a cause" are dependent on context. Notice that this context-relativity of what counts as a cause is no mere verbal matter. It really counts in ethics, law and politics. If you kill someone by replacing the kevlar in his vest with cotton, you can be convicted of murder. The bullet permeability of his vest caused his death. To quantify causation, to ascribe $X\%$ of the causation to the bullet and $Y\%$ to the bullet permeability of his vest, would require some way of standardizing contexts and interests, and then the notion would not be very useful for other contexts and interests.

But wait! Heritability is a causal notion too! It is the ratio of variation *caused by* genetic differences to total variation. So doesn't the same point apply to heritability? Why is heritability quantifiable? The answer is that the actual methods for measuring heritability involve the *tacit acceptance* of a uniform policy as to what will count as a cause and what will not that has nothing to do with our ordinary socially important ideas of causation and is often violently in conflict with them.

An example (Jencks *et al.* 1972) will help to make this point. Consider a culture in which red-haired children are beaten over the head regularly, but all other children are treated well. This effect will increase the heritability of IQ because red-haired identical twins will tend to resemble one another in IQ (because they will both have low IQs) no matter what the social class of the family in which they are raised. The effect of a red-hair gene on red hair is a "direct" genetic effect because the gene affects the color via an internal biochemical process. By contrast, a gene affects a characteristic *indirectly* by producing a direct effect which interacts with the environment so as to affect the characteristic (see Fig. 3). In the hypothetical example, the red-hair genes affect IQ indirectly. In the case of IQ, no one has any idea how to separate out direct from indirect genetic effects because no one has much of an idea how genes and environment affect IQ. For that reason, we don't know whether or to what extent the roughly 60% heritability of IQ found in white populations is *indirect heritability* as opposed to direct heritability. (I coined the term "indirect heritability" many years ago (Block and Dworkin 1974),

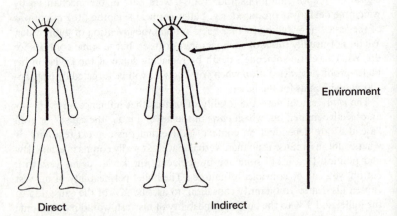

Fig. 3. A gene affects IQ directly via an internal biochemical process. A gene affects IQ indirectly by having a direct effect on something else (hair) which interacts with the environment so as to affect IQ

but it is now sometimes called reactive heritability (Tooby and Cosmides 1990).)

As I mentioned, we typically think of some but not other events or conditions in a causal chain as causes. The methodology used to measure heritability counts differences in characteristics as caused by genetic differences if there is a genetic difference, even if there is *also an environmental difference*, thus distorting the ways in which we normally think about causation. For instance, the heritability methodology focuses on the difference between the red-hair genes and genes for other hair colors, not on the fact that red-haired children—unlike blond children—are beaten.

Recall that earlier I said that wearing earrings used to be highly heritable because differences were "due" to the XY/XX difference. I put "scare quotes" around "due" because it is a by-product of the methodology for measuring heritability to adopt a tacit convention that *genes are taken to dominate environment*. Variation in ear-rings was as much a social matter as a genetic matter, but it still counted as highly heritable. If there is a genetic difference in the causal chains that lead to different characteristics, the difference counts as genetically caused even if the environmental differences are just as important. If we adopted the opposite convention, the convention that any environmental difference in two causal chains shows that the difference counts as environmentally caused, then we could not use current methodology for measuring heritability, because we have no general method of detecting indirect genetic effects using current techniques. Heritabilities using the two different conventions would be radically different if there are substantial indirect genetic effects.

Recall the examples mentioned earlier about the *measured heritabilities* of such quantities as number of hours of watching TV. No one should suppose that there is variation in genes for watching TV; this is a matter of indirect effects. Here is a good example of the never-never land of indirect heritability. A recent questionnaire study showed large heritabilities for many surprising "environmental" variables. (The method used was comparisons of one-egg and two-egg twins in non-adoptive environments. The more similar one egg twins are to one another compared to how similar two egg twins are to one another, the higher the heritability.) The twins were asked to indicate "things you have done during the past year". For "baby sat" the heritabilities were 35% for males and 47% for females. For "had your back rubbed", heritabilities were 92% for males and 21% for females (Schöne-mann and Schönemann 1991, 1994). How could heritability be different for males and females? Suppose (just for illustration) that male babysitters are chosen on the basis of weight and female babysitters are chosen on the basis of height. Height is more highly heritable than weight, so the indirect pathway would explain the difference. The result is *intelligible*, but it does show that heritability is a *strange* statistic.

Consider the fact that no one would do a heritability study on a mixed black/white population. I mentioned earlier that if you place a pair of black one-egg twins in different homes, you automatically fail to randomize environments, because the black twins will bring part of their environment with them; they are both black and will be treated as black. This is an indirect genetic effect *par excellence*. Implicitly, everyone in this field recognizes that, yet more subtle possibilities of indirect effects are typically ignored.

Recall that heritability is defined as a fraction: variation due to genetic differences divided by total variation. The measure of variation that is always used (though alternatives are available) is a statistical quantity known as variance. One factor that raises variance is a positive correlation between genetic and environmental variables. Consider, for example, a phenomenon of double advantage and double disadvantage (Jencks *et al.* 1972). Suppose that children whose genes give them an advantage in musical talent tend to have parents who provide them with an environment conducive to developing that talent, music lessons, concerts, a great CD collection, musical discussion over dinner, etc. Suppose further that other children who have a genetic disadvantage also have an environment that stultifies their musical talents. Hence there will be a correlation between genes and environment that will move children towards the extremes of the distribution, increasing the variance in musical skills. Variance due to gene/environment correlation (gene/environment "covariance") should not be counted in the genetic component of the variance, and there are a variety of methods of separating out such variance. It is common in behavior genetics to distinguish among a number of different types of covariance (Loehlin and DeFries 1987; Plomin *et al.* 1977; Plomin 1990*a*). The kind just mentioned in which parents provide genes for musical talent and an environment that develops it is called "passive" covariance because it doesn't depend on what the child does. Reactive covariance is a matter of the environment reacting to the child's qualities, as when a school gives extra music classes to musically talented children. Active covariance is a matter of the child creating a gene–environment correlation, as when a musically talented child practices musical themes in the imagination or pays attention to the musical environment. Passive covariance can be controlled in heritability calculations by attention to adoption studies in which the double-advantage/double-disadvantage does not exist. But reactive and active covariance cannot be measured without specific hypotheses about how the environment affects IQ. And it is just *a fact about IQ that little is known* about how the environment affects it. So reactive and active covariance is on the whole beyond the reach of the empirical methods of our era's "behavior genetics", for those methods do not include an understanding of what IQ *is* (e.g., whether it is information-processing capacity) or how the environment affects it.

Perhaps you think that my claim that no one understands very much about how the environment affects IQ would be hotly contested by behavior geneticists who agree with Herrnstein and Murray. *I doubt it!* Recall that earlier I mentioned that most of the environmental variation that affects IQ variation (in whites) is *within* families rather than *between* families. I mentioned the low correlations of adopted children raised in the same families. And I quoted Herrnstein and Murray agreeing that, of the environmental variation in IQ, "relatively little can be traced to the shared environments created by families. It is, rather, a set of environmental influences, *mostly unknown at present*, that are experienced by individuals as individuals." (*Bell*, 108; emphasis added.) Recall also that Herrnstein and Murray concede that no one has explained the Flynn effect.

The points about covariance just made assume that there are genes *for IQ* and that these genes may affect the environment so as to produce effects on IQ that are correlated with the ones that the genes themselves produce. But to think of the issue this way is to very seriously underestimate its significance. For as the red-hair example illustrates, indirect genetic effects needn't work through anything that should be thought of as "IQ genes".

Since we don't know much about how variation in environment differentially affects IQ, we can only guess about how variation in genes differentially affects IQ indirectly, via the environment. Suppose, for example, that a child's perceived attractiveness and self confidence strongly affect how adults interact with children in a way that largely accounts for the variation in IQ. Scarr and McCartney (1983), for example, say "It is quite likely that smiley, active babies receive more social stimulation than sober, passive infants. In the intellectual area, cooperative, attentive preschoolers receive more pleasant instructional interactions from the adults around them than uncooperative distractible children [p. 427]. ... The social psychology literature on attractiveness ... would seem to support our view that some personal characteristics evoke differential responses" (p. 433). Of course, adults could give some children more attention than others without making a difference to the children's IQs. That is, differential response on the part of adults does not show differential effect on IQ. But it could be so.

Suppose further that personal attractiveness and self confidence are highly heritable. Then we would have an indirect effect *par excellence*, and such an effect could, for all we know, largely account for the heritability of IQ. Without an understanding of how the environment affects IQ, we simply have no way of determining how much of the variance in IQ is indirect genetic variance of this sort. Of course, if we knew that some specific adult behavior that is triggered by some specific heritable property of children was responsible for a large component of IQ variation, then we could measure that behavior. But there is no theory of intelligence or IQ that would allow us to have any synoptic grip on such factors. The point is underscored by the possibility that the differences in environment might be partly *internal* to the child's interaction with stimuli rather than a matter of differences in the stimuli themselves. As Scarr and McCartney (1983) note, "The toddler who has 'caught on' to the idea that things have names and who demands the names for everything is experiencing a fundamentally different verbal environment from what she experienced before, even though her parents talked to her extensively in infancy" (p. 425).

This point is often (at least partially) acknowledged by behavior geneticists. For example, Plomin *et al.* (1977: 321) say: "Because it is not possible to measure all aspects of the environment (including everybody and everything) that might correlate with childrens' genotypes, it will probably never be possible to assess completely the effects of active and reactive genotype-environment correlations."

The upshot is that there may be a large component of heritability due to indirect genetic effects, including (but not limited to) gene–environment correlation, that is outside the boundaries of what can be measured given the mainly atheoretical approach that is available today. Where does the "gene–environment covariance" show up in heritability calculations? Answer: active and reactive effects that we don't know how to measure inevitably are included in the genetic component. This is often regarded by behavior geneticists as perfectly OK. In an often quoted passage, Roberts (1967) says:

The genotype may influence the phenotype either by means of biochemical or other processes, labelled for convenience as "development", or by means of influencing the animal's choice of environment. But this second pathway, just as much as the first, is a genetic one; formally it matters not one whit whether the effects of the genes are mediated through the external environment or directly through, say, the ribosomes. (p. 218)

Jensen (1973) notes "Generally, CovGE [i.e., gene–environment covariance] is included in h^2 [heritability] . . . either on the assumption that the covariance is due to the genotype and/or because the particular method of estimating h^2 does not permit separation of V_G [genetic variance] and CovGE" (p. 369). Indeed, Jensen argues that "much if not most, of this effect should be included in the genetic variance, because, in part, r_{GE} [the correlation of genes and environment] is a result of the genotype's selective utilization of the environment" (p. 54). In practice, if researchers were actually to identify an "un-meritocratic" effect such as the red-hair indirect effect mentioned earlier, they would no doubt ignore Roberts' advice, counting the variance produced by the effect as covariance rather than genetic variance. Of course, we have *no idea* how much of the 60% of the variance in IQ that is said to be genetic is of this sort. So in actual practice, covariance due to indirect effects that people actually know how to measure—at least if it is flagrantly non-meritocratic—is not counted in the heritability. But other indirect effects are counted as genetic. So what counts as genetic variance (inflating heritability) is a matter of *value judgements* and a matter of what effects we actually know about. Surely this makes heritability a lousy scientific concept.

In effect, the field has adopted as an axiom that *heritability of IQ can be measured by current methods*. Without this assumption, the right conclusion would be that since we cannot separate indirect genetic effects (including certain kinds of gene/environment covariance) from pure genetic variance, no heritability estimate can be made. Why does the field adopt this axiom? I cannot help thinking that part of the explanation is that behavior genetics is a young field (see Plomin 1990*a*) struggling for acceptance and funding, and heritability is a flag that attracts attention to it.

Let us return to the speculation mentioned above that the 60% heritability of IQ (within whites) is entirely indirect and due to differential treatment of children on the basis of heritable characteristics. Then the direct heritability of IQ would be zero and we would have no reason to think that anything that could be called genes *for* IQ (e.g., genes for information-processing capacity) vary in the white population, and no reason to look for such differences to explain the 15-point difference between blacks and whites.

Indeed, we would have reason to look for differences in the ways adults interact with children to explain the black–white IQ difference. So indirect heritability suggests an environmental hypothesis about the measured black–white IQ difference, maybe one that could be the object of social policy. Are there reasons to expect indirect genetic effects in the black-white difference? I mentioned the obvious example of genes for skin color above. But there may be less obvious indirect effects as well. I mentioned earlier that there are many more low birth weight black babies than white babies. Nothing known appears to rule out a genetic explanation (Lieberman 1995). If blacks are more likely to have genes for low birth weight babies, perhaps the effect could be neutralized by diet or by drug intervention in pregnancy.

Certainly, no one should think of genes for low birth weight as "IQ genes".[12]

Let us return to the topic of the last section, the issue of whether heritability within groups yields any probability judgement about the genetic differences between groups. I commented that (for all I'd said so far) if we knew nothing at all about two groups *except* that they differed by 15 points in IQ and that IQ is heritable in both, and we had to *guess* the causes, it would make sense to guess that the lower scoring group was disadvantaged *both* genetically and environmentally. But the points I've just made about indirect heritability show that any such guess would be misguided. The reasoning behind the guess assumed that the heritability of IQ within whites reflected differences in IQ caused by differences in *IQ genes*. But what the points about indirect heritability show is that we don't know whether *any* of the variation within whites is due to variation in IQ genes. If we have no real grip on what kinds of causal mechanisms result in the 60% heritability within whites, we can have no confidence in any extrapolation to blacks. Here is a very closely related point: the Jensen–Herrnstein–Murray reasoning assumed that there was a well-defined space of alternative genotypes for IQ that vary within whites and that can be used to apportion probabilities. Any reasoning about probability in the absence of data requires some way of dividing the possibilities into equi-probable alternatives. But what the direct/indirect distinction reveals is that the well-behaved space of IQ genotypes that would be required for such reasoning cannot be assumed to exist.

Let's call a person's genome (his total set of genes) genetically inferior with respect to IQ if that genome yields low IQ in any normal environment. But what is to count as a normal environment? In the example discussed earlier, genes for red hair yield low IQ within environments that are normal in the environment of the hypothetical society, but in environments that we would consider normal, the red-hair genes are irrelevant to IQ. What if the heritabilities observed for IQ are a result of indirect effects that can be changed by changing social practice? Then phrases like "genetically inferior in IQ" and "genetic disadvantage in IQ" will only apply to genomes such as that of Down's syndrome that yield low IQ no matter what the social practices.

Another consequence of the point about indirect heritability is to cast doubt on Herrnstein and Murray's ideas about genetic social stratification

---

[12] This is an oddball case but I still count it as an an indirect genetic effect. The mother's genes produce a direct effect on her reproductive system that has an additional effect on the environment of the baby. It should be noted that the direct/indirect distinction, as with any distinction involving causation, is itself context-relative. All direct genetic effects involve the environment in some way (if the environment had been different in the appropriate way the effect would have been different) so in some contexts such environmental dependencies can make the effect indirect.

within whites based on IQ. If the 60% heritability does not reflect IQ genes, then there is no reason to suppose that social classes differ at all in IQ genes. Herrnstein and Murray worry about pollution of the gene pool by immigrants and by large numbers of children of low-IQ parents. But if the heritability of IQ is mainly indirect, their emphasis on genes is misdirected. If we lived in a culture that damages the brains of red-haired children, should we complain about genetic pollution when large numbers of red-haired immigrants arrived? No, we should try to change the social practices that deprive those with certain genes of an equal chance.[13]

5. GENETIC BUCKET THEORY

Though IQ is not genetically determined, something close to it might be said to be genetically determined: namely *potential IQ*. The genes, it might be said, determine the size of the mental bucket and then the environment fills the bucket to one level or another. (Herrnstein and Murray are far from alone in talking this way. Vernon 1969, for example, introduced the term "intelligence A" for the size of the bucket.)

To see what is wrong with this idea, and also to see why heritability is much less relevant to social policy than many have supposed, we need the concept of a *norm of reaction*. Suppose that of the many plants growing on a mountain, some do well at high altitudes but poorly at low altitudes, and others are exactly the opposite. We could graph the situation as in Fig. 4.

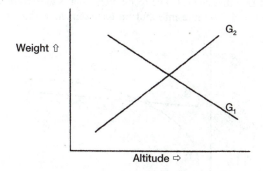

Fig. 4. One genetic type of plant does better at high altitudes, another does better at low altitudes

---

[13] The ideas in this section were developed from my contribution to Block and Dworkin (1974, sect. 1) in lectures that I gave in the 1970s, and in part stimulated by Jencks *et al.* (1972). While this paper was in press I read Jencks (1980), which makes a number of overlapping points.

140   NED BLOCK

One type of plant, genotype G_1 thrives at low altitudes (as measured by the weight of the plant) and the other thrives at high altitudes. The norm of reaction is simply the function from environment to phenotype for a specific genotype. Two norms of reaction, one for each type of plant, are illustrated in the diagram.

What is most truly genetically determined is the norm of reaction for a trait rather than any specific trait, as every population geneticist knows. The concept of the norm of reaction allows us to see that heritability data can tell us nothing about the genetic bucket theory. Consider some *hypothetical* norms of reaction for IQ as in Fig. 5. (Note: G_1 and G_2 are not intended as a guess about any actual races.)

One point illustrated is that current environments may have nothing to do with anything that could be thought of as *maximum* capacity, the potential size of the genetic bucket. That might be a ceiling we bump up against only in environments very different from ones available to us now (or perhaps there is no ceiling at all). If this seems unlikely to you, remember the Flynn effect. The IQ gap between us now and ourselves and our relatives of 1950 is about the same as between blacks and whites now. Another point that doesn't depend on IQ: when Gödel's theorem and general relativity were young, it was said that there were only a handful of people smart enough to understand them. Now any reasonably industrious and with-it college undergraduate has a good grasp of both within his reach. The change is improved understanding on the part of the intellectual community which allows difficult ideas to be made digestible. A similar point could be made with respect to athletic skills. The techniques (diet, shoes, training regime) required to run a 4-minute mile put an achievement within the reach of

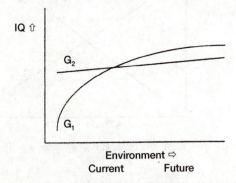

Fig. 5. Two hypothetical genotypes show a large difference in IQ in current environments, but the difference decreases and the order changes in another environment

many runners that was not available to the very top runners of a hundred year ago.

A second point illustrated by the graph is a much more significant one. Consider a population clustered on the left-hand side in the current environments section. If the population is equally split between G_1 and G_2, we can expect substantial heritability. But as the environment improves and moves into future environments, we get the following results: heritability decreases, IQ increases and G_1 and G_2 reverse. The point of course is not that anyone knows that this is what norms of reaction for IQ look like. The point is just the opposite—that no one does know how any human geno-types may react to environments that involve new intellectual machinery, new software for the brain. As Lewontin (1974; see also Feldman and Lewontin 1975) has emphasized, heritability gives a local analysis that depends on the environmental conditions and the distribution of genotypes that happens to exist at a given time. It tells us nothing about the effect of introducing environments that are either new or not now common. If we want to know the effects of a new or uncommon environment, we should *ignore heritability* and just try changing the environments. This is yet another reason why heritability is a bad statistic.

A third point (closely connected to the previous two) is that the talk of genetic advantage and disadvantage that I allowed at the outset of this paper is problematic. Even if some genotypes determine lower IQs than others in some environments, that tells us nothing about what will happen in other environments. Perhaps in ideally favorable environments most genotypes yield more or less the same phenotype. Talk of part of the black/white difference being genetic is even more problematic. We could try to make sense of the notion of part of an IQ difference being genetic as follows. Suppose there is a 10-point IQ difference between you and me. If we were both raised in an average environment, the difference would have been only 2 points. Then we might be tempted to say that the environmental part is 80% of the difference and the genetic part is 20%. But as we can see from the curves of the last figure, if our actual environment is far from the average, what happens at the average environment may have little or nothing to do with the actual causes of our IQ difference. Indeed, you may have a "genetic advantage" in our actual environments, but I may have a "genetic advan-tage" in the average environment. Further, any statistic that depends on the average environment has the problem of the heritability statistic—that it provides a local analysis that may have nothing to do with environments outside the current range.

Genetic determinists often react to data like those that I mentioned earlier on the large IQ changes in Holland by saying that though IQ scores are very environmentally malleable, the relative positions of individuals and groups are not. In effect, what they are supposing is that the norms of reaction are always parallel. There is some evidence for this within a very narrow range of environments of the current correlational studies. (See Plomin 1990*b* for the standard behavior genetics point of view on this, but see also Wahlsten 1990 for a discussion of problems with this point of view.) But there is no evidence at all outside that range. I think the right thing to say is that we don't know what the shape of the norms of reaction are, and if we are curious we should ignore heritability statistics and simply *try out improved environments*.

Further, it is not difficult to think of possibilities in which norms of reaction for IQ might not be parallel. Suppose, for example, that the brain is in a certain respect like a muscle: the activity of abstract thinking makes dendrites sprout whereas not thinking makes them shrivel. Then the more one *does* think, the better one *can* think. (Perhaps this would help to explain why college graduates appear to be at lower risk for Alzheimer's disease.) Then over the long run, differences in confidence and motivation will make for differences in ability. If there are environments that encourage some genotypes but discourage others, then we could expect to see norms of reaction for cognitive abilities that are far from parallel (and to the extent that IQ tests tap cognitive abilities, we could expect to see the same for IQ norms).

I mentioned earlier Kitcher's observation that though it was once said that PKU was a form of genetic retardation, we now feel that what is genetic in the case of PKU is the inability to metabolize phenylalanine properly. More generally, the more we know about the mechanisms of causation, the more we tend to see that what is genetic is not any specific phenotypic characteristic, but rather a tendency to develop it in certain environments. The notion of a norm of reaction allows us to see why that is the right way to think. Generally, what is genetic is simply a mapping from environment to actual (phenotypic) characteristics.

I would like to end with a brief comment on affirmative action. Herrnstein and Murray suppose that affirmative action policies depend on an assumption of genetic equality. But the main justifications for affirmative action do not so depend. Affirmative action is justified as a remedy for current discrimination, to make up for past discrimination and for the provision of role models. Issues about a genetic involvement in race differences have no relevance to these justifications.[14]

[14] I am grateful to the following people for their comments on earlier drafts: Alex Byrne, Susan Carey, Noam Chomsky, Josh Cohen, Delia Graff, Ned Hall, Michael Hardimon, Paul Horwich, Emily Jenkins, Johanna Jenkins, Philip Kitcher, Leonard Katz, Peter Klein, Amy Lang, Richard Lewontin, Karen Neander, Charles Nesson, Wayne O'Neil, Steven Pinker, Georges Rey, Sandra Scarr, Elliott Sober, Judith Thomson and an anonymous referee for *cognition*.

REFERENCES

Arvey, R., *et al.* (1994), "Mainstream Science on Intelligence", *Wall Street Journal* (Dec. 13).

Block, N., and Dworkin, G. (1974), "IQ, Heritability and Inequality", pt. II, *Philosophy and Public Affairs*, 4/1: 40–99; repr. in Block and Dworkin (1976).

—— (1976), *The IQ Controversy* (New York: Pantheon).

Chomsky, N. (1975), "On Cognitive Capacity", in Chomsky, *Reflections on Language* (New York: Pantheon); repr. in N. Block, *Readings in Philosophy of Psychology*, ii (Cambridge, Mass.: Harvard University Press, 1981), 305–23.

Feldman, M., and Lewontin, R. (1975), "The Heritability Hangup", *Science*, 190: 1163–8.

Flynn, J. R. (1987a), "Massive IQ Gains in 14 Nations: What IQ Tests really Measure", *Psychological Bulletin*, 101: 171–91.

—— (1987b), "Race and IQ: Jensen's Case Refuted", in S. Modgil and C. Modgil (eds.), *Arthur Jensen: Consensus and Controversy* (London: Falmer Press), 221–32.

Fodor, J., Bever, T., and Garrett, M. (1974), "The Specificity of Language Skills", in Fodor, Bever, and Garrett (eds.), *The Psychology of Language* (New York: McGraw-Hill), 436–41, 449–62; repr. in N. Block, *Readings in Philosophy of Psychology*, ii (Cambridge, Mass.: Harvard University Press, 1981), 324–38.

Gates, H. L., Jr. (1994), "Why Now"?, *New Republic* (Oct. 31), 211/18, issue 4163: 10.

Gould, S. J. (1994), "Curveball", *New Yorker*, 70: 139–49; repr. in S. Fraser (ed.), *The Bell Curve Wars* (New York: Basic Books, 1995), 11–22; and in R. Jacoby and N. Glauberman (eds.), *The Bell Curve Debate* (New York: Random Books, 1995), 3–13.

Herbert, R. (1994), "Throwing a Curve", *New York Times*, Oct. 26.

Herrnstein, R. J., and Murray, C. (1994), *The Bell Curve* (New York: Free Press).

Hofer, M. (1994), "Behind the Curve", *New York Times*, Dec. 26.

Holt, J. (1994), "Anti-social Science", *New York Times*, Oct. 19.

Jencks, C. (1980), "Heredity, Environment and Public Policy Reconsidered", *American Sociological Review*, 45: 723–36.

—— Smith, M., Acland, H., Bane, M., Cohen, D., Gintis, H., Heyns, B., and Michelson, S. (1972), *Inequality: A Reassessment of the Effect of Family and Schooling in America* (New York: Basic Books).

Jensen, A. R. (1969), "How much can we Boost IQ and Scholastic Achievement?", *Harvard Educational Review*, 39: 1–123.

—— (1970), "Race and the Genetics of Intelligence: A Reply to Lewontin", *Bulletin of the Atomic Scientists*; repr. in Block and Dworkin (1976: 93–107).

—— (1973), *Educability and Group Differences* (New York: Harper & Row).

Kamin, L. (1995), "Lies, Damned Lies, and Statistics", in R. Jacoby and N. Glauberman (eds.), *The Bell Curve Debate* (New York: Random House), 81–105.

Kitcher, P. (1996), "Fascinating Genetalk", in Kitcher, *An Unequal Inheritance* (New York: Simon & Schuster).

Leo, J. (1994), "Why IQ isn't Destiny/The Return of the IQ Wars", *US News and World Report*, 73–80/24.

Lewontin, R. (1970), "Race and Intelligence", *Bulletin of the Atomic Scientists*, 26/3: 2–8; repr. in Black and Dworkin (1976).

—— (1974), "The Analysis of Variance and the Analysis of Causes", *American Journal of Human Genetics*, 26: 400–11; repr. in Block and Dworkin (1976).

—— (1982), *Human Diversity* (New York: Scientific American Library).

Lieberman, E. (1995), "Low Birth Weight: Not a Black-and-White Issue", *New England Journal of Medicine*, 332: 117–18.

Loehlin, J., and DeFries, J. (1987), "Genotype–Environment Correlation and IQ", *Behaviour Genetics*, 17/3: 263–77.

Lynn, R. (1992), "Lynn Replies to Flynn", in J. Lynch, C. Modgil, and S. Modgil (eds.), *Cultural Diversity and the Schools* (London: Falmer Press).

Murray, C. (1994), "The Real Bell Curve", *Wall Street Journal*, Dec. 2.

—— (1995), Letters to the Editors, *New Republic*, Jan. 30, 5.

Nisbett, R. (1995), "Race, IQ and Scientism", S. Fraser (ed.), *The Bell Curve Wars* (New York: Basic Books), 36–57.

Ogbu, J. (1986), "The Consequences of the American Caste System", in U. Neisser (ed.), *The School Achievement of Minority Children: New Perspectives* (Hillsdale, NJ: Lawrence Erlbaum), 19–56.

Pedersen, N. L., Plomin, R., Nesselroade, J., and McClearn, G. (1992), "A Quantitative Genetic Analysis of the Cognitive Abilities during the Second Half of the Life Span", *Psychological Science*, 3: 346–53.

Plomin, R. (1989), "Environment and Genes", *American Psychologist*, 44: 105–111.

—— (1990*a*), *Nature and Nurture* (Pacific Grove, Calif.: Brooks-Cole).

—— (1990*b*), "Trying to Shoot the Messenger for his Message", *Behavioural and Brain Sciences*, 13: 144.

—— and Bergeman, C. (1991), "The Nature of Nurture: Genetic Influence on 'Environmental' Measures", *Behavioral and Brain Sciences*, 14: 373–86.

—— and Daniels, D. (1987), "Why are Children in the Same Family so Different from One Another?", *Behavioral and Brain Sciences*, 10: 1–60.

—— DeFries, J., and Loehlin, J. (1977), "Genotype–Environment Interaction and Correlation in the Analysis of Human Behavior", *Psychological Bulletin*, 84: 309–22.

—— —— and McClearn, G. (1990), *Behavioral Genetics: A Primer* (New York: Freeman).

—— Loehlin, J., and DeFries, J. (1985), "Genetic and Environmental Components of 'Environmental Influences'", *Developmental Psychology*, 21: 391–402.

Roberts, R. C. (1967), "Some Concepts and Methods in Quantitative Genetics", in J. Hirsch (ed.). *Behavior–Genetic Analysis* (New York: McGraw-Hill), 214–57.

Scarr, S. (1995), "Human Differences and Political Equality: The Dilemma of Group Differences", *Issues in Science and Technology*.

—— and McCartney, K. (1983), "How People Make their Own Environments: A Theory of Genotype → Environment Effects", *Child Development*, 54: 424–35.

Schönemann, P., and Schönemann, S. (1991), "We Wondered where the Errors Went", *Behavioral and Brain Sciences*, 14: 404–5.

—— —— (1994), "Environmental versus Genetic Models for Osborne's Personality Data on Identical and Fraternal Twins", *Cahiers de Psychologie Cognitive/European Bulletin of Cognitive Psychology*, 13: 141–67.

Sober, E. (1988), "Apportioning Causal Responsibility", *Journal of Philosophy*, 85: 303–18.

—— (1993), *Philosophy of Biology* (Boulder, Colo.: Westview Press).

Tooby, J., and Cosmides, L. (1990), "On the Universality of Human Nature and the Uniqueness of the Individual: The Role of Genetics and Adaptation", *Journal of Personality*, 58: 17–67.

Vernon, P. (1969), *Intelligence and Cultural Environment* (London: Methuen).

Wahlsten, D. (1990), "Insensitivity of the Analysis of Variance to Heredity–Environment Interaction", *Behavioral and Brain Sciences*, 13: 109–20.

Wright, R. (1995), "Has Charles Murray Read his Own Book?", *New Republic*, Jan. 2, 6.

6

RESPONSES TO RACE DIFFERENCES IN CRIME

MICHAEL LEVIN

I

It is widely agreed that young black males are significantly more likely to commit crimes against persons than are members of any other racially identified group. Approximately one black male in four is incarcerated at some time for the commission of a felony, while the incarceration rate for white males is between 2 and 3.5%.[1] Absolutely speaking, blacks commit most of the crime in the US, accounting for half of all arrests for assault and rape and two-thirds of arrests for robbery.[2] Blacks are in fact proportionally more heavily represented in all categories of felony except those requiring access to large amounts of money, such as stock fraud.[3] These figures parallel prevalence rates by race according to victims' reports,[4] so they do not represent bias in arrests. Some criminologists use the rule of thumb that a black male is ten times more likely than his white counterpart to be a criminal.[5]

While few people are familiar with these statistics, widespread intuitive awareness of the reality they report creates the familiar contemporary phenomenon of fear of black crime. The present paper examines some of the philosophical issues about risk assessment and rights of risk avoidance raised by this phenomenon.

From Michael Levin, 'Responses to Race Differences in Crime', *Journal of Social Philosophy*, 23 (Spring 1991).

[1] "The Black-on-Black Crime Plague," *US News and World Report*, Aug. 22, 1988, 54.

[2] J. Philippe Rushton, "Race Differences in Behavior: A Review and Evolutionary Analysis," *Personality and Individual Differences*, 9/6 (1988), 1016; also see James Q. Wilson and R. J. Herrnstein, *Crime and Human Nature* (New York: Basic Books, 1985), 461–6.

[3] Rushton, "Race Differences in Behavior."

[4] Ibid. 1016–17; also see Michael J. Hindelang, "Race and Involvement in Common Personal Crime," *American Sociological Review*, 4 (Feb. 1978), 100–1.

[5] "Marvin E. Wolfgang, a criminologist at the University of Pennsylvania, said that perceptions about who is more likely to commit a crime have some statistical basis. For four violent offenses— homicide, rape, robbery and aggravated assault—the crime rates for blacks are at least 10 times as high as they are by whites." Joseph Berger, *New York Times News Service*, June 19, 1987.

Black crime is obviously a problem for both blacks and whites, and most of my remarks will apply equally to black and white apprehension about it. Two considerations should be noted, however, which distinguish them. One is the ability of whites to flee black crime to an extent unavailable to blacks. Blacks, particularly young black males, cannot altogether avoid (other) young black males. It is therefore more pertinent to ask whether whites are entitled to flee black crime than it is to ask the same question of blacks. (Indeed, although black crime might no more threaten blacks than whites if the demographic distribution of the races were made random, such a distribution might—while reducing black exposure to black crime—inequitably increase white exposure.) The second factor is the asymmetry in interracial crime rates. It is commonly known that blacks are more likely than whites to be crime victims[6] and that their victimizers are more likely to be black than white: in 1987, for instance, 81.7% of aggravated assaults against blacks were committed by blacks, and 13.1% by whites.[7] However, more than 97% of white crime is committed against whites, while one-half to two-thirds of black crime is also committed against whites.[8] Since blacks are 12% of the population, 88% of the victims of black (and white) crime would be expected to be white if victim choice were random. Thus, whites attack blacks at about one-quarter of the rate predicted by random choice, while blacks attack whites at more than three-fifths of the predicted rate. Taking the ratio of these fractions as a measure of preference by race, black preference for white victims is at least 2.4 times that of white preference for black victims. Whether this figure indicates a greater propensity on the part of black criminals to seek white rather than black, victims depends on questions of opportunity, but current residential patterns do not seem to present blacks with disproportionately many contacts with whites. The data are thus consistent with a greater preference for white victims on the part of black criminals, and to that extent warrant greater white than black apprehension about black crime.

It is for behavioral scientists to explain black crime, although I pass some methodological remarks below on some proposed explanations. What philosophy can do best is to assess the conflicting epistemic and, especially, moral intuitions such an issue is bound to produce. A system of a priori moral standards would be helpful, but I will not assume any here and I am

---

[6] Between 1979 and 1986, 44.3 out of 1,000 blacks, as opposed to 34.5 out of 1,000 whites, were victims of violent crime; *Black Victims*, Special Report, Bureau of Justice Statistics, United States Department of Justice, Apr. 1990, table 1.

[7] National Crime Survey, Department of Justice, telephone interview, June 28, 1990.

[8] In 1987, 50.2% of simple assaults by blacks had white victims (National Crime Survey); between 1979 and 1986, 2,416,696 of the 4,088,945 simple assaults committed by blacks were directed against whites (*Black Victims*, tables 1, 16).

inclined to doubt any exist.[9] I will confine myself to what I take to be the criteria of rational acceptability already implicit in our commitments on other issues, and noting the application of these criteria in a new, disputed case. (Such applications may of course react back on the initial judgments and commitments until reflection stabilizes at new judgments and commitments.) Indeed, this "our" might well be replaced by "your," with me trying to persuade *you* of something by showing *you* your commitment to it. Whether or not there is some less ad hominem role for reason in ethics is a meaningless question for you the persuades, since you *endorse* your own standards. Deducing an individual judgment from principles will *convince* anyone already convinced of the principles, and likewise for extracting, principles from antecedently accepted judgments. From within your own moral framework—the perspective you cannot help but take—a deduction from your actual standards is perceived as proof, and a showing of inconsistency with those standards is perceived as refutation. (In my view, moral philosophy can do no more than articulate extant value systems and moral argument is essentially ad hominem, but I can't defend these large theses here and I won't assume them [but see n. 9].)

To be as explicit as possible about ground rules, then, "justified" and its cognates as used here mean "justified modulo general principles and particular judgments I expect the reader to hold with some tenacity"—"ordinary standards," for short.

II

My central claim is that a white (or black) encountering a young black male in isolated circumstances is more warranted in believing himself in danger, and in taking precautions, than when encountering a white in similar circumstances. This differential warrant is both epistemic and moral. Epistemically, one is more justified in believing oneself in danger in the former case, and, absolutely speaking, in believing oneself in some danger in the former but not the latter case. Morally, one is justified in the former case in seeking to escape.

This section discusses the epistemic justification, the next one the moral justification.

The usual rule in statistical decision theory is to reject those hypotheses whose probability falls below .05. If you know that one in four Acme

[9] See my "Further Reflections on a Philosophical Problem," in Peter Suedfeld (ed.), *Torture: Interdisciplinary Perspectives* (Washington, DC: Westview Press, 1990).

automobiles will break down in traffic, you cannot reject the hypothesis that the Acme you are stepping into will break down. There is a 25% chance it will. The failure of the hypothesis is "too remote to take seriously" only if fewer than 5 Acmes in 100 break down. Common sense is not quantitative, and is rarely called upon to evaluate statistical hypotheses, but it too recognizes fairly low credibility levels above which hypotheses become "likely enough" to be taken seriously. Note that the statistical rule (like common sense) distinguishes non-rejection from acceptance, which is demanded only of those hypotheses whose probability exceeds 95%.

There is nothing magic about .05. Textbook orthodoxy regards statistical hypotheses as never disproved, only shown to be less probable than some arbitrary confidence level—typically .05, but lower when rejection of truth is especially undesirable.[10] Nor does the pragmatist construal of acceptance as action as if a hypothesis were true, and non-rejection as allowance for its possibility when planning, select a natural confidence level. Perhaps the least arbitrary approach when forming expectations is pure Bayesianism, which incorporates a term for every hypothesis with non-zero probability. Rigorous Bayesianism also makes sense of eliminativism, at least about doxastic states. Eliminativism just sounds silly when taken to assert that nobody believes anything, but it is not silly when taken to assert that the binary notion of belief corresponds to nothing in the mind, being merely an abstraction from a Bayesian continuum of degrees of commitment. So there is something to be said for a revisionary theory of belief without confidence levels. Bear in mind, though, that rigorous Bayesianism preserves comparative acceptability judgments. As it should, it remains *more* reasonable to expect an Acme to break down than a Mercedes. Since most of the risk assessment issues raised by black crime are comparative, adopting Bayesianism would make little difference in the present context. In any case, Harman and Goldman have lately criticized Bayesianism on pragmatic, empirical and verific grounds,[11] so we may be stuck with confidence levels after all. In that case, .05 is as good as any.

[10] Thus R. L. Larsen and M. L. Marx: "*in many situations the beginning of reasonable doubt is taken as that critical value that is equalled or exceeded only 5% of the time* (when H_0 [the null hypothesis] *is true*" (*Statistics* [Englewood Cliffs, NJ: Prentice-Hall, 1990], 380). Also see e.g. William Feller, *An Introduction to Probability Theory and its Applications*, 3rd edn. (New York: Wiley, 1968), 189; more typical in its *va sans dire* use of a confidence level of .95 is Dennis Aigner, *Principles of Statistical Decisions Making* (New York: Macmillan, 1968), chs. 5 and 6.

[11] Harman stresses the unavailability of epistemic resources for the assignment of precise probabilities; see *Change of View* (Cambridge, Mass.: MIT Press, 1986), 22–6. Goldman cites experimental evidence of widespread de facto violations of the probability axioms, and discusses simple neurological models for transforming information into binary yes/no belief "decisions": see *Epistemology and Cognition* (Cambridge, Mass.: Harvard University Press, 1986), 90, 324–43. A judicious discussion of whether belief is analytically connected to behavior is F. Dretske, *Knowledge and the Flow of Information* (Cambridge, Mass.: MIT Press, 1981), 19ff.

This standard decision rule applies immediately to black crime. Suppose, jogging alone after dark, you see a young black male ahead of you on the running track, not attired in a jogging outfit and displaying no other information-bearing trait. Based on the statistics cited earlier, you must set the likelihood of his being a felon at .25. Of course, "felon" is a dispositional predicate, so the probability of his being prepared at that moment to attack you will generally be less than .25. At the same time, circumstances like the one described may raise the conditional probability of his attacking you if he is a felon above .5, in which case the "absolute" probability of danger is still a significant .125 or more. In any event felons are dangerous, so it is rational to take into account the possibility that you are in the presence of one, and irrational not to do so. On the other hand it would be rational to trust a white male under identical circumstances, since the probability of his being a felon is less than. 05. Since whatever factors affect the probability of the black attacking you—the isolation, your vulnerability—presumably affect the probability of a white attacking you as well, it remains rational to be more fearful of the black than of the white. Assuming ordinary confidence levels, there will many occasions on which it is noncomparatively rational to fear the black but not the white, but that conclusion is independent of the rank-ordering by danger.

To be sure, the odds are 3 out of 4 that the approaching black is not a felon. But you do not violate probabilities by acting as if he might be. The odds are 3 out of 4 that the beckoning Acme will hold up in traffic, but you do not violate probabilities by insuring access to other means of transportation. Confused expressions of this statistical intuition should be interpreted charitably. People may *say* "You can't trust Acmes," but what they probably mean is that sufficiently *many* Acmes break down to warrant regarding any one of them with suspicion. By the same token, while (some) people may unthinkingly say "Most blacks are criminals," their aversive behavior reflects the correct probability assessment that a black is likely *enough* to be a criminal for blackness to signify danger.

. The black in the park is definitely a felon or definitely not. Ideally, you would base your expectations about him on knowledge of which, just as your expectations about the Acme in front of you would ideally reflect complete knowledge of its characteristics. But you do not know. Relative to your state of knowledge, he is a typical member of a class one fourth of whose members are felons, and the probability to be assigned to a random member of that class being a felon is .25. So doing assumes some version of the principle of indifference, but under conditions which resist its abuse. This probability assignment does not asymmetrically partition the reference class of black males or humans generally, any more than the corresponding inference about Acmes asymmetrically partitions the class of Acmes or automobiles generally. The assignment does not illegitimately conjure knowledge from ignorance, since it does not say anyone is a felon. You are indeed reasoning under conditions of ignorance, but when reasoning under conditions of ignorance about the Acme, when it is known only to come from the Acme factory, common sense treats the car *as if* it were randomly chosen.[12] The assignment moves from an "objective" observed relative frequency to a "subjective" credal assessment, but frequencies standardly support subjective assessments despite what may be deep conceptual differences between them; once again, the move is unproblematic in the Acme case. Finally, the assignment obeys the constraints on information-seeking discussed in the post-Gettier literature. Two that might seem to impugn the snap credal decision in the park are: Seek more information when it is available, and, seek more information when judgment from current evidence would be immoral (as when current total evidence appears to condemn a friend). But such obligations may be overridden. Perhaps all Acmes that last 100 hours hold up for five years, but you may reasonably form a snap judgment about the Acme in front of you if you need a car *right now*, or if the salesman won't let you drive it for 100 hours unless you promise to buy expensive options. In general, you need not gather more information before deciding whether p if doing so costs more than error about p. The exemption in the park case would seem to be that you need not do A as a means to deciding whether p if the point of deciding whether p is to help reach a decision about doing A. Your park problem is whether to close the gap between yourself and the black male, but closing the gap is necessary for finding out more. So acting on present knowledge violates no informational constraints.

III

It is natural to treat the justification of private action separately from that of state action, and I do so in the present section. Ideally, discussion of state action should be flagged, in somewhat the way set theorists notationally

---

[12] To see why, consider arbitrary Acme A. If there are n Acmes, some subset of size $n/4$ are the detectives. There are $n!-(n-n/4)!$ such subsets *if* A is assumed to be in 25% of them. Assuming A to be in any other proportion of $n/4$-tuples of defective Acmes reduces the number of realizations of a 25% distribution of defective Acmes. So, if the distribution of defectives is known to be 25%, the "maximum entropy" distribution is more likely to be realized than any other. This is one approach to what Bayesians call the problem of "informationless priors." For a highly general discussion of this argument, see Roger Rosenkrantz, *Inference, Method and Decision* (Dordrecht: Reidel, 1977), ch. 2.

distinguish theorems requiring the axiom of choice. Trusting such precautions are not necessary, I subsequently treat the two issues in the same breath to avoid stilted exposition.

Private Morality. Precautions against the anonymous black of the last section are also morally justified. Since flight from perceived danger is ordinarily permissible so long as it harms no innocent bystander, you are allowed to turn on your heels. Indeed, the perception of danger is not ordinarily required to be rational. Acrophobes who have wandered onto the observation deck of the Empire State Building are entitled to flee so long as they don't trample anyone on the way down. Anyway, as noted, the perception of danger in the running track case is rational.

It may be objected that, by possibly offending an innocent black, flight does risk harming an innocent. But this harm, should it occur, is (arguably) not imposed by you and is in any case outweighed by the right to safety. Certainly, flight did not cause the innocent black's chagrin in the sense of "cause" appropriate to blameworthiness. Responsibility for harm is ordinarily borne by the author of the original wrong in the chain of events necessitating it, and the events necessitating flight were initiated by other black criminals. The innocent black wouldn't have been offended had you not run away, but you would not have run away were it not for those prior wrongful acts. You flee voluntarily more or less as Aristotle's storm-beset captain voluntarily jettisons his cargo. So responsibility for harm to the innocent black is most naturally assigned to other black criminals, not you. Indeed, the innocent black is epistemically obligated to realize that you are not judging him *dere*, since you do not know anything about *him*. You are avoiding a statistical possibility he represents.

But even if *you* are responsible for insulting *him*, the expected moral cost incurred by continuing ahead exceeds the expected moral cost imposed by flight. As a first approximation, the expected moral cost of continuing is .25× the evil of assault, while the cost imposed by flight on the black ahead of you is .75× the evil of insult. (Insulting criminals is not an evil.) If assault is more than three times worse than insult, calculations of expected morality favor flight. This calculation overstates the expected evil of continuing ahead since, as noted earlier, a black convicted felon may not intend harm to you, but it *also* overstates the cost of flight, since an innocent black may not notice or care about your running away; he may even be understanding. Because the large moral difference between insult and assault is invariant, more refined estimates of the moral cost of flight and continuing ahead may also be expected to favor flight.

State Action. The right of individuals to use racial classification in preemptively seeking safety would seem to extend to the state.

The state's regular use of other information-bearing traits to prevent serious crime sets a precedent for state use of information supplied by race for the same purpose, in the same manner, and to the same extent. Consider, in particular, suspect profiles and search for probable cause. It is uncontroversial that customs agents may subject violin possessors to special scrutiny if possession of a violin suitable for hiding contraband is known to increase the probability that its possessor is a smuggler. A glimpse of a rifle and a stack of car radios in the back seat of an automobile similarly entitles the highway patrol to search it. The state may "discriminate" on the basis of such traits as possession of a violin and occupancy of a car with a stack of radios, i.e. it may calibrate its treatment of individuals on the basis of these traits even when they do not indicate specific wrongful acts. Indeed, the authorities charged with preventing and detecting crime are *obligated* to use relevant information in screening.

Race is an information-bearing trait. Knowledge of race redistributes probabilities about past and potential commission of crimes. So, unless countervailing considerations can be brought, the state is entitled to use race in screening. The New Jersey Highway Patrol, for instance, reportedly stops young black males in expensive new cars for drug searches. The reasoning behind the violin case covers this practice as well, if most drug couriers are young black males driving expensive cars, and few blacks not involved in drug trafficking or other illicit activity own expensive cars (as the low average income and high unemployment rates of young black males would suggest is the case). Given that the presence of a young black male in an expensive car is a better predictor of drug involvement than that of a young white male, ordinary standards sanction and possibly mandate searches of black males under circumstances in which searching white males would be impermissible. If the race of a driver affects the probability of finding drugs in his vehicle, agents of the state may stop vehicles on the basis of their drivers' skin color, just as state agents may search violin owners at airports if most violins at airports contain contraband and most smugglers use violins.

To repeat, these precedents create (modulo ordinary standards) a *presumption* favoring racial screening, rebuttable by some relevant difference between race and other information-bearing traits. A number of such proposed differences will be reviewed presently. Prior to that review, however, it is well to reinforce the permissibility of racial screening by a systematic argument.

This argument begins with a reminder of what the state is *for*. All currently favored theories of the state assign provision of security as its raison d'etre. Lockeans base the state on protection of antecedent natural rights to property, which includes one's person: Hobbesians base the state on amoral interest in avoiding general war.[13] (Anarchists, who believe the state illegitimate, don't [vacuously] regard any state function as preceding security. Marxists, who expect the state to disappear, evidently regard state-enforced redistribution of property to its rightful owners as a temporary necessity.) Locke and Hobbes are both contractarians, deriving the state from an agreement between individuals to transfer their right of self-defense (Hobbes speaks of a "natural liberty") to some one enforcer. Now, part of that transferred right of self-defense is the use of information to gauge threats to oneself. Traces of this right can be discerned even in civil society, in the right of each individual to pre-empt clear and present dangers to himself. (If I see someone next to me draw a gun, I may disarm him.) Locke seems to accord each man in the state of nature the right to enforce the rights of another. On this view, although my right to use information in civil society does not extend to my entering a car if I see a stack of radios in the back seat, I presumably did have this right in the state of nature, since I had a right to act against perceived threats to anyone as well as myself. The state's right to pre-empt both non-specific threats (a man carrying burglar's tools) and threats to unknown targets (the burglar keeping his destination secret) does not emerge from or supervene upon individual rights. I myself am less confident of Locke's general executive right, and would prefer to derive the state's right by existentially generalizing over the individual rights it has received. Individual I_i can transfer only his right to pre-empt threats to I_i but the state, having acquired the rights to pre-empt threats to $I_i \ldots I_n$, takes upon itself the right to pre-empt threats to $I_l \text{ v} \ldots \text{v } I_n$, and thence threats whose target can be characterized only as "some I_i." However the state's right is derived, we *do* think the police may stop a car with a rifle on the back seat even if they cannot specify who the driver is threatening.

To be sure, the contractarian cannot argue that the state assumes an *obligation* to enforce individual rights by agreeing to do so. Individuals do not transfer their rights to the state by an agreement with *the state*, but by an agreement with each other to form a state. The effect, however, is much the same. The state acquires the rights of the individuals, with the understanding (between individuals) that this creature of their own will enforce those

---

[13] The Hobbesian state aims at least at security, but is often thought to go farther. For a reconstruction of a libertarian Hobbes, and an attempt to explain why security is a special value, see Michael Levin, "A Hobbesian Minimal State," *Philosophy and Public Affairs*, 11 (Fall 1982), 338–53; also J. Ronald Penock, "Correspondence," *Philosophy and Public Affairs*, 13/3 (Summer 1984), 255–62; Levin, "Reply to Pennock," ibid. 263–7; Christopher Morris, "A Hobbesian Welfare State?," *Dialogue*, 27 (1988), 653–63; David Schmidtz, "Contractarianism without Foundations," *Philosophia*, 19/4 (Dec. 1989), 461–70; Levin, "To the Lighthouse," ibid. 471–4. Also see Gregory Kavka, *Hobbesian Moral and Political Philosophy* (Princeton, NJ: Princeton University Press, 1986).

rights. Individuals acquire a right to have their rights enforced by the state, although this right is not against the state. (The salesman's promise that the vacuum cleaner will work gives me a right to a reliable vacuum cleaner, although it is not the vaccum cleaner that owes me proper functioning.) Moreover, since the state needs *agents* to achieve effective existence, these agents—the police—may literally be viewed as promising the rest of society to enforce their rights. So the state, as embodied in its agents, is *obligated* (because it has obligated itself) to provide security. Since what is obligatory is permissible, and the right to an end implies a right to otherwise permissible means, the state may use any otherwise permissible means to prevent attacks against individuals. Given the empirical salience of race in the commission of crime, attention to race is, absent some independent countervailing reason, permitted and indeed required by the state's protective function.

It is useful, in pursuing this argument, to follow theorists of the 14th Amendment in distinguishing two rationales for government classification of individuals corresponding to two "levels of scrutiny." (There is also an "intermediate" level of scrutiny, but as the philosophical questions are whether race can survive *any* scrutiny, or the *highest* degree of scrutiny, intermediate scrutiny may be ignored.) A classification is "benign" if, in the language of the Supreme Court's *Metro Broadcasting v FCC* (1990) decision, it "serve[s] important governmental objectives [and is] substantially related to the achievement of those objectives." "Benign" here does not mean "kindly"; it means "not intended to burden any individual or group on the basis of race." In fact, as in *Metro*—where the court permitted preferences for blacks competing for broadcast licenses to serve the state's interest in "diversity in broadcasting"—the US Supreme Court has countenanced benign racial classifications. The argument from Locke and Hobbes is that if the state may identify individuals by race to enhance diversity, it surely may identify individuals by race for its more essential purpose of controlling aggression.

At the same time, however, the Court has held that race is a "suspect" category, that classification by race must be "strictly" scrutinized and permitted only when shown to be necessary for the achievement of a "compelling state interest." (The Court apparently resolves this inconsistency by construing as benign those racial classifications beneficial to blacks, and suspect those racial classifications burdensome to blacks; see below.) Insistence on this more stringent standard will not daunt Hobbes or Locke. Clearly, they say, protecting citizens from attack is a compelling state interest; it is in fact the state's primary function. Crime statistics strongly suggest that race-consciousness can reduce attack, and might well be *necessary* for its adequate control. In all-white states like Utah and Idaho, the rate of death by homicide is about 1 per 100,000, comparable to European rates. In predominantly black areas like Detroit and Washington, D.C., the rate of death by homicide exceeds 70 per 100,000. It is difficult to deny that a greater police readiness to stop and search groups of young black males would decrease the murder rate. Perhaps all crime could be prevented by race-neutrally stationing policemen every fifty feet, but short of turning society into an armed camp, the marked black propensity to violence may be controllable only by attention to factors extensionally equivalent to race.

The court has offered reasons for striking down virtually all race-based classifications burdensome to blacks; its chief reason, as expressed in *Korematsu*, another recent decision, is that such classifications may reflect "racial antagonism [rather than] pressing public necessity." This language suggests that, in the Court's view, such classifications *merely* express racial antagonism, and cannot serve any other purpose. This is at bottom an empirical claim about the motives behind such classifications and their possible uses; in fact, the claim about the malign motive behind racial classifications is in large measure an inference from their presumed inutility. The point of the crime statistics is precisely that special police attention to (say) groups of young black males is not a baseless expression of "racial antagonism." Stopping acts which, as a matter of objective fact young black males are more likely to commit, by perhaps an order of magnitude, is a "pressing public necessity" if anything is.

Mention of these recent Supreme Court decisions is apt to raise the point that the impermissibility of state racial screening has indeed become a "fixed point of moral intuition." As observed, the Court, a reasonable guide to contemporary standards, strictly scrutinizes and by this standard rejects many racial classifications. To be sure, not all state racial classifications are deemed impermissible by this guide. There are laws (e.g. sec. 8a of the Small Business Administration Act) reserving funds for black-owned businesses and National Science Foundation Fellowships reserved for blacks, and, as also noted, the Supreme Court scrutinizes less closely, and permits, some racial classifications (in the preferential assignment of broadcast licenses to blacks in *Metro*, for instance). What appears to have become a fixed point is the impermissibility of classifications burdening blacks. If this appearance is accurate, then, in conjunction with the methodological resolve of Sec. I, it outweighs the analogies and arguments lately deployed.

Before looking more closely at this appearance, I'll reformulate it less tendentiously. Certainly, the Court prefers to term "benign" those classifications, like *Metro*'s, whose *purpose* is not burdening whites but some other end such as helping the disadvantaged or increasing diversity. But whatever the state's *purpose* when classifying by race (or classifying in any other way, for that matter), some individuals are better off and some worse off than they would have been had the state not so classified. Under some racial classifications permitted by the Court, for example those giving preference to blacks in the acquisition of broadcast companies in *Metro*, whites are worse off than they would have been had the classification been struck down. And here is the point of substance: the Court has *not* been as ready to permit classifications under which blacks would be worse off than otherwise. It is this asymmetry I mean when I speak of the impermissibility of only those classifications burdening blacks. Those who accept the doctrine of "disparate impact"—that any practice which adversely affects blacks is, however intended, prima facie discriminatory—should have no trouble with this terminology.

The distinction registered, let me underscore some important differences between strict scrutiny for racial classifications burdening blacks and such paradigm fixed moral points as the wrongness of lying. First, strict scrutiny is new—less than three decades old—whereas lying seemed as wrong to the Greeks as it does to us. Thirty years is too little time to establish an intuition's fixity. Second, the paradigm fixed points as a class give hope of immediate subsumption under some one sweeping characteristic, such as 'maximizing happiness' or 'being driven by a universalizable maxim.' Strict scrutiny for classifications burdening blacks lacks that same logical lucidity. A related point, or perhaps the same one differently expressed, is that the strict scrutiny rule is complex and asymmetrical in ways that paradigm fixed points are not. Lower levels of scrutiny are permitted for racial classifications benefitting blacks and burdening whites; the intuitive rule against lying recognizes exceptions, but not a large class of lies seemingly similar in principle to the lies it forbids. How can legal classifications burdening blacks be distinguished morally from symmetrical classifications exchanging "black" for "white"? There are reasons commonly cited, of course, but, ironically, these reasons generate the deepest difference between strict scrutiny and paradigm fixed points. Unlike the imperative of honesty, the imperative of color-consciousness when and only when not burdensome to blacks is commonly based on a number of contingent and historically limited assumptions, among them: that the state seriously mistreated blacks in the past, that racial classifications burdening blacks reflect wrong and harmful "stereotypes," that such classifications can be motivated only by racial hostility. The wrongness of lying also has its empirical presuppositions, but such as are taken to be *self-evident* and *universal*: that lying destroys trust, that co-operation requires reliance on the words of others, that (a la Wittgenstein and Davidson) universal lying is impossible because the meanings of words are determined by their conditions of use. I am not now denying the factual presuppositions of strict scrutiny or their ability to support strict scrutiny itself, although I will later address "stereotypes," and I earlier suggested that crime statistics allow racial classifications burdening blacks to survive strict scrutiny. I am asserting, rather, that these factual presuppositions do *too much* work. The value of strict scrutiny is not *inherent*, as the value of truth-telling is, but a consequence of more fundamental values (no needless state burdens, no catering to hatred) presumed to apply to a particular sort of racial classification. Classifications burdensome to blacks are thought wrong because blacks were once enslaved, and (moral axiom) slavery is wrong; because such classifications indulge hatred, and the indulgence of hatred is self-evidently wrong and leads to further (self-evident) wrongs.[14] Color con-sciousness does not remain immediately and intuitively impermissible when the associated factual assumptions are relaxed, as they may easily be in imagination. Indeed, racial classifications burdening whites are thought more permissible precisely because the parallel factual assumptions are known to be untrue of whites. By contrast, it's more difficult to imagine lying not causing distrust or not destroying communication. The wrongness of lying is integral to the human condition, while the wrongness of racial classifications burdening blacks is not.

In any case, the "fixed point" objection is pertinent only if racial screen-ing in fact is found to fail the Court's strict scrutiny test. At the time this is written, the Court is admittedly unlikely actually to permit measures like those under discussion. But times change. It is conceivable that at some point the Court might find black violence so threatening to public order, and its control so compelling a state interest, as to permit race-conscious measures while maintaining its doctrine that racial classifications are "suspect."

IV

The permissibility of private and especially state race-consciousness in seek-ing security will draw a number of objections, which I will consider in order of increasing intuitive force. But the burden of proof, as I have noted, rests on the objector. The statistical prevalence of black crime in conjunction with the rest of our ordinary moral beliefs may not force acceptance of race-consciousness, but the precedents cited together with the argument from the

---

[14] See Michael Levin, "Is Racial Discrimination Special?," *Journal of Value Inquiry*, 15 (1981), 225–32. The specialness of past racial discrimination is a theme that recurs in the Objections section of the present paper.

purpose of the state create a presumption favoring race-consciousness. Failure to rebut this presumption leaves race-consciousness permissible.

(1) *Basing treatment on race is racist.*

Much of the force of this objection depends on an ambiguity in "racism." If "racism" means *unjustified* race-consciousness, race-based differentiations need not be racist. In particular, race-based screening is not "racist" if justified by differential crime rates, and calling it "racist" in this sense simply begs the question. On the other hand, if—as it sometimes seems to— "racism" denotes any race-consciousness, racism is not automatically objectionable. Practices "racist" in *this* sense must be evaluated on their own merits. For those who favor them, affirmative action and the casting of white actors as Hamlet are unobjectionable forms of "racism," as the casting of female Ophelias is presumably an acceptable form of "sexism". Race-based screening is indeed "racist" in this sense, but must be evaluated on its merits.[15]

Of course, one might hold that in fact all forms of racism in this *second* sense are wrong, a claim both non-trivial and sweeping enough to bar racial screening. However, the moral objection it mounts to racial screening is not that it uses racial factors, but that all use of racial factors is wrong. Because this is the most penetrating and philosophically interesting objection, I am deferring it to last, as objection (5) below.

(2) *Rights precede utility.* Rights against screening by race override the possible benefits of screening.

This argument can easily beg the question, since the very issue at hand is the existence of a strong right against screening by race. But I won't press that point very hard at this stage, since the argument implicit in common sense for ordinary (and by extension racial) screening is not utilitarian at all, but "rights maximizing".[16] Maximum protection of rights permits local rights invasion which minimize invasion overall. Rights-maximizers admit the wrongness of detention without specific evidence of wrongdoing, but see such detention as most efficiently protecting citizens' net rights against aggression. Screening is not a matter of preferences vs. rights, but of rights

---

[15] It is sometimes argued that "racism" must by definition disadvantage blacks. Since whites occupy a dominant position, race-conscious distinctions by or favoring blacks must therefore proceed from the good desire to create equality, while race-conscious distinctions burdening blacks must proceed from the bad desire to oppress. Whatever else may be said about this refinement of the second sense of "racism," it reinforces the point that the wrongness of race-consciousness depends upon its nature and purpose.

[16] The phrase is Nozick's; he contrasts it with a Kantian morality of "side constraints" against doing wrong. See Robert Nozick, *Anarchy, State and Utopia* (New York: Basic Books, 1975), 28–33.

vs. more rights. Criticizing racial screening for favoring *utility* is thus an ignoratio.

The distinction between rights- and preference-maximizing suffices to turn the present objection, but its contribution to the intrinsic plausibility of screening, and thereby racial screening, deserves to be noted. "Utilitarianism of rights," which is deontological in its fashion, takes the more attractive side of the rights-vs.-utility debate and withstands the counterexamples that blow away classical preference-maximizing utilitarianism. (Act-utilitarianism tells you to rescue ten strangers instead of your own child from a burning building; the implications of rule-utilitarianism are less clear. Aggression-minimizing allows you in no uncertain terms to ignore the strangers, since refusal to rescue is not aggression.)

Objection (2) might be modified to an endorsement of an absolute ban on rights violations as against any brand of maximizing. This again begs the question when applied to race, but, again, there are more illuminating replies which concede arguendo a right of indeterminate strength against racial screening. The maximizer might boldly adapt the utilitarian idea that ordinary morality really is maximizing but *appears* Kantian to get us to maximize successfully.[17] The maximizing character of morality is revealed (the maximizer continues) when maximizing is preferred to Kantianism in hard cases—such as probable cause detention. Or, the maximizer may reply more concessively that if ordinary morality is indeed Kantian, the pre-theoretical acceptability of screening shows such measures to be consistent with Kantianism. (The maximizer gladly leaves to the Kantian the job of reconciling Kantianism with screening.) And if screening is consistent with Kantianism, another argument is needed to show that *racial* screening is not.

In connection with the general case for "rights utilitarianism" against side-constraint Kantianism, it is instructive to recall the role of "minimizing" pre-emption in Nozick's rights-based derivation of the state.[18] A seeming absolutist about the obligation not to aggress, Nozick insists that the state is legitimate only if it can emerge from anarchy without aggression. He easily derives a dominant voluntary protective association, but he cannot get it to achieve an enforcement monopoly, the defining characteristic of the state, without its aggressively imposing its rules on "independents." To permit this imposition, Nozick cites, rather plausibly, the anxiety created in association members by the prospect of independents conducting affairs according to their own rules. This anxiety is deemed great enough to justify

---

[17] See "Further Reflections."
[18] Notick, *Anarchy, State and Utopia*, 78–84, 110–13.

the association in imposing *its* rules on the independents, so long as it compensates ex-independents for this imposition by protecting them as well. Nozick's argument thus requires levels of merely potential aggression that justify limited preemptive aggression by the (proto)state, pretty much the principle I take to underlie extent screening practices. (State protection of the other rights of screening detainees realizes the compensation proviso.) Nozick's reluctant appeal to maximizing indicates the extent which maximizing intuitions permeate our conception of permissible state action.

Insofar as Objection (2) mounts a challenge to screening per se, it effectively concedes that racial screening is permissible if screening in general is. Not surprisingly, this Objection proves too sweeping. The impermissibility of race-based measures must rest on specifically racial factors, if on anything. An obvious one is:

(3) *Slippery slope.* Once race-based screening is countenanced, where does use of racial criteria stop? Doesn't it grease the slope down to concentration camps?

Drawing the line on uses of race raises no issue of principle. Just as the use of race in screening is governed by general norms governing the traits to be used in screening, permissible uses of race are limited by the norms which govern the use of all classification.

I have already mentioned two principles that may be used to govern state classification, namely substantial relation to an important government objective, and service of a compelling state interest. These principles can be abused, but so can any principles. A bad will could interpret "reasonable" search and seizure to cover anything, yet, recognizing this danger, we permit wiretapping. The philosophical rights-utilitarian, certainly, has a clear standard: a race-conscious policy A is permissible if A maximizes *expected morality*, the sum over world-states W_i of the products $p(W_i)m(A/W_i)$, where $m(A/W)$ is the net respect for rights achieved by following A in W and $p(W)$ is the probability of W holding. Now, if objection (3) is an expression of the worry that the expected morality of race-based action is *always* suboptimal, always less than some race-blind alternative, it becomes a version of objection (5), the wrongness of any use of race whatever. So (3) is best interpreted as referring to possible misuses, particularly by the state, of racial classifications.

It is difficult to respond to the Hitler comparison, since mention of Hitler seems to paralyze thought. (Max Hocutt and George Graham call this ploy "argumentum ad Nazium."[19]) Nazis persecuted an inoffensive population, the Jews, for being too clever and for imagined anti-German conspiracies.

[19] Max Hocutt, "Must Relativism Tolerate Evil?," *Philosophical Forum*, 17 (Spring 1986), 188–200.

The historical situation of blacks in the US is entirely dissimilar. It is a fact, not fantasy, that the murder rate in US cities has increased almost tenfold in the last half century as their black population has increased. Here are real innocent deaths, not hypothetical ones. Ordinary morality would demand that something be done about so large an increase if it were unrelated to race; it seems perverse to do nothing because it involves a factor reminiscent of something of concern to Hitler. Hitler's minions invented the multi-stage rocket—does this mean NASA should not use them?

To have any bite, objection (3) must explain without hyperbole why race is so amenable to abuse that, unlike abusable factors that are used, it must be ignored. The most familiar such explanation is the reinforcement of racial stereotypes by public or private use of racial factors. I now turn to that worry, but under the more general heading "race is special," which also permits discussion of a number of other important issues. In fact, so many topics arise that this objection merits its own section.

V

(4) *Race differs from other screening criteria.*

(4i) *Causal irrelevance.*

Standard probable causes, such as concealed rifles and stacks of car radios, are *causally relevant* to the commission of crime, while skin color is not. A stack of car radios, unlike race, carries information because it *results from* crime. (Car radios are *specific symptoms*; few crimes produce stacks of car radios in the back seat, but most stacks of car radios in the back seat are produced by crime.) The presence of a gun informatively correlates with the occurrence of a crime because both are effects of a common cause, criminal intent. Alternatively, a gun might be thought of as a factor likely to *cause* a crime. But race is not a characteristic cause of crime, or effect of crime, or co-effect with crime of some underlying cause. What is sometimes called the "unfairness" of race-based screening derives in part from this causal irrelevance.

This difference between race and many standard screening criteria is irrelevant to its informational value. Standard criteria are used because they carry information, *whatever* the source of this informativeness. *Why* they carry information is the separate issue of *why* they are criteria. To ask this is not to question, indeed it is to assume, that they are. Even though the rifle carries information due to its causal role, it is the information the rifle carries, not the reason that it carries information, that warrants a search when a rifle is noticed. Concealed weapons redistribute probabilities, and it is the redistributed probabilities that justify the state in stopping a man with a concealed weapon. Citing the causal relations between concealed weapons, criminal intent and crime is necessary to justify the revised probabilities, but it is the probabilities themselves, so long as they *are* justified, that warrant the search. By parity of reasoning, any factor which redistributes probabilities equally reliably is an equally legitimate probable cause. In general, A becomes a sign of B when $p(B/A)$ is high enough. That $P(B/A)$ is often determined by causal relations between A and B fosters confusion between warrant and its (usual) causal basis. It is the magnitude of $p(B/A)$, *whatever* its basis, that warrants an inference from A to B, and would warrant the inference if it held in virtue of unexplained but projectable correlations.

Suppose Borsalinos become popular among drug couriers and almost no one else because most couriers come from the one city where Borsalinos are in fashion. Neither cause nor effect nor co-effect of drug trafficking, Borsalinos at an airport become a reliable sign of involvement in drug traffic. Now, even though it is *accidental* that most drug couriers wear Borsalinos—or "lucky," as the Aristotle of the *Categories* would say—the state would surely be justified in using Borsalinos as a basis for search. Of course, so doing would be irrational if the correlation between headwear and smuggling were expected to break down at any moment. The correlation between race and crime has held for decades, however, long enough to be considered projectable. It is difficult to imagine smugglers ignoring the conspicuousness of their Borsalinos for decades, but if they did the hat/crime correlation would also be projectable. (Strictly speaking, of course, it is the predicates "wears a Borsalino" and "is black" that are [or are not] projectable.)

(4ii) *Race is a biological trait not chosen by its possessors.* People should not be penalized for what they cannot help. In this sense too race-based screening is unfair.

If screening is regarded as a punishment, the major premise is absurd. Were there a killer on the loose with a conspicuous, ineradicable birthmark, monitoring such men would be permissible even though birthmarks are not chosen. It would be absurd to forgo knowledge that might turn up a murderer because the murderer can't help providing it. In fact, however, the use of identifying traits is not a penalty. (So we can keep the axiom that people shouldn't be penalized for what they can't help.) The killer will be penalized for murder, not possession of a birthmark. The involuntariness of the tip-off is irrelevant to the need to identify him; by the same token, the involuntariness of race has nothing to do with the propriety of race-based screening. If race cannot be used because it is biological, neither should birthmarks, eye color, or—if there is a genetic predisposition to obesity—weight.

Consider the use of age, typically 16, in licensing drivers. Not only is one's age not chosen and a denial of the right to drive arguably a state burden, but the age criterion produces injustice. There are individuals under 16 mature enough to drive and individuals over 16 who are not. But testing every adolescent for maturity is impossible, and traffic accidents (many of which involve rights-violations) must be minimized, so age is used as a reasonably accurate proxy for physical and psychological maturity. Protecting the innocent from reckless drivers is felt to offset the attendant injustice. To be sure, 15-year-olds eventually become 16-year-olds, but the unalterability of race does not destroy the analogy. There will be mature 15-year-olds who, dying before their 16th birthday, are never licensed. We regard an age proxy as proper despite the inevitability of such injustices. What is more, justice delayed is said to be justice denied, so the injustice of denying an able 15-year-old his license is not cancelled when he gets his license on his 16th birthday. That a biological condition may change is evidently irrelevant to the permissibility of imposing a burden on the basis of that condition before it changes. If mutability still seems crucial in the licensing case, it is well to re-emphasize the immutability of birthmarks and inherited obesity, which the state can use in classifying suspects.

It might be allowed that involuntary tests, including race, may be used to identify perpetrators of known acts, but not merely potential malefactors. That an act's ontological status should determine the traits to be used in identifying perpetrators seems quite ad hoc, but assume it so. This ontological feature of racial screening, as well as the immutability of race, is also found in the use of genetic predictors of aggression, should they be found, to track potential criminals from birth. Thought experiments involving such predictors might seem at first to decide against racial screening, since many people now say they would reject tracking. Yet it is very far from clear that tracking would be widely rejected were it actually, concretely available. Imagine genetic information on file but disregarded, while every year post-conviction tests showed that 10,000 murderers (committing about half the murders in the US annually) had the crime gene. Would tracking still be considered wrong if we could *see* the victims who would not have been murdered had potential criminals been tracked?[20] To intensify the problem, instead of supposing 50% of murders are committed by possessors of a crime gene, suppose that 50%, or 90%, of unsupervised possessors of the

---

[20] Cf. Roger Wertheimer's discussion of visible fetuses in "Understanding the Abortion Problem," in Marshall Cohen, Thomas Nagel, and Thomas Scanlon (eds.), *The Rights and Wrongs of Abortion* (Princeton, NJ: Princeton University Press, 1974).

crime gene eventually commit murder. Would tracking *still* be considered impermissible because nobody chooses his genes? It seems to me likely that at some point the average person would endorse tracking, and even restrictions on the freedom of carriers. Intuitions about genetic tracking may thus prove to reinforce racial screening.

(4iii*a*) *Racial screening will strengthen stereotypes and mistrust of blacks.* Indeed, since white suspicions are in considerable part responsible for black crime, racial screening unfairly hounds blacks for their reaction to being hounded.

Whether racial screening will cause rights violations comparable to those it prevents, and encourage private acts of injustice as whites become irrationally mistrustful of blacks, is an empirical issue which cannot be decided by quasi-a priori speculation. As my doubts about the incipiency of Nazism might suggest, I am somewhat skeptical about this prediction, and in fact there are reasons for skepticism which also bear on the second part of the objection. The stereotype of black criminality is indeed already strong, but there is no evidence that it depends significantly on any variable other than the black crime rate itself. This point is unnecessary for meeting objection (4iii*a*) if, as I go on to argue, racial screening is permissible even if it self-fulfillingly predicts black crime. (I eventually argue that the etiological question as a whole is virtually irrelevant.) Nonetheless, many people seem certain that black crime is caused by white attitudes and actions, so that burdening blacks for black criminality impermissibly "burdens the victim." The self-fulfilling stereotype idea thus requires some discussion.

The most apparent shortcoming of this theory is methodological. It is not to be denied that many people privately view blacks as less intelligent, industrious and self-restrained than members of other groups, or that black educational and economic attainment, and obedience to law, conforms to this stereotype. Indeed, denying *either* point surrenders the self-fulfilling prophecy idea, by denying the prophecy or its fulfillment. As is widely recognized, however, the direction of the causal arrows between social phenomena is not self-evident, and in fact explaining stereotyped behavior by expectations quickly runs in a circle. Such an explanation renders inexplicable both the origin of stereotypes themselves and the assignment of particular stereotyped traits to particular groups. Group traits once *in place* may be supposed without circularity to be partly or wholly sustained by the expectations they confirm. But what starts the cycle? Whence the initial expectations? Positing a human propensity to stereotype, if it is just an aspect of the tendency to generalize experience, presupposes the stereotyped behavior. Stereotypes so construed are summaries of antecedently observed—perhaps misinterpreted but nonetheless observed—behavior. Including in the tendency to stereotype a need by the ingroup to ascribe disvalued traits to outgroups, the account favored by Sartre and Bettelheim, still fails to explain the ascription of *particular* traits to *particular* outgroups. If the array of outgroups is initially a *tabula rasa*, observation of which does not constrain ingroup ascriptions, these ascriptions must be supposed to be determined *arbitrarily*. Such a theory cannot explain why blacks are considered financially improvident and Jews canny, for instance, rather than vice-versa. And lacking an account of the choice of permutation among group/trait assignments we have no account of the origin of the feedback process, so no account of group traits *or* stereotypes. (It might also be noted that some racial stereotypes, such as Japanese efficiency and Jewish legal skill, are positive and do not obviously favor a need to feel superior.[21])

Reversing the causal arrow, by taking perceived group/trait correlations as independent variables and stereotypes as the dependent variables, explains stereotypes and leaves the cause of the correlations themselves an open question instead of a cul-de-sac. Such a "paradigm," in addition to permitting inquiry to continue,[22] would be consistent with the kernel of empirical truth in most stereotypes.[23] And I think many critics of racial screening would, after some reflection, admit as much. However, as suggested earlier, the black behavior empirically validating stereotypes is itself often attributed to white misdeeds. To distinguish the idea that black crime is caused by the expectation

[21] The self-fulfilling prophecy theory also fails to explain the cross-cultural robustness of stereotypes. 15th-century Arab slave-owners, with no prior direct or indirect contact with blacks, regarded them as highly sexed, highly rhythmic, and unintelligent. This perception cannot be explained by the servile status of the blacks with whom the Arabs were familiar, since Arabs stereotyped their Jewish slaves as very clever (as did the Romans); see Bernard Lewis, *Race And Slavery in the Middle East* (Oxford: Oxford University Press, 1990).

[22] For a discussion of the idea that explanations should never limit further inquiry, see Michael Slote, *Reason and Scepticism* (New York: Humanities Press, 1970), ch. II. A further methodological defect of the stereotype theory is the non-existence of any detailed, well-confirmed model of the transformation of perceived white mistrust into omnidirectional black aggression. Nor is it clear how such a model could be consistently constructed. Self-hate caused by disdain and mistreatment might explain black-on-black crime, but not black-on-white crime, while black resentment of whites does not easily explain black-on-white crime.

[23] Of the theoretical works on prejudice known to me, only William Helmreich's *The Things they Say behind your Back* (New York: Doubleday, 1982) attempts to gauge the empirical correctness of stereotypes. Helmreich examines 75 generalizations about Jews, blacks, Italians and other groups, and decides that one-third are true and "about half have a factual basis" (p. 244). Already considerably more than would be predicted by the psychological-needs theory, this number increases upon examination of Helmreich's examples. Many of Helmreich's assessments tend to treat wrongly caused group traits as not really there (calling to mind Russell's definition of a metaphysician as someone who says that something does not exist, and defines evil as the counterexamples). For instance, he discounts the stereotype of black oversensitivity by explaining this oversensitivity as a response to oppression. But a phenomenon cannot simultaneously be explained and denied, since the explanans of an explanation must be true and (at least on the DN model) entail the explanandum.

thereof from the idea that black crime is caused by more general forms of racial thinking and acting, it is useful at this point to register objection (4iii*b*):

(4iii*b*)   *Even if stereotypes about black crime reflect rather than cause black criminal behavior, this behavior is a consequence of past racism.*

Other information-bearing traits like birthmarks and Borsalinos differ from race because their association with crime was not wrongfully caused. Anyone who would screen blacks on the basis of race resembles the Potter of the *Rubaiyat* "who threatens he will toss to Hell the luckless Pots he marr'd in making."

Indeed, since racism and poverty are often mentioned in the same breath as the "root causes" of black crime, it is also important to mention objection (4iii*c*):

(4iii*c*)   *Root causes.* Society has a special responsibility to address the causes of black crime, not take it as a given to be handled by standard means.

(4iii*c*) can be treated in passing because it is an ignoratio. The legitimacy of racial screening and other race-conscious responses to black crime does not require their being the *best* or *only* legitimate responses. So long as race-conscious measures do not conflict with other legitimate measures, the existence of these other measures does not discredit race-consciousness. The root cause of arson may be depressed real estate values, but the urgency of buoying the real estate market does not forbid otherwise acceptable methods for foiling arson. Similarly, if poor education amplifies black crime, the need to improve schools has no bearing on what may be done to control the present criminal tendencies which past poor education has, unfortunately, already produced. Indeed, the very deployment *of* (4iii*c*) is special pleading unless measures against crime associated with other ethnic groups (the Mafia, Chinese tongs, Jewish insider trading) are also to be assessed by their attention to root causes, a yardstick seldom applied. Deploying (4iii*c*) has the further disadvantage of opening the door to "root cause" hypotheses other than white racism, some of which, especially those involving genetic factors, are often deemed offensive. Since disconfirmation of the racism hypothesis would raise the probability of offensive alternatives, I note that inclusion of (4iii*c*) is a response to insistence on it by many readers.

Recurring to (4iii*a–b*), I view (4iii*b*) like (4iii*a*) as a non sequitur. Race-conscious state measures are permitted even if white racism has caused black crime. However, as with (4iii*a*), the empirical assumption behind (4iii*b*) is so often viewed as both obvious and morally dispositive that failure to discuss it might seem to ignore everything important. Once again, then, some remarks, primarily methodological, are in order.

Slavery, and subsequent public and private discrimination against blacks, certainly occurred. However, neither the direction nor even the existence of any causal relation between these actions, contemporary black crime and correlates like poverty immediately follows therefrom. In fact, two morally salient causal distinctions must be observed. The first separates the endogenous/exogenous question—whether the cause(s) of black crime lie(s) within or without the black population—from the fault question. The cause of wrongdoing need not itself be wrongdoing, much as our sense of fitness might prefer it so. Perhaps some environmental factor unrelated to past mistreatment differentially affects blacks. Perhaps some accidental, unintended and unsuspected, byproduct of past wrongs differentially produces black crime. In neither case would whites be responsible for the higher black crime rate—nobody would be—and restraints on race-consciousness imposed by such responsibility would fall away. (It would of course be imperative to remove the environmental factor.) Or, disproportionate black crime might be produced by some non-moral factor within the black population, such as genetically greater average aggressiveness.[24] Since people are not responsible for their genes, neither blacks nor whites would be to blame for black crime in that case either.[25]

---

[24] "Population P is genetically more prone to X than population Q" can be taken to mean "P is phenotypically more X than Q in any environment." The weaker definiens "P is phenotypically more X than Q in all likely environments" accommodates the possibility that there are some environments in which P is more X than Q and some in which P is less X. (Any theoretically satisfactory definition should include the proviso that phenotypic X was more adaptive in the environment in which P evolved than that in which Q evolved.) Block and Dworkin ("IQ, Heritability, and Inequality," in N. Block and G. Dworkin (eds.), *The IQ Controversy* [New York: Pantheon, 1976], 479–85], like many authors, emphasize gene/environment interaction vis-a-vis race differences in intelligence, but cite no evidence of environments in which the norms of reaction for black and white genotypes yields similar phenotypes. The point of the well-formedness of both definitions and their rough extensional equivalence is that talk of genotypic differentiation is not impugned by the need for environmental mediation of genotypes.

It might be wondered how blacks can be more prone to aggression than whites, given that the most destructive wars have been waged by Europeans and Asians. One natural answer is a white advantage in organizational ability and technology. Although tribal conflict runs through African history, Africans were unable to form themselves into large armies with any regularity or develop weapons of mass destruction. The crime data is consistent with blacks being on average more *individually* aggressive than whites. Counterfactuals about what blacks would have done had they formed million-man armies runs into cotenability problems, since high levels of individual aggressiveness may impede cooperative enterprises.

[25] The degree to which individual black criminals would then be responsible for their crimes is one aspect of the perennial determinism puzzle, which warrants four specific comments here. First, environmental causes are no more in the control of the agents affected than are genetic causes, so if genetic causation diminishes criminal responsibility, so does environmental causation. If genetic causation diminishes responsibility, so does any cause short of noumenal agency. Second, genetic factors diminish the responsibility of black criminals only if a genetic predisposition to race hatred diminishes the responsibility of bigots, an implication many will be reluctant to draw. Third, compatibilists such as the present author distinguish freedom to desire from freedom to act on one's possibly unfree desires. The consequent possibility of free action from desires not freely

The response of dismissing such possibilities as absurd in light of history necessitates the second distinction, between the thesis that white mistreatment has causally contributed to black crime and its correlates, and the thesis that white mistreatment is its sole cause. The causal relevance of state action or white mistreatment generally to some aspect of black crime (or socioeconomic attainment) does not imply that that mistreatment has caused *all* the discrepancy between black and white crime rates (or other behaviors). Black crime may resemble many social phenomena in being a vector sum; in statistical terms, the question bearing on (4iii*b*) is the "proportion of variance explained" by white misconduct. If race-conscious responses to crime are held to be illegitimate *because* black crime is the result of racism, such responses are illegitimate only *to the extent* that black crime is the result of racism. Race-conscious measures regain legitimacy with decreases in the proportion of variance white racism explains. The reasoning behind (4iii*b*) even seems to admit moral thresholds. If for instance white misdeeds account for 10% of the difference between black and white crime rates, white responsibility might be too slight to restrain race-conscious measures to any extent at all. So white causal contributions to black crime do not by themselves show race-consciousness to be just more of what originally caused black crime, or to "burden the victim" impermissibly.

It may again seem obvious that white misdeeds directly or indirectly explain *all* the variance in crime rates, but a number of writers have begun to question this hypothesis. First, black crime rates in other countries, including all-black countries, are comparable to those in the US.[26] White racism, while still perhaps a sufficient or INUS condition, is thus not necessary for the black crime rate. Second, however, black crime has increased since the passage of the Civil Rights Act in 1964 and the inception of affirmative action in 1965. The racism hypothesis predicts a decrease in black crime with more equitable treatment of blacks, and it is difficult to argue that white racism has increased in the US since 1965.[27] Indeed, most black crime is

chosen reconciles genetic determination of high aggressiveness with responsibility for aggressive acts. However—and this fourth comment moves against the trend of the first three—the more refined compatibilism of Frankfort, Davidson, Sen, Davis and myself construes fully free action as action proceeding from desires the agent finds acceptable. (See my *Metaphysics and the Mind–Body Problem* [Oxford; Oxford University Press, 1979], ch. 7; also Lawrence Davis, *Philosophy of Action* [Englewood Cliffs, NJ: Prentice-Hall, 1979], for a graceful statement of this view.) Since aggressive emotions tend to preclude second-order reflection—indeed reflection of any sort—congenital aggression may well diminish freedom and responsibility.

[26] See Rushton, and Herrnstein and Wilson.

[27] This point is made in William Junius Wilson, *The Truly Disadvantaged* (Chicago: University of Chicago Press, 1987), 1ff. Wilson explains relative black poverty in terms of the disappearance of manufacturing jobs, but he does not explain why blacks have not adapted to an economy more geared to service and information.

committed by black males under 25 who have never experienced Jim Crow and have been raised in a society in which preferences for blacks is public policy. The idea that blacks have had insufficient time to recover from slavery and Jim Crow predicts similar crime patterns and recovery times for similarly mistreated groups, but this prediction is also unsustained. One may insist on the uniqueness of the black experience in America, but the Jewish experience worldwide certainly looks comparable. In much of Europe Jews were legally confined to ghettos and forbidden to engage in certain trades. The accepted estimate of the number of Jews killed by the Nazis is 6,000,000; the highest estimate I have seen of the number of blacks lynched in the American South between 1900 and 1954 is 5,000. According to T. E. Reed,[28] at most 400,000 slaves were shipped to America during the slave trade, most of them during the 18th century. If one is assumed to have died for every two who survived, the resultant death rate remains three orders of magnitude smaller than that of the Holocaust.

Turn of the century Jewish immigrants fleeing European anti-Semitism lived in extreme poverty in New York, and Jewish crime of the period supports the poverty/oppression/crime link to some extent. However, while Jewish crime was then high relative to Jewish norms elsewhere, it was not, as is black crime, disproportional to the number of Jews in the overall population.[29] Moreover, Jewish crime was directed primarily against property rather than persons, as is black crime.[30] Finally, even the relative prevalence of Jewish crime subsided by World War II,[31] the period 1900–1939 being about equal in length to that between *Brown* (1954) and the present.

Positing ever more obscure forms of racism to explain away such data yields a theory vulnerable as a whole to the question Hume so devastatingly asks of theism in the *Dialogues*: Is the world as we would expect it to be if all we knew beforehand was that this theory were true? Does the world look as if blacks and whites are equally behaviorally restrained but for white racism? Additional assumptions may reconcile the racism theory with ubiquitously

---

[28] T. E. Reed, "Caucasian Genes in American Negroes," *Science*, 165 (1969), 762–8.

[29] "[A]t no time during the prewar period did Jews have more lawbreakers than their proportion of the population warranted. Rather, Jews were consistently underrepresented among those charged with committing felonies with, on occasion, half as many felony arrests as their numbers allowed. From a purely statistical perspective, Jews did not exceed admissible levels of criminal behavior." Jenna Weissman Joselit, *Our Gang: Jewish Crime and the New York Jewish Community, 1900–1940* (Bloomington: University of Indiana Press, 1983), 32.

[30] "Close to 80 percent of all felony charges brought against Jews between 1900 and 1915 had to do with the commission of property crimes: burglary, larceny, arson, horse-poisoning, and receiving stolen goods. In contrast, only 12 percent of these arrests related to the commission of a violent crime, such as assault, murder, or rape." Ibid. 33.

[31] "[F]or New York Jews, crime was a one-generation phenomenon, a social and economic consequence of the immigrant experience." Ibid. 158–9.

high black crime rates and increases in black crime upon passage of protective legislation, but the theory does not predict these phenomena. The theory
becomes "conjecture piled atop hypothesis" without independent support.[32]

[32] Another popular explanation of black crime is low self-esteem caused by whites, but the
boundary condition in this explanation appears to be a non-fact. In a survey of the literature as of
1966, Audrey Shuey found "at the preschool level there seems to be some evidence of awareness of
color differences and a feeling of inferiority associated with dark skin, but at the grade school level
and continuing through high school and college there is no consistent evidence of lower self
esteem in Negroes; if there is a difference, it would appear to be more likely that Negroes have a
greater sense of personal worth, rather than the reverse" (*The Testing of Negro Intelligence*, 2nd
edn. [New York: Social Science Press, 1966], 512; italic in original). A recent study of adolescent
girls by Carol Gilligan indicated, to its author's apparent surprise, that black adolescent females
enjoy *higher* self-esteem than white adolescent females. (The survey has not been published at this
writing; but see Suzanne Daley, "Little Girls Lose their Self-Esteem on Way to Adolescence, Study
Finds," *New York Times*, Jan. 9, 1991). The evidence for low black self-esteem most commonly
cited (by, among others, the Supreme Court in *Brown v. Board of Education*) is the experimentally
observed preference of American black children for white dolls in the United States. This experiment has been replicated in the all-black Dominican Republic, however, and the reply that racism
has eroded the self-esteem even of blacks who have little contact with whites seems ad hoc. It
should be remembered that self-esteem reflects one's idea of one's own abilities and, to a decreas-
ing extent with a sharp gradient, those of one's immediate circle. But, as Nozick has perceptively
remarked (*Anarchy, State and Utopia*, 240–4), ability is comparative; to be good at something is to
be better at it than most members of a reference group. Most blacks in racially mixed societies find
themselves worse than average at most socially expected cognitive tasks, like reading. Cosmopolitan blacks elsewhere know that their societies have developed none of the technology
developed by Europeans and Asians. (Whether good or evil, technology requires traits not displayed by black societies.) *If* contact with whites has lowered black self-esteem, this perceived
disparity in achievement is the simplest explanation.

The cause of black crime, then, is likely to be endogenous, but explanations in terms of the
values reinforced by black culture are circular. Perhaps young black males are socialized to defy
authority, but why does black culture produce this particular value? Even if psychosocial explanation is autonomous in the sense that its characteristic predicates are not coextensive with any
finite Boolean functions of biological predicates, as anti-reductivists claim, treating it as absolutely
autonomous amounts to treating society or culture as an Unmoved Mover. Any non-circular
account of culture, or a specific culture, must eventually appeal to noncultural, presumably biological factors. There is obviously no genetic proneness to commit crime, since crime is socially
defined. What you get when you subtract the motion of a hand from an act of forgery is a legal
norm. The well-formed empirical hypothesis is that blacks are genetically more prone than whites
(see n. 24) to actions which in fact tend to be criminalized in societies with legal codes. Among
such actions are those intended to cause physical injury. A readiness on the part of other members
of the same social group to "punish" (i.e. negatively reinforce) such behavior is apparently found
even in non-human primates (see L. Ellis, "Evolution and the Nonlegal Equivalent of Aggressive
Behavior," *Aggressive Behavior*, 12 [1987], 57–71).

Genetic proneness requires a mediating physiological mechanism, and this may be found in the
higher average level in black males of serum testosterone, a known facilitator of aggression: see R.
Ross *et al.*, "Serum Testosterone Levels in Healthy Young Black and White Men," *Journal of the
National Cancer Institute*, 76 (1986), 45–8; L. Ellis and H. Nyborg, "Racial Ethnic Variations in
Male Testosterone Levels: A Probable Contributor to Group Differences in Health," *Steroids*, 57
(Feb. 1992), 1–4. There is some discrepancy between the Ross *et al.* and Ellis–Nyborg estimates of
the race difference, which Ellis and Nyborg attribute to age differences in the samples. It could
of course be argued that higher black levels of serum testosterone is itself an effect of the stresses
of racism, but, according to Ellis and Nyborg, "recent evidence has shown that black men exhibit
biochemical responses to stress that are, on average distinct from white men" (Ellis and Nyborg).
These differences in response readiness are themselves presumably non-social in origin.

But race-conscious safety-seeking measures remain proper even if white racism, or stereotyping, or some combination of the two, is the cause of black crime. So much seems unarguable in the case of "private" safety-seeking. That the black male on the running track is more likely than a white to attack a jogger *because* of the jogger's suspicions, or because his father suffered discrimination, does not diminish the jogger's danger or his right to avoid it. This right might be challenged on grounds of the jogger's obligation to break the vicious cycle, a challenge arising from (4iii*a*) particularly. However, his obligation to weaken the cycle cannot be greater than his contribution to it, weighted by his chances of weakening it by running ahead, and this is less than the danger of continuing. So the jogger's flight remains "subjectively" permissible and probably objectively permissible as well. A more general obligation not to flee a danger by means which might sustain or increase it, on the other hand, seems not to exist. Even if the burning of fossil fuel has so poisoned my city's air that I must leave immediately or asphyxiate, most people would permit me to escape by car. Despite the appearance of involving a ban on the use of means to avoid evils caused by those very means, both principles actually derive what plausibility they enjoy from the general rule that flight must not injure the innocent. My automotive flight imposes some pollution on others, and my flight from the running path, we are supposing, to some slight extent sustains black crime. Yet the reflexive character of these acts does not enter into their evaluation, which consists entirely in balancing my right to safety against the harm I may impose. (In my own non-philosophical view, continuing to run toward the black man is the cowardly subordination of one's own instinct for survival to a heteronomous fear of violating taboos against "racism.")

State action raises facially additional issues, since the fleeing jogger does not interfere with the black, while a police search does actively burden him. Yet this distinction does no work, since, as observed earlier, the state is usually understood to have acquired a right to use information to intervene preemptively from each individual's right or natural liberty to seek security. If some state intervention is permissible, (4iii*a*) and (4iii*b*) purport to show why it cannot be based on race. (4iii*a*) is the logically more compelling argument, in effect plausibly generalizing the rule against entrapment, namely: Do not punish a wrong caused by that very punitive act. The right to detain does not permit detaining someone for breaking a window in the room in which he is being held for breaking that window, since it is the state that has created the wrong on which it is basing detention. This is why acting on race-based suspicion seems wrong, on the self-fulfilling prophecy model. The cop on the beat is justifiably suspicious of black teenagers, but only because his suspicions dispose them to crime (by lowering their self-esteem or convincing them they have nothing to lose). But this objection loses its force when *specific* self-fulfillment is distinguished from *generic* self-fulfillment. Let us call an expectation-token E specifically self-fulfilling if E creates E-fulfilling conditions, whereas E is *generically* self-fulfilling if other tokens of E's type have created E-fulfilling conditions. The generalized rule against entrapment applies to specifically self-fulfilling suspicions but not to generically self-fulfilling ones. If this black's criminal propensity was not caused by this policeman's present suspicions of him, but only by past suspicions of blacks, possibly including him, this policeman's very suspicions are not responsible for the behavior which justifies them, and the policeman's acting on them does not impose a burden for a wrong created by the act of imposition. Perhaps those other suspicions should not have been harbored, but they *were* harbored and *have* had their effect on the black's character. These suspicions, we are assuming, have made him more likely to commit a crime. As an agent of the state the policeman is obligated to prevent those effects from manifesting themselves as criminal acts. The wrongness of the earlier suspicions bar the policeman from acting on his present ones only if he may never take preventive action in the light of *any* suspicions which are justified by (behavior produced by) some past wrong.

The response that the wrongs which cause black crime were not just any wrongs, but race-conscious wrongs, returns us to (4iii*b*): race-based measures are impermissible now because the purported need for them was created by past race-based injustice. But the character of those past causes, whatever they are, has turned out to be irrelevant so long as present race-based measures are not the specific causes of the behavior these measures are intended to prevent. Indeed, limited race-conscious screening is not even generically similar to the race-conscious measures said to have caused black crime. Stopping a group of black males because they are especially likely to be carrying guns is not slavery, lynching, separate drinking facilities or segregated schools. Such a measure does not resemble segregation in "reflecting racial antagonism," if this expression means that the measure exists only to express racial antagonism, without any further purpose. The crime statistics show such a measure to serve the independently justified purpose of controlling crime. To insist on an analogy between screening and segregation is simply to ignore the empirical fact that race predicts crime, and crime, to an even greater extent, predicts race.

Weakening (4iii*b*) to the impermissibility of race-based measures now because black crime was caused by *some* (perhaps distinct) unjust race-based measures, leaves it a non sequitur. Crime, like everything else, has causes, some of which are injustices, and the presence of a wrong in the causal chain leading to a crime does not normally constrain state action. It doesn't matter that I plan to steal your car because a swindle in 1950 impoverished my family, so long as my mental capacity is otherwise undiminished. It doesn't matter if the state abetted the swindle by finding the swindler innocent in a fixed trial. The state doesn't care *why* I plan to steal your car. (My theft might acquire some immunity if you had been the swindler and I meant to retaliate, but black criminals give no evidence of harboring retaliatory motives.) Our occasional tendency to think past wrongs mitigate their present effects may be due to a tendency to collapse causal chains—to think that when *A* causes *B* and *B* causes *C* it is really *A* that causes *C*, with *B* a sort of epiphenomenal intermediary. This fallacy is particularly tempting when *A* and *C* are actions and *B* is the desire which caused *C*. Because my desire to steal was caused by wrongful action, we think, *I* am not the real criminal; the real criminal is the agent behind *A*. That this is sheer confusion is, I trust, obvious.

If in general the presence of wrongs in the causal history of behavior is irrelevant to state treatment of it, it is hard to see how the *racial* character of those wrongs can create relevance. The intuition that it does, the intuition behind (4iii*b*), is that race-consciousness is special because race-consciousness is what caused all the trouble in the first place. The counter-vailing intuition is: so what? Suppose the Holocaust turned many Jews into bank robbers. The police see a man with a Mogen David and a concentration-camp mark on his arm eyeing a bank vault. Should they disregard these factors in deciding whether to enhance surveillance because these factors and perhaps the crime being plotted were the result of anti-Semitism? Consider race-consciousness from the perspective of you, the social contractor in the street, attacked by a black male. Imagine a police-man arriving just too late to save you who confides: "I saw the black approach you and suspected he might attack, but I didn't intercede even to the minimal extent of showing myself to discourage him because my belief that he might attack was *race*-based. I would have felt no impulse to inter-cede had your attacker been white. But I shouldn't act on thoughts I shouldn't think, and I shouldn't think that way. I shouldn't think that way because your attacker's turn to crime was a result of his great-grandfather's enslavement, his father's inferior education and his own constricted opportunities, circumstances based on racial thinking. Doing *anything* because of his race is just the sort of thinking that caused him to attack you." If you retained your composure, you would surely note your personal innocence with respect to your attacker's history. You would insist that seg-regation was based on factual errors, while his suspicion of the black was based on empirical realities. In signing the social contract, you would con-tinue, you created the office of policeman to prevent such attack. When he agreed to take this office, the constable assumed the enforcement of your right to self-defense and thereby obligated himself to protect you. You would admit to having limited his protective activities—no third degree, perhaps, no unreasonable invasion of privacy, no generalized entrapment. But the information that race predicts crime is untainted, because innocently acquired. Why couldn't he use it? Is it enough that use of that information bears a family resemblance to the thinking of segregationists?

VI

Even those who admit the irrelevance of the "root cause" issue may balk at the use of racial information because

(5) *People should be treated as individuals, not as members of groups.*

The alleged right of each person to be treated solely on the basis of his own traits rather than the category to which he belongs, particularly his racial category, is the fundamental objection.

I will eventually argue that Objection (5) rests on a confusion about "treating people as individuals," but let me first, dialectically, deny the objection to supporters of affirmative action. I take it as uncontroversial that affirmative action favors individual blacks (and women) solely on the basis of their race (and sex), without attention to the specifically demonstrated claims of any particular black or female beneficiaries. This is clear enough for the most familiar justification of affirmative action, the need to compensate or "remedy" blacks (and women) for the disabilities they now carry as a consequence of wrongs to themselves and their ancestors.[33] The presumption that a black favored over a better-qualified white has suffered from white misdeeds is applied to him not on the basis of his known individual circumstances and history, but on the racial group to which he belongs. Affirmative action entitlements to individuals are thus probability judgments based on empirical generalizations about classes, just as avoidance of an anonymous black is an implicit probability judgment about an individual based on empirical generalizations about classes. A black applying for a job is deemed so *likely* to bear the burdens of discrimination, because a high but unspeci-

---

[33] "But the remedy is necessarily designed, as all remedies are, to restore the victims of discriminatory conduct to the position they would have occupied in the absence of such conduct," *Milliken v. Bradley* (1974). A clear statement of the compensation argument is George Sher, "Justifying Reverse Discrimination in Employment," *Philosophy and Public Affairs*, 4 (Winter 1975). A very recent statement of the same argument is Sterling Harwood, "Fullenwider on Affirmative Action as Compensation," Abstract, *Proceedings of the American Philosophical Association*, 64 (Feb. 1991), 68.

fied proportion of blacks do, that favoring him now "makes him whole." Even if, the replies to (4iiia–b) notwithstanding, it is insisted that every American black has been harmed by white racism, it must also be admitted, I think, that the extent of the harm cannot be exactly determined in any concrete case. It cannot be shown specifically, for instance, that the less-senior blacks promoted over Brian Weber in the *Weber* case would have been *senior to Brain Weber* had there been no racism. So preference for a particular black over a better-qualified white, since it cannot rest on a showing that that black would have been better qualified than that white absent racism, must rest on the statistical inference that that black *probably* suffered an injury as great as the difference in their qualifications.

Other arguments extant for affirmative action also involve classifying by race. If, for instance, more black role models are needed because there aren't as many inspiring blacks as there would have been absent discrimination, we have not advanced beyond the compensation argument. (Many role-model theorists seem not to realize this.) If on the other hand more black role models are needed because the presence of more blacks in different walks of life is not a requirement of justice but a good thing by some more general criterion, the question shifts to why it is good. "Diversity" might be considered good in itself, like pleasure or acting from universalizable maxims. Whatever the merits of such a view—as a justification of affirmative action it is circular, "diversity" being another name for what affirmative action seeks to achieve[34]—diversity as an end in itself self-evidently requires racial consciousness. Blacks become fungible if the end is proportionality per se, with no black being chosen because of any individual trait (except race). Or, one might justify "diversity" and derivatively affirmative action in terms of some values that blacks can distinctively contribute.[35] In that case, however, unless one is prepared to specify a desirable trait possessed by every black and no white, one must believe certain desirable traits more prevalent in the black population, so that preferring a

[34] See Lino Graglia, "The 'Remedy' Rationale for Permitting otherwise Prohibited Discrimination: How the Court Overcame the Constitution and the 1964 Civil Rights Act," *Suffolk University Law Review*, 22/3 (Fall 1988), 581.

[35] This maneuver triggers a series of awkward questions. It forces one to ask, first, whether there are any race differences, for, absent race differences, it is hard to see why one black/white ratio in a situation is better than another. But if there are race differences, is discrimination their cause? If these differences are not caused by discrimination—if they are endogenous to the black population—they may explain the very black attainment shortfall usually attributed to white racism and used to justify affirmative action in the first place. And where do these endogenous differences come from? "Culture," we saw, is circular. But if, to avoid calling these differences biological, we recur to discrimination, we must explain how the psychological residue of racism—said to be low self-esteem, mistrust, aggrievement, poor academic attainment—can improve the university or workplace. Anyone basing affirmative action on "diversity" must answer these questions.

black over a better-qualified white on the basis of his race is *likely* to inject that trait into a given situation. By contrast, a racial classification may be justified, as in the *Metro* case, as helping the disadvantaged—which once again selects individuals because of presumed correlates of group membership rather than individual traits. (The Federal Communication Commission policy sanctioned in *Metro* did not extend preference to possibly disadvantaged white purchasers, or demand a showing by individual black purchasers that *they* had been disadvantaged.) On its face, the argument that preference-generated diversity will destroy stereotypes is a "distinctive black virtue" argument, since it takes all and only blacks to have the desirable characteristic of 'tending to contribute to the destruction of stereotypes.' But this property itself may involve appeal to a probabilistic assessment, the *likely* effect of a preferred black on stereotypes; more significantly, the thinking that is to be encouraged by affirmative action so justified—that blacks are more talented than might have been supposed—classifies individuals by race.[36]

It appears, then, that affirmative action however defended distributes benefits and burdens on the basis of group membership.[37] (This conclusion should not be surprising.) Proponents of affirmative action therefore cannot consistently deploy individualism—the principle that the distribution of

[36] Appeal to the destruction of stereotypes is self-defeating without the assumption that less-qualified blacks will perform as well as better-qualified whites. This assumption is plausible if the usual selection criteria—grades, scores on standardized tests, and the like—are biased against blacks, but in fact these predictors are as valid for blacks as for whites; see Alexandra K. Wigdor and Wendel R. Garner (eds.), *Ability Testing: Uses Consequences and Controversies* (Washington, DC: National Academy Press, 1982), 477.

[37] Ronald Dworkin's non-compensatory "utilitarian and ideal" rationale for preference (*Taking Rights Seriously* [Cambridge, Mass.: Harvard University Press, 1977], 223–39) parallels the reasoning of *Metro*-like decisions. Since Dworkin apparently cannot conceive a utilitarian basis for discriminating against blacks beyond the "external preferences" of whites for black frustration, he does not see the Pandora's box opened by utilitarian arguments for discriminating against whites. Suppose the presence of more than a threshold number of black children in a classroom impedes the intellectual development of white children. (There is some evidence for this: see Shuey, *The Testing of Negro Intelligence*, 120.) Here would be a utilitarian argument for school segregation appealing only to the "personal" preferences of white parents and children for academic success. Black males rape almost as many white females as they do black females, and (proportion of population held constant) rape white females twice as frequently as white males do. (Applying the rates given in *Black Victims* for single offender victimization [table 16, p. 1] to the aggregated number of victimizations [table 1], black males rape 25,000 white females annually and 26,700 black females; the corresponding numbers for white males are 105,000 and 3,300. Applying the rates for multiple offender victimizations [table 16, p. 2] to any proportion of aggregate victimizations decreases white-on-white rape and increases black-on-white rape.) Given the opportunity for unplanned contact created by residence patterns, these figures indicate a pronounced preference by black rapists for white females. If separating black men from white women would sharply decrease the incidence of rape among white women without raising its incidence among black women correspondingly, the personal preference of white women to avoid rape would be utilitarian grounds for such separation.

benefits and burdens should never be based upon membership in racial groups—against racial screening, or anything else.[38]

In contrast, a proponent of racial classification in the service of individual security can consistently oppose affirmative action. He may claim that, because assaults are far worse than uncompensated discrimination, the expected morality of screening (the probabilistically weighted value of assaults prevented less the disvalue of detaining innocent blacks) exceeds the expected morality of affirmative action (the probabilistically weighted value of compensating discrimination-induced disabilities less the disvalue of penalizing innocent whites).[39] The burden imposed by affirmative action on possibly innocent whites is heavy, he may say, and the probability of a given white's actually having contributed to a given black's present position not clearly high. As noted, the harm of not compensating discriminatory injury certainly seems less than the harm of an assault. But the harm of an assault is very great and the burden imposed on blacks by race-based measures to prevent it—the inconvenience of search—is lighter than the burden whites are made to bear by affirmative action. A great enough difference between the expected moralities of screening and affirmative action would justify endorsement of screening and rejection of affirmative action. After a time, affirmative action without screening may come to seem intuitively absurd. To be sure, the value of affirmative action can be raised above that of screening by suitable assumptions about the extent of discriminatory injury to blacks, the moral cost of not compensating it, and the harm to innocent blacks of screening. Nor would the screening proponent necessarily reject those assumptions. It is no part of his argument to call affirmative action *unjustified*, or to *deny* the remedial rationale for it. (Nor need he deny any of the other rationales, although he finds it strange that the state may use race-conscious measures thought to be related to subsidiary state goals like diversity, but not race-conscious measures more clearly related to the more fundamental state goal of security.) But even given empirical and normative assumptions favorable to affirmative action, the screening proponent regards it as hypocritical to advocate affirmative action while opposing race-based responses to crime *on the principle that individuals should always be treated solely as individuals*. The advocate of racial screening, having accepted no such principle, can be accused of no comparable hypocrisy. He

---

[38] Strictly speaking, the expected morality $e(A_i)$ of any affirmative action program A_i is $\Sigma_{jk} p(B_{jk}) m(A_i/B_{jk})$, where $p(B_{jk})$ is the probability that black j has been damaged by discrimination to degree k. When B_{jk} is sufficiently near 0, $m(A_i/B_{jk})$ will fall below 0 because of the attendant injustice to whites.

[39] A point made by Dworkin; see his "Why Bakke has no Case," in R. Wasserstrom (ed.), *Today's Moral Problems*, 3rd edn. (New York: MacMillan, 1985), 141–2.

accepts race-based classifications rationally related to basic moral goods, chiefly prevention of aggression.

Now, I have been arguing thus far as if there is an acceptable principle of individualism, the only question being who has a right to it. There is in fact no such principle. People are and must always be judged by the classes to which they belong, the traits they share with others. What are called individual or intrinsic traits are simply traits which, given past experience with others possessing those traits, are known to have high predictive value. "Judging" an individual consists largely in anticipating his behavior and personality on the basis of observed correlations between traits he is known to have and further traits he may then be presumed to have. "Natural kind" traits, which seem a distinctively appropriate basis for judgment, are simply traits whose predictive value and role in quasi-laws has made reliance on them second nature.

Both proponents and opponents of race-based classification would probably agree in contrasting a student's high-school grades with his race as, respectively, an "individualistic" and a "group" criterion for college admission. Use of grades, especially, would be thought to illustrate judging a student "on his own merits." But why are grades an *intrinsic* trait, and a permissible basis of judgment? Simply because of the reliable correlation between high school grades and success in college. Simplifying greatly, there is a correlation coefficient of .5 between high school and college grade point averages; i.e. 75% of those with high school g.p.a.'s of 3.5 or above achieve the same g.p.a. in college.[40] College admissions officers favor an applicant with a 3.5 g.p.a. because most other applicants with that same g.p.a. have performed well. Admitting an applicant with high grades, then, is a probabilistic judgment based on the group to which he belongs. Grades are unlike race in reflecting effort and choice, and thus are susceptible of moral evaluation. So, we feel, students deserve what their grades, but not their race, earn them. But other expressions of effort and choice, such as a student's physique from years of body-building or his splendid collection of beer cans, play no role in admissions' deliberations because they do not predict academic performance.

It is in fact sheer error to look to voluntariness for a way of distinguishing individual from group traits. Many intuitively "individual" traits are acquired as involuntarily as group traits like race. A 5'4" 125-lb. freshman will be made waterboy rather than linebacker because of his size (as opposed to his race) and we would agree that the coach had judged him on an "individual" trait, his size. But size is largely beyond one's control. And here, too,

<hr />

[40] For more precise data, see Robert Linn, "Ability Testing: Individual Differences, Prediction, and Differential Prediction," in Wigdor and Garner (eds.), *Ability Testing*, ii. 335–88.

the coach's basis for judgment is statistical: very few boys that size have ever succeeded as linebacker. There are exceptions, but that is the reasonable expectation—a conclusion dovetailing with that of (4ii) about the irrelevance of the biological character of race.

VII

It would be tempting but misguided to dismiss the cluster of problems I have discussed as "racist." Some of them are significant enough to reach all of social philosophy. While I am fairly confident of the conclusions I've presented here, many problems remain to be explored. We need to determine the limits of race consciousness. If there are race differences in maturation rates[41] would it be permissible to treat blacks as adult offenders at an earlier age than whites? If reinforcement schedules strongly differentiate by race, would different average deterrent effects for the same punishment on the three main racial groups justify race-based punishment schedules? Is a presumed narrowness in the variance of responses to punishment the only reason punishments are not individually tailored *now*? The courts do have discretion in sentencing and in setting bail, with the likely effect on the individual an important determinant of the latter especially. Perhaps the idea of equal treatment under law does not mean that everyone should receive the same punishment for the same crime, but that everyone should receive an equally aversive punishment, a punishment with the same deterrent effect, for the same crime. These questions are as interesting as they are disturbing, and I would hope to see philosophers take them up.

I would also hope these discussions treat black crime for what it is—a difficult, many-sided dilemma like abortion, capital punishment or euthanasia. There is no need to falter in following the argument as if one has stepped onto holy ground.

[41] For evidence of a relatively accelerated black life cycle, see Rushton, "Race Differences in Behavior," 1012–13 and references therein.

7

RIGHTS, HUMAN RIGHTS, AND RACIAL DISCRIMINATION

RICHARD A. WASSERSTROM

The subject of natural, or human, rights is one that has recently come to enjoy a new-found intellectual and philosophical respectability. This has come about in part, I think, because of a change in philosophical mood—in philosophical attitudes and opinions toward topics in moral and political theory. And this change in mood has been reflected in a renewed interest in the whole subject of rights and duties. In addition, though, this renaissance has been influenced, I believe, by certain events of recent history—notably the horrors of Nazi Germany and the increasingly obvious injustices of racial discrimination in both the United States and Africa. For in each case one of the things that was or is involved is a denial of certain human rights.

This concern over the subject of natural rights, whatever the causes may be, is, however, in the nature of a reinstatement. Certainly there was, just a relatively few years ago, fairly general agreement that the doctrine of natural rights had been thoroughly and irretrievably discredited. Indeed, this was sometimes looked upon as the paradigm case of the manner in which a moral and political doctrine could be both rhetorically influential and intellectually inadequate and unacceptable. A number of objections, each deemed absolutely dispositive, had been put forward: the vagueness of almost every formulation of a set of natural rights, the failure of persons to agree upon what one's natural rights are, the ease with which almost everyone would acknowledge the desirability of overriding or disregarding any proffered natural rights in any one of a variety of readily familiar circumstances, the lack of any ground or argument for any doctrine of natural rights.

Typical is the following statement from J. B. Mabbott's little book, *The State and the Citizen*:[1]

From Richard A. Wasserstrom, 'Rights, Human Rights and Racial Discrimination', *Journal of Philosophy*, 61/20 (Oct. 1964).

Presented in a symposium on "Human Rights" at the sixty-first annual meeting of the American Philosophical Association, Eastern Division, Dec. 27, 1964.

[1] (London: Arrow, 1958).

[T]he niceties of the theory [of natural rights] need not detain us if we can attack it at its roots, and there it is most clearly vulnerable. Natural rights must be self-evident and they must be absolute if they are to be rights at all. For if a right is derivative from a more fundamental right, then it is not natural in the sense intended; and if a right is to be explained or defended by reference to the good of the community or of the individual concerned, then these "goods" are the ultimate values in the case, and their pursuit may obviously infringe or destroy the "rights" in question. Now the only way in which to demonstrate the absurdity of a theory which claims self-evidence for every article of its creed is to make a list of the articles. . . .

Not only are the lists indeterminate and capricious in extent, they are also confused in content . . . [T]here is no single "natural right" which is, in fact, regarded even by its own supporters as sacrosanct. Every one of them is constantly invaded in the public interest with universal approval. (pp. 57–58)

Mabbott's approach to the problem is instructive both as an example of the ease with which the subject has been taken up and dismissed, and more importantly, as a reminder of the fact that the theory of natural rights has not been a single coherent doctrine. Instead, it has served, and doubtless may still serve, as a quite indiscriminate collection of a number of logically independent propositions. It is, therefore, at least as necessary here as in many other situations that we achieve considerable precision in defining and describing the specific subject of inquiry.

This paper is an attempt to delineate schematically the form of one set of arguments for natural, or human rights.[2] I do this in the following fashion. First, I consider several important and distinctive features and functions of rights in general. Next, I describe and define certain characteristics of human rights and certain specific functions and attributes that they have. Then, I delineate and evaluate one kind of argument for human rights, as so described and defined. And finally, I analyze one particular case of a denial of human rights—that produced by the system of racial discrimination as it exists in the South today.

I

If there are any such things as human rights, they have certain important characteristics and functions just because rights themselves are valuable and distinctive moral "commodities." This is, I think, a point that is all too often overlooked whenever the concept of a right is treated as a largely uninteresting, derivative notion—one that can be taken into account in wholly

---

[2] Because the phrase 'natural rights' is so encrusted with certain special meanings, I shall often use the more neutral phrase 'human rights'. For my purposes there are no differences in meaning between the two expressions.

satisfactory fashion through an explication of the concepts of duty and obligation.[3]

Now, it is not my intention to argue that there can be rights for which there are no correlative duties, nor, that there can be duties for which there are no correlative rights—although I think that there are, e.g., the duty to be kind to animals or the duty to be charitable. Instead, what I want to show is that there are important differences between rights and duties, and, in particular, that rights fulfill certain functions that neither duties (even correlative duties) nor any other moral or legal concepts can fulfill.

Perhaps the most obvious thing to be said about rights is that they are constitutive of the domain of entitlements. They help to define and serve to protect those things concerning which one can make a very special kind of claim—a claim of right. To claim or to acquire anything as a matter of right is crucially different from seeking or obtaining it as through the grant of a privilege, the receipt of a favor, or the presence of a permission. To have a right to something is, typically, to be entitled to receive or possess or enjoy it now,[4] and to do so without securing the consent of another. As long as one has a right to anything, it is beyond the reach of another properly to withhold or deny it. In addition, to have a right is to be absolved from the obligation to weigh a variety of what would in other contexts be relevant considerations; it is to be entitled to the object of the right—at least *prima facie*—without any more ado. To have a right to anything is, in short, to have a very strong moral or legal claim upon it. It is the strongest kind of claim that there is.

Because this is so, it is apparent, as well, that the things to which one is entitled as a matter of right are not usually trivial or insignificant. The objects of rights are things that matter.

Another way to make what are perhaps some of the same points is to observe that rights provide special kinds of grounds or reasons for making moral judgments of at least two kinds. First, if a person has a right to something, he can properly cite that right as the *justification* for having acted in accordance with or in the exercise of that right. If a person has acted so as to exercise his right, he has, without more ado, acted rightly—at least *prima facie*. To exercise one's right is to act in a way that gives appreciable assurance of immunity from criticism. Such immunity is far less assured when one

[3] See, e.g., S. I. Benn and R. S. Peters, *Social Principles and the Democratic State* (London: Allen & Unwin, 1959), 89: "Right and duty are different names for the same normative relation, according to the point of view from which it is regarded."

[4] There are some rights as to which the possession of the object of the right can be claimed only at a future time, e.g., the right (founded upon a promise) to be repaid next week.

leaves the areas of rights and goes, say, to the realm of the permitted or the nonprohibited.

And second, just as exercising or standing upon one's rights by itself needs no defense, so invading or interfering with or denying another's rights is by itself appropriate ground for serious censure and rebuke. Here there is a difference in emphasis and import between the breach or neglect of a duty and the invasion of or interference with a right. For to focus upon duties and their breaches is to concentrate necessarily upon the person who has the duty; it is to invoke criteria by which to make moral assessments of his conduct. Rights, on the other hand, call attention to the injury inflicted; to the fact that the possessor of the right was adversely affected by the action. Furthermore, the invasion of a right constitutes, as such, a special and independent injury, whereas this is not the case with less stringent claims.

Finally, just because rights are those moral commodities which delineate the areas of entitlement, they have an additional important function: that of defining the respects in which one can reasonably entertain certain kinds of expectations. To live in a society in which there are rights and in which rights are generally respected is to live in a society in which the social environment has been made appreciably more predictable and secure. It is to be able to count on receiving and enjoying objects of value. Rights have, therefore, an obvious psychological, as well as moral, dimension and significance.

II

If the above are some of the characteristics and characteristic functions of rights in general, what then can we say about human rights? More specifically, what is it for a right to be a human right, and what special role might human rights play?

Probably the simplest thing that might be said of a human right is that it is a right possessed by human beings. To talk about human rights would be to distinguish those rights which humans have from those which nonhuman entities, e.g., animals or corporations, might have.

It is certain that this is not what is generally meant by human rights. Rather than constituting the genus of all particular rights that humans have, human rights have almost always been deemed to be one species of these rights. If nothing else about the subject is clear, it is evident that one's particular legal rights, as well as some of one's moral rights, are not among one's human rights. If any right is a *human* right, it must, I believe, have at least four very general characteristics. First, it must be possessed by all human beings, as well as only by human beings. Second, because it is the same right that all human beings possess, it must be possessed equally by all human beings. Third, because human rights are possessed by all human beings, we can rule out as possible candidates any of those rights which one might have in virtue of occupying any particular status or relationship, such as that of parent, president, or promisee. And fourth, if there are any human rights, they have the additional characteristic of being assertable, in a manner of speaking, "against the whole world." That is to say, because they are rights that are not possessed in virtue of any contingent status or relationship, they are rights that can be claimed equally against any and every other human being.

Furthermore, to repeat, if there are any human *rights*, they also have certain characteristics as rights. Thus, if there are any human rights, these constitute the strongest of all moral claims that all men can assert. They serve to define and protect those things which all men are entitled to have and enjoy. They indicate those objects toward which and those areas within which every human being is entitled to act without securing further permission or assent. They function so as to put certain matters beyond the power of anyone else to grant or to deny. They provide every human being with a ready justification for acting in certain ways, and they provide each person with ready grounds upon which to condemn any interference or invasion. And they operate, as well, to induce well-founded confidence that the values or objects protected by them will be readily and predictably obtainable. If there are any human rights, they are powerful moral commodities.

Finally, it is, perhaps, desirable to observe that there are certain characteristics I have not ascribed to these rights. In particular, I have not said that human rights need have either of two features: absoluteness and self-evidence, which Mabbott found to be most suspect. I have not said that human rights are absolute in the sense that there are no conditions under which they can properly be overridden, although I have asserted—what is quite different—that they are absolute in the sense that they are possessed equally without any special, additional qualification by all human beings.[5]

Neither have I said (nor do I want to assert) that human rights are self-evident in any sense. Indeed, I want explicitly to deny that a special manner of knowing or a specific epistemology is needed for the development of a theory of human rights. I want to assert that there is much that can be said in defense or support of the claim that a particular right is a human right. And

---

[5] For the purposes of this paper and the points I wish here to make, I am not concerned with whether human rights are *prima facie* or absolute. I do not think that anything I say depends significantly upon this distinction. Without analyzing the notion, I will assume, though, that they are *prima facie* rights in the sense that there may be cases in which overriding a human right would be less undesirable than protecting it.

I want to insist, as well, that to adduce reasons for human rights is consistent with their character as human, or natural, rights. Nothing that I have said about human rights entails a contrary conclusion.

III

To ask whether there are any human, or natural rights is to pose a potentially misleading question. Rights of any kind, and particularly natural rights, are not like chairs or trees. One cannot simply look and see whether they are there. There are, though, at least two senses in which rights of all kinds can be said to exist. There is first the sense in which we can ask and answer the empirical question of whether in a given society there is intellectual or conceptual acknowledgment of the fact that persons or other entities have rights at all. We can ask, that is, whether the persons in that society "have" the concept of a right (or a human right), and whether they regard that concept as meaningfully applicable to persons or other entities in that society. And there is, secondly, the sense in which we can ask the question, to what extent, in a society that acknowledges the existence of rights, is there general respect for, protection of, or noninterference with the exercise of those rights.[6]

These are not, though, the only two questions that can be asked. For we can also seek to establish whether any rights, and particularly human rights, ought to be both acknowledged and respected. I want now to begin to do this by considering the way in which an argument for human rights might be developed.

It is evident, I think, that almost any argument for the acknowledgment of any rights as human rights starts with the factual assertion that there are certain respects in which all persons are alike or equal. The argument moves typically from that assertion to the conclusion that there are certain human rights. What often remains unclear, however, is the precise way in which the truth of any proposition about the respects in which persons are alike advances an argument for the acknowledgment of human rights. And what must be supplied, therefore, are the plausible intermediate premises that connect the initial premise with the conclusion.

One of the most careful and complete illustrations of an argument that does indicate some of these intermediate steps is that provided by Gregory

---

[6] This is an important distinction. Incontintinece in respect to rights is a fairly common occurrence. In the South, for example, many persons might acknowledge that Negroes have certain rights while at the same time neglecting or refusing (out of timidity, cowardice, or general self-interest) to do what is necessary to permit these rights to be exercised.

Vlastos in an article entitled, "Justice and Equality."[7] Our morality, he says, puts an equal intrinsic value on each person's well-being and freedom. In detail, the argument goes like this:

There is, Vlastos asserts, a wide variety of cases in which all persons are capable of experiencing the same values.

Thus, to take a perfectly clear case, no matter how A and B might differ in taste and style of life, they would both crave relief from acute physical pain. In that case we would put the same value on giving this to either of them, regardless of the fact that A might be a talented, brilliantly successful person, B "a mere nobody". . . . [I]n all cases where human beings are capable of enjoying the same goods, we feel that the intrinsic value of their enjoyment is the same. In just this sense we hold that (1) *one man's well-being is as valuable as any other's.* . . . [Similarly] we feel that choosing for oneself what one will do, believe, approve, say, read, worship, has its own intrinsic value, the same for all persons, and quite independently of the value of the things they happen to choose. Naturally we hope that all of them will make the best possible use of their freedom of choice. But we value their exercise of the freedom, regardless of the outcome; and we value it equally for all. For us (2) *one man's freedom is as valuable as any other's.* . . . [Thus], since we do believe in equal value as to human well-being and freedom, we should also believe in the *prima facie* equality of men's *right* to well-being and to freedom. (pp. 51–2)

As it is stated, I am not certain that this argument answers certain kinds of attack. In particular, there are three questions that merit further attention. First, why should anyone have a right to the enjoyment of any goods at all, and, more specifically, well-being and freedom? Second, for what reasons might we be warranted in believing that the intrinsic value of the enjoyment of such goods is the same for all persons? And third, even if someone ought to have a right to well-being and freedom and even if the intrinsic value of each person's enjoyment of these things is equal, why should all men have the equal right—and hence the human right—to secure, obtain, or enjoy these goods?

I think that the third question is the simplest of the three to answer. If anyone has a right to well-being and freedom and if the intrinsic value of any person's enjoyment of these goods is equal to that of any other's, then all men do have an equal right—and hence a human right—to secure, obtain, or enjoy these goods, just because it would be irrational to distinguish among persons as to the possession of these rights. That is to say, the principle that no person should be treated differently from any or all other persons unless there is some general and relevant reason that justifies this difference in treatment is a fundamental principle of morality, if not of rationality itself. Indeed, although I am not certain how one might argue for this, I think it could well be said that all men do have a "second-order"

---

[7] In Richard B. Brandt (ed.), *Social Justice* (Englewood Cliffs, NJ: Prentice-Hall, 1962), 31–72.

human right—that is, an absolute right—to expect all persons to adhere to this principle.

This principle, or this right, does not by itself establish that there are any specific human rights. But either the principle or the right does seem to establish that well-being and freedom are human rights if they are rights at all and if the intrinsic value of each person's enjoyment is the same. For, given these premises, it does appear to follow that there is no relevant and general reason to differentiate among persons as to the possession of this right.

I say "seem to" and "appear to" because this general principle of morality may not be strong enough. What has been said so far does not in any obvious fashion rule out the possibility that there is some general and relevant principle of differentiation. It only, apparently, rules out possible variations in intrinsic value as a reason for making differentiations.

The requirement of *relevance* does, I think, seem to make the argument secure. For, if *the reason* for acknowledging in a person a right to freedom and well-being is the intrinsic value of his enjoyment of these goods, then the nature of the intrinsic value of any other person's enjoyment is the only relevant reason for making exceptions or for differentiating among persons as to the possession of these rights.[8]

As to the first question, that of whether a person has a right to well-being and freedom, I am not certain what kind of answer is most satisfactory. If Vlastos is correct in asserting that these enjoyments are *values*, then that is, perhaps, answer enough. That is to say, if enjoying well-being is something *valuable*—and especially if it is intrinsically valuable—then it seems to follow that this is the kind of thing to which one ought to have a right. For if anything ought to be given the kind of protection afforded by a right, it ought surely be that which is valuable. Perhaps, too, there is nothing more that need be said other than to point out that we simply do properly value well-being and freedom.

I think that another, more general answer is also possible. Here I would revert more specifically to my earlier discussion of some of the characteristics and functions of rights. There are two points to be made. First, if we are asked, why ought anyone have a right to anything? or why not have a system in which there are not rights at all? the answer is that such a system

---

[8] See, e.g., Bernard Williams, "The Idea of Equality," in P. Laslett and W. G. Runeiman (eds.), *Philosophy, Politics and Society*, ii (Oxford: Blackwell, 1962), 111–13.

Professor Vlastos imposes a somewhat different requirement which, I think, comes to about the same thing: "An equalitarian concept of justice may admit just inequalities without inconsistency if, and only if, it provides grounds for equal human rights *which are also grounds for unequal rights of other sorts*" (Vlastos, "Justice and Equality," 40; italics in text).

would be a morally impoverished one. It would prevent persons from assert-ing those kinds of claims, it would preclude persons from having those types of expectations, and it would prohibit persons from making those kinds of judgments which a system of rights makes possible.

Thus, if we can answer the question of why have rights at all, we can then ask and answer the question of what things—among others—ought to be protected by *rights*. And the answer, I take it, is that one ought to be able to claim as entitlements those minimal things without which it is impossible to develop one's capabilities and to live a life as a human being. Hence, to take one thing that is a precondition of well-being, the relief from acute physical pain, this is the kind of enjoyment that ought to be protected as a right of some kind just because without such relief there is precious little that one can effectively do or become. And similarly for the opportunity to make choices, examine beliefs, and the like.

To recapitulate. The discussion so far has indicated two things: (1) the conditions under which any specific right would be a human right, and (2) some possible grounds for arguing that certain values or enjoyments ought to be regarded as matters of right. The final question that remains is whether there are any specific rights that satisfy the conditions necessary to make them human rights. Or, more specifically, whether it is plausible to believe that there are no general and relevant principles that justify making distinctions among persons in respect to their rights to well-being and freedom.

Vlastos has it that the rights to well-being and freedom do satisfy these conditions, since he asserts that we, at least, do regard each person's well-being and freedom as having equal intrinsic value. If this is correct, if each person's well-being and freedom does have *equal* intrinsic value, then there is no general and relevant principle for differentiating among persons as to these values and, hence, as to their rights to secure these values. But this does not seem wholly satisfactory. It does not give us any reason for supposing that it is plausible to ascribe equal intrinsic value to each person's well-being and freedom.

The crucial question, then, is the plausibility of ascribing equal intrinsic value to each person's well-being and freedom. There are, I think, at least three different answers that might be given.

First, it might be asserted that this ascription simply constitutes another feature of our morality. The only things that can be done are to point out that this is an assumption that we do make and to ask persons whether they would not prefer to live in a society in which such an assumption is made.

While perhaps correct and persuasive, this does not seem to me to be all that can be done. In particular, there are, I think, two further arguments that may be made.

The first is that there are cases in which all human beings *equally* are capable of enjoying the same goods, e.g., relief from acute physical pain,[9] or that they are capable of deriving equal enjoyment from the same goods. If this is true, then if anyone has a right to this enjoyment, that right is a human right just because there is no rational ground for preferring one man's enjoyment to another's. For, if all persons do have equal capacities of these sorts and if the existence of these capacities is the reason for ascribing these rights to anyone, then all persons ought to have the right to claim equality of treatment in respect to the possession and exercise of these rights.

The difficulty inherent in this argument is at the same time the strength of the next one. The difficulty is simply that it does seem extraordinarily difficult to know how one would show that all men are equally capable of enjoying any of the same goods, or even how one might attempt to gather or evaluate relevant evidence in this matter. In a real sense, interpersonal comparisons of such a thing as the ability to bear pain seems to be logically as well as empirically unobtainable. Even more unobtainable, no doubt, is a measure of the comparative enjoyments derivable from choosing for oneself.[10] These are simply enjoyments the comparative worths of which, as different persons, there is no way to assess. If this is so, then this fact gives rise to an alternative argument.

We do know, through inspection of human history as well as of our own lives, that the denial of the opportunity to experience the enjoyment of these goods makes it impossible to live either a full or a satisfying life. In a real sense, the enjoyment of these goods differentiates human from nonhuman entities. And therefore, even if we have no meaningful or reliable criteria for comparing and weighing capabilities for enjoyment or for measuring their quantity or quality, we probably know all we need to know to justify our refusal to attempt to grade the value of the enjoyment of these goods. Hence, the dual grounds for treating their intrinsic values as equal for all persons: either these values are equal for all persons, or, if there are differences, they are not in principle discoverable or measurable. Hence, the argument, or an argument, for the human rights to well-being and freedom.

---

[9] See, Williams, "The Idea of Equality," 112: "These respects [in which men are alike] are notably the capacity to feel pain, both from immediate physical causes and from various situations represented in perception and in thought; and the capacity to feel affection for others, and the consequences of this, connected with the frustration of this affection, loss of its objects, etc."

[10] At times, Vlastos seems to adopt this view as well as the preceding one. See, e.g., Vlastos, "Justice and Equality," 49: "So understood a person's well-being and freedom are aspects of his individual existence as unique and unrepeatable as is that existence itself. . . . "

Because the foregoing discussion has been quite general and abstract, I want finally to consider briefly one illustration of a denial of human rights and to delineate both the several ways in which such a denial can occur and some of the different consequences of that denial. My example is that of the way in which Negro persons are regarded and treated by many whites in the South.

The first thing that is obvious is that many white Southerners would or might be willing to accept all that has been said so far and yet seek to justify their attitudes and behavior toward Negroes.

They might agree, for example, that all persons do have a right to be accorded equal treatment unless there is a general and relevant principle of differentiation. They would also surely acknowledge that some persons do have rights to many different things, including most certainly well-being and freedom. But they would insist, nonetheless, that there exists a general and relevant principle of differentiation, namely, that some persons are Negroes and others are not.

Now, those who do bother to concern themselves with arguments and with the need to give reasons would not, typically, assert that the mere fact of color difference does constitute a general and relevant reason. Rather, they would argue that this color difference is correlated with certain other characteristics and attitudes that are relevant.[11] In so doing, they invariably commit certain logical and moral mistakes.

First, the purported differentiating characteristic is usually not relevant to the differentiation sought to be made; e.g., none of the characteristics that supposedly differentiate Negroes from whites has any relevance to the capacity to bear acute physical pain or to the strength of the desire to be free from it. Indeed, almost all arguments neglect the fact that the capacities to enjoy those things which are constitutive of well-being and freedom are either incommensurable among persons or alike in all persons.

Second, the invocation of these differentiating characteristics always violates the requirement of relevance in another sense. For, given the typical definition of a Negro (in Alabama the legal definition is any person with "a drop of Negro blood"), it is apparent that there could not—under any plausible scientific theory—be good grounds for making any differentiations between Negroes and whites.[12]

Third, and related to the above, any argument that makes distinctions as to the possession of human rights in virtue of the truth of certain empirical

[11] See, Williams, "The Idea of Equality," 113.

[12] This is to say nothing, of course, of the speciousness of any principle of differentiation that builds upon inequalities that are themselves produced by the unequal and unjust distribution of *opportunities*.

generalizations invariably produces some unjust denials of those rights. That is to say, even if some of the generalizations about Negroes are correct, they are correct only in the sense that the distinguishing characteristics ascribed to Negroes are possessed by some or many Negroes but not by all Negroes. Yet, before any reason for differentiating among persons as to the possession of human rights can be a relevant reason, that reason must be relevant in respect to *each person* so affected or distinguished. To argue otherwise is to neglect the fact, among other things, that human rights are personal and of at least *prima facie* equal importance to each possessor of those rights.

A different reaction or argument of white Southerners in respect to recent events in the South is bewilderment. Rather than (or in addition to) arguing for the existence of principles of differentiation, the white Southerner will say that he simply cannot understand the Negro's dissatisfaction with his lot. This is so because he, the white Southerner, has always treated his Negroes very well. With appreciable sincerity, he will assert that he has real affection for many Negroes. He would never needlessly inflict pain or suffering upon them. Indeed, he has often assumed special obligations to make certain that their lives were free from hunger, pain, and disease.

Now of course, this description of the facts is seldom accurate at all. Negroes have almost always been made to endure needless and extremely severe suffering in all too many obvious ways for all too many obviously wrong reasons. But I want to assume for my purposes the accuracy of the white Southerner's assertions. For these assertions are instructive just because they reveal some of the less obvious effects of a denial of human rights.

What is wholly missing from this description of the situation is the ability and inclination to conceptualize the Negro—any Negro—as the possible possessor of rights of any kind, and *a fortiori* of any human rights. And this has certain especially obnoxious consequences.

In the first place, the white Southerner's moral universe illustrates both the fact that it is possible to conceive of duties without conceiving of their correlative rights and the fact that the mistakes thereby committed are not chiefly mistakes of logic and definition. The mistakes matter morally. For what this way of conceiving most denies to any Negro is the opportunity to assert claims as a matter of right. It denies him the standing to protest against the way he is treated. If the white Southerner fails to do his duty, that is simply a matter between him and his conscience.

In the second place, it requires of any Negro that *he* make out his case for the enjoyment of any goods. It reduces all of *his* claims to the level of requests, privileges, and favors. But there are simply certain things, certain goods, that nobody ought to have to request of another. There are certain things that no one else ought to have the power to decide to refuse or to grant. To observe what happens to any person who is required to adopt habits of obsequious, deferential behavior in order to minimize the likelihood of physical abuse, arbitrary treatment, or economic destitution is to see most graphically how important human rights are and what their denial can mean. To witness what happens to a person's own attitudes, aspirations, and conceptions of himself[13] when he must request or petition for the opportunity to voice an opinion, to consult with a public official, or to secure the protection of the law is to be given dramatic and convincing assurance of the moral necessity of a conception of human rights.

And there is one final point. In a real sense, a society that simply lacks any conception of human rights is less offensive than one which has such a conception but denies that some persons have these rights. This is so not just because of the inequality and unfairness involved in differentiating for the wrong reasons among persons. Rather, a society based on such denial is especially offensive because it implicitly, if not explicitly, entails that there are some persons who do not and would not desire or need or enjoy those minimal goods which all men do need and desire and enjoy. It is to read certain persons, all of whom are most certainly human beings, out of the human race. This is surely among the greatest of all moral wrongs.

I know of no better example of the magnitude of this evil than that provided by a lengthy account in a Southern newspaper about the high school band program in a certain city. The article described fully the magnificence of the program and emphasized especially the fact that it was a program in which *all high school students* in the city participated.

Negro children neither were nor could be participants in the program. The article, however, saw no need to point this out. I submit that it neglected to do so not because everyone knew the fact, but because in a real sense the writer and the newspaper do not regard Negro high school students as children—persons, human beings—at all.

What is the Negro parent who reads this article to say to his children? What are his children supposed to think! How does a Negro parent even begin to demonstrate to the world that his children are really children, too? These are burdens no civilized society ought ever to impose. These are among the burdens that an established and acknowledged system of human rights helps to eliminate.

---

[13] Vlastos puts what I take to be the same point this way: "Any practice which tends to so weaken and confuse the personal esteem of a group of persons—slavery, serfdom or, in our own time racial segregation—may be morally condemned on this one ground, even if there were no other for indicting it" (Vlastos, "Justice and Equality," 71).

8

TWO KINDS OF DISCRIMINATION

ADRIAN M. S. PIPER

The two kinds of discrimination I want to talk about are political discrimination and cognitive discrimination. By *political discrimination*, I mean what we ordinarily understand by the term "discrimination" in political contexts: A manifest attitude in which a particular property of a person which is irrelevant to judgments of that person's intrinsic value or competence, for example his race, gender, class, sexual orientation, or religious or ethnic affiliation, is seen as a source of disvalue or incompetence; in general, as a source of inferiority.[1] I will call any such arbitrary property so perceived a *primary disvalued property*; and conversely, any such arbitrary property perceived as a source of value or superiority a *primary valued property*.

By *cognitive discrimination*, I mean what we ordinarily understand by the term "discrimination" in cognitive contexts: A manifest capacity to distinguish veridically between one property and another, and to respond appropriately to each. When we say of someone that she is a discriminating person, for example, or that she has discriminating judgment, we mean, in part, that she is a person of refined tastes or subtle convictions; that she exercises a capacity to make fine distinctions between properties

From Adrian M. S. Piper, 'Two Kinds of Discrimination', *Yale Journal of Criticism*, 6/1 (1993).

Work on this paper was supported in part by a National Endowment for the Humanities Summer Stipend and a Woodrow Wilson International Scholars' Fellowship. Portions are excerpted from a manuscript in progress, *Rationality and the Structure of the Self*, and from other articles (as indicated) in which I have addressed these issues.

[1] Thus I shall not be considering cases in which race, gender, etc., *are* relevant to judgments of a person's value or competence, e.g., as a role model in a classroom, or to provide a unique and needed perspective in a business venture or court of law. I restrict the discussion to consideration of *intrinsic* value or competence as determined by principles of justice and equality. The contrast is with *instrumental* value or competence in furthering some specified social or institutional policy, of the sort that would figure in arguments that would justify, e.g., refusing to sell real estate in a certain neighbourhood to a black family solely because doing so would lower property values, or hiring a woman to a professional position solely in order to meet affirmative action quotas, or refusing to serve Asians at one's family diner solely because it would be bad for business. Whether these should be included under the rubric of first-order political discrimination, hypocrisy, prudence, or mere moral pusillanimity is too large a topic to address here.

of a thing, and bases her positive or negative valuations on these actual properties.[2]

I want to explore the relation between these two kinds of discrimination, and to argue that the first type of discrimination depends upon a failure of the second. Judging a person as inferior because one perceives his race as a primary disvalued property depends upon failing to distinguish finely enough between properties he has and those he does not have, and between those which are relevant to such a judgment and those which are not. I begin by arguing that, on a Kantian conception of the self, we instinctively resist the challenge of cognitive discrimination by confining our range of judgments to those objects and properties that conform to preexisting categories and concepts that structure not only our experience, but thereby our selves. I suggest that we are compelled either to conceptualize the objects of our experience in familiar terms, or else not to register them at all; and that this is a necessary condition of preserving the unity and internal coherence of the self against anomalous data that threaten it. I invoke this model of the self to explain the phenomenon of xenophobia, i.e., fear of another who fails to satisfy our provincial preconceptions about *bona fide* persons; and xenophobia, in turn, to explain the phenomenon of political discrimination. I distinguish between two kinds of political discrimination: *first-order political discrimination* as defined above, and *higher-order political discrimination* as a refinement introduced by pangs of conscience that result in even more radical failures of cognitive discrimination: of the other, of oneself, and of the situation. Finally, I conclude by suggesting some ways in which works of art might combat political discrimination by cultivating cognitive discrimination.

I. THE KANTIAN RATIONALISM THESIS

In the first *Critique*,[3] Kant tells us repeatedly that if a perception does not conform to the fundamental categories of thought that ensure the unity and

---

[2] Notice that the veracity of the discrimination—and hence the reality of the properties—is presupposed in this use of the term. Someone who draws such distinctions in their absence is said to draw a "distinction without a difference;" or to be "seeing things." Of such a person we say not that he is discriminating, but rather that he is deluded. See my "'Seeing Things'," *Southern Journal of Philosophy*, 29, suppl. vol.: *Moral Epistemology* (1990), 29–60.

[3] Immanuel Kant, *Kritik der Reinen Vernunft*, ed. Raymund Schmidt (Hamburg: Felix Meiner Verlag, 1976). All references to this work are parenthesized in the text. Translations from the German are my own. Cognoscenti will find my translations to be generally more literal than Kemp Smith's, and (I think) more accurate in conveying not only the substance of Kant's claims, but his manner of expression. Despite Kant's tendency to indulge in run-on sentences, he is by and large a plain speaker with a fondness for the vernacular, not the stilted, pretentious Prussian Kemp Smith

coherence of the self, they cannot be part of our experience at all (A 112, 122, and B 132, 134).[4] Kant describes these fundamental categories as "*a priori* transcendental concepts of understanding," by which he means innate rules of cognitive organization that any coherent, conscious experience must presuppose. The table of transcendental categories he offers in the Metaphysical Deduction are drawn largely from Aristotle, with considerable additional tinkering by Kant. They include substance, totality, reality, possibility, causality, and community, to name just a few. Some commentators have rightfully concluded that the most significant candidate for this elevated cognitive status is the subject–predicate relation in logic, from which Kant derives the relational category of substance and property in the Table of Categories (Kant regards this as the result of fleshing out the subject–predicate relation or "judgment form" with "transcendental content," i.e., the sensory data our experience presupposes rather than the sensations we perceive as a result of them; A 70/B 95–A 79/B 105).[5] The idea, then, would be that organizing sensory data in terms of this relation is a necessary condition of experience. On this view, if we do not experience something in a way that enables us to make sense of it by identifying properties of it—for example, in propositions such as,

That car is dark red,

or

I am tired,

we cannot consciously experience that thing at all.

This thesis—call it the *Kantian Rationalism Thesis*—has the merit of plausibility over the archaic list of categories Kant originally furnished. It does not seem too controversial to suppose that any viable system of concepts should enable its user to identify states of affairs by their properties, since concepts just are of corresponding properties, and to ascribe a property to an object just is to subsume that object under the corresponding

makes him out to be. But the major objection to Kemp Smith's translation is that he obscures important philosophical issues by overinterpreting Kant so as to resolve them before the monolingual reader can become aware that there is anything to dispute.

[4] This thesis may be viewed as the resolution of a *Gedankenexperiment* Kant earlier conducts at A 89–91, in which he entertains the possibility of unsynthesized appearance. In any case, his ultimate commitment to this thesis is clear. See Robert Paul Wolff, *Kant's Theory of Mental Activity* (Cambridge, Mass.: Harvard University Press, 1968) for a discussion.

[5] See, for example, P. F. Strawson, *The Bounds of Sense* (London: Methuen, 1968), ch. II. 2. In hindsight Kant himself grudgingly admits that hypothetical and disjunctive syllogisms contain the same "matter" as the categorical judgment, but refuses to budge on their essential difference in form and function. See Kant's *Logic*, trans. Robert Hartman and Wolfgang Schwarz (New York: Bobbs-Merrill, 1974), paras. 24–9, 60 n. 2, esp. pp. 111 and 127.

concept. So any system of concepts should enable its user to ascribe to objects those properties of which she has concepts. The Kantian Rationalism Thesis—henceforth the KRT—is so weak that it may even be defensible in the face of anthropological evidence that languages considerably remote from Indo-European ones evince a cognitive structuring to the user's experience that is so different from our own as to be almost unintelligible to us. It would be an argument in favor of the KRT if it could be shown that the subject–predicate relation held regardless of the other ways in which culturally specific conceptual organizations of experience differed among themselves.

More precisely formulated, then, the KRT says that if we do not experience something in such a way as to allow us to make sense of it in terms of a set of coherent concepts that structure our experience, *whatever those concepts are*, we cannot consciously experience that thing at all. On this thesis the innate capacity would consist in a disposition to structure experience conceptually as such, but not necessarily to do so in accordance with any particular list of concepts,[6] provided that the particular, culturally specific set S of concepts c_1, c_2, c_3, ... c_n that did so satisfied the following requirements:

(A) S observes the law of noncontradiction, i.e. the members of S are internally and mutually consistent in their application;

(B) Any particular c_n in S is either
  (1) an instantiation of some other c_j in S; or
  (2) instantiated by some other c_k in S;
  i.e. S is minimally coherent;

(C) For any cognitively available particular p, there is a c_j in S that p instantiates.

The suggestion would be that we can understand particular states of affairs only if (A) the concepts by which we recognize them are neither internally nor mutually contradictory; (B) those concepts are minimally coherent with one another in that each particular identified by them satisfies the subject–predicate relationship with respect to at least one other of them; and (C) that particular itself instantiates at least one of them. I develop this suggestion at length elsewhere.[7] It says, roughly, that in order for something to register as a

---

[6] This thesis is elaborated in the contemporary context by Gerald M. Edelman, *Neural Darwinism: The Theory of Neuronal Group Selection* (New York: Basic Books, 1987) and *The Remembered Present: A Biological Theory of Consciousness* (New York: Basic Books, 1989). See the review of Edelman and others by Oliver Sacks in "Neurology and the Soul," *New York Review of Books*, 37/18 (Nov. 22, 1990), 44–50.

[7] Piper, "Rationality and the Structure of the Self," excerpted from *Rationality and the Structure of the Self* and delivered to the Association for the Philosophy of the Unconscious, American Philosophical Association Eastern Division Convention, Boston, Mass., 1986.

conscious experience at all for us, we have to be able to make sense of it in terms of some such concepts in the set; and that if we can't, it won't.

Suppose, for example, that we were to be confronted with some particular such that the concepts it instantiates satisfied (A) but violated (B), i.e., such that we could invoke a concept in identifying it consistently with the application of our other concepts; but that that concept itself bore no instantiation-relation to others in the set (i.e., aside from that of being a concept in the set). In this case, that which we invoked as a "concept" would in fact not be one at all, since the corresponding predicate would by definition denote only the single state of affairs it had been invoked to identify. Since there would be no further concepts in terms of which we might understand the meaning of that denoting term, it could not enter into any analytic truths. In short, this would be like cooking up a special noise to denote only one state of affairs on the single occasion of its occurrence. The enterprises of denotation and meaning themselves would fail.

Alternately, imagine what it would be like to be confronted by a particular such that its concept satisfied (B) but not (A), i.e., such that it enabled us to identify its properties in terms of concepts in the set, but the application of those concepts themselves was internally or mutually inconsistent. In that event, it would be possible to ascribe to the thing the conjunction of some predicate F and some other one, G, that implied the negation of F.[8] Again the enterprise of identification itself would fail. If we were finally to fail to identify the thing or state of affairs in question as having a consistent set of properties, we would fail to identify it altogether. And then it could not be part of our conscious experience. If such cases characterized all of our encounters with the world, we would have no experiences of it at all and therefore no unified sense of self either.

These are the sorts of failures Kant has in mind when he avers, in the A Deduction, that

> without such unity, which has its rule a priori, and which subjects appearances to it, thoroughgoing, universal, and therefore necessary unity of consciousness would not be found in the manifold of perceptions. These would then not belong to any experience, therefore would be without object, and nothing but a blind play of representations, that is, less even than a dream. (A 112)

Kant is saying that if we do not organize cognitively the data of our senses according to consistent and coherent rules, we cannot be rationally unified subjects. "For otherwise," he adds in the B Deduction, "I would have as many-colored and diverse a self as I have representations of which I am conscious" (B 134). I would, that is, lack a sense of myself as the subject in

---

[8] Piper, "Rationality and the Structure of the Self."

whose consciousness those representations occur. For a Kantian rationalist, then, the cognitive organization of experience according to consistent and coherent concepts is a necessary condition of being a rationally unified subject. Anomalous particulars or properties that fail to satisfy (A)–(C) cannot be objects of experience for us at all.

Elsewhere I have argued that the resistance to integrating anomaly is a general feature of human intellection that attempts to satisfy a Kantian requirement of rational self-preservation.[9] And Thomas Kuhn has documented the inherent impediments to paradigm shift in the natural sciences— their conservatism and constitutional insensitivity to the significance of new data, and their resistance to revising deeply entrenched theories in light of experimental anomaly.[10] Relative to this scheme, xenophobia is a particular example of a perfectly general disposition to defend the self against anomalous informational assaults on its internal coherence. Xenophobia is fear, not of strangers generally, but rather of certain kinds of strangers, namely, those who do not conform to one's preconceptions about how persons ought to look or behave. In what follows I want to argue that xenophobia explains political discrimination in the sense defined above. Our inability to make fine-grained cognitive discriminations in judging a person is the result of a fear reaction to the anomalous perceptual data that person presents, and the cause of a corresponding inability to evaluate her veridically as a person.

II. XENOPHOBIA

I will use the terms *person* and *personality* to denote particular empirical instantiations of the concept of personhood, which I assume to be innate for purposes of this discussion.[11] Thus when we refer to someone as a person, we ordinarily mean to denote at the very least a social being whom we presume—as Kant did—to have consciousness, thought, rationality, and agency. The term "person" used in this way also finds its way into jurisprudence, where we conceive of a person as a rational individual who can be held legally and morally accountable for his actions. Relative to these related

---

[9] Piper, "Two Conceptions of the Self," *Philosophical Studies*, 48/2 (Sept. 1985), 173–97; repr. in *Philosopher's Annual*, 8 (1985), 222–46; see also "Pseudorationality," in Amelie O. Rorty and Brian McLoughlin (eds.), *Perspectives on Self-Deception* (Los Angeles: University of California Press, 1988), 297–323.

[10] Thomas Kuhn, *The Structure of Scientific Revolutions* (Chicago: University of Chicago, 1971), chs. 6–8.

[11] I defend this assumption at length in sects. II and III of "Xenophobia and Kantian Rationalism," *Philosophical Forum*, 24/1–3 (Fall–Spring 1992–3), 188–232. The analysis offered in this and the following section of the present discussion is excerpted from sect. V of that article.

usages, an individual who lacks to a significant degree the capacities to reason, plan for the future, detect causal and logical relations among events, or control action according to principles applied more or less consistently from one occasion to the next is ascribed diminished responsibility for her actions, and her social and legal status as a person is diminished accordingly.

Similarly, when we call someone a "bad person," we communicate a cluster of evaluations that include, for example, assessing his conscious motives as corrupt or untrustworthy, his rationality as deployed for maleficent ends, and his actions as harmful. And when we say that someone has a "good personality" or a "difficult personality," we mean that the person's consciousness, thought, rationality, and agency are manifested in pleasing or displeasing or bewildering ways that are particular to that individual. We do not ordinarily assess a being who lacks any one of these components of personhood in terms of their personality at all. Persons, then, express their innate personhood in their empirical personalities.

With these stipulations in place, I now turn to an analysis of the concept of xenophobia. Xenophobia is not simply an indiscriminate fear of strangers in general: it does not include, for example, fear of relatives or neighbors whom one happens not to have met. It is more specific than that. Xenophobia is a fear of individuals who look or behave differently than those one is accustomed to. It is a fear of what is experientially unfamiliar, of individuals who do not conform to one's empirical assumptions about what other people are like, how they behave or how they look. Ultimately it is a fear of individuals who violate one's empirical conception of persons and so one's self-conception. So xenophobia is an alarm reaction to a threat to the rational coherence of the self, a threat in the form of an anomalous other who transgresses one's preconceptions about people. It is a paradigm example of reacting self-protectively to anomalous data that violate one's internally consistent conceptual scheme.

Recall that on the KRT, if we cannot make sense of such data in terms of those familiar concepts, we cannot register it as an experience at all. I have argued elsewhere[12] that *pseudorationality* is an attempt to make sense of such data under duress, i.e., to preserve the internal rational coherence of the self, when we are baldly confronted by anomaly but are not yet prepared to revise or jettison our conceptual scheme accordingly. It is in the attempt to make sense of anomalous data in terms of empirically inadequate concepts that the mechanisms of pseudorationality—rationalization, dissociation and denial—kick in to secure self-preservation. But they succeed in preserving only the appearance of rational coherence. In *rationalization*, we misapply a

---

[12] Piper, "Two Conceptions of Self" and "Pseudorationality."

concept to a particular by distorting its scope, magnifying the properties of the thing that instantiate the concept, and minimizing those that fail to do so. So, for example, conceiving of a slave imported from Africa as three-fifths of a person results from magnifying the properties that appear to support this diminished concept of personhood—the slave's environmental and psychological disorientation, lack of mastery of a foreign language, lack of familiarity with local social customs, incompetence at unfamiliar tasks, etc.; and minimizing the properties that disconfirm it—her capacity to learn, to forge innovative modes of communication and expression, to adapt and flourish in an alien social environment, to survive enslavement and transcend violations of her person, etc. In *dissociation*, we identify something in terms of the negation of the concepts that articulate our theory: Identifying Jews as subhuman, blacks as childlike, women as irrational, gays as perverts, or working-class people as animals, for example, conceives of them as lacking essential properties of personhood, and so are ways of defining these groups of individuals out of our empirical concepts of people. In *denial*, we suppress recognition of the anomalous particular or property altogether, by ignoring it or suppressing it from awareness. For example, ignoring a woman's verbal contributions to a discussion, or passing over a black person's intellectual achievements, or forgetting to make provisions at a Christmas celebration for someone who is a practicing Jew are all ways of eradicating the anomalous other from one's domain of awareness.

Thus through the pseudorational mechanisms of rationalization and dissociation, xenophobia engenders various forms of stereotyping—racism, sexism, anti-Semitism, homophobia, class elitism—that are discriminatory in both the perceptual and the political sense. It selects certain perceptually familiar properties of the person for primary disvalue, and distorts or obliterates those which remain. It thereby reduces the complex singularity of the other's properties to an oversimplified but conceptually manageable subset, and this in turn diminishes one's full conception of personhood. For the xenophobe, this results in a provincial self-conception and conception of the world, from which significant available data are excluded. And this provincial theory is sustained with the aid of denial, by enforcing those stereotypes through such tactics as exclusion, ostracism, scapegoating, tribalism, and segregation in housing, education, or employment. My thesis is that xenophobia is the originating phenomenon to which each of these forms of political discrimination is a response.

Nevertheless, even if it is true that we are innately cognitively disposed to respond to any conceptual and experiential anomaly in this way, it does not follow that our necessarily limited empirical conception of people must be so limited and provincial so as to invite it. A person could be so cosmopolitan and intimately familiar with the full range of human variety that only The Alien would rattle him. On the other hand, his empirical conception of people might be so limited that any variation in race, nationality, gender, sexual preference, or class would be cause for panic. How easily one's empirical conception of people is violated is one index of the scope of one's xenophobia; how central and pervasive it is in one's personality is another. In what follows I will focus primarily on cases of political discrimination midway between such extremes: for example, of a white person who is thoughtful, well-rounded, and well-read about the problems of racism in the United States, but who nevertheless feels fearful at being alone in the house with a black television repairman. In all such cases, the range of individuals in fact identifiable as persons is larger than the range of individuals to whom one's empirical conception of people apply. In all such cases, I will argue, political discrimination can be understood in terms of certain corrigible cognitive errors that characterize prereflective xenophobia.

A. The Error of Confusing People with Personhood

Xenophobia is fueled by a perfectly general condition of subjective consciousness, namely the first/third person asymmetry: Although I must identify myself as a person because of my necessary, enduring first-personal experience of rationally unified selfhood, my experience of you as a person, necessarily lacking that first-personal experience, can have no such necessity about it:

Identity of person is . . . in my own consciousness unfailingly to be found. But when I view myself from the standpoint of another (as object of his outer intuition), this external observer considers me first and foremost in time. . . . So from the I, which accompanies all representations at all times in my consciousness, and indeed with full identity, whether he immediately concedes it, he will not yet conclude the objective continuity of my self. For because the time in which the observer situates me is not the same as that time to be found in my own, but rather in his sensibility, similarly the identify that is necessarily bound up with my consciousness, is not therefore bound up with his, i.e. with the outer intuition of my subject. (A 362–3)

Kant is saying that the temporal continuity I invariably perceive in my own consciousness is not matched by any corresponding temporal continuity I might be supposed to have as the object of someone else's consciousness. Since I am not always present to another as I am to myself, I may appear discontinuously to her consciousness in a way I cannot to my own. And similarly, another may appear discontinuously to my consciousness in a way I cannot to my own.

Thus although personhood is a necessary concept of mine, whether or not any other empirical individual instantiates it is itself, from my point of view, a contingent matter of fact—as is the concept of that particular individual herself. Though you may exhibit rationality in your behavior, I may not know that, or fail to perceive it, or fail to understand it. Nor can you be a necessary feature of my experience, since I might ignore or overlook you, or simply fail to have any contact with you. In any of these cases, you will fail to instantiate my concept of personhood in a way I never can. Because the pattern of your behavior is not a necessary and permanent, familiar concomitant of my subjectivity in the way my own unified consciousness and ratiocinative processes are, I may escape your personhood in a way that I cannot escape my own. For me the innate idea of personhood is a concept that applies necessarily to me, but, from my perspective, only contingently and empirically to you. Hence just as our experience of the natural world is limited relative to the all-inclusive, transcendent idea of its independent unity, similarly our empirical experience of other persons is limited relative to our all-inclusive, transcendent idea of personhood.

But there is an important disanalogy between them that turns on the problem of other minds and the first/third person asymmetry. For any empirical experience of the natural world we have, we must, according to Kant, be able to subsume it under the transcendent concept of a unified system of nature of which it is a part, even if we do not know what that system might be. By contrast, it is not necessarily the case that for any empirical experience of other people we have, we must be able to subsume them under the transcendent idea of personhood. This is because although they may, in fact, manifest their personhood in their personality, we may not be able fully to discern their personhood through its empirical manifestations, if those manifestations fall outside our empirical conception of what people are like.

Suppose, for example, that within my subculture, speech is used to seek confirmation and promote bonding, whereas in yours it is used to protect independence and win status;[13] and that our only interpersonal contact occurs when you come to fix my TV. I attempt to engage you in conversation about what is wrong with my TV, to which you react with a lengthy lecture. To you I appear dependent and mechanically incompetent, while to me you appear logorrheic and socially inappropriate. Each of us perceives the other as deficient in some characteristic of rationality: you perceive me as lacking in autonomy and basic mechanical skills, whereas I perceive you as lacking

---

[13] This is the main thesis of Deborah Tannen's fascinating *You just don't Understand: Women and Men in Conversation* (New York: William Morrow, 1990), a popularization of her research in linguistics on gender differences in language use.

in verbal control and basic social skills. To the extent that this perceived deficit is not corrected by further contact and fuller information, each of us will perceive the other as less of a full-fledged person because of it. This is the kind of perception that contributes to one-dimensional stereotypes, for example of women as flighty and incompetent or of men as aggressive and barbaric, which poison the expectations and behavior of each toward the other accordingly. This is how gender becomes a primary disvalued property.

Or take another example, in which the verbal convention in my subculture is to disclose pain and offer solace, whereas in yours it is to suppress pain and advert to impersonal topics; and that our only interpersonal contact occurs when I come to work as your housemaid. Again each of us perceives the other as deficient in some characteristic of rationality: you perceive me as dull and phlegmatic in my lack of responsiveness to the impersonal topics you raise for discussion, whereas I perceive you as almost schizophrenically dissociated from the painful realities that confront us. Again, unless this perceived deficit is corrected by further contact and fuller information, each of us will perceive the other as less of a person because of it, thereby contributing to one-dimensional stereotypes of, for example, blacks as stupid, or of whites as ignorant and out of touch with reality, that similarly poison both the expectations and the behavior of each toward the other. This is how race becomes a primary disvalued property.

In such cases there are multiple sources of empirical error. The first one is our respective failures to discriminate cognitively between the possession of rationality as an active capacity in general, and particular empirical uses or instantiations of it under a given set of circumstances and for a given set of ends. Because your particular behavior and ends strike me as irrational, I surmise that you must be irrational. Here the error consists in equating the particular set of empirical behaviors and ends with which I am familiar from my own and similar cases with unified rational agency in general. It is as though I assume that the only rational agents there are are the particular people I identify as such. Kant might put the point by saying that each of us has conflated his empirically limited conception of people with the transcendent concept of personhood.

B. The Error of Assuming Privileged Access to the Self

But now suppose we each recognize at least the intentionality of the other's behavior, if not its rationality. Since each of us equates rational agency in general exclusively with the motives and actions of her own subculture in particular, each also believes that the motives and ends that guide the other's actions—and therefore the evidence of conformity to the rule and order of rationality—nevertheless remain inaccessible in a way we each believe our own motives and ends not to be inaccessible to ourselves. This third-personal opacity yields the distinction between the appearance and the reality of the self: You, it seems, are an appearance to me behind which is hidden the reality of your motives and intentions, whereas I am not similarly an appearance that hides my own from myself. The less familiar you are to me, the more hidden your motives and intentions will seem and the less benevolent I will assume them to be.

Of course whom we happen to recognize as familiar determines whose motives are cause for suspicion and whose are not. There is no necessary connection between actual differences in physical or psychological properties between oneself and another, and the epistemic inscrutability we ascribe to someone we regard as anomalous. It is required only that the other seem anomalous relative to our familiar subculture, however cosmopolitan that may be, in order to generate doubts and questions about what it is that makes him tick. Stereotypes of women as enigmatic or of Asians as inscrutable or of blacks as evasive all express the underlying fear of the impenetrability of the other's motives. And someone who conceives of Jews as crafty, blacks as shiftless, or women as devious expresses particularly clearly the suspicion and fear of various third-personal others as mendacious manipulators that are consequent on falsely regarding them as more epistemically inaccessible to one than one is to oneself.

Thus our mutual failure to identify the other as a person of the same status as oneself is compounded by scepticism based on the belief that each of us has the privileged access to her own personhood that demonstrates directly and first-personally what personhood really is. The inaccessibility and unfamiliarity of the other's conception of her own motives to our consciousness of her may seem conclusive justification of our reflexive fear and suspicion as to whether her motives can be trusted at all.

Now Kant argues (B 68–9, 153–6, 157–8a, A 551a/B 579a)[14] that from the first-personal relation I bear to my empirical self-conception which I lack to yours, it does not follow that my actual motives are any more accessible to me than yours are. Therefore, regardless of how comfortable and familiar my own motives may seem to me, it does not follow that I can know that my own motives are innocuous whereas yours are not. In fact, it is difficult to imagine how I might gain any understanding of the malevolent motives I reflexively ascribe to you at all, without having first experienced them in

---

[14] See also "Xenophobia and Kantian Rationalism," sect. IV: "Self-Knowledge," for a fuller discussion.

myself. Of course this is not to say that I cannot understand what it means to be the victim of maleficent *events* without having caused them myself. But it is to say that I must derive my understanding of the malevolent *intentionality* I ascribe to you from my own firsthand experience of it. Therefore your epistemic opacity to me furnishes no evidence for my reflexive ascription to you of malevolent or untrustworthy motives, although that ascription itself does furnish evidence for a similar ascription of them to myself. Thus Kant might put this second error by saying that we have been fooled by the first/ third person asymmetry into treating the ever-present "dear self" as a source of genuine self-knowledge on the basis of which we make even faultier and more damaging assumptions about the other.

C. The Error of Failing Rationally to Conceive Other Minds

These two errors are interconnected with a third one, namely our respective failures to imagine each other's behavior as animated by the same elements of personhood that animate our own, i.e., consciousness, thought, and rationality. Our prior failure to recognize the other's behavior as manifesting evidence of these properties—a failure compounded by conceptual confusion and misascription of motives—then further undermines our ability to bridge the first/third person asymmetry by imagining the other to have them. Since, from each of our first-personal perspectives, familiar empirical evidence of the presence of these properties is lacking in the other, we have no basis on which to make the ascription, and so no basis for imagining what it must be like from the other's perspective. Our respective, limited empirical conceptions of people, then, themselves the consequence of ignorance of others who are thereby viewed as different, delimit our capacity for empathy. This is part of what is involved in the phenomenon feminists refer to as objectification, and what sometimes leads men to describe some women as self-absorbed. Kant might put this point by saying that by failing to detect in the other's behavior the rule and order of rationality that guides it, we fail to surmise or imagine the other's motives and intentions.

This error, of failing to conceive the other as similarly animated by the psychological dispositions of personhood, is not without deleterious consequences for the xenophobe himself. Elsewhere I have described the self-centered and narrowly concrete view of the world that results from the failure to imagine empathically another's inner states, and its interpersonal consequences.[15] From the first-personal perspective, this error compounds

---

[15] Piper, "Impartiality, Compassion and Modal Imagination," *Ethics*, 101/4: Symposium on Impartiality (July 1991), 726–57.

the seeming depopulation of the social environment of persons and its repopulation by impenetrable and irrational aliens. This is to conceive one's social world as inhabited by enigmatic and unpredictable disruptions to its stability, to conjure chimaeras of perpetual unease and anxiety into social existence. Relative to such a conception, segregation is no more effective in banishing the threat than is leaving on the nightlight to banish ghosts, since both threats arise from the same source. Vigilance and a readiness to defend oneself against the hostile unknown may become such intimately familiar and constitutive habits of personality that even they may come to seem necessary prerequisites of personhood.

III. FIRST-ORDER POLITICAL DISCRIMINATION

The three foregoing errors involve failures of cognitive discrimination for which a well-intentioned individual could correct. For example, someone who regularly confuses people with personhood might simply take a moment to formulate a general principle of rational behavior that both applies to all the instances with which she is familiar from her particular community and has broader application as well; and remind herself, when confronted by anomalous behavior, at least to try to detect the operation of that principle within it. Similarly, it does not require excessive humility on the part of a person who falsely assumes privileged access to the self to remind himself that our beliefs about our own motives, feelings, and actions are exceedingly fallible and regularly disconfirmed; and that it is therefore even more presumptuous to suppose any authority about someone else's. Nor is it psychologically impossible to gather information about others' inner states—through research, appreciation of the arts, or direct questioning and careful listening, so as to cultivate one's imaginative and empathic capacities to envision other minds.

Thus it is possible for someone to have such xenophobic reactions without being a full-blown xenophobe, in the event that she views them as causes for concern rather than celebration. She may experience these cognitive failures without being a first-order political discriminator in the event that she has no personal investment in the defective empirical conception of people that results; and is identifiable as a *bona fide* first-order political discriminator to the extent that she does. A person has a *personal investment* in a conception or theory if

    (1) that theory is a source of personal satisfaction or security to her;
    (2) to revise or reject it would elicit in her feelings of dejection, deprivation or anxiety; and

(3) these feelings are to be explained by her identification with this theory.

She *identifies with* this theory to the extent that she is disposed to identify it as personally meaningful or valuable to her.[16] A person could make the first three cognitive errors without taking any satisfaction in her provincial conception of people ("Is this really all there is?" she might think to herself about the inhabitants of her small town), without identifying with it (she might find them boring and feel ashamed to have to count herself among them), and without feeling the slightest reluctance to enlarge and revise it through travel or exploration or research.

What distinguishes a first-order political discriminator is his personal investment in his provincial conception of people. His sense of self-preservation requires his conception to be veridical, and is threatened when it is disconfirmed. He exults in the thought that only the people he knows and is familiar with (whites, blacks, WASPs, Jews, residents of Waco, Texas, members of the club, etc.) are persons in the full, honorific sense. This is the thought that motivates the imposition of politically discriminatory stereotypes, both on those who confirm them and those who do not.

To impose a *stereotype* on someone is to view her as embodying a limited set of properties falsely taken to be exclusive, definitive, and paradigmatic of a certain kind of individual. I will say that a stereotype

(*a*) equates one contingent and limited set of primary valued properties that may characterize persons under certain circumstances with the universal concept of personhood;

(*b*) restricts that set to exclude divergent properties of personhood from it;

(*c*) withholds from these who violate its restrictions the essential properties of personhood; and

(*d*) ascribes to them the primary disvalued properties of deviance from it.

Thus a stereotype identifies as persons those and only those who manifest the primary valued properties in the set (*a*) and (*b*), and subsidiary ones consistent with it (such as minor personality quirks or mildly idiosyncratic personal tastes). Call this set the *honorific stereotype*, and an individual who bears such primary valued properties the *valuee*. And reciprocally, the honorific stereotype by implication identifies as deviant all those who manifest any properties regarded as inconsistent with it (*c*) and (*d*). Call this second

---

[16] The concept of personal investment is discussed in my "Moral Theory and Moral Alienation," *Journal of Philosophy*, 84/2 (Feb. 1987), 102–18. See also Piper, "Two Conceptions of Self" and "Pseudorationality."

set of primary disvalued properties the *derogatory stereotype*, and an individual who bears such primary disvalued properties the *disvaluee*.

So, for example, an individual who bears all the primary valued properties of the honorific stereotype as required by (*a*) may be nevertheless disqualified for status as a valuee according to (*b*), by bearing additional primary disvalued ones as well—being related by blood or marriage to a Jew, for example; or having bisexual inclinations; or, in the case of a black person, an enthusiasm for classical scholarship. In virtue of violating (*b*), one may then fail to qualify as a full-fledged person at all (*c*), and therefore may be designated as deviant by the derogatory stereotype according to (*d*). The derogatory stereotype most broadly includes all the primary disvalued properties that fall outside the set defining the honorific stereotype (i.e., "us versus them"), or may sort those properties into more specific subsets according to the range of individuals available for sorting.

A politically discriminatory stereotype generally is therefore distinguishable from an inductive generalization by its provincialism, its oversimplification, and its rigid imperviousness to the complicating details of singularity. Perhaps most importantly, a discriminatory stereotype is distinguishable from an inductive generalization by its function. The function of an inductive generalization is to guide further research, and this requires epistemic alertness and perceptual sensitivity to the possibility of confirming or disconfirming evidence in order to make use of it. An inductive generalization is no less a generalization for that: it would not, for example, require working-class blacks living in the Deep South during the 1960s to dismantle the functionally accurate and protective generalization that white people are dangerous. What would make this an inductive generalization rather than a stereotype is that it would not preclude recognition of a white person who is safe if one should appear. By contrast, the function of a stereotype is to render further research unnecessary. If the generalization that white people are dangerous were a stereotype, adopting it would make it cognitively impossible to detect any white people who were not.

Thus Kant might describe the reciprocal imposition of stereotypes as the fallacy of equating a partial and conditional series of empirical appearances of persons with the absolute and unconditioned idea of personhood that conceptually unifies them. Whereas the first error—of confusing one's empirical conception of people with the transcendent concept of personhood—involves thinking that the only persons there are are the people one knows, this fourth error—of equating personality with personhood—involves thinking that the kind of persons one knows are all there can ever be. So unlike inductive generalizations, the taxonomic categories of a stereotype are closed sets that fundamentally require the binary operation of sorting individuals and properties into those who fall within them and those who do not.[17]

As a consequence of his personal investment in an honorific stereotypical conception of persons, a first-order political discriminator has a personal investment in an honorific stereotypical self-conception. This means that that self-conception is a source of personal satisfaction or security to him; that to revise or disconfirm it would elicit in him feelings of dejection, deprivation, or anxiety; and that these feelings are to be explained by his identification with this self-conception. In order to maintain his honorific self-conception, a first-order political discriminator must perform the taxonomic binary sorting operation not only on particular groups of ethnic or gendered others, but on everyone, including himself. Since his self-conception as a person requires him and other *bona fide* persons to dress, talk, look, act, and think in certain highly specific and regimented ways in order to qualify for the honorific stereotype, everyone is subject to scrutiny in terms of it.

This is not only prejudicial to a disvaluee who violates these requirements and thereby earns the label of the derogatory stereotype. It is also prejudicial to a valuee who satisfies them, just in case there is more to his personality than the honorific stereotype encompasses and more than it permits. Avoidance of the negative social consequences of violating the honorific stereotype—ostracism, condemnation, punishment, or obliteration—necessitates stunting or flattening his personality in order to conform to it (for example, by eschewing football or night-clubs, and learning instead to enjoy scholarly lectures as a form of entertainment because one is given to understand that that is the sort of thing real academics typically do for fun); or bifurcating his personality into that part which can survive social scrutiny and that "deviant" part which cannot (as, for example, certain government officials have done who deplore and condemn homosexuality publicly on the one hand, while engaging in it privately on the other). One reason it is important not to equate personality with personhood is so that the former properties can flourish without fear that the latter title will be revoked.

Truncating his personality in order to conform to an honorific stereotype in turn damages the political discriminator's self-esteem and also his capacity for self-knowledge. Someone who is deeply personally invested in the honorific stereotype but fails fully to conform to it (as everyone must, of course) views himself as inherently defective. He is naturally beset by feelings of failure, inferiority, shame and worthlessness which poison his relations with others in familiar ways: competitiveness, dishonesty, defensiveness,

---

[17] I am indebted to Rüdiger Bittner for pressing this question in discussion.

envy, furtiveness, insecurity, hostility, and self-aggrandizement are just a few of the vices that figure prominently in his interpersonal interactions. But if these feelings and traits are equally antithetical to his honorific stereotype, then they, too, threaten his honorific stereotypical self-conception and so are susceptible to pseudorational denial, dissociation or rationalization. For example, a first-order political discriminator might be blindly unaware of how blatantly he advertises these feelings and traits in his behavior; or he might dissociate them as mere peccadilloes, unimportant eccentricities that detract nothing from the top-drawer person he essentially is. Or he might acknowledge them but rationalize them as natural expressions of a Nietzschean, *übermenschliche* ethic justified by his superior place in life. Such pseudorational habits of thought reinforce even more strongly his personal investment in the honorific stereotype that necessitated them, and in the xenophobic conception of others that complements it. This fuels a vicious downward spiral of self-hatred and hatred of anomalous others from which it is difficult for the political discriminator to escape. Thus the personal disadvantage of first-order political discrimination is not just that the discriminator devolves into an uninteresting and malevolent person. He damages himself for the sake of his honorific stereotype, and stunts his capacity for insight and personal growth as well.

A sign that a person's self-conception is formed by an honorific stereotype is that revelation of the deviant, primary disvalued properties provokes shame and denial, rather than a reformulation of that self-conception in such a way as to accommodate them. For example, a family that honorifically conceives itself as white Anglo-Saxon Protestant may deny that its most recent offspring in fact has woolly hair or a broad nose. Similarly, a sign that a person's conception of another is formed by a derogatory stereotype is that revelation of the other's nondeviant, primary valued properties provokes hostility and denial, rather than the corresponding revision of that conception of the other in such a way as to accommodate them. For example, a community of men that honorifically conceives itself in terms of its intellectual ability may dismiss each manifestation of a woman's comparable intellectual ability as a fluke.

These two reactions are reciprocal expressions of the same dispositions in the first- and third-personal cases respectively. Shame involves the pain of feeling publicly exposed as defective, and denial is the psychological antidote to such exposure: for example, if the purportedly WASP offspring does not have negroid features, there is nothing for the family to feel ashamed of. So a person whose self-conception is defined by an honorific stereotype will feel shame at having primary disvalued properties that deviate from it, and will attempt to deny their existence to herself and to others. By contrast, hostility toward another's excellence is caused by shame at one's own defectiveness, and denial of the excellence is the social antidote to such shame: for example, if the woman is not as intelligent as the men are purported to be, then there is no cause for feeling shamed by her, and so none for hostility toward her. So a person whose self-conception is formed by an honorific stereotype will feel hostility toward a disvaluee who manifests valued properties that violate the derogatory stereotype imposed on him; and will attempt to deny the existence of those valued properties in the other to herself and to others.

In the first-personal case, the objects of shame are primary disvalued properties that deviate from one's honorific stereotypical self-conception. In the third-personal case, the objects of hostility are valued properties that deviate from one's derogatory stereotypical conception of the disvaluee. But in both cases the point of the reactions is the same: to defend one's stereo-typical self-conception against attack, both by first-personal deviations from it and by third-personal deviations from the reciprocal stereotypes this requires imposing on others. And in both cases, the xenophobic reactions are motivated in the same way: the properties regarded as anomalous relative to the stereotype in question are experienced by the first-order political discriminator as an assault on the rational coherence of his theory of the world—and so, according to Kant, on the rational coherence of his self.

Indeed, left untreated, all four of these cognitive errors more generally—the conflation of the transcendent concept of personhood with one's provincial conception of people that another happens to violate, the ascription to the other of malevolent motives on the basis of an epistemically unreliable self-conception, the inability to imagine the other as animated by familiar or recognizably rational motives, and the equation of personality with personhood inherent in the imposition of reciprocal stereotype—combine to form a conception of the other as an inscrutable and malevolent anomaly that threatens that theory of the world which unifies one's experience and structures one's expectations about oneself and other people. If this were an accurate representation of others who are different, it would be no wonder that xenophobes feared them.

IV. RECIPROCAL FIRST-ORDER POLITICAL DISCRIMINATION

So far I have argued that first-order political discrimination involves the reciprocal imposition of honorific and derogatory stereotypes, on oneself and on the anomalous other respectively. But is it not possible to value properties ordinarily taken to be irrelevant to judgments of a person's value or competence without eliciting the charge of honorific stereotyping? Are such primary valued properties ever relevant to judgments of a person's noninstrumental value or competence? By *reciprocal first-order political discrimination*, I will mean a manifest attitude in which a particular property of a person that is irrelevant to judgments of that person's noninstrumental value or competence, for example her race, gender, class, sexual orientation, or religious or ethnic affiliation, is seen as a source of value or competence, in general, as a source of superiority. Primary valued properties are those perceived as elevating its bearers accordingly.

Take the case in which we are particularly drawn to befriend a valuee with whom we share a similar ethnic background, because we expect to have more in common (lifestyle, tastes, sense of humor), share similar values, or see the world from a similar perspective. In this kind of case the primary valued property is not, say, being Jewish; but rather having the same ethnic background, whatever that may be. Is similarity of ethnic background a property that is relevant to our judgments of how valuable the valuee is as a friend? No, for it does not form any part of the basis for such a judgment. That a friendship is better, richer, or more valuable in proportion to the degree of similarity of the friends' ethnic backgrounds is a judgment few would be tempted to make.

In these cases, it is not the valuee's similar ethnicity itself that is the source of value, but rather the genuinely valuable properties—for example, similarity of values or worldview—*with which we expect similar ethnicity to be conjoined*. Rather than making a normative judgment about his value or competence as a friend in this case, we in fact make an epistemic judgment about the probability that, given the valuee's ethnic identity, he will bear properties susceptible of such normative judgments. These epistemic rules of thumb are defeasible, and may have disappointing consequences for personal relationships. For they ascribe primary value to a kind of property at the expense of others that are in fact more important for friendship—such as sensitivity, similarity of tastes or experiences, or mutual respect—with which that kind of property is only contingently, if ever, conjoined. (Presumably something like this may explain the malaise of someone who has chosen all the "right" friends, married the "right" spouse, and landed the "best" job, yet feels persistently unhappy, disconnected, and dissatisfied in his social relationships.)

If similarity of race, gender, sexual orientation, class background, or religious or ethnic affiliation are in themselves irrelevant to judgments of a person's noninstrumental value or competence, primary valued properties such as being of a particular race, gender, etc., are even more obviously so. At least it has yet to be demonstrated that any particular racial, ethnic, gender, class or religious group possesses the properties necessary for, e.g., friendship to an outstanding degree.[18] Epistemic probability judgments about the concatenation of any such primary valued properties with genuinely valuable traits, such as sensitivity or similarity of interests, also may bias our ability to perceive clearly the properties a particular individual actually has—as when a wife minimizes the reality and seriousness of her husband's physical abuse of her, because of the weight she accords his class background. This would be a case of reciprocal first-order discrimination, according to the above definition, because she sees a primary valued property—class background—that is irrelevant to judgments of the valuee's noninstrumental value or competence as a spouse as a (compensating) source of superiority.

It might be objected that such epistemic rules of thumb are inductive generalizations, however irrational or poorly grounded, that we need in order to survive in a world of morally opaque others: How ought one behave, for example, alone in a subway car with four black male teenagers carrying ghetto blasters and wearing running shoes? Even if it were true that most muggers were black male teenagers in running shoes, it still would not follow that most black male teenagers in running shoes were muggers. This epistemic rule of thumb is a stereotype, not an inductive generalization, if it leads one to react to every black male teenager in running shoes one encounters as though he were a mugger when there is no independent justification for thinking he is.

Alternately, one may make a judgment of value about some such property abstractly and independently considered. One may value being black, or of working-class origins, for its own sake. Or one may choose a partner from the same religion because one views that religion and its traditions themselves as intrinsically valuable, independently of one's partner's compatibility with respect to lifestyle, values, or worldview. Here the judgment of value is directed not at the valuee's value or competence, but rather at the property he bears and to the preservation or affirmation of which one's choice of him is instrumental. Nothing in the following discussion addresses or precludes such judgments, although there is much to say about them. My target is judgments of noninstrumental value about individuals, not about properties of individuals abstractly and independently considered, to which individuals themselves are instrumental.

Is it humanly possible to value a person just and only because she bears

---

[18] The thesis that women make better friends is often supported by arguments to the effect that they *become closer confidantes more quickly*. But there are many other properties that contribute to friendship—trustworthiness, loyalty, dependability, honesty, mutual respect, etc.—that such arguments ignore.

some such primary valued property—not because of the further properties with which we expect that one to be conjoined, but just for the sake of that property in itself? It is difficult to make sense of this. Suppose I value Germanness because the Germans I have known tend to have deep passions and an amusingly fatalistic sense of humor; and that I then meet a shallow and phlegmatic German with no sense of humor at all. In the absence of other, unexpectedly attractive personality characteristics I may appreciate, just what is it about being German in itself that is supposed to confer worth on this particular individual? Either we must be able to spell out an answer to this question in terms of other properties that are only contingently connected, if at all, to this one—e.g., having been socialized within a certain culture "from the inside," being part of a certain historical tradition, etc.— or else we are appealing to a mysterious and ineffable, non-natural quality of Germanness.[19] Then suppose there are such qualities, and that we may arguably appeal to them. To what degree might Germanness outweigh the person's other properties that, by hypothesis, I deplore? Surely the mere fact of Germanness can provide no consolation at all, in practice, for other properties of the person that offend me. It will not compensate, for example, for a failure to laugh at my jokes, or a tendency to discuss the weather at excessive length, or to fall asleep at the opera. And then it is hard to see in what its purported value consists.

Independently of the other, genuinely valuable properties with which they are only contingently, if at all, conjoined, properties such as race, gender, sexual orientation, class background, or religious or ethnic affiliation are in themselves always irrelevant to judgments of a person's noninstrumental value or competence. This holds whether they are considered as primary disvalued or valued properties, and even where they are used as epistemic rules of thumb for detecting such properties. We may in fact feel compelled to make such judgments, in the service of expediency, or what we imagine to be our self-interest, and screen our circle of associates accordingly. But it is nothing to be proud of.

---

[19] For purposes of this discussion I ignore the range of cases in which my valuation of, e.g., Germanness is rooted in the status or worth I expect my choice of German friends to confer on *me*. This kind of case occurs both in situations in which the primary valued property is one shared by oneself, and in those cases in which it is not. Thus it may happen that one's choice of a white, Anglo-Saxon Protestant spouse is made in part with an eye to reinforcing the primary value to others and to oneself of one's own status as a white, Anglo-Saxon Protestant: or alternately, that one's contrasting choice of an African-American spouse is made with an eye to proving to others and to oneself one's "cool," sophistication, or commitment to civil rights. These are all cases in which the property is valued as a source of *instrumental* value or competence, namely for its ability to confer value on the reciprocal first-order political discriminator. Therefore I leave them aside here.

V. HIGHER-ORDER POLITICAL DISCRIMINATION

Now I want to examine a more sophisticated manifestation of political discrimination that is supervenient on the first-order political discrimination just discussed. I shall call this *higher-order political discrimination*.[20] As in first-order political discrimination, a higher-order discriminator manifests in behavior the attitude in which a particular property of a person that is irrelevant to judgments of that person's intrinsic value or competence, e.g., her race, gender, class, sexual orientation, or religious or ethnic affiliation, is seen as a source of disvalue or inferiority, i.e., as a primary disvalued property. By *second-order political discrimination*, I will understand the attitude within which a primary disvalued or valued property in turn confers disvalue or value respectively on further properties of the disvaluee or valuee respectively. I shall refer to these latter as *secondary disvalued (or valued) properties*.

Second-order political discrimination works in the following way. A disvaluee's primary disvalued property, say, being a male homosexual, causes the second-order political discriminator to view some *further* property of the disvaluee, say, being an eloquent speaker, in a negative light. The respect in which this further property is seen as negative depends on the range of possible descriptions it might satisfy, as well as the context in which it appears. Thus, for example, the second-order political discriminator might view the disvaluee's eloquence as purple prose, or empty rhetoric, or as precious, flowery, or mannered. These predicates are not interchangeable for the second-order political discriminator. Nor are they taken to be arbitrarily applied. The second-order political discriminator will choose from among them to express his disvaluation in response to contingencies of the situation and individuals involved. He may, in all sincerity, explain his disvaluation with reference to impartially applied aesthetic standards, or to his ingrown, native suspicion of big words. But the crucial feature of second-order political discrimination is that the actual explanation for his disvaluing the person's eloquence, *in whatever respect he disvalues it*, is the person's primary disvalued property of being a male homosexual.

Does second-order political discrimination as thus defined ever actually occur? Some familiar examples of it include attaching disvalue to a person's having rhythm, by reason of its putative connection with her being black; or attaching disvalue to a person's being very smart, by reason of its putative connection with his being Jewish. Both of these cases are examples of politically discriminatory stereotyping, in which some arbitrary property is

---

[20] The analysis of higher-order political discrimination in Sects. V through VII is excerpted from "Higher-Order Discrimination," in Amelie O. Rorty and Owen Flanagan (eds.), *Identity, Character and Morality* (Cambridge, Mass.: MIT Press, 1990), 285–309.

falsely taken to be characteristic of persons of a particular race or ethnic or religious affiliation. But I mean to call attention to a slightly different feature of these examples. Someone who practices second-order political discrimination regards a black person who has rhythm as vulgar, salacious, or offensive; at the very least, undignified. Similarly, such a person regards a Jewish person who is very smart as sophistical, glib, or crafty, or as subversive or ungentlemanly; at the very least, untrustworthy. In both cases, properties that are in themselves salutary, or at least neutral, are castigated by the second-order political discriminator, by reason of the disvalue conferred on them by the primary disvalued property. This is what makes them examples of second-order political discrimination.

These familiar, stereotypic examples of second-order political discrimination do not exhaust the repertoire of higher-order political discrimination, for many reasons. First, orders of discrimination can, in theory, be multiplied indefinitely. So, for example, a case of *third-order political discrimination* would involve what I shall call *tertiary disvalued properties*: The primary disvalued property (say, being black) confers disvalue on a further, secondary disvalued property (having rhythm), which in turn confers disvalue on yet a further property of the person (say, being a good dancer). Having rhythm is seen as vulgar, by reason of its association with being black, and being a good dancer is then seen as exhibitionistic (say), by reason of its association with having rhythm. In any such case, the primary property is in fact irrelevant to judgments of a person's value or competence. Hence the value or disvalue it confers on secondary, tertiary, etc., properties is bogus.

The n-order disvalue relation is *transitive*, in that, for example, if being black confers disvalue on having rhythm, and having rhythm confers disvalue on being a good dancer, then being black confers disvalue on being a good dancer. The n-order disvalue relation is also *inclusive*, in that the primary disvalued property poisons the higher-order political discriminator's evaluations of all further properties of the disvaluee. For example, the primary disvalued property of being black may confer disvalue, alternatively, on a dancer's classical styling: Classical styling in a black dancer may be seen as inappropriate, or as an obscene parody of traditional ballet.[21] The primary disvalued property also confers disvalue on other,

---

[21] Of course there are other, more convoluted cases of higher-order political discrimination that represent epicyclic variations on the straightforward cases I shall be examining. For example, being black may wildly exaggerate the value attached to classical styling in a black dancer, if classical styling is perceived as something the person had to overcome great innate and cultural obstacles to achieve. In either case, being black functions as a primary disvalued property because it carries a presumption of inferiority into the evaluation of further properties of the person.

unrelated properties of the disvaluee: her appearance, accent, mode of dress, etc.[22]

The inclusiveness of the n-order disvalue relation underscores a second reason why stereotypical cases of second-order discrimination do not exhaust the repertoire of higher-order discrimination: Nonstereotypical traits are also recruited to receive value or disvalue from primary properties to suit particular occasions. We do not ordinarily think of classical styling in dance as a property about which discriminators might have any particular attitude. But this may be mistaken. Higher-order discrimination is not concerned solely with *stereotypical* secondary, tertiary, etc., disvalued properties. It may be concerned with *any* further properties of the person on which the primary disvalued property itself confers disvalue. Thus, for example, being Jewish (or black, or a woman) may confer disvalue on being smart, which in turn may confer disvalue on being intellectually prolific: A person's intellectual prolificity may be seen as evidence of logorrhea, or lack of critical conscience, and may thus poison the evaluation of those intellectual products themselves. A first test for ascertaining whether the disvalue of some property of a person is to be explained as a case of higher-order political discrimination is to ascertain whether or not that property is disvalued uniformly across individuals, regardless of anything that might count as a primary disvalued property for a higher-order political discriminator. If someone is just as contemptuous of Fred Astaire's having rhythm as they are of Michael Jackson's, or just as contemptuous of intellectual prolificity in Balzac as in Isaac Asimov, then the charge of higher-order political discrimination may be defeated.[23]

---

[22] Is it perhaps too strong to claim that a primary disvalued property poisons the higher-order political discriminator's evaluation of *all* of the disvaluee's other properties? Can't a higher-order political discriminator respect a disvaluee's traits of character in a certain restricted area, *despite* his disvalued status? I am inclined to think not. For this seems to occur almost exclusively when the "valued" property itself conforms to the higher-order political discriminator's stereotypes. For example, a black man may be admired for his athletic prowess but encounter hostility when he runs for political office. In such cases, the higher-order political discriminator's admiration and respect for the stereotypical trait is not unalloyed. It is tempered by a certain smug complacency at the disvaluee's confirmation of his disvalued status in the very cultivation and expression of that stereotypical trait. To sustain the above objection, we would need to see a higher-order political discriminator exhibiting *unalloyed* admiration and respect for *non*stereotypical traits, such that *these positive feelings did not, in turn, positively reform the higher-order political discriminator's prejudicial attitude toward the person's primary disvalued property*: Someone who sincerely respects and admires a disvaluee for nonstereotypical reasons, without feeling threatened or invaded, has already begun to weaken the psychological edifice on which her politically discriminatory evaluation of the person as a disvaluee is based.

[23] It might be thought that this first test is inherently self-limiting for the case in which the person happens to dislike just the property that is most typically associated with, e.g., a certain race—say, dark skin—but nevertheless passes the first test in that she disvalues it uniformly across individuals, whether it occurs in blacks, East Indians, Jews, Arabs, Aborigines, or Coppertone-soaked Californians. I think what we should say about this kind of case is that it does not present a

Stereotypes change in accordance with changes in the objects of political discrimination, as different populations seek access to the goods, services and opportunities enjoyed by the advantaged; and primary and higher-order disvalued properties change accordingly. For instance, the anti-Semitic response to the attempts of Jewish intellectuals to achieve full assimilation to the institutions of higher education in this country frequently found expression in the disvaluative description of assertively ambitious Jewish academics as pushy or opportunistic. Now similarly situated blacks and women frequently enjoy that title. Conversely, those with such primary disvalued properties who attempt to substitute diplomacy for assertion are characterized by higher-order political discriminators as manipulative, obsequious, or sycophantic. A second test for ascertaining whether or not the disvalue of some property of a person is to be explained as a case of higher-order political discrimination is to ascertain whether there is any alternative property, conduct or manner, directed toward the same goal—i.e. of gaining access to unjustly withheld social advantages, that avoids or deflects the disvalue conferred by the primary disvalued property. If there is not—if, that is, whatever your strategy, you're damned if you do and damned if you don't, then the charge of higher-order political discrimination is *prima facie* justified.

Other arbitrary properties, not just the familiar political ones, can function as primary disvalued properties to a higher-order political discriminator. Physical appearance, style of diction, social bearing, familial, educational, or professional pedigree, circle of associates, manner of dress, are among the more familiar, if less widely acknowledged, objects of higher-order political discrimination. Some of these properties are often assumed to go hand in hand with, or even be partially definitive of, more widely recognized primary disvalued properties. For example, higher-order political discriminators may tend to assume that ethnic identity is inherently

problem. The fact that someone is acquitted of being a racist doesn't imply that her evaluations are therefore admirable or enlightened. Any predicate or combination of predicates that *fails* the first test is either a rigged definite description of a particular disvalued group, e.g., "ova-producing featherless bipeds," or else describes a discriminatory stereotype, e.g., "dark-skinned, dark-eyed, woolly-haired individuals with rhythm." Of course, a person might just happen to disvalue only individuals who fit such a stereotype and not those who violate it. But since this disvaluation would not be independent of anything that might count as a primary disvalued property for such a person, it would not defeat the charge of higher-order political discrimination.

Note, however, that the first test does *not* work for identifying a distinct but related attitude, which we might call *generalized higher-order political discrimination*, in which a person comes to disvalue some constellation of higher-order properties across the board *specifically because of its original association with* a primary disvalued property stereotypically ascribed to a certain group. Someone who finds having rhythm vulgar in any dancer, regardless of racial or ethnic affiliation, because he associates having rhythm with blacks, whom he fears and despises, would exemplify such an attitude.

connected with a certain physical appearance (Jews have dark, curly hair and long noses), that racial identity is connected with a certain style of diction and class background (blacks speak Black English and come from the ghetto), or that gender identity is connected with a certain social bearing (women are sympathetic, passive, and emotional). This is how a stereotype is formed. But again I mean to call attention to a slightly different point: These properties themselves may be seen as sources of disvalue, *independently* of their possible connection with such stereotypically primary disvalued properties. Someone who has all of the valued race, ethnic, religious, class, and gender properties, but lacks the valued style of diction, mode of self-presentation, or educational or professional pedigrees may be subject to higher-order political discrimination just as fully as someone who lacks all of the former properties but has all of the latter. In both cases, this means that their other properties—their personality characteristics, interests, or achievements—will be seen as higher-order disvalued properties, by reason of their association with these equally arbitrary primary disvalued properties.

This shows that the first-order political discrimination with which we are familiar is merely a special case of a more general psychological phenomenon which is not limited to first-order *political* discrimination at all. However, higher-order political discrimination as defined above usually includes it; for it would be psychologically unusual, to say the least, to find an individual who is in general corrupt in his evaluations of a person's other properties in the ways just described, yet impartial and scrupulous in his evaluations of blacks, Jews, women, gays, etc. and *their* properties. Someone who is apt to dislike a person because of her hair texture or accent or mode of dress can hardly be expected to be genuinely judicious when it comes to judging her gender, race, class, sexual orientation, or ethnic or religious affiliation. Hence we can expect that first-order political discrimination and higher-order political discrimination in general are to be found together.[24]

---

[24] There is another reason that favors retaining the label of higher-order *political* discrimination, despite its application to primary disvalued properties less widely recognized as political in nature, corresponding to a broader conception of political behavior. We can think of politically discriminatory stereotyping more generally as a means of sorting individuals into those with whom one is willing to share available power and resources versus those with whom one is not. In this broader sense, any disvalued property can become a criterion for excluding the disvaluee from the discriminator's circle of honorifically stereotyped valuees.

VI. RECIPROCAL HIGHER-ORDER POLITICAL
DISCRIMINATION

Higher-order political discrimination as so far described implies a companion phenomenon, which I shall call *reciprocal higher-order political discrimination*. Here properties irrelevant to judgments of a person's competence or worth are seen as primary *valued* properties, as sources of value which confer value on the person's secondary, tertiary, etc., properties. Any one of the primary properties enumerated so far may have this function. For example, a person's gender may be perceived as conferring value on secondary properties, such as his competence to hold a certain professional position. Or a person's familial lineage may be perceived as conferring value on her admissability to an institution of higher education. Or a person's class background may be perceived as conferring value on his manner of dress. Or a person's educational pedigree may be perceived as conferring value on her political pronouncements, which in turn confers value on her personal lifestyle; and so on. Each of these examples have an arbitrary and irrational quality to them. That is because reciprocal higher-order political discrimination, like higher-order political discrimination itself, is an arbitrary and irrational attitude.

Higher-order political discrimination and reciprocal higher-order political discrimination are materially interdependent. If a person's having a particular racial identity is a source of disvalue for a higher-order political discriminator, then if someone lacks that racial identity, they are not seen as tainted by that disvalue. For example, if a person's being Asian confers disvalue on his attempts at tact, i.e., if he is therefore perceived as particularly evasive and inscrutable, then if he were white, he would not be perceived as similarly evasive and inscrutable. For if a higher-order political discriminator recognized that one can be just as evasive and inscrutable without being Asian, say, if one has a hidden agenda or lacks social skills, then it would have to be recognized that those properties, *rather* than his being Asian, might be conferring disvalue on his attempts at tact. Conversely, if a person's having a particular racial identity is a source of value for a higher-order political discriminator, then someone who lacks that racial identity is not blessed by that value. For example, if a person's being white confers value on his attempts at tact, i.e., if he is therefore viewed as sensitive and reasonable, then if he were Asian, he would not be perceived as similarly sensitive and reasonable. For if a higher-order political discriminator recognized that one can be just as sensitive and reasonable without being white, say, if one has no personal investment in the issue or has thought hard about it, then it would have to be recognized that those properties, rather than his being white, might be conferring value on his attempts at tact.

The two tests for higher-order political discrimination apply analogously to reciprocal higher-order political discrimination: (1) Ascertain whether or not the higher-order valued property is valued uniformly across individuals, regardless of anything that might count as a primary valued property for the discriminator. If a person's perceived competence to hold a certain professional position would not be in any way diminished if she were black—if, that is, blacks with comparable competence have been hired to such positions, then the charge of reciprocal higher-order political discrimination may be defeated. (2) Ascertain whether there is any alternative property, conduct or manner, directed toward the same goal—of gaining access to some social advantage—that avoids or deflects the value conferred by the primary valued property. If there is not—if, for example, whether you are assertively ambitious or carefully diplomatic, intellectually prolific or intellectually fallow, you can do no wrong, then the charge of reciprocal higher-order political discrimination is *prima facie* justified.[25] Henceforth I shall take higher-order political discrimination to include reciprocal higher-order political discrimination. These two phenomena demonstrate that one need not be a blatant racist, sexist, anti-Semite, or homophobe—let us describe such an individual as a *simple first-order political discriminator*—in order to practice political discrimination. Higher-order political discrimination is given fullest expression indirectly, by implication, in seemingly unrelated tastes, preferences, and behavior.

---

[25] Here it might be objected that the second test is inadequate to ascertain the existence of reciprocal higher-order political discrimination, since the explanation for why "you can do no wrong" may be, not that all such higher-order properties receive value from primary valued properties, but rather that all such higher-order properties are in any case irrelevant to judgments of a person's competence. However, remember that the second test applies specifically to properties directed toward that goal of gaining access to some social advantage. This includes not only properties irrelevant to the question of one's entitlement to that advantage, such as those pertaining to the manner or quality of one's self-promotion, but also properties directly relevant to that question, such as those pertaining to one's status, potential, training, experience, etc. The second test sifts out those cases in which irrelevant higher-order properties are made the basis for conferring the advantage, e.g., one's manner of self-promotion, and in which relevant higher-order properties are discounted as the bases for conferring the advantage, e.g., one's previous professional experience. In both kinds of cases, higher-order political discrimination is marked by the *relaxation or modification* of the criteria of competence for receiving the advantage, in order to accommodate the particular properties of the valuee.

VII. HIGHER-ORDER POLITICAL DISCRIMINATION:
A CASE OF PSEUDORATIONALITY

So far I have used locutions such as, "seen as conferring value/disvalue on" and "by reason of its association with" to describe the relation between primary and higher-order disvalued or valued properties, without saying in any detail in what I take that relation to consist. It does *not* consist in the set of beliefs held by the higher-order political discriminator to the effect that

(A) (1) agent A has primary disvalued property P;
      (2) agent A has n-ary property N; and
      (3) P confers negative value on . . . N.

(A) is faulty because of (3): Only the most perverse and unrepentant higher-order political discriminator would admit—even to herself—that it is P that confers negative value on N. On the other hand, only the most absurdly consistent higher-order political discriminator would affirm the belief that, in virtue of (A. 1) and (A. 2),

(3′) therefore N is of negative value, period.

This would be the plight of the higher-order political discriminator who, in virtue of his contempt for Isaac Asimov's intellectual prolificity, would feel compelled to abjure Balzac as well. Instead, (3) must be replaced by

(3″) N, in the way in which it is borne by A, is of negative value.

(3″) is better because it incorporates that locution that scrupled higher-order political discriminators are so reluctant or unable to further define: For the higher-order political discriminator, there is just something about *the way in which* a person dances rhythmically that is vulgar; something about the way in which a person manifests their intelligence that is glib or sophistical; something about the way in which they attempt to gain access to social advantages that is unctuous or opportunistic. The higher-order political discriminator would vehemently reject the suggestion that this "something" might have anything to do with the person's race, gender, class, sexual orientation, or ethnic or religious affiliation. But in fact, it is precisely this primary disvalued property from which the blemish spreads. Let us then take the following set of beliefs

(B) (1) agent A has primary disvalued property P;
      (2) agent A has n-ary property N; and
      (3″) N, in the way in which it is borne by A, is of negative value,

plus the following stipulation

(4) For the higher-order political discriminator, A's possession of P is what in fact confers negative value on N

as characteristic of the typical, i.e. scrupulous higher-order political discriminator.

What makes higher-order political discriminators so scrupulous? What, that is, explains the higher-order political discriminator's tendency to suppress (B. 4)? Part of the answer lies in the nature of first-order political discrimination. As we have seen, first-order political discrimination can be understood as a species of pseudorationality which relies heavily on the mechanisms of rationalization and dissociation. The perception of someone's race, gender, class, sexual orientation, ethnic or religious affiliation, etc., as a source of disvalue or value is the consequence of applying value concepts like "person," "human being," "citizen," "member of the community," "rational and responsible agent," etc., too narrowly, to include only those individuals who have the primary valued property, and exclude those individuals who lack it. And similarly, dissociating Jews as subhuman, blacks as childlike, gays as perverts, working-class people as animals, or women as irrational are ways of obscuring one's identification of these individuals as fully mature, responsible human beings, and thereby obscuring one's recognition of these individuals as full members of the community with which one identifies.[26]

Higher-order political discrimination then adds to this the pseudorational mechanism of *denial*, in which we suppress recognition of an anomalous thing or property altogether, in order to preserve the internal consistency of our beliefs or theory about the world, ourselves, and other people. I have already argued that typically, higher-order political discriminators are likely to be first-order political discriminators as well; that is, they have the same prejudices that incline them to view individuals with the primary disvalued

---

[26] The irony in the case of racism is that there is a substantial literature in biology and the social sciences that indicates that almost all purportedly white Americans have between five and twenty percent black ancestry—hence are, according to this country's entrenched "just one trace" convention of racial classification, black. See F. James Davis, *Who is Black?* (University Park: Pennsylvania State University Press, 1991); Virginia R. Dominguez, *White by Definition: Social Classification in Creole Louisiana* (New Brunswick, NJ: Rutgers University Press, 1986); Joel Williamson, *A New People* (New York: Free Press, 1980); L. L. Cavalli-Sforza and W. F. Bodmer, *The Genetics of Human Populations* (San Francisco: W. H. Freeman, 1971), 490–9; T. E. Reed, "Caucasian Genes in American Negroes," *Science*, 165 (1969), 762–8; P. L. Workman, B. S. Blumberg and A. J. Cooper, "Selection, Gene Migration and Polymorphic Stability in a U.S. White and Negro Population," *American Journal of Human Genetics*, 15/4 (1963), 429–37; Bentley Glass and C. C. Li, "The Dynamics of Racial Admixture—An Analysis of the American Negro," *American Journal of Human Genetics*, 5 (1953), 1–20; and in general, *Genetic Abstracts* from about 1950. For these references and discussion on this matter I am indebted to Professor Monro S. Edmonson of Tulane University's Department of Anthropology.

properties as inferior, not fully members of their community. The simple first-order political discriminator experiences no conflict in categorizing disvaluees as inferior beings to be suppressed and exploited. Therefore, she has no need to exercise denial, either of her own discriminatory responses or of the disvaluees' existence. By contrast, higher-order political discriminators must deny both, in order to preserve the consistency of their beliefs. Because they are deeply affected, but not fully reformed, by arguments and experiences that suggest that political discrimination is unjust, both their own discriminatory responses and the objects of those responses are anathema to higher-order discriminators. Because they do not want to believe that their responses are politically discriminatory, they deny them altogether. The higher-order political discriminator may deny, for example, that the primary disvalued property in question is a disvalue at all, and yet helplessly deplore the "fact" that nevertheless there are no competent or worthy candidates bearing this property to be found; or hold any such candidate to a much higher standard of acceptance or performance than that he ordinarily applies, relative to which her secondary properties can be disparaged. He may denigrate her intelligence as cleverness; or ridicule her for working too hard when she exhibits energy and commitment to her work; or disparage her professional recognition as achieved through hustling or connections.

These discriminatory responses suggest that the higher-order political discriminator in fact categorizes such members of the disvalued group themselves in similarly demeaning terms with respect to their primary properties, but experiences a conflict of conscience about doing so. Faced with the conflict between first-order politically discriminatory habits of thought and the dictates of conscience, the higher-order political discriminator exercises denial, above all in order to avoid this conflict, by eradicating its source from awareness. The higher-order political discriminator often fails to acknowledge the very existence or presence of members of the disvalued groups, in order to circumvent his own, first-order politically discriminatory responses to them.[27] For instance, he may ignore or fail to acknowledge a disvaluee's contribution to a general discussion, or respond to that contribution as though someone else had made it. Or he may relegate a disvaluee to marginal or peripheral tasks in a professional setting. Or he may simply ignore the disvaluee altogether, avoiding all social interaction not strictly required by social or institutional obligations. In behaving in this fashion, the higher-

---

[27] This may contribute to an explanation of the phenomenon, noted by Schuman, Steeh, and Bobo (*Racial Attitudes in America: Trends and Interpretations* (Cambridge, Mass.: Harvard University Press, 1985)), that in the last twenty years, white support for the *principles* of equality and fairness for blacks have increased, concurrently with white opposition to the *implementation* of those principles.

order political discriminator does not give vent to any sort of malevolent impulse. His aim is not to insult or injure the disvaluee in any way. Rather, his aim is to avoid the painfully conflicting feelings—of disgust or contempt on the one hand, and the pangs of conscience on the other—that acknowledgment of the disvaluee provokes.[28]

When social or institutional obligations make denial of the disvaluee's presence impossible, denial of (at the very least) her primary disvalued property, and of its perceived disvalue, supplies a second-best resolution to this conflict of conscience: Denial of the disvaluee's primary disvalued property suppresses from awareness the discriminatory habits of thought elicited by it, hence similarly preserves consistency, by placating the requirements of conscience. Thus the higher-order political discriminator is guilty of an even greater failure of cognitive discrimination than that of the simple first-order political discriminator. For whereas the latter fails merely to perceive the disvaluee's personhood through her difference, the former fails to perceive either her or her difference altogether. This is why the higher-order political discriminator tends to suppress (B. 4). Unfortunately, to suppress habits of thought from awareness is not to eradicate their influence, any more than to suppress the disvaluee's existence from awareness is to eradicate her influence. Higher-order political discrimination is characterized by that attitude in which a certain habit of thought, namely first-order political discrimination, poisons one's evaluations and behavior, whether one acknowledges this or not.

The higher-order political discriminator is inclined, moreover, *not* to acknowledge this, no matter how obviously incriminating his evaluations and behavior may be to a disinterested observer. For this would expose the painful conflict of conscience the higher-order political discriminator's behavior attempts to suppress. To acknowledge this conflict, in turn, would be to acknowledge the need to resolve it, i.e., the need to work through and overcome the first-order prejudices that gave rise to it. But it is precisely in virtue of those first-order prejudices themselves that such a project of self-

---

[28] Here the joke characterizing the difference between first-order racism in the South and in the North is relevant: In the South, it is said, whites don't mind how close a black person gets, as long as he doesn't get too big; whereas in the North, whites don't mind how big a black person gets, as long as he doesn't get too close. Only the higher-order political discriminator of either region is compelled to deny the existence of the black person altogether.

Denial of a person's presence as a way of avoiding conflicting feelings about them is fairly common. A very handsome man may be the object of denial, when others' feelings of attraction to him conflict with their conviction that these feelings are inappropriate; a very fortunate or charismatic person may be the object of denial, when others' feelings of envy or resentment conflict with a similar conviction. Or a homely person may be the object of denial when others' feelings of repugnance conflict with their kindness or social good will. Higher-order political discrimination is most analogous to this last-described case.

improvement stands very low on the higher-order political discriminator's list of priorities. Unlike the resolution of Oedipal conflicts, emotional problems, tensions in one's personal relationships, or career dilemmas, coming to terms with one's prejudices and learning not to inflict them inadvertently on others just is not, in the last analysis, seen as terribly important by the higher-order political discriminator. That is part of what makes him a political discriminator in the first place.[29]

As I have painted it, then, higher-order political discrimination is peculiarly the sickness of thoughtful, well-intentioned and conscientious individuals who nevertheless have failed adequately to confront and work through their own prejudices, or who perhaps have been too quickly satisfied by their ability to marshall arguments on behalf of doing so. Such individuals are being neither disingenuous nor hypocritical when they deny that a person's race, gender, class, sexual orientation, or ethnic or religious affiliation affects their judgment of her competence or worth. They vehemently insist that this is so, they want it to be so, and they genuinely believe it to be so. They are, nevertheless, mistaken. Their efforts to explain away each manifest expression of higher-order political discrimination on different and inconsistent grounds are unconvincing. And their behavior exhibits a degree of otherwise inexplicable arbitrariness and idiosyncracy that severely strains our attempts to apply the principle of charity in making sense of it. Hence, in order to understand the behavior of higher-order political discriminators, we must watch what they *do*, not what they *say*.[30]

For example, these attitudes may find expression in an expectation of greater deference or genuflection from a member of the disvalued group. The simple first-order political discriminator expresses his anger at the violation of this expectation in certain familiar stereotypes: the "uppity nigger" whose refusal to behave subserviently is seen as impudence or disrespect; or the "Jewish-American Princess," whose assertiveness, presumption of self-worth, and expectation of attention and respect are seen as signs of being

---

[29] Here I think it would be wrong to interpret the higher-order political discriminator as concerned only with personal problems and not with social ones. Rather, the higher-order political discriminator belittles the importance of addressing a certain *personal* problem.

[30] One implication of characterizing higher-order political discrimination as a sickness rather than a fault is that higher-order political discriminators are, in the last analysis, not morally responsible for their behavior. This conclusion seems unpalatable in many respects. Nevertheless, I am reluctantly pessimistic about the efficacy of direct appeals to reason in higher-order political discriminators. Because their reason—or rather, their dogged pseudorationality—is so inherently a part of the problem. I am inclined to think that the solution should be sought in the adoption of some version of Strawson's "objective attitude" toward them; i.e. that higher-order political discriminators must be *managed*—perhaps psychotherapeutically—rather than *addressed*. I suggest an explanation for this kind of intractability in "Two Conceptions of the Self" and "Pseudorationality," and suggest certain artistic strategies that may have a beneficial effect on higher-order political discriminators in Sect. VIII, below.

spoiled, selfish, or imperious. But for the higher-order political discriminator, such anger is displaced into more subtle but similar reactions: Such an individual may just feel angered or personally affronted by a woman's presumption of equality—in personal, social, or intellectual status, or professional worth, or as a competitor for social or professional rewards; or unduly irritated by her failure to defer or back down in argument. She may be viewed as forward in conversation, when in fact she contributes no more and no less than anyone else; or stubborn, unresponsive, or impervious to well-intentioned criticisms, when in fact the only acceptable response to those criticisms, in the eyes of the higher-order political discriminator, would be for her to concur with them wholeheartedly and apologize for her dereliction. Or, to take another example, the higher-order political discriminator may feel invaded or compromised by a black person's jocularity or willingness to trade friendly insults that one accepts as a matter of course from those considered to be one's peers. The black person may be viewed as overly familiar, insolent, or presumptuous. In all such cases, the disvaluee's behavior is seen as a *presumption*, not a right or an accepted practice.[31] The higher-order political discriminator is tortured by the suspicion that he is somehow being ridiculed, or shown insufficient respect, or that the disvaluee's conduct bespeaks contempt.

In a recent compelling analysis of anger,[32] N. J. H. Dent suggests that anger is based ultimately on feelings of personal inferiority: These lead one to overestimate the importance of others' expressions of regard and esteem for one, which in turn multiplies the number of occasions upon which one feels slighted or demeaned when such expressions are not forthcoming, or are of insufficient magnitude relative to one's importunate requirements. This oversensitivity to being slighted in turn provokes the desire to rectify one's situation through retaliation, by lashing out at the offender. This analysis by itself does not, I think, cover all cases of anger; nor does it explain the origins of simple first-order political discrimination. But it does provide insight into why higher-order political discriminators, like simple first-order political discriminators, are apt to become so angry, so often, at imagined slights from seemingly arrogant disvaluees. The more inferior one feels, the more expressions of esteem one requires. And the more inferior one perceives a disvaluee to be, the more elaborate the disvaluee's expression of esteem of one is required to be. Whereas a friendly nod from a perceived

---

[31] The view of the disvaluee's assumption of equality as a *pre*sumption may explain the higher-order political discriminator's otherwise inexplicable umbrage at being complemented by a disvaluee: An inferior is in no position to confer favors of any kind.

[32] N. J. H. Dent, *The Moral Psychology of the Virtues* (Cambridge: Cambridge University Press, 1984), 155–60.

superior is sufficient to transport one to a state of grace, anything less than a full-length obeisance from a perceived inferior appears to be an insult.[33] In all such cases, irascibility regularly directed at particular members of disvalued groups should not be dismissed as simply an idiosyncracy of character, even if it is not intentionally directed at members of disvalued groups *as such*. It is, nevertheless, an overt expression of higher-order political discrimination.

A second, related example of behavior and judgments distorted by higher-order political discrimination is the treatment of disvaluees in a way that would constitute a clear insult or *faux pas*, if the person so treated were one's recognized peer. For example, a white Gentile may privately make an anti-Semitic remark to a black colleague, in a misguided effort to establish rapport, when such a remark would be seen as a serious social lapse even among other white Gentiles. Or a heterosexual may make gratuitous disparaging remarks to a gay colleague about her work or job performance, of a sort designed to "cut her down to size" rather than provide constructive criticism. Or a man may make offensively personal remarks to a woman colleague about her physical appearance, personal life, or manner of dress, of a sort that would be highly inappropriate if they were made to another man. Or he might expect from a woman colleague extra forbearance for fits of temper, irresponsible conduct, or extraordinary professional demands that he would not from a man. The higher-order political discriminator, in other social contexts, may be acclaimed quite rightly as a "prince among men;" to disvaluees, however, he reveals himself as Mr. Hyde.[34] Yet unlike former President Lyndon Johnson, who conferred with his cabinet through an open bathroom door, while uninhibitedly and indiscreetly performing his morning ablutions, the higher-order political discriminator cannot be supposed to commit these boorish excesses with any offensive intent. Rather, he regards his response to a person's disvalued properties as socially innocuous; as an acceptable variation in social etiquette, keyed to the variations among the personality traits of different individuals.

---

[33] In the deep South up to the mid-1960s, for example, for a black person to meet the gaze of a white person was perceived as an offense; and for a black man even to look at a white woman was to invite lynching.

[34] This often creates additional difficulties in identifying cases of higher-order political discrimination for what they are. The testimony of a disvaluee suffers a credibility problem at the outset. This problem is severely exacerbated if the testimony concerns a higher-order political discriminator whom others have every reason to regard as a saint. Under these circumstances, any charge of inconsistency—whether it comes from others and targets the disvaluee, or comes from the disvaluee and targets the higher-order political discriminator—is in the eye of the beholder. For higher-order political discriminators regard coarse, tasteless, or brutal behavior toward disvaluees as called forth by them and so warranted; hence as fully consistent with the most highly refined manners and courtly civility toward others.

A third example of such distorted behavior is the implicit treatment of disvaluees as being obligated by different rules of conduct than the ones which govern oneself and those considered to be one's peers. One may apply different criteria of interpretation to the behavior of disvaluees: Whereas enigmatic behavior by valuees is excused, overlooked, or given the benefit of the doubt, similar behavior on the part of disvaluees is interpreted as proof of vice or malevolence. This interpretation motivates the higher-order political discriminator not only to avoid, but also to justify the avoidance of direct interaction with the disvaluee, and thus avoid the conflict of conscience described earlier. Or one may apply rules of honor, loyalty, and responsibility only to those considered to be one's peers, but have no scruples about betraying the trust or confidentiality of a disvaluee, who is implicitly viewed as unentitled to such consideration. Alternately, one may hold disvaluees to far more stringent moral standards than the members of one's own community in fact practice among themselves. Any violation of these standards by the disvaluee then creates an irradicable moral blemish to which the valuees are invulnerable, by reason of their status as valuees. These cases express quite clearly the conviction that disvaluees just do not have quite that same status, hence are not to be subject to the same standards of treatment, as members of one's recognized community—at the same time that the higher-order political discriminator vehemently and in all honesty denies that any such discrimination is taking place. Indeed in all of these examples, the higher-order political discriminator may sincerely deny that the person's race, gender, sexual orientation, ethnic or religious affiliation, etc., arbitrarily influences his evaluations, when his behavior shows patently that they do.

VIII. FAILURES OF COGNITIVE DISCRIMINATION: CAUSES AND CURES

There are many forces that may intensify higher-order political discrimination and its social consequences. Among them are, first and foremost, complicitous institutional practices. Individuals in positions of responsibility often rank their personal and social allegiances ahead of their professional obligation to protect disvaluees from the pernicious effects of higher-order political discrimination. Or they effectively reward it, by regularly interpreting instances of it as expressions of professional autonomy, and refusing in principle to scrutinize suspected instances of it, on the grounds that doing so would be unwarranted interference in an organization's internal affairs. These institutions often comply with the letter of antidiscriminatory policies, by hiring members of disvalued groups to temporary positions of high public visibility. Since such individuals are regularly replaced by other, equally competent but equally transient members of the same disvalued group, that group's visibility within the institution can be maintained, without infiltrating the entrenched system of political discrimination through permanent or seniority status. This is to abdicate the responsibility for enforcing those antidiscriminatory policies to which such institutions publicly claim to be committed.

Second, there is the intellectual resourcefulness of the higher-order political discriminator: Someone who is in fact deeply invested in the disvaluational status of some primary property may always recruit some further, equally irrelevant property to explain her seemingly irrational judgment, and thus deflect the charge of higher-order political discrimination. It may be said, for example, that the disvalued property is not a person's race, gender, sexual orientation, class, ethnic or religious affiliation, etc., but rather his inability to "fit in," to "get along with others," or to "be a team player." This is a particularly familiar and dependable response, because the evidence for ascribing this property may be materially coextensive with the evidence for disvaluing the primary property at issue: Since the disvaluee is in theory held to the same standards of conduct that govern others in the community, but in fact expected to conform to different ones, tailored to his disvalued status, his inability to "fit in" can be guaranteed at the outset.[35]

A third force that intensifies higher-order political discrimination are the repressive pseudorational habits of rationalization, dissociation, and denial already discussed. Earlier I suggested that higher-order political discriminators were generally well-intentioned individuals who had failed to come to terms with their own prejudices. I also mentioned some possible reasons for this failure: avoidance of conflicts of conscience, feelings of personal inferiority, and first-order political discrimination being among them. Another reason that should not be neglected is that higher-order political discriminators tend to rationalize, dissociate, or deny the very existence of higher-order political discrimination itself. They might claim, for example, that the phenomenon I have described is in truth perceptual sensitivity to subtle variations and qualities among individuals, all of which might be relevant to questions of value or competence in a sufficiently broad sense. Or they might agree that higher-order political discrimination exists, but dissociate it from

---

[35] Under these circumstances, the disvaluee, too, may be accused rightly of pseudorationality, if his personal investment in the theoretical standards of equal treatment is so great that he rationalizes, dissociates, or denies the facts of discrimination that blatantly confront him. But I argue elsewhere ("The Meaning of 'Ought' and the Loss of Innocence," unpublished paper, 1989) that self-preservation *requires* that, although such ideals ultimately must die, they must not do so without a long and painful struggle.

their own motives and behavior, as an anomalous phenomenon that is too rare to merit further scrutiny. Or they might just flatly deny the existence of anything like what I have described as higher-order political discrimination, and deny as well the undeniably familiar instances of it which I have invoked to anchor the foregoing analysis. These tactics reinforce the tendencies of higher-order political discriminators to deny their own collusion in the practice of higher-order political discrimination, and to deny or minimize their need to come to terms with it. Higher-order political discriminators are adept at the tactics of pseudorationality because they have so much self-esteem to lose by modifying their beliefs. But *we* must not be taken in. For above all, higher-order political discriminators need to understand that no one is fooled by their tactics. With the aid of this understanding, they may someday learn to stop fooling themselves.

How might higher-order political discriminators come to such an understanding? How might they achieve self-awareness of the pseudorational tactics that buttress their political discrimination? In closing, I want to limn a set of strategies for cultivating more fine-grained cognitive discriminations in general, through exposure to contemporary works of art, and suggest some ways in which these might provide an antidote to higher-order political discrimination in particular.[36] I will not mean to suggest that works of art are capable of *curing* higher-order political discrimination. As we have seen, higher-order political discrimination is supervenient on first-order political discrimination; and first-order political discriminators are ashamed, not of their political discrimination, but of themselves as inadequate to the honorific stereotypes they reciprocally impose on themselves. In so far as a higher-order political discriminator retains a personal investment in that honorific stereotype, she will be unpersuaded by its deleterious effects on others to renounce it. This means that it is not just her cognitive habits that are in need of reform, but her more central conception of herself. This is a task for social reconditioning or psychotherapy, not art. Nevertheless, art has an important role to play in intensifying a viewer's self-awareness of these matters. Art can highlight pseudorational failures of cognitive discrimination as themselves objects of aesthetic examination; and it can heighten a viewer's level of cognitive sensitivity to a wide range of complex situations, of which political discrimination is only one.

In the contemporary setting, galleries and museums announce themselves to the public as arenas in which cognitive alertness is required, and in which

---

[36] None of my remarks here should be construed as an account of my own motivations, which are generally obscure to me, in producing the type of art I produce. Instead they should be regarded as providing a rationale for a certain kind of work, an interpretation that situates it in the context of my own conscious concerns.

the viewer's capacity to understand and situate an anomalous object in its singularly appropriate context will be tested. In earlier historical periods, galleries and museums had different roles: pedagogical or inspirational, for example. But in this one, their primary role, and the role of the artworks they exhibit, is to challenge the limitations of the viewer's conceptual scheme— her presuppositions about reality, the human condition, and social and personal relationships, as well as her presuppositions about what art is and what an exhibition space is supposed to do. By introducing into a specialized cognitive context singular objects that defy easy categorization, galleries and museums signal themselves to their audience as purveyors of heightened awareness through the objects and artifacts they display. Generated by a culture that values innovation for its own sake as well as for its ability to create its own market, these contemporary artifacts function primarily to provoke or stimulate in the viewer more flexible and inclusive conceptualizations of reality that can encompass them. In this sense, contemporary art is a paradigmatic experience of cognitive anomaly. It offers one the opportunity to reorganize the conceptual structure of the self in order to accommodate it, and to test and develop one's capacity for cognitive discrimination in order to grasp it.

Some works of art satisfy this *desideratum* better than others. Some choose instead to reaffirm traditional values, or the social and political *status quo*, or prevailing comfortable convictions and perceptions of human nature. But since Impressionism and perhaps before, but most explicitly since Duchamp, the most significant works of art in the Western tradition[37] have taken seriously the challenge of heightened cognitive discrimination, i.e., the challenge to compel the viewer to see what he did not see before, and to add these anomalous, newly discovered properties of objects and events to his permanent cognitive repertoire. Contemporary artists who are serious about art take seriously their responsibility to question and extend the limits of knowledge by offering anomalous objects, innovative in form, content, or both, as an antidote to provincial and conventional habits of thought.

Minimal art of the 1960s offers a particularly compelling example of this. For the first time in the history of Modernism, artists were taken seriously as critics and theorists of contemporary art. And what many Minimal artists explicitly averred in their writings was that no such theory was adequate to an understanding of the work; that the point of presenting geometrically, materially, and formally reductive objects was to draw the viewer's attention

---

[37] By "the Western tradition" in art, I understand not only the Euroethnic canon itself, but also the contributions of colonialized, marginalized, or non-Western cultures to it (as for example, Tahitian art influenced Gauguin, Japanese art influenced Van Gogh, African art influenced Picasso, or American jazz influenced Stuart Davis).

away from extrinsic associations and toward the specificity and materiality of the particular object itself. In its aesthetic strategies, Minimalism repudiated the imposition of abstract theory—psychoanalytic, social, or aesthetic—as cognitively inadequate to a full comprehension of the work. Instead it emphasized the uniqueness, singularity, and indexical immediacy of the art object itself. The category of art itself functioned as a catchall term signifying the object's inherent resistance to extrinsic conceptualization, and so its aesthetic interest as an otherwise anomalous entity in its own right. This stance itself was, of course, a theoretical one. But Minimalism differed from earlier theoretical stances in stipulating the properties of the specific object in question as the origin and locus of theorizing about it. It embedded the object in an abstract symbolic system of its own making.

Conceptual and Performance Art of the late 1960s and early 1970s extended this strategy further, by subordinating the medium in which the work was realized to the concepts it embodied or explored. It was even more clearly the intrinsic meaning of the work, and not the cognitive preconceptions the viewer brought to it, that dictated its appropriate conceptualization. In subordinating medium to concept, Conceptual Art not only reaffirmed the conceptual fluidity and inclusiveness of art, as originally introduced by Duchamp's urinal. It also opened the door to the use of any medium, event, or object deemed appropriate to the particular concepts the artist chose to explore. Thus Conceptual Art repudiated all remaining traditional restrictions on content and subject matter as well as on medium. And in so doing, it created the possibility of seeing any object as a conceptual anomaly relative to the conceptual scheme within which it was conventionally embedded. Any such object became a potential locus of original conceptual investigation, and all such objects became potential threats to the conceptual unity of a rigidly or provincially structured self.

Under these circumstances, the role of the gallery or museum as a site of cognitive provocation has become clear. Beyond a few extremely vague and uninformative terms of classification, such as "installation art," "performance art," "object art," etc., there are no longer any expectations or preconceptions a viewer may legitimately bring to such work regarding what kind of viewing experience is in store—except that she will be required to discriminate cognitively a variety of elements, and fashion for herself a coherent interpretation of the experience that at the same time respects the intrinsic conceptual integrity of the work. A viewer of contemporary art must be prepared for media that include foodstuffs, bodily fluids, chemical compounds, and industrial materials, as well as traditional art media; and for content that may be highly autobiographical, social, sexual, political, or philosophical, as well as realistic or abstract. No viewer who insists on maintaining excessively rigid, provincial, or philistine views about art will survive in the contemporary art world for very long.

This is to suggest that the contemporary art-going public is self-selected to consist, not in a specialized educational and economic elite (as though there were no working-class artists, self-made millionaire collectors, or scholarship students among the art critics!); but rather of those individuals who are psychologically prepared and sophisticated enough to engage in the hard work of cognitive discrimination in general. For all of the above reasons, the contemporary art-going public is likely to be particularly receptive to the conceptual challenge presented by cognitively anomalous objects or properties in general, and, *a fortiori*, by cognitively anomalous persons in particular. The arena of contemporary art, then, is a particularly apt one for addressing the cognitive failures of political discrimination.

Now to return to the plight of the higher-order political discriminator, taken in by his own pseudorational attempts to eradicate awareness of his xenophobic attitudes and behavior. With its latitude in the use of media, content, and subject matter, contemporary art may offer a variety of approaches for reducing this cognitive disingenuity and enhancing self-awareness. Take, for example, *mimesis*: A work of art may incorporate into its subject matter these very pseudorationalizations as an ironic commentary or distancing device. These pseudorationalizations not only impose politically discriminatory stereotyping on others. They are themselves stereotypical reactions, conditioned habitual responses that are part of a behavioral repertoire as limited as that which the political discriminator imposes on anomalous others. Indeed, they embody such stereotypes even as they express them. It is in the nature of deeply instilled habits of thought and action to seem, not only deeply private and individualized; but also fixed, natural, and part of the objective order of things—so much so that voluntarily bringing them to light as objects of self-conscious scrutiny on one's own is exceedingly difficult. One scarcely knows what to question or scrutinize. But hearing or seeing them echoed back to one by an impersonal art object can make it clear to one that these phrases or habits of reasoning are not uniquely one's own, but rather crude and common slogans that short-circuit the hard work of self-scrutiny. Thus mimesis can be an effective way of distancing oneself from such pseudorational slogans, and of illuminating their stereotypical character and function. By demonstrating their indiscriminate and simplistic application to a range of circumstances that clearly demand great sensitivity to specifics, such a work can encourage greater cognitive discrimination of particular persons and circumstances for what they are.

A second device that may be useful as an antidote to higher-order political discrimination is *confrontation*: As we have seen, a higher-order political discriminator escapes from the meaning of her behavior into a thicket of abstract pseudorational theorizing that detaches her from the actual personal and social consequences of her actions. Because she denies the existence of the object of her higher-order political discrimination, in addition to her own responses to it, the higher-order political discriminator often lacks a sense of the hurtfulness of her behavior, or of the harmfulness of its consequences for others. An art object that confronts a higher-order political discriminator with the human repercussions of these consequences can help restore to the higher-order political discriminator a sense of reality, and a sense of cognitive responsibility for the human effects of her unreflective stereotyping of anomalous others. Moreover, a confrontational art object can draw the higher-order political discriminator's attention away from the abstract realm of theoretical obfuscation, and back to the reality of her actual circumstances at the moment. It can help resituate her in the indexical present of her immediate, one-to-one relation to the object and the issues it embodies.

Finally, consider the strategy of *naming*: We have seen that pseudorationality for the higher-order discriminator consists in the construction of an elaborate edifice of euphemisms designed to obscure from himself and others the true meaning of his attitudes, actions, and policies toward others, and of the painful social realities to which his behavior in fact responds. This willed unconsciousness can be penetrated by concepts and symbols that speak plainly to the ugly realities these euphemisms conceal. An art object that draws the viewer's attention to these realities, and leaves no room for ambiguity in their identification, can be an assaultive and disturbing experience. It blocks escape into abstract speculation concerning the denotations and connotations of the terms or symbols deployed as referents, and may reinforce the vividness and objectivity of the realities brought forward through confrontation, with the legitimating imprimature of linguistic or representational acknowledgement. At the same time, through repetition and repeated viewing, it can help accustom the higher-order political discriminator to the existence of these realities, and conceptually defuse them to psychologically manageable proportions.

Of course each of these strategies, as well as many others I have not mentioned, can be deployed outside the contemporary art context as well as within it: in psychotherapy, encounter groups, or organizational training sessions, for example. But one benefit of utilizing art objects in this role is that, unlike psychotherapists, group leaders, or other human subjects, an art object can elicit different reactions from different viewers *while maintaining exactly the same phenomenological presence to all of them*. It does not itself react personally to any particular viewer, or differently to one viewer than it

does to another, or alter its presentational aspect to suit the tastes or dispositions of particular viewers. Because the logic of its internal structure and
external appearance depends on its personal history and interactive relationship with the artist rather than with the viewer, its final form is fixed and
immutable relative to any particular viewer in a way other human subjects
cannot be. Thus a viewer's relation to an art object can be both direct and
individual on the one hand, and *impersonal* on the other.

The impersonality, impenetrability, and inherent internal equilibrium of
an art object can be a distinct advantage in attacking political discrimination
through cognitive discrimination. A human subject who deploys these strategies in other interpersonal contexts is vulnerable to criticism by a participant who feels that the leader, trainer, or therapist is "reacting personally" to
her: just doesn't like her, is personally attacking her, manipulating her, or
projecting his own problems onto her. And in this type of situation, such
criticisms may be justified. But in an art context, they cannot be. For unlike
human subjects, an art object cannot have reactions to, intentions toward, or
designs of any kind on a viewer; and *a fortiori*, cannot have *personal* reactions, intentions or designs on any *particular* viewer. So although it may
happen that a particularly insecure or provincial viewer initially may feel
moved to accuse the work of art of manipulating him, ridiculing him,
trying to pull the wool over his eyes, guilt-tripping him, attacking him, etc.,
it will not require too much reflection on the viewer's part to conclude,
finally, that this is not the kind of thing an art object, unlike a human
subject, has the capacity to do. Nor will it require much more reflection of
the viewer's part to conclude that, if he does indeed feel that the work is
doing these things to him, these feelings can only be the result of magical
thinking and personal projection of his own emotions onto the object; and
that this response itself is worth his scrutiny.[38] An important benefit of

---

[38] Can the same claims be made for media advertising? Is it not clearly manipulative in intent?
Here I think we need to distinguish, in the case of art as well as of advertising, between the
creator's intentions in producing the work, and its psychological effects on its viewers. Like advert-
isers, artists of course have intentions in producing a particular work. Typically, an advertiser's
intention in producing a commercial is to get the consumer to buy the product, whereas an artist's
intention in producing a work of art may be to get the viewer to reflect on his political or aesthetic
attitudes. In both cases, these intentions can be distinguished from the psychological effects of the
work on its recipient. An advertiser who pairs a beautiful woman with a certain make of car in
order to get consumers to buy that make of car may intend to enhance the appeal of that make of
car to consumers. That a particular consumer comes to hate his wife because he has a different
make of car is not necessarily part of the advertiser's intention. Similarly, an artist who pairs
depiction of the homeless with standard stereotypical rationalizations for ignoring them may
intend to get viewers to reflect on their economic priorities. That a particular viewer feels guilt-
stricken because she has been making contributions to her alma mater instead of to the homeless
is not necessarily part of the artist's intention. Any individual who engages in an act of communication of any kind intends to have an effect on her audience, at least minimally that it understand

utilizing art objects to combat higher-order political discrimination, then, is that they enable the viewer to discriminate cognitively between what he sees and what he is.

her. This does not imply that she intends the actual effect on her audience her communication has. A consumer as well as an art viewer may examine their reactions to a commercial and a work of art respectively, in order self-consciously to discern and differentiate their personal areas of vulnerability or uncertainty from the intended act of impersonal communication the object represents.

9

'DIFFERENCE', CULTURAL RACISM AND ANTI-RACISM

TARIQ MODOOD

A NEW RACISM?

During the 1980s, several sociologists and anti-racists discerned the growing presence of a British 'new racism' (Barker 1981; Gordon and Klug n.d.; Gilroy 1987). It was argued that, following the Holocaust and the comprehensive discrediting of nineteenth-century scientific racism, racism based upon biological theories of superior and inferior races was no longer intellectually and politically viable as a public discourse. Instead, what had emerged was a racism based upon cultural differences, upon the 'natural' preference of human beings for their own cultural group, and the incompatibility between different cultures, the mixing or coexistence of which in one country, it was alleged, was bound to lead to violent social conflict and the dissolution of social bonds. It was a racism which was said to have been first articulated in the speeches of Enoch Powell in the late 1960s, was nurtured in the New Right intellectual circles of the 1970s, burst into prominence in the early 1980s with the publicity accorded to the polemical output of writers associated with the radical right-wing journal the *Salisbury Review*, and was then disseminated by many newspaper columnists and leader writers in both the broadsheets and the tabloids.

Several commentators have seen that this 'new racism' is not peculiar to the English New Right, but is part of a much larger intellectual and political movement. Étienne Balibar, for example, has argued that it is part of 'a racism in the era of "decolonisation", of the reversal of population movements between the old colonies and the old metropolises' (Balibar 1991: 21). It has developed in a way that gives expression to the perceived problem of assimilating or integrating culturally primitive and backward peoples into modern civilisations; into, for example, the France of the 'land of the Rights

From Tariq Modood, '"Difference", Cultural Racism and Anti-Racism', in Pnina Werbner and Tariq Modood (eds.), *Debating Cultural Hybridity: Multi-Cultural Identities and the Politics of Anti-Racism* (London: Zed Books, 1997).

of Man' (ibid. 24). He sees its prototype in modern anti-Semitism, of which he writes: 'Admittedly, bodily stigmata play a great role in its phantasmatics, but they do so more as signs of a deep psychology, as signs of a spiritual inheritance rather than a biological heredity' (ibid. 24). Such an interpretation of racism, Balibar points out, is particularly helpful in explaining the French colonial oppression of Muslims and contemporary Muslimophobia, and he borrows a term from Pierre-André Taguieff to identify it as 'differentialist racism'. David Goldberg, too, is surely right in his judgement that '[s]ince World War II, and especially in the past fifteen or twenty years, the cultural conception of race had tended to eclipse all others. It has become paradigmatic' (Goldberg 1993: 71).

A culturalist racism, then, should not be supposed to have originated with the British New Right. It has a much greater international and historical depth. It could indeed be said that in the long history of racism, it is nineteenth-century biologism that is the exception, and certainly Europe's oldest racisms, anti-Semitism and Islamophobia, are culturalist (Ballard 1996). Even the contemporary version of culturalist racism identified as 'new racism' certainly predates the speeches and writings of New Right politicians and intellectuals, who in fact gave an ideological expression to an extreme version of a common-sense or folk racism that has been around for some time. It is surely as old as the New Commonwealth immigration and settlement in Britain against which it was directed and which gave rise to its development, although it has become more explicit as the presence of these settlements, and the multicultural challenge they pose, has become more evident. I shall call this folk sentiment, as well as the culturally grounded, differential treatment, practices, policies and ideologies which it has given rise to or is part of, 'cultural racism', to distinguish it from biological racism, which it presupposes.

While biological racism is the antipathy, exclusion and unequal treatment of people on the basis of their physical appearance or other imputed physical differences—saliently in Britain their non-'whiteness'—cultural racism builds on biological racism a further discourse which evokes cultural differences from an alleged British or 'civilised' norm to vilify, marginalise or demand cultural assimilation from groups who also suffer from biological racism. Postwar racism in Britain has been simultaneously culturalist and biological, and while the latter is essential to the racism in question it is, in fact, the less explanatory aspect of a complex phenomenon. Biological interpretations have not governed what white British people, including racists, have thought or done; how they have stereotyped, treated and related to non-whites; and biological ideas have had increasingly less force both in the context of personal relationships and in the conceptualisation of groups.

As white people's interactions with non-white individuals increased, they did not become necessarily less conscious of group differences but they were far more likely to ascribe group differences to upbringing, customs, forms of socialisation and self-identity than to biological heredity.

A central feature of this combined racism was that the non-white presence in Britain was conceived of in terms of a double contrast. The first, a contrast between White/European/British and 'coloured'/Black/non-European, was a distinction based on skin colour. A further subdivision—of the 'coloured' group into Asians and West Indians—was also essential to the identification and definition of racial groups, and constituted the second dualism. As I shall soon show, these dualisms exist in common-sense or folk topologies as well as in the New Right discourse. But before we explore these contrasts, let us briefly consider what kind of anti-racist response was made to them.

ANTI-RACISMS AND ASIAN IDENTITIES

There have, in fact, been two different anti-racisms, an earlier and a later version. The early response—exemplified by the Campaign Against Racial Discrimination (CARD) in the 1960s, and influenced by the American Civil Rights Movement under the leadership of Martin Luther King Jnr—was to repudiate biological racism by arguing that all human beings are equal, irrespective of colour, and are entitled to the same civic rights within the nation-state. This colour-blind humanism gave way—again, first in the United States and more gradually in Britain, where it became prominent in the 1980s—to two forms of colour-conscious anti-racisms. One form consisted in the recognition of the essential need to monitor the socioeconomic disadvantages of non-whites, and the structural bias against them, in all the public institutions of a white society, in order to identify discrimination and measure both inequality and the extent of progress made towards its elimination.

The second form of anti-racism consisted in raising black consciousness, in getting black people to emphasise their blackness and pride in their roots, their solidarity with other black people and their struggles, and to organise as black people in mutual self-help and collective empowerment (Malcolm X 1966; Cleaver 1968; Blauner 1972). This movement was, in effect, to create a new black identity or black political ethnicity. The result was that the racists' first contrast, the black–white opposition, was accepted, even sharpened by racism-awareness, but reinterpreted. When this American anti-racist movement was pursued in Britain, it highlighted a problem, for in Britain there was also a second cleavage: a West Indian–Asian dualism. Despite the different political and cultural histories that this cleavage represented, British anti-racism, having accepted the first opposition between black and white, continued to deny any political or anti-racist strategic significance to this internal division (see, for example, Gordon and Klug n.d.: 23). I have argued in a series of articles that this denial has been a politically naive sociological falsification which has had a deleterious effect upon the ability of Asians to mobilise for anti-racist struggles (Modood 1992, 1994). Since the source of my feeling that British anti-racism has not taken sufficiently seriously the existence and nature of cultural racism is not merely sociological, but a matter of personal experience as an Asian living in Britain, it may be helpful to say a little about that starting point.

The effect of these anti-racisms upon Asians (initially, to be told—or to argue—that there were no real black–white differences, and later that 'colour' was the basis of ethnic pride and political solidarity) was to create a schizophrenic contradiction in many Asians' sense of identity. For during the period in which these were the dominant public anti-racist views, young British Asians were being brought up by their families and communities to feel that we *were* different *qua* Asians and *qua* specificities of religion, language, caste, national/regional origins, and so forth. We came to notice over time that it was our continued cultural differences that were resented by many of the British as alien, and made us a target of harassment and attack. Initially, the migrant generation were unsure of how long they expected to be in Britain; many expected and wished to return to their homelands in due course, and few sought any public policy of multiculturalism; but the general feeling was that even if our modes of living were to be modified through a process of settling into, and adaptation to life in Britain, some essential core of continuity had to be maintained. This was not, it must be stressed, a crudely conservative view; Asian parents knew, even if they did not always relish the prospect, that changes would occur if their children and grandchildren were to be accepted, as indeed they wished them to be, by white British people, and to succeed in the new society.

Different parents, different Asian communities, had different views on the pace of change and what should and must not be changed. In my family, national origins (Pakistan) and language (Urdu) were considered to be of lesser importance and hence detachable from the core values, which was defined as Islam (for an account of my father's Islam, see M. S. Modood 1990). This did not mean a rigid 'fundamentalist', anti-Western, anti-modernist religiosity (it particularly did not mean this in the 1960s and 1970s), but it did mean that the new ways of living, the gradually becoming a part of British society, had to be ultimately justified in terms compatible with a Muslim faith and the welfare of Muslim people. The ultimate form of 'selling out', of self-abnegation, I was taught, was to be a traitor to Islam and to be indifferent to the fate of Muslims.

Of course, only about half of the South Asians in Britain are Muslim, and not all Muslims are equally committed to a Muslim identity (which is certainly open to a number of interpretations). Some Pakistanis see their cultural heritage and Pakistani identity as being inseparable from—and hence not of lesser value than—their Muslim lifestyle. Some valorise only their Punjabi or North Indian cultural identity, while others valorise their common past struggle against British imperialism. My point is not to reduce the complexity and range of identities and commitments in the South Asian communities to the religious, though I do believe that religion is much more central to British Asian ethnicity than many anti-racists would like to acknowledge. My point is that South Asian immigrants to Britain believed, and taught their children to believe, in the uniqueness of their culturally distinct beliefs and practices, and felt that this cultural heritage was of value and under threat (Modood et al. 1994).

The threat did not come just from racism. It also arose from the fact of migration and settlement in a society very different from the one in which one had roots—in which, for example, religion played a very different role in structuring collective identities. Yet the anti-racisms of both the earlier and the later periods ignored these issues, and with them the significance of Asian ethnicities. This meant that one was denied a language in which to debate cultural difference and the extent to which Asian cultural differences were increasingly being racialised; a language in which to give expression to ethnicity while seeking, at the same time, to oppose racist stereotyping and public expressions of contempt, as well as right-wing 'culturalist' constructions of identity; a form of words to express loyalty to one's own minority community within a public discourse of equality and civic integration.

In some ways, the second form of anti-racism was an advance on the first in that it brought issues of representation as well as policy under critical political scrutiny; it was a less defensive anti-racism which did not assume that cultural homogeneity was a prerequisite of common citizenship. It highlighted the crucial issue of identity. Yet from an Asian point of view, the black consciousness movement was in other ways less preferable to the earlier civic anti-racism, for the assertive identity it promoted to unite the victims of racism focused on colour. Ironically, this was at a time when it was cultural racism that was on the increase, eclipsing other forms, and when Asians were asking themselves what were the core identities they felt were under threat and most worth preserving, and hence were least interested in defining themselves in terms of a global colour identity.

The second anti-racism, therefore, excluded Asians and other victims of racism who did not see their primary identity and incorporation into British society in terms of colour; or at least, it was an anti-racism that was insensitive to the concerns and vulnerabilities of such groups. Yet the secondary status of Asians in anti-racism went further. For as I have suggested, there was one ethnic identity with which this second anti-racism was compatible—indeed, they usually went hand in hand. This was black consciousness or a black pride movement where 'black' meant African roots and origins in the enslavement of African peoples in the 'New World'. Hence the 1980s anti-racism consisted of (in the case of white people, a solidarity with) an oppositional blackness based on an inversion of the racist white–black/coloured divide, together with a celebration of the positive elements of the black diasporic African heritage of struggle, and of the achievements of the contemporary bearers of that heritage. There was tension between these two versions of blackness—political solidarity of all non-whites, and a black diasporic African ethnicity—but no real anti-racist criticism of what was perceived as a natural and benign conflation. Yet my experience in racial equality work was that the assertion of any other non-white minority identity—Asian, Indian or Muslim—was condemned as culturalism, as racism(!) or as divisive of the anti-racist effort and minority unity (Modood 1994). This created an anti-racism that failed to acknowledge the existence of cultural racism, and therefore to contend with the specificities of anti-Asian racism. An absurd situation had emerged in which anti-racists were encouraging self-pride and assertiveness in the racially subordinated, but were intolerant of Asians defining themselves, their circumstances, frustrations and aspirations, except in approved ways.

In fact this opposition to Asian ethnicity has been anomalous within the broader left-wing politics of the last two decades, in which the solidarities of class or social citizenship have been superseded by an ideal of equality based on the view that 'a positive self-definition of group difference is in fact more liberatory' (I. M. Young 1990: 157). It is a politics that has informed not just black power anti-racism but the gay pride movement and, above all, radical feminism. Those elements of the Old Left that thought such politics divisive have found themselves having to accommodate it or risk irrelevance. Yet the intolerance of Asian self-definition did not come only or even primarily from the Old Left; the charge that Asian self-definition is divisive is heard as frequently from advocates of the politics of difference (Gilroy 1987).

THE COMPLEXITIES OF RACISM

More recently—not unrelated to a hypothesising of the existence of a new racism, and partly following the lead of some in the field of Cultural Studies (e.g. Gilroy 1987, 1990)—a reappraisal of anti-racism as strategy and mode of discursive representation has been initiated. One of the arguments for a reappraisal is that contemporary racism was, but no longer is, a unitary phenomenon: that Britain has become 'multi-racist'. Support for this diversity is evidenced by the fact that white people who are racist towards some ethnic groups can nevertheless admire other ethnic groups because of, for example, aspects of their subcultural styles:

Most typically, of course, many White working-class boys discriminate positively in favour of Afro-Caribbean subcultures as exhibiting a macho, proletarian style, and against Asian cultures as being 'effeminate' and 'middle-class'. Such boys experience no sense of contradiction in wearing dreadlocks, smoking ganja and going to reggae concerts whilst continuing to assert that 'Pakis Stink'. (Cohen 1988: 83)

Les Back found these insights confirmed in his ethnographic study of a large South London council estate in 1985–87 (Back 1993). He observed among the young whites on the estate a 'neighbourhood nationalism', side by side and in tension with a British nationalism. While the latter was understood as a preserve of whites, the former was based on racially mixed groups of friends and the prestigious position of black youth cultures and styles in the area, and embraced blacks as well as whites. The Vietnamese on the estate were, however, excluded from both these local patriotisms, and therefore incurred 'the full wrath of the new racism which defines "outsiders" in terms of "cultural" difference' (ibid. 228). Back believes that this situation is interestingly new. Indeed, it is relatively new in terms of British sociology and anti-racist discussions. I would suggest, however, that, like the 'new racism' itself, these inconsistent and differential racisms are as old as the immigration and settlement they are attempting to make sense of and live with.

British race relations policies and anti-racisms are premissed on the assumption that the problem is of an exclusionism typified by the notice that some landladies in the 1950s put in their front windows: 'No Coloureds' (the fuller version being 'No Irish, No Coloureds, No Dogs') (Cohen 1988: 14); notices evoking memories for those newly arrived immigrants like my father of signs outside the clubs of the British in India: 'No Indians, No Dogs'. The imagined solution to this exclusionary tendency is symbolised by the black-and-white handshake that serves as the logo of the Commission for Racial Equality. But neither the problem nor the solution was ever quite so simple. The 'No-Coloureds' racism was not unitary: racists always distinguished between the groups they rejected, and while the likelihood of someone who discriminated against one group discriminating against other groups was probably high, the culturally constructed grounds of rejection varied depending upon the immigrant group.

Alastair Bonnett cites a BBC interview with some 'Teddy Boys' just after the 1958 racist attacks in Notting Hill (Bonnett 1993: 19–20, using an interview transcript in Glass 1961). He observes that while there is a reductionist, homogenising racialism, 'They're all spades'—it is constantly qualified, as particular groups (notably Jamaicans and Maltese) are identified and 'extricated from the "racial"/colour based logic involved in drawing a clear line between "spades" and "us" (Bonnett 1993: 20). My own memories of my secondary modern, working-class school in North West London in the second half of the 1960s are very much in line with Back's South London observations, making doubtful the suggestion that he has discovered a new phenomenon. While there was indiscriminate racist name-calling, the black and white boys had interracial friendships and a respect for each other, focused, above all, on football, which was greater than either had for Asian boys. The school roll included many skinheads and other adherents of the cult of Paki-bashing who appeared to me at the time to have a very clear perception of an elemental difference between 'Pakis' (a.k.a. Indians and Asians) and 'non-Pakis'. The contrast that Cohen referred to, cited above, between 'pushover' Asians and 'hard' West Indians was certainly in place, though the more recent contrast between academic, obedient Asians and disruptive, dull (male, but not female) Afro-Caribbeans was, with Asians still struggling with the English language, as yet in its infancy. Mac an Ghail, on the basis of observation in a Midlands working-class secondary school in the 1980s, has argued that this pair of stereotypes is fostered by (racist) teachers (Mac an Ghail 1988). I certainly do not remember it being confined to the teachers, or actively led by them (see also Gillborn 1990; Willis 1977).

This perception of 'coloured immigrants' as coming not in one but in two kinds, 'black'/'Jamaican'/'West Indian'/'Afro-Caribbean' and 'Paki'/'Indian'/'Asian', is not confined to schools, youth or the working class. Despite the way in which anti-racists represent racist discourse, the actual speeches and literature of, say, Enoch Powell, the National Front, the Conservative New Right or the British National Party constantly make this distinction, and this is evident even in the quotes that some anti-racists use (e.g. Gordon and Klug n.d.: 17–19; Gilroy 1987: 45–6). In the only in-depth research of how racial stereotypes work in job selection (Jenkins 1986), Richard Jenkins undertook a study of middle managers across a range of public- and private-sector organisations. Through interviews, he identified eight stereotypes in what the managers said (the percentage indicates the number of times this comment came up in the interviews):

1. West Indians are lazy, happy-go-lucky, or slow   43%
2. Asians are hard workers   34%
3. Asians are more ambitious and academic   14%
4. West Indians are aggressive and excitable   12%
5. West Indians mix better with whites   13%
6. Asians are clannish and don't mix   13%
7. West Indians have a chip on their shoulders   11%
8. Asians are lazy, less willing   11%

None of these stereotypes is about—to use the managers' favoured term—'coloured people' as such. What emerges once again are two groups, and what is interesting is that there is only one stereotype, 'laziness', that applies to both (points 1 and 8), and even there, the votes cast suggest contrast rather than similarity. In this respect racism, especially British racism, is quite different from sexism. Of course there are stereotypes about different kinds of women: for example, the bossy, the demure, and the man-hater. But—unlike the case with non-whites—there are some fundamental stereotypes about women *as such*: they are less rational, more emotional; physically weak and lacking in toughness; more caring, and so on. While the managers' categories could exist only in the context of a society in which racism was present, it would be quite wrong to suppose that stereotypes such as these are confined to a special group of people: racists, or white people. A Runnymede Trust survey found that about the same number (nearly 50 per cent) of Afro-Caribbeans as whites assented to the proposition 'Asian people work harder than white people' (the Asian figure was nearly 70 per cent); similarly, about 15 per cent of whites and nearly the same number of Asians agreed with the proposition 'White people are more intelligent than black people' (Amin and Richardson 1992: 44).

These fundamentally contrasting images and generalisations about Asians and West Indians are not hidden away in private conversations, to be teased out through subtle research. They are commonly found in the mass media, especially in the tabloid press. Alastair Bonnett has interestingly brought out how, in the 1980s, even among opponents of non-white immigration such as the *Sun*, there is a softening of a blanket rejectionism as worthwhile qualities are found in one or other minority group (Bonnett 1993: 25–9). Usually such positive qualities are attributed to one group but not to the other, so that the two groups are not just distinguished, but implicitly contrasted. From the examples Bonnett offers, two sets of contrasts can be identified: one favouring Afro-Caribbeans, the other Asians.

1. Asians are law-abiding, hard-working, resourceful and respectful of

traditional family values; blacks lack the discipline and structures to resist an inner-city underclass culture of drugs, vice, crime and violence.

2. Asians have a profoundly alien culture; they do not share and do not want to share the Judaeo-Christian outlook and/or a democratic individualism; black people, typified by the celebration of the boxer Frank Bruno as a 'Great Briton', are patriotic Britons who enrich a shared popular culture and bring honour to national sporting teams.

Bonnett goes on to point out that while these sweet–sour contrasts are based on very old, long-standing stereotypes and cultural relationships, they nevertheless more than hint at a new right-wing redefinition of Britishness by de-emphasising 'whiteness' in favour of characteristics such as 'law abiding', 'family-loving', 'individualism', and so on, which minorities may already have or can learn (or be taught) to emulate. It is a vision that claims to be colour-blind, while it propagates a culturally intolerant British nationalism, suggesting that contemporary racist sentiment is capable not just of the kind of 'neighbourhood nationalism' of a working-class council estate but of effacing colour racism while reinforcing cultural racism at a macro-level (not that cultural intolerance is confined to the Right; see Weldon 1989). Moreover, as Bonnett also notes, in the late 1980s and early 1990s a third racialised grouping emerged in public discourse as a target for racist graffiti and attacks, a group apparently particularly suited to focus the unease evoked by alien cultures and their seeming lack of respect for, and incompatibility with, the British way of life. I refer here, of course, to Muslims. As I argue elsewhere, I believe that Muslimphobia is at the heart of contemporary British and European cultural racism (Modood 1990, 1992).

THE RISE OF CULTURAL RACISM

The implications of the development of a seemingly 'colour-blind' nationalism, which appears to be gaining support, need to be spelled out. While it is just possible that it will give us a post-biological racist cultural intolerance, it is much more likely that the hostility against perceived cultural difference will be directed primarily against non-whites rather than against white minorities. That is to say, even if it should be the case that colour racism may become negligible in its own right, it is still possible for it to operate in conjunction with cultural racism. What we would have is a situation in which colour racism is triggered by, and becomes potent only in combination with, cultural antagonisms and prejudices. It is by no means an impossible development for colour prejudice to decline, while discourses attacking the collective cultures of minority groups rise. At this point, cultural racism would have come into its own. In my view it is quite possible that we shall witness in the next few decades an increasing de-racialisation of, say, culturally assimilated Afro-Caribbeans and Asians, along with, *simultaneously*, a racialisation of other culturally 'different' Asians, Arabs and non-White Muslims.

Having anything but a European physical appearance may be enough in contemporary European societies to make one a possible object of racist treatment (not that only European societies can be racist; see, for example, Dikötter 1990). But such phenotypical racism can also be the foundation of a more complex form of racism. I am not, however, arguing that wherever there is biological racism there must be cultural racism too, or that cultural exclusionism occurs only in the context of racism, or should be re-labelled 'racism'. Ethnic hierarchies and religious discrimination, for example, can and do exist in all-white or all-black societies—in societies where groups are not differentiated by physical appearance. My argument is that racialised groups which have distinctive cultural identities, or a community life defined as 'alien', will suffer an additional dimension of discrimination and prejudice. The hostility against the non-white minority is likely to be particularly sharp if that minority is sufficiently numerous to reproduce itself as a community, and has a distinctive and cohesive value system which can be perceived as an alternative, and possible challenge, to the norm. It is particularly important to recognise that racism constitutes opposition to, discrimination against, not just individuals but, above all, communities or groups.

Racism normally makes a linkage between a difference in physical appearance and a (perceived) difference in group attitudes and behaviour. In contemporary settings this linkage is not usually crudely genetic or biological, but is likely to rest on history, social structure, group norms, values and cultures. The causal linkage is unlikely to be perceived as scientific or determining but as probabilistic, and therefore allowing of exceptions. Thus, European people can have good personal relations with certain non-white people and yet have stereotypes about the groups those persons are from, believing that the groups in question have major adjustment problems (chips on their shoulders, etc.). These whites are likely to deny that they are racists ('my best friend is black . . . '). Indeed, this denial can be genuine, for it is possible not to be a racist in individual relationships or in the context of shared cultural assumptions, yet be a racist in one's attitudes towards groups. Such collective racism can be overridden in the course of interracial friendships and shared lifestyles where a non-white friend, for example, can demonstrate that he or she is the exception to the stereotype; yet on the other hand, it is also clear that despite such one-to-one relationships, stereotypes may continue to be held by the white friend (and, of course, not only by whites) to apply to the group as a whole.

Cultural racism is likely to be particularly aggressive against those minority communities that want to maintain—and not just defensively—some of the basic elements of their culture or religion; if, far from denying their difference (beyond the colour of their skin), they want to assert this difference in public, and demand that they be respected just as they are. Some of the early researchers on racial discrimination in England were quite clear about the existence of a colour and cultural component in racial discrimination, yet thought the former much the more important. A leading study by W. W. Daniel, for example, concluded: 'The experiences of white immigrants, such as Hungarians and Cypriots, compared to black or brown immigrants, such as West Indians and Asians, leaves no doubt that the major component in the discrimination is colour' (Daniel 1968: 209). This was further confirmed for Daniel by the finding that West Indians experienced more discrimination than Asians, and he takes the view that people who physically differ most from the white population were discriminated against most; therefore, he argues, 'prejudice against Negroes is most deep-rooted and widespread' (ibid. 209). In contrast, he thought that lighter-skinned Asians suffered from some discrimination for cultural reasons, but that this would tend to decrease for British-educated second-generation Asians. While his prediction appears, on the surface, reasonable, it overlooked the increasing significance that cultural racism was to play in determining attitudes to ethnic minorities.

The annual Social Attitudes Survey, which began in 1982, has consistently recorded, as have other surveys, that the English think there is more extreme prejudice against Asians than against Afro-Caribbeans. The differences are minor, though widening: in 1991, 58 per cent of whites thought that there was considerable prejudice against Asians, and 50 per cent against West Indians (K. Young 1992: 181). The more detailed breakdown, available in the 1986 survey report, shows that the difference is mainly accounted for by those under the age of 35 and those in social classes III (manual), IV, V and other (Airey and Brook 1986: 163). In other words, anti-Asian racism appears to be on the increase. Perhaps an even better measure of the difference between attitudes to these two major ethnic groups can be found among the white respondents who admitted to being prejudiced themselves: 14 per cent said they were prejudiced against Asians as against only 5 per cent against black people; the figures for the under-35s were 20 per cent and 5 per cent respectively, and the factorial difference was even greater in the North and Midlands (ibid. 164). A Policy Studies Institute survey conducted in 1994 found that all ethnic groups believe that prejudice against Asians in general, and Muslims in particular, is much the highest of all ethnic, racial or religious prejudices, and it is believed by Asian people themselves that the prejudice against Asians is primarily a prejudice against Muslims (Modood *et al.* 1997).

These survey findings are confirmed by several qualitative or personal accounts—for example, by Dervla Murphy in her documentation of racism in Bradford and Birmingham (Murphy 1987), and by the Scottish-Nigerian writer Adewale Maja-Pearce in his travels around Britain (Maja-Pearce 1990). Both found that white people expressed more hostility towards Asians, especially Pakistanis, than any other group (see Murphy 1987: 214). Maja-Pearce was indeed moved to write: 'This obsessive hatred of people from the Indian subcontinent is paralleled in recent [pre-Bosnia] history by a well-known event in central Europe' (Maja-Pearce 1990: 72). Part of the explanation for the failure of Daniel's prediction may be found in Michael Banton's observation, made just a decade later: 'the English seemed to display more hostility towards the West Indians because they sought a greater degree of acceptance than the English wished to accord; in more recent times there seemed to have been more hostility towards Asians because they are insufficiently inclined to adopt English ways' (Banton 1979: 242).

INDIRECT DISCRIMINATION

My attempt thus far to establish that there is such a thing as 'cultural racism' has focused on stereotypes, prejudices and discourse, on perceptions and attitudes which are not only part of a climate of opinion but lead to direct acts and practices of racial discrimination in areas of social life such as employment, housing, schools, social services, electoral politics, and so on. There is also, however, a dimension of indirect discrimination involved in this racism. I take my idea of indirect discrimination from the British Race Relations Act (1976). A practice or policy may make no reference to race or ethnic groups, but may nevertheless disproportionately disadvantage some groups more than others. For example, a company policy that gives preference in filling jobs to local people is formally non-racist (and even may date from the time when Britain was not multiracial), but if the local population happens to be predominantly white, the policy disadvantages minority groups. If there are no countervailing justifiable reasons in favour of this policy—related, for example, to the efficiency of the business—then this constitutes indirect discrimination.

It should be clear that many kinds of non-racist forms of socioeconomic inequalities, especially forms of class exclusivity—for example, a bias in favour of Oxbridge graduates for certain kinds of elite jobs—are *prima facie* cases of indirect racial discrimination (see, for instance, Commission for Racial Equality 1987). Cultural differences too, however, can be the basis for unintended discrimination. Every society has ways of doing things— customs, norms, cultural preferences and rewards—which reflect a majority view, or that of a particularly prized cultural group. Membership of a non-dominant cultural group can deprive one of, say, excellence in the dominant language and its modes of representation, or access to certain useful social networks. A member of any group which has failed to master or accept the established norms may find it systematically and cumulatively more difficult to meet the target those norms underwrite. Such norms may vary from the unwillingness to engage in the social drinking of alcohol to wearing what counts as acceptable, professional and appropriate clothing, to accent or manner of speech. To be disadvantaged because of one's religion or culture is to suffer discrimination. The English custom that requires staff to work on Fridays, the day of collective worship for Muslims, while recognising that it is unreasonable to demand work on Sundays, may have no justifiable grounds other than local custom. What is taught in schools, the character and delivery of medical and social services, the programme schedules of television and radio, the preference for certain forms of entertainment and culture, can all be sites of culture-blind indirect discrimination.

I cannot possibly pursue here the different kinds of issues that have arisen in these different fields and that, together, give substance to what I might call the outer, indirect part of the concept of cultural racism. A very good example of a debate about the kind of ethnocentrism I have in mind has been raging in American academia and elsewhere, regarding the demands by feminists and ethnic minority activists that university curricula and intel-lectual canons reflect a multiculturalism appropriate to the country as a whole, encompassing groups which have been historically marginalised and culturally denuded, 'written out' as agents (as opposed to objects) of intel-lectual inquiry (for an attempt to moderate the debate, see Barber 1992). My own focus has been on how South Asians, and especially South Asian Muslims, have been marginalised and written out of equality debates and anti-racist perspectives.

A MORE PLURAL ANTI-RACISM

I am aware that the concept of cultural racism as elaborated here will seem perverse to some. It will seem yet another example of what Robert Miles calls an 'inflation of the meaning of racism' (Miles 1989) created by bringing together two things—racism proper and cultural prejudice or ethno-centricism—that are apparently quite distinct, thereby obscuring the real nature of racist thinking and practices. Against that I would argue that while it is true that there is no logical connection between cultural prejudice and colour racism, by the same token there is no logical connection between racial discrimination and class inequalities, yet when the two do come together, the concept of racial disadvantage is a good one to describe the situation. Or again, there is no necessary connection between racism and sexism (for the opposite view, see Balibar 1991: 49), but we know they can be connected, and when they are, a distinctive phenomenon is created in the form of stereotypes about submissive Asian women or the strong black woman who cannot keep her man (Anthias and Yuval-Davis 1992: 125). Similarly, there may be only a contingent, matter-of-fact connection between colour prejudice and cultural prejudice, true for only certain times and places; nevertheless, when the two kinds of exclusionism and oppression come together, we have a distinctive phenomenon worthy of its own name and conceptualisation.

In this conceptualising, far from obscuring racism, we learn something about it: namely, that—contrary to just about everybody who writes about racism, including those who emphasise the specificities of different kinds of racism and its articulations with nation, gender, class, and so on (Miles 1989; Anthias and Yuval-Davis 1992)—contemporary British racism is not dependent upon any (even unstated) form of biological determinism. True, there is always some reference to differences in physical appearances and/or a legacy of the racism of earlier centuries, but the reference is not necessarily to a deep biology; minor phenotypical differences are all that is required to mark out racial groups, stereotype them and treat them accordingly. Being able to pick individuals out on the basis of their physical appearance and to assign them to a racial group may be an essential aspect of the definition of racism, but physical appearance stands only as a marker of race, not as the explanation of a group's behaviour. Racists impute inferiority, undesir-ability, distinctive behavioural traits, and so on, to a group distinguished by their appearance; but this does not imply an assumption on their part that the behavioural qualities are produced by biology rather than by history, culture, upbringing, by certain norms or their absence.

In the extreme case, cultural racism—as I have argued above—does not necessarily hinge on colour racism, merely a colour racism *at the point* of cultural racism. Ironically, then, it is not the contemporary racists who make biology the cause of culture, but those anti-racists who define the 'new racism' as the view exposed by some anti-racists 'that there are biologically-determined differences between groups of people which are so fundamental as to lead to unbridgeable gaps in culture and lifestyle' (Gordon and Klug n.d.: 22). Perhaps the tactic of understating the cultural dimensions of racism is intended to have a simpler thesis to refute, and to focus energy and debate merely on colour racism. But if so, it is to fail to oppose racism and to create the basis of a movement which all racially victimised groups can identify with.

For if the New Right's 'new racism' of Enoch Powell and the *Salisbury Review* did anything, it was to make explicit and to elaborate a *cultural* determinism, without apparent biological claims, the purpose being to raise doubts about the possibility of assimilating cohesive 'alien' minorities into the nation, and to challenge the feasibility of the reformist goal of a pluralist, multicultural British nationality. To interpret a thesis of cultural determinism directed at phenotypically identified groups as a disguised form of biological determinism, as some anti-racists have done, is to understate its persuasiveness for those who are unmoved by a crude biologism. An antiracism narrowly focused on colour racism is, therefore, at best a partial, at worst a misdirected, riposte to the New Right and the complex and damaging racism in contemporary Britain. It is an anti-racism which, by failing to meet discourse with counter-discourse, fails also to connect with many British South Asians' anxieties and energies.

The growing calls to revise and update anti-racism by pluralising the concept of political blackness are to be welcomed (Hall 1988: 28; Parekh 1994: 102). An element of this project depends on the argument that a 'black' political identity does not compete with or replace other identities—for example, 'Asian'; for, it is argued, different identities refer to different aspects of a person's subjectivity, or are emphasised in different situations—say, one in politics, the other to do with culture. As no one has yet given this idea any content, I am unsure what is being proposed. Who, for example, is to decide what is a political situation and what a cultural one? As a matter of fact, most of the minority of Asians who think of themselves as 'black' think this in relation not to specific contexts but to what they perceive as a pervading fact of social existence (Modood *et al.* 1997). Moreover, is 'blackness' really available to Asians when some of the most thoughtful and acclaimed contributions to the development of 'blackness' are not about downgrading the cultural content but about increasing the reference to African roots and the Atlantic experience (Gilroy 1987; 1993)? Can political blackness, emotionally and intellectually, really hope to replace an ethnic blackness, with all its powerful resonances and appeals to self-pride, with a notion that is supposed to unite in certain limited contexts for pragmatic purposes? It is because I think that 'blackness' contains so much of the history, sorrow, hopes and energy of descendants of African enslavement in the Atlantic world that I do not think it can be turned into a politics that is neutral between different non-white groups. It cannot have the same meaning for, or equally give strength to, those who can identify with that history and those who cannot.

There is in racial discrimination and colour racism quite clearly a commonality of circumstance among people who are not white. It is partly what gives sense to the term 'ethnic minorities' and to suggestions for a 'rainbow coalition' (Modood 1988: 402). The question is not whether coalitional anti-racism is desirable, but of what kind. My personal preference and commitment is for a plural politics that does not privilege colour identities. We must accept what is important to people, and *we must be even-handed between the different identity formations*. Political blackness is an important constituent of this pluralism, but it cannot be *the* overarching basis of unity. The end of its hegemony is not without its problems and dangers, but is not to be regretted. A precondition for creating/re-creating a coalitional pluralism is the giving up of the corrupting ideal of a solidaristic monism.

A new public philosophy of racial equality and pluralism must aspire to bring into harmony the pluralism and hybridity that exist on the ground, not to pit them against themselves by insisting that some modes of collectivity trump all others. That was the error of the anti-racism of the 1980s.

REFERENCES

Airey, Colin, and Brook, Lindsay (1986), 'Interim Report: Social and Moral Issues', in Roger Jowell *et al.* (eds.), *British Social Attitudes* (Aldershot: SCPR, Gower).

Amin, Krutika, and Richardson, Robin (1992), *Politics for All: Equality, Culture and the General Election 1992* (London: Runnymede Trust).

Anthias, Floya, and Yuval-Davis, Nira (1992), *Racialised Boundaries: Race, Nation, Gender, Colour and Class and the Anti-Racist Struggle* (London: Routledge).

Back, Les (1993), 'Race, Identity and Nation within an Adolescent Community in South London', *New Community*, 19: 217–33.

Balibar, Étienne (1991), 'Is there a 'Neo-Racism?', in Étienne Balibar and Immanuel Wallerstein, *Race, Nation, Class: Ambiguous Identities* (London: Verso), 17–28.

Ballard, Roger (1996), 'Islam and the Construction of Europe', in W. A. R. Shadid and Van Koningsveld (eds.), *Islam, Hinduism and Political Mobilization in Western Europe* (Kampen: Kok Pharos).

Banton, Michael (1979), 'It's our Country', in Robert Miles and Annie Phizacklea (eds.), *Racism and Political Action in Britain* (London: Routledge), 223–46.

Barber, Benjamin R. (1992), *An Aristocracy for Everyone: The Politics of Education and the Future of America* (New York: Ballantine).

Barker, Martin (1981), *The New Racism: Conservatives and the Ideology of the Tribe* (London: Junction Books).

Blauner, Robert (1972), *Racial Oppression in America: Essays in Search of a Theory* (New York: Harper & Row).

Bonnett, Alastair (1993), *Radicalism, Anti-Racism and Representation* (London: Routledge).

Cleaver, Eldridge (1968), *Soul on Ice* (New York: McGraw-Hill).

Cohen, Philip (1988), 'The Perversions of Inheritance: Studies in the Making of Multi-Racist Britain', in Philip Cohen and Harbajan S. Bains, *Multi-Racist Britain* (London: Macmillan).

Commission for Racial Equality (1987), *Chartered Accountancy Training Contracts: Report of a Formal Investigation into Ethnic Minority Recruitment* (London: CRE).

Daniel, W. W. (1968), *Racial Discrimination in England* (London: Penguin).

Dikötter, F. (1990), 'Group Definition and the Idea of "Race" in Modern China', *Ethnic and Racial Studies*, 13: 420–31.

Gillborn, David (1990), *'Race', Ethnicity and Education: Teaching and Learning in Multi-Ethnic Schools* (London: Routledge).

Gilroy, Paul (1987), *There Ain't No Black in the Union Jack: The Cultural Politics of Race and Nation* (London: Hutchinson).

—— (1990), 'The End of Anti-Racism', *New Community*, 17: 71–83.

—— (1993), *The Black Atlantic: Modernity and Double Consciousness* (London: Verso).

Glass, R. (1961), *London's Newcomers: The West Indian Migrants* (Cambridge, Mass.: Harvard University Press).

Goldberg, David T. (1993), *Racist Culture: Philosophy and the Politics of Meaning* (Cambridge, Mass.: Blackwell).

Gordon, Paul, and Klug, Francesca (n.d., probably 1986), *New Right, New Racism* (London: Searchlight).

Hall, Stuart (1988), 'New Ethnicities', in Kobena Mercer (ed.), *Black Film, British Cinema* (London: Institute of Contemporary Arts); also in J. Donald and A. Rattansi (eds.) (1992), *'Race', Culture and Difference* (London: Sage).

Jenkins, Richard (1986), *Racism and Recruitment* (Cambridge: Cambridge University Press).

Mac an Ghail, Mairtin (1988), *Young, Gifted and Black* (Milton Keynes: Open University Press).

Maja-Pearce, Adewale (1990), *How Many Miles to Babylon?* (London: Heinemann).

Malcolm X (1966), *The Autobiography of Malcolm X*, written with Alex Hailey (New York: Hutchinson/Collins).

Miles, Robert (1989), *Racism* (London: Routledge).

Modood, M. S. (1990), 'My Faith: A Personal Statement', in Frances Gurnley and Brian Redhead (eds.), *The Pillars of Islam* (London: BBC Books).

Modood, Tariq (1988), '"Black", Racial Equality and Asian Identity', *New Community*, 14/3: 297–404.

—— (1990), 'British Asian Muslims and the Rushdie Affair', *Political Quarterly*, 61/2: 143–60; also in J. Donald and A. Rattansi (eds.), *'Race', Culture and Difference* (London: Sage).

—— (1992), *Not Easy Being British: Colour, Culture and Citizenship* (Stoke-on-Trent: Trentham for the Runnymede Trust).

—— (1994), 'Political Blackness and British Asians', *Sociology*, 28: 4.

—— Berthoud, Richard, Lakey, Jane, Nazroo, James, Smith, Patten, Virdee, Satnam, and Beishon, Sharon (1997), *Ethnic Disadvantage in Britain: The Fourth National Survey of Ethnic Minorities* (London: Policy Studies Institute).

—— Beishon, Sharon, and Virdee, Satnam (1994), *Changing Ethnic Identities* (London: Policy Studies Institute).

Murphy, Dervla (1987), *Tales from Two Cities* (London: John Murray).

Parekh, Bikhu (1994), 'Minority Rights, Majority Values', in D. Milliband (ed.), *Reinventing the Left* (Cambridge: Polity Press).

Weldon, Fay (1989), *Sacred Cows* (London: Chatto Press).

Willis, Paul (1977), *Learning to Labour* (Aldershot: Gower).

Young, Iris Marion (1990), *Justice and the Politics of Difference* (Princeton, NJ: Princeton University Press).

Young, Ken (1992), 'Class, Race and Opportunity', in Roger Jowell *et al.*, *British Social Attitudes*, 9th Report (Aldershot: SCPR).

10

THE HEART OF RACISM

J. L. A. GARCIA

The phenomenon of racism having plagued us for many centuries now, it is somewhat surprising to learn that the concept is so young. The second edition of *The Oxford English Dictionary* (1989) dates the earliest appearances of the term 'racism' only to the 1930s.[1] During that decade, as the shadow of Nazism lengthened across Europe, social thinkers coined the term to describe the ideas and theories of racial biology and anthropology to which the Nazi movement's intellectual defenders appealed in justifying its political program. Thus, Ruth Benedict, in a book published in 1940, called racism "the dogma that one ethnic group is condemned by nature to congenital inferiority and another group is destined to congenital superiority"[2] (Benedict 1940).

These origins are reflected in the definition that the *O.E.D.* still offers: "The theory that distinctive human characteristics and abilities are determined by race."[3] Textbook definitions also echo this origin: "Racism—a doctrine that one race is superior" (Schaefer 1990: 27). Recently, however, some have argued that these definitions no longer capture what people mean when they talk of racism in the moral and political discourse that has become the term's primary context. Some on the political left argue that definitions reducing racism to people's beliefs do not do justice to

From J. L. A. Garcia, 'The Heart of Racism', *Journal of Social Philosophy*, 27/1 (Spring 1996).

[1] The same dictionary dates the cognate 'racist', as both adjective and noun, to the same period, but places the first appearances of 'racialism' and 'racialist' three decades earlier.

[2] Miles begins a summary of his review of the first uses of the term in the effort of certain intellectuals to attack the pseudo-scientific defenses of the Nazi movement by saying that "the concept of racism was forged largely in the course of a conscious attempt to withdraw the sanction of science from a particular meaning of the idea of 'race'"; and he chides these early critics on the grounds that their interpretation of racism, "by focusing on the product of nineteenth century scientific theorizing, tended to presume that racism was always, and therefore was only, a structured and relatively coherent set of assertions . . . Such a definition [is problematic insofar as it] excludes less formally structured assertions, stereotypical ascriptions and symbolic representations . . . " (Miles 1986: 47, 48).

[3] Merriam-Webster's *Ninth New Collegiate Dictionary* offers a secondary definition: "racial prejudice or discrimination."

racism as a sociopolitical reality. Robert Miles records the transition in the thought of Ambalvaner Sivanandan, director of Britain's Institute of Race Relations, who abandoned his earlier account of racism (1973) as "an explicit and systematic ideology of racial superiority" because later (1983) he came to think that "racism is about power not prejudice." Eventually (1985), he saw racism as "structures and institutions with power to discriminate" (1985; quoted at Miles 1989: 54).[4] From the right, the philosopher Antony Flew has suggested that, to identify racism with "negative beliefs" about "actual or alleged matters of fact" is a "sinister and potentially dangerous thing"—it "is to demand, irrespective of any evidence which might be turned up to the contrary, that everyone must renounce certain disapproved propositions."[5] Flew worries that this poses a serious threat to intellectual freedom, and proposes a behavioral understanding of 'racism' as "meaning the advantaging or disadvantaging of individuals for no better reason than that they happen to be members of this racial group rather than that."

I agree with these critics that in contemporary moral and political discourse and thought, what we have in mind when we talk of racism is no longer simply a matter of beliefs.[6] However, I think their proposed reconceptions are themselves inadequate. In this paper, I present an account of racism that, I think, better reflects contemporary usage of the term, especially its primary employment as both descriptive and evaluative, and I sketch some of this view's implications for the morality of race-sensitive discrimination in private and public life. I will also briefly point out some of

[4] For a negative appraisal of Sivanandan's thought, see David Dale, "Racial Mischief: The Case of Dr. Sivanandan," in Palmer (1986: 82–94).

[5] Discussing an account of racism offered by Britain's Commission for Racial Equality, Flew writes: "[a] sinister and potentially dangerous thing here is the reference to actual or alleged matters of fact—to 'negative beliefs'. . . . For this is to demand, irrespective of any evidence which might be turned up to the contrary, that everyone must renounce certain disapproved propositions about average or universal differences and similarities as between races and racial groups: difference and similarities, that is, either in respect of biology or in respect of culture. To concede such a demand to the often Marxist militants of race relations is to open the door to purges: not only of libraries and of textbooks and of curricula; but also of people. It is not ten years since many a campus in the U.S.A. was ringing with calls to 'Sack' and even to 'Kill Jensen'—Jensen being a psychologist who dared to publish evidence suggesting that there may be genetically determined average differences between different races and racial groups in respect of other than their racial defining characteristics" (Flew 1986: 22). I critically examine Flew's view of racism at the end of this essay.

[6] Banton suggests that we should restrict our usage of the term, withholding its application from many people we nowadays call racists. In his view, these people are not racists because they use arguments of cultural superiority in preference to the doctrines of biologically based superiority the term was coined to pick out (Banton 1970). This proposal is unrealistic, and serves to illustrate what makes unacceptable the excessively conservative approach to word meaning of those who still insist that racism consists solely in certain beliefs, ideology, doctrines, and theories.

this account's advantages over various other ways of thinking about racism that we have already mentioned—racism as a doctrine, as a socioeconomic system of oppression, or as a form of action. One notable feature of my argument is that it begins to bring to bear on this topic in social philosophy points made in recent criticisms of modernist moral theory offered by those who call for increased emphasis on the virtues. (This voice has hitherto largely been silent in controversies within practical social philosophy.)

I. A VOLITIONAL CONCEPTION OF RACISM

Kwame Anthony Appiah rightly complains that, although people frequently voice their abhorrence of racism, "rarely does anyone stop to say what it is, or what is wrong with it" (Appiah 1990: 3). This way of stating the program of inquiry we need is promising, because, although racism is not essentially "a moral doctrine," *pace* Appiah, it is always a moral evil[7] (Appiah 1990: 13). No account of what racism is can be adequate unless it at the same time makes clear what is wrong with it. How should we conceive racism, then, if we follow Appiah's advice "to take our ordinary ways of thinking about race and racism and point up some of their presuppositions" (Appiah 1990: 4)? My proposal is that we conceive of racism as fundamentally a vicious kind of racially based disregard for the welfare of certain people. In its central and most vicious form, it is a hatred, ill-will, directed against a person or persons on account of their assigned race. In a derivative form, one is a racist when one either does not care at all or does not care enough (i.e., as much as morality requires) or does not care in the right ways about people assigned to a certain racial group, where this disregard is based on racial classification. Racism, then, is something that essentially involves not our beliefs and their rationality or irrationality, but our wants, intentions, likes, and dislikes and their distance from the moral virtues.[8] Such a view helps explain racism's conceptual ties to various forms of *hatred* and contempt. (Note that 'contempt' derives from 'to contemn'—not to care (about someone's needs and rights.)

---

[7] That is not to say that its definition must include a moral evaluation. The act-utilitarian must hold that nonoptimific behavior is always wrong simply in virtue of what it is and what morality is, but she need not think the term 'nonoptimific' includes a moral evaluation in its definition. Similarly, a divine command theorist may judge every act against God's will to be immoral *eo ipso*, without thinking this wrongness analytically derivable from the meaning of 'against God's will'.

[8] According to Miles, the term 'racism' originally denoted certain pseudo-scientific doctrines. I think the term changed its meaning, and speculate that this change occurred as race became important less for the discredited beliefs than for attitudes and resultant social practices. (See Miles 1989; chs. 2, 3.) On the linguistic history, also see the *Oxford English Dictionary*, 2nd edn.

It might be objected that there can be no such thing as racism because, as many now affirm, "there are no races." This objection fails. First, that 'race' is partially a social construction does not entail that there are no races. One might even maintain, though I would not, that race-terms, like 'person', 'preference', 'choice', 'welfare', etc., and, more controversially, such terms as 'reason for action', 'immoral', 'morally obligatory', etc. may be terms that, while neither included within nor translatable into, the language of physics, nevertheless arise in such a way and at such a fundamental level of social or anthropological discourse that they should be counted as real, at least, for purposes of political and ethical theory.[9] Second, as many racial anti-realists concede, even if it were true that race is unreal, what we call racism could still be real (Appiah 1992: 45). What my account of racism requires is not that there be races, but that people make distinctions in their hearts, whether consciously or not on the basis of their (or others') racial classifications. That implies nothing about the truth of those classification." [10]

Lawrence Blum raises a puzzling question about this. We can properly classify a person S as a racist even if *we* do not believe in races. But what if S herself does not believe in them? Suppose S is a White person who hates Black people, but picks them out by African origin, attachment to African cultures, residence or rearing in certain U. S. neighborhoods, and so on. Should we call S racist if she does not hate Black people *as* such (i.e., on the basis of her assigning them to a Black race), but hates all people she thinks have been corrupted by their internalizing undesirable cultural elements from Harlem or Watts, or from Nairobi, or the Bunyoro? I think the case

[9] Compare David Wiggins and John McDowell on Kantian moral realism. (See Wiggins, "Truth, Invention, and the Meaning of Life," in Wiggins 1987; and McDowell 1986.) Although in conversation with me he has denied any such dependence, there is reason to worry that Appiah's position may covertly rely on a form of scientism, the supposition that no serious use of a once-pseudo-scientific term is permissible if it plays no role within legitimate science. In any case, he seems to allow that neither the fact that the concept of 'race' is inexact in its criteria and extension, nor the fact that it was the subject of a discredited science, nor the fact that it was used to justify unjust social practices, is by itself sufficient to show that the notion must be banished from speech. (Perhaps he thinks they are jointly sufficient, but that remains to be shown.) Moreover, he is willing to talk informally of this person being Black and that one White, so he and I are not so far apart. I do not see why this informal, but acceptable, way of speaking cannot be extended to allow us to call such talk acceptable (albeit informal) racial classification. Of course, informal talk of races cannot be accepted if racial terms must really be scientific. That, however, returns us to our question why anyone should think that.

Appiah's criticism of talk of races on the grounds that there are no "racial essences" suggests that he may presuppose a metaphysical essentialism that does not count against using racial terms on the looser bases of Wittgensteinian "family resemblances": perhaps a combination of surface and ancestral features, ordered in no one way, underlies the legitimate application of race terms to many but not all persons.

[10] Miles objects to some early accounts of the nature of racism on the grounds that they "tended to remain inextricably entangled with, and consequently to legitimate, the idea of 'race'" (Miles 1989: 48).

underdescribed. Surely, a person can disapprove of a culture or a family of cultures without being racist. However, cultural criticism can be a mask for a deeper (even unconscious) dislike that is defined by racial classification. If the person transfers her disapproval of the group's culture to contempt or disregard for those designated as the group's members, then she is already doing something morally vicious. When she assigns all the groups disliked to the same racial classification, then we are entitled to suspect racism, because we have good grounds to suspect that her disavowals of underlying racial classifications are false. If S hates the cultures of various Black groups for having a certain feature, but does not extend that disapproval to other cultures with similar features, then that strongly indicates racism.

Even if she is more consistent, there may still be racism, but of a different sort. Adrian Piper suggests that, in the phenomenon she calls 'higher order discrimination,' a person may claim to dislike members of a group because she thinks they have a certain feature, but really disapprove of the feature because she associates it with the despised group. This 'higher order discrimination' would, of course, still count as racist in my account, because the subject's distaste for the cultural element derives from and is morally infected by race-based disregard.

We should also consider an additional possibility. A person may falsely attribute an undesirable feature to people she assigns to a racial group because of her disregard for those in the group. This will often take the forms of exaggeration, seeing another in the worst light, and withholding from someone the benefit of the doubt. So, an anti-Semite may interpret a Jew's reasonable frugality as greed; a White racist may see indolence in a Black person's legitimate resistance to unfair expectations of her, and so on.

Thinking of racism as thus rooted in the heart fits common sense and ordinary usage in a number of ways. It is instructive that contemptuous White racists have sometimes called certain of their enemies 'Nigger-lovers.' When we seek to uncover the implied contrast-term for this epithet, it surely suggests that enemies of those who "love" Black people, as manifested in their efforts to combat segregation, and so forth, are those who hate Black people or who have little or no human feelings toward us at all. This is surely born out by the behavior and rhetoric of paradigmatic White racists.

This account makes racism similar to other familiar forms of intergroup animosity. Activists in favor of Israel and of what they perceive as Jewish interests sometimes call anti-Semites 'Jew-haters.' Wistrich, for example, says that "'anti-Semitism,' which never really meant hatred of [all] Semites, but rather hatred of Jews, has come to be accepted in general usage as denoting all forms of hostility toward Jews and Judaism throughout history" (Wistrich 1992, p. xv). He opposes this expansion of meaning,

J. L. A. GARCIA

especially extending the term to cover opposition to the religion of Judaism. According to him, those who coined the term for their own doctrines were "not opposed to Jews on religious grounds, but claimed to be motivated by social, economic, political, or 'racial' considerations."[11] What is important for us is to note that *hostility* toward Jews is the heart of anti-Semitism.

It is also worth noting that, immediately prior to the coining of the term 'racism', even some of the early anti-Nazi polemicists referred to their subject as 'race hatred'.[12] This suggests such thinkers may have realized that the true problem was not so much the doctrines of the scientists of race-biology and race-anthropology, but the antipathy these doctrines rationalized and encouraged.

Racism also seems, intuitively, to be structurally similar to xenophobia and the anti-homosexual malice sometimes called 'homophobia'. However, xenophobia is commonly understood not primarily as consisting in holding certain irrational beliefs about foreigners, but in *hatred* or disregard of them. This suggests that racism should, as I here claim, be considered a form of disaffection.[13] The gay activists Kirk and Madsen urge that we reclassify some so-called 'homophobes' as 'homohaters'. They cite studies indicating that many people who detest homosexuals betray none of the telltale physiological signs of phobia, and remind us that what is at stake is primarily a hostility toward homosexual persons on account of their homosexuality.[14] Again, by analogy, racism should be deemed a form of disregard.

---

[11] After an Arab dismissed a charge of anti-Semitism by the late Meir Kahane, on the grounds that Arabs are themselves a Semitic people, I once heard Kahane sensibly (if not necessarily accurately) respond by amending his charge to that of 'Jew-hater'. Of course, Kahane himself was often described, with some justification, as an Arab-hater. The connection between racism and anti-Semitism may be more than analogical. It is sometimes said that anti-Semitism is itself a type of racism. Thus, Miles writes of "that form of racism which others label anti-Semitism" (Miles 1989: 68).

It is worth remarking that, whereas Wistrich thinks anti-Semitism "the longest hatred," Castoriadis claims that the Hebrew Bible is, because of its exaltation of the Jews, the oldest extant racist document (Castoriadis 1992: 3). I think that Castoriadis' view serves as a *reductio* of understanding racism as a matter of beliefs. Whether or not one thinks God selected the Jews for a special role in human salvation, this election hardly constitutes the sort of contemptuous or aversive dismissal of others that properly counts as racist.

[12] "Critics of scientific theories of race prior to this decade [the 1930s] did not use a concept of racism to identify their ideological object. For example, in a wide-ranging critique published in the late 1920s, Friedrich Hertz referred to 'race hatred'" (Miles 1989: 42).

[13] As I said at the outset, the term 'xenophobia' also suggests that this aversion to others is accompanied or caused by fear of them, but I do not think this association carries over to 'racism'.

[14] They write, "'Homophobia' is a comforting word, isn't it? It suggests that . . . all who oppose, threaten, and persecute us [that is, homosexuals] are actually scared of us! [However, f]ear need have nothing to do with it. A well-designed study . . . demonstrate[ed] that although some 'homonegative' males respond to homosexual stimuli with the 'tell-tale racing heart' of phobia, plenty of others don't." Kirk and Madsen condemn "the specious 'diagnosis'" of homophobia as a "medically exculpatory euphemism," and offer a proposal: "Let's reserve the term 'homophobia' for the psychiatric cases to which it really applies, and find a more honest label for the attitudes,

On my account, racism retains its strong ties to intolerance. This tie is uncontroversial. Marable, for example, writes of "racism, and other types of intolerance, such as anti-Semitism ... [and] homophobia ... " (Marable 1992: 3, 10). Intolerant behavior is to be expected if racism is hatred.[15] How, after all, can one tolerate those whom one wants to injure, and why ought one to trouble oneself to tolerate those whom one disregards?

Such an account of racism as I propose can both retain and explain the link between the two "senses of" racism found in some dictionaries: (i) belief in superiority of R1s to R2s, and (ii) inter-racial 'antagonism'.[16] I suggest that we think of these as two elements within most common forms of racism. In real racists, I think, (ii) is normally a ground of (i) (though sometimes the reverse is true), and (i) is usually a rationalization of (ii). What is more important is that (i) may not be logically *necessary* for racism. (In some people, it may nonetheless be a psychological necessity.) However, even when (ii) is a result of (i), it is (ii) and not (i), that makes a person a racist. (Logically, not causally.)

My view helps explain why racism is always immoral. As Stephen Nathanson says, "Racism, as we ordinarily speak of it, ... implies ... a special

---

words, and acts of hatred that are, after all, the real problem." As for their own linguistic procedure, "when we really do mean 'fear of homosexuals,' [then] 'homophobia' it will be; when we're talking about hatred of homosexuals, we'll speak (without the hyphen) of 'homohatred,' 'homo-hating,' and 'homohaters.' We urge the reader to follow suit." (See Kirk and Madsen 1989, pp. xxii–iii.) This is sensible advice, though some caveats are in order. First, we should bear in mind that not every fear is a phobia. Second, even the quasi-scientific term "homonegative" tends to lump together such very different matters as (i) a person's personal aversion to her own engaging in homosexual activities, (ii) her concern over perceived social effects of other peoples' homosexual conduct, and (iii) her holding the belief that such conduct is morally impermissible. Hatred of homosexual persons is immoral (although, as Kirk and Madsen point out, to see it simply as a medical condition tends to exculpate). Moral disapproval of homosexual practices, whether on medical, moral, or religious grounds, is a different matter, however, and it may often be an unrelated one. Third, to use the prefix 'homo' to mean 'homosexual' is objectionable for obvious reasons, so it seems preferable to speak of 'homosexual-haters' and 'homosexual-hatred,' retaining the hyphen. This would also make it clear, as the term 'homophobia' does not, that what is to be condemned is an attitude of ill-will or contempt toward certain people, and not a moral judgment on certain practices.

[15] The Freudian theorist Elizabeth Young-Bruehl, in an unpublished paper, argues that anti-Semitism differs from racism in that anti-Semitism, which she thinks rooted in a combination of assumed male Gentile sexual superiority and economic and intellectual inferiority, aims to exterminate its targets, while racism, which she thinks rooted in assumed White male sexual inferiority, seeks to keep its victims around for humiliation (Young-Bruehl 1992). I suspect all this wrong-headed. For our purposes, what is important is that no such causality is essential to racism or anti-Semitism, because we should label haters of Jews or Black people anti-Semite and racists even if we knew their haterd had different causes.

[16] I shall use such terms as 'R1' and 'R2' to refer to racial groups, and such expressions as 'R1s' and 'R2s' to refer to people assigned to such groups. This usage holds potential for some confusion, since the plural term 'R1s' is not the plural of the singular term 'R1', but I think the context will always disambiguate each instance of this usage.

disregard for other groups. Hence, there is a sense in which racism is necessarily immoral" (Nathanson 1992: p. 9).[17] Its immorality stems from its being opposed to the virtues of benevolence and justice. Racism is a form of morally insufficient (i.e., vicious) concern or respect for some others. It infects actions in which one (*a*) tries to injure people assigned to a racial group because of their XXXXX, or (*b*) objectionably fails to take care *not* to injure them (where the agent accepts harm to R1s because she disregards the interests and needs of R1s because they are R1s). We can also allow that an action is racist in a derivative and weaker sense when it is less directly connected to racist disregard, for example, when someone (*c*) does something that (regardless of its intended, probable, or actual effects) stems in significant part from a belief or apprehension about other people, that one has (in significant part) because of one's disaffection toward them because of (what one thinks to be their) race. Racism, thus, will often offend against justice, not just against benevolence, because one sort of injury to another is withholding from her the respect she is owed and the deference and trust that properly express that respect. Certain forms of paternalism, while benevolent in some of their goals, may be vicious in the means employed. The paternalist may deliberately choose to deprive another of some goods, such as those of (licit) freedom and (limited) self-determination in order to obtain other goods for her. Here, as elsewhere, the good end need not justify the unjust means. Extreme paternalism constitutes an instrumentally malevolent benevolence: one harms A to help her. I return to this below in my discussion of 'Kiplingesque' racism.

If, as I maintain, racism is essentially a form of racially focused ill-will or disregard (including disrespect), then that explains why "'Racism' is inescapably a morally loaded term. To call a person a racist is to impugn his character by suggesting deliberate, malign discrimination . . . " (Lichtenberg 1992: 5).

My account of racism suggests a new understanding of racist behavior and of its immorality. This view allows for the existence of both individual racism and institutional racism. Moreover, it makes clear the connection between the two, and enables us better to understand racism's nature and limits. Miles challenges those who insist on talking only of 'racism' in the plural to "specify what the many different racisms have in common" (Miles 1989: 65). This may go too far. Some philosophers have offered respected

---

[17] Two caveats. First, since our interest is in the central sense(s) of the term 'racism', I see little reason to add Cottingham's qualifier "there is a sense in which" to our claim that racism must be illicit. Any sense of the term in which racism is not illicit must be decidedly peripheral. Second, Cottingham seems to think of this "disregard" as primarily a matter of negative evaluative beliefs, while I reject any such doxastic account and construe 'disregard' as disaffection or malice.

accounts of common terms that seem not to require that every time A is an F and B is an F, then A and B must have some feature in common (other than that of being-an-F, if that *is* a feature). Nominalism and Wittgenstein's "family resemblance" view are two examples. However, if we are not dealing with two unrelated concepts the English terms for which merely happen to have the same spelling and pronunciation (like the 'bank' of a river and the 'bank' that offers loans), then we should be able to explain how the one notion develops out of the other.

Some think that institutions, etc. are racist when they are structures of racial domination, and that individual beliefs, etc. are racist when they express, support, or justify racial superiority. Both, of course, involve denying or violating the equal dignity and worth of all human beings independent of race. This sort of approach contains some insight. However, it leaves unclear how the two levels or types of racism are related, if they are related at all. Thus, such views leave us rather in the dark about what it is in virtue of which each is a form of racism. Some say that institutional racism is what is of central importance; individual racism, then, matters only inasmuch as it perpetuates institutional racism. I think that claim reverses the order of moral importance, and I shall maintain that the individual level has more explanatory importance.

At the individual level, it is in desires, wishes, intentions, and the like that racism fundamentally lies, not in actions or beliefs. Actions and beliefs are racist in virtue of their *coming from* racism in the desires, wishes, and intentions of individuals, not in virtue of their *leading to* these or other undesirable effects. Racism is, for this reason, an interesting case study in what we might call 'infection' (or 'input-centered' or backward-looking) models of wrongdoing, in contrast to the more familiar consequentialist and other result-driven approaches. Infection models of wrongdoing—according to which an action is wrong because of the moral disvalue of what goes into it rather than the nonmoral value of what comes out of it—seem the best approach within virtues-based ethics. In such ethical systems, actions are immoral insofar as they are greedy, arrogant, uncaring, lustful, contemptuous, or otherwise corrupted in their motivational sources.[18] Finally, desires, wishes, and intentions *are* racist when they either are, or in certain ways reflect, attitudes that withhold from people, on the basis of their being assigned to a particular race, levels or forms of good-will, caring, and well-wishing that moral virtue demands.[19] At its core, then, racism consists in

---

[18] See Slote (1994) and Garcia (1997).

[19] I will not try to identify minimal levels of good will such that having less is against the virtue of benevolence, nor minimal levels of respect such that less offends against justice. I doubt these levels can be identified in abstraction, and it will be difficult or impossible for us to determine them

vicious attitudes toward people based on their assigned race. From there, it extends to corrupt the people, individual actions, institutional behavior, and systemic operations it infects. Some, however, seem not to think of racism in this way, as something that, like cruelty or stupidity, can escalate from its primary occurrence in individual people to infect collective thought and decision-making of organizations and, from there, to contaminate the behavior of institutions as well. So to think of it is to see the term as not merely descriptive and evaluative, but also as having some explanatory force.

How is institutional racism connected to racism within the individual? Let us contrast two pictures. On the first, institutional racism is of prime moral and explanatory importance. Individual racism, then, matters (and, perhaps, occurs) only insofar as it contributes to the institutional racism which subjugates a racial group. On the second, opposed view, racism within individual persons is of prime moral and explanatory import, and institutional racism occurs and matters because racist attitudes (desires, aims, hopes, fears, plans) infect the reasoning, decision-making, and action of individuals not only in their private behavior, but also when they make and execute the policies of those institutions in which they operate. I take the second view. Institutional racism, in the central sense of the term, occurs when institutional behavior stems from (*a*) or (*b*) above or, in an extended sense, when it stems from (*c*). Obvious examples would be the infamous Jim Crow laws that originated in the former Confederacy after Reconstruction. Personal racism exists when and insofar as a person is racist in her desires, plans, aims, etc., most notably when this racism informs her conduct. In the same way, institutional racism exists when and insofar as an institution is racist in the aims, plans, etc., that people give it, especially when their racism informs its behavior. Institutional racism begins when racism extends from the hearts of individual people to become institutionalized. What matters is that racist attitudes contaminate the operation of the institution; it is irrelevant what its original point may have been, what its designers meant it to do. If it does not operate from those motives (at time T1), then it does not embody institutional racism (at T1). On this view, some phenomena sometimes described as institutionally racist will turn out not to be properly so describable, but others not normally considered to be institutionally racist will fit the description. (I return to this below.)

Not only is individual racism of greater explanatory import, I think it also

even in minutely described particular situations. Throughout, I generally restrict my talk of disrespect and other forms of disregard to cases where the levels are morally vicious, offending against the moral virtues of benevolence and justice, respectively.

more important morally. Those of us who see morality primarily as a matter of suitably responding to other people and to the opportunities they present for us to pursue value will understand racism as an offense against the virtues of benevolence and justice in that it is an undue restriction on the respect and goodwill owed people. (Ourselves as well as others; racism, we must remember, can take the form of self-hate.) Indeed, as follows from what I have elsewhere argued, it is hard to render coherent the view that racist hate is bad mainly for its bad effects. The sense in which an action's effects are bad is that they are undesirable. But that it is to say that these effects are evil things to want and thus things the desire for which is evil, vicious. Thus, any claim that racial disadvantage is a bad thing presupposes a more basic claim that race-hatred is vicious. What is more basic morally is also morally more important in at least one sense of that term.[20] Of course, we should bear in mind that morality is not the same as politics. What is morally most important may not be the problem whose rectification is of greatest political urgency.

II. IMPLICATIONS AND ADVANTAGES

There are some noteworthy implications and advantages of the proposed way of conceiving of racism.

First, it suggests that prejudice, in its strict sense of 'pre-judgment', is not essential to racism, and that some racial prejudice may not be racist, strictly speaking. Racism is not, on this view, primarily a cognitive matter, and so it is not in its essence a matter of how or when one makes one's judgments. Of course, we can still properly call prejudiced-based beliefs racist in that they *characteristically* either are rooted in prior racial disregard, which they rationalize, or they foster such disregard.[21] Whether having such a belief is immoral in a given case will depend in large part on whether it is a rationalization for racial disaffection. It may depend on *why* the individual is so quick to think the worst of people assigned to the other racial group. Of course, even when the order is reversed and the prejudice does not whitewash a prior and independent racial disaffection, but causes a subsequent one, the person will still be racist because of that disaffection, even if she is not racist

---

[20] See Garcia (1986, 1987).

[21] In a way similar to my nondoxastic account of racism, John Dewey seems to have offered an account of race-prejudice that is nondoxastic. Recent scholarship reminds us that, for Dewey, prejudice was not primarily a matter of hasty judgment, but of a fear of, and aversion to, what is unfamiliar. Gregory Pappas expounded Dewey's view in his paper "Dewey's Philosophical Interpretation of Racial Prejudice," presented at a session of the 1992 Ford Fellows Conference in Irvine, California.

in holding that belief, that is, even if she does not hold it for what we might call 'racist reasons.' My guess is that, in most people who have been racists for some expanse of time, the belief and the disregard will reinforce each other.

A person may hold prejudices about people assigned to a race without herself being racist and without it being racist of her to hold those prejudices.[22] The beliefs themselves can be called 'racist' in an extended sense because they are characteristically racist. However, just as one may make a wise move without acting wisely (as when one makes a sound investment for stupid reasons), so one may hold a racist belief without holding it for racist reasons. One holds such a belief for racist reasons when it is duly connected to racial disregard: when it is held in order to rationalize that disaffection or when contempt inclines one to attribute undesirable features to people assigned to a racial group. One whose racist beliefs have no such connection to any racial disregard in her heart does not hold them in a racist way and if she has no such disregard, she is not herself a racist, irrespective of her prejudices.

Second, when racism is so conceived, the person with racist feelings, desires, hopes, fears, and dispositions is racist even if she never acts on these attitudes in such a way as to harm people designated as members of the hated race. (This is not true when racism is conceived as consisting in a system of social oppression.) It is important to know that racism can exist in (and even pervade) societies in which there is no systematic oppression, if only because the attempts to oppress fail. Even those who think racism important primarily because of its effects should find this possibility of inactive racism worrisome for, so long as this latent racism persists, there is constant threat of oppressive behavior.

Third, on this view, race-based preference (favoritism) need not be racist. *Preferential* treatment in affirmative action, while race-based, is not normally based on any racial disregard. This is a crucial difference between James Meredith's complaint against the University of Mississippi and Allan Bakke's complaint against the University of California at Davis Medical School (see Appiah 1990: 15). Appiah says that what he calls "Extrinsic racism has usually been the basis [1] for treating people worse than we otherwise might, [2] for giving them less than their humanity entitles them to" (Appiah 1992: 18). What is important to note here is that (1) and (2) are not at all morally equivalent. Giving someone less than her humanity entitles her to is morally wrong. To give someone less than we could give her, and even to give her less than we would if she (or we, or things) were

---

[22] See Appiah (1992).

different is to treat her "worse [in the sense of 'less well'] than we otherwise might." However, the latter is not normally morally objectionable. Of course, we may not deny people even gratuitous favors out of hatred or contempt, whether or not race-based, but that does not entail that we may not licitly choose to bestow favors instead on those to whom we feel more warmly. That I feel closer to A than I do to B does not mean that I feel hatred or callousness toward B. I may give A more than A has a claim to get from me and more than I give B, while nevertheless giving B everything to which she is entitled (and even more). Thus, race-based favoritism does not have to involve (2) and need not violate morality.

Appiah recognizes this fact, saying that 'intrinsic racism,' because of its ties to solidarity, fraternity, and even "family feeling," is often merely "the basis for acts of supererogation, the treatment of others better than we otherwise might, better than moral duty demands of us" (Appiah 1990: 11). However, he warns ominously, "This is a contingent fact. There is no logical impossibility in the idea of racialists whose moral beliefs lead them to feelings of hatred for other races while leaving them no room for love for members of their own" (Appiah 1990: 12). But why should the fact that this remains a logical possibility incline us to condemn racial preference? When the possibility is actualized, and someone feels, not special regard for those who share assignment to her own racial group (along with adequate affection for people assigned to other groups), but hatred for those allocated to other groups (whether or not there is affection for people allocated to her own), then we have illicit antipathy not licit favoritism. When this ugly possibility is not actualized, however, then we need some independent argument against favoritism.[23] Appiah invokes Kant for this purpose (Appiah 1992: 18; 1990: 14, 15). However, the invocation is insufficient. There is no obvious inconsistency in willing that a moderate form of race preference, like other moderate forms of kinship preference, should be a

---

[23] Iris Young offers the interesting suggestion that modernist moral theory's aversion to partiality, like its aversion to appeals to feelings and its insistence on the irrelevance of gender, ethnicity, and other aspects of personal or group experience, history, and situatedness, originates as part of an endeavor to eliminate from the viewpoint of the moral judge those factors that are deemed inessential to her as a rational agent and that serve to differentiate her from others. This effort is perhaps most evident in Kant's famous insistence that an agent's moral requirements be rooted in her (universal) reason, and not be contingent upon her desires (unlike "hypothetical imperatives"), lest the requirements vary across persons and times, as he thought all substantive desires did. Young also thinks the impartialist unfairly presents impartiality as the only alternative to egoism (see Young 1990, ch. 4). If that is right, then the impartialist position rests upon several dubious assumptions, most notably, assumptions about the constituents of the moral agent's identity (or "essence"), about the irreducible variability of desires and feelings, and about the supposed gap between human passions and desires on the one hand and abstract reason on the other. All these assumptions are currently undergoing philosophical reconsideration. (See, especially, Blum 1994.)

universal law of nature, as Kant's own principal test of universalization requires.[24]

Discrimination *on the basis of* race, then, need not be immoral. It is discrimination *against* people because of their racial assignment that cannot but be immoral. Christopher Jencks says "we need formal discrimination in favor of blacks to offset the effects of persistent informal discrimination against them."[25] Suppose Jencks' claim about our need for discrimination is true. Can racial favoritism ever be justified? It will help to remind ourselves that discriminating *in favor of* R1s need not entail discriminating *against* R2s.[26] The latter consists in acting either (i) with intention of harming R2s, or (ii) with hard-hearted racist indifference to the action's foreseeable ill effects on R2s,[27] or (iii) from racist beliefs held because of racist disaffection. Similarly, racial self-segregation need not be immoral. It may be especially suspect when White people do it, because we have good historical reason to be suspicious that what is presented as merely greater-than-morally-required concern for fellow White people really involves less-than-morally-required concern for Black people. It may also be

---

[24] Note that action from maxims that pass Kant's universalizability test is therein permissible, not necessarily obligatory.

[25] Quoted in Hacker (1992*b*: 30).

[26] Arguing against some writers who use the slogan "Preference is not prejudice" to support their view that moderate racial preference is permissible, Miles complains, "[T]o prefer is to rank and to choose to value something or person or group, and therefore necessarily to preclude some other thing, person or group" (Miles 1989: 8). What Miles says is true, but it does nothing to prove the controverted point that excluding person S1 in the course of expressing greater-than-morally-required regard for S2 is the moral equivalent of excluding S1 out of less-than-morally-required concern for S1. That said, I do certainly not wish to associate myself with the further doctrines of the thinkers Miles is criticizing, who use the inflammatory example of preferring to marry within one race as an example of supposedly innocent preference. In a society such as ours, any such "preference" is likely to be informed by and to result in part from an aversion to interracial marriage as 'race-treachery' or 'miscegenation'. Such a preference is not at all innocent, in my view, having roots in deep-seated racial antipathy.

In personal correspondence, Glenn Loury has expressed misgivings about my view, reminding me that "what ends in personal viciousness towards the 'other' finds its beginning in the more benign celebration of the virtues of one's 'own kind'." I wonder whether, in fact, racial antipathy does *always* begin in such a benign attitude. However, even if it does, the danger that it may lead to racial antipathy is a reason to be cautious of racial favoritism. It is not a reason to condemn this partiality as malign nor, more to the point, as racist. Even the framers of a recent California measure proposing to outlaw racial preferences observe a distinction between discriminating against A and according B a preference. "The anti-affirmative action measure is essentially a simple declaration: 'Neither the State of California nor any of its political subdivisions shall use race, sex, color, ethnicity, or national origin as a criterion for either discriminating against or granting preferential treatment to, any individual or group in the operation of the state's system of public employment, public education, or public contracting'" (Schrag 1995: 18). The drafters may, however, make the distinction merely to close a possible linguistic loophole, and not deem it a distinction that marks any genuine and morally significant difference. With that, of course, I disagree.

[27] I say 'foreseeable' effects rather than 'foreseen' because S's racist contempt may be the reason she does not bother to find out, and thus does not foresee some of the bad effects of her behavior.

ill-advised even when it is Black people who do it. However, in neither case must it be immoral.[28] In neither case must it be racist.

According to this conception of racism, *de jure racial segregation* violates political morality primarily because (and, therefore, when) it expresses a majority's (or minority's) racial indifference, contempt, or ill-will. It is therein vicious, offending against the virtues of both benevolence and justice. However, it need not have such origin, a fact illustrated by recent suggestions to establish separate academies to deal with the educational challenges confronting young Black males, and by efforts to control the racial dem-

---

[28] I think this undermines an argument recently offered by Gomberg. He argues against what has been called "moderate patriotism," which "includ[es limited] preference for fellow nationals," on the grounds that any argument in defense of it will also legitimize what he calls "moderate racism," which allows someone to "discriminate against black or Hispanic people or against immigrants" so long as one is careful not to "violate their fundamental rights" (1990: 147). Assuming that such "moderate racism" is unjustifiable, then so too is moderate patriotism or any form of preference. The problem is that it is hard to see why Gomberg's "moderate racism" need be unjustifiable, or even why it is racism. His analogy with patriotism suggests that what Gomberg has in mind is merely a mild form of preference for people of one's own racial group. This will sometimes be suspicious morally, especially when the one discriminating on the basis of race belongs to a group that has enforced and benefited from forms of discrimination that are racist, that is, that are driven by racial disaffection. However, it is unclear that there is anything morally troubling in same-race favoritism by those on the bottom, or by those who live in a situation, unlike ours, where favoritism has been historically divorced from race hatred. Similarly, there seems to be nothing morally troubling in other-race favoritism; at least, there is nothing morally troubling where this favoritism is likely to be divorced from hatred of one's own racial group, as is the case with other-race favoritism by those from historically oppressing groups.

Indeed, while same-race favoritism by people considered members of the oppressing group and other-race favoritism by those allocated to the oppressed group are disturbing morally, I think that, to the extent this discomfort is legitimate, it will be rooted in our suspicion that it is really race-hatred masking as mere favoritism, or in our worry that such a practice, should it become widespread, will have the bad effect of exacerbating the comparatively disadvantaged position of those assigned to the historically oppressed group. The latter worry may be serious, but it is a concern about the general effects of a social (or personal) policy, not a concern that individuals may be treated unjustly. As such, it is much less significant morally.

(Since first writing this, I have seen a similar point made in Stephen Nathanson's response to Gomberg. Nathanson sensibly writes that "a racial preference might not be inherently wrong or evil. American Blacks have been an oppressed group that has needed special attention. Whites are not similarly oppressed as a group. Thus, a person with a special affection and concern for whites might not be equally justified in promoting their interests . . . " Actions done from such favoritism will even "be wrong if they require neglect of the much more pressing need of others" (Nathanson 1992: 10, 11)).

In this connection, it is worth noting that Appiah rejects what he calls "intrinsic speciesism," adherents of which think it would be morally permissible "to kill cattle for beef, even if cattle exercised all the complex cultural skills of human beings" (Appiah 1992: 19). Such a position is to be condemned, of course, but we can condemn it without necessarily rejecting the view ("moderate speciesism"?) that even in the world of Appiah's cosmopolitan cattle, we may, and perhaps even should, show greater concern for members of our own species simply because of their relation to us. The impermissibility of such favoritism does not follow from the recognition that there are moral limits on the ways in which we may treat the various others outside the favored group. I can think morality allows and even demands that I care specially for my family without thereby committing myself to thinking that we may slaughter, butcher, and eat the folks next door.

ography of public housing projects in order to avoid problems that have sometimes arisen when such projects became virtually all-Black or virtually all-White. Whatever the social merit of such proposals, in cases like these, even if the segregation in the end proves immoral, this is not intrinsic. There must be some special additional factor present that makes it immoral. De facto racial segregation (mere separation or disproportional representation) need not be morally problematic at all when it happens to result from decently and responsibly motivated individual or social actions.[29] However, it will be immoral if its bad effects on, say, R1s are accepted out of racist hard-heartedness, that is, out of racist indifference to the harm done R1s. This will sometimes, but not always, be the case when harms are disproportionally distributed across the various racial groupings to which people are assigned.

Fourth, on this view of racism, racist discrimination need not always be conscious. The real reason why person P1 does not rent person P2 a room may be that P1 views P2 as a member of a racial group R2, to whose members P1 has an aversion. That may be what it is about P2 that turns P1 off, even if P1 convinces herself it was for some other reason that she did not rent. As racist discrimination need not always be conscious, so it need not always be intended to harm. Some of what is called 'environmental racism,' especially the location of waste dumps so as disproportionally to burden Black people, is normally not intended to harm anyone at all. Nevertheless, it is racist if, for example, the dumpers regard it as less important if it is 'only,' say, Black people who suffer. However, it will usually be the case that intentional discrimination based on racist attitudes will be more objectionable morally, and harder to justify, than is unintentional, unconscious racist discrimination. Ra*cial* discrimination is not always ra*cist* discrimination. The latter is always immoral, because racism is inherently vicious and it corrupts any differentiation that it infects. The former—racial discrimination—is not inherently immoral. Its moral status will depend on the usual factors—intent, knowledge, motive, and so on—to which we turn to determine what is vicious.

This understanding of racism also offers a new perspective on the controversy over efforts to restrict racist "hate speech." Unlike racially *offensive* speech, which is defined by its (actual or probable) effects, racist *hate* speech is defined by its origins, i.e., by whether it expresses (and is thus an act of) racially directed hate. So we cannot classify a remark as racist hate speech simply on the basis of *what* was said, we need to look to *why* the speaker said it. Speech laden with racial slurs and epithets is presumptively hateful, of

---

[29] See Carter (1991).

course, but merely voicing an opinion that members of R1 are inferior (in some germane way) will count as racist (in any of the term's chief senses, at least) only if, for example, it expresses an opinion held from the operation of some predisposition to believe bad things about R1s, which predisposition itself stems in part from racial disregard.[30] This understanding of racist hate speech should allay the fears of those who think that racial oversensitivity and the fear of offending the oversensitive will stifle the discussion of delicate and important matters beneath a blanket of what is called 'political correctness.' Racist hate speech is defined by its motive forces and, given a fair presumption of innocence, it will be difficult to give convincing evidence of ugly motive behind controversial opinions whose statement is free of racial insults.

III. SOME DIFFICULTIES

It may seem that my view fails to meet the test of accommodating clear cases of racism from history. Consider some members of the southern White aristocracy in the antebellum or Jim Crow periods of American history— people who would never permit racial epithets to escape their lips, and who were solicitous and even protective of those they considered 'their Negroes' (especially Black servants and their kin), but who not only acquiesced in, but actively and strongly supported the social system of racial separatism, hierarchy, and oppression. These people strongly opposed Black equality in the social, economic, and political realms, but they appear to have been free of any vehement racial hatred. It appears that we should call such people racists. The question is: Does the account offered here allow them to be so classified?[31]

This presents a nice difficulty, I think, and one it will be illuminating to grapple with. There is, plainly, a kind of hatred that consists in opposition to a person's (or group's) welfare. Hatred is the opposite of love and, as to love someone is to wish her well (i.e., to want and will that she enjoy life and its benefits), so one kind of hatred for her is to wish her ill (i.e., to want and will that she not enjoy them). It is important to remember, however, that not all hatred is wishing another ill for its own sake. When I take revenge, for

---

[30] For a helpful discussion of the controversy surrounding efforts to identify and regulate hate speech, and of the different grounds offered for these restrictions, see Simon (1991).

[31] Lichtenberg reminds us that such figures are often seen as paradigms of racism, though, unfortunately, she ties this to her claim that Black people and White people tend to have fundamentally different understandings of the nature of racism. "The white picture of the racist is the old-time southern white supremacist" (1992: 3). Sure it is not merely what is sometimes disparaged as "thinking White" to see such people as plausible instances of racism.

example, I act from hate, but I also want to do my enemy ill for a purpose (to get even). So too when I act from envy. (I want to deprive the other of goods in order to keep her from being better off than I, or from being better off than I wish her to be.) I have sometimes talked here about racial "antipathy" ("animosity," "aversion," "hostility," etc.), but I do not mean that the attitude in question has to be especially negative or passionate. Nor need it be notably ill-mannered or crude in its expression. What is essential is that it consists in either opposition to the well-being of people classified as members of the targeted racial group or in a racially based callousness to the needs and interests of such people.

This, I think, gives us what we need in order to see part of what makes our patricians racists, for all their well-bred dispassion and good manners. They stand against the advancement of Black people (as a group, even if they make an exception for 'their Negroes'). They are averse to it as such, not merely doing things that have the *side* effect of setting back the interests of Black people.[32] Rather, they *mean* to retard those interests, to keep Black people "in their place" relative to White people. They may adopt this stance of active, conscious, and deliberate hostility to Black welfare either simply to benefit themselves at the expense of Black people or out of the contemptuous belief that, because they are Black, they merit no better. In any event, these aristocrats and their behavior can properly be classified as racist.

Recall, too, that even if the central case of racism is racial hatred (malevolence), the racial disaffection that constitutes racism also extends to racial callousness, heartlessness, coldness, or uncaring. (We might group these as the vice of nonbenevolence). These too are racism, for it is surely vicious morally to be so disposed toward people classified as belonging to a certain racial group that one does not care whether they prosper or suffer, and is thus indifferent to the way in which the side effects of one's action disadvantage them. Indeed, I think that, as described, our genteel, oppressive members of the gentry go beyond this to manifest a kind of practical hostility: they consciously and actively act to suppress Black people. However, even those who do not go that far are still racist. (Dr. King famously reminded us that to the extent that the good are silent in the face of evil, they are not (being) good). Morally, much will depend on what these agents mean to do. Do they seek to deprive Black people of various positions and opportunities

---

[32] Contrast a religious school that (like the Westminster Academy, in the newspapers a few years back) refuses to hire non-Christians. This policy deprives those who would otherwise have been hired of prestige and salary. However, this deprivation is incidental to the policy's purpose, benign or benighted as it may be, of securing a certain sort of instruction by hiring only instructors with certain relevant convictions.

precisely because they wish Black people not to have these things because the things are good? If so, this is a still deeper type of race malice.

It may not be clear how the understanding of racism offered here accommodates the common-sense view that the attitudes, rhetoric, behavior, and representatives of the mindset we might characterize as the 'white man's burden'-view count as racist.[33] One who holds such a Kiplingesque view (let's call her K) thinks non-Whites ignorant, backward, undisciplined, and generally in need of a tough dose of European 'civilizing' in important aspects of their lives. This training in civilization may sometimes be harsh, but it is supposed to be for the good of the 'primitive' people. Moreover, it is important, for our purposes, to remember that K may think that, for all their ignorance, lack of discipline, and other intellectual and moral failings, individuals within the purportedly primitive people may in certain respects, and even on the whole, be moral superiors to certain of their European 'civilizers.' Thus, Kipling's notorious coda to "Gunga Din."[34]

The matter is a complex one, of course, but I think that, at least in extreme instances, such an approach can be seen to fit the model of racism whose adoption I have urged. What is needed is to attend to and apply our earlier remarks about breaches of respect and the vice of injustice. An important part of respect is recognizing the other as a human like oneself, including treating her like one. There can be extremes of condescension so inordinate they constitute degradation. In such cases, a subject goes beyond more familiar forms of paternalism to demean the other, treating her as utterly irresponsible. Plainly, those who take it upon themselves to conscript mature, responsible, healthy, socialized (and innocent) adults into a regimen of education designed to strip them of all authority over their own lives and make them into 'civilized' folk condescend in just this way.[35] This abusive paternalism borders on contempt and it can violate the rights of the subjugated people by denying them the respect and deference to which their status

[33] Philip Kitcher directed my attention to this topic.

[34] "Though I've belted you and flayed you, By the livin' Gawd that made you, You're a better man than I am, Gunga Din." Rudyard Kipling, "Gunga Din," in *Kipling: A Selection of his Stories and Poems* (Garden City: Doubleday, n.d.).

[35] It is in the form of Kiplingesque, "white man's burden"-racism that racism most nearly approaches the structure of sexism. Sexism is, of course, a form of social bias to which many assume racism is structurally similar, and those who introduced the notion of sexism as a concept of social explanation explicitly modeled it on (their understanding of) racism. In general, however, I think the similarity is not great. Sexism appears *normally* to be a form of condescension, wherein males deprive women of authority and power in order to protect them from the consequences of their supposed immaturity and weakness. This sort of disrespect can violate the virtue of justice in just the ways I have been describing. However, noticing that racism in certain peripheral forms can resemble what sexism seems to be in its most central forms helps reveal a significant dissimilarity between these two social vices. (For a sophisticated comparative account of racism and sexism, see Thomas 1980.)

entitles them. By willfully depriving the oppressed people of the goods of freedom, even as part of an ultimately well-meant project of 'improving' them, the colonizers act with the kind of instrumentally malevolent benevolence we discussed above. The colonizers stunt and maim in order to help, and therein plainly will certain evils to the victims they think of as beneficiaries. Thus, their conduct counts as a kind of malevolence insofar as we take the term literally to mean willing evils.[36]

Of course, the Kiplingesque agent will not think of herself as depriving responsible, socialized people of their rights over their lives; she does not see them that way and thinks them too immature to have such rights. However, we need to ask why she regards Third World peoples as she does. Here, I suspect, the answer is likely to be that her view of them is influenced, quite possibly without her being conscious of it, by her interest in maintaining the social and economic advantages of having her group wield control over its subjects. If so, her beliefs are relevantly motivated and affected by (instrumental) ill-will, her desire to gain by harming others. When this is so, then her beliefs are racist not just in the weak sense that their content is the sort that characteristically is tied to racial disaffection, but in the stronger and morally more important sense that her own acceptance of these beliefs is partially motivated by racial disaffection. She is *being* racist in thinking as she does. I conclude that the account of racism offered here can allow that, and help explain why, many people who hold the 'white man's burden'-mentality are racist, indeed, why they may be racist in several different (but connected) ways.

Having said all this about some who are what I have called Kiplingesque racists and about some 'well-meaning' southern aristocrats, I must admit that my account suggests that some people in these situations, some involved in racially oppressive social systems, will not themselves be racist in their attitudes, in their behaviour, or even in their beliefs (at least, in the stronger sense of being racist in holding her beliefs). I do not shrink from this result, and think it should temper our reliance on the concept of collective responsibility. There are real cases where people share in both wrongdoing and blameworthiness, but collective responsibility for racism is philosophically problematic (in ways I cannot here pursue) and, I think, it is neither so common nor so important morally as some maintain (see May 1992).

---

[36] See Garcia (1987).

IV. SOME CASES

John Cottingham asks us to imagine that "walking down the street, I come across two beggars, both equally in need of assistance, and I have only a single banknote, so that I cannot assist both." If, moreover, "one of the mendicants is white and the other black, may not a black passer-by legitimately choose to give his banknote to the latter for no other reason than 'he's one of my race'?" (Cottingham 1986: 359, 362). He also asks us to imagine ourselves in a position heroically to rescue only one of two people trapped in a burning building. If they are of different races, may I legitimately direct my supererogatory efforts to saving the one who is of my own race?[37]

The view of racism suggested here can help us see how to think about such cases. It indicates, at least, that its being done from nonmalicious racial partiality need not tend to render an action wrong. For a Black person, or a White one, to give to the Black mendicant out of racial preference seems to me unobjectionable, so long as the gift is not likely to mean the difference between life and death. Giving preferentially to the White mendicant is more suspicious, but there is no more vicious ('wrong-making,' as some say) tendency *inherent* in this preference than there is in the other. (I see little or none in the other.) However, if 'Because he's Black [like me or like the ones I prefer]' states a morally acceptable answer to the question why someone gave to the Black beggar when she acts from the pro-Black preference, then do we not have to say that 'Because he's Black' (or 'Because he isn't White [as I am and as are the ones I prefer]') is a legitimate answer to the question why one did not give to the Black beggar when she acts from a different preference? And mustn't we avoid being committed to this, and admit that the latter answer is clearly racist and illegitimate? Well, no; we do not have to admit that. To explain a failure to help someone by saying 'Because he's Black' sounds ugly because, given the history of anti-Black attitudes and behavior in this society, it sounds as if the agent were acting in order to deprive Black people of certain goods. This is likely racist. In our case, however, this answer is merely a misleading way of saying that this person lost out, not on his rights, but on special favors, and not because of ill-will toward Black people but because of extra good will toward some other group. Once the explanation 'Because he's Black' is itself explained, I think, some of our initial suspicion of racism evaporates. (Of course, we might still deem the conduct undesirable and insensitive.)

What of the rescues from the burning building? Even here, I suspect,

---

[37] I follow him in assuming that the prospective agent stands in no special personal relationship to either of the trapped people (e.g., son) and occupies no role that specially calls for impartiality (e.g., paid village fire-fighter).

appeals to race are not as such immoral. They may, however, be inappropriate to the gravity of what is at stake. Surely, it would be objectionable to make the two trapped people play a game, or pick a number, to decide who gets saved. For similar reasons, it would be improper to subject them to a questionnaire and then save the one whose answers were "correct" in matching one's own trivial preferences. No one should lose her life even in part because her favorite color, or football team, or musical performer is different from mine. That is not because there is anything wrong with my having such preferences or, normally, with acting from them. It is because it mocks the seriousness of what is at stake and demeans the persons involved to bring such frivolous matters into these deliberations. By the same token, it may be that strictly racial preference, though innocent in itself, remains too trifling a basis for choice to be made the crux in so weighty a matter. Exactly what seems objectionable about these procedures is hard to specify, but surely it centers on the contrast between the comparative insignificance of the decisive factor (race) and the gravity of what is to be decided (life and death). It makes it more difficult to attend to the importance and solemnity of the end when we must deal with means we have properly trained ourselves to take none too seriously.[38] Race, of course, is a more serious matter in our society than are sports or color preferences, primarily because of its historical over-emphasis in programs of oppression and their rationalization. In itself, and more properly, it forms no deep part of one's identity, I think; but, like rooting for the sports teams of one's neighborhood or hometown or school, it may be associated psychologically with interpersonal connections of a more serious nature.

Nonetheless, while perhaps racial classification as such cannot bear the moral weight of life and death choices, the notions of race and of shared race may be masking work done by more serious features and affinities: e.g., heightened compassion for those with a history of shared or comparable suffering, a sense of kinship, shared community (not of race but) of social/political connection, and so on. In any case, within a properly virtues-based ethical theory, the important question is not (i) what has B done that legitimizes A's abandoning her? but (ii) in what way is A vicious toward B (cruel? unjust? callous?) if A prefers to help C even when that precludes her also helping B? It is not at all clear that or how attending to affinities connected with the admittedly crude notion of race must always suffice to render A's choice vicious.

---

[38] I think this problem also besets various schemes of randomization, such as flipping a coin and throwing dice, though this drawback is seldom noticed by philosophers so blinded by their attachment to the goal of impartiality that they cannot see the grotesquerie of the means sometimes suggested for achieving it. (Hursthouse makes a similar point in Hursthouse 1990.)

Consider the related problem of disfavoritism.[39] Suppose Persons D and E both have more regard for people assigned to every race than morality requires of them. D plays favorites, however, loving (people she considers to be) members of R1 more than she loves those of any other racial group. E plays disfavorites (as we might say), specially reserving (people she considers to be) members of R1 for *less* concern than she has for others. Is what E does/feels racism? Is it morally permissible?

It seems to me that what E does is not racism, because her so-called "disfavoritism" is only a special case of favoritism. She picks out all (people she considers to be) *non*members of R1 for preferential good treatment. (I.e., better than that she accords R1s.) This is likely to be more dangerous socially than are standard cases of favoritism, because it threatens more easily to degenerate into insufficient regard for R1s (or even into antipathy toward them). It is thus a dangerous business, but it lacks the moral ugliness of true racism.

Perhaps it would be a better world without any such racial favoritism. The more important human interconnections, after all, are those founded on joint projects, shared understandings, and common commitments. In short, they are ones that help more fully to humanize us, that bind us one to another in binding us to what is greater than ourselves. All that is a separate matter, however, and one that has no direct bearing on our question of whether acting from such favoritism is permissible.[40]

What should we say of some different cases, discussed by Andrew Hacker and Gertrude Ezorsky, among others, in which a person who herself harbors no racial disregard or disrespect, nonetheless accedes to others' racism by refusing to hire, promote, or serve those assigned to a targeted racial group? Here the agent's action is infected, poisoned by racial hatred. It has such hate in its motivational structure, and that is the usual hallmark of racist behavior. I think what crucially distinguishes this agent's behavior is that it is not *the agent's own* hatred. I suggest that in addition to the two forms of racist disaffection we have already identified—the core concept of racial malevolence and the derivative concept of a race-based insufficiency of good-will—we can allow that an action may be called racist in an extended sense of the term when it is poisoned by racism, even where the racial disaffection that corrupts it does not lie in the agent's own heart but in those to whom the agent accedes. Thus, the agent in our example, while not herself racist, performs an action that is in an important way infected by other people's racism. I doubt we should simply say without qualification that her

[39] Robert Audi raised this problem with me in conversation.
[40] A world without partiality to family members, in contrast, would surely be a worse one, less rich in virtues and in other goods.

280   J. L. A. GARCIA

own action is racist, but it is surely morally objectionable.[41] Her action
reflects the racial disaffection that constitutes racism, although it may not
express or manifest any racist motivation in the agent. (It may, as I note
below, but also it may not.) Actions of this sort are morally objectionable,
but the moral objection to them will not normally be so severe as is that to
actions in which the agent's own racial antipathy motivates her to try to
harm members of the targeted group. They may reflect an insufficiency of
good-will, but they may also fall short of actual malevolence.[42] We should,
however, note different and more vicious cases. Consider a person who
denies service, or promotion, or admission, or employment to people
assigned to group G1 in order to appease people with a racial disaffection
directed against them. Now suppose further that she herself cooperates in
the latter's malevolence by *trying* to harm those classified as G1s in order to
placate their enemies. (This would be a form of what moral theologians have
called "formal cooperation.") When the agent goes that far, she has internalized racist malice into her own intentions, and thus corrupted her actions in
a more grievous way than has the person who merely goes along with neigh-
boring racists in her external actions. This is so whether or not her *feelings*
toward people assigned to G1 are hostile.

What should we say of a case Judith Lichtenberg raises, in which, acting
from racial fear, a White person crosses the street to avoid Black pedestrians
she perceives as possible dangers?[43] Lichtenberg thinks it acceptable for the
fearful (and prejudiced?) White person to cross the street in order to avoid
proximity with the Black teenagers who approach her at night (Lichtenberg
1992: 4). She sensibly suggests that this is not racist if the person would
respond in the same way with White teenagers. "She might well do the same
if the teenagers were white. In that case her behavior does not constitute
racial discrimination." (Of course, her behavior now raises a question of age

[41] I am inclined to think we should say a racist act in the strict sense is one that is done from
racist attitudes (in the agent, whether settled dispositions or a passing episode of nasty whimsy),
rather than merely being one done in acquiescence to others' racist attitudes. A's act is not
cowardly merely because it is one in which A accedes to B's cowardice. (Consider the remark:
"OK, we'll take the longer way to school if it will calm you down, but I still say there's no real
danger we would be attacked by dogs if we took the shortcut." Here the speaker accedes to the
listener's cowardice, but does not therein act from her own cowardice.) Likewise with racism.
[42] This action of hers reflects an insufficiency of good-will, whether or not she does something
or feels something else (e.g., regret, sympathy) that manifests some measure of fellow-feeling. It
just is not enough. (I am, of course, aware that at this point I am relying merely on intuition; I offer
here no suggestion of how much good-will morality requires, let alone any theoretical justification
for drawing this line at one place rather than another.)
[43] Reflecting on this case should help inform our answers to related questions: What should we
say of those, White or Black, who lock car doors when driving through Black neighborhoods but
not White ones? Or of store-owners (again, White or Black) who will not admit Black teenagers to
their premises?

discrimination, but, like Lichtenberg, I will not pursue that topic.) Helpfully, Lichtenberg cites several factors she thinks relevant to deciding when it is unjust to take race into account. How much harm does the victim suffer? How much does the agent stand to suffer if she does not discriminate? Is the person who discriminates acting in a public or official capacity?

Lichtenberg maintains that the Black teenagers suffer "a minimal slight—if it's even noticed." She even suggests that the White person might spare their feelings "by a display of ulterior motivation, like [pretending to] inspect the rosebushes on the other side" of the street in order to make it look as if it were her admiration for the flowers, and not her fear of Black people, that motivated her to cross the street. The latter pretense is, in my judgment, insulting and unlikely to succeed. More important, this appears to be a guilty response, as if the person is trying to cover up something she knows is wrong. I think that fact should cause Lichtenberg and her imagined agent to reconsider the claim that the action is unobjectionable. It is also quite wrong-headed to think that the harm of insult is entirely a matter of whether a person has hurt feelings. Does it make a difference that the victims suffer little direct and tangible harm? Some, but not much. After all, by that criterion, egregiously racist behavior such as engaging in caricatures or telling jokes that mock Black people would be justified if done in an all-White setting.

According to Lichtenberg, it is acceptable for the White woman to try to avoid the Black teenager on the street, but much harder to justify her racially discriminating when he applies for a job. It will be difficult to maintain this position, however. How is this woman—so terrified of contact with young Black males that she will not walk on the same side of the street with them—simply to turn off this uneasiness when the time comes for her to decide whether to offer a job to the Black male? Suppose that the job is to help out in her family's grocery store, and that this is likely to mean that the woman and the teenager will be alone in the store some evenings? Lichtenberg's advice, that the woman indulge her prejudice in her private life but rigorously exclude it from their official conduct, seems unstable. Indeed, Lichtenberg seems to assume that the woman can take refuge in bureaucracy, that she will be the personnel officer who does the hiring, while it is other people who will actually have to work in proximity with the new employee. It is the worst of liberal bad faith, however, for this woman to practice her tolerance in official decision-making, but only on the condition that it is other people who will have to bear the burden of adjusting to the pluralistic environment those decisions create and of making that environment work. (Compare the liberal politician who boldly integrates the public schools while taking care to "protect" her own kids in all-White private schools.)

Lichtenberg assumes that private discrimination is less serious morally, but this is doubtful. The heart is where racism, like all immorality, begins and dwells. Even if some moral *virtue*-traits were differentially distributed along racial lines (and even if that were for genetic rather than historical reasons), each individual would still retain the right to be given the benefit of the probability that she is *not* herself specially inclined toward vice. Of course, this sort of racial discrimination need not be racist, since it can be entirely unconnected to any racial disaffection, just as it may not be irrational if it is a response to a genuine statistical disparity in risk. (Similarly, there need be nothing immoral in age-based discrimination should the woman seek to avoid being on dark streets alone with teenagers but not with the elderly.) Nevertheless, such conduct runs substantial risk of reinforcing some of the ugly racial stereotypes that are used to rationalize racial antipathy, and there is reason to avoid relying upon it.

Our view of institutional racism is both narrower and wider than some others that have been offered. To see how it is narrower, that is, less inclusive, let us consider the practice of 'word-of-mouth' job-recruitment, in which people assigned to a privileged racial group, who tend to socialize only with one another, distribute special access to employment benefits to social acquaintances similarly assigned. Some deem this institutional racism, because of its adverse impact on those considered members of the disadvantaged group. (See, for example, Ezorsky 1991.) Miles protests against those who expansively identify institutional racism with, as he puts it, "all actions or processes (whatever their origin or motivation) which result in one group being placed or retained in a subordinate position by another." In his eyes, the practice of 'word-of-mouth' recruitment is not racist because, although it has an admittedly disproportionally adverse impact on people assigned to the disadvantaged racial group (e.g., African-Americans), it has similar impact on members of other groups—ethnic, gender, economic—that are underrepresented among the elite (Miles 1989: 52, 61).

One can, however, respond that this fact does not show the practice is not an instance of institutional racism. It may be an instance of institutional racism and, at the same time, an instance of institutional sexism, of institutional 'classism,' etc.[44] Miles' critics have a point. I think, however, what this shows is that we go wrong when we try to identify institutional racism merely by examining the effects of institutional practices. On the view taken here, the practice, while possibly undesirable and perhaps even unjust, is not racist unless it stems from racist antipathy or lack of empathy or from

---

[44] It was Larry Blum who pointed out to me the availability of this line of response to Miles.

negative beliefs born of such disaffection, in the hearts of the people who carry out the practice.[45]

Consider, similarly, the so-called 'old boy network.'[46] Person F, upon hearing of an opening at his place of employment, tells the people he thinks of (who are all White males like himself) about the job and recommends one of them (Person G) to the boss, who hires him. Ignoring the exaggeration in calling anything so informal an 'institution,' let us explore whether this 'institution' of the 'old boy network' is racist. Is F (or F's behavior) racist? Is G (or G's behavior) racist? Some are ready to offer affirmative answers. What should we say? First, G cannot be racist just for receiving the job; that's not sufficiently active. What about G's act of *accepting* the job? That can be racist. I think, however, that it is racist only in the exceptional circumstance where the institutions are so corrupt that G should have nothing to do with them. Second, F may be racist insofar as his mental process skips over some possible candidates simply because the stereotypes he uses (perhaps to mask his racial disaffection from himself and others) keep him from thinking of them as possible job candidates. Third, one needs some further reason not yet given to label racist the practice of the 'old boy network.' It may work 'systematically' to the detriment of Black people. That, however, merely shows that, in our society, with our history of racism, Black people can be disadvantaged by many things other than race-based factors. (Glenn Loury offers several other examples of this, interestingly including the custom of endogamy among both White and Black people.[47]) What is important to note is that it is misleading to call all these things racist, because that terminology fails to differentiate the very different ways in which and reasons for which they disadvantage people. This classification and broad use of the term, then, fails adequately to inform us and, of more practical importance, it fails to direct our attention (and efforts) to the source of the

---

[45] It is also doubtful whether such an informal practice, not tied to any organizational structure in particular and part of no determined policy, properly counts as institutional behavior at all. However, I will not pursue that classificatory matter here. Philosophers and other social thinkers nowadays use the term 'institution' in quite a broad and vague way, and this is not the place to try to correct that practice. (That 'institution'? For a step toward a more discriminate use, see the brief discussion of 'institutions' and 'practices' in MacIntyre 1984, ch. 14.)

[46] This phenomenon is closely related to that of word-of-mouth job recruiting. There are, however, some distinctions. The 'old boy network' is defined by an educational elite of private schools (which often embeds a still more restricted elite who are members of secret societies, dining halls, and special clubs). This educationally elite network may also extend its privileging beyond recruitment to include admission to restricted social occasions and establishments where business is conducted, employment advancement, informal help and advice, and the wielding of influence to gain preference in academic admissions and fellowships, the awarding of contracts and consultantships, immunity from having to pay for misconduct, and other social and economic privileges.

[47] Loury (1992).

difficulty. It doesn't identify for us *how* things are going wrong and thus *what* needs to be changed.

Some accounts of institutional racism threaten to be excessively broad in other ways. Some implicitly restrict institutional racism to operations *within* a society—they see it as one group maintaining its social control over the other.[48] This is too narrow, since it would exclude, for example, what seem to be some clear cases of institutional racism, such as discrimination in immigration and in foreign assistance policies. However, if this restriction to intra-group behavior is simply removed from these accounts, then they will have to count as instances of institutional racism some actions which do not properly fall within the class. Suppose, for example, the government of a hostile planet, free of any bigotry toward any Earthling racial group, but unenamored of all Earthlings, launches a missile to destroy the Earth. Suppose it lands in Africa. This institutional (governmental) action has a disproportionally adverse impact on Black people, but it is silly to describe it as racist. (It remains silly even if the aliens decide to target *all* their attacks on the same continent—say, because its size or subterranean mineral deposits make it easier for their tracking systems to locate—and the effect thus becomes 'systematic'.) Talk of racism here is inane because the action, its motivation, and its agents are entirely untainted by any racial disaffection or prejudice. By the same token, however, although the agents of many earthly institutions *are* tainted by racism (e.g., in the U.S. government), that fact cannot suffice, even in combination with adverse impacts, to make its actions institutionally racist. The racism has first to *get into* the institutional conduct somehow by informing the conduct of individual agents. In contrast, proponents of expansive accounts of institutional racism, by focusing on the action's effects, end up in the untenable position of claiming that racism somehow *comes out of* institutional behavior, while simultaneously denying that it must ever even get into the action at the action's source in the aims, beliefs, desires, hopes, fears, and so on of the agents who execute institutional policy.[49]

---

[48] For instance, "[T]he essential feature of racism is . . . the *defense* of a system from which advantage is derived on the basis of race" (D. Wellman, quoted at Miles 1989: 52; emphasis added).

[49] This reflection illuminates a further example. Young-Bruehl says, "A current law [in the United States] which has as its known consequence that women using federally funded family planning clinics—a majority of whom are women of color—will be deprived of information to make informed reproductive choices is, simply, racist" (Young-Bruehl 1992: 10). The law she seems to have had in mind was an executive order, which, because of court action, was never enforced and was later rescinded.

Young-Bruehl clearly assumes that this information would have been given outside the context of a clerisy of family planning professionals trying to encourage poor, predominantly Black, women to terminate their pregnancies for what the professionals see as their own good. She also

We can also profitably turn our account to an interesting case Skillen offers. He writes:

Suppose Dr Smythe-Browne's surgery has been ticking over happily for years until it is realized that few of the many local Asians visit him. It turns out that they travel some distance to Dr Patel's surgery. Dr Smythe-Browne and his staff are upset. Then they realise that, stupidly, he has never taken the trouble to make himself understood by or to understand the Asians in his area. His surgery practices have had the effect of excluding or at least discouraging Asians. Newly aware, he sets out to fix the situation.

By the same token as his practices have been 'consequentially', not 'constitutively' discriminatory, they have been 'blind', lacking in awareness.

The example shows the possibility of a certain sort of 'racism' that, if we must attribute blame, is a function of a lack of thought (energy, resources, etc.). If that lack of thought is itself to be described as 'discriminatory' it would need to be shown Dr Smythe-Browne showed no such lack of attention when one of the local streets became gentrified . . . In such cases, it is not racial sets as such that are the focus of attention, but race as culturally 'inscribed'. In other words, one is concerned with people in respect of how they identify themselves and are identified by others (for example, intimidating institutions or outright racists). (Skillen 1993: 81)

Despite what Skillen implies, that an institution intimidates some racial groups ("sets") does not make it racist. Flew is right about the insufficiency (even the irrelevance) of mere effects to establish racism, as he is right about

---

seems to assume that it is somehow wrong for the state to try to discourage such choices and that withholding this information about where to get an abortion is objectionable in a way that depriving women of detailed information about the effects of abortion on the developing life within is not. She sees the effects of the regulation as a harm to poor, Black women as individuals, while it is, arguably, better to understand the provision as a protection of poor Black people as a group. I do not here challenge her assumptions. Permit me to observe only that she does not argue for them, that they are not at all obvious, and that I think them all implausible and some plainly false.

Young-Bruehl's classification of the law as racist is highly implausible. Presumably, the requirement was part of a general policy of getting the government out of the provision and support of abortion—a policy which also militates against funding overseas abortion-"providers" through foreign aid, against federal facilities performing abortions on government property (such as military bases) or in U.S. protectorates or the federal district, against using federal payments to employees' insurance funds to pay for abortions, and against using federal insurance payments to provide abortions. Some of these restrictions will wind up having statistically disportionate impact on minority women and children; some will not. (Some will interpret this impact as specially burdening minority women, others as specially protecting minority children.)

It does not appear, however, that any beliefs or feelings or desires about race enter into these policies in their design or execution. Thus, those who agree with Young-Bruehl, if they mean to rise above nasty rhetoric to serious argument, need to reveal to us where, when, and how the racism gets into this institutional practice, if they are going to back up their claim that this law is a manifestation or instance of institutional racism. Of course, they might instead claim that the law is racist because of the racist conduct of those who execute it. This will probably be true of some administrators. In just the same way, however, it is true of some of the law's opponents that they are motivated by a racist desire to reduce the numbers of Black people, especially the poor female ones who are most likely to be lost should the government make abortion cheap and easy while it leaves the having and rearing of children a disproportionally heavy financial burden. Advocacy of facilitated abortion access, no less than opposition to it, *can* be marked by both racism and sexism. That fact does nothing to support Young-Bruehl's one-sided criticism.

the sufficiency of racism to establish immorality.[50] Otherwise, the inter-planetary attacks in our earlier example would count as instances of institutional racism. Moreover, that Smythe-Browne was thoughtless about what might be needed to attract Asians in no way shows his conduct was racist, not even if he was more sensitive and interested in how to attract 'yuppies' brought close by local gentrification. Insensitivity to certain race-related differences is not racist, even if one is sensitive to class-related differences or to differences associated with other racial differences. Smythe-Browne does not so much "discourage" Asians as fail to encourage them. Psychologically and ontologically, that is a very different matter, and those differences are likely to correlate with moral differences as well. (Failure to encourage is likely merely to be at worst an offense of *non*benevolence rather of *mal*evolence.) *Perhaps* the Asians were 'invisible' to Smythe-Browne in a way that he is culpable for. To show this, however, more would need to be said about why he did not notice them, their absence, and their special interests. Is it that he cares so little about Asians and their well-being? If there is nothing like this involved, then there is no racism in Smythe-Browne's professional behavior, I say. And if there is something like this involved, then Smythe-Browne's conduct is not purely " 'consequentially' . . . discriminatory." It is corrupted by its motivation in racial disaffection.

When it comes to defending racial preferences against Flew's strictures, however, Skillen shows more insight. He adds further detail to his case, asking us to suppose that Dr. Smythe-Browne "decides that the only way to cope with the situation is to get an Asian doctor, preferably female, onto the staff. He advertises the job and, finding a good person of the sort he needs, she joins the practice, whereas a number of, in other respects at least, equally good applicants (white, male for the most part) do not. Is this 'racism'?" Skillen thinks not, and I think he argues his point well. "Is it not, in Flew's terms, a case of 'discriminating in favor of a racially defined subset out of a total set'? Well, not necessarily. Dr. Smythe-Browne's criteria remain medical. His selection is legitimate insofar as we accept that medicine is a human and communicative 'art' in respect of which socially significant variables are relevant. In that sense it is simply not the case that bypassed candidates with better degree results were necessarily 'better candidates' " (Skillen 1993: 82).

With this understanding and assessment, I agree wholeheartedly. Dr. Smythe-Brown's hiring preference here seems to me to exemplify the sort of

---

[50] It is nor clear what Skillen thinks about the latter point. I agree that some people with racist beliefs should not be condemned morally, but that is because I think that racist beliefs don't make one a real racist and that the beliefs are 'racist' only in a derivative sense. Does Skillen agree?

race-based distinction that is in its nature and its morality quite different from racist discrimination.[51]

As I mentioned, this account of institutional racism is also more inclusive than some. Flew's account, for example, is too narrow in ways I shall point out below. Usually, people apply the term institutional racism only to practices that reinforce existing inter-group power relations. However, a company of people, all of whom are assigned to an oppressed racial group, may harbor reactive racist attitudes toward all those designated as members of the dominant group, and may institutionalize their racism in such institutions as they control: excluding people considered members of the resented group from access to certain schools, scholarships, employment positions, memberships, etc., not out of fraternal/sororal solidarity with others similarly oppressed, nor out of a concern to realize more just distribution of benefits, but simply from resentful racial antipathy. That is racism in the operations of a social organization, institutionalized racism, and should therefore count as institutional racism. This bears out an observation of Randall Kennedy's. "Some argue that, at least with respect to whites, African Americans cannot be racist because, as a group, they lack the power to subordinate whites. Among other failings, this theory ignores nitty-gritty realities. Regardless of the relative strength of African-American and Jewish communities, the African Americans who beat Jews in Crown Heights for racially motivated reasons were, at the moment, sufficiently powerful to subordinate their victims. This theory, moreover, ignores the plain fact African Americans—as judges, teachers, mayors, police officers, members of Congress and army officers—increasingly occupy positions of power and influence from which they could, if so minded, tremendously damage clients, coworkers, dependents, and beyond, the society as a whole" (Kennedy 1994).

The approach taken here opens the door to the sort of research H. L. Gates has recently called for. He writes, "[W]e have finessed the gap between rhetoric and reality by forging new and subtler definitions of the word 'racism.' Hence a new model of institutional racism is one that can operate in the absence of actual racists. By redefining our terms we can always say of the economic gap between black and white America: the problem is still racism . . . and by stipulation it would be true. But the grip of this vocabulary has tended to foreclose the more sophisticated models of political economy we so desperately need" (Gates 1994).

---

[51] One must, however, take care not to proceed too far down this path. One must assure that the White candidates are not victims of reverse racism. For it would normally be wrong to keep out Black candidates even if the White patients related better to White physicians. One may not bow to primary racism by becoming illicitly collaborative in its workings. See the discussion in Sect. IV above.

V. OTHER VIEWS

This way of understanding the nature of racism contrasts with certain other views from the literature. Elizabeth Young-Bruehl and Cornel West have recently articulated the common view that White male sexual insecurity is at the heart of White racism. "White fear of black sexuality is a basic ingredient of white racism . . . Social scientists have long acknowledged that interracial sex and marriage is the most *perceived* source of white fear of black people—just as the repeated castrations of lynched black men cries out for serious psychocultural explanation" (West 1992: 86–7; also see Young-Bruehl 1992).

Suppose that West and Young-Bruehl are right to think that most of the White racists around today (or in history) were driven to their racism through fear of Black male sexuality. Even if this claim about the psychological causes of racism is true, it leaves unaffected our claim about what racism consists in. It is implausible to think such insecurity essential to (a necessary condition for) racism, even for White racism, because if we came across someone who hated Black people, thought us inherently inferior, worked to maintain structures of White domination over us, and so on, but came to all this for reasons other than sexual insecurity, we would and should still classify her attitude as racism. Nor is this hypothesis a near-impossibility; we may come across such people quite often, especially when we consider other forms of racism—hostility against Asians, for example. "Psychocultural explanation" is unlikely to reveal (logically) necessary truths about the nature of racism.

Finally, let us examine the views offered by Antony Flew and Anthony Skillen in the recent exchange to which we have already several times attended (Skillen 1993; Flew 1990). Skillen writes[52]

According to Antony Flew, when people, beliefs or practices are spoken of as "racist," one of three sorts of thing is usually being said. These express three concepts of racism. But only one of the them, the first, is valid.

(1) Racism as "unjust discrimination." In this first of Flew's senses, to be "racist" is to discriminate *in favor of* [emphasis added] or against people for no other or better reason than that they belong to one particular racial set and not another. Since the "defining characteristics" of a race are "skin pigmentation, shape of skull, etc." and since such attributes are strictly superficial and properly irrelevant to (almost) all questions of social status and employment, racism in this sense is as grotesquely unfair as to disqualify competing candidates because they are bald, or blond, or red-

---

[52] Throughout this discussion, I have had to rely on Skillen for a presentation of Flew's views. Flew's paper is difficult to locate and the periodical in which it appeared is no longer published. Fortunately, Skillen is aware of the difficulty, and takes extra care to present Flew's views at length, separating summary from interpretation or critique. I follow his practice in presenting sometimes extensive verbatim passages quoted from Flew.

headed. So this is a valid use of the term "racist", which both picks out a recognizable practice, color discrimination, and indicates why it is abominable.

(2) Racism as "heretical belief." In this second sense, to be racist is to *believe* that there are substantial inherited differences among racial sets in attributes relevant to important practical questions. Such differences in accompanying characteristics might be differences in intelligence . . . in aggressiveness, etc. . . . But, Flew contends, the person accused of racism in this sense (provided they are not simply aiming to throw up a smoke-screen for true racism—racism 1), is accused wrongly. (p. 73)

(3) "Institutionaliz*ed* racism." [emphasis added] In this third sense, "institutions" (schools, firms, government, courts) are said to be racist when their routine practices, however "legitimated" have the *effect* [Skillen's emphasis] of and typically, it is alleged, the unadmitted purpose, of excluding or disadvantaging racial sets. Against this Flew argues, again apriori, that institutions cannot have intentions and hence cannot be the target of moral blame. (p. 74)

In Flew's terms, then, "racism 3" (pervasive "disadvantage") is falsely represented as a function of "racism 1" by representing the claims of inherited inferiorities ("racism 2") as a legitimating smoke-screen. Thus armed, "anti-racism" becomes the ideology of a genuine and abhorrent racism with blacks getting preference simply on the basis of the color of their skin . . . [According to Flew's p. 66: "discriminating in favor of a racially defined subset out of the total set of all those worse off than the majority . . . is paradigmatically racist" (quoted at Skillen 1993: 74.)]

Skillen rejects Flew's narrow view of what properly counts as racism in favor of his own more expansive conception.

On the contrary, I [Skillen] see racism, which is by no means peculiar to Europeans, as being like misogyny, bigotry, and chauvinism in its *straddling the theory–practice (belief–action) dichotomy* essential to Flew's scheme of things. *Racism, in my view, is a belief-validated or "ideological" disposition or attitude.* As such, *racism is not just a feature of this or that individual but a largely cultural matter.* (emphases added, except Skillen emphasizes 'cultural'; Skillen 1993: 75.)

[R]acism is a complex of ideological attitudes and practices, more or less bound up with institutionalized barriers . . . In all cases there is an exercise, through ideology, of power. (Skillen 1993: 87)

The volitional account of racism, advocated here, captures what is valuable in the views of Flew and Skillen, while helping to identify and correct their difficulties. As regards Flew, it is not clear what counts as "discrimination" for him. Does a mere differentiation I make in my mind count? (E.g., thinking all Xs are stupid, corrupt, lazy, greedy, conniving? Thinking they tend disproportionally to be stupid, etc.?) Or must I go on to *do* things to some Xs? If the latter, then what kinds of things? Must it involve withholding real benefits? (How about just keeping away from them?) What if I do things, but don't really do much of anything to Xs? (Suppose I malign the intelligence or character of Xs when I speak to my fellow Ys.) What counts as "discriminating" for Flew? I suspect his criterion is too behavioral and insufficiently centered in the racists' desires and goals. Further, Flew's rejection as racist of discrimination in favor even of those socially assigned to an oppressed racial group merely misses the distinction made above between *racist* discrimination and modes of discriminating that are merely race-based. In addition, one wonders about Flew's concession that someone accused of racism for holding so-called "heretical" beliefs will not escape the charge if, in offering factual claims to defend her position, she is "simply aiming to throw up a smoke-screen for [unjust discrimination]." What if she throws out a smoke-screen without aiming to? Or without consciously aiming to?

Contra Skillen's position, it is not clear that a "belief-validated disposition or attitude" does straddle the belief–action divide. If the "attitude" is the doxastic attitude of belief, then racism doesn't straddle, it's just a belief. Nor need it straddle if the "disposition" is a disposition to perform certain (which?) actions. Much depends on how one understands dispositions (and beliefs) but, assuming that a belief is not just a disposition to act, then that would place racism on the action/practice side. (The disposition would count as racist, however, only if it stood in the right relationship to certain beliefs.)

Skillen nicely counters Flew by pointing out that expressing a negative view of the capabilities of Blacks "is paradigmatic of racism. [However] Flew excludes it from racism proper ... [Such] utterances ... can't, on Flew's view, be racist at all, because racism by proper definition is morally abominable, whereas [Flew thinks that] morally to condemn a belief is to be categorically mistaken" (Skillen 1993: 77). So, "not only can beliefs be racist but racism typically entails a belief 'system'. Hence Flew's dissection of 'racism in the second sense' [i.e., as belief] involves considerable misdirection" (Skillen 1993: 79). Skillen adds that "the person who sees the world in terms of the sort of essentialising divisions [drawn by those who think races like species or natural kinds] is at least suffering from a shortfall of vision. If his racism is sincere, he ought not to be 'condemned' and vilified ... though he may need to be argued with, contested and, if he is in position of power, fought" (Skillen 1993: 79). For me, typically holding such beliefs is racist because one holds them in part to justify racial antipathy, ill-will, or disregard. So, some people can be condemned for holding these beliefs, pace both Flew and Skillen. In any case, someone with such beliefs is likely to have racist desires and volitions whether they cause, or are caused by, the beliefs. It is important to observe, pace Skillen, first, that racism need entail no 'system' of beliefs and, second, while various institutions and other elements of the cultural environment may nurture racism and derived racist beliefs, racism nevertheless lies fundamentally in individuals.

Racism has, according to Skillen, an "institutional character."

If it is the case that individuals, not institutions, have intentions or goals, we need to say that institutions operate through individuals, that our intentions are structured by institutions (going home, teaching, keeping the country or the club white and so on) ... Racism, like sexism or confessional discrimination can be an implicit thing, taken for granted, a traditional part of the way we've always done things. (Skillen 1993: 80)

[A]s Flew's ... objection charging the opponent of "institutionalized racism" with definition in terms of "consequences" bears out, his main concern is not with institutions whose racism is more or less constitutive of their identity [as in a club or school founded to give Whites refuge from integration], ... [but] with regulative practices: tests, entry requirements, employment practices, which, *as it turns out*, result in poor outcomes for members of certain racial sets. (p. 81; original emphasis)

This is wrong-headed for reasons that should by now be clear. No institutional practices can be racist—nor malicious, dishonest, or in any other way morally vicious—merely because "as it turns out" they have undesirable effects. Flew is right that an institution can be racist in the way it is constituted, and Skillen is right that institutions can also be racist in their operations, even when innocently founded. However, Skillen goes too far that its effects alone can suffice to make an institution racist. Institutional racism exists, as we said, when the racism in individuals becomes institutionalized. To become institutionalized, racism must infect the institution's operations by informing the ends it adopts, or the means it employs, or the grounds on which it accepts undesirable side effects (as is normally the case in 'environmental racism'), or the assumptions on which it works. Failing any such basis, Skillen is unable to explain how racism gets into the institution to corrupt its behavior. Any suggestion that it gets into the institution and its behavior after the fact from the behavior's effects is incoherent. Skillen's error is to confuse output-driven concepts, such as being dangerous or harmful or lethal, with a moral concept such as racism. Output-driven concepts can be useful for moral judgment, because they help us to ask the right questions about why the agent (here: the institution) acted as it did and why it did not abandon its plans in favor of some less harmful course of action. Answers to these questions can help us to decide whether the action is negligent or malicious or otherwise vicious. However, output-driven concepts cannot suffice to ground assigning any moral status, because vice and virtue are by nature tied to the action's motivation. Effects can only be (defeasible) evidence of motivation.[53]

Finally, Skillen is correct to observe that oftentimes institutions shape individual intentions and actions. Institutional racism will often exist in

---

[53] I am aware that the charge I here level against Skillen would also militate against all forms of direct, optimizing consequentialism, and against other result-driven accounts of wrongdoing, such as the satisficing consequentialism Slote discussed. (For more on this, see Garcia 1990, 1992 and Slote 1995.)

reciprocal relation to individual racism. The racism of some Individual (or individuals) first infects the institution, and the institution's resultant racism then reinforces racism in that individual or breeds it in others. Once individual racism exists, institutional racism can be a powerful instrument of its perpetuation. This reciprocity of causal influence, however, should not blind us to the question of origins. Individual racism can come into the world without depending on some prior institutionalization. (It could come to be, say, as a result of some twist in one person's temperament.) The converse is not true. Institutional racism can reinforce and perpetuate individual racism. Unless an institution is corrupted (in its ends, means, priorities, or assumptions) by a prior and independent racism in some individual's heart, however, institutional racism can never come to exist.

Nevertheless, we should take care not to overstate the dependence of institutional racism upon individual. Institutional racism appears to be capable of continuing after individual racism has largely died out. Think of a case where, for example, officials continue, uncomprehendingly, to implement policies originally designed, and still functioning, to disadvantage those assigned to a certain racial group. Indeed, I strongly doubt that the qualifier 'and still functioning' is necessary. Institutional racism can exist without actually functioning to harm anyone. Suppose, a few generations back, some R1s designed a certain institutional procedure P specifically to harm R2s, an oppressed racial group, though the designers were never explicit about this aim. Later, anti-R2 feeling among R1s faded away, and in time real social equality was achieved. The R1s, however, are a traditionalist lot, and they continue faithfully to execute P out of deference to custom and their ancestors. P no longer specially harms R2s. (Perhaps it excludes from various privileges those who come from some specific, traditionally poor R2 neighborhoods, and R2s are no longer disproportionally represented in those neighborhoods, which, perhaps, are also no longer disproportionally poor.)

In that case, it appears that the racism of the earlier generation persists in the institutional procedure P, even though P no longer specially harms R2s. This indicates that institutional racism, no less than individual racism, can be either effective or ineffective, either harmful or innocuous. Institutional racism, then, is a bad thing; but it is a bad thing not because of its actual effects, but sometimes merely because of its aims. The study of people's aims directs the social theorist's attention into their hearts, to what they care about, to what they have set themselves on having, or being, or making, or doing. Such is the stuff of the moral virtues, of course. Neither the social theorist nor the moral theorist can continue to neglect them if she wishes to understand the world. Or to change it.

VI. CONCLUSION

These reflections suggest that an improved understanding of racism and its immorality calls for a comprehensive rethinking of racial discrimination, of the preferential treatment programs sometimes disparaged as 'reverse discrimination,' and of institutional conduct as well. They also indicate the direction such a rethinking should take, and its dependence on the virtues and other concepts from moral psychology. That may require a significant change in the way social philosophers have recently treated these and related topics.[54]

[54] I am grateful to many people who discussed these matters with me. Henry Richardson, Martha Minow, David Wilkins, David Wong, Anthony Appiah, Susan Wolf, Dennis Thompson, Glenn Loury, and Judith Lichtenberg offered thoughtful comments on earlier drafts of some of this material. Discussions with Russell Hittinger, Ken Taylor, and others also profited me greatly. I am especially indebted to Lawrence Blum for repeated acts of encouragement and assistance, including reading and discussing my manuscripts and letting me read from his unpublished work, and I thank him and an audience at Rutgers' 1994 conference on philosophy and race, for making suggestions and raising forceful objections.

My work was made possible by generous sabbatical support from Georgetown University, by research assistance from Rutgers University, and by grants from the National Endowment for the Humanities and from Harvard's Program in Ethics and the Professions. This paper would not have been written without the stimulation and the opportunity for reflection afforded me at the annual Ford Foundation Fellows conferences. To all these institutions I am indebted.

REFERENCES

Adams, Robert (1987), "The Virtue of Faith," in Adams, *The Virtue of Faith* (Oxford: Oxford University Press), 9–24.

Appiah, Anthony (1990), "Racisms," in D. T. Goldberg (ed.), *Anatomy of Racism* (Minneapolis: University of Minnesota Press).

—— (1992), *In My Father's House: Africa in the Philosophy of Culture* (Oxford: Oxford University Press).

Banton, Michael (1970), "The Concept of Racism," in Sami Zubaida (ed.), *Race and Racialism* (New York: Barnes & Noble), 17–34.

—— and Miles, Robert (1988), "Racism," in E. Ellis Cashmore (ed.), *Dictionary of Race and Ethnic Relations*, 2nd edn. (London: Routledge).

Blum, Lawrence (1991), "Antiracism, Multiculturalism, and Interracial Community: Three Educational Values for a Multicultural Society," Office of Graduate Studies and Research, University of Massachusetts at Boston.

—— (1994), *Moral Perception and Particularity* (Cambridge: Cambridge University Press).

—— (1993), "Individual and Institutional Racism," Paper read at Smith College, Feb.

Carter, Stephen (1991), *Reflections of an Affirmative Action Baby* (New York: Basic Books).

Castoriadis, Cornelius (1992), "Reflections on Racism," *Thesis Eleven*, no. 32: 1–12.

Cohen, Marshall, *et al.* (eds.) (1980), *Marx, Justice, and History* (Princeton: Princeton University Press).

Cottingham, John (1986), "Partiality, Favouritism and Morality," *Philosophical Quarterly*, 36: 357–73.

Ezorsky, Gertrude (1991), *Racism and Justice* (Ithaca, NY: Cornell University Press).

Flew, Antony (1986), "Clarifying the Concepts," in Palmer (1986: 15–31).

—— (1990), "Three Concepts of Racism," *Encounter*, 73 (Sept.).

Garcia, J. L. A. (1986), "The Tunsollen, the Seinsollen, and the Soseinsollen," *American Philosophical Quarterly*, 23: 267–76.

—— (1987), "Goods and Evils," *Philosophy and Phenomenological Research*, 47: 385–412.

—— (1990), "The Primacy of the Virtuous," *Philosophia*, 20: 69–91.

—— (1992), "African-American Perspectives, Cultural Relativism, and Normative Issues," in Edmund Pellegrino and Harley Flack (eds.), *African-American Perspectives on Biomedical Issues: Philosophical Issues* (Washington: Georgetown University Press).

—— (1993), "The New Critique of Anti-Consequentialist Moral Theory," *Philosophical Studies*, 71: 1–32.

—— (1995), "Virtue Ethics," in Robert Audi (ed.), *Cambridge Dictionary of Philosophy* (Cambridge: Cambridge University Press).

—— (1997), "Current Conceptions of Racism," *Journal of Social Philosophy*, 28/2 (Fall 1997), 6–42.

Gates, Henry Louis, Jr. (1993), "Let Them Talk: A Review of 'Words that Wound: Critical Race Theory, Assaultive Speech and the First Amendment,' by Mari J. Matsuda, Charles R. Lawrence III, Richard Delgado, and Kimberle Williams Crenshaw," *New Republic* (Sept. 20 and 27) (double issue), 37–49: 48.

Gilligan, Carol (1982), *In a Different Voice* (Cambridge, Mass.: Harvard University Press).

Goldberg, David Theo, "The Social Formation of Racist Discourse," in D. T. Goldberg (ed.), *Anatomy of Racism* (Minneapolis: University of Minnesota Press), 295–318.

—— (1992), "The Semantics of Race," *Ethnic and Racial Studies*, 15: 543–69.

—— (1994), "Racist Exclusions," *Philosophical Forum*, 26: 21–32.

Gomberg, Paul (1990), "Patriotism is Like Racism," *Ethics*, 101: 144–50.

Green, Judith (1992), "King's Historical Location of Political Concepts," *APA Newsletter on Philosophy and the Black Experience*, 91: 12–14.

Hacker, Andrew (1992*a*), *Two Nations: Black and White, Separate, Hostile, Unequal* (New York: Scribner's).

—— (1992*b*), "The New Civil War," *New York Review of Books*, Apr. 23: 30–3.

Hursthouse, Rosalind (1993), "Virtue Theory and Abortion," *Philosophy and Public Affairs*, 20: 223–46.

Kamm, F. M. (1992), "Non-Consequentialism, the Person as an End-in-Itself, and the Significance of Status," *Philosophy and Public Affairs*, 21: 35–89.

Kennedy, Randall (1994), "Some Good may yet Come of This," *Time*, Feb. 28, 34.

Kirk, Marshall, and Madsen, Hunter (1989), *After the Ball: How America will Conquer its Fear and Hatred of Gays in the '90s* (New York: Doubleday).

Larrabee, Mary Jane (ed.) (1993), *An Ethic of Care* (New York: Routledge).

Lichtenberg, Judith (1992), "Racism in the Head, Racism in the World," *Philosophy and Public Policy* (Newsletter of the Institute for Philosophy and Public Policy, University of Maryland), 12.

Loury, Glenn (1987–8), "Why should we Care about Group Inequality?" *Social Philosophy and Policy*, 5: 249–71.

—— (1992) "The Economics of Discrimination," *Harvard Journal of African-American Public Policy*, 1: 91–110.

—— (1993), "The New Liberal Racism: A Review of Andrew Hacker's *Two Nations*," *First Things* (Jan.), 39–42.

Lukes, Stephen (1987), *Marxism and Morality* (Oxford: Oxford University Press).

Lyas, Colin (ed.) (1969), *Philosophy and Linguistics* (New York: St Martin's Press).

MacIntyre, Alasdair (1984), *After Virtue*, 2nd edn. (Notre Dame: University of Notre Dame Press).

Marable, Manning (1992), *Black America: Multicultural Democracy in the Age of Clarence Thomas and David Duke*, Open Magazine Pamphlet Series, no. 16 (Westfield, NY).

May, Larry (ed.) (1992), *Collective Responsibility* (Lanham, Md.: Rowman & Littlefield).

McDowell, John (1985), "Values and Secondary Qualities," in Ted Honderich (ed.), *Morality and Objectivity* (London: Humanities Press), 110–29.

Miles, Robert (1989), *Racism* (London: Routledge).

Murphy, Jeffrie, and Hampton, Jean (1988), *Forgiveness and Mercy* (New York: Cambridge University Press).

Nathanson, Stephen (1992), "Is Patriotism Like Racism?" *APA Newsletter on Philosophy and the Black Experience*, 91: 9–11.

Noddings, Nell (1986), *Caring* (Berkeley: University of California Press).

Okin, Susan Miller (1989), *Justice, Gender and the Family* (New York: Basic Books).

Palmer, Frank (ed.) (1986), *Anti-Racism: An Assault on Education and Value* (London: Sherwood).

Piper, Adrian M. (1990), "Higher Order Discrimination," in Owen Flanagan and Amelie Rorty (eds.), *Identity, Character, and Morality* (Cambridge, Mass.: MIT Press), 285–309.

Rothenberg, Paula (1988), *Racism and Sexism: An Integrated Study* (New York: St Martin's Press).

Schaefer, Richard (1990), *Racial and Ethnic Groups*, 4th edn. (Glenview: Scott, Foresman).

Schrag, Peter (1995), "Son of 187," *New Republic*, Jan. 30, 16–19.

Sheehan, Thomas (1992), "A Normal Nazi," *New York Review of Books*, Jan. 14.

Simon, Thomas (1994), "Fighting Racism: Hate Speech Detours," in Mortimer Sellers (ed.), *An Ethical Education: Community and Morality in the Multicultural University* (Oxford: Berg).

Skillen, Anthony (1993), "Racism: Flew's Three Concepts of Racism," *Journal of Applied Philosophy*, 10: 73–89. Skillen quotes from and cites Flew (1990). I have had to rely on Skillen's careful summary for the presentation of Flew's views. The publication in which Flew's article appeared is no longer published and is difficult to find.

Slote, Michael (1985), *Common-Sense Morality and Consequentialism* (London: Routledge & Kegan Paul).

—— (1994), "Agent-Based Virtue Ethics," Paper presented at a University of Santa Clara conference on virtue ethics, Mar.

Thomas, Laurence (1980), "Racism and Sexism: Some Conceptual Differences." *Ethics*, 90: 239–250.

Ture, Kwame, and Hamilton, Charles (1992), *Black Power*, reissue, with new afterword, of 1967 edn. (New York: Vintage Books).

West, Cornel (1993), *Race Matters* (Boston: Beacon).

Wiggins, David (1987), *Needs, Value, Truth* (New York: Blackwell).

Williams, Patricia (1991), *The Alchemy of Race and Rights* (Cambridge, Mass.: Harvard University Press).

Wistrich, Robert (1992), *Antisemitism: The Longest Hatred* (New York: Pantheon).

Young, Iris (1990), *Justice and the Politics of Difference* (Princeton: Princeton University Press).

Young-Bruehl, Elizabeth (1992), "Kinds of Types of Prejudices."

11

BAKKE'S CASE: ARE QUOTAS UNFAIR?

RONALD DWORKIN

On October 12, 1977, the Supreme Court heard oral argument in the case of *The Regents of the University of California v. Allan Bakke*. No lawsuit has ever been more widely watched or more thoroughly debated in the national and international press before the Court's decision. Still, some of the most pertinent facts set before the Court have not been clearly summarized.

The medical school of the University of California at Davis has an affirmative action program (called the "task force program") designed to admit more black and other minority students. It sets sixteen places aside for which only members of "educationally and economically disadvantaged minorities" compete. Allan Bakke, white, applied for one of the remaining eighty-four places; he was rejected but, since his test scores were relatively high, the medical school has conceded that it could not prove that he would have been rejected if the sixteen places reserved had been open to him. Bakke sued, arguing that the task force program deprived him of his constitutional rights. The California Supreme Court agreed, and ordered the medical school to admit him. The university appealed to the Supreme Court.

The Davis program for minorities is in certain respects more forthright (some would say cruder) than similar plans now in force in many other American universities and professional schools. Such programs aim to increase the enrollment of black and other minority students by allowing the fact of their race to count affirmatively as part of the case for admitting them. Some schools set a "target" of a particular number of minority places instead of setting aside a flat number of places. But Davis would not fill the number of places set aside unless there were sixteen minority candidates it considered clearly qualified for medical education. The difference is therefore one of administrative strategy and not of principle.

So the constitutional question raised by *Bakke* is of capital importance for higher education in the United States, and a large number of universities and

From Ronald Dworkin, 'Bakke's Case: Are Quotas Unfair?', in Ronald Dworkin, *A Matter of Principle* (Cambridge, Mass.: Harvard University Press, 1985).

schools have entered briefs *amicus curiae* urging the Court to reverse the California decision. They believe that if they are not free to use explicit racial criteria in their admissions programs, they will be unable to fulfill what they take to be their responsibilities to the nation.

It is often said that affirmative action programs aim to achieve a racially conscious society divided into racial and ethnic groups, each entitled as a group to some proportionable share of resources, careers, or opportunities. That is a perverse description. American society is currently a racially conscious society; this is the inevitable and evident consequence of a history of slavery, repression, and prejudice. Black men and women, boys and girls, are not free to choose for themselves in what roles—or as members of which social groups—others will characterize them. They are black, and no other feature of personality or allegiance or ambition will so thoroughly influence how they will be perceived and treated by others, and the range and character of the lives that will be open to them.

The tiny number of black doctors and other professionals is both a consequence and a continuing cause of American racial consciousness, one link in a long and self-fueling chain reaction. Affirmative action programs use racially explicit criteria because their immediate goal is to increase the number of members of certain races in these professions. But their long-term goal is to *reduce* the degree to which American society is overall a racially conscious society.

The programs rest on two judgments. The first is a judgment of social theory: that the United States will continue to be pervaded by racial divisions as long as the most lucrative, satisfying, and important careers remain mainly the prerogative of members of the white race, while others feel themselves systematically excluded from a professional and social elite. The second is a calculation of strategy: that increasing the number of blacks who are at work in the professions will, in the long run, reduce the sense of frustration and injustice and racial self-consciousness in the black community to the point at which blacks may begin to think of themselves as individuals who can succeed like others through talent and initiative. At that future point the consequences of nonracial admissions programs, whatever these consequences might be, could be accepted with no sense of racial barriers or injustice.

It is therefore the worst possible misunderstanding to suppose that affirmative action programs are designed to produce a balkanized America, divided into racial and ethnic subnations. They use strong measures because weaker ones will fail; but their ultimate goal is to lessen not to increase the importance of race in American social and professional life.

According to the 1970 census, only 2.1 percent of American doctors were black. Affirmative action programs aim to provide more black doctors to serve black patients. This is not because it is desirable that blacks treat blacks and whites treat whites, but because blacks, through no fault of their own, are now unlikely to be well served by whites, and because a failure to provide the doctors they trust will exacerbate rather than reduce the resentment that now leads them to trust only their own. Affirmative action tries to provide more blacks as classmates for white doctors, not because it is desirable that a medical school class reflect the racial makeup of the community as a whole, but because professional association between blacks and whites will decrease the degree to which whites think of blacks as a race rather than as people, and thus the degree to which blacks think of themselves that way. It tries to provide "role models" for future black doctors, not because it is desirable for a black boy or girl to find adult models only among blacks, but because our history has made them so conscious of their race that the success of whites, for now, is likely to mean little or nothing for them.

The history of the campaign against racial injustice since 1954, when the Supreme Court decided *Brown v. Board of Education*, is a history in large part of failure. We have not succeeded in reforming the racial consciousness of our society by racially neutral means. We are therefore obliged to look upon the arguments for affirmative action with sympathy and an open mind. Of course, if Bakke is right that such programs, no matter how effective they may be, violate his constitutional rights, then they cannot be permitted to continue. But we must not forbid them in the name of some mindless maxim, like the maxim that it cannot be right to fight fire with fire, or that the end cannot justify the means. If the strategic claims for affirmative action are cogent, they cannot be dismissed on the ground that racially explicit tests are distasteful. If such tests are distasteful, it can only be for reasons that make the underlying social realities the programs attack more distasteful still.

It is said that, in a pluralistic society, membership in a particular group cannot be used as a criterion of inclusion or exclusion from benefits. But group membership is, as a matter of social reality rather than formal admission standards, part of what determines inclusion or exclusion for us now. If we must choose between a society that is in fact liberal and an illiberal society that scrupulously avoids formal racial criteria, we can hardly appeal to the ideals of liberal pluralism to prefer the latter.

Archibald Cox of Harvard Law School, speaking for the University of California in oral argument, told the Supreme Court that this is the choice the United States must make. As things stand, he said, affirmative action programs are the only effective means of increasing the absurdly small number of black doctors. The California Supreme Court, in approving Bakke's claim, had urged the university to pursue that goal by methods that do not explicitly take race into account. But that is unrealistic. We must distinguish, Cox said, between two interpretations of what the California Court's recommendation means. It might mean that the university should aim at the same immediate goal, of increasing the proportion of black and other minority students in the medical school, by an admissions procedure that on the surface is not racially conscious.

That is a recommendation of hypocrisy. If those who administer the admissions standards, however these are phrased, understand that their immediate goal is to increase the number of blacks in the school, then they will use race as a criterion in making the various subjective judgments the explicit criteria will require, because that will be, given the goal, the only right way to make those judgments. The recommendation might mean, on the other hand, that the school should adopt some non-racially conscious goal, like increasing the number of disadvantaged students of all races, and then hope that that goal will produce an increase in the number of blacks as a by-product. But even if that strategy is less hypocritical (which is far from plain), it will almost certainly fail because no different goal, scrupulously administered in a non-racially conscious way, will significantly increase the number of black medical students.

Cox offered powerful evidence for that conclusion, and it is supported by the recent and comprehensive report of the Carnegie Council on Policy Studies in Higher Education. Suppose, for example, that the medical school sets aside separate places for applicants "disadvantaged" on some racially neutral test, like poverty, allowing only those disadvantaged in that way to compete for these places. If the school selects those from that group who scored best on standard medical school aptitude tests, then it will take almost no blacks, because blacks score relatively low even among the economically disadvantaged. But if the school chooses among the disadvantaged on some basis other than test scores, just so that more blacks will succeed, then it will not be administering the special procedure in a non-racially conscious way.

So Cox was able to put his case in the form of two simple propositions. A racially conscious test for admission, even one that sets aside certain places for qualified minority applicants exclusively, serves goals that are in themselves unobjectionable and even urgent. Such programs are, moreover, the only means that offer any significant promise of achieving these goals. If these programs are halted, then no more than a trickle of black students will enter medical or other professional schools for another generation at least.

If these propositions are sound, then on what ground can it be thought that such programs are either wrong or unconstitutional? We must notice an important distinction between two different sorts of objections that might be made. These programs are intended, as I said, to decrease the importance of race in the United States in the long run. It may be objected, first, that the programs will harm that goal more than they will advance it. There is no way now to prove that that is not so. Cox conceded in his argument that there are costs and risks in these programs.

Affirmative action programs seem to encourage, for example, a popular misunderstanding, which is that they assume that racial or ethnic groups are entitled to proportionate shares of opportunities, so that Italian or Polish ethnic minorities are, in theory, as entitled to their proportionate shares as blacks or Chicanos or American Indians are entitled to the shares the present programs give them. That is a plain mistake: the programs are not based on the idea that those who are aided are entitled to aid, but only on the strategic hypothesis that helping them is now an effective way of attacking a national problem. Some medical schools may well make that judgment, under certain circumstances, about a white ethnic minority. Indeed it seems likely that some medical schools are even now attempting to help white Appalachian applicants, for example, under programs of regional distribution.

So the popular understanding is wrong, but so long as it persists it is a cost of the program because the attitudes it encourages tend to a degree to make people more rather than less conscious of race. There are other possible costs. It is said, for example, that some blacks find affirmative action degrading; they find that it makes them more rather than less conscious of prejudice against their race as such. This attitude is also based on a misperception, I think, but for a small minority of blacks at least it is a genuine cost.

In the view of the many important universities which have such programs, however, the gains will very probably exceed the losses in reducing racial consciousness overall. This view is hardly so implausible that it is wrong for these universities to seek to acquire the experience that will allow us to judge whether they are right. It would be particularly silly to forbid these experiments if we know that the failure to try will mean, as the evidence shows, that the status quo will almost certainly continue. In any case, this first objection could provide no argument that would justify a decision by the Supreme Court holding the programs unconstitutional. The Court has no business substituting its speculative judgment about the probable consequences of educational policies for the judgment of professional educators.

So the acknowledged uncertainties about the long-term results of such programs could not justify a Supreme Court decision making them illegal. But there is a second and very different form of objection. It may be argued that even if the programs *are* effective in making our society less a society dominated by race, they are nevertheless unconstitutional because they violate the individual constitutional rights of those, like Allan Bakke, who lose places in consequence. In the oral argument Reynold H. Colvin of San Francisco, who is Bakke's lawyer, made plain that his objection takes this second form. Mr. Justice White asked him whether he accepted that the goals affirmative action programs seek are important goals. Colvin acknowledged that they were. Suppose, Justice White continued, that affirmative action programs are, as Cox had argued, the only effective means of seeking such goals. Would Colvin nevertheless maintain that the programs are unconstitutional? Yes, he insisted, they would be, because his client has a constitutional right that the programs be abandoned, no matter what the consequences.

Colvin was wise to put his objections on this second ground; he was wise to claim that his client has rights that do not depend on any judgment about the likely consequences of affirmative action for society as a whole, because if he sustains that claim, then the Court must give him the relief he seeks.

But can he be right? If Allan Bakke has a constitutional right so important that the urgent goals of affirmative action must yield, then this must be because affirmative action violates some fundamental principle of political morality. This is not a case in which what might be called formal or technical law requires a decision one way or the other. There is no language in the Constitution whose plain meaning forbids affirmative action. Only the most naive theories of statutory construction could argue that such a result is required by the language of any earlier Supreme Court decision or of the Civil Rights Act of 1964 or of any other congressional enactment. If Colvin is right, it must be because Allan Bakke has not simply some technical legal right but an important moral right as well.

What could that right be? The popular argument frequently made on editorial pages is that Bakke has a right to be judged on his merit. Or that he has a right to be judged as an individual rather than as a member of a social group. Or that he has a right, as much as any black man, not to be sacrificed or excluded from any opportunity because of his race alone. But these catch phrases are deceptive here, because, as reflection demonstrates, the only genuine principle they describe is the principle that no one should suffer from the prejudice or contempt of others. And that principle is not at stake in this case at all. In spite of popular opinion, the idea that the *Bakke* case presents a conflict between a desirable social goal and important individual rights is a piece of intellectual confusion.

Consider, for example, the claim that individuals applying for places in medical school should be judged on merit, and merit alone. If that slogan means that admissions committees should take nothing into account but scores on some particular intelligence test, then it is arbitrary and, in any case, contradicted by the long-standing practice of every medical school. If it means, on the other hand, that a medical school should choose candidates that it supposes will make the most useful doctors, then everything turns on the judgment of what factors make different doctors useful. The Davis medical school assigned to each regular applicant, as well as to each minority applicant, what it called a "benchmark score." This reflected not only the results of aptitude tests and college grade averages, but a subjective evaluation of the applicant's chances of functioning as an effective doctor, in view of society's present needs for medical service. Presumably the qualities deemed important were different from the qualities that a law school or engineering school or business school would seek, just as the intelligence tests a medical school might use would be different from the tests these other schools would find appropriate.

There is no combination of abilities and skills and traits that constitutes "merit" in the abstract; if quick hands count as "merit" in the case of a prospective surgeon, this is because quick hands will enable him to serve the public better and for no other reason. If a black skin will, as a matter of regrettable fact, enable another doctor to do a different medical job better, then that black skin is by the same token "merit" as well. That argument may strike some as dangerous; but only because they confuse its conclusion—that black skin may be a socially useful trait in particular circumstances—with the very different and despicable idea that one race may be inherently more worthy than another.

Consider the second of the catch phrases I have mentioned. It is said that Bakke has a right to be judged as an "individual," in deciding whether he is to be admitted to medical school and thus to the medical profession, and not as a member of some group that is being judged as a whole. What can that mean? Any admissions procedure must rely on generalizations about groups that are justified only statistically. The regular admissions process at Davis, for example, set a cutoff figure for college grade-point averages. Applicants whose averages fell below that figure were not invited to any interview, and therefore rejected out of hand.

An applicant whose average fell one point below the cutoff might well have had personal qualities of dedication or sympathy that would have been revealed at an interview, and that would have made him or her a better doctor than some applicant whose average rose one point above the line. But the former is excluded from the process on the basis of a decision taken for administrative convenience and grounded in the generalization, unlikely to hold true for every individual, that those with grade averages below the cutoff will not have other qualities sufficiently persuasive. Even the use of standard Medical College Aptitude Tests (MCAT) as part of the admissions procedure requires judging people as part of groups, because it assumes that test scores are a guide to medical intelligence, which is in turn a guide to medical ability. Though this judgment is no doubt true statistically, it hardly holds true for every individual.

Allan Bakke was himself refused admission to two other medical schools, not because of his race but because of his age: these schools thought that a student entering medical school at the age of thirty-three was likely to make less of a contribution to medical care over his career than someone entering at the standard age of twenty-one. Suppose these schools relied, not on any detailed investigation of whether Bakke himself had abilities that would contradict the generalization in his specific case, but on a rule of thumb that allowed only the most cursory look at applicants over (say) the age of thirty. Did these two medical schools violate his right to be judged as an individual rather than as a member of a group?

The Davis medical school permitted whites to apply for the sixteen places reserved for members of "educationally or economically disadvantaged minorities," a phrase whose meaning might well include white ethnic minorities. In fact several whites have applied, though none has been accepted, and the California Court found that the special committee charged with administering the program had decided, in advance, against admitting any. Suppose that decision had been based on the following administrative theory: it is so unlikely that any white doctor can do as much to counteract racial imbalance in the medical professions as a well-qualified and trained black doctor can do that the committee should for reasons of convenience proceed on the presumption no white doctor could. That presumption is, as a matter of fact, more plausible than the corresponding presumption about medical students over the age of thirty, or even the presumption about applicants whose grade-point averages fall below the cutoff line. If the latter presumptions do not deny the alleged right of individuals to be judged as individuals in an admissions procedure, then neither can the former.

Colvin, in oral argument, argued the third of the catch phrases I mentioned. He said that his client had a right not to be excluded from medical school because of his race alone, and this as a statement of constitutional right sounds more plausible than claims about the right to be judged on merit or as an individual. It sounds plausible, however, because it suggests the following more complex principle. Every citizen has a constitutional right that he not suffer disadvantage, at least in the competition for any public benefit, because the race or religion or sect or region or other natural or artificial group to which he belongs is the object of prejudice or contempt.

That is a fundamentally important constitutional right, and it is that right that was systematically violated for many years by racist exclusions and anti-Semitic quotas. Color bars and Jewish quotas were not unfair just because they made race or religion relevant or because they fixed on qualities beyond individual control. It is true that blacks or Jews do not choose to be blacks or Jews. But it is also true that those who score low in aptitude or admissions tests do not choose their levels of intelligence. Nor do those denied admission because they are too old, or because they do not come from a part of the country underrepresented in the school, or because they cannot play basketball well, choose not to have the qualities that made the difference.

Race seems different because exclusions based on race have historically been motivated not by some instrumental calculation, as in the case of intelligence or age or regional distribution or athletic ability, but because of contempt for the excluded race or religion as such. Exclusion by race was in itself an insult, because it was generated by and signaled contempt.

Bakke's claim, therefore, must be made more specific than it is. He says he was kept out of medical school because of his race. Does he mean that he was kept out because his race is the object of prejudice or contempt? That suggestion is absurd. A very high proportion of those who were accepted (and, presumably, of those who run the admissions program) were members of the same race. He therefore means simply that if he had been black he would have been accepted, with no suggestion that this would have been so because blacks are thought more worthy or honorable than whites.

That is true: no doubt he would have been accepted if he were black. But it is also true, and in exactly the same sense, that he would have been accepted if he had been more intelligent, or made a better impression in his interview, or, in the case of other schools, if he had been younger when he decided to become a doctor. Race is not, in *his* case, a different matter from these other factors equally beyond his control. It is not a different matter because in his case race is not distinguished by the special character of public insult. On the contrary, the program presupposes that his race is still widely if wrongly thought to be superior to others.

In the past it made sense to say that an excluded black or Jewish student was being sacrificed because of his race or religion; that meant that his or her exclusion was treated as desirable in itself, not because it contributed to any goal in which he as well as the rest of society might take pride. Allan Bakke is being "sacrificed" because of his race only in a very artificial sense of the word. He is being "sacrificed" in the same artificial sense because of his level of intelligence, since he would have been accepted if he were more clever than he is. In both cases he is being excluded not by prejudice but that he is any less entitled to concern or respect than any black student accepted in the program. He has been disappointed, and he must have the sympathy due that disappointment, just as any other disappointed applicant—even one with much worse test scores who would not have been accepted in any event—must have sympathy. Each is disappointed because places in medical schools are scarce resources and must be used to provide what the more general society most needs. It is not Bakke's fault that racial justice is now a special need—but he has no right to prevent the most effective measures of securing that justice from being used.

12

RACISM AND SEXISM

RICHARD A. WASSERSTROM

I

Racism and sexism are two central issues that engage the attention of many persons living within the United States today. But while there is relatively little disagreement about their importance as topics, there is substantial, vehement, and apparently intractable disagreement about what individuals, practices, ideas, and institutions are either racist or sexist—and for what reasons. In dispute are a number of related questions concerning how individuals and institutions ought to regard and respond to matters relating to race or sex.

Much of the confusion in thinking and arguing about matters concerning race and sex and in trying to determine which institutions, practices, attitudes, or beliefs are either racist or sexist results, I believe, from a failure to see that there are different domains of inquiry within which any of these matters can be examined. As a result, any inquiry concerned with the question of racism or sexism, or the question of the relevance of persons' race or sex, can most profitably begin by distinguishing these domains and getting clear about which questions one is or is not seeking to answer. What I offer in this essay is, first, a general theory about the proper places or contexts within which to discuss and assess the varieties of issues and arguments which arise within this general topic, and second, a rather detailed examination of the primary questions that arise within several of these contexts. To call the overall structure a general theory is to use a somewhat pretentious phrase for marking what seem to me to be the essentially different and distinct questions that can be asked about such things as the relevance of race or sex and the defensibility or indefensibility of programs, practices, attitudes, or beliefs which take into account or concern a person's race or sex. I call it a general theory chiefly because it provides an analytic

From Richard A. Wasserstrom, 'Racism and Sexism', in Richard A. Wasserstrom, *Philosophy and Social Issues: Five Studies* (Notre Dame, Ind.: University of Notre Dame Press, 1980).

framework within which to investigate a large number of issues concerning any characteristic, like race or sex. That is to say, while this inquiry is concerned solely with issues relating to race or sex, it is my belief that this same schema—this same way of marking off questions and contexts—works just as well and in just the same manner for a consideration of comparable issues that might be addressed in respect to socioeconomic class, or religion, or any other comparable characteristic of individuals.

There are four questions, or domains of inquiry, that I think it essential to distinguish and keep separate. The first is what I call the question of the social realities. Within this domain, one is concerned with asking what is the correct, complete description of the existing social arrangements in respect to either the characteristic of race or sex. Under the category of social arrangements I mean to include such things as the existing institutional structures, laws, practices, places in society, attitudes, and ideologies—and within the idea of an ideology I include both beliefs about the facts and beliefs about the appropriateness of the existing set of arrangements.

The second question is devoted to the task of explanation. Given a description of what the social reality at any given time and place is, one can certainly ask how things got that way and by what mechanisms they tend to be perpetuated or changed. There can be, and typically is, an array of competing explanatory theories concerning the causes of the social reality and the determinants of social change and stability. For example, much of the literature about the social relations between men and women is focused upon this question of explanation. Complex and sophisticated theories utilizing the ideas of Freud, Levi-Strauss, and Marx have been developed to explain the past and present oppression of women.[1] Alternative theories, drawing upon such things as the behavior of animals, the nature of early human societies, and the psychological and physiological differences between men and women, have also been offered to explain the dominance of males.[2]

The third question is what I call the question of ideals. Within this domain one is concerned with asking the question of how things ought be arranged: if we had the good or the just society in respect to race or sex, if the social reality were changed so that it in fact conformed to our vision of what the social arrangements ought to be as to these characteristics, what would that society's institutions, practices, and ideology be in respect to matters of racial and sexual differentiation? In other words, what, if anything, would be the social significance of race or sex in a society which got things right as to

---

[1] For an example of this kind of theory see Rubin, "The Traffic in Women," in Rayna R. Reiter (ed.), *Toward an Anthropology of Women* (New York: Monthly Review Press, 1975), 157–210.

[2] For an example of this kind of theory see Lionel Tiger, *Men in Groups* (New York: Random House, 1969).

these two characteristics; when, if at all, would either individuals or institutions ever care about and make social decisions concerning the race or sex of the individuals in that society?

The fourth and final question is that of instrumentalities. Once one has developed the correct account of the social realities, and the most defensible conception of the nature of the good society, and the most adequate theory of how the social realities came about and are maintained, then the remaining question is the broadly instrumental one of the appropriate vehicle of social change. How, given all of this, might a society most effectively and fairly move from the existing state of affairs to a closer approximation of the ideal?

It is a central part of my thesis that many of the debates over matters pertaining to race or sex are less illuminating than they otherwise would be because they neglect to take into account these four different domains, each of which is important and deserving of separate consideration, and to identify clearly which of these four questions is in fact being addressed. While I do not claim that all the significant normative and conceptual questions concerning race and sex can be made to disappear or be rendered uncontroversial once these distinctions are fully grasped, I do believe that an awareness and use of these distinctions can produce valuable insights that contribute to their resolution. In particular, it can, for example, be seen quite readily that the often-asked question of whether race or sex is relevant is not as straightforward or unambiguous as may appear at first. The question may be about social realities, about how the categories of race or sex in fact function in the culture and to what effect. Or the question may be about explanations, about the theory which most adequately explains what has caused the social realities in respect to race or sex, or about the theory which most accurately identifies the features, if any, which underlie the social realities in respect to race or sex. Or the question may be about ideals, about what the good society would make of race or sex. Or the question may be about instrumentalities, about how to achieve a closer approximation of the ideal, given the social realities and the most adequate explanatory theories. When the issues are properly disentangled, one thing that is possible is that what might be an impermissible way to take race or sex into account in the ideal society, may nonetheless be a desirable and appropriate way to take race or sex into account, given the social realities.

It is these different domains and these underlying issues that I endeavor to explore. The framework is employed to clarify a number of central matters that are involved in thinking clearly about the topics of racism and sexism and the relevance of race and sex. Within this structure some of the analogies and disanalogies between racism and sexism, and race and sex, are examined—the ways they are and are not analytically interchangeable phenomena and characteristics. In this essay I look first and relatively briefly at the social realities in respect to race and to sex. Then, in the remainder of the piece I examine a good deal more fully some competing ideals concerning what the meaning and significance of race and sex would be in the good society. I set out three different conceptions of the way or degree to which any person's race or sex would be viewed as an important characteristic in the good society. I next examine various arguments which purport to establish the relevance and significance of determining whether these characteristics have a natural, as opposed to a socially created, foundation. And I then consider some moral arguments in favor of rendering both race and sex insignificant features of the social existence of persons. In the essay that follows, "Preferential Treatment," I examine, as primarily an issue to be located within the context of instrumentalities, the question of the justifiability of programs of preferential treatment. I view the entire inquiry as providing a map that helps to identify where a number of the key issues and considerations concerning race and sex belong and what further types of investigations need to be undertaken.

II

One way to think and talk about race and sex is, as I have indicated, to concentrate upon the domain of the social realities. Here one must begin by insisting that to talk about either is to talk about a particular social and cultural context.

In our own culture the first thing to observe is that race and sex are socially important categories. They are so in virtue of the fact that we live in a culture which has, throughout its existence, made race and sex extremely important characteristics of and for all the people living in the culture.[3]

---

[3] In asserting the importance of one's race and sex in our culture I do not mean to deny the importance of other characteristics—in particular, socioeconomic class. I do think that in our culture race and sex are two very important facts about a person, and I am skeptical of theories which "reduce" the importance of these features to a single, more basic one, e.g., class. But apart from this one bit of skepticism I think that all of what I have to say is compatible with several different theories concerning why race and sex are so important—including, for instance, most versions of Marxism. See, e.g., the account provided in Juliet Mitchell, *Woman's Estate* (New York: Pantheon Books, 1971).

As I have indicated, the correct causal explanation for the social realities is certainly an important question, both in its own right and for some of the issues I address. It is particularly significant for the development of an adequate program for altering the social realities to bring them closer to the ideal. Nonetheless, I have limited the scope of my inquiry to exclude a consideration of this large, difficult topic.

It is surely possible to imagine a culture, for instance, in which race would be an unimportant, insignificant characteristic of individuals. In such a culture race would be largely if not exclusively a matter of superficial physiology; a matter, we might say, simply of the way one looked. And if it were, then any analysis of race and racism would necessarily assume very different dimensions from what they do in our society. In such a culture, the meaning of the term "race" would itself have to change substantially. This can be seen by the fact that in such a culture it would literally make no sense to say of a person that he or she was "passing."[4] This is something that can be said and understood in our own culture and it shows at least that to talk of race is to talk of more than the way one looks.[5]

Sometimes, for instance, when people talk about what is wrong with affirmative action programs, or programs of preferential hiring, they say that what is wrong with such programs is that they take a thing as superficial as an individual's race and turn it into something important.[6] They say that a person's race doesn't matter; other things do, such as qualifications. Whatever else may be said of statements such as these, as descriptions of the social realities they seem to be simply false. One complex but correct empirical claim about our society is that the race of an individual is much more than a fact of superficial physiology. It is, instead, one of the dominant characteristics that affects both the way the individual looks at the world and the way the world looks at the individual. That surely need not be the case. It may in fact be very important that we work toward a society in which that would not be the case, but it is the case now and it must be understood in any adequate and complete discussion of racism and the relevance of race. That is why, too, it does not make much sense when people sometimes say, in talking about the fact that they are not racists, that they would not care if an individual were green and came from Mars, they would treat that

---

[4] Passing is the phenomenon in which a person who in some sense knows himself or herself to be black "passes" as white because he or she looks white. A version of this is described in Sinclair Lewis' novel *Kingsblood Royal* (New York: Random House, 1947), where the protagonist discovers when he is an adult that he, his father, and his father's mother are black (or, in the idiom of the late 1940s, Negro) in virtue of the fact that his great grandfather was black. His grandmother knew this and was consciously passing. When he learns about his ancestry, one decision he has to make is whether to continue to pass or to acknowledge to the world that he is in fact "Negro."

[5] That looking black is not in our culture a necessary condition for being black can be seen from the phenomenon of passing. That it is not a sufficient condition can be seen from the book *Black Like Me* (Boston: Houghton Mifflin, 1961) by John Howard Griffin, where "looking black" is easily understood by the reader to be different from being black. I suspect that the concept of being black is, in our culture, one which combines both physiological and ancestral criteria in some fairly complex, yet imprecise fashion.

[6] Justice Douglas suggests something like this in his dissent in *DeFunis*: "The consideration of race as a measure of an applicant's qualification normally introduces a capricious and irrelevant factor working an individuous discrimination." DeFunis v. Odegaard, 416 U.S. 312. 333 (1974).

individual the same way they treat people exactly like themselves. For part of *our* social and cultural history is to treat people of certain races in a certain way, and we do not have a social or cultural history of treating green people from Mars in any particular way. To put it simply, it is to misunderstand the social realities of race and racism to think of them simply as questions of how some people respond to other people whose skins are of different hues, irrespective of the social context.

The point can be put another way: Race does not function in our culture in the way eye color does. Eye color is an irrelevant category; nobody cares what color people's eyes are; it is not an important cultural fact; nothing turns on what eye color you have. It is essential to see that race is not like that at all. This truth affects, among other things, what will and will not count as cases of racism. In our culture to be nonwhite—and especially to be black[7]—is to be treated as and seen to be a member of a group that is different from and inferior to the group of standard, fully developed persons, the adult white males.

In our society, to be black is to be at a disadvantage in terms of virtually every conceivable measure of success or satisfaction—be it economic, vocational, political, or social. To see that this is so one need only conduct a simple thought experiment. If one wanted to maximize one's chances of being wealthy, satisfied with one's employment, politically powerful, secure from arbitrary treatment within the social institutions, and able to pursue one's own goals and develop one's own talents to the fullest, and if one could choose to be born either white or black, which race would one choose to be born?

An emphasis upon the actual character of the social realities was central to Mr. Justice Marshall's analysis of the way to think about the constitutionality of the program of preferential treatment at issue in the *Bakke* case. In his opinion in that case Mr. Justice Marshall sought to remind both his colleagues and the country that

[t]he position of the Negro today in America is the tragic but inevitable consequence

---

[7] There are significant respects in which the important racial distinction is between being *white* and being *nonwhite*, and there are other significant respects in which the fact of being *black* has its own special meaning and importance. My analysis is conducted largely in terms of what is involved in being black. To a considerable extent, however, what I say directly applies to the more inclusive category of being nonwhite. To the extent to which what I say does not apply to the other nonwhite racial distinctions, the analysis of those distinctions should, of course, be undertaken separately.

One unsatisfactory aspect of the position of the dissenters in the *Bakke* case is their failure to discuss the social realities in respect to the other nonwhite groups included in the Davis Medical School preferential treatment program. See, "Preferential Treatment," in Wasserstrom, *Philosophy and Social Issues*, 78–9 n. 8.

of centuries of unequal treament. Measured by any benchmark of comfort or achievement, meaningful equality remains a distant dream for the Negro.

A Negro child today has a life expectancy which is shorter by more than five years than that of a white child. The Negro child's mother is over three times more likely to die of complications in childbirth, and the infant mortality rate for Negroes is nearly twice that for whites. The median income of the Negro family is only 60% that of the median of a white family, and the percentage of Negroes who live in families with incomes below the poverty line is nearly four times greater than that of whites.

When the Negro child reaches working age, he finds that America offers him significantly less than it offers for his white counterpart. For Negro adults, the unemployment rate is twice that of whites, and the unemployment rate for Negro teenagers is nearly three times that of white teenagers. A Negro male who completes four years of college can expect a median annual income of merely $110 more than a white male who has only a high school diploma. Although Negroes represent 11.5% of the population, they are only 1.2% of the lawyers and judges, 2% of the physicians, 2.3% of the dentists, 1.1% of the engineers and 2.6% of the college and university professors.

The relationship between those figures and the history of unequal treatment afforded to the Negro cannot be denied. At every point from birth to death the impact of the past is reflected in the still disfavored position of the Negro.[8]

In short, to be black is to be a member of what was once a despised minority and what is still a disliked and oppressed one. That is part of the awful truth of our cultural and social history, and a significant feature of the social reality of our culture today.[9]

It is even easier to see that the two sexual categories, male and female, like the racial ones, are also of major social significance. Like one's race, one's sex is not merely or even primarily a matter of physiology. To appreciate this we need only realize that we can understand the idea of a transsexual. A transsexual is someone who would describe himself or herself either as a person who is essentially a female but through some accident of nature is trapped in a male body, or a person who is essentially a male but through some accident of nature is trapped in the body of a female. His (or her) description is some kind of a shorthand way of saying that he (or she) is more comfortable with the role allocated by the culture to people who are

---

[8] Regents of the University of California v. Bakke, 98 S. Ct. 2733 (1978).

[9] See, e.g., James Baldwin, *The Fire Next Time* (New York: Dial Press, 1963); W. E. B. Du Bois, *The Souls of Black Folks* (Chicago: A. C. McClurg, 1903); Ralph Ellison, *Invisible Man* (New York: Random House, 1952); John Franklin, *From Slavery to Freedom*, 3rd edn. (New York: Alfred A. Knopf, 1967); Stokley Carmichael and Charles V. Hamilton, *Black Power* (New York: Random House, 1967); *Report of the National Advisory Commission on Civil Disorders* (Washington, DC: US Government Printing Office, 1968); Kilson, "Whither Integration?" 45 *Am. Scholar* 360 (1976); and many other sources such as these that describe a great variety of features of the black experience in America: such things as the historical as well as the present-day material realities and the historical as well as present-day ideological realities—the way black people have been and are thought about within the culture. In *Kingsblood Royal* Lewis provides a powerful account of what he calls the "American Credo" about the Negro, circa 1946. Wasserstrom, *Philosophy and Social Issues*, 194–7, n. 4.

physiologically of the opposite sex. The fact that we regard this assertion of the transsexual as intelligible shows something of how deep the notion of sexual identity is in our culture and how little it has to do with physiological differences between males and females. Because people do pass in the context of race and because we can understand what passing means; because people are transsexuals and because we can understand what transsexuality means, we can see that the existing social categories of both race and sex are in this sense fundamentally social rather than natural categories.[10]

It is even clearer in the case of sex than in the case of race that one's sexual identity is a centrally important, crucially relevant category within our culture. If anything, it seems even more important and more fundamental than one's race. It is evident that there are substantially different role expectations and role assignments to persons in accordance with their sexual physiology, and that the positions of the two sexes in the culture are distinct. We have a patriarchal society of sorts in which it matters enormously whether one is a male or a female.[11] Just as with the case of race, by almost all important measures it is more advantageous to be a male rather than a female.

---

[10] I discuss the meaning and significance of "social" versus "natural" categories further in Sect. III below.

[11] One very good general account of the structure of patriarchy and of its major dimensions and attributes is that found in the chapter "Theory of Sexual Politics," in Kate Millett, *Sexual Politics* (Garden City, NY: Doubleday, 1970), 23–58. The essay seems to me to be a major contribution to an understanding of the subject. I draw upon Millett's analytic scheme in my description of the social realities of sex.

Something of the essence of the thesis is contained in the following: "[A] disinterested examination of our system of sexual relationship must point out that the situation between the sexes now, and throughout history, is a case of that phenomenon Max Weber defined as *Herrschaft*, a relationship of dominance and subordinance. What goes largely unexamined, often even unacknowledged (yet is institutionalized nonetheless) in our social order, is the birthright priority whereby males rule females. Through this system a most ingenious form of 'interior colonization' has been achieved. It is one which tends moreover to be sturdier than any form of segregation and more rigorous than class stratification, more uniform, certainly more enduring. However muted its present appearance may be, sexual dominion obtains nevertheless as perhaps the most pervasive ideology of our culture and provides its most fundamental concept of power.

"This is so because our society, like all other historical civilizations, is a patriarchy. The fact is evident at once if one recalls that the military, industry, technology, universities, science, political office, and finance—in short, every avenue of power within the society, including the coercive force of the police, is entirely in male hands. . . .

"Sexual politics obtains consent through the 'socialization' of both sexes to basic patriarchal politics with regard to temperament, role, and status. As to status, a pervasive assent to the prejudice of male superiority guarantees superior status in the male, inferior in the female. The first item, temperament, involves the formation of human personality along stereotyped lines of sex category ('masculine' and 'feminine'), based on the needs and values of the dominant group and dictated by what its members cherish in themselves and find convenient in subordinates: aggression, intelligence, force and efficacy in the male; passivity, ignorance, docility, 'virtue,' and ineffectuality in the female. This is complemented by a second factor, sex role, which decrees a consonant and highly elaborate code of conduct, gesture and attitude for each sex. In terms of activity, sex role assigns domestic service and attendance upon infants to the female, the rest of

The roles, status, and opportunities of men and women are different. We learn very early and forcefully that we are either males or females and that much turns upon which sex we are. A woman's success or failure in life is still defined largely in terms of her activities within the family. It is important for her that she marry, and when she does she is expected to take responsibility for the wifely tasks: the housework, the child care, and the general emotional welfare of the husband and children.[12] Her status in society is determined in substantial measure by the vocation and success of her husband.[13] Economically, women are substantially worse off than men. They do not receive pay for the work that is done in the home. As members of the labor force their wages are significantly lower than those paid to men, even when they are engaged in similar work and have similar educational backgrounds.[14] The higher the prestige or the salary of the job, the less likely it is that a woman will fill that job. And, of course, women are conspicuously absent from most positions of authority and power in the major political institutions of our society.

In the case of both race and sex the correct description of the social realities is provided through the rendering of a complete, composite account of the role of race or sex in the culture under examination. In this sense, the

human achievement, interest and ambition to the male. . . . Were one to analyze the three categories one might designate status as the political component, role as the sociological, and temperament as the psychological—yet their interdependence is unquestionable and they form a chain." Ibid. 24–6; footnotes omitted.

[12] "For the married woman, her husband and children must always come first; her own needs and desires, last. When the children reach school age, they no longer require constant attention. The emotional-expressive function assigned to the woman is still required of her. Called the 'stroking function' by sociologist Jessie Bernard, it consists of showing solidarity, raising the status of others, giving help, rewarding, agreeing, concurring, complying, understanding, and passively accepting. The woman is expected to give emotional support and comfort to other family members, to make them feel like good and worthwhile human beings." Deckard, *The Women's Movement* (New York: Harper & Row, 1975), 59.

"Patriarchy's chief institution is the family. It is both a mirror of and a connection with the larger society; a patriarchal unit within a patriarchal whole. Mediating between the individual and the social structure, the family effects control and conformity where political and other authorities are insufficient." Millett, *Sexual Politics*, 33.

[13] "Even if the couple consciously try to attain an egalitarian marriage, so long as the traditional division of labor is maintained, the husband will be 'more equal.' He is the provider not only of money but of status. Especially if he is successful, society values what he does; she is just a housewife. Their friends are likely to be his friends and co-workers; in their company, she is just his wife. Because his provider function is essential for the family's survival, major family decisions are made in terms of how they affect his career. He need not and usually does not act like the authoritarian paterfamilius [*sic*] of the Victorian age. His power and status are derived from his function in the family and are secure so long as the traditional division of labor is maintained." Deckard, *The Women's Movement*, 62.

[14] In 1970, women workers were, on the average, paid only 59 percent of men's wages. And when wages of persons with similar educational levels are compared, women still were paid over 40 percent less than men. Ibid. 79–81.

methodology is identical for the two characteristics. In respect to the particulars of the culture under investigation the resulting analysis may, however, reveal important differences in focus and emphasis. Such seems to be the case for race and sex in our culture. In the case of race, for example, in the case of trying to decide what it means, in terms of the kind of life one is apt to live and to be able to live if one is white or black, the significant variables seem to be such things as: formal legal and institutional rights, access to economic resources, practices relating to racial separation in such things as housing and social interaction, and the significance which the dominant ideology attaches to being black rather than white. And these are also important when it comes to trying to develop a comparable composite picture of the kind of life one is apt to live and to be able to live if one is female or one is male. But there are also other kinds of things which seem important to an answer to this question where sexual identity is concerned that are less significant where race is the relevant characteristic. There are, as has been indicated, important differences in status between males and females just as there are between blacks and whites. Concomitantly, there are important differences in the political, institutional, and economic opportunities readily open to individuals depending upon whether they are male or female. But there are also major differences in role and role expectations in the case of sex that seem less central today in the case of race. There are conventions, idealized models of behavior, and norms of what is appropriate to and expected of persons that have a much more central place in the sexual sphere than they have any longer in the racial one. The significance of race today seems to be maintained primarily through relatively impersonal institutional mechanisms, and its ideological backing and dependence upon a conception of role is weak and changing. That is why, for instance, one can today locate few if any persons who overtly and unashamedly announce themselves to be racists or who refer to the appropriate existence of different roles for blacks and whites. Sexual differences, on the other hand, are much more heavily and directly connected with and fostered by norms of appropriate behavior and the expectations these norms develop and nourish concerning the correct, natural, or proper way for males and females to seek to live their lives and interact with one another. Sex roles are a central part of the society's ideology as well as a part of its formal or material structure.

Closely connected with, and perhaps a part of this idea of sex roles, is the matter of temperament—those personal, largely psychological, attributes and characteristics that are associated with being either male or female and which are thought by the culture to be properly or appropriately displayed, depending upon the sex of the individual and the propriety of the temperament at issue. The evidence seems to be overwhelming and well documented that both sex roles and expectations concerning temperament play a fundamental role in our society in the way persons think of themselves as either male or female.[15] Men and women are socialized to see men as essentially independent, capable, powerful, active, rational, and unemotional. Men and women are socialized to view women as more limited in abilities, passive, emotional, dependent, intuitive, and weak.

Another thing that distinguishes the ideology of sex from the ideology of race is that a female, as opposed to a black, is not conceived of as simply a creature of less worth. That is an important respect in which the sexual categories are differentiated from the racial ones: the ideology of sex, as opposed to the ideology of race, is a good deal more complex and confusing. Women are both put on a pedestal and deemed not fully developed persons. They are idealized; their approval and admiration are sought; and they are at the same time regarded as less competent than men and less able to live fully developed, fully human lives—for that is what men do.[16] Because the sexual ideology is complex, variable, and even inconsistent, it does not unambiguously proclaim the lesser value attached to being female, nor does it as unambiguously correspond to the existing more material parts of the social realities. For these, among other reasons, the sexual categories could plausibly be regarded as deeper than the racial ones. They are more deeply embedded in the culture; hence they are less visible. In a corresponding

[15] See, e.g., Arlie Russell Hochschild, "A Review of Sex Role Research," 78 Am. J. Soc. 1011 (1973), which reviews and very usefully categorizes the enormous volume of literature on this topic. See also Stewart, "Social Influences on Sex Differences in Behavior," in Teitelbaum (ed.), Sex Differences (Garden City, NY: Anchor Press/Doubleday, 1976); Weitzman, "Sex-Role Socialization," in Jo Freeman (ed.), Women: A Feminist Perspective (Palo Alto, Calif.: Mayfield, 1975), 105. A number of the other pieces in Women: A Feminist Perspective also describe and analyze the role of women in the culture, including the way they are thought of by the culture.
The Women's Room by Marilyn French (New York: Harcourt Brace Jovanovich, 1977) is a powerful literary portrayal of a number of these same matters.
[16] "It is generally accepted that Western patriarchy has been much softened by the concepts of courtly and romantic love. While this is certainly true, such influence has also been vastly overestimated. In comparison with the candor of 'machismo' or oriental behavior, one realizes how much of a concession traditional chivalrous behavior represents—a sporting kind of reparation to allow the subordinate female certain means of saving face. While a palliative to the injustice of woman's social position, chivalry is also a technique for disguising it. One must acknowledge that the chivalrous stance is a game the master group plays in elevating its subject to pedestal level. Historians of courtly love stress the fact that the raptures of the poets had no effect upon the legal or economic standing of women, and very little upon their social status. As the sociologist Hugo Beigel has observed, both the courtly and the romantic versions of love are 'grants' which the male concedes out of his total powers. Both have the effect of obscuring the patriarchal character of Western culture and in their general tendency to attribute impossible virtues to women, have ended by confining them in a narrow and often remarkable conscribing sphere of behavior. It was a Victorian habit, for example, to insist the female assume the function of serving as the male's conscience and living the life of goodness he found tedious but felt someone ought to do anyway." Millett, Sexual Politics, 36–7.

fashion, sexism may be deeper than racism. Being harder to detect, it is harder to eradicate. Moreover, it is less unequivocally regarded as unjust and unjustifiable. That is to say there is less agreement within the dominant ideology that sexism even implies an unjustifiable practice or attitude.[17] For these and other reasons sexism may be a more insidious evil than racism, but there is little merit, surely, in trying to decide which of two seriously objectionable practices is worse.

Viewed from within the perspective of social reality it should be clear, too, that racism and sexism should not be thought of as phenomena that consist simply in taking a person's race or sex into account, or even simply in taking a person's race or sex into account in an arbitrary way. Instead, racism and sexism consist in taking race and sex into account in a certain way, in the context of a specific set of institutional arrangements and a specific ideology which together create and maintain a *system* of institutions and beliefs and attitudes. That system is and has been one in which political, economic, and social power and advantage are concentrated in the hands of those who are white and male.[18]

One way to bring this out, as well as to show another respect in which racism and sexism are different in their ideologies, concerns segregated bathrooms. We know, for instance, that it is wrong, clearly racist, to have racially segregated bathrooms. There is, however, no corresponding conception that it is wrong, clearly sexist, to have sexually segregated ones. How is this to be understood? The answer to the question of why it was and is racist to have racially segregated bathrooms can be discovered through a consideration of the role that this practice played in that system of racial segregation we had in the United States—from, in other words, an examination of the social realities of race. For racially segregated bathrooms were an important part of that system. That is because a part of that system was its ideology; this ideology was complex and perhaps not even wholly internally consistent. A significant feature of this ideology was that blacks were not only less than fully developed humans, but that they were also dirty and impure. They were the sorts of creatures who could and would contaminate white persons if they came into certain kinds of contact with them—in the bathroom, at the dinner table, or in bed, although it was at the same time appropriate for blacks to prepare and handle food, and even to nurse white infants. This ideology was intimately related to a set of institutional arrangements and power relationships in which whites were politically, economically, and socially dominant. The ideology supported the institutional arrangements, and the institutional arrangements reinforced the ideology. Racially

---

[17] I discuss the reasons for this in Sect. III, below.
[18] I return to this point, too, in Sect. III.

segregated bathrooms were both a part of the institutional mechanism of oppression and an instantiation of this ideology of racial taint. The point of maintaining racially segregated bathrooms was not in any simple or direct sense to keep both whites and blacks from using each other's bathrooms; it was to make sure that blacks would not contaminate bathrooms used by whites. The practice also taught both whites and blacks that certain kinds of contacts were forbidden because whites would be degraded by the contact with the blacks.

The failure to understand the character of these institutions of racial oppression is what makes some of the judicial reasoning about racial discrimination against blacks so confusing and unsatisfactory. At times when the courts have tried to explain what is constitutionally wrong with racial segregation, they have said that the problem is that race is an inherently suspect category. What they have meant by this, or have been thought to mean, is that any differentiation among human beings on the basis of racial identity is inherently unjust, because arbitrary, and therefore any particular case of racial differentiation must be shown to be fully rational and justifiable.[19] But the primary evil of the various schemes of racial segregation against blacks that the courts were being called upon to assess was not that such schemes were a capricious and irrational way of allocating public benefits and burdens. That might be the primary evil of a system of racial segregation in some other society, different in important respects from our own. Within our society, however, the primary evil of *these* schemes was that they designedly and effectively marked off all black persons as degraded, dirty, less than fully developed persons who were unfit for full membership in the political, social, and moral community.[20]

[19] Thus, in Bolling v. Sharpe, 347 U.S. 497 (1953), the Supreme Court said that what was wrong with preventing black children from attending the all white schools of the District of Columbia was that "[s]egregation in public education is not reasonably related to any proper governmental objective, and thus it imposes on Negro children of the District of Columbia a burden that constitutes an arbitrary deprivation of their liberty in violation of the Due Process Clause." Ibid. 500.

[20] Others have made this general point about the nature of the evil of racial segregation in the United States. See, e.g., John Hart Ely, "The Constitutionality of Reverse Discrimination," 41 *U. Chi. L. Rev.* 723 (1974); Owen Fiss, "Groups and Equal Protection," 5 *Phil. & Pub. Aff.* 107 (1976); Irving Thalberg, "Reverse Discrimination and the Future," 5 *Phil. Forum* 268 (1973).

The failure fully to understand this general point seems to me to be one of the things wrong with Professor Wechsler's famous article "Toward Neutral Principles of Constitutional Interpretation," 73 *Harv. L. Rev.* 1 (1959). Near the very end of the piece Wechsler reports, "In the days when I joined with Charles H. Houston [a well-known black lawyer] in a litigation in the Supreme Court, before the present building was constructed, he did not suffer more than I in knowing that we had to go to Union Station to lunch together during the recess." Ibid. 34. If the stress in that sentence is wholly on the fact of *knowing*, no one can say for certain that Professor Wechsler is wrong. But what is certain is that Charles H. Houston suffered more than Professor Wechsler from living in a system in which he, Charles H. Houston, could only lunch at Union Station because *he* was black.

It is worth observing that the social realities of sexually segregated bathrooms appear to be different. The idea behind such sexual segregation seems to have more to do with the mutual undesirability of the use by both sexes of the same bathroom at the same time. There is no notion of the possibility of contamination from use; or even directly of inferiority and superiority. What seems to be involved—at least in part—is the importance of inculcating and preserving a sense of secrecy concerning the genitalia of the opposite sex. What seems to be at stake is the maintenance of that same sense of mystery or forbiddenness about the other sex's sexuality which is fostered by the general prohibition upon public nudity and the unashamed viewing of genitalia.

Sexually segregated bathrooms play a different role in our culture than did racially segregated ones. But that is not to say that the role they play is either benign or unobjectionable—only that it is different. Sexually segregated bathrooms may well be objectionable, but here too, the objection is not on the ground that they are prima facie capricious or arbitrary. Rather, the case against them now would rest on the ground that they are, perhaps, one small part of that scheme of sex-role differentiation which uses the mystery of sexual anatomy, among other things, to maintain the primacy of hetero-sexual sexual attraction central to that version of the patriarchal system of sexual relationships we have today.[21] Whether sexually segregated bathrooms would be objectionable, because irrational, in the good society depends once again upon what the good society would look like in respect to sexual differentiation.

I do not think the brief description of our society that I have provided is either inaccurate or especially controversial. It is certainly the case, though, that the claims I have made have been stated rather imprecisely and substan-tiated with comparatively little evidence. Because I take the question of social realities to be a complex kind of empirical question, the rendering of a detailed, comprehensive answer is not within my purview as a philosopher. In a crude way, though, we are capable, I believe, both of understanding the basic assertions and seeing their essential correctness by reflecting seriously and critically upon our own cultural institutions, attitudes and practices. But in a more refined, theoretical way, I assume that a more precise and correct description of the social reality would be rendered by that composite, descriptive account of our society which utilized the relevant social sciences to examine such things as the society's institutions, practices, attitudes, and

---

[21] This conjecture about the role of sexually segregated bathrooms may well be inaccurate or incomplete. The sexual segregation of bathrooms may have more to do with privacy than with patriarchy. However, if so, it is at least odd that what the institution makes relevant is the sex of the individuals rather than merely the ability to perform the eliminatory acts in private.

ideology—if the social sciences could be value free and unaffected in outlook or approach by the fact that they, themselves, are largely pursued and conducted by persons who are white and male. Such an account would at a minimum include: (1) a description of the economic, political, and social positions of blacks and whites, and males and females in the culture; (2) a description of the sexual and racial roles, i.e., the rules, conventions, and expectations concerning how males and females, blacks and whites, should behave, and the attitudes and responses produced by these roles; and (3) a description of the existing ideology pertaining to racial and sexual differences. This would include popular beliefs about how males and females, and blacks and whites, differ, as well as the beliefs as to what accounts for these differences, these roles, and the concomitant economic, political, and social features.

The problem of empirical objectivity is, however, made difficult by the fact that part of the dominant ideology contains the belief that white males are the one group in society whose members are able to be genuinely detached and objective when it comes to things like an understanding of the place of race and sex in the culture. The hold of this ideological component is reflected, for example, in the conduct of a sex-discrimination suit that was brought against a prominent law firm. The case was assigned to Judge Constance Motley of the Federal District Court. The defendant law firm filed a motion that she be disqualified partly because, as a woman judge, she would be biased in favor of the plaintiff. Judge Motley denied the motion. Explaining her decision, Judge Motley pointed out: "[I]f background or sex or race of each judge were, *by definition*, sufficient grounds for removal, no judge on this court could hear this case, or many others, by virtue of the fact that all of them were attorneys, of a sex, often with distinguished law firm or public service backgrounds."[22]

As long as this belief in the detachment and objectivity of white males remains either an explicit or implicit part of the dominant ideology concerning inquiries into issues related to race or sex, many accounts provided by the social sciences will be suspect on this special ground, and not, for example, because of more generic methodological doubts concerning the objectivity of the social sciences. Beliefs and assumptions such as these are themselves a part of the social reality and must be understood as such.[23]

---

[22] Blank v. Sullivan and Cromwell, 418 F. Supp. 1, 4 (S.D.N.Y. 1975) writ of mandamus denied sub nom. Sullivan and Cromwell v. Motley No. 75–3045 (2d Cir. Aug. 26, 1975) (emphasis added).

[23] I discuss one respect in which this phenomenon is relevant to the justifiability of programs of preferential treatment in "Preferential Treatment," in Wasserstrom, *Philosophy and Social Issues*, 57–60.

III

Just as we can and must ask what is involved in our or any other culture in being of one race or one sex rather than the other, and how individuals are in fact viewed and treated, we can also ask a different question, namely, what would the good or just society make of an individual's race or sex, and to what degree, if at all, would racial and sexual distinctions ever properly be taken into account there? Indeed, it could plausibly be argued that we could not have a wholly adequate idea of whether a society was racist or sexist unless we had some conception of what a thoroughly nonracist or nonsexist society would look like. This question is an extremely instructive as well as an often neglected one. Comparatively little theoretical literature that deals with either racism or sexism has concerned itself in a systematic way with this issue, but as will be seen it is in some respects both a more important and a more complicated one where sex is concerned than where race is involved.[24] Moreover, as I shall argue, many discussions of sexual differences which touch upon this question do so inappropriately by concentrating upon the relatively irrelevant question of whether the differences between males and females are biological rather than social in origin.

The inquiry that follows addresses and seeks to answer two major questions. First, what are the major, plausible conceptions of what the good society would look like in respect to the race and sex of individuals, and how are these conceptions to be correctly characterized and described? And second, given a delineation of the alternatives, what is to be said in favor or against one or another of them? Here, the focus is upon two more specific issues. One concerns the relevance and force of the various arguments founded upon nature and the occurrence of natural differences for the preservation of sex roles and sexual or racial differences in the good society. The other concerns some of the central moral arguments for the elimination of sex roles and the diminution, if not elimination, of the importance of distinctions connected with one's sex or race.

In order to ask more precisely what some of the possible ideals are of desirable racial or sexual differentiation, it is necessary to ask: Differentiation in respect to what? And one way to do this is to distinguish in a crude way among three levels or areas of social and political arrangements and activities. First, there is the area of basic political rights and obligations, including such things as the rights to vote and to travel, and the obligation to pay taxes. Second, there is the area of important, but perhaps less primary

---

[24] One of the few thorough and valuable explorations of this question as it relates to sexual difference is Jaggar's "On Sexual Equality," 84 *Ethics* 275 (1974). The article also contains a very useful analysis of the views of other feminist writers who have dealt with this topic.

institutional benefits and burdens of both governmental and nongovern-
mental types. Examples are access to and employment in the significant
economic markets, the opportunity to acquire and enjoy housing in the
setting of one's choice, the right of persons who want to marry each other to
do so, and the duties (nonlegal as well as legal) that persons acquire in
getting married. And third, there is the area of individual, social interaction,
including such matters as whom one will marry, have as friends, and, perhaps, what aesthetic preferences one will cultivate and enjoy.

As to each of these three areas we can ask, for example, whether in a
nonracist or a nonsexist society it would be thought appropriate ever to take
the race or sex of an individual into account. It is, for instance, a widely held,
but by no means unanimously accepted, view that we would have the good
society in respect to race if race were to be a wholly unimportant characteristic of individuals—if, that is, race were to function in the lives of
individuals in the way in which eye color now does.

Thus, one conception of a nonracist society is that which is captured by
what I shall call the assimilationist ideal: a nonracist society would be one in
which the race of an individual would be the functional equivalent of the eye
color of individuals in our society today.[25] In our society no basic political
rights and obligations are determined on the basis of eye color. No important institutional benefits and burdens are connected with eye color. Indeed,
except for the mildest sort of aesthetic preferences, a person would be
thought odd who even made private, social decisions by taking eye color into
account. It would, of course, be unintelligible, and not just odd, were a
person to say today that while he or she looked blue-eyed, he or she regarded
himself or herself as really a brown-eyed person. Because eye color functions differently in our culture than does race, there is no analogue to passing for eye color. Were the assimilationist ideal to become a reality, the same
would be true of one's race. In short, according to the assimilationist ideal, a
nonracist society would be one in which an individual's race was of no more
significance in any of these three areas than is eye color today.

What is a good deal less familiar is an analogous conception of the good
society in respect to sexual differentiation—one in which an individual's sex
were to become a comparably unimportant characteristic. An assimilationist
society in respect to sex would be one in which an individual's sex was of
no more significance in any of the three areas than is eye color today.
There would be no analogue to transsexuality, and, while physiological or

---

[25] There is a danger in calling this ideal the "assimilationist" ideal. That term often suggests the
idea of incorporating oneself, one's values, and the like into the dominant group and its practices
and values. No part of that idea is meant to be captured by my use of the term. Mine is a
stipulative definition.

anatomical sex differences would remain, they would possess only the kind and degree of significance that today attaches to the physiologically distinct eye colors persons possess.

It is apparent that the assimilationist ideal in respect to sex does not seem to be as readily plausible and obviously attractive here as it is in the case of race. In fact, many persons invoke the possible realization of the assimilationist ideal as a reason for rejecting the Equal Rights Amendment and indeed the idea of women's liberation itself. The assimilationist ideal may be just as good and just as important an ideal in respect to sex as it is in respect to race, but it is important to realize at the outset that this appears to be a more far-reaching proposal when applied to sex rather than race and that many more persons think there are good reasons why an assimilationist society in respect to sex would not be desirable than is true for the comparable racial ideal. Before such a conception is assessed, however, it will be useful to provide a somewhat fuller characterization of its features.

To begin with, it must be acknowledged that to make the assimilationist ideal a reality in respect to sex would involve more profound and fundamental revisions of our institutions and our attitudes than would be the case in respect to race. On the institutional level we would, for instance, have to alter significantly our practices concerning marriage. If a nonsexist society is a society in which one's sex is no more significant than eye color in our society today, then laws which require the persons who are getting married to be of different sexes would clearly be sexist laws.

More importantly, given the significance of role differentiation and ideas about the psychological differences in temperament that are tied to sexual identity, the assimilationist ideal would be incompatible with all psychological and sex-role differentiation. That is to say, in such a society the ideology of the society would contain no proposition asserting the inevitable or essential attributes of masculinity or feminity; it would never encourage or discourage the ideas of sisterhood or brotherhood; and it would be unintelligible to talk about the virtues or the disabilities of being a woman or a man. In addition, such a society would not have any norms concerning the appropriateness of different social behavior depending upon whether one were male or female. There would be no conception of the existence of a set of social tasks that were more appropriately undertaken or performed by males or by females. And there would be no expectation that the family was composed of one adult male and one adult female, rather than, say, just two adults—if two adults seemed the appropriate number. To put it simply, in the assimilationist society in respect to sex, persons would not be socialized so as to see or understand themselves or others as essentially or significantly who they were or what their lives would be like because they were either male or female. And no political rights or social institutions, practices, and norms would mark the physiological differences between males and females as important.[26]

Were sex like eye color, these kinds of distinctions would make no sense. Just as the normal, typical adult is virtually oblivious to the eye color of other persons for all significant interpersonal relationships, so, too, the normal, typical adult in this kind of nonsexist society would be equally as indifferent to the sexual, physiological differences of other persons for all significant interpersonal relationships. Bisexuality, not heterosexuality or homosexuality, would be the typical intimate, sexual relationship in the ideal society that was assimilationist in respect to sex.[27]

To acknowledge that things would be very different is, of course, hardly to concede that they would thereby be undesirable—or desirable for that matter. But still, the problem is, perhaps, with the assimilationist ideal. And the assimilationist ideal is certainly not the only possible, plausible ideal.

There is, for instance, another one that is closely related to, but distinguishable from that of the assimilationist ideal. It can be understood by considering how religion rather than eye color tends to be thought about in our culture today and incorporated within social life today. If the good society were to match the present state of affairs in respect to one's religious identity, rather than the present state of affairs in respect to one's eye color, the two societies would be different, but not very greatly so. In neither would we find that the allocation of basic political rights and duties ever took an individual's religion into account. And there would be a comparable indifference to religion even in respect to most important institutional benefits

---

[26] Allison Jaggar describes something fairly close to the assimilationist view in this way: "The traditional feminist answer to this question [of what the features of a nonsexist society would be] has been that a sexually egalitarian society is one in which virtually no public recognition is given to the fact that there is a physiological sex difference between persons. This is not to say that the different reproductive function of each sex should be unacknowledged in such a society nor that there should be no physicians specializing in female and male complaints, etc. But it is to say that, except in this sort of context, the question whether someone is female or male should have no significance.

" . . . In the mainstream tradition, the nonsexist society is one which is totally integrated sexually, one in which sexual differences have ceased to be a matter of public concern." Jaggar, "On Sexual Equality," 276–7.

[27] In describing the assimilationist society in this fashion, I do not mean thereby to be addressing the question of how government and laws would regulate all of these matters, or even whether they would. I am describing what laws, practices, attitudes, conventions, ideology, behavior, and the like one would expect to find. These might be reasons, for example, why it would be undesirable to have laws that regulated interpersonal relationships and personal preferences. We have no such laws concerning eye color and interpersonal relationships and yet it is generally irrelevant in this area. If the entire cultural apparatus were different from what it now is in respect to race or sex, we can imagine that race and sex would lose their significance in the analogous ways, even in the absence of laws which regulated all dimensions of social life.

and burdens—for example, access to employment in the desirable vocations, the opportunity to live where one wished to live, and the like. Nonetheless, in the good society in which religious differences were to some degree socially relevant, it would be deemed appropriate to have some institutions (typically those which are connected in an intimate way with these religions) which did in a variety of ways properly take the religion of members of the society into account. For example, it would be thought both permissible and appropriate for members of a religious group to join together in collective associations which have religious, educational, and social dimensions, and when it came to the employment of persons who were to be centrally engaged in the operation of those religious institutions (priests, rabbis and ministers, for example), it would be unobjectionable and appropriate explicitly to take the religion of job applicants into account. On the individual, interpersonal level, it might also be thought natural and possibly even admirable, were persons to some significant degree to select their associates, friends, and mates on the basis of their religious orientation. So there is another possible and plausible ideal of what the good society would look like in respect to a particular characteristic in which differences based upon that characteristic would be to some degree maintained in some aspects of institutional and interpersonal life. The diversity of the religious beliefs of individuals would be reflected in the society's institutional and ideological fabric in a way in which the diversity of eye color would not be in the assimilationist society. The picture is a more complex, somewhat less easily describable one than that of the assimilationist ideal.

There could be at least two somewhat different reasons why persons might think it preferable to have some ideal different from that of the assimilation-ist one in respect to religion. They might, for instance, think that heterodoxy in respect to religious belief and practice was a positive good. On this view they would see it as a loss—they would think it a worse society—were every-one to be a member of the same religion. Or they might, instead, view heterodoxy in respect to religious belief and practice more as a necessary, lesser evil. On this view they would see nothing intrinsically better about diversity rather than uniformity in respect to religion, but they might also think that the evils of achieving anything like homogeneity far outweighed the possible benefits. That is to say, persons holding this position might believe, for instance, that there was one correct religion and that it would be good were everyone to accept and be a member of that religion, but they might also believe that it would be undesirable and wrong to try to structure the social and political institutions, or the socialization of persons in the society, in such a way that social benefits and burdens were distributed in accordance with one's religion or that significantly different norms of social behavior ought to be connected with being of one religion or the other. Because persons favoring religious diversity for either reason would desire and expect different religions to exist in the good society, and because religions themselves are composed of and require certain institutional structures of varying degrees of formality and complexity, the good society modeled upon this ideal would necessarily contain some acceptable social and interpersonal differentiation based upon the religious identity of the individuals in the society. As such, the rendering of the precise description of the right degree of differentiation based upon religion would be a more complex and more difficult undertaking than is true for the assimilationist ideal.

Nonetheless, it may be that in respect to sex, and conceivably, in respect to race, too, something more like this ideal of diversity in respect to religion is the right one. But one problem then—and it is a more substantial one than is sometimes realized—is to specify with a good deal of precision and care what that ideal really comes to in the matter of sexual or racial identity and degree of acceptable sexual or racial differentiation. Which institutional and personal differentiations would properly be permissible and which would not be? Which attiudes, beliefs, and role expectations concerning the meaning and significance of being male or female would be properly introduced and maintained in the good society and which would not be? Which attitudes, beliefs, and practices would continue in the good society to constitute the meaning of ethnicity as a racial concept and which would have to be purged? Part, but by no means all, of the attractiveness of the assimilationist ideal is its clarity and simplicity. In the good society of the assimilationist sort we would be able to tell easily and unequivocally whether any law, practice, attitude, or form of socialization was in any respect either racist or sexist. Part, but by no means all, of the unattractiveness of any more pluralistic ideal concerning sex or race is that it makes the question of what is racist or sexist a much more difficult and complicated one to answer. But although simplicity and lack of ambiguity may be virtues, they are not the only virtues to be taken into account in deciding among competing ideals. We quite appropriately take other considerations to be relevant to an assessment of the value and worth of alternative, possible conceptions of nonracist and nonsexist societies. What has been said so far by no means settles the question.

Nor do I even mean to suggest that all persons who reject the assimilationist ideal in respect to sex would necessarily embrace something like the kind of pluralistic ideal I have described as matching something like our present arrangements and ideas concerning the relevance of religious identity— although these do seem to exhaust the plausible ideals in respect to race.

Some persons might think the right ideal was one in which substantially greater sexual differentiation and sex-role identification were retained than would be the case within a good society of that general type. Thus, someone might believe, for instance, that the good society was, perhaps, essentially like the one they think we now have in respect to sex: equality of basic political rights, such as the right to vote, but all of the sexual differentiation in both legal and nonlegal, formal and informal institutions, all of the sex-role socialization and all of the differences in matters of temperament that are characteristic of the way in which our society has been and still is ordered. And someone might also believe that the prevailing ideological concomitants of these arrangements are the correct and appropriate ones to perpetuate.[28]

This could, of course, be regarded as a version of the pluralistic ideal described above, with the emphasis upon the extensive character of the institutional, normative, and personal differences connected with sexual identity. Whether it is a form of this pluralistic ideal or a different ideal altogether turns, I think, upon two things: first, how pervasive the sexual differentiation is in terms of the number, importance, and systemic interconnectedness of the institutions and role expectations connected with being of one sex or the other, and, second, whether the ideal contains within it a conception of the appropriateness of significant institutional and interpersonal inequality, e.g., that the woman's job is in large measure to serve and be dominated by the male. The more either or both of these features is present, the clearer is the case for regarding this as an ideal, distinctively different from either of the other two described so far. I shall indicate later why I think these two features make such a difference.

But the next question is that of how a choice is rationally to be made among these different, possible ideals. One general set of issues concerns the empirical sphere, because the question of whether something is a plausible and attractive ideal does turn in part on the nature of the empirical world. If

---

[28] Thus, for example, a column appeared a few years ago in the *Washington Star* concerning the decision of the Cosmos Club to continue to refuse to permit women to be members. The author of the column (and a member of the club) defended the decision on the ground that women appropriately had a different status in the society. Their true distinction was to be achieved by being faithful spouses and devoted mothers. The column closed with this paragraph:

"In these days of broken homes, derision of marriage, reluctance to bear children, contempt for the institution of the family—a phase in our national life when it seems more honorable to be a policewoman, or a model, or an accountant than to be a wife or mother—there is a need to reassert a traditional scale of values in which the vocation of homemaker is as honorable and distinguished as any in political or professional life. Such women, as wives and widows of members, now enjoy in the club the privileges of their status, which includes [*sic*] their own drawing rooms, and it is of interest that they have been among the most outspoken opponents of the proposed changes in club structure." Groseclose, "Now—Shall we Join the Ladies?" *Washington Star*, Mar. 13, 1975.

it is true, for example, that any particular characteristic, such as an individual's race or sex, is not only a socially significant category in our culture but that it is largely a socially created one as well, then for many people a number of objections to the assimilationist ideal appear immediately to disappear. The other general set of issues concerns the relevant normative considerations. Here the key questions concern the principles and considerations by which to assess and evaluate different conceptions of how persons ought to be able to live and how their social institutions ought to be constructed and arranged. I begin with the empirical considerations and constraints, although one heuristic disadvantage in doing so is that this decision may appear to give them greater weight than, as I shall argue, they in fact deserve.

What opponents of assimilationism and proponents of schemes of strong sexual differentiation seize upon is that sexual difference appears to be a naturally occurring category of obvious and inevitable relevance for the construction of any plausible conception of the nature of the good society.[29] The problems with this way of thinking are twofold. To begin with, a careful and thorough analysis of the social realities would reveal, I believe, that it is the socially created sexual differences which constitute most of our conception of sex differences and which tend in fact to matter the most in the way we live our lives as persons of one sex or the other. For, it is, I think, sex-role differentiation and socialization, not the physiological and related biological differences—if there are any—that make men and women as different as they are from each other, and it is these same sex-role-created differences which are invoked to justify the necessity or the desirability of most sexual differentiation proposed to be maintained at any of the levels of social arrangements and practices described earlier.[30]

[29] This is not to deny that certain people believe that race is linked with characteristics that prima facie are relevant. Such beliefs persist. They are, however, unjustified by the evidence. See, e.g., N. Block and R. Dworkin, "IQ, Heritability and Inequality," 3 *Phil. & Pub. Aff.* 331 (1974); 4 *Phil. & Pub. Aff.* 40 (1974). More to the point, even if it were true that such a linkage existed, none of the characteristics suggested would require that political or social institutions, or interpersonal relationships, would have to be structured in a certain way.

[30] See, e.g., authorities cited in n. 15, above; M. Mead, *Sex and Temperament in Three Primitive Societies* (New York: Morrow, 1935).

"These three situations [the cultures of the Anapesh, the Mundugumor, and the Tchambuli] suggest, then, a very definite conclusion. If those temperamental attitudes which we have traditionally regarded as feminine—such as passivity, responsiveness, and a willingness to cherish children—can so easily be set up as the masculine pattern in one tribe, and in another to be outlawed for the majority of women as well as for the majority of men, we no longer have any basis for regarding such aspects of behaviour as sex-linked.

" . . . We are forced to conclude that human nature is almost unbelievably malleable, responding accurately and contrastingly to contrasting cultural conditions. . . . Standardized personality differences between the sexes are of this order, cultural creations to which each generation, male and female is trained to conform." Ibid. 190–1.

It is important, however, not to attach any greater weight than is absolutely necessary to the truth or falsity of this causal claim about the source of the degree of sexual distinctions that exist in our or other cultures. For what is significant, although seldom recognized, is the fact that the answer to that question almost never goes very far in settling the question of what the good society should look like in respect to any particular characteristic of individuals. And the answer certainly does not go as far as many persons appear to believe it does to settle that question of the nature of the good society.

Let us suppose that there are what can be called "naturally occurring" sexual differences and even that they are of such a nature that they are in some sense of direct prima facie social relevance. It is essential to see that this would by no means settle the question of whether in the good society sex should or should not be as minimally significant as eye color. Even if there are major or substantial biological differences between men and women that are in this sense "natural" rather than socially created, this does not determine the question of what the good society can and should make of these differences—without, that is, begging the question by including within the meaning of "major" or "substantial" or "natural" the idea that these are things that ought to be retained, emphasized, or otherwise normatively taken into account. It is not easy to see why, without begging the question, it should be thought that this fact, if it is a fact, settles the question adversely to anything like the assimilationist ideal. Persons might think that truths of this sort about nature or biology do affect, if not settle, the question of what the good society should look like for at least two different reasons.

In the first place, they might think the differences are of such a character that they substantially affect what would be *possible* within a good society of human persons. Just as the fact that humans are mortal necessarily limits the features of any possible good society, so, they might argue, the fact that

---

A somewhat different view is expressed in Julia Ann Sherman, *On the Psychology of Women* (Springfield, Ill.: C. C. Thomas, 1975). There the author suggests that there are "natural" differences of a psychological sort between men and women, the chief ones being aggressiveness and strength of sex drive. See ibid. 238. However, even if she is correct as to these biologically based differences, this does little to establish what the good society should look like.

Almost certainly the most complete discussion of this topic is Eleanor Macoby and Carol Nagy Jacklin, *The Psychology of Sex Differences* (Stanford, Calif.: Stanford University Press, 1974). The authors conclude that the sex differences which are, in their words, "fairly well established," are: (1) that girls have greater verbal ability than boys; (2) that boys excel in visual-spacial ability; (3) that boys excel in mathematical ability; and (4) that males are aggressive. Ibid. 351–2. They conclude, in respect to the etiology of these psychological sex differences, that there appears to be a biological component to the greater visual-special ability of males and to their greater aggressiveness. Ibid. 360.

males and females are physiologically or biologically different limits in the same way the features of any possible good society.[31]

In the second place, they might think the differences are of such a character that they are relevant to the question of what would be *desirable* in the good society. That is to say, they might not think that the differences determine or affect to a substantial degree what is possible, but only that the differences are appropriately taken into account in any rational construction of an ideal social existence.

The second reason seems to be a good deal more plausible than the first. For there appear to be very few, if any, respects in which the ineradicable, naturally occurring differences between males and females *must* be taken into account. The industrial revolution has certainly made any of the general differences in strength between the sexes capable of being ignored by the good society for virtually all significant human activities.[32] And even if it were true that women are naturally better suited than men to care for and nurture children, it is also surely the case that men can be taught to care for and nurture children well.[33] Indeed, the one natural or biological fact that seems *required* to be taken into account is the fact that reproduction of the human species requires that the fetus develop *in utero* for a period of

---

[31] As H. L. A. Hart has observed in a different context, if humans had a different physical structure such that they were virtually invulnerable to physical attack or assault by other humans, this would alter radically the character or role of substantial segments of the criminal and civil law. H. L. A. Hart, *The Concept of Law* (Oxford: Clarendon Press. 1961), 190. But humans are, of course, not like this at all. The fact that humans are vulnerable to injury by others is a natural fact that affects the features of any meaningful conception of the good society.

[32] As Sherman observes, "Each sex has its own special physical assets and liabilities. The principal female liability of less muscular strength is not ordinarily a handicap in a civilized, mechanized, society. . . . There is nothing in the biological evidence to prevent women from taking a role of equality in a civilized society." Sherman, *On the Psychology of Women*, 11.

There are, of course, some activities that would be sexually differentiated in the assimilationist society, namely, those that were specifically directed toward, say, measuring unaided physical strength. Thus, I think it likely that even in this ideal society, weight-lifting contests and boxing matches would in fact be dominated perhaps exclusively so, by men. But it is hard to find any significant activities or institutions that are analogous. And it is not clear that such insignificant activities would be thought worth continuing, especially since sports function in existing patriarchal societies to help maintain the dominance of males. See Millett, *Sexual Politics*, 48–9.

It is possible that there are some nontrivial activities or occupations that depend sufficiently directly upon unaided physical strength that most if not all women would be excluded. Perhaps being a lifeguard at the ocean is an example. Even here, though, it would be important to see whether the way lifeguarding had traditionally been done could be changed to render such physical strength unimportant. If it could be changed, then the question would simply be one of whether the increased cost (or loss of efficiency) was worth the gain in terms of equality and the avoidance of sex-role differentiation. In a nonpatriarchal society very different from ours, where sex was not a dominant social category, the argument from efficiency might well prevail. What is important, once again, is to see how infrequent and peripheral such occupational cases are.

[33] Once again, though, I believe there is substantial evidence that to sex-role socialization and not to biology is far more plausibly attributed the dominant causal role in the relative child-rearing capacities and dispositions of men and women in our and other societies.

months. Sexual intercourse is not necessary, for artificial insemination is available. Neither marriage nor the nuclear family is necessary either for conception or child rearing. Given the present state of medical knowledge and what might be termed the natural realities of female pregnancy, it is difficult to see why any important institutional or interpersonal arrangements are constrained to take the existing biological differences as to the phenomenon of *in utero* pregnancy into account.

But to say all this is still to leave it a wholly open question to what degree the good society *ought* to build upon any ineradicable biological differences, or to create ones in order to construct institutions and sex roles which would thereby maintain a substantial degree of sexual differentiation. The way to answer that question is to consider and assess the arguments for and against doing so. What is significant is the fact that many of the arguments for doing so are less persuasive than they appear to be upon the initial statement of this possibility.

It might be argued, for instance, that the fact of menstruation could be used as a premise upon which to base the case for importantly different social roles for females than for males. But this could only plausibly be proposed if two things were true: first, that menstruation would be debilitating to women and hence relevant to social role even in a culture which did not teach women to view menstruation as a sign of uncleanliness or as a curse;[34] and, second, that the way in which menstruation necessarily affected some or all women was in fact necessarily related in an important way to the role in question. But even if both of these were true, it would still be an open

---

[34] See, e.g., Paige, "Women Learn to Sing the Menstrual Blues," in C. Tavis (ed.), *The Female Experience* (Del Mar, Calif.: CRM, 1973), 17.

"I have come to believe that the 'raging hormones' theory of menstrual distress simply isn't adequate. All women have the raging hormones, but not all women have menstrual symptoms, nor do they have the same symptoms for the same reasons. Nor do I agree with the 'raging neurosis' theory, which argues that women who have menstrual symptoms are merely whining neurotics, who need only a kind pat on the head to cure their problems.

"We must instead consider the problem from the perspective of women's subordinate social position, and of the cultural ideology that so narrowly defines the behaviors and emotions that are appropriately 'feminine.' Women have perfectly good reasons to react emotionally to reproductive events. Menstruation, pregnancy and childbirth—so sacred, yet so unclean—are the woman's primary avenues of achievement and self-expression. Her reproductive abilities define her femininity; other routes to success are only second-best in this society.

"... My current research on a sample of 114 societies around the world indicates that ritual observances and taboos about menstruation are a method of controlling women and their fertility. Men apparently use such rituals, along with those surrounding pregnancy and childbirth, to assert their claims to women and their children.

"... The hormone theory isn't giving us much mileage, and it's time to turn it in for a better model, one that looks to our beliefs about menstruation and women. It is no mere coincidence that women get the blue meanies along with an event they consider embarrassing, unclean—and a curse." Ibid. 21.

question whether any sexual differentiation ought to be built upon these facts. The society could still elect to develop institutions that would nullify the effect of these natural differences and it would still be an open question whether it ought to do so. Suppose, for example, what seems implausible—that some or all women will not be able to perform a particular task while menstruating, e.g., guard the border of a country. It would be possible, even easy, if the society wanted to, to arrange for substitute guards for the women who were incapacitated. We know that persons are not good guards when they are sleepy, and we make arrangements so that persons alternate guard duty to avoid fatigue. The same could be done for menstruating women, even given the implausibly strong assumptions about menstruation.

The point that is involved here is a very general one that has application in contexts having nothing to do with the desirability or undesirability of maintaining substantial sexual differentiation. It has to do with the fact that humans possess the ability to alter their natural and social environment in distinctive, dramatic, and unique ways. An example from the nonsexual area can help bring out this too seldom recognized central feature. It is a fact that some persons born in human society are born with congenital features such that they cannot walk or walk well on their legs. They are born naturally crippled or lame. However, humans in our society certainly possess the capability to devise and construct mechanical devices and institutional arrangements which render this natural fact about some persons relatively unimportant in respect to the way they and others will live together. We can bring it about, and in fact are in the process of bringing it about, that persons who are confined to wheelchairs can move down sidewalks and across streets because the curb stones at corners of intersections have been shaped so as to accommodate the passage of wheelchairs. And we can construct and arrange buildings and events so that persons in wheelchairs can ride elevators, park cars, and be seated at movies, lectures, meetings, and the like. Much of the environment in which humans live is the result of their intentional choices and actions concerning what that environment shall be like. They can elect to construct an environment in which the natural incapacity of some persons to walk or walk well is a major difference or a difference that will be effectively nullified vis-à-vis the lives that they, too, will live.

Nonhuman animals cannot do this in anything like the way humans can. A fox or an ape born lame is stuck with the fact of lameness and the degree to which that will affect the life it will lead. The other foxes or apes cannot change things. This capacity of humans to act intentionally and thereby continuously create and construct the world in which they and others will live is at the heart of what makes studies of nonhuman behavior essentially irrelevant to and for most if not all of the normative questions of social, political, and moral theory. Humans can become aware of the nature of their natural and social environment and then act intentionally to alter the environment so as to change its impact upon or consequences for the individuals living within it. Nonhuman animals cannot do so. This difference is, therefore, one of fundamental theoretical importance. At the risk of belaboring the obvious, what it is important to see is that the case against any picture of the good society of an assimilationist sort—if it is to be a defensible critique—ought to rest on arguments concerned to show why some other ideal would be preferable; it cannot plausibly rest in any significant respect upon the claim that the sorts of biological differences typically alluded to in contexts such as these require that the society not be assimilationist in character.

There are, though, several other arguments based upon nature, or the idea of the "natural" that also must be considered and assessed. First, it might be argued that if a way of doing something is natural, then it ought to be done that way. Here, what may be meant by "natural" is that this way of doing the thing is the way it would be done if culture did not direct or teach us to do it differently. It is not clear, however, that this sense of "natural" is wholly intelligible; it supposes that we can meaningfully talk about how humans would behave in the absence of culture. And few if any humans have ever lived in such a state. Moreover, even if this is an intelligible notion, the proposal that the natural way to behave is somehow the appropriate or desirable way to behave is strikingly implausible. It is, for example, almost surely natural, in this sense of "natural," that humans would eat their food with their hands, except for the fact that they are, almost always, socialized to eat food differently. Yet, the fact that humans would naturally eat this way, does not seem in any respect to be a reason for believing that that is thereby the desirable or appropriate way to eat food. And the same is equally true of any number of other distinctively human ways of behaving.

Second, someone might argue that substantial sexual differentiation is natural not in the sense that it is biologically determined nor in the sense that it would occur but for the effects of culture, but rather in the sense that substantial sexual differentiation is a virtually universal phenomenon in human culture. By itself, this claim of virtual universality, even if accurate, does not directly establish anything about the desirability or undesirability of any particular ideal. But it can be made into an argument by the addition of the proposition that where there is a widespread, virtually universal social practice or institution, there is probably some good or important purpose served by the practice or institution. Hence, given the fact of substantial sex-role differentiation in all, or almost all, cultures, there is on this view some reason to think that substantial sex-role differentiation serves some important purpose for and in human society.

This is an argument, but it is hard to see what is attractive about it. The premise which turns the fact of sex-role differentiation into any kind of a strong reason for sex-role differentiation is the premise of conservatism. And it is no more or less convincing here than elsewhere. There are any number of practices or institutions that are typical and yet upon reflection seem without significant social purpose. Slavery was once such an institution; war perhaps still is.

More to the point, perhaps, the concept of "purpose" is ambiguous. It can mean in a descriptive sense "plays some role" or "is causally relevant." Or, it can mean in a prescriptive sense "does something desirable" or "has some useful function." If "purpose" is used descriptively in the conservative premise, then the argument says nothing about the continued desirability of sex-role differentiation or the assimilationist ideal. If "purpose" is used prescriptively in the conservative premise, then there is no reason to think that premise is true.[35]

To put it another way, the question that seems fundamentally to be at issue is whether it is desirable to have a society in which sex-role differences are to be retained in the way and to the degree they are today—or even at all. The straightforward way to think about the question is to ask what would be good and what would be bad about a society in which sex functioned like eye color does in our society; or alternatively, what would be good and what would be bad about a society in which sex functioned in the way in which religious identity does today; or alternatively, what would be good and what would be bad about a society in which sex functioned in the way in which it does today. We can imagine what such societies would look like and how they might work. It is hard to see how thinking about answers to this question is substantially advanced by reference to what has typically or always been the case. If it is true, for instance, that the sex-role-differentiated societies that have existed have tended to concentrate power and authority in the hands of males, have developed institutions and ideologies that have perpetuated that concentration, and have restricted and prevented women from living the kinds of lives that persons ought to be able to live for themselves, then this, it seems to me, says far more about what may be wrong with any strongly nonassimilationist ideal than does the conservative premise say what may be right about any strongly nonassimilationist ideal.

This does not, however, exhaust the reasons why persons might think that the question of whether sex differences are naturally occurring differences is

---

[35] See also Joyce Trebilcot, "Sex Roles: The Argument from Nature," 85 *Ethics* 249 (1975).

an important or relevant one. There are at least two others. First, if the differences are natural, rather than socially created, it might be thought that there is less of an obligation to correct or alter the impact or effect that those differences will play in the lives people will be able to live in the society. That is to say, if it is nature, or biology, that accounts for the differences that result, then the society is not causally responsible and for that reason is not to blame for or accountable for those differences. The cause is not society, but nature. If society were the cause, and if the differences produced arrangements that seemed unequal or unfair, then the fault would be society's and its obligation to remedy the situation would be clearer, more direct, and more stringent. But since it is not, the causal chain is different and society is, for this reason, off the hook of accountability. An argument such as this one is seldom made explicit, but it underlies, I suspect, much of the motivation for the belief in the relevance of the search for natural as opposed to social causation.

The difficulty here is that only if the question is cast in terms of a certain very particular conception of compensatory justice does the causal issue assume genuine relevance or importance. What remains unexplained is why that perspective should be seen to be the obviously correct or appropriate one from which to look at matters. For if the question were to be cast, instead, in terms of a conception of distributive justice—one that was, say, founded upon the importance of a *resulting* equality of distributional treatment—then the cause of the initial differences or inequalities becomes a substantially less significant issue. And, if the focus were to be on the more general question of what kind of society it would be desirable to have, then the correct causal explanation would be still less important. Consider again the fact that some persons are born lame while others are not. Even though social institutions did not cause the lameness at all, it is difficult to understand how that is at all decisive to the question of what the good society would do in the way of seeking to nullify the natural consequences of lameness through having certain institutions and arrangements rather than others. If the cause of undesirable existing inequalities or differences is socially created, then there is an additional argument of a compensatory sort of requiring that the society make the alterations necessary to change the operative social mechanisms. But the absence of such an argument in no way implies that things may therefore be appropriately or justly left the way nature has produced them.

The other argument is that if the differences are natural, then there are considerations of efficiency that come into play. If some persons are naturally less equipped or suited to do some things, then it will be less efficient than would otherwise be the case to bring it about that they will end up being able to do those things—either because they will not be able to do them as well as others, or because it will be most costly to bring it about that they will be able to do them as well as others who are differently endowed can do them. Here, too, there is, I think, something to the argument, but not as much as is typically supposed. If it is possible to arrange things so that the natural differences can be nullified, and if there are reasons of justice (or reasons of morality) for doing so, then it is as hard here, as elsewhere, to see why considerations of efficiency should necessarily be thought overriding.

There are, in fact, several different issues and arguments that may be involved here, and it is worthwhile trying to disentangle them. One issue is whether what underlies this line of thought is the view that all persons ought to be *required* to do whatever it is they are naturally endowed to do, and that, therefore, the social institutions should be designed so as to bring that state of affairs into being. On this view, if a person were naturally endowed to be a brain surgeon, or a garbage collector, the social institutions ought to at least direct if not require the person to end up in that role or place—irrespective of the person's desires and irrespective of the kind and quality of life allotted to the persons with differing natural endowments. A society organized in this fashion would, doubtless, be highly efficient in terms of the correspondence between natural endowments and places in society and the degree to which each person was living the life he or she was "naturally" suited for, but I do not see how one could easily argue that such a "naturally" ordered society would be either just or morally desirable. Apart from everything else, if one wanted a nice philosophical example of a case of viewing persons wholly as a means—a case of using persons as objects—a society organized and justified along these lines would seem to be an obvious candidate.

But the argument about nature and efficiency may not be this sweeping. Perhaps instead the claim is only that in the good society at least those persons who are especially able or competent ought to be permitted to do what they are naturally able or competent to do. This is a substantially weaker thesis, and I shall assume for purposes of argument that it is defensible. This thesis is not, however, fundamentally at issue. The primary question is whether the society ought to be organized so that the less well endowed will be able to do things, live their lives, in a way that is more fully adequate and satisfactory. If some are naturally able to do certain things well, while others are less able naturally to do them, one complaint the better endowed could have about attempts to increase the abilities and opportunities of the less well endowed is that based upon the overall social cost involved in doing so. But the better endowed do not have a claim that, just because they happen to be better endowed by nature, they *alone* should have the opportunity to participate in institutions that depend upon or require certain abilities, talents, dispositions, and the like. They can claim that different social structures may be less efficient in terms of overall cost of having those social structures than ones in which they alone participate. But if there are considerations of justice or morality that favor these alternative "more expensive" arrangements, it seems plausible that considerations of efficiency should at least to some degree give way.

Perhaps, though, they have one other argument, namely, that if alternative social arrangements are to be preferred, then the society will be one in which the institutions do not permit them to utilize their natural talents to the fullest extent. This may be just a restatement of the argument from efficiency, or it may be an argument that the better endowed deserve to be able always to utilize their natural talents to the fullest.[36]

I do not think they can claim to deserve to be able always to utilize their natural talents to the fullest. They cannot claim this because, *ex hypothesi* since these are natural talents or capabilities, they manifestly did nothing to deserve these natural attributes.[37] And while it may be good to permit them to utilize their talents—in terms of the happiness of those who are naturally better endowed—there is no reason to give their claims any greater weight than the claims of others on the ground that their talents or characteristics are naturally rather than socially produced. And it even seems plausible, for reasons analogous to those offered by Rawls for the difference principle, that if there are sacrifices of any sort to be made, it is fairer that they be made or borne by the naturally better rather than naturally worse off.

So, even supposing that there is a clear sense of natural endowments or capabilities based on sexual physiology, and even supposing that the natural differences between males and females were as strongly present "in nature" as the preceding arguments require, the conclusions to be drawn vis-à-vis the character of the good society would be appreciably weaker and more indeterminate than is typically supposed by those who focus upon the possible existence of biological differences between the sexes. The primary point that emerges is that the question of whether there are natural differences (in any of the above senses) between males and females (or even persons of different races) tends to get disputed on the wrong grounds. The debate tends to focus upon whether biology or society is the cause of the differ-

---

[36] Thomas Nagel suggests that the educationally most talented deserve, as a matter of "educational justice," the opportunity to develop their talents to the fullest. Thomas Nagel, "Equal Treatment and Compensatory Discrimination," 2 *Phil. & Pub. Aff.* 348, 356 (1973).

I do not find the concept of educational justice a clear or even wholly intelligible one. Nor, I think, has Nagel adequately explained why this is a matter of desert at all.

[37] What, if anything, the most qualified deserve because they are the most qualified is an issue I discuss more fully in "Preferential Treatment," in Wasserstrom, *Philosophy and Social Issues*, 68–77.

ences. The debate ought to attend instead to the question of why it matters. The debaters ought to address first the unasked question of within what theoretical inquiry the issue is even relevant. When the question is one of ideals, of what the good society would make of sexual or racial character- istics, the issue of natural as opposed to social causation is a strikingly irrelevant one. There do not, therefore, appear to be any very powerful, let alone conclusive, arguments against something like the assimilationist society that can be based on any of the different, possible appeals to nature and the natural.

If the chief thing to be said in favor of something like the assimilationist society in respect to sex is that some arguments against it are not very relevant, that does not by itself make a very convincing case. Such is not, however, the way in which matters need be left. There is an affirmative case of sorts for something like the assimilationist society.

One strong, affirmative moral argument on behalf of the assimilationist ideal is that it does provide for a kind of individual autonomy that a sub- stantially nonassimilationist society cannot provide. The reason is because any substantially nonassimilationist society will have sex roles, and sex roles interfere in basic ways with autonomy. The argument for these two proposi- tions proceeds as follows.

Any nonassimilationist society must have some institutions and some ideology that distinguishes between individuals in virtue of their sexual physiology, and any such society will necessarily be committed to teaching the desirability of doing so. That is what is implied by saying it is nonassimilationist rather than assimilationist. And any substantially nonassimilationist society will make one's sexual identity an important characteristic so that there will be substantial psychological, role, and status differences between persons who are male and those who are female. That is what is implied by saying that it is substantially nonassimilationist. Any such society will necessarily have sex roles, a conception of the places, character- istics, behaviors, etc., that are appropriate to one sex or the other but not both. That is what makes it a *sex* role.

Now, sex roles are, I think, morally objectionable on two or three quite distinct grounds. One such ground is absolutely generic and applies to all sex roles. The other grounds are less generic and apply only to the kinds of sex roles with which we are familiar and which are a feature of patriarchal societies, such as our own. I begin with the more contingent, less generic objections.

We can certainly imagine, if we are not already familiar with, societies in which the sex roles will be such that the general place of women in that society can be described as that of the servers of men. In such a society individuals will be socialized in such a way that women will learn how properly to minister to the needs, desires, and interests of men; women and men will both be taught that it is right and proper that the concerns and affairs of men are more important than and take precedence over those of women; and the norms and supporting set of beliefs and attitudes will be such that this role will be deemed the basic and appropriate role for women to play and men to expect. Here, I submit, what is objectionable about the connected set of institutions, practices, and ideology—the structure of the prevailing sex role—is the role itself. It is analogous to a kind of human slavery. The fundamental moral defect—just as is the case with slavery—is not that women are being arbitrarily or capriciously assigned to the social role of server, but that such a role itself has no legitimate place in the decent or just society. As a result, just as is the case with slavery, the assignment on *any* basis of individuals to such a role is morally objectionable. A society arranged so that such a role is a prominent part of the structure of the social institutions can be properly characterized as an *oppressive* one. It consigns some individuals to lives which have no place in the good society, which restrict unduly the opportunities of these individuals, and which do so in order improperly to enhance the lives and opportunities of others.

But it may be thought possible to have sex roles and all that goes with them without having persons of either sex placed within a position of general, systemic dominance or subordination. Here, it would be claimed, the society would not be an oppressive one in this sense. Consider, for example, the kinds of sex roles with which we are familiar and which assign to women the primary responsibilities for child rearing and household maintenance. It might be argued first that the roles of child rearer and household maintainer are not in themselves roles that could readily or satisfactorily be eliminated from human society without the society itself being deficient in serious, unacceptable ways. It might be asserted, that is, that these are roles or tasks that simply must be filled if children are to be raised in a satisfactory way. Suppose this is correct, suppose it is granted that society would necessarily have it that these tasks would have to be done. Still, if it is also correct that, relatively speaking, these are unsatisfying and unfulfilling ways for humans to concentrate the bulk of their energies and talents, then, to the degree to which this is so, what is morally objectionable is that if this is to be a *sex* role, then women are unduly and unfairly allocated a disproportionate share of what is unpleasant, unsatisfying, unrewarding work. Here the objection is the degree to which the burden women are required to assume is excessive and unjustified vis-à-vis the rest of society, i.e., the men. Unsatisfactory roles and tasks, when they are substantial and pervasive, should surely be allocated and filled in the good society in a way which seeks to distribute the burdens involved in a roughly equal fashion.

Suppose, though, that even this feature were eliminated from sex roles, so that, for instance, men and women shared more equally in the dreary, unrewarding aspects of housework and child care, and that a society which maintained sex roles did not in any way have as a feature of that society the systemic dominance or superiority of one sex over the other, there would still be a generic moral defect that would remain. The defect would be that any set of sex roles would necessarily impair and retard an individual's ability to develop his or her own characteristics, talents, capacities, and potential life-plans to the extent to which he or she might desire and from which he or she might derive genuine satisfaction. Sex roles, by definition, constitute empirical and normative limits of varying degrees of strength—restrictions on what it is that one can expect to do, be, or become. As such, they are, I think, at least prima facie objectionable.

To some degree, all role-differentiated living is restrictive in this sense. Perhaps, therefore, all role differentiation in society is to some degree troublesome, and perhaps all strongly role-differentiated societies are objectionable. But the case against sex roles and the concomitant sexual differentiation they create and require need not rest upon this more controversial point. For one thing that distinguishes sex roles from many other roles is that they are wholly involuntarily assumed. One has no choice about whether one shall be born a male or female. And if it is a consequence of one's being born a male or a female that one's subsequent emotional, intellectual, and material development will be substantially controlled by this fact, then it is necessarily the case that substantial, permanent, and involuntarily assumed restraints have been imposed on some of the most central factors concerning the way one will shape and live one's life. The point to be emphasized is that this would necessarily be the case, even in the unlikely event that substantial sexual differentiation could be maintained without one sex or the other becoming dominant and developing oppressive institutions and an ideology to support that dominance and oppression. Absent some far stronger showing than seems either reasonable or possible that potential talents, abilities, interests, and the like are inevitably and irretrievably distributed between the sexes in such a way that the sex roles of the society are genuinely congruent with and facilitative of the development of those talents, abilities, interests, and the like that individuals can and do possess, sex roles are to this degree incompatible with the kind of respect which the good or the just society would accord to each of the individual persons living within it. It seems to me, therefore, that there are persuasive reasons to believe that no society which maintained what I have been describing as *substantial* sexual differentiation could plausibly be viewed as a good or just society.

What remains more of an open question is whether a society in which sex functioned in the way in which eye color does (a strictly assimilationist society in respect to sex) would be better or worse than one in which sex functioned in the way in which religious identity does in our society (a nonoppressive, more diversified or pluralistic one). For it might be argued that especially in the case of sex and even in the case of race much would be gained and nothing would be lost if the ideal society in respect to these characteristics succeeded in preserving in a nonoppressive fashion the attractive differences between males and females and the comparably attractive differences among ethnic groups. Such a society, it might be claimed, would be less bland, less homogeneous and richer in virtue of its variety.

I do not think there is any easy way to settle this question, but I do think the attractiveness of the appeal to diversity, when sex or race are concerned, is less alluring than is often supposed. The difficulty is in part one of specifying what will be preserved and what will not, and in part one of preventing the reappearance of the type of systemic dominance and subservience that produces the injustice of oppression. Suppose, for example, that it were suggested that there are aspects of being male and aspects of being female that are equally attractive and hence desirable to maintain and perpetuate: the kind of empathy that is associated with women and the kind of self-control associated with men. It does not matter what the characteristic is, the problem is one of seeing why the characteristic should be tied by the social institutions to the sex of the individuals of the society. If the characteristics are genuinely ones that all individuals ought to be encouraged to display in the appropriate circumstances, then the social institutions and ideology ought to endeavor to foster them in all individuals. If it is good for everyone to be somewhat empathetic all of the time or especially empathetic in some circumstances, or good for everyone to have a certain degree of self-control all of the time or a great deal in some circumstances, then there is no reason to preserve institutions which distribute these psychological attributes along sexual lines. And the same is true for many, if not all, vocations, activities, and ways of living. If some, but not all persons would find a life devoted to child rearing genuinely satisfying, it is good, surely, that that option be open to them. Once again, though, it is difficult to see the argument for implicitly or explicitly encouraging, teaching, or assigning to women, as opposed to men, that life simply in virtue of their sex. Thus, while substantial diversity in individual characteristics, attitudes, and ways of life is no doubt an admirable, even important feature of the good society, what remains uncertain is the necessity or the desirability of continuing to link attributes or behaviors such as these to the race or sex of individuals. And for the reasons I have tried to articulate there are significant moral arguments against any conception of the good society in which such connections are pursued and nourished in the systemic fashion required by the existence and maintenance of *sex* roles.

13

SEXISM AND RACISM: SOME CONCEPTUAL DIFFERENCES

LAURENCE THOMAS

How should we understand the difference between sexism and racism? Is the difference merely that we have women as victims of the former and blacks (or some other minority group) as victims of the latter? Or, are there differences of a deeper sort?

Consider: If a black were to report to his colleagues (all of whom are white) that he had just been called a "nigger," one could be reasonably certain that, since he is black, his colleagues would convey considerable sympathy toward him for having been subjected to such extreme verbal abuse. But if a woman were to report to her colleagues (all of whom are male) that she had just been called a "chick," "fox," or even a "dumb broad," I suspect that her colleagues—and it is the reaction of her male colleagues which should concern us—would not be likely to suppose that she had been subjected to equally extreme verbal abuse;[1] and, therefore, they would be less inclined to view her as deserving of or in need of sympathy, let

From Laurence Thomas, 'Sexism and Racism: Some Conceptual Differences', *Ethics*, 90/2 (Jan. 1980).

I was first prompted to think about the topic of this paper in the fall of 1976 when I received an invitation from Stanley M. Browne, on behalf of Talladega College (Alabama), to give a talk on it. Versions of this paper have since been read at Georgia State University, Tuskegee Institute, Union College, Western Michigan University, and the American Philosophical Association meetings (Pacific Division). Lawrence Alexander saved me from a number of slips and stylistic infelicities. Lyla H. O'Driscoll and Alison M. Jagger forced me to be more careful than I would have been in my remarks about the sexual identity of men. Section III of this paper was extensively revised in the light of the very forthright criticisms of my APA commentator, Robert C. Williams. Among others who have been kind enough to offer extensive comments are: C. Freeland, D. Jamieson, H. McGary, J. Narveson, J. Nickel, and A. Soble. A special word of thanks goes to Sandra Bartky and Connie Price for their encouragement in writing this paper from the very start. The completion of later drafts of this paper was facilitated by my having an A. W. Mellon Faculty Fellowship at Harvard University for the 1978–9 academic year.

[1] A sexual parallel here would have to be denigrating, but not vulgar. Thus, words such as 'bitch' and 'cunt' do not parallel the racial epithet 'nigger.' Indeed, in certain contexts, the word 'nigger' is not even denigrating: a black woman may call a black man with whom she is in love her "sweet nigger." Of the three expressions mentioned in the text, I suspect that "dumb broad," suggested to me by A. Soble, is the closest parallel to "nigger," though it still misses the mark.

alone considerable sympathy. I believe that the different reactions that we would get here are indicative of some fundamental differences between sexism and racism. In this essay, I shall argue that the following are two such differences: (*a*) Sexism, unlike racism, readily lends itself to a morally unobjectionable description. (*b*) The positive self-concept of men has been more centrally tied to their being sexists than has been the positive self-concept of whites to their being racists. An unfortunate consequence of *a* and *b*, I am afraid, is that racist attitudes are relatively easier to give up than sexist ones. This perhaps is what one would expect given the different reactions that we would get from the two parallel situations which I have just described. Before getting underway, though, I want to make a few preliminary remarks.

1. Sexism and racism are obviously very large topics to try to cover in a single essay. My discussion, therefore, will be extremely one sided in that I shall be concerned with the attitude of the sexist and the racist qua perpetrator only and not qua victim. This, of course, is not to say that a person cannot be on both sides of the fence.[2] Thus, I shall make no attempt, except in passing, to give an account of the self-concept which a victim of either sexism or racism has. It seems to be a fact that women are less likely to see themselves as victims of sexism than blacks (say) are to see themselves as victims of racism.[3] I believe that what I shall have to say on these two topics will be compatible with this fact.

2. Undoubtedly, there are different conceptions of sexism and racism, just as there are different conceptions of justice.[4] However, my aim is not to defend a particular conception of either social phenomenon: instead, I shall offer only a skeletal account of both which others, no doubt, will flesh out in different ways.

3. I mean only to be explaining the difference between sexism and racism. I do not in any way suppose that either can be morally justified. Moreover, I shall not be concerned with whether one is more morally objectionable than the other. For both are sufficiently objectionable, on moral grounds, that everyone should be equally concerned to perpetuate neither.

4. Finally, although I hardly think that blacks constitute the only ethnic group which has been the victim of racism, I am going to limit the discussion

---

[2] Marabel Morgan, it would seem, is a woman who is on both sides of the fence. The "total woman" classes organized by her are based on the view that for a married woman "love is *unconditional* acceptance of him [her husband] and his feelings" (emphasis added) (see *The Total Woman* [New York: Pocket Books, 1975], 161).

[3] See Eugene D. Genovese, *Roll, Jordon, Roll: The World Slaves Made* (New York: Pantheon Books, 1974).

[4] On the difference between the concept and a conception of justice, see John Rawls, *A Theory of Justice* (Cambridge, Mass.: Harvard University Press, 1971), 5–11.

to blacks nonetheless. Not only will this make the discussion more manageable; I am, for the most part, concerned with racism (and sexism) in the United States—and it is fair to say that, because of both their physical features and numbers, blacks have been the primary target of racism in the United States.

I

Obviously enough, if *a* and *b* are true, then sexism and racism must differ in the way in which each views its victims. The following social phenomenon sheds some light on the matter. In response to the demands of liberated women, men are forming groups in order to come to grips with their conception of themselves as men, that is, in order to understand what the male role comes to.[5] However, whereas the struggle against sexism has sent men back to the drawing board, as it were, in order to redefine their maleness, the struggle against racism has not resulted in a similar reaction on the part of whites. Whites have not found themselves at a loss to understand themselves qua white persons. The point here is not that the lives of whites have gone unaffected in this regard. Rather, it is that, although men often perceive the women's movement as an affront to their masculinity, the black movement has not been perceived in a similar vein by whites. Whites have not taken being less of a racist to mean being less of a white in the way that men have taken being less of a sexist to mean being less of a man (see Section III). Why is this? The answer which readily recommends itself is that the conception which men have of women is much more central to the conception which men have of themselves than is the case for whites with respect to blacks. I shall refer to this view as the racial and sexual identity (RSI) thesis. Lest there be any misunderstanding, I should note that it no more follows from the truth of this thesis that sexism exists than it does that racism does not.

The truth of the RSI thesis is, I believe, well supported by the following considerations: (1) Since the beginning of humanity, women and men have had to interact for the purpose of procreation in order for the human species to survive. (2) There are male and female members of every race; hence, no race is dependent upon the members of any other race for its survival. (3) Any male and female member of any race can have offspring. (4) Whereas

---

[5] Cf. David Gelman *et al.*, "How Men are Changing," *Newsweek*, Jan. 16, 1978, and Peter Knobler, "Is it More Difficult to be a Man Today?" *New York Times*, May 27, 1978. Also, there is Gene Marine, *A Male Guide to Women's Liberation* (New York: Avon Books, 1972), and many other books of this genre.

one can be racially mixed, one's gender is an all-or-nothing matter. A person is either male or female, taking the sexual organs to be the determining factor.[6] (5) The races are not regarded as biological complementaries of one another, but the two sexes are. Thus, it suffices that there exists some race or other which is different from a person's own race in order for it to be possible for that person to have a racial identity; such identity does not require the existence of a particular race. Our sexual identity, however, is clearly predicated upon the existence of a particular sex, namely, the opposite one. I shall assume that the RSI thesis is well supported by these five considerations. The thesis will be central to the account which I shall give of the way in which sexism and racism each conceives of its object: women and blacks, respectively.

Now, I should note that sexism and racism are commonly taken to be quite similar. This is because both racist and sexist attitudes rest upon the view that, respectively, there are innate differences between whites and blacks, on the one hand, and men and women, on the other, which in each case make it natural for the latter to be subordinate to the former.[7] For instance, blacks and women have been stereotyped as being both intellectually and emotionally inferior to whites and men, respectively. But closer inspection reveals that even this similarity is not without a fundamental difference. For whereas the woman's lack turns out to make her naturally suited for the home and raising children and, therefore, natural for her to be around, the conclusion that it is natural for blacks to be around is not forthcoming. Indeed, it has been said by blacks and whites alike that things would be better if all blacks were back in Africa.[8] So we encounter a difference between sexism and racism even in the respect in which they are thought to be most similar. It takes only a moment of reflection to see that this difference can be explained by reference to the considerations offered in support of the RSI thesis. There is no biological role for blacks to play in the reproduction of white offspring, however much whites may find it desirable to have blacks around for other reasons. It is in this light that the remarks of this paragraph must be understood.

Taking my cue from the preceding discussion, the way in which sexism

---

[6] Among persons and other higher animals, there can only be what is called pseudohermaphroditism, i.e., genetic abnormalities or hormonal imbalances (see *The Encyclopedia Americana*, international edn., s.v. "hermaphrodite").

[7] In connection with sexism, two of the most sophisticated writers whom I have come across are Mary Wollstonecraft, *A Vindication of the Rights of Women* (1792), and Dorothy L. Sayers, *Unpopular Opinions* (New York: Harcourt Brace, 1947).

[8] Among blacks who have held this view, Marcus Garvey comes foremost to mind (see Edmund David Cronon, *Black Moses: The Story of Marcus Garvey and the Universal Negro Improvement Association* [Madison: University of Wisconsin Press, 1969]).

and racism each conceives of its object can be put as follows: Sexism entails the view that, although (*a*) women are inferior to men in some sense, (*b*) biological considerations dictate that women ought to be around in order to insure the survival of the human species. Moreover, in view of *a* and *b*, (*c*) it is appropriate for women to cater to the wants and needs of men; indeed, women are understood as complementing men. Racism entails the view that (*a*) blacks are in some sense inferior to whites and that, in view of this, (*b*) it is appropriate for blacks to cater to the wants and needs of whites, but not the view that (*c*) biological considerations dictate that blacks ought to be around whites and, therefore, that blacks complement whites. It goes without saying that I am merely stating what I take to be the core of a sexist conception of women and a racist conception of blacks; in no way do I mean to be endorsing either.

Some explanatory remarks are in order. What I mean by the claim that women complement men is aptly expressed by the saying, "Behind every man there is a good woman." Women are supposed to possess or excel at those virtues which make them naturally suited for being supportive of and bringing out the best in men.[9] For instance, women are supposed to possess a greater capacity than men for being understanding, encouraging, and sympathetic. (The first capacity, which has to do with patience and tolerance, is not to be confused with the capacity to understand, which has to do with intellectual ability.) Thus, it is thought to be a man's benefit to associate himself with the right woman, since the right woman, so the view goes, will be a man's constant source of support and encouragement, thereby enabling him to excel at what he does. Women, then, are thought to play a central role in the self-development of men and, thus, in men having a positive conception of themselves. Nothing of the sort is thought to be true of blacks vis-à-vis whites. There are no time-honored sayings to the effect that "behind every white there is a good black." It has not been thought that by associating with the right black whites will enhance their chances of excelling at whatever they do, of being their best as whites.[10]

We now have before us a skeletal account of the way in which sexism and racism construe women and blacks, respectively. As I have remarked, others may wish to flesh out these accounts in different ways. In any event, we are in the position to make good the claim that the following are two of the fundamental differences between sexism and racism: (*a*) Sexism, unlike racism,

[9] Cf. Morgan. Wollstonecraft speaks of men having the pleasure of commanding flattering sycophants (see p. 13 of the edition of *A Vindication of the Rights of Women* edited by Carol H. Post [New York: W. W. Norton, 1975]). Wollstonecraft's point is developed in a contemporary vein by L. Blum *et al.*, "Altruism and Women's Oppression," *Philosophical Forum*, 5 (1973), 196–221.

[10] During the times of slavery American whites did not think that European whites needed to find themselves the right black in order to better themselves.

readily lends itself to a morally unobjectionable description. (*b*) The positive self-concept of men has been more centrally tied to their being sexists than has been the positive self-concept of whites to their being racists. In the order mentioned, I turn to these two claims in the sections which follow.

II

I shall proceed in this section by arguing first that sexism readily lends itself to a morally unobjectionable description and then for the claim that racism does not.

A major aspect of the traditional male role is what I shall call the benefactor role. It is the role of men to protect women and to provide them with the comforts of life. That men should be the benefactors of women (in the sense described) is, it should be observed, a natural outcome of a sexist conception of women. For it will be recalled that, according to that conception, women play a central role in the self-development of men. And, of course, any person has good reasons to protect and provide for that which plays a central role in her or his self-development. But it goes without saying that this aspect of the traditional male role hardly seems morally objectionable.[11] For we do not normally suppose that a person does that which is morally wrong in benefiting someone. And on the face of it, surely, providing a person with the comforts of life would hardly seem to be a morally objectionable thing to do. After all, are they not desired by nearly everyone? At first blush, then, the traditional male role seems quite immune to moral criticism, which explains why the charge of sexism often seems to be lacking in moral force. Indeed, it is not uncommon to hear a man boast of being a sexist—even nowadays!

Now, of course, an arrangement where men benefit women is not morally

---

[11] In order to keep down the length of this essay, I have deliberately not said anything about the traditional male role in connection with sex. The sexual exploitation of women is surely one of the worst aspects of the traditional male role. In the work compiled by the Sex Information and Educational Council of the United States, *Sexuality and Man* (New York: Charles Scribner's Sons, 1970), we find the following remarks: "Four major premarital sexual standards exist today: Abstinence, the formal standard of forbidding intercourse to both sexes; the Double Standard, the Western world's oldest standard, which allows males to have greater access to coitus than females; Permissiveness with Affection . . . and Permissiveness without Affection . . . " (p. 40). And this is to say nothing of the humiliation to which women have been subjected in connection with rape. It was once common practice for men to sexually abuse the women they captured. And, even today, many rapes go unreported because of the humiliation to which the victims are subjected (see Gerda Lerna, *The Female Experience: An American Documentary* [Indianapolis: Bobbs-Merrill, 1977], pp. 433ff.). It goes without saying that I have also left aside the traditional female role in connection with sex and childbearing. For an excellent discussion in connection with the former, see Christopher Lasch, "The Flight From Feeling: Sociopsychology of Sexual Conflict," *Marxist Perspectives*, I (1978), 74–95. This essay was brought to my attention by Eugene Rivers.

objectionable—in and of itself, that is. What is morally objectionable, though, are the presuppositions behind it, one of the most important of them being that this sort of arrangement is ordained by nature.[12] From this presupposition, a number of things are thought to follow, such as that men should earn more money than women (period) and that the work which women do around the home is not as important as the work which men do on the job. These matters could be pursued at length, but I shall not do so here. For my concern has been to show that sexism readily lends itself to a morally unobjectionable description. And to show that it is a natural outcome of a sexist conception of women that men should be the benefactors of women (in the sense described) is to show this much.

Let us now look at racism. The first thing we should observe is that a racist conception of blacks does not naturally give rise to the view that whites should be the benefactors of blacks. This should come as no surprise, for it will be remembered (a) that blacks and whites alike have thought that things would be better if all blacks were back in Africa and (b) that blacks have not been thought to play a central role in the self-development of whites. For blacks were thought to be too inferior for that. Whites, then, have never conceived of it as their role qua whites to be the benefactor of blacks. And, as history shows,[13] the benefit of blacks has hardly been the concern of racist arrangements. For the most part, the benefit of blacks was incidental to (an unintended side effect of) such arrangements or, in any case, up to the whim of those responsible for such arrangements. These facts, alone, make it very difficult for racism to be viewed in a morally unobjectionable light.

Now it might be objected that racism can be so viewed if we suppose that whites held blacks to be inferior in their moral status to whites.[14] But not so. For one thing, the case of women shows that persons can have what I called the benefactor role even with respect to living things presumed to be of inferior moral status. After all, it is impossible to understand the doctrine of coverture (e.g.) without supposing that according to it women are inferior in

---

[12] I am indebted to Linda Patrik (Union College) for much of the way that I have put this paragraph.

[13] See Genovese.

[14] In my "Rawlsian Self-Respect and the Black Consciousness Movement" (*Philosophical Forum*, 9 [1978], 303–14), I have distinguished between having full, partial, and no moral status. A thing has no moral status (e.g., stones) if there are no rights which it can have and there no duties which it can have or which can be owed to it. A thing has only partial moral status (e.g., animals) if there are duties which can be owed to it, but there are no duties which it can have. A thing has full moral status (e.g., persons) if there are rights and duties which it can have. As for whether or not animals can have rights, suffice it to say that they cannot, unlike persons, have rights against one another. A dog does not violate any rights of the squirrel which it catches and kills or hurts.

their moral status to men.[15] For another, the cruel treatment of living things of inferior moral status is morally wrong in any event, as the case of animals shows. Racism, though, has often called for the cruel treatment of blacks, whose moral status has most certainly not been thought to be inferior to the moral status of animals. So the objection fails.

A satisfactory case, I believe, has been made for the claim that sexism, unlike racism, readily admits of a morally unobjectionable description.

III

The task of this section is to show that the positive self-concept of men has been more centrally tied to their being sexists than has been the positive self-concept of whites to their being racists. I shall first say a few words about what a person's positive self-concept comes to.

There are various aspects of a person's positive self-concept. However, the one which is germane to our discussion is what is called self-esteem.[16] It is the attitude which we have toward ourselves regarding our ability to interact effectively with our social environment, to achieve the goals which we set for ourselves. Respectively, our self-esteem is positive or negative if we have a reasonably favorable or unfavorable attitude toward ourselves in this regard. No person without deep psychological problems desires to have a negative conception of her- or himself. Thus, those activities which we believe will enhance our self-esteem have a natural attraction for us. So we are disinclined to give up those activities the successful pursuit of which enhances our self-esteem unless we have reason to believe that we can maintain our self-esteem by engaging in other activities. Obviously enough, the range of our abilities is very relevant here. The wider it is the more options there are that are open to us.

But now it is our values which determine the sorts of activities whose successful pursuit will enhance our self-esteem. Hence, having an excellent

[15] The doctrine reads thus: "By marriage the husband and the wife are one person in law: that is, the very being or legal existence of the woman is suspended during the marriage, or at least incorporated and consolidated into that of the husband; under whose wing, protection, and cover, she performs everything" (see William Blackstone, *Commentaries on the Laws of England*, reprint edn. [London: Dawsons of Pall Mall, 1966], 430).

[16] See, among others, Stanley Coopersmith, *The Antecedents of Self-Esteem* (San Francisco: W. H. Freeman, 1967); I. Edward Well and Gerald Marwell, *Self-Esteem: Its Conceptualization and Measurement* (Beverly Hills, Calif.: Sage, 1976); and Robert W. White, "Ego and Reality in Psychoanalytic Theory," *Psychological Issues*, 3, monograph 11 (1963). I have tried to show the importance of distinguishing between self-esteem and self-respect, which I have defined in terms of having the conviction that one has and is deserving of full moral status (see my "Morality and our Self-Concept," *Journal of Value Inquiry*, 12 [1978], 258–68).

voice for classical music will do little to enhance our self-esteem if we have no interest in such music. On the other hand, if being able to sing classical music well is very important to us, then our self-esteem will suffer a severe blow if we are told by someone whose opinion we highly respect that this is an end which is beyond our reach. In large measure the social institutions among which we live determine the sorts of values which we come to have. And those values which have been instilled in us since childhood by our familial, educational, and religious institutions may have such a tenacious hold upon us that we find ourselves unable to give them up even when the ends which they call for prove to be beyond our reach. These few remarks about self-esteem, as sketchy as they are, should give us enough of a handle on the concept to permit us to proceed with the task of showing that the positive self-concept (self-esteem) of sexists is more centrally tied to the fact that they are sexists than is the positive self-concept (self-esteem) of racists to the fact that they are racists. (Throughout the remainder of this essay, I shall use the term 'self-esteem' instead of 'self-concept.')

If the RSI thesis is sound, then our sexual identity is clearly central to the conception which we have of ourselves. As things stand, though, while our gender is clearly relevant to our sexual identity, it is far from being the sole determiner of it.[17] Our beliefs about the sorts of roles we should play have a most powerful influence in this regard. There is, we might say, as much a social sense of the terms 'woman' and 'man' as there is a biological one. A person is a woman or man in the biological sense merely in virtue of having the appropriate biological properties. But to be a woman or man in the social sense not only must one have the appropriate biological properties; one must also have the appropriate aspirations and social behavior. The traditional female and male roles define a social sense of the terms 'woman' and 'man'. Hence, a woman's self-esteem can turn upon the fact that she measures up to the traditional female role; a man's self-esteem can turn upon the fact that he measures up to the traditional male role.

Now we have seen that, according to the traditional male role, men have what I have called the benefactor role with respect to women: they are supposed to protect women and provide them with the comforts of life. That men should have this role with respect to women is, without a doubt, one of the most deeply entrenched views of our society. A "real" man is one who "wears the pants around the house." He is the breadwinner. Indeed, the

---

[17] In a nonsexist society, perhaps the difference between gender identity and sexual identity would collapse (see Richard Wasserstrom, "Racism, Sexism, and Preferential Treatment: An Approach to the Topics," *UCLA Law Review*, 24 [1977], 581–622). For some illuminating discussions concerning the roles of women, see the collection of articles in Jo Freeman (ed.), *Woman: A Feminist Perspective* (Palo Alto, Calif.: Mayfield, 1975); and Michele Garskof (ed.), *Roles Women Play* (Belmont, Calif.: Brooks/Cole, 1971).

benefactor role is not an optional feature of the traditional male role—
something which a man may take or leave as it pleases him. For it will be
remembered that it is supposedly ordained by nature that men should have
the benefactor role with respect to women. Unless there is some excuse, such
as that of being a priest, it follows, according to the traditional male role,
that men ought to be the benefactors of women. Thus, men believe that it is
appropriate for their conception of themselves to turn upon how well they
live up to the benefactor role. And, in the cases of those men who do so
reasonably well, their self-esteem is enhanced precisely because their success
in this regard constitutes an affirmation of their ability to be men in the
social sense of the term. In view of the considerations advanced in this and
the preceding paragraph, there is no getting around the fact that the positive
self-esteem of men has been centrally tied to their being sexists.

We do not encounter an analogous situation between the black and white
races. One very important reason why this is so is that there is only a biological sense of the races and, so, the black and white races. Thus, racial
identity for whites, and any other race, is something which has been more or
less entirely settled by biological considerations. To be a full-fledged white
person one has never had to own black slaves or even to hate blacks. This
latter point is well illustrated by the case of the nigger lover. To be sure, many
whites looked rather disparagingly upon the nigger lover. But this is not
because whites considered her or him to be a white person *manqué*. The
nigger lover was not a mulatto! A mulatto can no more be a nigger lover
than a male a tomboy or a female a sissy. As for the first point, suffice it to
say that American slaveowners were hardly of the opinion that European
whites were less than full-fledged whites on account of the fact that black
slavery was not a very prominent feature of European white societies.

Of course, I do not mean to deny the obvious fact that whites have perceived there to be fundamental differences among themselves, as, for
example, class differences.[18] Nor do I mean to deny that whites have thought
certain forms of conduct to be inappropriate for them, as, for example, the
conduct of a nigger lover. What I do mean to deny, however, is that the racial
identity of whites turned upon any of these differences. And if I am right
about this, then it follows with impeccable logic that the racial identity of
whites has not turned upon their being racists.

Now, to be sure, there have been many whites whose self-esteem has been
enhanced by the fact that they were racists. At one point in his life George
Wallace was certainly such an individual. It is significant to note, though,

[18] See, e.g., Patricia Hollis (ed.), *Class and Conflict in Nineteenth-Century England, 1815–1850*
(London: Routledge & Kegan Paul, 1973).

that the word 'racist' is not the name of an institutional role, as are, say, the words 'teacher,' 'governor,' and 'spouse.'[19] Moreover, the definitions of such roles do not make any reference to the sorts of activities which, under some description or other, are properly characterized as racist. No one, for instance, supposes that a person cannot be a teacher, governor, or spouse unless she or he is a racist,[20] though, to be sure, many may think that only racists should occupy such roles. If, therefore, it is true that for any institutional role K a person S can perform K without being a racist, under some description or other, then it has to be equally true that, if S were a racist, then S could cease to be one without S's self-esteem being jeopardized with respect to the performance of K. When this consideration is coupled with the fact that the racial identity of whites has not turned upon their being racists, what follows most straightforwardly is that the self-esteem of whites has not been centrally tied to their being racists.

Now, the word 'sexist' is not the name of an institutional role either. However, there is at least one institutional role, namely that of being a spouse (traditionally understood), which by definition makes reference to the sorts of activities which are sexist under at least some description. For the attitudes which the traditional male spouse has toward women (his wife, in particular) are, needless to say, dictated by the traditional male role, as what I have called the benefactor role should make clear. And, as we have seen, in their endeavors to measure up to the benefactor role, the self-esteem of men has been centrally tied to their being sexists.

I should conclude this section by noting that nothing I have said implies that the self-esteem of slavemasters did not or could not have turned upon their owning slaves. For their slaves were their property; and one's self-esteem can turn upon how much property one owns, whether that property is land, cattle, houses, or black slaves. Thus, it would be a mistake to suppose that the fact that the self-esteem of slave owners turned upon their owning slaves militates against the arguments of this section. For being a slave holder was not, surely, a defining characteristic of either a racist or a white person during the times of slavery; and so, a fortiori, it has not been since the passing of slavery.

---

[19] In the use of the word 'institutional,' I follow John Rawls, "Two Concepts of Rules," *Philosophical Review*, 64 (1955), 3–32.

[20] Indeed, it would seem that this is true even of the role of slavemaster. Aristotle thought it natural that there should be slaves. I do not see, though, that he thought it natural that the slaves should be black (see *Politics*, bk. 1).

IV

Throughout this essay, I have assumed that the traditional male role can be described in a morally objectionable way. I do not now want to argue the case. Rather, I would like for the reader to engage in a brief thought experiment with me. Suppose that men were the victims of sexism and that

[everything a man] wore, said, or did had to be justified by reference to female approval; if he were compelled to regard himself, day in day out, not as a member of society, but merely ... as a virile member of society. If the centre of his dress-consciousness were the cod-piece, his education directed to making him a spirited lover and meek paterfamilias; his interests held to be natural only in so far as they were sexual. If from school and lecture-room, press and pulpit, he heard the persistent outpouring of a shrill and scolding voice, bidding him remember his biological function. If he were vexed by continual advice how to add a rough male touch to his typing, how to be learned without losing his masculine appeal, how to combine chemical research with education, how to play bridge without incurring the suspicion of impotence. If, instead of allowing with a smile that "women prefer cavemen," he felt the unrelenting pressure of a whole social structure forcing him to order all his goings in conformity with that pronouncement.[21]

I have no doubt that most men would find a world thus described quite objectionable—and on moral grounds. If so, then there is indeed a morally objectionable way of describing the traditional male role in this world.

The differences between sexism and racism go much deeper than, as is commonly supposed, the fact that women are victims of the former and blacks of the latter. If I have argued soundly in this essay, then we have seen that sexism and racism are not two ways of referring to the same social monster, but two rather different ones.

V

My objective in this essay has been to show that there are at least two fundamental differences between sexism and racism: (a) Sexism, unlike racism, readily lends itself to a morally unobjectionable description. (b) The positive self-concept of men has been more centrally tied to their being sexists than has been the positive self-concept of whites to their being racists. As I said at the outset of this essay, it is, I believe, a consequence of the truth of a and b that racist attitudes are relatively easier to give up than sexist ones.

---

[21] Sayers, *Unpopular Opinions*, 143–5. A later paragraph reads as follows: "If, after a few centuries of this kind of treatment, the male was a little self-conscious, a little on the defensive, I should not blame him. If he traded a little upon his sex, I could forgive him. If he presented the world with a major social problem, I would scarcely be surprised. It would be more surprising if he retained any rag of sanity and self-respect."

I shall not attempt a defense of this claim at this point. Suffice to say, first of all, that persons must see that something is morally objectionable before they take themselves to have a moral reason for giving it up. We have seen that sexism presents a greater difficulty than racism in this regard. Second, it is a fact that people are disinclined to alter their behavior if they have reason to believe that in doing so they would jeopardize their self-esteem.[22] And we have seen that sexism presents a greater difficulty than racism in this regard as well.

In this essay, I have argued that there are some fundamental differences between sexism and racism. I have not denied that there are any similarities between the two; nor have I meant to do so.

---

[22] The fact that a person's self-esteem may be enhanced by the successful pursuit of morally unacceptable ends is often proffered as an explanation as to why those for whom street crime is a way of life do not accept the more traditional moral values (see, e.g., Charles Silberman, *Criminal Violence, Criminal Justice* [New York: Random House, 1978], chs. 2 and 3).

14

GROUP AUTONOMY AND NARRATIVE IDENTITY: BLACKS AND JEWS

LAURENCE THOMAS

Any attempt to compare the suffering of blacks and Jews would seem likely to be felled by the waves of invidious comparisons. That is because any such comparison is likely to be seen, however obliquely, as an endeavor to answer the question: Which group has suffered more—blacks or Jews? And the feeling, of course, is that the suffering of both has been (and is) so heinous that to be concerned with answering that question is to embark upon a most despicable kind of moral enterprise. Be that as it may, there can be instructive comparisons regarding the suffering of Jews and blacks. I shall attempt such a comparison in this essay. At the very end of this essay, I shall speak to why it has seemed so natural to compare Jews and blacks.

I

My thesis is that *despite* the Holocaust contemporary Jews have group autonomy, whereas *on account* of American slavery contemporary blacks do not. An identifiable group of people has group autonomy when its members are generally regarded by others not belonging to the group as the foremost interpreters of their own historical-cultural traditions. I take it to be obvious that group autonomy, understood in that way, is a moral good of enormous importance. On an individual level the most significant indication that others take us seriously is that they regard us as the foremost interpreters of who we are: our desires, aims, values, beliefs, and so on. Suppose I were to ask a person about her aims and so forth—but only as a matter of courtesy, it being evident that I have already satisfied myself as to what the person is like. If the person has any self-respect at all, she would rightly feel insulted, resentful, and angry. The importance of group autonomy is analogous. Normally, it is only because a group has an extraordinary command of its

From Laurence Thomas, 'Group Autonomy and Narrative Identity: Blacks and Jews', in Paul Berman (ed.), *Blacks and Jews: Alliances and Arguments* (New York: Delacorte Press, 1994).

own history and experiences that it has group autonomy. It is logically possible that a group could have such autonomy and yet lack a command of these things, if the group is regarded as having mastery of its historical-cultural traditions when, in actuality, it does not. On the other hand, it is not sufficient for group autonomy that a group has such mastery, since having the mastery is quite compatible with other groups not acknowledging that it does.

To be sure, it is a consequence of my account that group autonomy is contingent upon being held in a certain regard by others. This is true of self-regarding attitudes in general. Insofar as we respect ourselves as individuals, it is precisely because we have been respected often enough by others. If respect from others has been adequate at the very formative stages of our lives, then it is possible to endure a considerable amount of disrespect from others for a period of time without losing our respect for ourselves, even if our self-respect shows signs of wearing out. And massive displays of respect after the ordeal would be crucial to repairing the damage done—to strengthening the paths of self-respect that had worn thin. Our own self-respect is not thereby diminished because it is anchored in the respect that we receive from others. By parity of reasoning, then, group autonomy is not diminished because it is anchored in the respect that a group receives from other groups.

I maintain that despite the Holocaust contemporary Jews have group autonomy, whereas on account of American slavery contemporary blacks do not. At any rate, blacks have considerably less group autonomy than Jews. What fuels my thinking are the following considerations: (1) Given the evil of the Holocaust for Jews and the evil of slavery for blacks, if any two groups should interact in harmony with one another it is Jews and blacks. (2) It is clear that they do not. And (3) I do not find the prevailing explanation that there is enormous economic disparity between blacks and Jews to be a complete explanation for the disharmony between the two groups. I do not wish to discount the reality of the economic disparity between blacks and Jews as a factor in black–Jewish tensions; rather, I believe that the disharmony between the two groups can be explained in a different and morally more satisfying way.

I suggest that some of the negative feelings toward Jews that are so prevalent among blacks can be attributed to the fact that Jews have considerably more group autonomy than blacks. This difference has given rise to resentment born of envy on the part of blacks toward Jews. At the end of this essay, I shall say something about racism on the part of Jews toward blacks.

Group autonomy is an indisputable moral good. It is understandable that every group should want to have it. Likewise, if a group which has been egregiously wronged should fail to have it, then it is understandable, though in no way justifiable, that the members of that group should be envious of the members of groups which have it, especially the members of groups which have also been egregiously wronged. For envy is a function of the uncomfortably small distance that we find between ourselves and others who possess goods that we prize. It does not require any wrongdoing on anyone's part. As social beings, we inevitably have a comparative conception of ourselves, and sometimes we cannot prevent or blunt the force of a stark comparison between ourselves and those who possess a prized good. It is perfectly understandable, for instance, that a person without legs might experience envy from time to time toward persons with legs. Envy is no less understandable when it can be attributed to a prized good that is moral, as group autonomy certainly is.

When we see the negative feelings that blacks have toward Jews derives, in large part, from the disparity in group autonomy between the two groups rather than from the economic disparity between them, we thereby view those negative feelings from a different part of the moral landscape. Of course, understandable envy is no less envy, and we should do all that we can to dissipate it. But our attitude toward understandable envy should be different from our attitude toward envy born of rapaciousness. And this holds all the more when the envy can be attributed to a failure to possess the prized moral good of group autonomy owing to social victimization. I do not want to deny the existence of anti-Semitism on the part of blacks toward Jews. It is very real indeed. Rather, I have tried to show that not all negative feelings that blacks might have toward Jews are properly characterized as anti-Semitic. I take it to be obvious that resentment on the part of blacks toward Jews owing to the differential between them with respect to group autonomy is far more morally palatable than resentment owing to the economic success of Jews.

Needless to say, I am no more blaming blacks for lacking group autonomy than I am crediting Jews for having it. Neither situation can be construed as a matter of choice.

It is perhaps tempting to suppose that group autonomy comes in the wake of economic success. This temptation should be resisted, however. In *A Certain People* (1986), Charles E. Silberman paints a glowing picture of the success of American Jews. Well, the success of Jews should not blind us to the reality that in general Jews did not arrive in America well-off. On the contrary, many were quite poor when they came here. Yet they had group autonomy.

It was not too long ago that Jews had considerable difficulty getting into so venerable an institution as Harvard University, as Bruce Kuklick has shown in *The Rise of American Philosophy* (1977). Indeed, the Harvard philosophy department has come a very long way since the days of Harvard University's president, Lawrence Lowell, who wrote that "Cambridge could make a Jew indistinguishable from an Anglo-Saxon; but not even Harvard could make a black man white." But even in those days—when Harvard philosophy professors could write, in a letter on behalf of a Jew, that "he has none of the traits calculated to excite prejudice" (Ralph Perry), and that his Jewishness is "faintly marked and by no means offensive" (James Wood)—the Jews, I submit, still had group autonomy.

On the other hand, it is far from obvious that economically well-off blacks have group autonomy. In the area of sports and entertainment, numerous blacks are making millions upon millions of dollars. All the same, there is no reason to suppose that, collectively or individually, blacks in sports and entertainment have more group autonomy than other blacks. Together, these considerations show that economic good fortune is neither a necessary basis for group autonomy nor a sufficient basis for it. What then is? The answer, I suggest, is a narrative.

II

By a narrative, I mean a set of stories which defines values and entirely positive goals, which specifies a set of fixed points of historical significance, and which defines a set of ennobling rituals to be regularly performed. A goal is entirely positive only if it is not in any way defined in terms of avoiding some harm. Thus, simply eliminating sexism, or racism, or anti-Semitism does not constitute a positive goal, as important as these objectives are. Learning Swahili, by contrast, can be a positive goal, even if it turns out to help one avoid some harm, since the goal itself can be entirely specified independently of avoiding any harm. A narrative can be understood as a group's conception of its good. The stories which constitute a narrative may very well be true, but they need not be—though perhaps they cannot be blatantly inconsistent with the facts. For example, the Jewish narrative (as well as the Muslim one) holds that Abraham circumcised himself in his old age, with a stone no less. Can this be true? Well, it simply does not matter at this point. For circumcision has been required of Jewish males down through the ages. What Abraham actually did does not change one iota the fact that this has been an ennobling ritual among Jewish males down through the ages.

Now, given the character of American slavery, it can hardly be surprising that this institution and its racist legacy left blacks bereft of a narrative, and so of group autonomy. The Holocaust did not leave Jews bereft of a narrative, and so of their conception of the good. This is not because the Holocaust was a less nefarious institution than American slavery, but because the Holocaust was a radically different kind of nefarious institution. The telos of American slavery was utter dependence; the telos of the Holocaust was the extermination of the Jews. The former is best achieved by depriving the victims of any sense of their history. As a matter of logic, the latter, of course, is achieved by death. But Hitler did not succeed in exterminating the Jews; and his failure made it possible for the Jewish narrative to survive. Reflection upon the extent to which he almost succeeded, and the means that he employed to achieve that end, leaves any morally decent person numb. But that he did not succeed is an unvarnished truth. The survival of the Jewish narrative owes to that fact. Many will insist that surely blacks have a narrative, as shown by black music and art. I think not, a point to which I shall return in due course (Section III).

Now, I believe that it is impossible for a people to flourish in a society that is hostile toward them without a narrative that is essentially isomorphic with respect to them. A narrative is essentially isomorphic when, taken in its totality, it cannot be shared by others. There are primarily two reasons why a narrative is crucial to the flourishing of a people in a hostile society. One is the obvious truth that genuine cooperation is necessary if a people is to be successful in the face of systematic hostility. The other is that there can be no genuine cooperation among a people in the absence of a narrative, for a narrative provides the basis for trust.

Having a common enemy does not, in and of itself, suffice to ensure cooperating among a people, precisely because it cannot be a basis for trust. If a member of an oppressed group has good reason to believe that she can entirely avoid social hostility without cooperating with others in her group, or that she can avoid as much hostility on her own as she would avoid if she cooperated, then she has no rationally compelling reason to cooperate with others like herself. For if one's only aim is to avoid harm, then it is totally irrelevant whether one does so with one's group or on one's own, since in either case one avoids the harm in question. What is more, there will always be the incentive to avoid the harm on one's own, regardless of what might happen to the group. Naturally, a person could be motivated by altruistic considerations to help others in his group. But the motive of altruism is something distinct from and additional to the motive that stems purely from having a common enemy.

A common enemy makes for very unstable cooperation, if any at all, among a people. We can trust people when they have given us a good reason to believe that they will do their part, although they could refrain from doing so without bearing any loss whatsoever—that is, they will do their part whether they are being observed by others or not. A common enemy alone does not deliver such a basis for trust.

By contrast, when a people has a narrative, then their self-identity is tied to a set of goals and values that is independent of a common enemy. What is more, there is what I shall call contributory pride. Contributory pride is no more mysterious than pride itself or than the delight we generally take in doing things that reflect well upon our talents. Even when alone, and there is no chance of being heard by someone, a person who can play the piano well will want to do so because she delights in playing up to her level of competence. Likewise, we want our lives to reflect those values and goals which are dear to us, and it is a source of pleasure to us when this is so.

Because a narrative provides a basis for contributory pride, it allows for the possibility of genuine cooperation, in that others who belong to the group—and so identify with the narrative—can be counted on to do their part even if no one is observing their performances. Sometimes, in fact, people can be counted on to do their part even when this is at some cost to them. Such is the power of identification with an ideal. The moral of the story, then, is this. There can be no genuine cooperation among a people who belong to the same group simply on account of their desire to overcome the same hostile social forces, since the existence of the same social forces cannot suffice as a basis for mutual trust. What is needed is a set of positive values and goals which are constitutive of the self-identity of persons who belong to the group. For positive values and goals have their own motivational force, as the case of contributory pride makes abundantly clear.

III

Let me now apply the account of a narrative, with its implications for group trust, directly to the situation of blacks and Jews. I take it to be obvious that there is an isomorphic narrative for Jews. Even people who do not like Jews are prepared to acknowledge that the Old Testament is primarily about the history of the Jews. What is more, there is a universal set of ennobling rituals which, when practiced, define being a good Jew or, at any rate, are the reference point against which a good Jew is defined, such as keeping kosher and mastering the Torah. These ennobling rituals are defined by the narrative and are entirely independent of the culture in which Jews happen to find themselves (the State of Israel aside). Wearing a yarmulke is an ennobling Jewish ritual. And notice that a non-Jew who outside of a synagogue generally wore what was unmistakably a yarmulke would be showing utter disrespect for Judaism. This speaks to the point that a narrative cannot be readily appropriated by nonmembers of the group.

Do blacks have a narrative, their conception of the good? Clearly, there is no denying the influence of African traditions upon the lives of black Americans. In voice, music, and dance the influence of Africa is unshakably there. Martin Luther King's speech, "I Have a Dream," surely owes some of its majesty to the cadence of voice, with its indelible African influence. It is impossible to listen to black gospel music and preaching without seeing—nay, feeling—the distinctiveness and richness. But form does not a narrative make. I want to say that blacks do not have a narrative—at least not as yet, anyway.

It is important to distinguish between culture and what I am calling a narrative. A narrative can be part of a culture, but it is quite possible to have a culture without a narrative. And even where a narrative is part of a culture, not everything in the culture is part of the narrative. Although bagels are very much identified with Jewish American culture, they are not part of the Jewish narrative. There are various Jewish cultures, but one Jewish narrative—though various disagreements over that narrative. While it is manifestly obvious that there is a black culture in America, that culture is not underwritten or guided by a narrative. Black music and style do not constitute an ennobling ritual. Neither rap music nor braids constitute ennobling rituals, although both are deep aspects of black culture. Things do not change with black gospel music and preaching. The distinctiveness here is indicative of black culture, and not to some ennobling ritual that black gospel music and preaching exemplify. Blacks have no special claim to preaching and gospel music, only to the style of performance.

Let me acknowledge the role of black Christianity in the lives of black Americans and black slaves. It stands to reason that without Christianity both American slavery and racism in general would have taken a much greater toll upon the lives of black people. Some of the great Negro spirituals such as "Swing Low, Sweet Chariot" and "Let My People Go" were surely an emotional balm in a very harsh world. Notwithstanding this moral reality, the truth of the matter is that blacks do not have any isomorphic relationship to Christianity. Christianity is a universal doctrine. Even if Jesus is given a black face, that will not change the fact that Christianity remains a universal doctrine. There are no texts in the Christian writings that blacks can claim as applying specifically to them. Nor have blacks gone on either to produce a reading of Christianity that applies specifically to blacks or to produce a set of ennobling rituals that only black Christians lay claim to performing. No basis for such rituals can be found in the Christian writings themselves.

So, in denying that blacks have a narrative, I do not mean to be taking anything away from the richness of black culture—just as in claiming that Jews do have narrative, I do not mean to be taking anything away from the suffering that Jews have endured. What is more, if it seems reasonable that blacks do not have group autonomy owing to American slavery and its racist legacy, then it should also stand to reason that blacks do not have a narrative, given the nature of slavery and racism. While I have maintained that it is possible to have a culture without a narrative, the converse is not true: a people with a narrative will have a culture. The idea that slavery robbed blacks of a narrative helps us to appreciate just how devastating the effect was that slavery had upon blacks. To be sure, there were whips and chains. There were even deaths. But the real pain of slavery, I suggest, is not to be located here but in the fact that it robbed blacks of a narrative. This makes it clear that I am using the notion of narrative in a very technical sense. The slave narratives—that is, the memoirs written by the slaves themselves—do not constitute what I have called a ritual. These are primarily accounts of the experience of slavery. The slave narratives do not specify ennobling rituals or fixed points of historical reference nor do they define a set of positive goals and values to be achieved by blacks independently of racism. As I have said, I regard the fact that black slaves were robbed of a narrative to be the very essence of the real pain of American slavery.

On the other hand, from just the fact that Hitler failed in his attempt to exterminate the Jews, and the Jewish narrative survived, we can see the hope that can arise out of the utter ashes of despair, and so appreciate all the more Emil Fackenheim's so-called 614th Commandment: Lest Hitler be handed a posthumous victory, every Jew must continue being a Jew in practice.

Jews have both group autonomy and a narrative, whereas blacks have neither—so I have claimed. All the same, the picture is somewhat more complicated than I have allowed. It is not just that Jews have a narrative, but that the Jewish narrative is an indispensable aspect of the Christian narrative, since the Christ story is inextricably tied to the Jewish narrative. The Christian narrative, by its very own account, is conceptually tied to the Jewish narrative (see also Section V). But if the Jewish narrative is an ineliminable part of the Christian narrative, then the Jewish narrative is also an ineliminable part of the narrative of Western culture, because of the place of Christianity in Western culture. Thus, insofar as Christianity takes itself seriously, it is conceptually bound to acknowledge that at the very least Judaism once had an indisputable claim to being meritorious. So, while Christianity may insist that Jews are now quite mistaken about the importance of their rituals and traditions, it must concede the importance of these things at an earlier time. And it must concede that Jews are rightly an authority on those rituals and traditions.

By contrast, neither the Western nor the Christian narrative is conceptually required to take the black experience seriously. Lest there be any misunderstanding, I do not deny that there have been gross distortions of the contributions of blacks to Western thought. But, as I have already observed, truth as such is not the defining feature of a narrative. I am not here debating whether Christianity and Western culture have discounted the accomplishments of blacks. My point, instead, is that as these two narratives, the Christian and the Western, have been formulated, they are not conceptually bound, by their very own formulations, to take blacks seriously at any point in time, in the way that Christianity is required to take Judaism seriously.

From these considerations it might be thought to follow that Western culture has been more racist than anti-Semitic. But not so. While I shall not argue the case here, suffice it to say that having to take a people seriously is perfectly compatible with despising them to the very core. Indeed, one may despise them precisely because one has to take them seriously.

In the next section, I shall look at some of the practical implications of the account of group autonomy and narrative which I have offered.

IV

Recall the 1967 Six-Day War, when Israel fought Egypt, Syria, and Jordan. Jews of virtually every stripe and persuasion banded together in support of Israel. This was no accident, because in the face of an imminent threat, a narrative—a group's conception of its good—orders priorities. For Orthodox Jews, kashrut laws are extremely important; for Reform Jews, nothing could be further from the truth. But during the 1967 war, a good Jew was most certainly one who supported the State of Israel, regardless of her or his other shortcomings. A common threat can be most galvanizing. But it is a narrative that gives directions that amount to more than avoiding harm.

For just about every Jew, including quite secular Jews, the existence of synagogues and the State of Israel is a good thing. It is regarded as a good thing by just about every Jew that there are Talmudic scholars and rabbis. One may define a secular Jew as one who wants nearly all aspects of Jewish life to flourish, but who does not want to be an active or regular participant in any aspect of Jewish religious life. In any case, the point that I am concerned to bring out in these observations is that there are goods that Jews want, and these goods are quite independent of a common enemy. These goods are delivered by the Jewish narrative.

Do we find a comparable set of goods among blacks? I think not. Aside from the elimination of racism, it is not clear what blacks in general can be said to want, from the standpoint of being black. But I want to bring out the significance of a group's having a narrative, and the significance of its not having one, in another way.

Consider the black church. It is widely regarded as the most influential institution in the black community. What is more, it is relatively independent of white influence. Now, there are approximately 30 million blacks in America, and let us suppose that 4 million black adults regularly go to church each Sunday. If each were to give fifty cents to the United Negro College Fund, say, that would be $2 million. Over a year that would be $104 million to UNCF. For years now, fifty cents has been barely enough to buy a cup of coffee. And I assume that anyone who attends church regularly can afford to part with fifty cents. So, the most obvious question is: Why is something like this not being done? The answer cannot possibly be racism, if only because the black church is as independent of white influence as any institution in the black community can be. And if a common enemy—racism, in this instance—were a sufficient basis for cooperative endeavors, then one would have thought that a practice analogous to the one that I have proposed would have been in place quite some time ago.

I want to say that lack of a narrative can explain the absence of cooperative practices of the sort sketched above. In order for a people in a hostile society to flourish as a people, their self-identity must be anchored by a conception of the good that is independent of the hostility that they wish to avoid. What prevents us from seeing this, I suspect, is that there are times when eliminating a harm counts as an end in its own right, and it is irrelevant what other objectives a person might have.

To view struggling against oppression as the equivalent of eliminating an imminent life-threatening harm is to make an egregious error. By its very nature, oppression is about being deprived of some options rather than others. The struggle of a people against oppression can only be properly understood in the context of what it means for them to get on with their lives as a people. And that requires a narrative which anchors their self-identity.

Thus, we must distinguish between a racist society with overt structural inequality (such as American slavery and Jim Crow practices) and a society with structural equality that is coupled with widespread racist presuppositions of inferiority on the part of the powerful toward an identifiable group of individuals who are less well-off. In either case, we have an unjust society, and the latter, of course, may owe its origins to the former. However, combating the former does not require a narrative, whereas combating the latter does. For in the first instance, there is a rigorously specifiable set of harms or wrongs the elimination of which is called for. Their elimination is called for regardless of the aims that a people might otherwise have in society. What is more, while the elimination of the harms of overt structural inequality is no doubt a precondition for flourishing, just as being alive is a precondition for flourishing, their elimination does not constitute flourishing; nor does their elimination point to what a people's flourishing might consist of, just as being alive does not.

By contrast, eliminating the coupling of structural equality with widespread presuppositions of the other's inferiority is a different matter entirely, if only because in such an instance there is no rigorously specifiable set of harms or wrongs to be eliminated and there is no socially acceptable procedure for getting the dominant group to change their pejorative beliefs. Moreover, while it is conceptually possible to have no beliefs at all about an oppressed people, in other words a null set of beliefs, what is wanted is not a case where the null set of beliefs replaces the beliefs that a people are inferior. What is wanted, rather, is for the beliefs of inferiority to be replaced by a positive set of beliefs about the people in question. But which positive set? More to the point, who determines which positive set of beliefs replaces the beliefs about inferiority? Nothing better positions an oppressed people to answer these two questions than their having a narrative. For we have equality at its very best not simply when a people must be precisely like others in order to command the respect of others, but when a people can command the respect of others for being who they are. Equality across sameness is one thing; equality across differences is quite another. And the virtue of equality is truly showcased only in the latter instance. The latter equality is a more affirming equality that is inescapably predicated upon a people having a narrative—not just a culture—of their own.

The role of a narrative in equality simply presupposes what we already know, namely that there is all the difference in the world between being moved to help someone out of pity and being moved to help someone out of respect for their conception of the good. The latter is a more affirming kind of assistance. Things are no different at the level of groups.

I have claimed that without a narrative a people cannot flourish in a hostile society. Initially, I focused on how a narrative provides a basis for cooperation among a people. As should be obvious, I want also to say that it is only in having a narrative that, in a hostile society, a people can have assistance born of respect instead of pity. It has been said that the Creator helps those who help themselves. It would be stunning if human beings were much different. And nothing enhances self-help like a goal. Things can be no different for a group; hence, the importance of a narrative. We can best understand the success of Jews in America if we see them as having a narrative in a society with structural equality coupled with widespread presuppositions of inferiority. In the face of widespread presuppositions of (moral) inferiority, Jews had a conception of their good—that is, a narrative. This narrative anchored their lives and provided a basis for affirmation that was (and continues to be) independent of the values of society at large, not readily appropriated by mainstream American society. Again, I submit that the pain of slavery can be seen in the fact that it robbed blacks of a narrative.

V

A narrative is the cornerstone that secures group autonomy. In claiming that Jews, on the one hand, have both group autonomy and a narrative and that blacks, on the other, have neither, have I made an invidious comparison? It is true that I have drawn attention to a differential between blacks and Jews of extraordinary significance. But that does not make the comparison invidious. After all, it is generally agreed that Jews as a people have flourished in American society, whereas blacks as a people have languished. Yet, few would call that comparison invidious. Why? Because by any reasonable assessment, that differential between Jews and blacks would seem to be the truth of the matter—a truth that neither distorts the present social reality of either group nor requires distorting the historical experiences of either group. If this should be the guide to whether a comparison is invidious or not, then the differential between blacks and Jews regarding group autonomy and a narrative is not invidious.

Furthermore, there is the explanatory power of the account offered. Some insight is gained into why Jews have flourished and blacks have languished without denying the reality of the horrors that have occurred in the history of the Jews. If anything, some insight has been gained regarding the toll that American slavery and racism has taken upon the lives of blacks in the United States—an insight that is not gained by focusing upon the horrors of chains, whips, and lynchings or even upon the horror of how many blacks lost their lives due to slavery. These horrors are not to be diminished. Thus, those who would object to the account that I have offered as favoring Jews might want to think again; for the account gives us a better handle on the evil of racism without detracting from the horrendous evil that others have suffered.

Finally, the account sheds some light on the tension between blacks and Jews. I have already spoken to the negative feelings of blacks regarding Jews.

I want to conclude with a word about racism on the part of Jews towards blacks.

Racism is the belief, immune to a wide range of evidence and explanatory considerations to the contrary, that blacks are inferior. Nothing better invites the suspicion of inferiority than the following line of reasoning: Although Jews and blacks have suffered equally, the Jews have flourished and the blacks have languished. What can explain this differential between Jews and blacks other than that blacks are lacking in some way?

In *Vessels of Evil*, I observed that there are two ways of understanding the claim that X is an ultimate evil: (1) No evil can be more horrible than X; (2) All other evils are less horrible than X. Far too often, in talking about the difference between the Holocaust and American slavery, people have said the first, but in their heart of hearts have meant the second. Blacks have often supposed that understanding American slavery in the second sense of ultimate evil helps to explain the plight of blacks in the United States today. I suggest that the account of group autonomy and narrative does much better in that regard. Let me observe that when the Holocaust is understood by Jews as an ultimate evil in the second sense, then in light of the comparative success of Jews vis-à-vis blacks, the result is an interpretation of the respective sufferings of both groups that is easily carried along by the winds of racist ideology. By contrast, the account of group autonomy and narrative is not.

But why do we think of drawing the contrast between Jews and blacks instead of Jews and some other group, or blacks and some other group? The obvious answer, it might seem, is the extraordinary suffering that both groups have endured. The problem with this answer, though, is that is does not take seriously the suffering of still other groups—Native Americans, the Armenians, and so on. I should like to conclude this essay with a different answer.

As the label suggests, American slavery stands as America's most brazen, systematic, and enduring institution of oppression. It is an evil that America actively sought to sustain. This it did, even as it took itself to be a Christian nation, which brings me to Judaism. According to the Christian narrative, Christianity is flanked by the experience of the Jews: The Jewish people gave birth to Christianity, and the fulfillment of Christianity is tied to the experience of the Jewish people. For many fundamentalist Christians, Israel's winning the Six-Day War was an occasion to rejoice, as this could only mean that the Second Coming was near. Thus, for radically different reasons— reasons that have nothing whatsoever to do with the comparative success of Jews and blacks, these two peoples are—or at least have been—an extremely deep part of the very psyche of Americans. It is most unfortunate that this has turned into a race for the who-has-suffered-the-most award. With the accounts of group autonomy and narrative offered in this essay, I should like to think we have a basis for leaving behind that useless competition and entering into a dialogue of understanding.

15

AFRICAN IDENTITIES

KWAME ANTHONY APPIAH

It is, of course true that the African identity is still in the making. There
isn't a final identity that is African. But, at the same time, there *is* an
identity coming into existence. And it has a certain context and a certain meaning. Because if somebody meets me, say, in a shop in Cambridge, he says "Are you from Africa?" Which means that Africa means
something to some people. Each of these tags has a meaning, and a
penalty and a responsibility.[1]

(Chinua Achebe)

The cultural life of most of black Africa remained largely unaffected by
European ideas until the last years of the nineteenth century, and most
cultures began our own century with ways of life formed very little by direct
contact with Europe. Direct trade with Europeans—and especially the slave
trade—had structured the economies of many of the states of the West
African coast and its hinterland from the mid-seventeenth century onward,
replacing the extensive gold trade that had existed at least since the Carthag-
inian empire in the second century B.C.E. By the early nineteenth century, as
the slave trade went into decline, palm nut and groundnut oils had become
major exports to Europe, and these were followed later by cocoa and coffee.
But the direct colonization of the region began in earnest only in the later
nineteenth century, and European administration of the whole of West
Africa was only accomplished—after much resistance—when the Sokoto
caliphate was conquered in 1903.

On the Indian ocean, the eastward trade, which sent gold and slaves to
Arabia, and exchanged spices, incense, ivory, coconut oil, timber, grain, and
pig iron for Indian silk and fine textiles, and pottery and porcelain from
Persia and China, had dominated the economies of the East African lit-
toral until the coming of the Portuguese disrupted the trade in the late

From Kwame Anthony Appiah, 'African Identities', in Kwame Anthony Appiah, *In my Father's
House: Africa in the Philosophy of Culture* ((New York: Oxford University Press, 1992).

[1] Achebe, Interview.

fifteenth century. From then on European trade became increasingly pre-dominant, but in the mid-nineteenth century the major economic force in the region was the Arab Omanis, who had captured Mombasa from the Portuguese more than a century earlier. Using slave labor from the African mainland, the Omanis developed the profitable clove trade of Zanzibar, making it, by the 1860s, the world's major producer. But in most of East Africa, as in the West, extended direct contact with Europeans was a late-nineteenth-century phenomenon, and colonization occurred essentially only after 1885.

In the south of the continent, in the areas where Bantu-speaking people predominate, few cultures had had any contact with Europeans before 1900. By the end of the century the region had adopted many new crops for the world economy; imports of firearms, manufactured in the newly industrial-ized West, had created a new political order, based often on force; and European missionaries and explorers—of whom David Livingstone was, for Westerners, the epitome—had traveled almost everywhere in the region. The administration of southern Africa from Europe was established in law only by the ending, in 1902, of the Boer War.

Not surprisingly, then, European cultural influence in Africa before the twentieth century was extremely limited. Deliberate attempts at change (through missionary activity or the establishment of Western schools) and unintended influence (through contact with explorers and colonizers in the interior, and trading posts on the coasts) produced small enclaves of Euro-peanized Africans. But the major cultural impact of Europe is largely a product of the period since the First World War.

To understand the variety of Africa's contemporary cultures, therefore, we need, first, to recall the variety of the precolonial cultures. Differences in colonial experience have also played their part in shaping the continent's diversities, but even identical colonial policies identically implemented work-ing on the very different cultural materials would surely have produced widely varying results.

No doubt we can find generalizations at a certain abstract level, which hold true of most of black Africa before European conquest. It is a famil-iar idea in African historigography that Africa was the last continent in the old world with an "uncaptured" peasantry, largely able to use land without the supervision of feudal overlords and able, if they chose, to market their products through a complex system of trading networks.[2] While European ruling classes were living off the surplus of peasants and the newly developing industrial working class, African rulers were

---

[2] See, for example, Robert Harms, *Times Literary Supplement*, 29 Nov. 1985, 1343.

essentially living off taxes on trade. But if we could have traveled through Africa's many cultures in those years—from the small groups of Bushman hunter-gatherers, with their stone-age materials, to the Hausa kingdoms, rich in worked metal—we should have felt in every place profoundly different impulses, ideas, and forms of life. To speak of an African identity in the nineteenth century—if an identity is a coalescence of mutually responsive (if sometimes conflicting) modes of conduct, habits of thought, and patterns of evaluation; in short, a coherent kind of human social psychology—would have been "to give to aery nothing a local habitation and a name."

Yet there is no doubt that now, a century later, an African identity is coming into being. I have argued throughout these essays that this identity is a new thing; that it is the product of a history, some of whose moments I have sketched; and that the bases through which so far it has largely been theorized—race, a common historical experience, a shared metaphysics—presuppose falsehoods too serious for us to ignore.

Every human identity is constructed, historical; every one has its share of false presuppositions, of the errors and inaccuracies that courtesy calls "myth," religion "heresy," and science "magic." Invented histories, invented biologies, invented cultural affinities come with every identity; each is a kind of role that has to be scripted, structured by conventions of narrative to which the world never quite manages to conform.

Often those who say this—who deny the biological reality of races or the literal truth of our national fictions—are treated by nationalists and "race men" as if they are proposing genocide or the destruction of nations, as if in saying that there is literally no Negro race one was obliterating all those who claim to be Negroes, in doubting the story of Okomfo Anokye one is repudiating the Asante nation. This is an unhelpful hyperbole, but it is certainly true that there must be contexts in which a statement of these truths is politically inopportune. I am enough of a scholar to feel drawn to truth telling, *ruat caelum*; enough of a political animal to recognize that there are places where the truth does more harm than good.

But, so far as I can see, we do not have to choose between these impulses: there is no reason to believe that racism is always—or even usually—advanced by denying the existence of races; and, though there is some reason to suspect that those who resist legal remedies for the history of racism might use the nonexistence of races to argue in the United States, for example, against affirmative action, that strategy is, as a matter of logic, easily opposed. For, as Tvetzan Todorov reminds us, the existence of racism does not require the existence of races. And, we can add, nations are real enough, however invented their traditions.[3]

To raise the issue of whether these truths are truths to be uttered is to be forced, however, to face squarely the real political question: the question, itself, as old as political philosophy, of when we should endorse the ennobling lie. In the real world of practical politics, of everyday alliances and popular mobilizations, a rejection of races and nations in theory can be part of a program for coherent political practice, only if we can show more than that the black race—or the Shona tribe or any of the other modes of self-invention that Africa has inherited—fit the common pattern of relying on less than the literal truth. We would need to show not that race and national history are falsehoods but they are useless falsehoods at best or—at worst—dangerous ones: that another set of stories will build us identities through which we can make more productive alliances.

The problem, of course, is that group identity seems to work only—or, at least, to work best—when it is seen by its members as natural, as "real." Pan-Africanism, black solidarity, can be an important force with real political benefits, but it doesn't work without its attendant mystifications. (Nor, to turn to the other obvious exemplum, is feminism without its occasional risks and mystifications either.) Recognizing the constructedness of the history of identities has seemed to many incompatible with taking these new identities with the seriousness they have for those who invent—or, as they would no doubt rather say, discover—and possess them.[4] In sum, the demands of agency seem always—in the real world of politics—to *entail a misrecognition of its genesis*; you cannot build alliances without mystifications and mythologies. And this chapter is an exploration of ways in which Pan-African solidarity can be appropriated by those of us whose positions as intellectuals—as searchers after truth—make it impossible for us to live through the falsehoods of race and tribe and nation, whose understanding of history makes us skeptical that nationalism and racial solidarity can do the good that they can do without the attendant evils of racism—and other particularisms; without the warring of nations.

Where are we to start? I have argued often in these pages against the forms of racism implicit in much talk of Pan-Africanism. (And in other places, especially in "Racisms" and "Racism and Moral Pollution," I have offered further arguments against these racist presuppositions.)

---

[3] Tzvetan Todorov, "'Race,' Writing and Culture," in Henry Louis Gates Jr. (ed.), *Race, Writing and Difference* (Chicago: University of Chicago Press, 1986), 370–80. You don't have to believe in witchcraft, after all, to believe that women were persecuted as witches in colonial Massachusetts.

[4] Gayatri Spivak recognizes these problems when she speaks of "strategic" essentialisms. See *In Other Worlds: Essays in Cultural Politics* (New York: Routledge, 1988), 205.

But these objections to a biologically rooted conception of race may still seem all too theoretical: if Africans can get together around the idea of the Black Person, if they can create through this notion productive alliances with African-Americans and people of African descent in Europe and the Caribbean, surely these theoretical objections should pale in the light of the practical value of these alliances. But there is every reason to doubt that they can. Within Africa—in the OAU, in the Sudan, in Mauritania[5]— racialization has produced arbitrary boundaries and exacerbated tensions; in the diaspora alliances with other peoples of color, qua victims of racism—people of south Asian descent in England, Hispanics in the United States, "Arabs" in France, Turks in Germany—have proved essential.

In short, I think it is clear enough that a biologically rooted conception of race is both dangerous in practice and misleading in theory: African unity, African identity, need securer foundations than race.

The passage from Achebe with which I began this chapter continues in these words: "All these tags, unfortunately for the black man, are tags of disability." But it seems to me that they are not so much labels of disability as disabling labels; which is, in essence, my complaint against Africa as a racial mythology—the Africa of Crummell and Du Bois (from the New World) and of the *bolekaja* critics (from the Old); against Africa as a shared metaphysics—the Africa of Soyinka; against Africa as a fancied past of shared glories—the Africa of Diop and the "Egyptianists."

Each of these complaints can be summarized in a paragraph.

"Race" disables us because it proposes as a basis for common action the illusion that black (and white and yellow) people are fundamentally allied by nature and, thus, without effort; it leaves us unprepared, therefore, to handle the "intraracial" conflicts that arise from the very different situations of black (and white and yellow) people in different parts of the economy and of the world.

The African metaphysics of Soyinka disables because it founds our unity in gods who have not served us well in our dealings with the world—Soyinka never defends the "African World" against Wiredu's charge that since people die daily in Ghana because they prefer traditional herbal remedies to Western medicines, "any inclination to glorify the unanalytical [i.e. the traditional] cast of mind is not just retrograde; it is tragic." Soyinka has proved the Yoruba pantheon a powerful literary resource, but he cannot explain why Christianity and Islam have so widely displaced the old gods, or why an

---

[5] The violence between Senegalese and Mauritanians in the spring of 1989 can only be understood when we recall that the legal abolition of racial slavery of "Negroes," owned by "Moorish" masters, occurred in the early 1980s.

image of the West has so powerful a hold on the contemporary Yoruba imagination; nor can his mythmaking offer us the resources for creating economies and polities adequate to our various places in the world.

And the Egyptianists—like all who have chosen to root Africa's modern identity in an imaginary history—require us to see the past as the moment of wholeness and unity; tie us to the values and beliefs of the past; and thus divert us (this critique is as old as Césaire's appraisal of Tempels) from the problems of the present and the hopes of the future.

If an African identity is to empower us, so it seems to me, what is required is not so much that we throw out falsehood but that we acknowledge first of all that race and history and metaphysics do not enforce an identity: that we can choose, within broad limits set by ecological, political, and economic realities what it will mean to be African in the coming years.

I do not want to be misunderstood. We are Africans already. And we can give numerous examples from multiple domains of what our being African means. We have, for example, in the OAU and the African Development Bank, and in such regional organizations as SADDC and ECOWAS, as well as in the African caucuses of the agencies of the UN and the World Bank, African institutions. At the Olympics and the Commonwealth games, athletes from African countries are seen as Africans by the world—and, perhaps, more importantly, by each other. Being African already has "a certain context and a certain meaning."

But, as Achebe suggests, that meaning is not always one we can be happy with, and that identity is one we must continue to reshape. And in thinking about how we are to reshape it, we would do well to remember that the African identity is, for its bearers, only one among many. Like all identities, institutionalized before anyone has permanently fixed a single meaning for them—like the German identity at the beginning of this century, or the American in the latter eighteenth century, or the Indian identity at independence so few years ago—being African is, for its bearers, one among other salient modes of being, all of which have to be constantly fought for and rethought. And indeed, in Africa, it is another of these identities that provides one of the most useful models for such rethinking; it is a model that draws on other identities central to contemporary life in the subcontinent, namely, the constantly shifting redefinition of "tribal" identities to meet the economic and political exigencies of the modern world.

Once more, let me quote Achebe:

The duration of awareness, of consciousness of an identity, has really very little to do with how deep it is. You can suddenly become aware of an identity which you have been suffering from for a long time without knowing. For instance, take the Igbo people. In my area, historically, they did not see themselves as Igbo. They saw themselves as people from this village or that village. In fact in some place "Igbo" was a word of abuse; they were the "other" people, down in the bush. And yet, after the experience of the Biafran War, during a period of two years, it became a very powerful consciousness. But it was *real* all the time. They all spoke the same language, called "Igbo," even though they were not using that identity in any way. But the moment came when this identity became very very powerful . . . and over a very short period.

A short period it was, and also a tragic one. The Nigerian civil war defined an Igbo identity: it did so in complex ways, which grew out of the development of a common Igbo identity in colonial Nigeria, an identity that created the Igbo traders in the cities of northern Nigeria as an identifiable object of assault in the period that led up to the invention of Biafra.

Recognizing Igbo identity as a new thing is not a way of privileging other Nigerian identities: each of the three central ethnic identities of modern political life—Hausa-Fulani, Yoruba, Igbo—is a product of the rough-and-tumble of the transition through colonial to postcolonial status. David Laitin has pointed out that "the idea that there was a single Hausa-Fulani tribe . . . was largely a political claim of the NPC [Northern Peoples' Congress] in their battle against the South," while "many elders intimately involved in rural Yoruba society today recall that, as late as the 1930s, 'Yoruba' was not a common form of political identification."[6] Nnamdi Azikiwe—one of the key figures in the construction of Nigerian nationalism—was extremely popular (as Laitin also points out) in Yoruba Lagos, where "he edited his nationalist newspaper, the *West African Pilot*. It was only subsequent events that led him to be defined in Nigeria as an *Igbo* leader."[7] Yet Nigerian politics—and the more everyday economy of ordinary personal relations—is oriented along such axes, and only very occasionally does the fact float into view that even these three problematic identities account for at most seven out of ten Nigerians.

And the story is repeated, even in places where it was not drawn in lines of blood. As Johannes Fabian has observed, the powerful Lingala and Swahili-speaking identities of modern Zaire exist "because spheres of political and economic interest were established before the Belgians took full control, and continued to inform relations between regions under colonial rule."[8]

---

[6] David Laitin, *Hegemony and Culture: Politics and Religious Change among the Yoruba* (Chicago: University of Chicago Press, 1986), 7–8.

[7] Ibid. 8.

[8] This passage continues: "Increasingly also Lingala and Swahili came to divide functions between them. Lingala served the military and much of the administration in the capital of the lower Congo; Swahili became the language of the workers in the mines of Katanga. This created cultural connotations which began to emerge very early and which remained prevalent in Mobutu's Zaire. From the point of view of Katanga/Shaba, Lingala has been the undignified jargon of unproductive soldiers, government clerks, entertainers, and, recently, of a power clique, all of them

Modern Ghana witnesses the development of an Akan identity, as speakers of the three major regional dialects of Twi—Asante, Fante, Akuapem— organize themselves into a corporation against an (equally novel) Ewe unity.[9]

When it is not the "tribe" that is invested with new uses and meanings, it is religion. Yet the idea that Nigeria is composed of a Muslim North, a Christian South, and a mosaic of "pagan" holdovers is as inaccurate as the picture of three historic tribal identities. Two out of every five southern Yoruba people are Muslim, and, as Laitin tells us: "Many northern groups, especially in what are today Benue, Plateau, Gongola, and Kwara states, are largely Christian. When the leaders of Biafra tried to convince the world that they were oppressed by northern Muslims, ignorant foreigners (including the pope) believed them. But the Nigerian army . . . was led by a northern Christian."[10] It is as useless here, as in the case of race, to point out in each case that the tribe or the religion is, like all social identities, based on an idealizing fiction, for life in Nigeria or in Zaire has come to be lived through that idealization: the Igbo identity is real because Nigerians believe in it, the Shona identity because Zimbabweans have given it meaning. The rhetoric of a Muslim North and a Christian South structured political discussions in the period before Nigerian independence. But it was equally important in the debates about instituting a Muslim Court of Appeals in the Draft Constitution of 1976, and it could be found, for example, in many an article in the Nigerian press as electoral registration for a new civilian era began in July 1989.

There are, I think three crucial lessons to be learned from these cases. First, that identities are complex and multiple and grow out of a history of changing responses to economic, political, and cultural forces, almost always in opposition to other identities. Second, that they flourish despite what I earlier called our "misrecognition" of their origins; despite, that is, their roots in myths and in lies. And third, that there is, in consequence, no large place for reason in the construction—as opposed to the study and the management—

---

designated as *batoka chini*, people from down-river, i.e. from Kinshasa. Swahili as spoken in Katanga was a symbol of regionalism, even for those colonials who spoke it badly." Johannes Fabian, *Language and Colonial Power* (Cambridge: Cambridge University Press, 1986), 42–3. The dominance of Swahili in certain areas is already itself a colonial product (*Language and Colonial Power*, 6).

[9] Similarly, Shona and Ndebele identities in modern Zimbabwe became associated with political parties at independence, even though Shona-speaking peoples had spent much of the late precolonial period in military confrontations with each other.

[10] Laitin, *Hegemony and Culture*, 8. I need hardly add that religious identities are equally salient and equally mythological in Lebanon or in Ireland.

of identities. One temptation, then, for those who see the centrality of these fictions in our lives, is to leave reason behind: to celebrate and endorse those identities that seem at the moment to offer the best hope of advancing our other goals, and to keep silence about the lies and the myths. But, as I said earlier, intellectuals do not easily neglect the truth, and, all things considered, our societies profit, in my view, from the institutionalization of this imperative in the academy. So it is important for us to continue trying to tell our truths. But the facts I have been rehearsing should imbue us all with a strong sense of the marginality of such work to the central issue of the resistance to racism and ethnic violence—and to sexism, and to the other structures of difference that shape the world of power; they should force upon us the clear realization that the real battle is not being fought in the academy. Every time I read another report in the newspapers of an African disaster—a famine in Ethiopia, a war in Namibia, ethnic conflict in Burundi—I wonder how much good it does to correct the theories with which these evils are bound up; the solution is food, or mediation, or some other more material, more practical step. And yet, as I have tried to argue in this book, the shape of modern Africa (the shape of our world) is in large part the product, often the unintended and unanticipated product, of theories; even the most vulgar of Marxists will have to admit that economic interests operate *through* ideologies. We cannot change the world simply by evidence and reasoning, but we surely cannot change it without them either.

What we in the academy *can* contribute—even if only slowly and marginally—is a disruption of the discourse of "racial" and "tribal" differences. For, in my perfectly unoriginal opinion, the inscription of difference in Africa today plays into the hands of the very exploiters whose shackles we are trying to escape. "Race" in Europe and "tribe" in Africa are central to the way in which the objective interests of the worst-off are distorted. The analogous point for African-Americans was recognized long ago by Du Bois.[11] Du Bois argued in *Black Reconstruction* that racist ideology had

---

[11] That "race" operates this way has been clear to many other African-Americans: so, for example, it shows up in a fictional context as a central theme of George Schuyler's *Black No More* (New York: Negro Universities Press, 1931); see, for example, p. 59. Du Bois (as usual) provides— in *Black Reconstruction: An Essay toward a History of the Part which Black People Played in America, 1860–1880* (New York: Russel & Russel, 1935)—a body of evidence that remains relevant. As Cedric J. Robinson writes, "Once the industrial class emerged as dominant in the nation, it possessed not only its own basis of power and the social relations historically related to that power, but it also had available to it the instruments of repression created by the now subordinate Southern ruling class. In its struggle with labour, it could activate racism to divide the labour movement into antagonistic forces. Moreover, the permutations of the instrument appeared endless: Black against white; Anglo-Saxon against southern and eastern European; domestic against immigrant; proletariat against share-cropper; white American against Asian, Black, Latin American, etc." Cedric J. Robinson, *Black Marxism: The Making of the Black Radical Tradition* (London: Zed Books, 1983), 286.

essentially blocked the formation of a significant labor movement in the U.S., for such a movement would have required the collaboration of the 9 million ex-slave and white peasant workers of the South.[12] It is, in other words, because the categories of difference often cut across our economic interests that they operate to blind us to them. What binds the middle-class African-American to his dark-skinned fellow citizens downtown is not economic interest but racism and the cultural products of resistance to it that are shared across (most of) African-American culture.

It seems to me that we learn from this case what John Thompson has argued recently, in a powerful but appreciative critique of Pierre Bourdieu: namely, that it may be a mistake to think that social reproduction—the processes by which societies maintain themselves over time—presupposes "some sort of consensus with regard to dominant values or norms." Rather, the stability of today's industrialized society may require "a pervasive *fragmentation* of the social order and a proliferation of divisions between its members." For it is precisely this fragmentation that prevents oppositional attitudes from generating "a coherent alternative view which would provide a basis for political action."

Divisions are ramified along the lines of gender, race, qualifications and so on, forming barriers which obstruct the development of movements which could threaten the *status quo*. The reproduction of the social order may depend less upon a consensus with regard to dominant values or norms than upon a *lack of consensus* at the very point where oppositional attitudes could be translated into political action.[13]

Thompson allows us to see that within contemporary industrial societies an identification of oneself as an African, above all else, allows the fact that one is, say, not an Asian, to be used against one; in this setting—as we see in South Africa—a racialized conception of one's identity is retrogressive. To argue this way is to presuppose that the political meanings of identities are historically and geographically relative. So it is quite consistent with this claim to hold, as I do, that in constructing alliances *across* states—and

---

[12] See Robinson, *Black Marxism*, 313.

[13] John B. Thompson, *Studies in the Theory of Ideology* (Berkeley: University of California Press, 1984), 62–3. Again and again, in American labor history, we can document the ways in which conflicts organized around a racial or ethnic group identity can be captured by the logic of the existing order. The financial support that black churches in Detroit received from the Ford Motor Company in the 1930s was only a particularly dramatic example of a widespread phenomenon: corporate manipulation of racial difference in an effort to defeat labor solidarity. See, for example, James S. Olson, "Race, Class and Progress: Black Leadership and Industrial Unionism, 1936–1945," in M. Cantor (ed.), *Black Labor in America* (Westport, Conn.: Negro Universities Press, 1969); and David M. Gordon, Richard Edwards, and Michael Reich, *Segmented Work, Divided Workers: The Historical Transformation of Labor in the United States* (Cambridge: Cambridge University Press, 1982), 141–3, and Fredric Jameson, *The Political Unconscious* (Ithaca, NY: Cornell University Press, 1981), 54.

especially in the Third World—a Pan-African identity, which allows African-Americans, Afro-Caribbeans, and Afro-Latins to ally with continental Africans, drawing on the cultural resources of the black Atlantic world, may serve useful purposes. Resistance to a self-isolating black nationalism *within* England or France or the United States is thus theoretically consistent with Pan-Africanism as an international project.

Because the value of identities is thus relative, we must argue for and against them case by case. And given the current situation in Africa, I think it remains clear that another Pan-Africanism—the project of a continental fraternity and sorority, *not* the project of a racialized Negro nationalism— however false or muddled its theoretical roots, can be a progressive force. It is as fellow Africans that Ghanaian diplomats (my father among them) interceded between the warring nationalist parties in Rhodesia under UDI; as fellow Africans that OAU teams can mediate regional conflicts; as fellow Africans that the human rights assessors organized under the Banjul Declaration can intercede for citizens of African states against the excesses of our governments. If there is, as I have suggested, hope, too, for the Pan-Africanism of an African diaspora once it, too, is released from bondage to racial ideologies (alongside the many bases of alliance available to Africa's peoples in their political and cultural struggles), it is crucial that we recognize the independence, once "Negro" nationalism is gone, of the Pan-Africanism of the diaspora and the Pan-Africanism of the continent. It is, I believe, in the exploration of these issues, these possibilities, that the future of an intellectually reinvigorated Pan-Africanism lies.

Finally, I would like to suggest that it is really unsurprising that a continental identity is coming into cultural and institutional reality through regional and subregional organizations. We share a continent and its ecological problems; we share a relation of dependency to the world economy; we share the problem of racism in the way the industrialized world thinks of us (and let me include here, explicitly, both "Negro" Africa and the "Maghrib"); we share the possibilities of the development of regional markets and local circuits of production; and our intellectuals participate, through the shared contingencies of our various histories, in a common discourse whose outlines I have tried to limn in this book.

"ɔdɛnkyɛm nwu nsuo-ase mma yɛmmɛfrɛ kwakuo sɛ ɔbɛyɛ no ayie," goes an Akan proverb. "The crocodile does not die under the water so that we can call the monkey to celebrate its funeral." Each of us, the proverb can be used to say, belongs to a group with its own customs. To accept that Africa can be in these ways a usable identity is not to forget that all of us belong to multifarious communities with their local customs; it is not to dream of a single African state and to forget the complexly different trajectories of the continent's so many languages and cultures. "African solidarity" can surely be a vital and enabling rallying cry; but in this world of genders, ethnicities, and classes, of families, religions, and nations, it is as well to remember that there are times when Africa is not the banner we need.

16

SOCIAL MOVEMENTS AND THE POLITICS OF DIFFERENCE

IRIS MARION YOUNG

The idea that I think we need today in order to make decisions in political matters cannot be the idea of a totality, or of the unity, of a body. It can only be the idea of a multiplicity or a diversity. . . . To state that one must draw a critique of political judgment means today to do a politics of opinions that at the same time is a politics of Ideas . . . in which justice is not placed under a rule of convergence but rather a rule of divergence. I believe that this is the theme that one finds constantly in present day writing under the name "minority."

(Jean-François Lyotard)

There was once a time of caste and class, when tradition decreed that each group had its place, and that some are born to rule and others to serve. In this time of darkness, law and social norms defined rights, privileges, and obligations differently for different groups, distinguished by characteristics of sex, race, religion, class, or occupation. Social inequality was justified by church and state on the grounds that people have different natures, and some natures are better than others.

Then one day Enlightenment dawned, heralding a revolutionary conception of humanity and society. All people are equal, the revolutionaries declared, inasmuch as all have a capacity for reason and moral sense. Law and politics should therefore grant to everyone equal political and civil rights. With these bold ideas the battle lines of modern political struggle were drawn.

For over two hundred years since those voices of Reason first rang out, the forces of light have struggled for liberty and political equality against the dark forces of irrational prejudice, arbitrary metaphysics, and the crumbling towers of patriarchal church, state, and family. In the New World we had a head start in this fight, since the American War of Independence was fought on these Enlightenment principles, and our Constitution stood for liberty

From Iris Marion Young, 'Social Movements and the Politics of Difference', in Iris Marion Young, *Justice and the Politics of Difference* (Princeton: Princeton University Press, 1990).

and equality. So we did not have to throw off the yokes of class and religious privilege, as did our Old World comrades. Yet the United States had its own oligarchic horrors in the form of slavery and the exclusion of women from public life. In protracted and bitter struggles these bastions of privilege based on group difference began to give way, finally to topple in the 1960s.

Today in our society a few vestiges of prejudice and discrimination remain, but we are working on them, and have nearly realized the dream those Enlightenment fathers dared to propound. The state and law should express rights only in universal terms applied equally to all, and differences among persons and groups should be a purely accidental and private matter. We seek a society in which differences of race, sex, religion, and ethnicity no longer make a difference to people's rights and opportunities. People should be treated as individuals, not as members of groups; their life options and rewards should be based solely on their individual achievement. All persons should have the liberty to be and do anything they want, to choose their own lives and not be hampered by traditional expectations and stereotypes.

We tell each other this story and make our children perform it for our sacred holidays—Thanksgiving Day, the Fourth of July, Memorial Day, Lincoln's Birthday. We have constructed Martin Luther King Day to fit the narrative so well that we have already forgotten that it took a fight to get it included in the canon year. There is much truth to this story. Enlightenment ideals of liberty and political equality did and do inspire movements against oppression and domination, whose success has created social values and institutions we would not want to lose. A people could do worse than tell this story after big meals and occasionally call upon one another to live up to it.

The very worthiness of the narrative, however, and the achievement of political equality that it recounts, now inspires new heretics. In recent years the ideal of liberation as the elimination of group difference has been challenged by movements of the oppressed. The very success of political movements against differential privilege and for political equality has generated movements of group specificity and cultural pride.

In this chapter I criticize an ideal of justice that defines liberation as the transcendence of group difference, which I refer to as an ideal of assimilation. This ideal usually promotes equal treatment as a primary principle of justice. Recent social movements of oppressed groups challenge this ideal. Many in these movements argue that a positive self-definition of group difference is in fact more liberatory.

I endorse this politics of difference, and argue that at stake is the meaning of social difference itself. Traditional politics that excludes or devalues some persons on account of their group attributes assumes an essentialist meaning of difference; it defines groups as having different natures. An egalitarian politics of difference, on the other hand, defines difference more fluidly and relationally as the product of social processes.

An emancipatory politics that affirms group difference involves a reconception of the meaning of equality. The assimilationist ideal assumes that equal social status for all persons requires treating everyone according to the same principles, rules, and standards. A politics of difference argues, on the other hand, that equality as the participation and inclusion of all groups sometimes requires different treatment for oppressed or disadvantaged groups. To promote social justice, I argue, social policy should sometimes accord special treatment to groups. I explore pregnancy and birthing rights for workers, bilingual-bicultural rights, and American Indian rights as three cases of such special treatment. Finally, I expand the idea of a heterogeneous public here by arguing for a principle of representation for oppressed groups in democratic decisionmaking bodies.

COMPETING PARADIGMS OF LIBERATION

In "On Racism and Sexism," Richard Wasserstrom (1980) develops a classic statement of the ideal of liberation from group-based oppression as involving the elimination of group-based difference itself. A truly nonracist, nonsexist society, he suggests, would be one in which the race or sex of an individual would be the functional equivalent of eye color in our society today. While physiological differences in skin color or genitals would remain, they would have no significance for a person's sense of identity or how others regard him or her. No political rights or obligations would be connected to race or sex, and no important institutional benefits would be associated with either. People would see no reason to consider race or gender in policy or everyday interactions. In such a society, social group differences would have ceased to exist.

Wasserstrom contrasts this ideal of assimilation with an ideal of diversity much like the one I will argue for, which he agrees is compelling. He offers three primary reasons, however, for choosing the assimilationist ideal of liberation over the ideal of diversity. First, the assimilationist ideal exposes the arbitrariness of group-based social distinctions which are thought natural and necessary. By imagining a society in which race and sex have no social significance, one sees more clearly how pervasively these group categories unnecessarily limit possibilities for some in existing society. Second, the assimilationist ideal presents a clear and unambiguous standard of equality and justice. According to such a standard, any group-related differentiation or discrimination is suspect. Whenever laws or rules, the division of labor, or other social practices allocate benefits differently according to group membership, this is a sign of injustice. The principle of justice is simple: treat everyone according to the same principles, rules, and standards. Third, the assimilationist ideal maximizes choice. In a society where differences make no social difference people can develop themselves as individuals, unconstrained by group norms and expectations.

There is no question that the ideal of liberation as the elimination of group difference has been enormously important in the history of emancipatory politics. The ideal of universal humanity that denies natural differences has been a crucial historical development in the struggle against exclusion and status differentiation. It has made possible the assertion of the equal moral worth of all persons, and thus the right of all to participate and be included in all institutions and positions of power and privilege. The assimilationist ideal retains significant rhetorical power in the face of continued beliefs in the essentially different and inferior natures of women, Blacks, and other groups.

The power of this assimilationist ideal has inspired the struggle of oppressed groups and the supporters against the exclusion and denigration of these groups, and continues to inspire many. Periodically in American history, however, movements of the oppressed have questioned and rejected this "path to belonging" (Karst 1986). Instead they have seen self-organization and the assertion of a positive group cultural identity as a better strategy for achieving power and participation in dominant institutions. Recent decades have witnessed a resurgence of this "politics of difference" not only among racial and ethnic groups, but also among women, gay men and lesbians, old people, and the disabled.

Not long after the passage of the Civil Rights Act and the Voting Rights Act, many white and Black supporters of the Black civil rights movement were surprised, confused, and angered by the emergence of the Black Power movement. Black Power advocates criticized the integrationist goal and reliance on the support of white liberals that characterized the civil rights movement. They encouraged Blacks to break their alliance with whites and assert the specificity of their own culture, political organization, and goals. Instead of integration, they encouraged Blacks to seek economic and political empowerment in their separate neighborhoods (Carmichael and Hamilton 1967; Bayes 1982, ch. 3; Lader 1979, ch. 5; Omi and Winant 1986, ch. 6). Since the late 1960s many Blacks have claimed that the integration successes of the civil rights movement have had the effect of dismantling the bases of Black-organized social and economic institutions at least as much as they have lessened Black–white animosity and opened doors of opportunity (Cruse 1987). While some individual Blacks may be better off than they would have been if these changes had not occurred, as a group, Blacks are no better off and may be worse off, because the Blacks who have succeeded in assimilating into the American middle class no longer associate as closely with lower-class Blacks (cf. Wilson 1978).

While much Black politics has questioned the ideal of assimilation in economic and political terms, the past twenty years have also seen the assertion and celebration by Blacks of a distinct Afro-American culture, both as a recovery and revaluation of an Afro-American history and in the creation of new cultural forms. The slogan "Black is beautiful" pierced American consciousness, deeply unsettling the received body aesthetic which I argued in Chapter 5[1] continues to be a powerful reproducer of racism. Afro-American hairstyles pronounced themselves differently stylish, not less stylish. Linguistic theorists asserted that Black English is English differently constructed, not bad English, and Black poets and novelists exploited and explored its particular nuances.

In the late 1960s Red Power came fast on the heels of Black Power. The American Indian Movement and other radical organizations of American Indians rejected perhaps even more vehemently than Blacks the goal of assimilation which has dominated white-Indian relations for most of the twentieth century. They asserted a right to self-government on Indian lands and fought to gain and maintain a dominant Indian voice in the Bureau of Indian Affairs. American Indians have sought to recover and preserve their language, rituals, and crafts, and this renewal of pride in traditional culture has also fostered a separatist political movement. The desire to pursue land rights claims and to fight for control over resources on reservations arises from what has become a fierce commitment to tribal self-determination, the desire to develop and maintain Indian political and economic bases in but not of white society (Deloria and Lytle 1983; Ortiz 1984, pt. 3; Cornell 1988, pt. 2).

These are but two examples of a widespread tendency in the politics of the 1970s and 1980s for oppressed, disadvantaged, or specially marked groups to organize autonomously and assert a positive sense of their cultural and experiential specificity. Many Spanish-speaking Americans have rejected the traditional assumption that full participation in American society requires linguistic and cultural assimilation. In the last twenty years many have developed a renewed interest and pride in their Puerto Rican, Chicano, Mexican, or other Latin American heritage. They have asserted the right to

---

[1] Of *Justice and the Politics of Difference*. All cross-references in this chapter are to this book.—Ed.

maintain their specific culture and speak their language and still receive the benefits of citizenship, such as voting rights, decent education, and job opportunities. Many Jewish Americans have similarly rejected the ideal of assimilation, instead asserting the specificity and positive meaning of Jewish identity, often insisting publicly that Christian culture cease to be taken as the norm.

Since the late 1960s the blossoming of gay cultural expression, gay organization, and the public presence of gays in marches and other forums have radically altered the environment in which young people come to sexual identity, and changed many people's perceptions of homosexuality. Early gay rights advocacy had a distinctly assimilationist and universalist orientation. The goal was to remove the stigma of being homosexual, to prevent institutional discrimination, and to achieve societal recognition that gay people are "no different" from anyone else. The very process of political organization against discrimination and police harassment and for the achievement of civil rights, however, fostered the development of gay and lesbian communities and cultural expression, which by the mid 1970s flowered in meeting places, organizations, literature, music, and massive street celebrations (Altman 1982; D'Emilio 1983; Epstein 1987).

Today most gay and lesbian liberation advocates seek not merely civil rights, but the affirmation of gay men and lesbians as social groups with specific experiences and perspectives. Refusing to accept the dominant culture's definition of healthy sexuality and respectable family life and social practices, gay and lesbian liberation movements have proudly created and displayed a distinctive self-definition and culture. For gay men and lesbians the analogue to racial integration is the typical liberal approach to sexuality, which tolerates any behavior as long as it is kept private. Gay pride asserts that sexual identity is a matter of culture and politics, and not merely "behavior" to be tolerated or forbidden.

The women's movement has also generated its own versions of a politics of difference. Humanist feminism, which predominated in the nineteenth century and in the contemporary women's movement until the late 1970s, finds in any assertion of difference between women and men only a legacy of female oppression and an ideology to legitimate continued exclusion of women from socially valued human activity. Humanist feminism is thus analogous to an ideal of assimilation in identifying sexual equality with gender blindness, with measuring women and men according to the same standards and treating them in the same way. Indeed, for many feminists, androgyny names the ideal of sexual liberation—a society in which gender difference itself would be eliminated. Given the strength and plausibility of this vision of sexual equality, it was confusing when feminists too began taking the turn to difference, asserting the positivity and specificity of female experience and values (see Young 1985; Miles 1985).

Feminist separatism was the earliest expression of such gynocentric feminism. Feminist separatism rejected wholly or partly the goal of entering the male-dominated world, because it requires playing according to rules that men have made and that have been used against women, and because trying to measure up to male-defined standards inevitably involves accommodating or pleasing the men who continue to dominate socially valued institutions and activities. Separatism promoted the empowerment of women through self-organization, the creation of separate and safe spaces where women could share and analyze their experiences, voice their anger, play with and create bonds with one another, and develop new and better institutions and practices.

Most elements of the contemporary women's movement have been separatist to some degree. Separatists seeking to live as much of their lives as possible in women-only institutions were largely responsible for the creation of the women's culture that burst forth all over the United States by the mid 1970s, and continues to claim the loyalty of millions of women— in the form of music, poetry, spirituality, literature, celebrations, festivals, and dances (see Jaggar 1983: 275–86). Whether drawing on images of Amazonian grandeur, recovering and revaluing traditional women's arts, like quilting and weaving, or inventing new rituals based on medieval witchcraft, the development of such expressions of women's culture gave many feminists images of a female-centered beauty and strength entirely outside capitalist patriarchal definitions of feminine pulchritude. The separatist impulse also fostered the development of the many autonomous women's institutions and services that have concretely improved the lives of many women, whether feminists or not—such as health clinics, battered women's shelters, rape crisis centers, and women's coffeehouses and bookstores.

Beginning in the late 1970s much feminist theory and political analysis also took a turn away from humanist feminism, to question the assumption that traditional female activity expresses primarily the victimization of women and the distortion of their human potential and that the goal of women's liberation is the participation of women as equals in public institutions now dominated by men. Instead of understanding the activities and values associated with traditional femininity as largely distortions and inhibitions of women's truly human potentialities, this gynocentric analysis sought to revalue the caring, nurturing, and cooperative approach to social relations they found associated with feminine socialization, and sought in women's specific experiences the bases for an attitude toward the body and nature healthier than that predominant in male-dominated Western capitalist cuture.

None of the social movements asserting positive group specificity is in fact a unity. All have group differences within them. The Black movement, for example, includes middle-class Blacks and working-class Blacks, gays and straight people, men and women, and so it is with any other group. The implications of group differences within a social group have been most systematically discussed in the women's movement. Feminist conferences and publications have generated particularly fruitful, though often emotionally wrenching, discussions of the oppression of racial and ethnic blindness and the importance of attending to group differences among women (Bulkin *et al.* 1984). From such discussions emerged principled efforts to provide autonomously organized forums for Black women, Latinas, Jewish women, lesbians, differently abled women, old women, and any other women who see reason for claiming that they have as a group a distinctive voice that might be silenced in a general feminist discourse. Those discussions, along with the practices feminists instituted to structure discussion and interaction among differently identifying groups of women, offer some beginning models for the development of a heterogeneous public. Each of the other social movements has also generated discussion of group differences that cut across their identities, leading to other possibilities of coalition and alliance.

EMANCIPATION THROUGH THE POLITICS OF DIFFERENCE

Implicit in emancipatory movements asserting a positive sense of group difference is a different ideal of liberation, which might be called democratic cultural pluralism (cf. Laclau and Mouffe 1985: 166–71; Cunningham 1987: 186–99: Nickel 1987). In this vision the good society does not eliminate or transcend group difference. Rather, there is equality among socially and culturally differentiated groups, who mutually respect one another and affirm one another in their differences. What are the reasons for rejecting the assimilationist ideal and promoting a politics of difference?

As I discussed in Chapter 2, some deny the reality of social groups. For them, group difference is an invidious fiction produced and perpetuated in order to preserve the privilege of the few. Others, such as Wasserstrom, may agree that social groups do now exist and have real social consequences for the way people identify themselves and one another, but assert that such social group differences are undesirable. The assimilationist ideal involves denying either the reality or the desirability of social groups.

Those promoting a politics of difference doubt that a society without group differences is either possible or desirable. Contrary to the assumption of modernization theory, increased urbanization and the extension of equal formal rights to all groups has not led to a decline in particularist affiliations. If anything, the urban concentration and interactions among groups that modernizing social processes introduce tend to reinforce group solidarity and differentiation (Rothschild 1981; Ross 1980; Fischer 1982). Attachment to specific traditions, practices, language, and other culturally specific forms is a crucial aspect of social existence. People do not usually give up their social group identifications, even when they are oppressed.

Whether eliminating social group difference is possible or desirable in the long run, however, is an academic issue. Today and for the foreseeable future societies are certainly structured by groups, and some are privileged while others are oppressed. New social movements of group specificity do not deny the official story's claim that the ideal of liberation as eliminating difference and treating everyone the same has brought significant improvement in the status of excluded groups. Its main quarrel is with the story's conclusion, namely, that since we have achieved formal equality, only vestiges and holdovers of differential privilege remain, which will die out with the continued persistent assertion of an ideal of social relations that make differences irrelevant to a person's life prospects. The achievement of formal equality does not eliminate social differences, and rhetorical commitment to the sameness of persons makes it impossible even to name how those differences presently structure privilege and oppression.

Though in many respects the law is now blind to group differences, some groups continue to be marked as deviant, as the Other. In everyday interactions, images, and decisions, assumptions about women, Blacks, Hispanics, gay men and lesbians, old people, and other marked groups continue to justify exclusion, avoidance, paternalism, and authoritarian treatment. Continued racist, sexist, homophobic, ageist, and ableist institutions and behavior create particular circumstances for these groups, usually disadvantaging them in their opportunity to develop their capacities. Finally, in part because they have been segregated from one another, and in part because they have particular histories and traditions, there are cultural differences among social groups—differences in language, style of living, body comportment and gestures, values, and perspectives on society.

Today in American society, as in many other societies, there is widespread agreement that no person should be excluded from political and economic activities because of ascribed characteristics. Group differences nevertheless continue to exist, and certain groups continue to be privileged. Under these circumstances, insisting that equality and liberation entail ignoring difference has oppressive consequences in three respects.

First, blindness to difference disadvantages groups whose experience, culture, and socialized capacities differ from those of privileged groups. The strategy of assimilation aims to bring formerly excluded groups into the mainstream. So assimilation always implies coming into the game after it is already begun, after the rules and standards have already been set, and having to prove oneself according to those rules and standards. In the assimilationist strategy, the privileged groups implicitly define the standards according to which all will be measured. Because their privilege involves not recognizing these standards as culturally and experientially specific, the ideal of a common humanity in which all can participate without regard to race, gender, religion, or sexuality poses as neutral and universal. The real differences between oppressed groups and the dominant norm, however, tend to put them at a disadvantage in measuring up to these standards, and for that reason assimilationist policies perpetuate their disadvantage. Later in this chapter and in Chapter 7 I shall give examples of facially neutral standards that operate to disadvantage or exclude those already disadvantaged.

Second, the ideal of a universal humanity without social group differences allows privileged groups to ignore their own group specificity. Blindness to difference perpetuates cultural imperialism by allowing norms expressing the point of view and experience of privileged groups to appear neutral and universal. The assimilationist ideal presumes that there is a humanity in general, an unsituated group-neutral human capacity for self-making that left to itself would make individuality flower, thus guaranteeing that each individual will be different. As I argued in Chapter 4, because there is no such unsituated group-neutral point of view, the situation and experience of dominant groups tend to define the norms of such a humanity in general. Against such a supposedly neutral humanist ideal, only the oppressed groups come to be marked with particularity; they, and not the privileged groups, are marked, objectified as the Others.

Thus, third, this denigration of groups that deviate from an allegedly neutral standard often produces an internalized devaluation by members of those groups themselves. When there is an ideal of general human standards according to which everyone should be evaluated equally, then Puerto Ricans or Chinese Americans are ashamed of their accents or their parents, Black children despise the female-dominated kith and kin networks of their neighborhoods, and feminists seek to root out their tendency to cry, or to feel compassion for a frustrated stranger. The aspiration to assimilate helps produce the self-loathing and double consciousness characteristic of oppression. The goal of assimilation holds up to people a demand that they "fit," be like the mainstream, in behavior, values, and goals. At the same time, as long as group differences exist, group members will be marked as different—

as Black, Jewish, gay—and thus as unable simply to fit. When participation is taken to imply assimilation the oppressed person is caught in an irresolvable dilemma: to participate means to accept and adopt an identity one is not, and to try to participate means to be reminded by oneself and others of the identity one is.

A more subtle analysis of the assimilationist ideal might distinguish between a conformist and a transformational ideal of assimilation. In the conformist ideal, status quo institutions and norms are assumed as given, and disadvantaged groups who differ from those norms are expected to conform to them. A transformational ideal of assimilation, on the other hand, recognizes that institutions as given express the interests and perspective of the dominant groups. Achieving assimilation therefore requires altering many institutions and practices in accordance with neutral rules that truly do not disadvantage or stigmatize any person, so that group membership really is irrelevant to how persons are treated. Wasserstrom's ideal fits a transformational assimilation, as does the group-neutral ideal advocated by some feminists (Taub and Williams 1987). Unlike the conformist assimilationist, the transformational assimilationist may allow that group-specific policies, such as affirmative action, are necessary and appropriate means for transforming institutions to fit the assimilationist ideal. Whether conformist or transformational, however, the assimilationist ideal still denies that group difference can be positive and desirable; thus any form of the ideal of assimilation constructs group difference as a liability or disadvantage.

Under these circumstances, a politics that asserts the positivity of group difference is liberating and empowering. In the act of reclaiming the identity the dominant culture has taught them to despise (Cliff 1980), and affirming it as an identity to celebrate, the oppressed remove double consciousness. I am just what they say I am—a Jewboy, a colored girl, a fag, a dyke, or a hag—and proud of it. No longer does one have the impossible project of trying to become something one is not under circumstances where the very trying reminds one of who one is. This politics asserts that oppressed groups have distinct cultures, experiences, and perspectives on social life with humanly positive meaning, some of which may even be superior to the culture and perspectives of mainstream society. The rejection and devaluation of one's culture and perspective should not be a condition of full participation in social life.

Asserting the value and specificity of the culture and attributes of oppressed groups, moreover, results in a relativizing of the dominant culture. When feminists assert the validity of feminine sensitivity and the positive value of nurturing behavior, when gays describe the prejudice of heterosexuals as homophobic and their own sexuality as positive and self-developing, when Blacks affirm a distinct Afro-American tradition, then the dominant culture is forced to discover itself for the first time as specific: as Anglo, European, Christian, masculine, straight. In a political struggle where oppressed groups insist on the positive value of their specific culture and experience, it becomes increasingly difficult for dominant groups to parade their norms as neutral and universal, and to construct the values and behavior of the oppressed as deviant, perverted, or inferior. By puncturing the universalist claim to unity that expels some groups and turns them into the Other, the assertion of positive group specificity introduces the possibility of understanding the relation between groups as merely difference, instead of exclusion, opposition, or dominance.

The politics of difference also promotes a notion of group solidarity against the individualism of liberal humanism. Liberal humanism treats each person as an individual, ignoring differences of race, sex, religion, and ethnicity. Each person should be evaluated only according to her or his individual efforts and achievements. With the institutionalization of formal equlity some members of formerly excluded groups have indeed succeeded, by mainstream standards. Structural patterns of group privilege and oppression nevertheless remain. When political leaders of oppressed groups reject assimilation they are often affirming group solidarity. Where the dominant culture refuses to see anything but the achievement of autonomous individuals, the oppressed assert that we shall not separate from the people with whom we identify in order to "make it" in a white Anglo male world. The politics of difference insists on liberation of the whole group of Blacks, women, American Indians, and that this can be accomplished only through basic institutional changes. These changes must include group representation in policy making and an elimination of the hierarchy of rewards that forces everyone to compete for scarce positions at the top.

Thus the assertion of a positive sense of group difference provides a standpoint from which to criticize prevailing institutions and norms. Black Americans find in their traditional communities, which refer to their members as "brother" and "sister," a sense of solidarity absent from the calculating individualism of white professional capitalist society. Feminists find in the traditional female values of nurturing a challenge to a militarist worldview, and lesbians find in their relationships a confrontation with the assumption of complementary gender roles in sexual relationships. From their experience of a culture tied to the land American Indians formulate a critique of the instrumental rationality of European culture that results in pollution and ecological destruction. Having revealed the specificity of the dominant norms which claim universality and neutrality, social movements of the oppressed are in a position to inquire how the dominant institutions must be changed so that they will no longer reproduce the patterns of privilege and oppression.

From the assertion of positive difference the self-organization of oppressed groups follows. Both liberal humanist and leftist political organizations and movements have found it difficult to accept this principle of group autonomy. In a humanist emancipatory politics, if a group is subject to injustice, then all those interested in a just society should unite to combat the powers that perpetuate that injustice. If many groups are subject to injustice, moreover, then they should unite to work for a just society. The politics of difference is certainly not against coalition, nor does it hold that, for example, whites should not work against racial injustice or men against sexist injustice. This politics of group assertion, however, takes as a basic principle that members of oppressed groups need separate organizations that exclude others, especially those from more privileged groups. Separate organization is probably necessary in order for these groups to discover and reinforce the positivity of their specific experience, to collapse and eliminate double consciousness. In discussions within autonomous organizations, group members can determine their specific needs and interests. Separation and self-organization risk creating pressures toward homogenization of the groups themselves, creating new privileges and exclusions, a problem I shall discuss in Chapter 8. But contemporary emancipatory social movements have found group autonomy an important vehicle for empowerment and the development of a group-specific voice and perspective.

Integration into the full life of the society should not have to imply assimilation to dominant norms and abandonment of group affiliation and culture (Edley 1986; cf. McGary 1983). If the only alternative to the oppressive exclusion of some groups defined as Other by dominant ideologies is the assertion that they are the same as everybody else, then they will continue to be excluded because they are not the same.

Some might object to the way I have drawn the distinction between an assimilationist ideal of liberation and a radical democratic pluralism. They might claim that I have not painted the ideal of a society that transcends group differences fairly, representing it as homogeneous and conformist. The free society envisaged by liberalism, they might say, is certainly pluralistic. In it persons can affiliate with whomever they choose; liberty encourages a proliferation of life styles, activities, and associations. While I have no quarrel with social diversity in this sense, this vision of liberal pluralism does not touch on the primary issues that give rise to the politics of difference. The vision of liberation as the transcendence of group difference seeks to abolish the public and political significance of group difference, while retaining and promoting both individual and group diversity in private, or nonpolitical, social contexts. In Chapter 4 I argued that this way of distinguishing public and private spheres, where the public represents universal citizenship and the private individual differences, tends to result in group exclusion from the public. Radical democratic pluralism acknowledges and affirms the public and political significance of social group differences as a means of ensuring the participation and inclusion of everyone in social and political institutions.

RECLAIMING THE MEANING OF DIFFERENCE

Many people inside and outside the movements I have discussed find the rejection of the liberal humanist ideal and the assertion of a positive sense of group difference both confusing and controversial. They fear that any admission by oppressed groups that they are different from the dominant groups risks justifying anew the subordination, special marking, and exclusion of those groups. Since calls for a return of women to the kitchen, Blacks to servant roles and separate schools, and disabled people to nursing homes are not absent from contemporary politics, the danger is real. It may be true that the assimilationist ideal that treats everyone the same and applies the same standards to all perpetuates disadvantage because real group differences remain that make it unfair to compare the unequals. But this is far preferable to a reestablishment of separate and unequal spheres for different groups justified on the basis of group difference.

Since those asserting group specificity certainly wish to affirm the liberal humanist principle that all persons are of equal moral worth, they appear to be faced with a dilemma. Analyzing W. E. B. Du Bois's arguments for cultural pluralism, Bernard Boxill poses the dilemma this way: "On the one hand, we must overcome segregation because it denies the idea of human brotherhood; on the other hand, to overcome segregation we must self-segregate and therefore also deny the idea of human brotherhood" (Boxill 1984: 174). Martha Minow finds a dilemma of difference facing any who seek to promote justice for currently oppressed or disadvantaged groups. Formally neutral rules and policies that ignore group differences often perpetuate the disadvantage of those whose difference is defined as deviant; but focusing on difference risks recreating the stigma that difference has carried in the past (Minow 1987: 12–13; cf. Minow 1985, 1990).

These dilemmas are genuine, and exhibit the risks of collective life, where the consequences of one's claims, actions, and policies may not turn out as one intended because others have understood them differently or turned them to different ends. Since ignoring group differences in public policy does not mean that people ignore them in everyday life and interaction, however, oppression continues even when law and policy declare that all are equal. Thus I think for many groups and in many circumstances it is more empowering to affirm and acknowledge in political life the group differences that already exist in social life. One is more likely to avoid the dilemma of difference in doing this if the meaning of difference itself becomes a terrain of political struggle. Social movements asserting the positivity of group difference have established this terrain, offering an emancipatory meaning of difference to replace the old exclusionary meaning.

The oppressive meaning of group difference defines it as absolute otherness, mutual exclusion, categorical opposition. This essentialist meaning of difference submits to the logic of identity. One group occupies the position of a norm, against which all others are measured. The attempt to reduce all persons to the unity of a common measure constructs as deviant those whose attributes differ from the group-specific attributes implicitly presumed in the norm. The drive to unify the particularity and multiplicity of practices, cultural symbols, and ways of relating in clear and distinct categories turns difference into exclusion.

Thus I explored in the previous two chapters how the appropriation of a universal subject position by socially privileged groups forces those they define as different outside the definition of full humanity and citizenship. The attempt to measure all against some universal standard generates a logic of difference as hierarchical dichotomy—masculine/feminine, civilized/savage, and so on. The second term is defined negatively as a lack of the truly human qualities; at the same time it is defined as the complement to the valued term, the object correlating with its subject, that which brings it to completion, wholeness, and identity. By loving and affirming him, a woman serves as a mirror to a man, holding up his virtues for him to see (Irigaray 1985). By carrying the white man's burden to tame and educate the savage peoples, the civilized will realize universal humanity. The exotic orientals are there to know and master, to be the completion of reason's progress in history, which seeks the unity of the world (Said 1978). In every case the valued term achieves its value by its determinately negative relation to the Other.

In the objectifying ideologies of racism, sexism, anti-Semitism, and homophobia, only the oppressed and excluded groups are defined as different. Whereas the privileged groups are neutral and exhibit free and malleable subjectivity, the excluded groups are marked with an essence, imprisoned in a given set of possibilities. By virtue of the characteristics the group is alleged to have by nature, the ideologies allege that group members have specific dispositions that suit them for some activities and not others. Difference in these ideologies always means exclusionary opposition to a norm. There are rational men, and then there are women; there are civilized men, and then there are wild and savage peoples. The marking of difference always implies a good/bad opposition; it is always a devaluation, the naming of an inferiority in relation to a superior standard of humanity.

Difference here always means absolute otherness; the group marked as different has no common nature with the normal or neutral ones. The categorical opposition of groups essentializes them, repressing the differences within groups. In this way the definition of difference as exclusion and opposition actually denies difference. This essentializing categorization also denies difference in that its universalizing norms preclude recognizing and affirming a group's specificity in its own terms.

Essentializing difference expresses a fear of specificity, and a fear of making permeable the categorical border between oneself and the others. This fear, I argued in the previous chapter, is not merely intellectual, and does not derive only from the instrumental desire to defend privilege, though that may be a large element. It wells from the depths of the Western subject's sense of identity, especially, but not only, in the subjectivity of privileged groups. The fear may increase, moreover, as a clear essentialism of difference wanes, as belief in a specifically female, Black, or homosexual nature becomes less tenable.

The politics of difference confronts this fear, and aims for an understanding of group difference as indeed ambiguous, relational, shifting, without clear borders that keep people straight—as entailing neither amorphous unity nor pure individuality. By asserting a positive meaning for their own identity, oppressed groups seek to seize the power of naming difference itself, and explode the implicit definition of difference as deviance in relation to a norm, which freezes some groups into a self-enclosed nature. Difference now comes to mean not otherness, exclusive opposition, but specificity, variation, heterogeneity. Difference names relations of similarity and dissimilarity that can be reduced to neither coextensive identity nor nonoverlapping otherness.

The alternative to an essentializing, stigmatizing meaning of difference as opposition is an understanding of difference as specificity, variation. In this logic, as Martha Minow (1985, 1987, 1990) suggests, group differences should be conceived as relational rather than defined by substantive categories and attributes. A relational understanding of difference relativizes the previously universal position of privileged groups, which allows only the oppressed to be marked as different. When group difference appears as a function of comparison between groups, whites are just as specific as Blacks or Latinos, men just as specific as women, able-bodied people just as specific as disabled people. Difference thus emerges not as a description of the attributes of a group, but as a function of the relations between groups and the interaction of groups with institutions (cf. Littleton 1987).

In this relational understanding, the meaning of difference also becomes contextualized (cf. Scott 1988). Group differences will be more or less salient depending on the groups compared, the purposes of the comparison, and the point of view of the comparers. Such contextualized understandings of difference undermine essentialist assumptions. For example, in the context of athletics, health care, social service support, and so on, wheelchair-bound people are different from others, but they are not different in many other respects. Traditional treatment of the disabled entailed exclusion and segregation because the differences between the disabled and the able-bodied were conceptualized as extending to all or most capacities.

In general, then, a relational understanding of group difference rejects exclusion. Difference no longer implies that groups lie outside one another. To say that there are differences among groups does not imply that there are not overlapping experiences, or that two groups have nothing in common. The assumption that real differences in affinity, culture, or privilege imply oppositional categorization must be challenged. Different groups are always similar in some respects, and always potentially share some attributes, experiences, and goals.

Such a relational understanding of difference entails revising the meaning of group identity as well. In asserting the positive difference of their experience, culture, and social perspective, social movements of groups that have experienced cultural imperialism deny that they have a common identity, a set of fixed attributes that clearly mark who belongs and who doesn't. Rather, what makes a group is a social process of interaction and differentiation in which some people come to have a particular *affinity* (Haraway 1985) for others. My "affinity group" in a given social situation comprises those people with whom I feel the most comfortable, who are more familiar. Affinity names the manner of sharing assumptions, affective bonding, and networking that recognizably differentiates groups from one another, but not according to some common nature. The salience of a particular person's group affinities may shift according to the social situation or according to changes in her or his life. Membership in a social group is a function not of satisfying some objective criteria, but of a subjective affirmation of affinity with that group, the affirmation of that affinity by other members of the group, and the attribution of membership in that group by persons identifying with other groups. Group identity is constructed from a flowing process in which individuals identify themselves and others in terms of groups, and thus group identity itself flows and shifts with changes in social process.

Groups experiencing cultural imperialism have found themselves objectified and marked with a devalued essence from the outside, by a dominant culture they are excluded from making. The assertion of a positive sense of group difference by these groups is emancipatory because it reclaims the definition of the group by the group, as a creation and construction, rather than a given essence. To be sure, it is difficult to articulate positive elements of group affinity without essentializing them, and these movements do not always succeed in doing so (cf. Sartre 1948: 85; Epstein 1987). But they are developing a language to describe their similar social situation and relations to one another, and their similar perceptions and perspectives on social life. These movements engage in the project of cultural revolution I recommended in the last chapter, insofar as they take culture as in part a matter of collective choice. While their ideas of women's culture, Afro-American culture, and American Indian culture rely on past cultural expressions, to a significant degree these movements have self-consciously constructed the culture that they claim defines the distinctiveness of their groups.

Contextualizing both the meaning of difference and identity thus allows the acknowledgment of difference within affinity groups. In our complex, plural society, every social group has group differences cutting across it, which are potential sources of wisdom, excitement, conflict, and oppression. Gay men, for example, may be Black, rich, homeless, or old, and these differences produce different identifications and potential conflicts among gay men, as well as affinities with some straight men.

RESPECTING DIFFERENCE IN POLICY

A goal of social justice, I will assume, is social equality. Equality refers not primarily to the distribution of social goods, though distributions are certainly entailed by social equality. It refers primarily to the full participation and inclusion of everyone in a society's major institutions, and the socially supported substantive opportunity for all to develop and exercise their capacities and realize their choices. American society has enacted formal legal equality for members of all groups, with the important and shameful exception of gay men and lesbians. But for many groups social equality is barely on the horizon. Those seeking social equality disagree about whether group-neutral or group-conscious policies best suit that goal, and their disagreement often turns on whether they hold an assimilationist or culturally pluralist ideal. In this section I argue for the justice of group-conscious social policies, and discuss three contexts in which such policies are at issue in the United States today: women's equality in the workplace, language rights of non-English speakers, and American Indian rights. Another category of group-conscious policies, namely, affirmative action, I will discuss in Chapter 7.

The issue of formally equal versus group-conscious policies arises primarily in the context of workplace relations and access to political power. I have already discussed one of the primary reasons for preferring group-conscious to neutral policies: policies that are universally formulated and thus blind to differences of race, culture, gender, age, or disability often perpetuate rather than undermine oppression. Universally formulated standards or norms, for example, according to which all competitors for social positions are evaluated, often presume as the norm capacities, values, and cognitive and behavioral styles typical of dominant groups, thus disadvantaging others. Racist, sexist, homophobic, ageist, and ableist aversions and stereotypes, moreover, continue to devalue or render invisible some people, often disadvantaging them in economic and political interactions. Policies that take notice of the specific situation of oppressed groups can offset these disadvantages.

It might be objected that when facially neutral standards or policies disadvantage a group, the standards or policies should simply be restructured so as to be genuinely neutral, rather than replaced by group-conscious policies. For some situations this may be appropriate, but in many the group-related differences allow no neutral formulation. Language policy might be cited as paradigmatic here, but as I will discuss shortly, some gender issues may be as well.

More important, however, some of the disadvantages that oppressed groups suffer can be remedied in policy only by an affirmative acknowledgement of the group's specificity. The oppressions of cultural imperialism that stereotype a group and simultaneously render its own experience invisible can be remedied only by explicit attention to and expression of that group's specificity. For example, removing oppressive stereotypes of Blacks, Latinos, Indians, Arabs, and Asians and portraying them in the same roles as whites will not eliminate racism from television programming. Positive and interesting portrayals of people of color in situations and ways of life that derive from their own self-perceptions are also necessary, as well as a great deal more positive presence of all these groups than currently exists.

These considerations produce a second reason for the justice of group-conscious policies, in addition to their function in counteracting oppression and disadvantage. Group-conscious policies are sometimes necessary in order to affirm the solidarity of groups, to allow them to affirm their group affinities without suffering disadvantage in the wider society.

Some group-conscious policies are consistent with an assimilationist ideal in which group difference has no social significance, as long as such policies are understood as means to that end, and thus as temporary divergences from group-neutral norms. Many people look upon affirmative action policies in this way, and as I shall discuss shortly, people typically understand bilingual education in this way. A culturally pluralist democratic ideal, however, supports group-conscious policies not only as means to the end of equality, but also as intrinsic to the ideal of social equality itself. Groups cannot be socially equal unless their specific experience, culture, and social contributions are publicly affirmed and recognized.

The dilemma of difference exposes the risks involved both in attending to and in ignoring differences. The danger in affirming difference is that the implementation of group-conscious policies will reinstate stigma and exclusion. In the past, group-conscious policies were used to separate those defined as different and exclude them from access to the rights and privileges enjoyed by dominant groups. A crucial principle of democratic cultural pluralism, then, is that group-specific rights and policies should stand together with general civic and political rights of participation and inclusion. Group-conscious policies cannot be used to justify exclusion of or discrimination against members of a group in the exercise of general political and civil rights. A democratic cultural pluralism thus requires a dual system of rights: a general system of rights which are the same for all, and a more specific system of group-conscious policies and rights (cf. Wolgast 1980, ch. 2). In the words of Kenneth Karst: "When the promise of equal citizenship is fulfilled, the paths to belonging are opened in two directions for members of cultural minorities. As full members of the larger society, they have the option to participate to whatever degree they choose. They also may look inward, seeking solidarity within their cultural group, without being penalized for that choice" (Karst 1986: 337). If "cultural minority" is interpreted to mean any group subject to cultural imperialism, then this statement applies to women, old people, disabled people, gay men and lesbians, and working-class people as much as it applies to ethnic or national groups. I will now briefly consider three cases in which group-specific policies are necessary to support social equality: women, Latinos, and American Indians.

1. Are women's interests best promoted through gender-neutral or group-conscious rules and policies? This question has been fiercely debated by feminists in recent years. The resulting literature raises crucial questions about dominant models of law and policy that take equality to mean sameness, and offers some subtle analyses of the meaning of equality that do not

assume identity (see Vogel 1990). Most of this discussion has focused on the question of pregnancy and childbirth rights in the workplace.

Advocates of an equal treatment approach to pregnancy argue that women's interests are best served by vigorously pressing for the inclusion of pregnancy leaves and benefits within gender-neutral leave and benefit policies relevant to any physical condition that renders men or women unable to work. The history of protective legislation shows that women cannot trust employers and courts not to use special classification as an excuse for excluding and disadvantaging women, and we are best protected from such exclusion by neutral policies (Williams 1983). Even such proponents of equal treatment, however, agree that gender-neutral policies that take male lives as the norm will disadvantage women. The answer, according to Nadine Taub and Wendy Williams, is a model of equality in the workplace that recognizes and accommodates the specific needs of all workers; such a model requires significant restructuring of most workplace policy (Taub and Williams 1986).

In my view an equal treatment approach to pregnancy and childbirth is inadequate because it either implies that women do not have any right to leave and job security when having babies, or assimilates such guarantees under the supposedly gender-neutral category of "disability." Such assimilation is unacceptable because pregnancy and childbirth are usually normal conditions of normal women, because pregnancy and childbirth themselves count as socially necessary work, and because they have unique and variable characteristics and needs (Scales 1981; Littleton 1987). Assimilating pregnancy and childbirth to disability tends to stigmatize these processes as "unhealthy." It suggests, moreover, that the primary or only reason that a woman has a right to leave and job security is that she is physically unable to work at her job, or that doing so would be more difficult than when she is not pregnant and recovering from childbirth. While these are important considerations, another reason is that she ought to have the time to establish breast-feeding and develop a relationship and routine with her child, if she chooses. At issue is more than eliminating the disadvantage women suffer because of male models of uninterrupted work. It is also a question of establishing and confirming positive public recognition of the social contribution of childbearing. Such recognition can and should be given without either reducing women to childbearers or suggesting that all women ought to bear children and are lacking if they do not.

Feminists who depart from a gender-neutral model of women's rights generally restrict this departure to the biological situation of childbirth. Most demand that parental leave from a job, for example, should be gender-neutral, in order not to perpetuate the connection of women with the care of children, and in order not to penalize those men who choose more than average childbearing responsibilities. I myself agree with gender-neutral policy on this issue.

Restricting the issue of group-conscious policies for women to childbirth, however, avoids some of the hardest questions involved in promoting women's equality in the workplace. Women suffer workplace disadvantage not only or even primarily because of their birthing capacity, but because their gender socialization and identity orients the desires, temperaments, and capacities of many women toward certain activities and away from others, because many men regard women in inappropriately sexual terms, and because women's clothes, comportment, voices, and so on sometimes disrupt the disembodied ideal of masculinist bureaucracy. Differences between women and men are not only biological, but also socially gendered. Such gender differences are multiple, variable, and do not reduce men and women to segregating essences. Perhaps such differences should not exist, but without doubt they do now. Ignoring these differences sometimes disadvantages women in public settings where masculine norms and styles predominate.

In a model she calls "equality as acceptance," Christine Littleton argues for a gender-conscious approach to policy directed at rendering femininely gendered cultural attributes costless for women. This model begins with the assumption of structured social gender differences—for example, gender-dominated occupational categories, woman-dominated childrearing and other family member caretaking, and gender differences in the sports people wish to pursue. None of these are essences; it is not as though all men or all women follow the gendered patterns, but the patterns are identifiable and apply broadly to many people's lives. Littleton's model of equality as acceptance supports policies which not only will not disadvantage women who engage in traditionally feminine activity or behavior, but which value the feminine as much as the masculine:

The focus of equality as acceptance, therefore, is not on the question of whether *women* are different, but rather on the question of how the social fact of gender asymmetry can be dealt with so as to create some symmetry in the lived-out experience of all members of the community. I do not think it matters so much whether differences are "natural" or not; they are built into our structures and selves in either event. As social facts, differences are created by the interaction of person with person or person with institution; they inhere in the relationship, not in the person. On this view, the function of equality is to make gender differences, perceived or actual, costless relative to each other, so that anyone may follow a male, female, or androgynous lifestyle according to their natural inclination or choice without being punished for following a female lifestyle or rewarded for following a male one. (Littleton 1987: 1297)

The acceptance model of equality, then, publicly acknowledges culturally based gender differences, and takes steps to ensure that these differences do not disadvantage. Though Littleton does not emphasize it, this model implies, first, that gender differences must not be used implicitly or explicitly as a basis for excluding persons from institutions, positions, or opportunities. That is, general rights to equal opportunity, as well as other civil and political rights, must obtain. Over and above this, equality as acceptance explicitly revalues femininely coded activity and behavior as the equal of masculine-coded activity.

Comparable worth policies are a widely discussed strategy for revaluing the culturally feminine. Schemes of equal pay for work of comparable worth require that predominantly male and predominantly female jobs have similar wage structures if they involve similar degrees of skill, difficulty, stress, and so on. The problem in implementing these policies, of course, lies in designing methods of comparing different jobs. Most schemes of comparison still choose to minimize sex differences by using supposedly gender-neutral criteria, such as educational attainment, speed of work, whether the work involves manipulation of symbols, pleasantness of work conditions, decisionmaking ability, and so on. Some writers have suggested, however, that standard classifications of job traits may be systematically biased to keep specific kinds of tasks involved in many female-dominated occupations hidden (Beatty and Beatty 1981; Treiman and Hartman 1981: 81). Many female-dominated occupations involve gender-specific kinds of labor—such as nurturing, smoothing over social relations, or the exhibition of sexuality—which most task observation ignores (Alexander 1987). A fair assessment of the skills and complexity of many female-dominated jobs may therefore involve paying explicit attention to gender differences rather than applying gender-blind categories of comparison (cf. Littleton 1987: 1312).

Littleton offers sports as another area of revaluation. An "equality as acceptance" approach, she suggests, would support an equal division of resources between male and female programs rather than divide up the available sports budget per capita (Littleton 1987: 1313). If the disparities in numbers of people involved were too great, I do not think this proposal would be fair, but I agree with the general principle Littleton is aiming at. Women who wish to participate in athletic activities should not be disadvantaged because there are not more women who currently wish to; they should have as many well-paid coaches, for example, as do men, their locker room facilities should be as good, and they should have access to all the equipment they need to excel. More importantly, femininely stereotyped sports, such as synchronized swimming or field hockey, should receive a level of support comparable to more masculine sports like football or baseball.

2. In November 1986 the majority of voters in California supported a

referendum declaring English the official language of that state. The ramifi-
cations of this policy are not clear, but it means at least that state institutions
have no obligation to print ballots and other government literature or provide services in any language other than English. The California success has
spurred a national movement to declare English the official language of the
United States, as well as many additional local movements, especially in
regions with fast-growing populations of people whose first language is not
English. In winter 1989, for example, an English-only proposal went before
the legislature of Suffolk County, Long Island, that even some English-first
advocates thought was too strong. Not only would it have made English the
official language of Suffolk County, but it would have forbidden public
service providers from speaking to clients in any language other than
English (Schmitt 1989).

Many English-only advocates justify their position as another of many
measures that should be taken to cut the costs of government. But the
movement's primary appeal is to a normative ideal of the unity of the polity.
As a nation, the United States was founded by English speakers; non-
English speakers are not "real" Americans, no matter how many generations
they can trace on American soil. A polity cannot sustain itself without
significant commonality and mutual identification among its citizens, this
argument goes, and a common language is one of the most important of
such unifying forces. Linguistic and cultural pluralism leads to conflict, divisiveness, factionalism, and ultimately disintegration. Giving public preference to English supports this unity and encourages non-English speakers to
assimilate more quickly.

There are at least three arguments against this appeal to the unity of a
single harmonious polity. First, it is simply unrealistic. From its beginnings
the United States has always harbored sizeable linguistic and cultural minorities. Its history of imperialism and annexation and its immigration policy
have resulted in more. In the past twenty-five years U.S. military and foreign
policy has led to a huge influx of Latin Americans and Asians. Some estimate, moreover, that by the year 2000 Hispanic and Asian populations in the
United States will have increased by 84 and 103 percent respectively (Sears
and Huddy 1987). Many individuals belonging to cultural minorities choose
to assimilate, as do some whole groups. But many do not. Even without
official support for their doing so and with considerable pressures against it,
many groups have retained distinct linguistic and cultural identities, even
some whose members have lived in the United States for several generations.
Spanish speakers may be the most salient here because their relative numbers
are large, and because their connections with Puerto Rico, Mexico, or other
parts of Latin America remain strong. Given the determination of many

linguistic and cultural minorities to maintain a specific identity even as they claim rights to the full benefits of American citizenship, a determination which seems to be increasing, the desire of the English-only movement to create unity through enforced language policy is simply silly.

Second, as I have already argued at several points, this norm of the homogeneous public is oppressive. Not only does it put unassimilated persons and groups at a severe disadvantage in the competition for scarce positions and resources, but it requires that persons transform their sense of identity in order to assimilate. Self-annihilation is an unreasonable and unjust requirement of citizenship. The fiction, poetry, and songs of American cultural minorities brim over with the pain and loss such demands inflict, documenting how thoroughly assimilationist values violate basic respect for persons.

Thus, third, the normative ideal of the homogeneous public does not succeed in its stated aim of creating a harmonious nation. In group-differentiated societies conflict, factionalism, divisiveness, civil warfare, do often occur between groups. The primary cause of such conflict, however, is not group difference per se, but rather the relations of domination and oppression between groups that produce resentment, hostility, and resistance among the oppressed. Placing a normative value on homogeneity only exacerbates division and conflict, because it gives members of the dominant groups reason to adopt a stance of self-righteous intractability.

I argued in Chapter 4 that a just polity must embrace the ideal of a heterogeneous public. Group differences of gender, age, and sexuality should not be ignored, but publicly acknowledged and accepted. Even more so should group differences of nation or ethnicity be accepted. In the twentieth century the ideal state is composed of a plurality of nations or cultural groups, with a degree of self-determination and autonomy compatible with federated equal rights and obligations of citizenship. Many states of the world embrace this ideal, though they often realize it only very imperfectly (see Ortiz 1984, pt. 2). English-only advocates often look with fear at the large and rapidly growing cultural minorities in the United States, especially the Spanish-speaking minority, and argue that only enforcing the primacy of English can prevent us from becoming a culturally plural society like Canada. Such arguments stubbornly refuse to see that we already are.

The difference between an assimilationist and a culturally pluralist ideal becomes particularly salient in educational policy. Bilingual education is highly controversial in the United States today, partly because of the different cultural meanings given to it. In 1974 the Supreme Court ruled that the state has an obligation to remedy the English-language deficiency of its students so they will have equal opportunity to learn all subjects; but the Court did not specify how this should be done. The Bilingual Education Act,

passed in 1978 and amended several times, sets aside federal funds for use by
school systems to develop bilingual education programs (see Minow 1985;
Kleven 1989). Even so, in 1980, 77 percent of Hispanic children in the
United States received no form of special programming corresponding to
their linguistic needs (Bastian *et al.* 1986: 46). In 1986 in Texas, 80 percent of
school districts were found out of compliance with a state-mandated
bilingual education program (Canter 1987).

There are several different models of language support programs. Some,
like English as a Second Language, provide no instruction in the student's
native language, and are often not taught by persons who can speak the
student's language. Others, called immersion programs, involve English-
language instruction primarily, but are taught by bilingual instructors whom
the student can question in his or her native language. Transitional bilingual
education programs involve genuinely bilingual instruction, with the proportions of English and native language changing as the student progresses.
Transitional programs instruct students in such subjects as math, science
and history in their native language at the same time that they develop
English-language skills; they aim to increase the amount of time of instruction in English.

All these programs are assimilationist in intent. They seek to increase
English proficiency to the point where native-language instruction is
unnecessary; none has the goal of maintaining and developing proficiency in
the native language. The vast majority of programs for students with limited
English proficiency in the United States take one of these forms. The use of
transitional bilingual programs instead of ESL or immersion programs is
hotly debated. The majority of Americans support special language programs for students with limited English, in order to help them learn English;
but the more programs instruct in a native language, especially when they
instruct in subjects like math or science, the more they are considered by
English speakers to be unfair coddling and a waste of taxpayer dollars
(Sears and Huddy 1987). Transitional bilingual educational programs, on
the other hand, are usually preferred by linguistic minorities.

Another model of bilingual education is rarely practiced in the United
States, and is hardly on the public agenda: bilingual-bicultural maintenance
programs. These aim to reinforce knowledge of the students' native language
and culture, at the same time that they train them to be proficient in the
dominant language, English. Few advocates of cultural pluralism and group
autonomy in the United States would deny that proficiency in English is a
necessary condition for full participation in American society. The issue is
only whether linguistic minorities are recognized as full participants in their
specificity, with social support for the maintenance of their language and

culture. Only bilingual-bicultural maintenance programs can both ensure the possibility of the full inclusion and participation of members of linguistic minorities in all society's institutions and at the same time preserve and affirm their group-specific identity (cf. Nickel 1987: 119).

3. American Indians are the most invisible oppressed group in the United States. Numbering just over one million, they are too small a proportion of most regional populations to organize influential pressure groups or threaten major disruptions of the lives of white society. Federal and state policy often can safely ignore Indian interests and desires. Many Indians live on reservations, where non-Indians have little contact with them. Even in cities Indians often form their own support systems and networks, mingling little with non-Indians (Cornell 1988: 132–7). Whether on or off the reservation, Indians suffer the most serious marginalization and deprivation of any social group; by every measure—income, unemployment rates, infant mortality, and so on—Indians are the poorest Americans.

At the same time, Indians are the most legally differentiated people in the United States, the only group granted formally special status and rights by the federal government. Indians represent the *arche*-difference that from the beginning subverts the claim to origin, to a New World, that founds the myth of America as the home of English-speaking farmers, traders, and inventors. Agents of the U.S. government have poisoned, burned, looted, tricked, relocated, and confined Indians many times over, in persistently genocidal policies, attempting to purge this difference within. Legal history and the string of federal treaties, however, also testify to a begrudging acknowledgment of the Indian peoples as independent political entities with which the government must negotiate. Until the twentieth century the special legal status of Indians was conceptualized almost entirely as a relation of wardship and dependence between an inferior savage people and a superior civilized sovereign, and the shadow of this conceptualization darkens even recent legal decisions (Williams 1987). As with women, Blacks, and the feebleminded, Indian difference was codified in normalizing law as an inferior infantile nature that justified less than full citizenship.

At the turn of the century policymakers assumed that an end to this position of tutelage and wardship implied assimilation to the dominant culture. Thus the land reallocation policies of the late 1800s were intended to encourage Indians to value private property and the virtues of yeoman husbandry. In the 1920s, when Congress voted to grant Indians full U.S. citizenship, federal policy forced assimilation by forbidding Indian children to speak their native language in the boarding schools to which they were transported, sometimes thousands of miles from home. During the same period Indians were prohibited from practicing many of their traditional religious rites.

In the 1930s the Indian Reorganization Act eliminated and reversed many of these policies, creating the contemporary system of federally recognized tribal governments. But in the 1950s the pendulum swung back with the effort by Congress to terminate the federal relationship with tribes, withdrawing all recognition of Indians as distinct peoples, and once again attempting to force Indians to assimilate into white society. This brutal seesaw history of U.S.-Indian relations caused Indians to change and adapt their values, practices, and institutions and even their identities. Many distinct Indian identities have disappeared, as Indian groups merged or reorganized their relations with one another under the oppression of white policies. Throughout this history, however, assimilation was not a live option for the Indians. While many individuals may have left their groups and successfully integrated into the dominant white culture, Indians as groups persistently preserved their differences from white society against the fiercest opposition. Many Indians today find much fault with the present organization of the tribes, the definition of their role, and their legal relationship with the U.S. government, but few would propose the elimination of the tribal system that formally recognizes specific independently defined Indian groups and guarantees them specific rights in defining and running tribal affairs.

The case of American Indians especially exemplifies the arguments of this chapter because it is perhaps clearest here that justice toward groups requires special rights, and that an assimilationist ideal amounts to genocide. Such special rights, however, should not justify exclusion from full participation in the American dream of liberty, equal opportunity, and the like. The justice of recognizing both specific needs of a group and rights of full participation and inclusion in the polity has clear precedence in U.S.-Indian law. Indians are the only group to have what almost amounts to a dual citizenship: as members of a tribe they have specific political, legal, and collective rights, and as U.S. citizens they have all the civil and political rights of other citizens (Deloria and Lytle 1984: 3–4). Recognized Indian tribes have specific rights to jurisdictional and territorial sovereignty, and many specific religious, cultural, and gaming rights (see Pevar 1983).

Many Indians believe this system of particular rights remains too much at the discretion of the federal government, and some have taken their claims for greater self-determination to international judicial bodies (Ortiz 1984: 32–46). Justice in the form of unambiguous recognition of American Indian groups as full and equal members of American society requires, in my view, that the U.S. government relinquish the absolute power to alter or eliminate Indian rights.

Even in the absence of full justice the case of Indians provides an important example of the combination of general rights and particular rights which, I have argued, is necessary for the equality of many oppressed or disadvantaged groups. The system of tribal rights, and their relation to general rights, is certainly complex, and there is often disagreement about the meaning and implications of these rights. Many Indians believe, moreover, that their rights, especially territorial rights to make decisions about land, water, and resources, are not sufficiently recognized and enforced because economic interests profit from ignoring them. I do not wish to argue that this system of particular rights, or the bureaucratic form it takes, should extend to other oppressed or disadvantaged social groups. The specificity of each group requires a specific set of rights for each, and for some a more comprehensive system than for others. The case of American Indians, however, illustrates the fact that there is a precedent for a system of particular rights that a group wants for reasons of justice, namely, because they enforce the group's autonomy and protect its interests as an oppressed minority.

THE HETEROGENEOUS PUBLIC AND GROUP REPRESENTATION

I have argued that participatory democracy is an element and condition of social justice. Contemporary participatory democratic theory, however, inherits from republicanism a commitment to a unified public that in practice tends to exclude or silence some groups. Where some groups are materially privileged and exercise cultural imperialism, formally democratic processes often elevate the particular experiences and perspectives of the privileged groups, silencing or denigrating those of oppressed groups.

In her study of the functioning of a New England town meeting government, for example, Jane Mansbridge demonstrates that women, Blacks, working-class people, and poor people tend to participate less and have their interests represented less than whites, middle-class professionals, and men. White middle-class men assume authority more than others, and they are more practiced at speaking persuasively; mothers and old people find it more difficult than others to get to meetings (Mansbridge 1980, ch. 9). In Chapter 3 I cited Amy Gutmann's example of how increasing democracy in some school systems led to increased segregation because the more numerous, materially privileged, and articulate whites were able to promote their perceived interests against Blacks' just demand for equal treatment in an integrated system (Gutmann 1980: 191–202).

In these and similar cases, the group differences of privilege and oppression that exist in society have an effect on the public, even though the public claims to be blind to difference. Traditionally political theory and practice have responded to evidence of such bias by attempting yet once again to institute a genuinely universal public. Such a pure perspective that transcends the particularity of social position and consequent partial vision, I argued in Chapter 4, is impossible. If the unified public does not transcend group differences and often allows the perspective and interests of privileged groups to dominate, then a democratic public can counteract this bias only by acknowledging and giving voice to the group differences within it.

I assert, then, the following principle: a democratic public should provide mechanisms for the effective recognition and representation of the distinct voices and perspectives of those of its constituent groups that are oppressed or disadvantaged. Such group representation implies institutional mechanisms and public resources supporting (1) self-organization of group members so that they achieve collective empowerment and a reflective understanding of their collective experience and interests in the context of the society; (2) group analysis and group generation of policy proposals in institutionalized contexts where decisionmakers are obliged to show that their deliberations have taken group perspectives into consideration; and (3) group veto power regarding specific policies that affect a group directly, such as reproductive rights policy for women, or land use policy for Indian reservations.

Specific representation for oppressed groups in the decisionmaking procedures of a democratic public promotes justice better than a homogeneous public in several ways, both procedural and substantial (cf. Beitz 1988: 168–9). First, it better assures procedural fairness in setting the public agenda and hearing opinions about its items. Social and economic privilege means, among other things, that the groups which have it behave as though they have a right to speak and be heard, that others treat them as though they have that right, and that they have the material, personal, and organizational resources that enable them to speak and be heard. As a result, policy issues are often defined by the assumptions and priorities of the privileged. Specific representation for oppressed groups interrupts this process, because it gives voice to the assumptions and priorities of other groups.

Second, because it assures a voice for the oppressed as well as the privileged, group representation better assures that all needs and interests in the public will be recognized in democratic deliberations. The privileged usually are not inclined to protect or advance the interests of the oppressed, partly because their social position prevents them from understanding those interests, and partly because to some degree their privilege depends on the continued oppression of others. While different groups may share many needs, moreover, their difference usually entails some special needs which the individual groups themselves can best express. If we consider just democratic decisionmaking as a politics of need interpretation, as I have already suggested, then democratic institutions should facilitate the public expression of the needs of those who tend to be socially marginalized or silenced by cultural imperialism. Group representation in the public facilitates such expression.

In the previous section I argued for the assertion of a positive sense of difference by oppressed groups, and for a principle of special rights for those groups. I discussed there the legitimate fears of many in emancipatory social movements that abandoning group-blind policies and adopting group-specific ones will restigmatize the groups and justify new exclusions. Group representation can help protect against such a consequence. If oppressed and disadvantaged groups can self-organize in the public and have a specific voice to present their interpretation of the meaning of and reasons for group-differentiated policies, then such policies are more likely to work for than against them.

Group representation, third, encourages the expression of individual and group needs and interests in terms that appeal to justice, that transform an "I want" into an "I am entitled to," in Hannah Pitkin's words. In Chapter 4 I argued that publicity itself encourages this transformation because a condition of the public is that people call one another to account. Group representation adds to such accountability because it serves as an antidote to self-deceiving self-interest masked as an impartial or general interest. Unless confronted with different perspectives on social relations and events, different values and language, most people tend to assert their perspective as universal. When social privilege allows some group perspective to dominate a public while others are silent, such universalizing of the particular will be reaffirmed by many others. Thus the test of whether a claim upon the public is just or merely an expression of self-interest is best made when those making it must confront the opinion of others who have explicitly different, though not necessarily conflicting, experiences, priorities, and needs (cf. Sunstein 1988: 1588). As a person of social privilege, I am more likely to go outside myself and have regard for social justice when I must listen to the voice of those my privilege otherwise tends to silence.

Finally, group representation promotes just outcomes because it maximizes the social knowledge expressed in discussion, and thus furthers practical wisdom. Group differences are manifest not only in different needs, interests, and goals, but also in different social locations and experiences. People in different groups often know about somewhat different institutions, events, practices, and social relations, and often have differing perceptions of the same institutions, relations, or events. For this reason members of some groups are sometimes in a better position than members of others to understand and anticipate the probable consequences of implementing particular social policies. A public that makes use of all such social knowledge in its differentiated plurality is most likely to make just and wise decisions.

I should allay several possible misunderstandings of what this principle of group representation means and implies. First, the principle calls for specific representation of social groups, not interest groups or ideological groups. By an interest group I mean any aggregate or association of persons who seek a particular goal, or desire the same policy, or are similarly situated with respect to some social effect—for example, they are all recipients of acid rain caused by Ohio smokestacks. Social groups usually share some interests, but shared interests are not sufficient to constitute a social group. A social group is a collective of people who have affinity with one another because of a set of practices or way of life; they differentiate themselves from or are differentiated by at least one other group according to these cultural forms.

By an ideological group I mean a collective of persons with shared political beliefs. Nazis, socialists, feminists, Christian Democrats, and anti-abortionists are ideological groups. The situation of social groups may foster the formation of ideological groups, and under some circumstances an ideological group may become a social group. Shared political or moral beliefs, even when they are deeply and passionately held, however, do not themselves constitute a social group.

A democratic polity should permit the expression of all interests and opinions, but this does not imply specific representation for any of them. A democratic public may wish to provide representation for certain kinds of interests or political orientations; most parliamentary systems, for example, give proportional representation to political parties according to the number of votes they poll. The principle of group representation that I am arguing for here, however, refers only to social groups.

Second, it is important to remember that the principle calls for specific representation only of oppressed or disadvantaged groups. Privileged groups are already represented, in the sense that their voice, experience, values, and priorities are already heard and acted upon. The faces of oppression explicated in Chapter 2 provide at least beginning criteria for determining whether a group is oppressed and therefore deserves representation. Once we are clear that the principle of group representation refers only to oppressed social groups, then the fear of an unworkable proliferation of group representation should dissipate.

Third, while I certainly intend this principle to apply to representative bodies in government institutions, its application is by no means restricted to that sphere. In earlier chapters I have argued that social justice requires a far wider institutionalization of democracy than currently obtains in American society. Persons should have the right to participate in making the rules and policies of any institution with authority over their actions. The principle of group representation applies to all such democratized publics. It should apply, for example, to decisionmaking bodies formed by oppressed groups that aim to develop policy proposals for a heterogeneous public. Oppressed groups within these groups should have specific representation in such autonomous forums. The Black caucus should give specific representation to women, for example, and the women's caucus to Blacks.

This principle of group representation, finally, does not necessarily imply proportional representation, in the manner of some recent discussions of group representation (see Bell 1987, ch. 3; Beitz 1988: 163). Insofar as it relies on the principle of "one person one vote," proportional representation retains the assumption that it is primarily individuals who must be represented in decisionmaking bodies. Certainly they must, and various forms of proportional representation, including proportional representation of groups or parties, may sometimes be an important vehicle for representing individuals equally. With the principle I argue for here, however, I am concerned with the representation of group experience, perspectives, and interests. Proportional representation of group members may sometimes be too little or too much to accomplish that aim. A system of proportional group representation in state and federal government in the United States might result in no seats for American Indians, for example. Given the specific circumstances and deep oppression of Indians as a group, however, the principle would certainly require that they have a specific voice. Allocating strictly half of all places to women, on the other hand, might be more than is necessary to give women's perspectives an empowered voice, and might make it more difficult for other groups to be represented.

A principle of group representation has been implicitly and sometimes explicitly asserted in several contemporary social movements struggling against oppression and domination. In response to the anger and criticism that women, Blacks, gays and lesbians, American Indians, and others have leveled against traditionally unitary radical groups and labor unions, many of them have implemented some form of group representation in their decisionmaking bodies. Some political organizations, unions, and feminist groups have formal caucuses for Blacks, Latinos, women, gay men and lesbians, disabled people, and old people, whose perspectives might be silenced without explicit representation. Frequently these organizations have procedures for giving the caucuses a voice in organization-wide discussion and caucus representation in decisionmaking. Some organizations also require representation of members of disadvantaged groups in leadership bodies.

At the height of efforts to occupy nuclear power construction sites, for example, many anti-nuclear power actions and organizations responded to criticisms by feminists or people of color that the movement was dominated by straight white men. Social group affinity groups formed and were generally encouraged, providing solidarity and representation to formerly invisible groups. The National Women's Studies Association, to take another example, has a complex and effective system of representation for group caucuses in its decisionmaking bodies.

The idea of a Rainbow Coalition expressed a heterogeneous public with forms of group representation. The traditional coalition corresponded to the idea of a unified public that transcends particular differences of experience and concerns. In traditional coalitions diverse groups work together for specific ends which they agree interest or affect them all in a similar way, and they generally agree that the differences of perspective, interests, or opinion among them will not surface in the public statements and actions of the coalition. This form ideally suits welfare state interest-group politics. In a Rainbow Coalition, by contrast, each of the constituent groups affirms the presence of the others as well as the specificity of their experience and perspective on social issues (Collins 1986). In the Rainbow public Blacks do not simply tolerate the participation of gays, labor activists do not grudgingly work alongside peace movement veterans, and none of these paternalistically concede to feminist participation. Ideally, a Rainbow Coalition affirms the presence and supports the claims of each of the oppressed groups or political movements constituting it, and arrives at a political program not by voicing some "principles of unity" that hide difference, but rather by allowing each constituency to analyze economic and social issues from the perspective of its experience. This implies that each group maintains significant autonomy, and requires provision for group representation. Unfortunately, the promise of the Jesse Jackson campaign to launch a viable grassroots organization expressing these Rainbow Coalition ideals has not been fulfilled.

A principle of representation for oppressed or disadvantaged groups has been implemented most frequently in organizations and movements that challenge politics as usual in welfare capitalist society. Some more mainstream organizations, however, also have implemented this principle in some form. The National Democratic Party has had rules requiring representation of women and people of color as delegates, and many state Democratic parties have had similar rules. Many nonprofit agencies call for representation of specific groups, such as women, Blacks, Latinos, and disabled people, on their boards of directors. In a program that some of them call "valuing difference," some corporations have instituted limited representation of oppressed social groups in corporate discussions. One can imagine such a principle of group representation extended to other political contexts. Social justice would be enhanced in many American cities, for example, if a city-wide school committee formally and explicitly represented Blacks, Hispanics, women, gay men and lesbians, poor and working-class people, disabled people, and students.

Some might object that implementing a principle of group representation in governing bodies would exacerbate conflict and divisiveness in public life, rendering decisions even more difficult to reach. Especially if groups have veto power over policies that fundamentally and uniquely affect members of their group, it seems likely, it might be claimed, that decisionmaking would be stalled. This objection presupposes that group differences imply essential conflicts of interest. But this is not so; groups may have differing perspectives on issues, but these are often compatible and enrich everyone's understanding when they are expressed. To the extent that group differences produce or reflect conflict, moreover, group representation would not necessarily increase such conflict and might decrease it. If their differences bring groups into conflict, a just society should bring such differences into the open for discussion. Insofar as structured relations of privilege and oppression are the source of the conflict, moreover, group representation can change those relations by equalizing the ability of groups to speak and be heard. Thus group representation should mitigate, though not eliminate, certain kinds of conflict. If, finally, the alternative to stalled decisionmaking is a unified public that makes decisions ostensibly embodying the general interest which systematically ignore, suppress, or conflict with the interests of particular groups, then stalled decisionmaking may sometimes be just.

A second objection might be that the implementation of this principle can never get started. For to implement it a public must be constituted to decide which groups, if any, deserve specific representation in decisionmaking procedures. What principles will guide the composition of such a "constitutional convention"? Who shall decide what groups should receive representation, and by what procedures shall this decision be made? If oppressed groups are not represented at this founding convention, then how will their representation be ensured at all? And if they are represented, then why is implementation of the principle necessary?

These questions pose a paradox of political origins which is not specific to this proposal, and which no philosophical argument can resolve. No program or set of principles can found a politics, because politics does not have a beginning, an original position. It is always a process in which we are already engaged. Normative principles such as those I have proposed in this chapter can serve as proposals in this ongoing political discussion, and means of envisioning alternative institutional forms, but they cannot found a polity. In actual political situations application of any normative principle will be rough and ready, and always subject to challenge and revision. If democratic publics in American society accept this principle of group representation, as I have suggested a few have, they also are likely to name candidates for groups within them that deserve specific representation. Such an opening might sensitize the public to the need for other groups to be represented. But if it does not, these groups will have to petition with arguments that may or may not be persuasive. I see no practical way out of this problem of origin, but that does not stand as a reason to reject this or any other normative principle.

One might ask how the idea of a heterogeneous public which encourages self-organization of groups and group representation in decisionmaking differs from the interest-group pluralism I criticized in Chapter 3. Interest-group pluralism, I suggest, operates precisely to forestall the emergence of public discussion and decisionmaking. Each interest group promotes its own specific interest as thoroughly and forcefully as it can, and need not consider the other interests competing in the political marketplace except strategically, as potential allies or adversaries in its own pursuit. The rules of interest-group pluralism do not require justifying one's interest as right, or compatible with social justice. A heterogeneous public, however, is a *public*, where participants discuss together the issues before them and come to a decision according to principles of justice. Group representation, I have argued, nurtures such publicity by calling for claimants to justify their demands before others who explicitly stand in different social locations.

Implementing principles of group representation in national and local politics in the United States, or in restructured democratic publics within particular institutions such as factories, offices, universities, churches, and social service agencies, would obviously require creative thinking and flexibility. There are no models to follow. European models of consociational democratic institutions, for example, cannot be removed from the contexts in which they have evolved, and even within them it is not clear that they constitute models of participatory democracy. Reports of experiments with institutionalized self-organization among women, indigenous peoples, workers, peasants, and students in contemporary Nicaragua offer an example closer to the conception I am advocating (Ruchwarger 1987).

Social justice entails democracy. Persons should be involved in collective discussion and decisionmaking in all the settings that depend on their commitment, action, and obedience to rules—workplaces, schools, neighborhoods, and so on. When such institutions privilege some groups over others, actual democracy requires group representation for the disadvantaged. Not only do just procedures require group representation in order to ensure that oppressed or disadvantaged groups have a voice, but such representation is also the best means to promote just outcomes of the deliberative process.

I have argued that the ideal of the just society as eliminating group differences is both unrealistic and undesirable. Instead justice in a group-differentiated society demands social equality of groups, and mutual recognition and affirmation of group differences. Attending to group-specific needs and providing for group representation both promotes that social equality and provides the recognition that undermines cultural imperialism.

REFERENCES

Alexander, David (1987), "Gendered Job Traits and Women's Occupations," Ph.D. diss., University of Massachusetts.

Altman, Dennis (1982), *The Homosexualization of American Society* (Boston: Beacon Press).

Bastian, Ann, Norm Fruchter, Marilyn Gittell, Colin Greer, and Kenneth Haskins (1988), *Choosing Equality. The Case for Democratic Schooling* (Philadelphia: Temple University Press).

Bayes, Jane H. (1982), *Minority Politics and Ideologies in the United States* (Novato, Calif.: Chandler & Sharp).

Beatty, Richard W., and James R. Beatty (1981), "Some Problems with Contemporary Job Evaluation Systems," in Helen Remick (ed.), *Comparable Worth and Wage Discrimination: Technical Possibilities and Political Realities* (Philadelphia: Temple University Press).

Beitz, Charles (1988), "Equal Opportunity in Political Representation," in Norman Bowie (ed.), *Equal Opportunity* (Boulder, Colo.: Westview Press).

Bell, Derek (1987), *And We Are Not Saved: The Elusive Quest for Racial Justice* (New York: Basic Books).

Boxill, Bernard (1984), *Blacks and Social Justice* (Totowa, NJ: Rowman & Allanheld).

Bulkin, Elly, Minnie Bruce Pratt, and Barbara Smith (1984), *Yours in Struggle: Three Feminist Perspectives on Anti-Semitism and Racism* (New York: Long Haul).

Canter, Norma, V. (1987), "Testimony from Mexican American Legal Defense and Education Fund," *Congressional Digest* (Mar.).

Carmichael, Stokley, and Charles Hamilton (1967), *Black Power* (New York: Random House).

Cliff, Michelle (1980), *Reclaiming the Identity they Taught me to Despise* (Watertown, Mass.: Persephone).

Collins, Sheila (1986), *The Rainbow Challenge: The Jackson Campaign and the Future of U.S. Politics* (New York: Monthly Review Press).

Cornell, Stephen (1988), *The Return of the Native: American Indian Political Resurgence* (New York: Oxford University Press).

Cruse, Harold (1987), *Plural but Equal: Blacks and Minorities and America's Plural Society* (New York: Morrow).

Cunningham, Frank (1987), *Democratic Theory and Socialism* (Cambridge: Cambridge University Press).

Deloria, Vine, and Clifford Lytle (1984), *The Nations Within* (New York: Pantheon).

D'Emilio, Joseph (1983), *Sexual Politics, Sexual Communities* (Chicago: University of Chicago Press).

Edley, Christopher, (1986), "Affirmative Action and the Rights Rhetoric Trap," in Robert Fullinwider and Claudia Mills (eds.), *The Moral Foundations of Civil Rights* (Totowa, NJ: Rowman & Littlefield).

Epstein, Steven (1987), "Gay Politics, Ethnic Identity: The Limits of Social Constructionism," *Socialist Review*, 17 (May–Aug.), 54.

Fischer, Claude (1982), *To Dwell among Friends: Personal Networks in Town and City* (Chicago: University of Chicago Press).

Gutmann, Amy (1980), *Liberal Equality* (Cambridge: Cambridge University Press).

Haraway, Donna (1985), "Manifesto for Cyborgs," *Socialist Review*, 80 (Mar.–Apr.), 65–107.

Irigaray, Luce (1985), *Speculum of the Other Woman* (Ithaca, NY: Cornell University Press).

Jaggar, Alison (1983), *Feminist Politics and Human Nature* (Totowa, NJ: Rowman & Allanheld).

Karst, Kenneth (1986), "Paths to Belonging: The Constitution and Cultural Identity," *North Carolina Law Review*, 64 (Jan.), 303–77.

Kleven, Thomas (1988), "Cultural Bias and the Issue of Bilingual Education," *Social Policy*, 19 (Summer), 9–12.

Laclau, Ernesto, and Chantal Mouffe (1985), *Hegemony and Socialist Strategy* (London: Verso).

Lader, Laurence (1979), *Power on the Left* (New York: W. W. Norton).

Littleton, Christine (1987), "Reconstructing Sexual Equality," *California Law Review*, 75 (July), 1279–1337.

Mansbridge, Jane (1980), *Beyond Adversarial Democracy* (New York: Basic Books).

McGary, Howard (1983), "Racial Integration and Racial Separatism: Conceptual Clarifications," in Leonard Harris (ed.), *Philosophy Born of Struggle* (Dubuque, Iowa: Hunt).

Miles, Angels (1985), "Feminist Radicalism in the 1980's," *Canadian Journal of Political and Social Theory*, 9:16–39.

Minow, Martha (1985), "Learning to Live with the Dilemma of Difference: Bilingual and Special Education," *Law and Contemporary Problems*, 48 (Spring), 157–211.

—— (1987), "Justice Engendered," *Harvard Law Review*, 101 (Nov.), 11–95.

—— (1990), *Making All the Difference* (Ithaca, NY: Cornell University Press).

Nickel, James (1988), "Equal Opportunity in a Pluralistic Society," in Ellen Frankel Paul, Fred D. Miller, Jeffrey Paul, and John Ahrens (eds.), *Equal Opportunity* (Oxford: Blackwell).

Omi, Michael, and Howard Winant (1986), *Racial Formation in the United States* (New York: Routledge & Kegan Paul).

Ortiz, Roxanne Dunbar (1984), *Indians of the Americas* (New York: Praeger).

Pevar, Stephen L. (1983), *The Rights of Indians and Tribes* (New York: Bantam).

Ross, Jeffrey (1980), Introduction to Jeffrey Ross and Ann Baker Cottrell (eds.), *The Mobilization of Collective Identity* (Lanham, Md.: University Press of America).

Rothschild, Joseph (1981), *Ethnopolitics* (New York: Columbia University Press).

Ruchwarger, Gary (1987), *People in Power: Forging a Grassroots Democracy in Nicaragua* (South Hadley, Mass.: Bergin & Garvey).

Said, Edward (1978), *Orientalism* (New York: Pantheon).

Sartre, Jean-Paul (1948), *Anti-Semite and Jew* (New York: Schocken Books).

Scales, Ann (1981), "Towards a Feminist Jurisprudence," *Indiana Law Journal*, 56 (Spring), 375–444.

Schmitt, Eric (1989), "As the Suburbs Speak More Spanish, English Becomes a Cause," *New York Times*, 26 Feb.

Scott, Jean (1988), "Deconstructing Equality-versus-Difference: Or the Uses of Post-Structuralist Theory for Feminism," *Feminist Studies*, 14 (Spring), 33–50.

Sears, David O., and Leonie Huddy (1987), "Bilingual Education: Symbolic Meaning and Support among Non-Hispanics," Paper presented at the Annual Meeting of the American Political Science Association, Chicago, Sept.

Sunstein, Cass R. (1988), "Beyond the Republican Revival," *Yale Law Journal*, 97 (July), 1539–90.

Taub, Nadine, and Wendy Williams (1985), "Will Equality Require More than Assimilation, Accommodation or Separation from the Existing Social Structure?", *Rutgers Law Review*, 37 (Summer), 825–44.

Treiman, Donald J., and Heidi I. Hartman (1981), *Women, Work and Wages* (Washington, DC: National Academy Press).

Vogel, Lisa (1990), "Debating Difference: The Problem of Special Treatment of Pregnancy in the Workplace," *Feminist Studies*.

Wasserstrom, Richard (1980), "On Racism and Sexism," in *Philosophy and Social Issues* (Notre Dame, Ind.: Notre Dame University Press).

Williams, Robert A. (1986), "The Algebra of Federal Indian Law: The Hard Trail of Decolonizing and Americanizing the White Man's Indian Jurisprudence," *Wisconsin Law Review*, 219–99.

Williams, Wendy (1983), "Equality's Riddle: Pregnancy and the Equal Treatment/Special Treatment Debate," *New York University Review of Law and Social Change*, 13: 325–80.

Wilson, William J. (1978), *The Declining Significance of Race* (Chicago: University of Chicago Press).

Wolgast, Elizabeth (1980), *Equality and the Rights of Women* (Ithaca, NY: Cornell University Press).

Young, Iris (1985), "Humanism, Gynocentrism and Feminist Politics," *Women's Studies International Forum*, 8: 173–83.

17

RACE, MULTICULTURALISM AND DEMOCRACY

ROBERT GOODING-WILLIAMS

INTRODUCTION

In this paper I bring into conversation two debates pertaining to identities in the contemporary United States. The debate about race has been prompted by the proposition that, as ordinarily conceptualized by most Americans, biological racial identities do not exist. This view is sometimes associated with the claim that historians and social scientists should expunge talk of race and racial identities from their vocabularies, a proposal that is often rejected by those who would defend a social constructionist account of racial identities. The debate about multiculturalism is less well focused, but generally concerns the justification of multicultural educational practices in the context of a so-called "politics of recognition." A central question, here, is whether multiculturalism should be embraced for the reason that it advances the self-esteem of individuals belonging to socially oppressed groups by enabling them to discover the reflection or representation of their identities in a reformed canon.[1]

Part I of the paper engages the first debate by addressing an important skeptical reply to the claim that racial identities are social constructs. Focusing in particular on black identity, I answer Walter Benn Michaels's objection that a nonbiological and social constructionist account of American

From Robert Gooding-Williams, 'Race, Multiculturalism and Democracy', *Constellations*, 5/1 (1998).

For helpful comments on earlier drafts of this paper I wish to thank Alexander George, Andy Parker, Jan Dizard, Amrita Basu, Mark Kesselman, Preston King, Stanley Fish, Gary Watson, Georgia Warnke, Paul Stern, David Wills, Anna Stubblefield, Tom Wartenberg, Jyl Gentzler, Iris Young, Donald Morrison, Nancy Gilson, Starry Schor, Judith Butler, George Kateb, Lorenzo Simpson, Michael Hardimon, Tom McCarthy, and Sara Gooding-Williams. I am also grateful to the Columbia University Seminar in Social and Political Thought, to Princeton University's University Center for Human Values, and to the Yale Political Theory Workshop for opportunities to present this paper.

[1] See Henry Louis Gates, Jr., *Loose Canons* (Oxford: Oxford University Press, 1992), 35.

racial identities is not possible because the practice of racial classification in America involves the idea that racial passing is possible.

Having met Michaels's objection, I proceed in Section II to detail a social constructionist view of black identity that builds on the work of Anna Stubblefield and Anthony Appiah. Here, I suggest that black identities have both a third-person and a first-person dimension. I also explore some of the implications of my interpretation of black identity, focusing in particular on the issues of racial authenticity, African-American identity, and mixed race identity.

In Section III of the paper I shift my attention to multiculturalism and, specifically, to a version of Afrocentrism often associated with multiculturalism. In particular, I argue that Molefi Asante's notion of Afrocentric "recentering" suggests a model of multicultural education that, because it rests on a questionable understanding of African-American identity, should be rejected. In addition, I propose that in rejecting Asante's Afrocentrism we should refuse to exchange it for an anti-Afrocentric nationalism of the sort that Arthur M. Schlesinger, Jr. articulates in *The Disuniting of America*. Despite their differences, Schlesinger and Asante each promotes an identity politics that makes identity into a form of kitsch.

Neither Afrocentric nor dependent on an argument from self-esteem, my defense of multicultural education in the fourth part of this essay rests on a normative claim about the point of public education in a democratic society. In elaborating that defense, I employ my social constructionist concept of black identity to show that multiculturalism in contemporary America should be race-conscious. More exactly, I argue for endorsing race-conscious multiculturalism as a pedagogical and research program for disseminating a "cultural capital" that fosters the capacity for democratic deliberation in contemporary America.[2]

Finally, in the fifth and concluding part of the paper, I summarize my argument for multiculturalism by recurring to W. E. B. Du Bois's seminal turn-of-the-century reflections on the nature and point of a politics of recognition.

I. MEETING THE SKEPTICAL OBJECTION

Let me begin by stipulating that, by 'racialism,' I mean a brand of nineteenth century biological essentialism according to which "there are

---

[2] This way of formulating my argument draws inspiration from John Guillory's excellent discussion of the current canon wars in his *Cultural Capital: The Problem of Literary Canon Formation* (Chicago: University of Chicago Press, 1993), 38–55.

heritable characteristics, possessed by members of our species, which allow us to divide them into a small set of races, in such a way that all members of those races share certain traits and tendencies with each other that they do not share with members of any other race."[3] The racialist thesis that having a racial identity is a matter of embodying a biological racial "essence" or "type" is widely regarded to be false due to post-Darwinian developments in population genetics.[4] Here, I mention this thesis, because it plays a central role in Walter Benn Michaels's critique of the social constructionist approach to racial identity. To be sure, Michaels does not deny that racialism is false. Rather his point is that a prior commitment to racial essentialism is implicit in any social constructionist account of American racial identities that acknowledges the possibility of racial passing. In Michaels's view, it is not possible to give a social constructionist account of American racial identities that acknowledges this possibility but is not parasitic on the assumption that biological racial essences exist.

Michaels begins his criticism of social constructionism by reviewing Michael Omi's and Howard Winant's influential attempt to develop a theory of racial formations that conceptualizes racial identity "without biology."[5] His critique concentrates not on Omi and Winant, however, but (1) on the 1985 Louisiana Fourth Circuit Court of Appeals' ruling that "Susie Phipps, 'who had always thought she was white, had lived as white, and had twice married as white,' was not in fact white because her parents . . . had thought of themselves and of her as 'coloured'"[6] and (2) on some remarks that Adrian Piper makes in her essay, "Passing for White, Passing for Black." According to Piper, "[w]hat joins me to other blacks . . . and other blacks to another, is not a set of shared physical characteristics. Rather it is the shared experience of being visually or cognitively *identified* as black by a white racist society, and the punitive and damaging effects of that identification."[7] Michaels responds to the Louisiana court ruling and to Piper's remarks as follows:

[3] Kwame Anthony Appiah, *In my Father's House: Africa in the Philosophy of Culture* (New York: Oxford University Press, 1992), 13. For Appiah's more detailed discussions of racialism, see his "Racisms," in David Goldberg (ed.), *Anatomy of Racism* (Minneapolis: University of Minnesota Press, 1990) and K. Anthony Appiah and Amy Gutmann, *Color Conscious* (Princeton: Princeton University Press), 54–6.

[4] On the population geneticist's conception of races as breeding populations, see Ernst Mayr, "Typological versus Population Thinking," in *Evolution and the Diversity of Life* (Cambridge, Mass.: Harvard University Press, 1975), 26–9, and Richard Goldsby, *Race and Races* (New York: MacMillan, 1971).

[5] See Michael Omi and Howard Winant, *Racial Formation in the United States* (New York: Routledge, 1986), 90, and Walter Benn Michaels, "The No-Drop Rule," *Critical Inquiry*, 20 (Summer 1994), 90.

[6] Ibid. 764.

[7] Adrian Piper, "Passing for White, Passing for Black," *Transition*, 58 (1992), 30–1.

This is the Louisiana standard: if you're *perceived* as black, you are black. [emphasis added] But Piper's account of her own experience makes the incoherence of this standard even more obvious than it is in the Phipps case. For Piper describes herself as so light skinned that she is constantly being treated as if she were white. She is thus made to feel that she is passing for white, and since passing for white seems to her 'a really authentically shameful thing to do' . . . she is led into strenuous efforts to identify herself as a black. But what consequences must these efforts have for her nonbiological definition of racial identity? The point of the definition is that being black means being identified by a white racist society as black. On what grounds, then, can someone who is not identified by that society as black be said to be black?

Piper makes this dilemma even clearer by going on to remark that she has 'white friends who fit the prevailing stereotype of a black person' and thus have 'experiences' 'similar' to ones that make blacks black . . . If they really do have such experiences, what can she mean by calling these friends 'white'? That they can be white even if they are treated as black; that she can be black even if she is treated as white —these facts are tributes to, not critiques of, racial essentialism. The very idea of passing—whether it takes the form of looking like you belong to a different race or of acting like you belong to a different race—requires an understanding of race as something separate from the way you look and act. If race really were nothing but culture, that is, if race were nothing but a distinctive array of beliefs and practices, then, of course, there could be no passing, since to believe and practice what the members of any race believed and practiced would, by definition, make you a member of that race.[8]

For Michaels, Piper's suggestion that black identity is a matter of being classified and thus identified as black makes explicit the social constructionist account of racial identity that is implicit in the Louisiana Court of Appeals ruling. As I read him, the argument he adduces in criticism of both Piper and the court can be reconstructed as follows:

(1) Premise: If racial identities in America can be coherently conceptualized as social constructs, absent the assumption that biological racial essences exist, then it is not true that the practice of racial classification in America permits the possibility of passing.

(2) Premise: The practice of racial classification in America permits the possibility of passing.

(3) Conclusion: It is not true that racial identities in America can be coherently conceptualized as social constructs, absent the assumption that biological racial essences exist.

Thus construed, Michaels's argument is valid. It is unsound, however, because the first premise is false. This premise is false because it is a conditional whose antecedent is true and consequent false. In other words, racial identities in America can be coherently conceptualized as social constructs, absent the assumption that biological racial essences exist, even

---

[8] Michaels, "The No-Drop Rule," 767–8.

though the practice of racial classification in America permits the possibility of passing.

We can begin to see why Michaels's argument is unsound by noting a confusion that animates his reading of Piper in the second paragraph I cite. For Michaels, Piper's suggestion that race is "nothing but culture" amounts to the claim that someone is black if, and only if, she subscribes to certain beliefs and participates in certain practices. More exactly, he reads Piper as defining black racial identity with reference to the idea of a culture that is common to and only to persons who have been designated as black. But this is precisely what she does *not* do. On the contrary, her approach is to conceptualize black identity with reference to a practice of racial classification to which blacks have been subjected by American society. Black identity is a consequence of *that* practice, Piper implies, and not of the beliefs and practices which are shared by or distinctive to the people whom that practice designates as black. Socially constructed racial identities *are* cultural phenomena (in this sense, race *is* culture), but, *pace* Michaels, two individuals can have the same socially constructed racial identity (e.g., both can be socially constructed as black) without having what an anthropologist would call "a common culture."[9]

Michaels's response to Piper in the first paragraph I cite is more to the point, though finally flawed. Given Piper's view of black racial identity, he asks, how can it make sense to say that blacks who pass for white are not white, or that whites who pass for black are not black? Michaels is prompted to raise these questions, I think, because he ignores a significant part of Piper's conception of black racial identity. Where Piper sees the American practice of racial classification as incorporating both visual *and cognitive* identifications, Michaels pays attention only to visual identifications, that is, to the *perception* of individuals as black ("[I]f you're *perceived* as black," Michaels writes, "you are black"). Piper's reference to cognitive identification is meant, I assume, to flag the fact that the American practice of racial classification involves criteria entailing that someone perceived to be white can be black and that someone perceived to be black can be white. For Piper, then, someone who would not be classified as black on the basis of visual criteria could still *be black* because Americans' conventional (though not universal) adherence to the one-drop rule *cognitively* identifies her as black.[10] For Michaels, of course, the thought that such a person could exist is contradictory and incoherent. Because Michaels understands racial classification with reference only to visual criteria, he equates not being perceived to

---

[9] Appiah makes a similar point in *Color Conscious*, 85–90.
[10] See Piper, "Passing for White, Passing for Black," 18–19.

be black with not being classified as black. He believes, then, that Piper contradicts herself in allowing that there exist persons (e.g., blacks passing as white) who, though they are not perceived to be black, are classified as black. The appearance of contradiction disappears, I have been arguing, if one bears in mind the distinction between visual and cognitive identification. Similarly, for Piper, there is no contradiction in claiming that someone classified as white could be perceived to be black and have experiences "similar" to those whom the American practice of racial classification counts as black.

Racial identities in America can be coherently conceptualized as social constructs, absent the assumption that biological racial essences exist, even though the American practice of racial classification permits the possibility of passing. Piper shows that this is so by offering a noncontradictory, social constructionist account of racial identities that, without presupposing the existence of racial essences, acknowledges that passing can occur. In treating black identity as the product of a rule-governed social practice of racial classification, Piper interprets it as a social construct.[11] Needless to say, she *does not* assert that being black amounts to satisfying the false and often pernicious notions of black identity that have historically informed the American practice of racial classification. She does not claim, for example, that to be black is to be psychologically indisposed to hard work or to be by innate constitution intellectually inferior to whites. Neither does she propose, explicitly or otherwise, that black identity is a consequence of satisfying the one-drop rule or of embodying a biological racial essence. Rather Piper suggests that black identity is an effect of being *designated as black* by a practice of racial classification that has adhered to the one-drop rule through much of this century[12] and promoted the belief that racial essences

---

[11] Here, I do not take up the important question of what it is that makes a practice of racial classification a practice of *racial* classification. The problem, here, is to identify the concepts and beliefs that distinguish practices of racial classification from other practices of social classification (e.g., practices of gender identification). This is *not* a question that Omi and Winant take up in either the first or the revised edition of *Racial Formation in the United States*. Nor does Winant take up the issue in his recent book, *Racial Conditions* (Minneapolis: University of Minnesota Press, 1994). Robert Miles does address the issue in his *Racism* (New York: Routledge, 1989), 73–5, but it is not obvious to me that his notion of racialization suffices to capture all the practices of social identification which we are inclined to call 'racial' (e.g., racial identification in Brazil, which proceeds on the basis of principles very different from those which obtain in the United States). In the final analysis, there may be no adequate general concept of practices of racial identification. Still, there may be significant family resemblances (in Wittgenstein's sense) between these different practices.

[12] Only in the twentieth century does the one-drop rule become the dominant rule of racial classification in the United States. Indeed, in much of the nineteenth century, it finds itself in competition with a rule that defines mulattoes as other than black. For a detailed recounting of the social and political history of the one-drop rule and of black and white challenges to the rule, see F. James Davis, *Who is Black* (University Park: Pennsylvania University Press, 1991). See, also, David Hollinger, *PostEthnic America* (New York: Basic Books, 1995), 32, 44–5.

exist. In her view, being black is a matter of being classified as black by a particular practice of racial classification, it is not a function of satisfying all the odd rules and beliefs that have animated that practice.[13]

II. ON BEING A BLACK PERSON

Thus far, my elaboration of a view that Piper only sketches has focused on defending that view from Michaels's critique. Here, however, I would like to shift ground. In particular, I would like to complicate Piper's conception of black identity by drawing a distinction between being black and being a black person. Piper, I wish to say, defines a necessary but not a sufficient condition of being a black person. Even if one considers her point that being black not only involves being identified as black, but, additionally, the negative effects of being thus identified, it seems clear that her stated "definition" of black identity expresses a third-person perspective intended to highlight the objectification of blacks *as blacks* by a racist society.[14] Anna Stubblefield's and Anthony Appiah's recent treatments of racial identity point in a similar direction when, in keeping with Piper's nominalist intuitions, they propose that racial identities result from criteria governed practices of racial classification through the application of racial labels.[15] In explaining the concept of a black person I aim to enrich this perspective with a first-person point of view that notes the ways in which individuals classified as black contribute to the construction of their racial identities. Following Appiah, I draw on Ian Hacking's essay "Making Up People"[16] to discuss the "identifications"[17] by which black people shape their projects in light of the racial labelings and classifications to which they have been subjected.

Hacking's central idea is a view he calls 'dynamic nominalism.' Dynamic nominalism, he says, is the "doctrine ... that numerous kinds of human beings and human acts come into being hand in hand with our invention of

---

[13] If, for Piper, being black were a function, say, of satisfying the one-drop rule, then she would be committed to the view that, even in the absence of a practice of racial classification wherein the rule found application (explicitly or implicitly), America would still contain its share of black folk. On my reconstruction of her position, this is a view she rejects.

[14] This is not to deny that the bulk of Piper's powerful autobiographical essay deftly expresses her own "first-person" perspective.

[15] See Anna Stubblefield, "Racial Identity and Non-Essentialism about Race," *Social Theory and Practice*, 21/3 (Fall 1995), and Appiah, *Color Conscious*, 76–83.

[16] See Ian Hacking, "Making Up People," in Thomas C. Heller, Morton Sosna, and David Wellbery (eds.), *Reconstructing Individualism* (Stanford, Calif.: Stanford University Press, 1986), 222–36.

[17] By "identification," Appiah means "the process through which an individual intentionally shapes her projects—including her plans for her own life and her conception of the good—by reference to available labels, available identities." See *Color Conscious*, 78.

the categories labeling them ... it contends that our spheres of possibility, and hence our selves, are to some extent made up by our naming and what that entails."[18] To be sure, Hacking is not proposing here that the sheer utterance or inscription of newly invented names suffices in itself to cause the existence of the human beings named. Rather his point is that our sense of ourselves and of the possibilities existing for us is, to a significant degree, a function of the descriptions we have available to us to conceptualize our intended actions and prospective lives. "What is curious about human action," Hacking remarks, "is that by and large what I am deliberately doing depends on the possibilities of description ... [h]ence if new modes of description come into being, new possibilities of action come into being in consequence."[19]

Hacking's dynamic nominalism helps to explain the concept of a black person because it provides a means of conceptualizing the contributions individuals make to the construction of their racial identities. In effect, it suggests that individuals classified as black become black persons just in case they begin to act in the world under a description of themselves as racially black. As I have previously suggested, being black—that is, being racially classified as black—is a necessary but not a sufficient condition of being a black person. One becomes a black person only if (1) one begins to identify (to classify) *oneself* as black and (2) one begins to make choices, to formulate plans, to express concerns, etc., in light of one's identification of oneself as black.

Though this way of explaining the concept of a black person may seem a bit abstract, it is best understood as a philosopher's gloss on the sort of experience which is described time and again in the letters and literature of black persons. Consider, for example, the scene of visiting-card exchanges which Du Bois describes near the beginning of *The Souls of Black Folk*. Only after his card is refused, "peremptorily, with a glance," does it dawn on Du Bois that he "was different from the others."[20] Only then, moreover, does Du Bois begin to live his life in light of the fact that he has been classified as racially black and different, recognizing possibilities and making choices that he could not have recognized or made before, including, for example, the choice to prove his racial worth by competing with his white school-mates: "But they should not keep their prizes, I said; some, all, I would wrest from them."[21] Or consider the reflections of James Weldon Johnson's

[18] See Hacking, "Making Up People," 236.
[19] Ibid. 231.
[20] W. E. B. Du Bois, *The Souls of Black Folk*, ed. David W. Blight and Robert Gooding-Williams (New York: Bedford Books, 1997), 38.
[21] Ibid.

protagonist in *The Autobiography of an Ex-Coloured Man* as he recalls the experience of having been labelled one "fateful day at school" for the first time as a "nigger" and then as "coloured":

I have often lived through that hour, that day, that week, in which was wrought the miracle of my transition from one world into another; for I did indeed pass into another world. From that time I looked out through other eyes, my thoughts were coloured, my words dictated, my actions limited by one dominating, all pervading idea which constantly increased its force and weight until I finally realized in it a great, tangible fact.

And this is the dwarfing, warping, distorting influence which operates upon each and every coloured man in the United States. He is forced to take his outlook on all things, not from the point of view of a citizen, or a man, or even human being, but from the point of view of a *coloured* man.[22]

For Du Bois and Johnson's protagonist alike, a new world of new possibilities and impossibilities is born when acts of objectifying racial classification move them to understand themselves, to formulate aspirations, and to plan the future courses of their lives under descriptions of themselves as black, or colored. By acting under these descriptions, both individuals actively contribute to the construction of their identities as black persons. Johnson's ex-colored man is a particularly interesting example of a black person who *becomes* a black person at a memorable moment in his life, for he is the sort of black person who learns to pass for white in the new world into which he passes.

Elsewhere I have argued that Du Bois, notwithstanding his insight into the social construction of black persons, errs in *The Souls of Black Folk* in supposing in an Hegelian vein that a single "folk spirit" or "social mind" pervades the lives of black Americans. I have also suggested that Du Bois himself speaks persuasively against this supposition by highlighting (in *Souls*) the multiple minds and sensibilities and modes of self-understanding that polyphonically characterize black identity in America. It would be a mistake, of course, to think that a rejection of the Du Boisian idea of a collective black *Geist*, along with the older notion of a biological black racial essence, entails a rejection of the view that one can speak of black identity in general terms. Generally speaking, to be black (in America) is, simply, to be subject to a practice of racial classification that counts one as black. Corresponding to being black, however, are numerous ways of being a black person; that is, numerous ways of interpreting and assigning

---

[22] James Weldon Johnson, *The Autobiography of an Ex-Coloured Man* (New York: Vintage, 1989), 20–1.

significance to being black.[23] In some cases, the significance one assigns to being black in identifying oneself as black bears centrally on one's view of oneself. In other cases, it does not. It should be noted, moreover, that many of the most politically salient modes of being a black person involve the assignment of a *collective* significance to being black, a fact to which I will return in my discussion of race-conscious multiculturalism.

Let me conclude my explanation of the concept of a black person by sketching a few of its consquences for our thinking about racial authenticity, African-American identity, and mixed race identity.

Racial Authenticity

The distinction between *being authentically a black person* and *being inauthentically a black person* makes no sense in my view, since one becomes a black person by, and only by, acting under certain descriptions. In other words, I postulate no black personhood *apart* from a black person's actions to which she or he could be true or untrue in the performance of those actions.[24] Put a bit differently, I do not suppose that, prior to the performance of discursively shaped actions, there exist black selves or persons that such actions could authentically or inauthentically express.[25] It would be a mistake, then, to assert that some black persons are more authentic in their black personhood than others.

The putative distinction between *being authentically black* and *being inauthentically black* requires separate consideration, given that I differentiate between being black and being a black person. In considering this distinction, it is useful to note the affinity between my notion of being black and Sartre's notion of being a Jew. According to Sartre, the anti-Semite creates the Jew by identifying him *as a Jew*. To be a Jew, Sartre proclaims, "is to be thrown into—*to be abandoned to*—the situation of a Jew."[26] Sartre posits a

---

[23] The position I sketch here is consistent, I think, with Stuart Hall's well-known remarks regarding the "end of the innocent notion of the essential black subject." "What is at issue," Hall argues, "is the extraordinary diversity of subject positions, social experiences, and cultural identities which compose the category 'black'." On my account, this diversity is in part a function of the numerous ways in which one can be a "black person." See Stuart Hall, "New Ethnicities," in James Donald and Ali Rattansi (ed.), *"Race", Culture and Difference* (Thousand Oaks, Calif.: Sage Publications, 1992), 254.

[24] In other words, I do not subscribe to the sort of philosophical realism that, as Appiah puts it, "seems inherent in the ways questions of authenticity are normally posed." See Appiah, *Color Conscious*, 96.

[25] By 'discursively shaped' I mean, simply, description-shaped. For a similar approach to the topic of gender identity, see Judith Butler, *Gender Trouble* (New York: Routledge, 1990).

[26] Jean-Paul Sartre, *Anti-Semite and Jew*, trans. George Becker, with an introduction by Michael Walzer (New York: Schocken Books, 1995), 89.

distinction between authentic and inauthentic Jews. I doubt the usefulness of this distinction, because I see no clearly defined criteria for distinguishing authentic choices and behaviors—said to express "a true and lucid consciousness of [one's] situation"—from the types of choices and behaviors (e.g., the Jewish rationalist's universalism) that Sartre, somewhat arbitrarily, brands as inauthentic.[27] For the same reason, I doubt the value of the distinction between being authentically black and being inauthentically black. What criteria could one persuasively invoke for distinguishing between existentially lucid and less-than-lucid responses to the fact that one has been thrown into a world shaped by a practice of racial classification classifying one as black? Even supposing that one could clearly define some such criteria, it would remain to be shown that they provided a basis for identifying some specific *types* of behavior as inauthentic.[28]

African-American Identity

On my account, being African-American is coextensive neither with being black nor with being a black person. Being African-American is being a native born American who is black—who is, in other words, racially classified as black—and who typically is a black person. Yet the class of blacks and black persons in America also includes West Indian, Nigerian, Eritrean, Ghanaian, and other individuals who are not African-Americans. As I shall argue in the next part of this paper, African-American identity is culturally complex. Yet it would be false to claim that a commitment to the perpetuation of cultural forms associated with African-Americans is either a necessary or a sufficient condition of being a black person in America. As is well known, there exist black persons in America who are not committed to the perpetuation of any of these cultural forms and many non-blacks—and thus non-black persons—who are devoted to jazz and who take delight in the art of signifying.

Mixed Race Identity

A few words, finally, about the politics of mixed race identity, which actively contests America's current practice of racial classification. Advocates of a

---

[27] Sartre, *Anti-Semite and Jew*, 90, 111.

[28] For a more detailed critique of Sartre's remarks about inauthentic Jews and about Jewish identity in general, see Michael Walzer's introduction to the edition of *Anti-Semite and Jew* cited above.

mixed race identity, though still classified as black by that practice, deliberately decline to live in the world as black persons. Refusing to act under
descriptions of themselves as black, they act, instead, under descriptions of
themselves as racially mixed. One could still say of these individuals that
they *are in fact black*, meaning simply that, regardless of their self-
descriptions, they remain subject to a practice of racial classification that, to
the extent that it is still governed by the one-drop rule, counts them as black.
Yet claims of this sort will seem increasingly odd as the politics of mixed
race gathers steam, if only because an essential element of that politics is its
repudiation of the one-drop rule (such claims will seem odd in just the way
that it would have seemed odd to say to Susie Guillory Phipps, in the face of
her challenge to the one-drop rule, that she was in fact black in virtue of the
rule). The politics of mixed race disturbs the current conventions of racial
classification with an eye to enacting and making pervasive a new convention providing social space for the appearance of dynamic nominalist
"mixed race persons."[29]

III. MULTICULTURALISM AND KITSCH

In the third part of this essay I turn my attention to multiculturalism, which
I view as both an educational and a political project. In particular, I proffer a
critique of the educational program implicit in Molefi Asante's Afrocentrism. I then proceed to a critical analysis of Arthur Schlesinger, Jr.'s
explicitly anti-Afrocentric American nationalism.

My critique of Afrocentrism has some affinity to Anthony Appiah's
repeated attack on what he describes, borrowing a term from Paulin Hountondji, as Afrocentrism's "unanimist" idea of Africa. By 'unanimism'
Appiah has in mind the view "that Africa is culturally homogeneous—the
belief that there is some central body of folk philosophy that is shared by
black Africans quite generally."[30] Against this view, he insists on "the extraordinary diversity of Africa's peoples and its cultures," remarking that it is
"surely preposterous to suppose that there is a single African culture, shared

---

[29] It is important to see that the politics of mixed race is, ambiguously, a politics of disturbance *and* enactment. To the extent that it aims to institute a new order of racial classification
conventions that still relies on a principle of descent (mixed race identity is, after all, a function of
the racial identities of one's parents), I find it difficult to see in this politics, as does David
Hollinger, a "fundamental challenge to the authority of descent-defined categories." See
Hollinger, *PostEthnic America*, 165. For an interesting argument to the effect that the very heart of
democratic politics is an ambiguous tension between disturbance and enactment see William E.
Connolly, *The Ethos of Pluralization* (Ithaca, NY: Cornell University Press, 1995), 75–104.

[30] Appiah, *In my Father's House*, 24.

by everyone from the civilizations of the Upper Nile thousands of years ago
to the thousand or so language-zones of contemporary Africa."[31] Afro-
centrists embrace a simplistic vision of Africa, Appiah argues, and so
obscure the radically heterogeneous character of Africa's cultural life. Here,
I likewise take issue with Afrocentrism's yearning for simplicity, though
not as regards its idea of Africa; rather my focus will be Afrocentrism's
conception of African-American identity.

In "Racism, Consciousness, and Afrocentricity," Asante identifies himself
as African-American and remarks that "a precondition of [his] fullness, a
necessary and natural part of [his] maturity [has been] the commitment to be
who [he is], to be Afrocentric."[32] "One becomes Afrocentric," Asante
continues, by:

exploring connections, visiting the quiet places, and remaining connected. The furious
pace of our dislocation, mislocation, displacement, off-centeredness, and marginalization, often brought on by the incredible conspiracy of the Eurocentric architection,
drives us further and further away from ourselves, reinforcing us in our dislocation
and affirming us in our out-of-placeness. In such a situation, in the fringes of the
European experience, pushed away from the center, we swirl around lost looking for
place, for location. Afrocentricity is the active centering of the African in subject place
in our historical landscape. This has always been my search; it has been a quest for
sanity. Therefore, it was unthinkable for me to entertain ideas of living in the margins,
being in the periphery of someone else's historical and cultural experiences. My aim
was more fundamental, basic, the essential quality of being normal, uncomplicated.
By being normal, I do not reject the other; I embrace that which I truly know, i.e., jazz,
blues, railroads, Obatala, roots, hoodoo, soul, rhythms, sweet mommas, Dunbar and
Hughes, Sanchez, Mari Evans, and Charles Fuller, and so on, in ways that I do not
know the products of the other, i.e., country music, mistletoe, Valhalla, Wotan, pale
blonds, Frost and Mailer. *I recognize these products as part of my experience in the
large but they do not impact on me in the same way as those which seem to grow from the
soil of my ancestors.* With my own products I can walk confidently toward the future
knowing full well that I can grasp whatever-else is out there because my own center is
secured.[33] (emphasis mine)

Eurocentrism, on this account, has alienated and de-centered the African-
American subject, driving him further and further away from himself and
leaving him lost and without sanity at the periphery of Europe's historical
and cultural experience. The aim of an Afrocentric re-centering and, Asante
suggests, re-education of the African-American subject is an identity whose

---

[31] Appiah, *In my Father's House*, 24. See also Appiah, "Europe Upside Down: Fallacies of the
New Afrocentrism," *SAPINA Newsletter* V (Jan.–June 1993), 5. Appiah makes a similar point in
the context of his critique of Afrocentrism in his "Afrocentrism, 'Difference,' Role Models and the
Construction of Race," *Salmagundi*, 104–5 (Fall 1994–Winter 1995), 93–4.

[32] Molefi Kete Asante, "Racism, Consciousness, and Afrocentricity," in Gerald Early (ed.),
Lure and Loathing: Essays on Race, Identity, and the Ambivalence of Assimilation (New York:
Penguin, 1993), 142.

[33] Asante, "Racism, Consciousness, and Afrocentricity," 142–3.

defining quality, essence and foundation is a state of being that is normal and uncomplicated. One can become "normal" and "uncomplicated," he proposes, by embracing what one *truly* knows. At first this suggestion might seem to present a problem, since what the African-American subject *appears* to know is the contents of an experience that has been *complicated* by the integration of African and European elements, of jazz and country music, of sweet mommas and pale blonds. Yet we soon discover that what the African-American subject apparently knows is a good deal more than what he truly knows, since what he truly knows is simply those elements in his experience that express his African heritage. On what basis, however, can this subject claim to know truly the African elements in his experience but *not* the European elements? Asante's answer is that the former, unlike the latter, *seem to grow from the soil of the African-American subject's ancestors.*

Although there is much to object to in Asante's argument, the issue on which I should like to focus is his rhetorical resolution of what he admits to be the phenomenological complexity of African-American experience. Asante's African-American experience is complicated, not only because it involves his African and European heritages alike, but because his African heritage harbors complexities that he does not explicitly acknowledge, e.g., its inseparability from things European in the example of the railroads, and its patchwork combination of the originally African Obatala and the originally African-American jazz. The complexity Asante addresses he quickly disowns by appropriating the rhetoric of organic, biological growth. In other words, it is the figure of plant-like connectedness to an ancestral soil that provides Asante the epistemological vehicle he requires to bifurcate his experience into what he truly and does not truly know. Here, the effect of his language is to resurrect the specter of the nineteenth century racial sciences and their view that cultural identities express biological racial essences.[34] For Asante, the naturalizing rhetoric of biological growth is a simplifying rhetoric by which he dissociates himself from what he (putatively) fails truly to know in order to represent himself as the normal, uncomplicated and secure product of a specifically Afrocentric *Bildung.*

I can summarize my reading of Asante's rhetoric by identifying it as the rhetoric of kitsch. According to Karsten Harries, kitsch in modern art is the art of a realism that "[u]nlike most modern art, which betrays the precariousness of its project . . . seems sure of itself. Kitsch pretends to be in

---

[34] For a good discussion of the theoretical commitments of the nineteenth-century racial sciences, see Michael Banton, *Racial Theories* (Cambridge: Cambridge University Press, 1987), ch. 2.

possession of an adequate image of man."[35] Asante speaks the language of
kitsch because he invokes the imagery of a fixed biological identity to construct a putatively adequate image of African-American cultural identity.
His language successfully secures a "normal" and normalizing vision of that
identity by obscuring the hybrid, complex and multidimensional character
of African-American life and experience.[36] We can think of Afrocentrism as
an Afro-kitsch, because it sacrifices a skeptical sensibility—a sense that
African-Americans are much too complicated culturally to be reduced to
whitewashed (or better, "blackwashed") images of unambiguous self-
possession—to the sentimental impulse to see them sure of themselves, strid-
ing "confidently" toward the future.[37] What African-American novelist
Charles Johnson says of the Negritude movement—that "[l]ike fascist art in
Germany . . . Negritude—all Kitsch—is a retreat from ambiguity"—can just
as well be said of Asante's program for the Afrocentric re-education and
re-centering of African-American subjects.[38]

If African-American identities are complicated, this is (in part) because
they have been constituted not only by African-American cultures and societies, but, likewise, by a perpetual dialogue and violent engagement with the
larger society to which they belong.[39] It is important to remember, moreover,
that the converse is true of the identities of Americans who are not African-
Americans. As Albert Murray puts the point, "American culture, even in its
most rigidly segregated precincts, is patently and irrevocably composite. It is,

---

[35] Karsten Harries, *The Meaning of Modern Art* (Evanston, Ill: Northwestern University
Press, 1968), 149.

[36] The production of normalizing norms and images of African-American identity is a staple
of African-American cultural nationalism. On this point, see William L. Van DeBurge, *New Day
in Babylon: The Black Power Movement and American Culture 1965–1975* (Chicago: University of
Chicago Press, 1992), 170 ff.

[37] Manthia Diawara has also interpreted Afrocentricity as Afro-kitsch in his "Afro-Kitsch,"
in Gina Dent (ed.), *Black Popular Culture* (New York: Dia Center for the Arts, 1992), 285–91.

[38] Charles Johnson, *Being and Race: Black Writing since 1970* (Bloomington: Indiana University Press, 1988), 20. Eve Sedgwick has suggested, if I read her correctly, that kitsch-attribution
is a supercilious gesture expressing an attitude of "self-exemption or cynicism but nothing much
more interesting than that." Harries's and Johnson's use of the term 'kitsch' seems to me to be
exempt from this criticism in that it relies on a clearly stated concept of kitsch (kitsch as a retreat
from ambiguity) rather than on the haughty pretension simply to be able to "recognize kitsch
when [one] sees it" (see Eve Kosofsky Sedgwick, *Epistemology of the Closet* [Berkeley: University
of California Press, 1990], 155–6). For a more recent and equally persuasive critique of the ideology of "negritude," see Tsenay Serequeberhan, *The Hermeneutics of African Philosophy* (New
York: Routledge, 1994), 42–53. For a critique of Afrocentric education that differs from (but is
complementary to) the one offered here, see Amy Gutmann, "Challenges to Multiculturalism in
Democratic Education," in Robert K. Fullinwide (ed.), *Public Education in a Multicultural Society*
(Cambridge: Cambridge University Press, 1996), 158–9.

[39] Appiah makes a similar point in his "Identity, Authenticity, Survival: Multicultural Societies and Social Reproduction," in Amy Gutmann (ed.), *Multiculturalism: Examining the Politics
of Recognition* (Princeton: Princeton University Press, 1994), 154–5.

regardless of all the hysterical protestations of those who would have it otherwise, incontestably mulatto."[40] Ralph Ellison makes a similar point when he remarks that "most American whites are culturally part Negro American without even realizing it."[41] In a more humorous vein, Ellison notes that the American language "began by merging the sounds of many tongues, brought together in the struggle of diverse regions. And whether it is admitted or not, much of the sound of that language is derived from the timbre of the African voice and the listening habits of the African ear. So there is a de'z and do'z of slave speech sounding beneath our most polished Harvard accents, and if there is such a thing as a Yale accent, there is a Negro wail in it—doubtlessly introduced there by Old Yalie John C. Calhoun, who probably got it from his mammy."[42]

It is a significant and valuable feature of Arthur Schlesinger, Jr.'s *The Disuniting of America* that it acknowledges the mulatto character of American culture that Murray and Ellison were once at such pains to stress. "Historically and culturally," Schlesinger writes, "this republic has had an Anglo-Saxon base; but from the start that base has been modified, enriched, and reconstituted by transfusions from other continents and civilizations. The movement from exclusion to inclusion causes a constant revision in the texture of our culture. The ethnic transfusions affect all aspects of American life—our politics, our literature, our music, our painting, our movies, our cuisine, our customs, our dreams. Black Americans in particular have influenced the ever-changing national culture in many ways. They have been here for centuries . . . "[43] Still, Schlesinger is not happy with contemporary American culture, as he fears that the differences animating its perpetually changing mosaic of multiple and heterogeneous hybridities may tear it apart: "If the republic now turns away from Washington's old goal of 'one people'", he worries, "what is its future?—disintegration of the national community, apartheid, Balkanization, tribalization?"[44]

Schlesinger would fend off the threat of "Balkanization" and "tribaliza-

---

[40] Albert Murray, *The Omni-Americans* (New York: Vintage, 1983), 22.

[41] Ralph Ellison, *Going to the Territory* (New York: Vintage, 1987), 108. Murray's and Ellison's central point is that American identities are *multicultural*. For a recent sounding of a similar theme that stresses the multicultural or "mélange" character of modern identities generally, see Jeremy Waldron, "Multiculturalism and Mélange," in Robert K. Fullinwider (ed.), *Public Education in a Multicultural Society* (Cambridge: Cambridge University Press, 1996), 90–118. For a recent discussion of the hybrid and syncretic character of African-American and other "black Atlantic" cultures, see Paul Gilroy, *The Black Atlantic: Double Consciousness and Modernity* (Cambridge: Harvard University Press, 1993), ch. 3.

[42] Ellison, *Going to the Territory*, 108–9.

[43] Arthur M, Schlesinger, Jr., *The Disuniting of America: Reflections on a Multicultural Society* (New York: W. W. Norton, 1992), 135.

[44] Ibid. 118.

tion" by having all Americans, despite their differences, affirm a "democratic faith" in certain common and unifying "political ideals."[45] These "ideals of democracy and human rights," which Schlesinger, following Myrdal, calls the "American Creed," "transcend ethnic, religious and political lines."[46] They are the stuff of an "overarching political commitment" that Schlesinger believes can provide "the solvent that will prevent differences from escalating into antagonism and hatred."[47] Reminiscent of Asante, whose educational proposals for strengthing the self-esteem of black students he harshly criticizes, Schlesinger's search for a solvent bespeaks a desire to dissolve the complications he associates with hybridity and difference. But where Asante seeks his solvent in a rhetoric of ancestral soil and biological growth, Schlesinger finds his in a fantastical vision of ideals that, to his mind, have a well-defined content and meaning that transcend the group-based disagreements of a complex and quarrelsome American society. No less than Asante's rhetoric, Schlesinger's vision is a kind of kitsch, precisely because its figure of a semantically fixed and stable creed abstracts from the ambiguities and, especially, the conflicts of interpretation that have historically constituted American's engagement with political ideals. The creed, and the laws Schlesinger thinks embody it—e.g., the antidiscrimination laws yielded by the civil rights movement—are not transparent in their meaning and admit of multiple and contradictory readings reflecting the various ways Americans understand themselves.[48] Schlesinger's flight from difference cannot escape difference, because difference reproduces itself in the contest over the disputed meanings of unifying democratic ideals. Granting that these ideals are in some sense constitutive of democracy, their precise content and scope remains ever open to democratic debate.[49]

I can summarize my critique of Schlesinger by saying that he only partially acknowledges what Michael Walzer aptly depicts as the doubly hyphenated character of American identities. "[I]t is not the case that Irish-Americans, say, are culturally Irish and politically American," writes Walzer,

---

[45] Schlesinger, *Disuniting of America*, 135–6.

[46] Ibid. 27, 118.

[47] Ibid. 135.

[48] On the ambiguities built into antidiscrimination legislation, see Kimberlé Williams Crenshaw, "Race, Reform, and Retrenchment: Transformation and Legitimation in Antidiscrimination Law," *Harvard Law Review*, 101 (May 1988), 1341–6.

[49] For more on this point, and on the hermeneutic circle that characterizes democratic debate about basic rights and liberties, see Seyla Benhabib, "Toward a Deliberative Model of Democratic Legitimacy," in Seyla Benhabib (ed.), *Democracy and Difference: Contesting the Boundaries of the Political* (Princeton: Princeton University Press, 1996), 77–80. See, in the same volume, Chantel Mouffe, "Democracy, Power, and the 'Political,'" 254. Also see Amy Gutmann, "Challenges of Multiculturalism in Democratic Education," 168–9.

"[r]ather, they are culturally Irish-American and politically Irish-American. Their culture has been significantly influenced by American culture, their politics is still, both in style and substance, significantly ethnic."[50] Schlesinger, though he admits and indeed insists on the American-Irish and American-African hybridity of Irish-American and African-American *ethnic* identities, still romances the prospect of an American political identity that has been purified of ethnic and racial difference, and hence cleansed of struggles over the meanings of political ideals. Somewhat like the Afrocentrist who yearns for a simple and normal African-American identity—and so refuses to embrace the cultural hybridity of African-American lives—Schlesinger yearns for a simple and normal American political identity.[51] In both cases, identity is fashioned as a safe and placid home, free of ambiguity, contradiction, and conflict.[52]

IV. RACE CONSCIOUS MULTICULTURALISM

In the fourth part of this paper I defend a version of multiculturalism that avoids the kitsch of Afro- and other ethno-centrisms, as well as the kitsch of a political nationalism that eschews difference. In particular, I make the case that multicultural education in contemporary America should be race conscious.

I begin with the assumption that fostering the capacity for democratic deliberation is a central aim of public education in a democratic society.[53] I also follow a number of contemporary political theorists in supposing that democratic deliberation is a form of public reasoning geared towards adducing considerations that all parties to a given deliberation can find

---

[50] Michael Walzer, "What Does it Mean to be an 'American'?," *Social Research*, 57 (Fall 1990), 612.

[51] For clear-sighted resistance to kitsch conceptions of American identity of the sort that Schlesinger's position represents, see Thomas L. Dumm's letter to Laurie Anderson in the first chapter of his *United States* (Ithaca, NY: Cornell University Press, 1994) and Anne Norton's "Engendering Another American Identity," in Frederick M. Dolan and Thomas L. Dumm (eds.), *Rhetorical Republic: Governing Representations in American Politics* (Amherst: University of Massachusetts Press, 1993), 125–42.

[52] Here, I mean to suggest that both Asante's Afrocentrism and Schlesinger's nationalism exemplify what Bonnie Honig has recently called "the politics of home." See Bonnie Honig, "Difference, Dilemmas, and the Politics of Home," in Seyla Benhabib (ed.), *Democracy and Difference: Contesting the Boundaries of the Political* (Princeton: Princeton University Press, 1996), 257–77.

[53] Following Amy Gutmann, I use public education to refer to "all publically subsidized and publically accredited institutions that satisfy a mandatory schooling requirement, whether they are actually controlled by public or private organizations." This includes publicly accredited private schools. See Amy Gutmann, "Challenges of Multiculturalism in Democratic Education," 176 n. 1.

compelling.[54] On this view, successful deliberation requires that co-deliberators cultivate a mutual understanding of the differences in conviction that divide them, so that they can formulate reasons (say, for implementing or not implementing a proposed policy) that will be generally acceptable despite those differences.[55] In the words of one theorist, "[d]eliberation encourages people with conflicting perspectives to understand each other's point of view, to minimize their moral disagreements, and to search for common ground."[56]

Lorenzo Simpson usefully glosses the pursuit of mutual understanding when he writes that it requires "a 'reversibility of perspectives,' not in the sense of my collapsing into you or you into me, but in the sense that I try to understand—but not necessarily agree with—what you take your life to be about and you do the same for me . . . [i]n such a . . . mutual understanding you may come to alter the way in which you understand yourself and I . . . may find that listening to you leads me to alter my self-understanding."[57] According to Simpson, the search for common ground need not leave us with the convictions with which we began. On the contrary, the process of democratic deliberation can be a source of self-transformation that enriches one's view of the issues at hand and even alters one's conception of the demands of social justice.[58]

---

[54] See, for example, Joshua Cohen, "Procedure and Substance in Deliberative Democracy," in Seyla Benhabib (ed.), *Democracy and Difference: Contesting the Boundaries of the Political* (Princeton: Princeton University Press, 1996), 95–119; Amy Gutmann and Dennis Thompson, *Democracy and Disagreement* (Cambridge, Mass.: Harvard University Press, 1996), esp. ch. 2; and Seyla Benhabib, "Towards a Deliberative Model of Democratic Legitimacy."

[55] Joshua Cohen is especially clear on this point: "In an idealized deliberative setting, it will not do simply to advance reasons that one takes to be true or compelling: such considerations may be rejected by others who are themselves reasonable. One must instead find reasons that are compelling to others, acknowledging those others as equals, aware that they have alternative reasonable commitments and knowing something about the kinds of commitments that they are likely to have." See Cohen, "Procedure and Substance in Deliberative Democracy," 100.

[56] Amy Gutmann, "The Challenge of Multiculturalism in Political Ethics," *Philosophy and Public Affairs*, 22 (Summer 1993), 199.

[57] Lorenzo C. Simpson, "Community and Difference: Reflections in the Wake of Rodney King," in C. C. Gould and R. S. Cohen (eds.), *Artifacts, Representations and Social Practice* (Deventer: Kluwer Academic Publishers, 1994), 531–2. Here, it is important to note that, for Simpson, "reversing perspectives" does not entail that one be able literally to put oneself in the position of the other; or that one find a way to live the history she has lived; or even that one be able adequately to imagine her perspective as one's own—none of which possibilities are *real* possibilities according to Iris Young. On the contrary, he seems to have in mind precisely the sort of listening and learning "across differences" that Young endorses. In this essay, I use the idea of reversing perspectives as Simpson uses it. For Young's discussion of this issue, see her "Asymmetrical Reciprocity: On Moral Respect, Wonder and Enlarged Thought," *Constellations*, 33 (Jan. 1997), 340–63.

[58] Iris Young makes a similar point in her essay "Difference as a Resource for Democratic Communication," in James Bohman and William Rehg (eds.), *Democracy and Deliberation* (Cambridge, Mass.: MIT Press, 1997).

In multicultural America, multicultural public education is a good that promotes mutual understanding across cultural differences, thereby fostering and strengthening citizens' capacities for democratic deliberation. In essence, multicultural education is a form of pedagogy whereby students study the histories and cultures of differently cultured fellow citizens, many of whose identities have a composite, multicultural character. More exactly, it is a form of cross-cultural hermeneutical dialogue, and therefore a way of entering into conversation with those histories and cultures.[59] By disseminating the cultural capital of cross-cultural knowledge, multicultural education can cultivate citizens' abilities to "reverse perspectives." By facilitating mutual understanding, it can help them to shape shared vocabularies for understanding their moral and cultural identities and for finding common ground in their deliberations.[60]

By strengthening a student's ability to reverse perspectives, multicultural education may bolster her disposition to engage the self-understandings of differently cultured others, even if the particulars of her multicultural education have not involved an engagement with the cultures of precisely *those* others (consider, e.g., someone whose multicultural education has included courses in Asian-American literatures, but who knows nothing of American Latino subcultures). Acquiring a know-how and a feel for cross-cultural hermeneutical conversation is likely to reinforce a student's inclination to understand and learn from the self-interpretations of cultural "others" in just the way that the cultivation of an athletic skill (e.g., the ability to "head" a soccer ball) tends to reinforce one's inclination to participate in the sports for which having that skill is an advantage (e.g. playing soccer). In the case of multicultural education, one cultivates a skill which is motivationally conducive to the sort of mutual understanding that is critical to the flourishing of deliberative democracy in a multicultural society.[61]

Let me summarize my argument so far. In contrast to Schlesinger, who yearns for a society in which the understanding of key political ideals remains immune from deliberative debate animated by cultural and other group differences, I have been suggesting that deliberative debate of this sort is an appropriate medium for seeking and forging common grounds and ideals. I have also been arguing (1) that a commitment to deliberative

---

[59] Here, I follow Gadamer in allowing that one can enter into dialogue, not only with persons, but with narratives and other forms of written expression.

[60] See Simpson, "Community and Difference," 532–3.

[61] For a related argument that, from a somewhat different perspective, raises the question of the connection between multicultural education and democratic citizenship, see Janet Farrel Smith, "A Critique of Adversarial Discourse: Gender as an Aspect of Cultural Difference," in Lawrence Foster and Patricia Herzog (eds.), *Contemporary Philosophical Perspectives on Pluralism and Multiculturalism* (Amherst: University of Massachusetts Press, 1994), 59–82.

democracy in multicultural America entails a commitment to promoting the mutual understanding of differences through cross-cultural dialogue and (2) that such a commitment justifies the institution of multicultural education. The promotion of mutual understanding avoids Schlesinger's and Asante's kitsch, because it is not predicated on an imperative to preserve an uncomplicated national or ethnic identity in the face of cultural and social complexity. Indeed, the ideal of mutual understanding invites *increasing* complexity by suggesting that cross-cultural educational insights, since they can effect changes in the self-understandings of persons who have benefitted from a multicultural education, may alter and further complicate those persons' identities, perhaps making them *more* multicultural. In what follows, I further explore the implications of this ideal by proposing that a commitment to deliberative democracy in multicultural America justifies a form of multicultural education that is, specifically, *race-conscious*.

Multicultural education in America should be race-conscious, because the mutual understanding of differences in America is impossible absent attention to race. As regards cross-cultural conversations with specifically African-American *cultures*,[62] this is perhaps obvious. To be sure, my claim here *is not* that these cultures are somehow reducible to black Americans' reactions to racial classification, or to the slavery and racism that have attended that classification. As Ralph Ellison once asked, "can a people . . . live and develop for over three hundred years simply by *reacting*?"[63] Still, it seems to me incontrovertible that any cross-cultural inquiry into African-American cultures will have to address the largely racialized character of African-Americans' self-understandings; that is, it will have to investigate the ways in which African-Americans, in describing themselves as black, have coped with racial classification and racial oppression, thereby modifying the character of African-American life, art, and politics. African-American cultures, notwithstanding their past and present diversity, have been and continue to be inflected by meanings and self-understandings that *black persons* have assigned to being black in a society that has been shaped by black slavery and antiblack racism. Because racism, the legacies of slavery, and black personhood cut across the cultural differences distinguishing African-Americans, cross-cultural education that engages the complexity of African-American cultures will *almost always* attend to the meanings that

---

[62] Here, I mean to flag the fact that, like Anthony Appiah, I remain skeptical of the view that there is a single culture shared in common by all African-Americans. On this point, see Appiah's recent contribution to Appiah and Gutmann, *Color Conscious*. See, also, Bernard Boxill, *Blacks and Social Justice* (Totowa, NJ: Rowman & Allenheld, 1984), 178.

[63] Ralph Ellison, "An American Dilemma: A Review," *Shadow and Act* (New York: Vintage, 1972), 315.

black persons, mindful of the slave past and of antiblack racism, ascribe to being black.

Let me develop this point by highlighting the role that the concept of a black person, like that of subjective gender identity, can play in historical inquiry. Using the latter concept, Joan Scott has shown how nineteenth-century French seamstresses, acting under descriptions of themselves as *women*, established a "distinctively feminine work identity" that significantly shaped their political actions. Similarly, Robin D. G. Kelley has argued that "[r]ace, particularly a sense of 'blackness,' . . . figures prominently in the collective identities of black working people." In effect, he implies that the concept of a black person—that is, of someone black who acts in the world under a description of himself as black—can make a valuable contribution to the historian's study of America's black working class, a point that he later bears out in his discussion of the African-Americans who fought in Spain with the Abraham Lincoln Brigade "out of their concern for *black people*."[64] Kelley's work is relevant to my argument, because it offers an indication of the sort of race-conscious insight that ought to inform American multicultural education. To be precise, it suggests that students' cross-cultural study of African-American working class cultures should focus, in part, on the ways in which the racialized self-understandings of black persons have informed and continue to inform those cultures.

Kelley's example stresses the *collective* significance that working class black persons have assigned to being black. This is significant, in my view, for I suspect that race-conscious multiculturalism will enhance nonblacks' capacity to find deliberative common ground with blacks—a ground that at times seems to be sorely missing from American public life (as, for example, in discussions of the million man march and of the "not guilty" verdict in the O. J. Simpson criminal trial)—just to the extent that it emphasizes African-American views of and debates about being black that develop the insight that black identity is a collective predicament. In the same vein, one could easily envision a race-conscious multicultural curriculum that investigated African-American history and political thought with the explicit aim of making sense of such views and debates.

Consider, for example, the view held by many (though not all) African-Americans that the (comparatively) low, average socioeconomic status of African-Americans, because it is due to the cumulative effects of racial slavery and antiblack racism, is an injustice for which African Americans deserve compensation. Some white Americans will dismiss this assertion of

[64] See Joan Wallach Scott, *Gender and the Politics of History* (New York: Columbia University Press, 1988), 44, 104, and Robin D. G. Kelley, *Race Rebels* (New York: Free Press), 4–5, 104.

injustice, largely because they are "reluctant to see the present social plight
of blacks as the result of American slavery."[65] Still, were these whites to
learn something of American racial slavery and of its impact on African-
American life, they could begin to see that the argument for reparations is
plausible, and begin to share with the African-Americans who advance that
argument a common moral ground for further deliberations. In other words,
through the study of African American social history, they could begin to
acknowledge the cogency of the considerations in light of which many
African-American black persons, in reflecting on that history, have insisted
that being black in America involves collective injustice. Supposing that they
augmented this study with inquiry into the central themes of African-
American political thought[66] (as it has evolved, say, from the writings of
Martin Delaney to those of Martin King), they could enlarge the common
ground by beginning to recognize the range and force of African-American
perspectives on other race-related issues.

It would be a mistake, of course, to think that multiculturalism needs to
be race-conscious only when addressing the self-understandings of black
persons or, by analogy, the self-understandings of racially classified but non-
black "persons of color." America is also a nation of racially classified
whites and white persons; and white personhood, we know, cuts across ethnic lines. Again, by analogy to blacks who become black persons, whites who
become white persons let their descriptions of themselves as white matter to
the ways in which they live their lives. David Roediger's work on the racial
formation of Irish-American workers is relevant here, as it provides a model
for historical inquiry that illuminates the social construction and ethnic cultural significance of white racial identities.[67] Also important, in this context,
is Toni Morrison's book *Playing in the Dark*. Reflecting on the nature of
American literature, Morrison writes:

that cultural identities are formed and informed by a nation's literature, and . . . what
seemed to be on the 'mind' of the literature of the United States was the self-conscious
construction of the American as a new white man. Emerson's call for this new man in
'The American Scholar' indicates the deliberateness of the construction, the conscious necessity for establishing the difference. But the writers who responded to this
call, accepting or rejecting it, did not look solely to Europe to establish a reference for
difference. There was a very theatrical difference underfoot. Writers were able to

[65] Bill E. Lawson, "Moral Discourse and Slavery," in Howard McGary and Bill E. Lawson
(eds.), *Between Slavery and Freedom: Philosophy and American Slavery* (Bloomington: Indiana
University Press, 1992), 85.

[66] For a brief but excellent introduction to the central themes of African-American political
thought, see Bernard Boxill, "Two Traditions in African-American Political Philosophy," *Philosophical Forum*, 24 (Fall–Spring 1992–3), 119–35.

[67] See David Roediger, *The Wages of Whiteness: Race and the Making of the American
Working Class* (London: Verso, 1991).

celebrate and deplore an identity already existing or rapidly taking a form that was elaborated through racial difference. That difference provided a huge payout of sign, symbol, and agency in the process of organizing, separating, and consolidating identity . . . [68]

For Morrison, reading American writers after Emerson (e.g., Poe and Twain) is a matter of engaging complicated constructions of white racial identities implicated in a racial ideology ("American Africanism" is Morrison's phrase) that assigns multiple meanings to the African presence in America. Self-consciously constructing a literature in light of descriptions of themselves as white, the "founding writers of young America" were white persons (in my sense of the term) for whom the figure of the black African became a "staging ground and arena for the elaboration of the quintessential American identity."[69] For my purposes, Morrison's short study is valuable, because it affords some excellent examples of the ways multicultural inquiry can explore the cultural construction of white racial identities and their connection to the promotion of racial ideologies. In America, multicultural education cannot avoid race, because socially constructed racial identities—those of black persons and white persons alike—come into view no matter what class or ethnic perspective one occupies in cross-cultural deliberations. And while one ought not to conflate multiculturalism with struggles against racism and economic injustice, or promote it as a substitute for such struggles, multicultural education, by being race conscious, can contribute to an understanding of the issues posed by these struggles.[70]

CONCLUSION: THE POLITICS OF RECOGNITION

Let me conclude this essay by returning to Du Bois.

In 1897, Du Bois sketched his position on the question of cultural recog-

[68] Toni Morrison, *Playing in the Dark: Whiteness and the Literary Imagination* (Cambridge, Mass.: Harvard University Press, 1992), 39.

[69] Ibid. 44, 51. See also, in this vein, Karen Sánchez-Eppler, *Touching Liberty* (Berkeley: University of California Press, 1993), especially her chapter on Walt Whitman.

[70] For an insightful and valuable discussion of the differences and possible connections between multiculturalism and antiracism, see Lawrence Blum, "Multiculturalism, Racial Injustice, and Community: Reflections on Charles Taylor's 'Politics of Recognition,'" in Lawrence Foster and Patricia Herzog (eds.), *Contemporary Philosophical Perspectives on Pluralism and Multiculturalism* (Amherst: University of Massachusetts Press, 1994), 175–205. On the dangers of letting the promotion of multiculturalism substitute for struggles against racism and other forms of social injustice, see Hazel Carby, "The Multicultural Wars," *Radical History*, 54 (Fall 1992), 10–11, as well as her unpublished paper "Cultural Integration/Political Apartheid," delivered at the Brown at Forty Conference, Amherst College, Dec. 2 and 3. For a related critique of an identity politics that "caresses the better-off female, gay, and/or minority self while consigning its working class sisters and brothers to their 'richly' deserved misery," see Micaela di Leonardo, "White Ethnicities, Identity Politics, and Baby Bear's Chair," *Social Text*, 41 (Winter 1994), 165–91.

nition in a paper he entitled "The Conservation of Races." In this essay, he argued that each race has a cultural or "spiritual" message for humanity, although some races, the Negro race among them, have yet fully to deliver themselves of their messages. Among the central themes of "The Conservation of Races" is Du Bois's effort to exhort his fellow Negroes, especially his fellow American Negroes, to act in concert to cultivate and bring to fruition the Negro's message for humanity. Here, however, I wish only to emphasize Du Bois's guiding assumption in this essay, that recognizing the cultural worth of a race's spiritual message is a matter of seeing that that message has something to say to all human beings. In 1897, then, Du Bois conceptualized cultural recognition as the predication of universal value.[71]

In *The Souls of Black Folk*, published just six years after "The Conservation of Races," Du Bois develops a somewhat different notion of recognition; not recognition as the predication of universal value, but what I shall call 'self-recognition'. The self of self-recognition is not, for the Hegelian Du Bois, the self taken by itself, but the self-conceived as socially mediated. For Du Bois, then, self-recognition is a form of cultural recognition that entails seeing one's own cultural identity in connection to the cultural identities of the other members of one's community. Where self-recognition is frustrated by racial prejudice, Du Bois proposes, the likely outcome is social tragedy.[72]

The emergence in Du Bois's writing of a second conception of cultural recognition marks a distinction that continues to play a role in debates about the politics of recognition. Charles Taylor, for example, in his influential essay on that topic, explicitly conceptualizes cultural recognition as the predication of universal value. For Taylor, one's hermeneutic engagement with cultures not one's own should be guided by the defeasible presumption that "all human cultures that have animated whole societies over some considerable stretch of time have something important to say to all human beings."[73] Now compare Taylor's understanding of recognition to the one Susan Wolf propounds in her critique of Taylor. According to Wolf, "[t]he politics of recognition urges us not just to make efforts to recognize the other more actively and accurately—to recognize those people and those cultures that occupy the world in addition to ourselves—it urges us to take a

---

[71] For the full text of "The Conservation of Races" see Howard Brotz (ed.), *Negro Social and Political Thought 1850–1920* (New York: Basic Books, 1966), 493–502.

[72] I explore the relation between recognition and tragedy in *Souls* in ch. 3 of an unpublished manuscript, "Recognizing Race: Du Boisian Meditations on Black Identity in America." A short version of this chapter appears under the title "Du Bois's Counter-Sublime," *Massachusetts Review*, 35 (Summer 1994), 202–24. See also the editors' introduction to the Bedford Books edition of *The Souls of Black Folk*.

[73] Charles Taylor, "The Politics of Recognition," in Amy Gutmann (ed.), *Multiculturalism: Examining the Politics of Recognition* (Princeton: Princeton University Press, 1994), 66.

closer, less selective look at who is sharing our cities, the libraries, the schools we call our own. There is nothing wrong with allotting a special place in the curriculum for the study of our history, our literature, our culture. But if we are to study our culture, we had better recognize who we, as a community, are."[74] Here, like the Du Bois of *Souls*, Wolf concerns herself with *self*-recognition, suggesting that one aim of multicultural education is a knowledge of one's community in its multifaceted complexity. Recognizing who *we* are, as distinct from recognizing that *they* have something valuable to say, is the critical element in her interpretation of the politics of recognition.

Now it is clear, I hope, that the conception of the politics of recognition which I have been defending is Wolf's "self-recognition" conception. Recognition, as I conceive it, is recognition gained through multicultural education oriented towards mutual understanding. Thus understood, recognition is, as it was for Du Bois, a matter of seeing one's cultural identity in connection to the cultural identities of other members of one's community. Sometimes this will involve seeing more clearly the point of the needs-interpretations of others; and sometimes it will lead to criticism and debate about the validity of those needs-interpretations. On still other occasions, recognition will move us to change our views of ourselves, or to see that our sense of what matters to us brings our culturally hybrid selves closer to culturally hybrid others than we ever expected. Whatever the case may be, the pursuit of socially mediated self-recognition is important to advancing the goal of deliberative democracy in America. "America's dilemma," Ronald Takaki reminds us, "has been our resistance to ourselves—our denial of our immensely varied selves."[75]

---

[74] Susan Wolf, "Comment," in Amy Gutmann (ed.), *Multiculturalism: Examining the Politics of Recognition* (Princeton: Princeton University Press, 1994), 85.

[75] Ronald Takaki, *A Different Mirror: A History of Multicultural America* (Boston: Little, Brown, 1993), 427.

18

KANT AND RACE

THOMAS E. HILL JR. AND BERNARD BOXILL

I. INTRODUCTION

Kant has been long recognized as one of the greatest philosophers of the West and recently his works have been increasingly influential. In the past it has been mainly his *Critique of Pure Reason* and *Groundwork of the Metaphysics of Morals* that were the focus of attention, but the later writings are now being taken more and more seriously (by friend and foe). Understandably, the enhanced attention paid to Kant's later writing has evoked a response from non-Kantians. There has been more vigorous criticism from many quarters. Some old familiar objections turn up repeatedly, and many of these rest on misunderstanding. But scholars well aware of Kant's later writings also raise new concerns that reflect sensitivity to contemporary problems and perspectives.[1] Specifically, feminists and African American philosophers raise objections focused on Kant's writings on law, politics, history, and anthropology.

There are a number of charges, many of which fall under the general heading of 'Kant was a racist and sexist'. For example, anecdotes, quotations and stories reported from others, and comments on particular blacks and women, or groups of them, seem to reflect racist and sexist beliefs and attitudes on Kant's part. Perhaps more seriously, aspects of Kant's published, and unpublished, *philosophical* work, it has been argued, are

---

[1] Objections raise questions that should be distinguished, for example: (1) Is Kant's allegedly racist idea an empirical claim, a specific attitude, or a philosophical thesis? (2) Is it an idea that is itself racist (in some specified sense) or merely one that tends (e.g. in the wrong hands) to facilitate the growth of racist ideas and attitudes? (3) Are the specific objections and charges directed to ideas or the man, e.g. the man's motivation by racist attitudes, the man's having been culpably influenced by racist ideas, or the man's culpably endorsing racist ideas? (4) In so far as the objections are to Kant's philosophy, broadly construed, are they objections to his basic ideas (e.g. the central and more foundational claims in the three Critiques and the *Groundwork*) or to aspects of Kant's philosophy that are separable parts (independent or falsely believed to be derivative) or to merely particular illustrations presented re philosophical points (perhaps falsely believed to be apt examples)? For example, in the latter two categories: Kant's claims about property, revolution, women, and, arguably, race.

themselves racist, or at least apt to facilitate the growth of racist ideas and attitudes. Often these objections stem from more specific political and anthropological claims, for example, that women are to be mere 'passive citizens' without a vote and that some races are permanently inferior. But sometimes the problem is thought to lie deeper, for example, in Kant's rationalism in moral theory and his ideas of teleology and race in anthropology. One concern that may (for some) lie behind these objections is a suspicion that Kant, the man, was himself so racist and sexist that his works should not receive the respect and favourable attention that they currently receive. (The thought may be the dubious one that we should not concern ourselves with the good ideas of bad people. On the other hand, it may instead be that the faults of attitude and judgement that show up in one aspect of a thinker's work is likely to infect his work as a whole.) Apart from the concern with Kant, the man, however, there remain the important questions about the ideas presented in his philosophical and other works, many of which have been and continue to be influential.

We will focus on Kant and race, referring to similar issues regarding gender only for comparison. We acknowledge that Kant expressed various beliefs and attitudes that are aptly called racist, in that they falsely (and perhaps culpably) affirm belief in the inferiority of non-white races and so are liable to encourage policies and attitudes towards them that are unjust, contemptuous, and callous. His failings, we suggest, were not only faults of commission (what he said) but also faults of omission (what he did not say but should have).[2] We deny, however, some of the exaggerated charges of radical and deep racism put forward by some notable recent critics. Kant's basic critical philosophy and moral theory, we believe, is not infected with racism. On the contrary, the moral theory can serve as a reasonable framework for addressing contemporary racial problems, provided it is suitably supplemented with realistic awareness of the facts about racism and purged from association with certain false empirical beliefs and inessential derivative theses. Our position, then, is that, while it is important to notice and block the influence of aspects of Kant's writings that reflect or might encourage racism, the charges of racism do not reach Kant's deep theory or undermine its potential for guiding deliberation about the problems of race.

Our discussion will be divided as follows.

---

[2] Whether or not the 'fault' was one for which Kant was morally culpable, given what he might and should have known at the time, is not the question on which we will focus. Our concern is whether his expressed ideas were faulty in any of the several ways that we consider, e.g. expressing racist beliefs and attitudes or encouraging, by his opinions (and what he fails to say), racist beliefs and attitudes in others.

First, we examine various contentions made by Emmanuel Eze, who charges on the basis of an extensive review of Kant's less known writings that Kant's racism is extensive and deeply embedded in his basic philosophy. The texts that he cites are indeed troublesome and not to be ignored, but Eze's conclusions, we argue, extend considerably beyond what the cited texts actually warrant. There are two sorts of problem: (*a*) the texts do not in fact support the extreme form of racist beliefs that Eze attributes to Kant, e.g. that some races are not human; and (*b*) Eze's charge that Kant's racist beliefs are inseparable from his basic critical philosophy rests on serious interpretative mistakes.

Second, we take up an important, and potentially troublesome, version of the suspicion that Kant's moral philosophy (not just his anthropological remarks) reflects a deep prejudice against people who do not share Kant's European, Enlightenment, male, professorial values. The suspicion is that by inflating the value of reason, as he conceived it, Kant in effect denigrated those who chose a more spontaneous life of passion or relaxed enjoyment. Even if Kant had not expressed his unfortunate views about hereditary racial inferiority, there is an aspect of his moral philosophy that may be called into question on the ground that it expresses, or at least may encourage, a contemptuous attitude towards certain non-European peoples simply because their lifestyles differ radically from that of the white, male, European models that Kant admired. Kant's enthusiasm for 'the life of reason' arguably extended beyond what his commitment to reason as the source of moral judgements warranted. Striving for perfection, contributing to civilization and high culture, planning, competing, controlling impulse and emotion apparently had value for Kant far beyond what is required to satisfy the basic demands of duty (and even beyond what is defensible as 'imperfect duty'). They are part of a controversial conception of the good life that Kant, unfortunately, seems ready to prescribe universally, not merely as a permitted lifestyle but as the only alternative to a worthless existence. The Tahitians, as he imagined them, symbolized for Kant this worthless alternative to the busy, productive, reason-dominated lifestyle that he apparently admired. Setting aside all issues of hereditary racial tendencies, Kant is at least suspect for encouraging contemptuous attitudes towards any people who, being talented or not, chose life closer to the Tahitians (as he pictured them). This objection, we think, has considerable force and gives reason for contemporary Kantians to dissociate themselves from some of Kant's excesses in adulation of the life of reason.

Third, although the last point is significant, it should not be confused with a more general condemnation of Kant's rationalism. In particular, his insistence on the crucial role of reason in moral deliberation and finding solutions to social problems is separable from the previous objection, and it seems quite right. Kant argued, rightly we think, that the development of deliberative reason is crucially important for groups, as well as individuals, to develop solutions to the problems of social justice. Although *more* than reason is required for moral living and decent communities, Kant seems right that people who tried to live as he (no doubt falsely) portrayed the Tahitians, without the use of reason and only for enjoyment, would be ill equipped to handle the social and moral problems inevitably presented by the hard realities of human life. Thus, while he arguably inflated the value of a lifestyle devoted to perfecting reason, his main message, the need for the use (and so adequate development of) deliberative reason, is still much needed.

Fourth, although (as just suggested) Kant's moral and political philosophy rightly emphasizes the need for the development and use of deliberative reason, he apparently did not fully recognize the powerful role that relatively intractable, gut-level, feelings about race (and other differences) play in human choices. He was keenly aware of ways in which self-serving desires tempt otherwise good people to 'make exceptions of themselves', and he acknowledged human frailty and self-deception. But his confidence that reason *can* overcome any assaults from our sensuous nature may have fostered over-confidence that rational arguments are sufficient and generally effective to resolve problems generated by feelings that lead to conflict. Although in theory, admittedly, Kant could acknowledge that divisive feelings, e.g. racial antagonisms, in fact colour our judgements and undermine the effectiveness of rational solutions, he did not seem to grasp the pervasiveness of the problem as an obstacle to progress through the use of rational arguments. This is not surprising, for, as we have seen, Kant apparently had prejudicial attitudes that influenced his own work without his awareness. This problem, we suggest, calls for supplementation of Kant's theory (as in principle he should approve) with a more thorough appreciation of the way racial feelings and beliefs actually function, i.e. realities of the sort to which African American philosophers such as Charles Mills so powerfully call our attention. Facing these problems with Kantian deliberative reason together with this fuller appreciation of the realities of racial consciousness, the solutions to which we must seriously turn our attention are ways of restructuring our social institutions and moral education to combat racism, not merely with rational arguments, but where it lives, underground, in gut-level antipathies and suspicions immune to overt assaults by rational moral argument.

II. EZE

In his essay 'The Color of Reason' Eze shows not only that Kant made comments that appear to reflect a racist attitude, but also that he had a carefully formulated racial theory that included the claim that the white race is superior to the other races. Indeed it is probably true, as Eze claims, that Kant gave 'the strongest, if not the only, sufficiently articulated theoretical philosophical justification of the superior/inferior classification of "races of man" of any European writer up to his time'.[3] Further, as if in anticipation of a rejoinder from Kant's friends that his racist attitudes and his possibly racist racial theory throw no light on, and fail to call into question, his main philosophical theories, Eze claims to have demonstrated that Kant's 'racial theories . . . belong in an "intimate" way to his transcendental philosophy, or at least cannot be understood without the acknowledgment of the transcendental grounding that Kant explicitly provides them'.[4] Eze succeeds in showing that Kant saw his racial theory as a serious philosophical project, that it was not an offhand, unreflective set of conjectures, and that it deserves philosophical attention. More particularly, he succeeds in showing that Kant thought his racial theory was an inherent part of his total philosophical system, and that he appealed to his general philosophical principles to derive and state it. As Eze says, one cannot understand Kant's racial theory without acknowledging the philosophical grounding that he tried to give it.

But these concessions do not imply that Kant's central philosophical principles are tainted with racism. Suppose we grant that his racial theory is racist. (Some argument is needed to establish this point. Kant's racial theory is not racist simply because it claims that there are superior and inferior races. Conceivably the evidence available to him supported that claim. A racial theory is racist only if it relies on a culpable neglect of evidence that could have disproved it, or expresses or encourages contempt or disregard for people because of the race they are alleged to belong to.) And suppose we grant that Kant appealed to his general philosophical principles to derive and state his racial theory. It would follow that these principles are tainted with racism only if they strictly entailed his racial theory. If Kant's racial theory depends on false factual assumptions, or if his attempt to derive it from his general philosophical principles is invalid, these principles need not be tainted with racism any more than genetic science is necessarily tainted with racism just because some racists try to use it to justify their views.

But although Kant's use of his general philosophical principles to derive

---

[3] Emmanuel Chukwudi Eze, 'The Color of Reason', in Eze (ed.), *Post Colonial African Philosophy: A Critical Reader* (Oxford: Blackwell, 1997), 129.
[4] Ibid. 130.

his racial theory does not prove that his general philosophical principles are tainted, it does raise the suspicion that they might be. Eze should therefore be commended for pointing out that Kant seems to have believed that his general philosophical principles supported his racial theory. He has suggested another critical way to test the soundness of these principles. They may be responsible for the possible racism of his racial theory, and if they are, then that should count against them. We argue, however, that Kant's general philosophical principles are not responsible for the possible racism in his racial theory. He may have appealed to them to derive his racial theory, but his derivation was invalid and seems to have relied on false factual assumptions.

Eze evidently thinks it very important to emphasize that Kant appealed to his transcendental philosophy and his theory of the a priori to formulate his racial theory. For example, he claims to have shown that for Kant 'racial differences and racial classifications are based a priori on the reason of the natural scientist';[5] that Kant assumed that his 'classification of humans according to race and racial distinctions (skin color assumed as external proof and evidence) is based on an idea "inevitably inherited by Nature"— that is, a priori, transcendentally grounded and immutable';[6] that the 'so-called subhuman, primitive, and characterological inferiority of the American Indian, the African, or the Asian, is a biologically *and* metaphysically inherited (arche)type';[7] and finally that Kant 'elevated' David Hume's 'literary and political speculations about the "Negro," and provided these speculations with "transcendental justifications"'.[8] The import of these claims seems to be that Kant believed that the racial classification he offered was a necessary truth, based on reason alone, and neither derived from experience nor revisable in the light of experience. But it is hard to make sense of the claim that Kant believed that the racial classification he offered was a necessary truth. It is true that in a central sense, for Kant, a priori truths about the world are necessary truths; examples are the truths of mathematics. Surely Eze cannot mean that Kant believed that statements about racial classifications are necessarily true like statements of mathematics! And if he does mean this, he does not make the slightest attempt to prove it. Kant also argued that space, time, and the categories are a priori forms of any possible experience, meaning that they are presupposed by any possible experience. But here too Eze surely cannot be trying to tell us that Kant believed that racial difference and racial classification are presuppositions of any possible experience. Nor is it any more plausible to say that Kant believed that racial difference and racial classification are

---

[5] Ibid. 122.   [6] Ibid. 124.   [7] Ibid. 125.   [8] Ibid. 122.

presuppositions of any experience of human beings. Certainly he knew that some of his contemporaries denied that there were such things as races.

Kant distinguished 'constitutive' from 'regulative' principles. Constitutive principles are the principles of the possibility of the objects of experience and determine how in general they must be. Regulative principles are maxims about how we ought to think about the objects of experience (A509 B537). Among these principles is the systematic unity of nature and that causes must not be multiplied needlessly. Kant says that in using these principles we 'presuppose a transcendental principle whereby such a systematic unity is a priori assumed to be necessarily inherent in the objects' (A651 B679). The idea here is that the assumption that causes are not needlessly multiplied is a priori in the sense that it is not derived from experience. Rather it is an assumption we ought to employ when we deal with the objects of experience, supposing that we want to construct a reasonable and humanly comprehensible theory about these objects.

Probably Kant relied on such a principle when he constructed his racial theory. For example, it seems to be the ground of his preference for monogenesis—the theory that the races are descended from a common stock—over polygenesis—the theory that the races have different origins. In this way a principle Kant identified as a priori was implicated in his racial theory. But this certainly does not support Eze's contention that Kant believed that the racial classification he offered was a necessary truth. Even if it is an a priori truth that causes should not be multiplied unnecessarily, and even if this leads us initially to prefer monogenesis over polygenesis, in the end monogenesis may still have to be withdrawn in the light of experience. No matter how carefully we refrain from multiplying causes unnecessarily, the facts may still force us to prefer polygenesis over monogenesis. And even if this is not the case, and monogenesis remains the preferable theory, experience alone can settle whether there are races or whether the racial classification Kant offers is correct. Finally, suppose that we hypothesize that there are races, and that the correct racial classification has a certain form. These hypotheses may be described as a priori in the sense that they are not generalizations based on experience. But it does not follow that Kant would have supposed that they are fixed or 'metaphysical' or 'immutable', as Eze seems to believe. A hypothesis that is not a generalization based on experience may still be fully revisable in the light of experience; it may not be derived from experience, but it may be falsified by experience.

Eze claims that Kant critiques Linnaeus's work on the ground it was not 'transcendentally grounded'. To back up this claim he cites a passage from Kant's 'Physical Geography', which goes as follows:

One should call the system of nature created up to now more correctly an aggregate of nature, because a system presupposes the idea (*Idee*) of a whole out of which the manifold character of thing is being derived. We do not have as yet a system of nature. In the existing so-called system of this type, the objects are merely put beside each other and ordered in sequence one after another . . . True philosophy, however, has to follow the diversity and the manifoldness of matter through all time.[9]

We grant that this passage shows that Kant believed that science involved more than mere classification, and that it had to take the form of a derivation from fundamental assumptions. And it follows that if Kant believed that a science of race was possible, then he would have believed that it would have to take the form of a derivation from fundamental assumptions. But Eze makes no attempt to show that this required Kant to believe that the racial classification he offered was a priori and transcendentally grounded in the sense that it was based on reason alone and was not revisable in the light of experience. Instead he launches into a discussion of Kant's *Observations of the Feeling of the Beautiful and Sublime*, claiming that the book shows Kant's 'theoretic transcendental philosophical position at work'. But although he cites some passages in it that certainly seem to express racist attitudes, Eze says nothing to suggest that Kant believed that these passages were any more than empirical a posteriori claims that could be falsified by experience. Certainly he makes no attempt to show that Kant thought of them as necessarily true, or based on reason alone, or a condition of experience.

Eze claims at another point that, on Kant's terms, 'The black person . . . can accordingly be denied full humanity, since full and "true" humanity accrues only to the white European'.[10] It is certainly true that Kant believed that whites were the most talented race. He writes, 'Humanity is at its greatest perfection in the race of the whites. The yellow Indians do have a meager talent. The Negroes are far below them and at the lowest point are a part of the American peoples'.[11] But this is a far cry from claiming that non-whites lack dignity, in the sense that they lack the capacity to act morally. One does have to be highly talented to have the capacity to act morally and consequently to have dignity. Kant often insisted on this. Further, he made many claims that indicated specifically that he did not endorse the view that non-whites were incapable of moral action or were without dignity. For example, in the *Metaphysics of Morals* Kant writes, concerning European settlement of lands inhabited by 'shepherds or hunters (like the Hottentots, the

[9] Eze, *Post Colonial African Philosophy*, 120.
[10] Ibid. 121.
[11] Immanuel Kant, selections from 'Physical Geography', in Emmanuel Chukwudi Eze (ed.), *Race and the Enlightenment: A Reader* (Oxford: Blackwell, 1997), 63.

Tungusi, or most of the American Indian nations) who depend for their sustenance on great open regions', that such settlement 'may not take place by force but only by contract, and indeed by a contract that does not take advantage of the ignorance of those inhabitants with respect to ceding their lands'.[12] It should be noted that only moral agents are capable of making contracts, and that Kant includes here the American Indians whom he had described as the least talented of the human races. He was clear, then, that even the race he believed to be the least talented was capable of moral action and had dignity. Similarly, in *Perpetual Peace* he denounces the 'appallingly great' 'injustice' of the European powers in their conquest of 'America, the negro countries, the Spice islands, and the Cape'; and blames them for inciting the Indian states to 'wars, famine, insurrection, treachery and the whole litany of evils which can afflict the human race'.[13]

Eze is on firmer ground when he claims that Kant believed that only Europeans have the capacity for self-perfection and are likely to contribute to the future progress of the human race.[14] This puts him in a position to argue that Kant believed that only Europeans are properly human, since the capacity for self-perfection is part of what it means to be human. But even if Kant believed that only Europeans have the capacity for self-perfection and are likely to contribute to human progress, the question is whether he was led to believe this by any central principles of his philosophy.

As Eze correctly notes, Kant used his universal history in order to argue for a theory of human nature, and was moved to do so probably as a result of studying Rousseau's earlier effort to do the same thing.[15] But Kant's universal history, and his theory of human nature, are very different from Rousseau's. Rousseau thought he had a theory that explained human wickedness. On his account, human beings are good when they come from the hand of nature, and most of them are wicked only because of the bad social conditions they are in. His conjectural history of human beings was the method he chose to justify that account. Starting from the assumption that human beings would be happy and good in a pre-social and solitary state of nature, he tried to show how they become wicked as they accidentally create and stumble into social conditions that make them wicked.[16] Kant's con-

---

[12] Immanuel Kant, *The Metaphysics of Morals*, trans. Mary Gregor (Cambridge: Cambridge University Press, 1991), hereafter abbreviated *MM*, p. 159 (vi: 353). Parenthetical numbers in Kant's works refer to the standard Prussian Academy edition volume and pages.

[13] Immanuel Kant, 'Perpetual Peace', in *Kant: Political Writings*, ed. Hans Reiss (Cambridge: Cambridge University Press, 1970), 106.

[14] Eze, 'The Color of Reason', 117.

[15] Ibid. 108–14.

[16] See e.g. J.-J. Rousseau, 'Discourse on the Origin and Foundations of Inequality among Men, or Second Discourse', in Rousseau, *The Discourses and Other Political Writings*, ed. Victor Gourevitch (Cambridge: Cambridge University Press, 1997), 111–222.

jectural history, on the other hand, was not an attempt to explain human wickedness, or to prove anything in particular about what human nature is when it comes unsullied from the hand of nature. Rather, it was an attempt to show what human nature has to be like, given that we have to interpret human history as mankind's long journey to the point where all human talents will be fully perfected.[17] Accordingly, although Kant agrees with Rousseau that people are wicked and engaged in a worsening spiral of competition and war, he insisted that we have to find a way to interpret this as eventually leading to good, and that we have to assume a view of human nature that supports that interpretation. Thus Kant argues that the war and competition that Rousseau deplores sharpens and deepens our understanding of nature and of ourselves, and that this, together with our natural prudence, will one day lead and enable us to design the republican constitutions and the world federation that will guarantee the conditions for peaceful competition and the eventual flowering of all human talents. Further, he argues that we have to take human nature to include a capacity for action that leads to self-perfection or self-improvement.

As far as we can tell, Eze tries to connect this fanciful, but otherwise innocent-sounding story to Kant's racial theory and transcendental philosophy by arguing that the claim that human nature includes a capacity for self-perfection is an a priori claim. That is, it is not established by experience, from the data at one's disposal, but is brought to experience as an organizing principle, to help make sense of the data at one's disposal and to direct empirical research. This point must be granted. The next step, however, is invalid. Eze seems to suggest that if we take the claim that human nature includes a capacity for self-perfection as a priori and notice that non-European peoples are not perfecting themselves, at least in the European way, then we will be led to conclude that they lack the capacity for self-perfection, and we will also take that conclusion to be a priori. This seems to be the argument he uses to press his claim that Kant thought it an a priori truth that non-Europeans are not fully human. But it is, as we said, invalid. Even if Kant was convinced that non-Europeans were not perfecting themselves in the European way, he could without the slightest contradiction have rejected the claim that such peoples lack the capacity for self-perfection. That is, Kant's teleology may have led him to take it to be an a priori truth that human nature included a capacity for self-perfection, but there was nothing in it to lead him to conclude that non-Europeans lacked that capacity, even if some of them, like the Tahitians, were not involved in the war

---

[17] See e.g. Immanuel Kant, 'Idea for a Universal History with a Cosmopolitan Purpose', 'Perpetual Peace', and 'Conjectures on the Beginning of Human History', in *Kant: Political Writings*.

and competition he thought of as necessary means to human perfection. It is perfectly possible for people to have capacities they fail to realize, because, for example, they fail to be in circumstances that provoke them to realize their capacities. Accordingly, even if Kant inferred that non-Europeans lacked the capacity for improvement, this was because he made factual assumptions that were not part of his central philosophical assumptions, or because his prejudice led him to draw unwarranted conclusions from his teleology.

Indeed it seems that if Kant had stuck to his central methodological principles, for example, that causes must not be multiplied unnecessarily, he would have been led to reject the idea that some peoples lack the capacity for self-perfection. To see this point, let us compare his theory of history with Rousseau's more streamlined account. Although Rousseau would have agreed with Kant that different physical conditions probably account for the different appearances of the races, he dispenses with the further and unnecessary assumption that these differences are correlated with differences in talent and motivation. And this, we may observe, is exactly what Kant should have argued if he had remained faithful to his principle not to multiply causes unnecessarily. Clearly, if we can explain apparent differences in talent and motivation in terms of social conditions, we can obviously cut back on the number of causes we have to appeal to in order to explain human history. Eze says that Kant described European history and imagined he was describing human history. But consider, for example, how Rousseau and Kant deal with European history. For Rousseau, it is a condition that human beings in Europe have stumbled into by accident. For reasons it would be tedious to repeat here in detail, Rousseau argued that the physical conditions of Europe led the people living there to devise certain social institutions that then inexorably, but without their understanding or intention, propelled them into the strife, competition, and 'progress' of Europe.[18] Other peoples not in Europe have escaped Europe's fate, simply because of accident, or because the physical conditions they were in led them to devise different social institutions that did not involve them in the strife of competition, and consequently the development of talents found in Europe. Specifically, Rousseau avoided multiplying causes. He argued that if Europeans do indeed have a disposition to unsocial sociability and therefore to competitiveness, this is a result of the social institutions they were led to devise by the physical conditions of their continent. On his account, any other people in the same conditions would have devised the same institutions

---

[18] Progress must be put in inverted commas here because Rousseau maintained that the progress of Europe was a moral disaster.

and would have developed the unsocial sociability and the competitiveness of Europeans. But Kant argued that European competitiveness is a result of innate European talent and unsocial sociability. We can only speculate that prejudice or gullibility led him to multiply causes needlessly and to violate his own philosophical principles. In any case, these principles cannot be blamed for his view that non-Europeans are less talented than Europeans and perhaps even lack the capacity for self-perfection.

III. THE TAHITIANS AND THE IDEAL OF REASON

Contemporary readers sensitive to persistent problems of Western bias towards Third World peoples will hardly be pleased by Kant's various references to South Sea Islanders.[19] Europe in Kant's day knew of Tahiti and other 'exotic' places from the reports of travellers, who mostly saw what they wanted to see through European eyes. Tahiti was romanticized as an idyllic land of peace and plenty, endless enjoyment without responsibility. Only a few, such as Forster, reported a more complex, perhaps more realistic picture. Kant's reaction was to accept the usual romantic stereotype without the customary admiration that accompanied it. He accepted the idea of the Tahitians as people completely devoted to the life of ease and pleasure, with no need to develop their reason and talents to satisfy their basic natural needs and immediate desires. Rather than envying them for this, however, Kant disapproved. In his view, they neglected the distinctive human powers that give life meaning and value. If their idleness were never to change, the world would not be a worse place, he suggests, if Tahiti sank.

One can try to make excuses for Kant on grounds of non-culpable ignorance of empirical fact, but there is reason to suppose that he should have known better because he engaged in public controversy with Forster, who reported a different story of the Tahitians from his travels with Captain Cook. Kant was less interested in the empirical facts, it seems, than in the occasion the Tahitians seemed to provide for a moral sermon to his readers. Whether he was culpable or not, it is hard to deny that his disapproving attitude and ready acceptance of the common stereotype fit with and could have encouraged European tendencies towards self-righteous domination and interference with non-Western cultures. To say this, however, is not yet to make a deep charge against Kant's moral and political theories. Are his philosophical ideas at fault, or is his attitude about the Tahitians something

[19] Immanuel Kant, *Groundwork of the Metaphysics of Morals*, ed. Mary Gregor (Cambridge: Cambridge University Press, 1997), hereafter abbreviated *G*, pp. 32–3 (iv: 422–3), 38–9 (iv: 430).

separable? There is reason to suspect that the problem goes deeper than suggested so far—though still, we believe, not to the core of his ethical and political theories. Echoing familiar concerns sometimes expressed by feminist, African American, and various postmodern critics of the Enlightenment, an extreme version of the objection might go like this. Kant disapproves of the Tahitians because they fail to meet a parochial, historically conditioned, European and male biased Enlightenment ideal of reason. Their failure, the ground of the alleged worthlessness of their lives, is their not working to 'perfect' themselves as demanded by the categorical imperative, an absolute requirement of pure practical reason. Their enjoyment is counted for nothing because they are not fulfilling the end of reason, which is to control passion, maintain a pure 'good will', and to contribute as far as one can to mankind's cultural and moral perfection. They are not as productive, competitive, and combative as Europeans, and so do not contribute to the perfection of humanity as reason demands. Thus, it is charged, Kant tries to justify the moral and cultural superiority of Enlightenment Europeans and excuse the imperialistic extension of their values, all from local bias masked as pure reason.

Now, though there is an important kernel of truth in this objection, the extreme version as expressed here contains several exaggerations and oversights that should be mentioned. First, it should be remembered that Kant regards the duty to develop one's talents only as an imperfect duty of 'wide obligation'.[20] That is, the development of talents is supposed to be an end prescribed by reason, but the duty is indefinite, not saying how much or how or when one is to promote that end. Other ends, including the happiness of others *and one's own*, are also commended by reason, and there is no formula for all as to how to balance these pursuits. The duty is also relative to one's talents, so the mere failure to meet high 'objective' standards of culture are not, in principle, grounds for disapproval of anyone as morally inferior.[21] For Kant moral disapproval of the Tahitians, for example, presupposes that they have talents. Further, the duty to perfect one's talents is only a 'duty to oneself'.[22] That is, it is unenforceable by law and only the ethical responsibility of each agent to himself, not the business of distant strangers or even his neighbours. Kant may not always keep this in mind, but he does at points

---

[20] *MM* 152–5 (vi: 388–93).

[21] 'When it is said that it is in itself a duty for a human being to make his end the perfection belonging to a human being as such (properly speaking, to humanity), this perfection must be put in what can result from his deeds, not in mere gifts for which he must be indebted to nature; for otherwise it would not be a duty. This duty can therefore consist only in *cultivating* one's faculties (or natural predispositions), the highest of which is understanding, the faculty of concepts and so too of those concepts that have to do with duty' (*MM* 150 (vi: 386–7); also see *G* 150 (iv: 423)).

[22] *MM* 174–5 (vi: 418–20), 194–7 (vi: 444–7).

object to the meddlesomeness of anthropologists in other cultures and the unjust incursions of European settlers on the lands of others (e.g. the Hottentots, Tungusi, and American Indians).[23] Even the idea that idle persons' exclusive devotion to enjoyment is 'unworthy of their humanity' is, for Kant, not a *practical* judgement that should guide our treatment of them.[24] Because of our ignorance of motives, moral worth, ultimately, can only be judged by God, according to Kant; our duties of respect and beneficence make no reference to the worthiness of the recipient. The primary place of judgements of deficient 'moral worth' is when we sense our own shortcomings, by comparison with an ideal (not other people) and this leads us to commit ourselves to greater effort.[25] Another point to note is that not everything in Kant's objectionable attitude to the Tahitians stems from his idea of reason. For example, his thought that human beings can progress to the ideal of humanity only through 'unsocial sociability' (and so by competitiveness, hard work driven by self-interest, etc.) is an empirical claim, no doubt an overgeneralization and not itself a philosophical thesis.[26]

All this said, there remains a serious objection. In brief, Kant does not merely call attention to the importance of deliberative reason for prudence and moral problem-solving, but, beyond this, he apparently endorses a particular rationalistic conception of the good life as a universal and necessary goal.[27] That is, the development of intellectual abilities, control of passions, conscious striving for determinate goals, critical thinking, etc. seem not merely recommended as prudentially advantageous and often useful for moral ends, but as valuable ends intrinsic to rational nature itself. Such a lifestyle, independent of its effect on happiness, accords with the *telos* of our nature as rational beings. Although other ends, such as the happiness of others, are also to be sought, morally good persons, Kant seems to think,

[23] *MM* 212 (vi: 466), 122 (vi: 353).

[24] See 'Kant's Anti-Moralistic Strain', in Thomas E. Hill Jr., *Dignity and Practical Reason in Kant's Moral Theory* (Ithaca, NY: Cornell University Press, 1992); also Thomas E. Hill Jr., 'Kant on Wrongdoing, Desert, and Punishment', *Law and Philosophy*, 18 (1999), 407–41. Note this too against spreading derogatory accounts of others: 'The intentional spreading of something that detracts from another's honor—even if it is not a matter of public justice, and even if what is said is true—diminishes respect for humanity as such, and so as finally to cast a shadow of worthlessness over our race itself, making misanthropy (shying away from human beings) or contempt the prevalent cast of mind . . . ' (*MM* 212 (vi: 466)). Cynics will doubtless say 'our race' here refers exclusively to European whites, but such charges are more reflective of critical zeal than careful survey of relevant evidence.

[25] Regarding comparing ourselves to an ideal standard rather than to other people, see *MM* 187 (vi: 435–6).

[26] See *Kant: Political Writings*, 44–5 (from 'Idea of a Universal History with a Cosmopolitan Purpose', 1784), and Alan Wood's commentary, 'Unsociable Sociability: The Anthropological Basis of Kantian Ethics', *Philosophical Topics*, 19/1 (Spring 1991), 325–51.

[27] *MM* 151 (vi: 387), 154 (vi: 391–2); 194–5 (vi: 444–6); 180–1 (vi: 427–8).

regard the perfection of their own higher powers as neither a mere means nor an optional end. Those who do nothing towards this ideal perfection, then, are either culpably neglectful of duty, morally ignorant, or devoid of the 'higher' powers of mind and soul. Thus Kant seems to be committed to a value judegment beyond what can plausibly be claimed as a necessary requirement of reason, and it is a value judgement that would be understandably annoying to those who prefer a style of life that is less intellectually oriented, though neither foolish nor immoral. Kant's model, then, seems suspiciously that of a male, northern European, Enlightenment professor in a time more hopeful than ours of progress through discipline, rigorous thinking, and competition. If people in less powerful cultures do not share these values—or are so perceived—then the suggestion is that they must be inferior in morality, knowledge, or talent. This is a suggestion naturally resented by people whose values have been misunderstood, and it is one that can easily play into the hands of people already prepared to exploit them.

This objection is not just that Kant made misjudgements in applying his philosophical ideas, but neither is it a deep problem at the core of his moral and political theories. To see this, we need to distinguish the following: (1) Kant's basic moral theory, the fundamental moral principles and their grounding,[28] (2) the hypothetical imperative, a rational requirement to take the necessary means to one's ends (or abandon the ends),[29] (3) teleological claims about the end of humanity, or rational nature, in persons, the end towards which history is progressing, etc.[30] and (4) specific applications of the above made on the basis of empirical assumptions.[31] Kant's basic moral theory holds that behind particular moral debates are certain formal general principles, the categorical imperative, that any fully rational autonomous person would accept. The hypothetical imperative requires us not only to be prudent, but to do what is necessary to achieve morally required ends. These together pose a significant 'demand of reason' at the core of Kant's theory. That, of course, is controversial enough, but it is separable from the objection under consideration. That problem depends crucially on Kant's teleological claims about the 'end' for which nature or God gave us reason, for Kant's moral ground for the duty to develop our powers of mind and soul is that these are means needed to contribute to the perfection of humanity—the end of rational nature in us. Kant's fundamental moral principles do

---

[28] See especially, *G* 29–66 (vi: 418–66), omitting Kant's examples.

[29] *G* 24–9 (vi: 413–19); Hill, *Dignity and Practical Reason*, 16–37, 124–31.

[30] e.g. *MM* 230 (vi: 488), 164 (vi: 405), 141 n. (vi: 376), 178–80 (vi: 424–6), 123–4 (vi: 354); *G* 8–10 (iv: 395–6), 32–3 (iv: 422–3), 38–9 (iv: 430).

[31] *MM* 176–218 (vi: 421–74); *G* 32–3 (iv: 422–3), 38–9 (iv: 430).

not, indeed cannot, depend on teleological claims, but his examples of specific moral duties often do. Contemporary philosophers are understandably sceptical about Kant's teleology, especially the claims (*a*) that we should regard history as progressing to the flourishing of humankind in culture, politics, and morality as well as happiness consonant with virtue, and (*b*) that intellectual powers are wrong to neglect because they are gifts of nature. But the contested points here, it is important to see, are distinct from Kant's more fundamental moral theory.

In sum, then, we share with Kant's critics the suspicion that he exaggerated the value that a moral and rational person must place on 'reason' in so far as he prescribed as a universal and necessary value an intellectual lifestyle with features, in kind and degree, beyond what basic prudence and morality require. The point, however, should not be confused with a much more radical charge about Kant's endorsement of 'Enlightenment reason', namely that it represents nothing but the parochial values of a particular historical era and class, with nothing more to recommend it than its corrupt origin and its adaptability to evil imperialistic aims. Virtually everything in philosophy is controversial, but the objections to Kant's teleological claims, which few contemporary philosophers accept, are not grounds for dismissing his emphasis on reason in his basic moral and political theories, elements of which in fact are widely accepted among many of his critics as well as his defenders. The basic theory, for example, holds that it is a reasonable aim to seek a world of justice, peace, and mutual respect in which all people can pursue their own happiness, with the aid of others, under mutually acceptable constraints. It implies, further, that it is rationally required to take the necessary means, when available, to this moral end. This does not make *intellectual and cultural perfection* of individuals or the human species an end in itself. What is required is whatever use of reason can help to promote the morally better world just described.

So, do these basic points support a moral requirement for people to use reason and to develop intellectual powers more than Kant imagined the Tahitians did? As a general rule, this seems obviously implied, but Kant grants that what specifically is required in each context varies with the circumstances (such as one's talents, opportunities, and other legitimate ends). Development of reason, in general, is important to counteract oppressive superstitions, to structure social institutions that foster mutual cooperation and respect, and to develop the means and strategies to provide for the security and basic needs of all in a fair way. Granted, reason alone, especially not instrumental reason alone, is not *sufficient* to solve these problems, but that is not the issue here. The point is just that, even after we abandon Kant's inflated view of the necessity of intellectual life style, there remains a plausible core to his insistence on the presumptive moral case for favouring the development and use of intellectual powers in the service of moral ends. To say this need not be a culturally biased disparagement of any group of people, though it implies that there are moral reasons not to devote oneself entirely to pleasure to the total neglect of one's talents (as Kant apparently imagined the Tahitians did). The minimal moral claim here is that one should develop one's powers of mind to serve moral ends and this (in Kant's official theory) is offered only as an indeterminate, unenforceable maxim for each person's moral consideration, to be applied by the responsible judgement of each according to his or her circumstances. If Kant had gone no further than this, it is hard to imagine how the claim could be construed as unduly disparaging except by those who hold the extreme relativistic view that it is necessarily disparaging to make any moral claim that challenges the preferred way of life of others. Although, as noted, the construal of Kant's minimal claim as unduly disparaging is hard to imagine, it must be admitted that the liability of philosophical ideas to distortion sometimes proves to be beyond imagination.

IV. DELIBERATIVE REASON AND VISCERAL RACISM

When we ask about the relevance of Kant's philosophical writings to contemporary problems of racism, there is more to consider than whether Kant himself had racist attitudes and beliefs and more even than whether his claims have implications likely to facilitate racism in others. There may be faults of omission as well as faults of commission. Or, to set aside assessment of personal blame, the point is that philosophical work, like any other, can by its omissions or incompleteness encourage its readers to rest content with deplorable attitudes not anticipated or strictly entailed by the content of the work. Such work stands in need of serious supplementation as well as more explicit clarification and warnings against appropriation for illegitimate purposes.

A natural worry of this kind about Kantian moral philosophy might be put as follows. Kant so emphasizes the role of reason in moral deliberation and motivation that he ignores, and encourages his readers to ignore, the hard reality that people are often moved by gut-level feelings that are impervious to rational argument. As has become horribly evident in the twentieth century, racial antagonisms are a paradigm of visceral attitudes that did not stem from reason and, it seems amply evident, are rarely extinguished by reason alone. Extolling rational arguments while ignoring the stubbornness of blind visceral racism has potentially disastrous consequences. It encourages us to approach the deeply rooted problems of contemporary racism with the largely ineffective tool of rationalistic moral argument. Or, to change the metaphor, it is like treating a disease with the wrong medicine, even a non-medical treatment, like a lecture or a sermon. The problem in Kant's case, the objection might continue, is not a minor surface problem, readily remedied; for he repeatedly implies that the way to fight the immorality prompted by feelings and impulses is to focus the mind and will on the moral law, a principle of reason that makes no appeal to our sentiments.

Although the objection summarized here raises serious problems that should not be dismissed, we must be careful not to exaggerate. For example, Kant was obviously well aware that people often do terrible things from blind sentiments and impulses. Even when their immoral acts are coldly calculating, Kant thought, they are merely taking means perceived as necessary to achieve ends prompted by their non-rational inclinations.[32] Because his project in the *Groundwork* and the *Critique of Practical Reason* was, to a large extent, to combat 'sentimentalist' theories such as those of Hutcheson and Hume, it is understandable that he would emphasize his belief in the possibility and importance of pure rational motivation; but this does not mean that he denied, or disregarded, the evident fact that much of human behaviour, for better or worse, proceeds as if reason were silent or offered only prudential counsel. Admittedly, Kant writes as if the main obstacle to our making moral choices were merely *self-serving* inclinations[33] and our tendency to 'make exceptions of ourselves' to principles that, in general, we acknowledge as valid.[34] He was apparently not aware of the influence of

---

[32] The coolness of a scoundrel, Kant says, makes him not only 'more dangerous but immediately abominable in our eyes than we would have taken him to be without it' (*G* 8 (iv: 394)). He follows merely 'hypothetical imperatives' to personal ends adopted on the basis of inclinations, contrary to 'categorical imperatives'. His principles are 'rules of skill' or 'technical precepts'. 'The precepts for a physician to make his man healthy in a well-grounded way, and for a poisoner to be sure of killing his, are of equal worth so far as each serves to bring about his purpose' (*G* 26 (iv: 415)).

[33] As Butler famously notes, we have 'particular passions' regarding many things, such as the good or ill of others, quite distinct from the second-level desire to be 'happy' or gratified by satisfying such first-order desires. Visceral racism commonly shows itself in such first-order desires to put down people of other races, to harm, dominate, or humiliate them. Contempt is felt for all who share certain group characteristics and, though the racist may enjoy oppressing them, the contempt precedes the enjoyment and partially explains it. The racist tendency to 'make exceptions' is thus often not initially and primarily a tendency to promote (perceived) self-interest but rather a disposition to exclude a despised 'other' group from the range of those to whom our moral consideration is owed.

[34] 'Now reason issues its precepts unremittingly, without promising anything to the inclinations. . . . But from this there arises a natural dialectic, that is, a propensity to rationalize against those strict laws of duty and to cast doubt upon their validity, or at least upon their purity and strictness, and where possible, to make them better suited to our wishes and inclinations . . .' (*G* 17–18 (iv: 405)); 'if we now attend to ourselves in any transgression of a duty, we find that we

deep visceral *racial* feelings, which are not simply self-regarding and may be as harmful to oneself as to others. Nevertheless, Kant can hardly be said to have been ignorant or indifferent to the fact that there are deep forces in human nature, evident throughout history, that work against our instituting practices that impartial reason would approve. For example, in the *Groundwork* (and elsewhere) Kant repeatedly expresses uncertainty that there ever existed a person with a purely good will.[35] In *The Metaphysics of Morals* he describes vividly characteristic temptations to vice,[36] acknowledges human frailty,[37] and allows that virtue is at best 'in progress' and 'considered objectively' an 'ideal' that is 'unattainable'.[38] In *Religion* he insists there is 'radical evil' in human nature, a innate tendency to subordinate the moral law to the pursuit of personal concerns, and in 'Idea for a Universal History with a Cosmopolitan Purpose' his metaphor is that human beings are made of 'crooked wood' that can never be made straight.[39]

Kant was also aware, to some degree, that to fulfil our moral ends it is helpful (even if not absolutely necessary) to cultivate our feelings as well as our rational nature.[40] There is no inconsistency between this common-sense point, which Kant admits, and his insistence that in principle we must presume that we can overcome any inner obstacles to doing our duty and must hold ourselves responsible if we fail.[41] But Kant understandably would be inclined to de-emphasize the admission, because a central theme of his was that acting from rational recognition of duty is possible and the distinctive mark of a morally good person. He apparently saw cultivation of feelings as a minor supplement to a moral agent's main tasks, not as a major project for the individual and not among the aims of the state.

Although the objection under consideration must be qualified by recognizing these aspects of Kant's writings, it nevertheless remains a serious problem that cannot be lightly dismissed. Admittedly Kant knew that blind impulses and feelings are obstacles to morality and some cultivation of

do not really will that our maxim should become a universal law, since that is impossible for us, but that the opposite of our maxim should indeed remain a universal law, only we take the liberty of making an exception to it for ourselves (or just for this once) to the advantage of inclination' (*G* 34–5 (iv. 424)).

[35]   *G* 19–8 (iv: 407); *MM* 196 (vi: 447).

[36]   *MM* 184–8, (vi: 432–3), 206–13.

[37]   *MM* 166 (vi: 408), 196 (vi: 446); see also *Religion with the Limits of Reason Alone* and *G* 19 (iv: 406).

[38]   *MM* 167–8 (vi: 410). In the *Critique of Practical Reason* Kant suggests that the ever-receding ideal of virtue towards which one must strive would take infinite time to approach, which is a reason, he proposes, for faith in immortality. See *Critique of Practical Reason*, 102–3 (v: 122–3).

[39]   *Political Writings*, 46.

[40]   *MM* 218 (vi: 473), 204–5 (vi: 456–7).

[41]   *Critique of Practical Reason*, 82–4 (v: 98–100).

feelings can be useful as a counterpoise to natural temptations, but it remains a fact that the main solution that he offers to moral and social problems is more extensive development and use of *reason*. He repeatedly suggests, for example, that merely holding the categorical imperative clearly before the mind, as a pure principle of reason, is all that we need to know and be moved to do what is right.[42] His idea of moral education, while not entirely neglectful of habit, feeling, and physical well-being, is almost a paradigm of a rationalistic approach, with an emphasis on maxims, rules, and above all cultivation of the mind.[43] The moral 'catechism' sketched at the end of *The Metaphysics of Morals* presents the teacher as drawing forth moral knowledge from the pupil in a manner reminiscent of Socrates and the slave boy in Plato's *Meno*.[44] Moreover, although Kant's idea that our moral ends with regard to others is to promote their happiness, not their moral perfection, is a commendable antidote to moral imperialism, it tends to discourage, if not forbid, systematic moral efforts to eliminate visceral racism by attacking the institutions and practices that foster it. Kant seems all too content to think that it is not a social problem but rather the responsibility of each individual to fight his or her own bad feelings and attitudes without significant outside aid.[45] Unlike Rousseau, from whom he otherwise learned much, Kant did not acknowledge the need to restructure social institutions to help cultivate the social sentiments that promote and preserve institutions that moral reason approves. He seems, for example, not to have questioned seriously his commitment to a virtually absolute property right, prior (in a sense) to government and constraining what it may justly do.

But what is the lesson to draw here? Surely it is not that Kant was wrong to think that we need reasonable deliberation and dialogue to address racial problems. Rather, it is that such use of reason must be informed by an adequate understanding of the empirical facts about racism, its genesis, its stubbornness, its hiding-places, its interplay with other factors, and the most effective means to combat it. Racist attitudes, as we have argued, are incompatible with Kant's basic principle of respect for humanity in each person. Moreover, tolerating or ignoring racism is a policy that reasonable mutually respecting persons cannot will as universal law, or even parochial law. Given this, reasonable moral deliberation must direct us to discover and use the most effective permissible means to combat racist attitudes. If, as we

---

[42] *G* 15–16 (iv: 403–4), etc.

[43] See Immanuel Kant, *Education* (Ann Arbor: University of Michigan Press, 1960), esp. 83–121.

[44] *MM* 222–8 (vi: 478–85).

[45] *MM* 150–2 (vi: 385–8).

believe, Rousseau was right in thinking that social institutions and practices tend to shape social attitudes and feelings, then we must turn our attention to those institutions and practices. For example, we must look for the seeds of racism, and the prospect of reducing it, in our economy, our courts and gaols, our educational system, zoning laws, political processes, and so on. What in particular needs to be done is, of course, a complex and controversial matter to determine, and there is no denying that individual self-scrutiny of the sort Kant prescribes is also important. The main point, however, now seems quite clear: a basic Kantian deliberative perspective characterized by impartiality and mutual respect combined with a realistic awareness of the realities of racism would demand a more thorough, systematic, and perhaps radical assault on racism than Kant, the historical man himself, could have endorsed, or even imagined.

To accept this conclusion seems to require contemporary Kantians to reject the extreme idea that our moral end regarding others is (only) to promote their happiness, not their moral goodness. But even this is not clear, for Kant's claim that our moral end is not to promote the perfection of others occurs in the context of an outline of our *most fundamental* 'ends which are duties', not a discussion of the application of those principles to the problems of our times. One can grant that it should not be regarded as our *basic* moral duty to make others morally better while still arguing forcefully, from Kantian premises, that we should structure social institutions as best we can to eliminate or reduce racism. We must oppose racist attitudes not in a moralistic, missionary spirit, with the aim to 'make others good' (implicitly 'like us'). We oppose them because, in innumerable ways, they stand as empirical obstacles to developing a world with more justice, peace, and mutual respect—the sort of world that Kant's basic theory requires us to seek.

Finally, we must face a more *radical* version of the objection that Kantians ignore the realities of visceral racism. One can imagine an impatient postmodern Thrasymachus making the complaint before storming away. Your solution fails, he might say, because it assumes that 'deliberative reason', which you say must prescribe solutions in the light of facts about racism, is itself uninfected by racist attitudes. You fail to draw the lesson of the 'facts' about racism that you admit must be taken seriously: that is, that in a racist culture there is no untainted power of deliberative reason. In other words, you are deceived, probably self-deceived, in thinking that you (your 'reason') can stand outside the racist perspectives that you aim to eliminate. Your man, Kant himself, was influenced by the racist attitudes and beliefs of his time, by your own admission. What makes you think that you, or your Kantian models of rational deliberation, can in the real world escape the subtle, unrecognized influences of the visceral racism that you acknowledge is our key problem?

We set aside the philosophically irrelevant *ad hominem* accusation in this complaint that Kant and his defenders are biased. It does, however, contain a respectable philosophical objection to Kant's views. Kant believed that the really difficult part about acting rightly is having the moral strength to overcome contrary inclinations and desires and do what we know to be right, although we can always succeed in overcoming such inclinations and desires and do our duty if we try hard enough. On this he was perhaps mistaken, for it seems that sometimes we are literally overcome by inclination and desire and cannot do what we know to be right. But, so the objection goes, he was mistaken in a more fundamental way about how our inclinations and desires, or, more precisely, our emotions, passions, and attitudes, can interfere with our acting rightly. He thought that knowing what the right thing to do is relatively easy: 'it would be easy to show', he says,

how common human reason knows very well how to distinguish in every case that comes up what is good and what is evil, what is in conformity with duty or contrary to duty if, without in the least teaching it anything new, we only, as did Socrates, make it attentive to its own principle; and that there is, accordingly, no need of science and philosophy to know what one ought to do in order to be honest and good, and even wise and virtuous.[46]

It may seem that this is mistaken, because there are cases where knowing what is in conformity with duty requires more sophisticated intellectual argumentation than is available to 'common human reason'. This may or may not be true. In any case, the objection now under consideration maintains that Kant's remark is mistaken for a different and perhaps more fundamental reason. It can allow that, suitably qualified, Kant's remark is right that 'common human reason' can always know what is in conformity with duty. The qualification is that to be able to know what is in conformity with duty common human reason must always have the morally relevant facts vividly before it. But, so the objection goes, emotions, passions, and attitudes often make it extremely difficult if not impossible for common human reason to have the morally relevant facts vividly before it. As Aristotle reminds us, the emotions, passions, and attitudes focus our attention on certain facts and distract our attention from other facts. The confident person tends to overlook facts that a fearful person notices; and an angry person tends to overlook facts that a happy person notices. In other words, emotions, passions, and attitudes tend to make certain facts vivid, and to make others obscure. Indeed they often make morally irrelevant facts vivid, and morally

---

[46] *G* 16 (iv: 404).

relevant facts obscure. But if common human reason must have the morally relevant facts vividly before it to know what is in conformity with duty, the emotions, passions, and attitudes can make it very difficult for common human reason to know what is in conformity with duty. We can see this in a case that Kant himself constructs: according to him, a person cannot will that his maxim not to assist others in need be made a law of nature because many cases could occur in which he would need the assistance of others. But this argument depends on the possibility of such cases being sufficiently vivid to the person in question, and we know that they will not be if he is very proud and self-confident. Generally, if the maxims we can will to be universal laws depend on the factual beliefs we have vividly before us, and the maxims we can will to be universal laws determine what we think is right, our emotions, passions, and attitudes can determine what we think is right. The problem is that if our emotions and passions can make morally irrelevant facts vivid, and morally relevant facts obscure, they can mislead us into thinking that what is right is wrong, and that what is wrong is right.

If this is correct, confident, complacent, well-positioned white people will not only find it difficult to do what they know to be right; they will find it still more difficult to know what is right, even when they sincerely claim that they are trying to do so. Indeed, such sincere people are likely to be particularly dangerous for, feeling their own sincerity, they will be unlikely to believe that they can be mistaken. We do not think that Kant was altogether unaware of this problem, for he frequently warned of the dangers of self-deception. His mistake seems to have been to suppose we can always overcome our self-deceptions, and bring the morally relevant facts vividly before us, by a sufficiently strenuous rational self-examination.

Still, the solution to this difficulty is not to abandon reliance on reason. On the contrary, we can only solve this difficulty if we rely even more on reason. It was reason that led us to appreciate that the emotions, passions, and attitudes can distort the results of reason's efforts to determine what is right; and it was reason that led us to see that rational self-examination alone may not always enable us to bring all the morally relevant facts vividly before us. Finally, it is reason that will enable us to solve the problem, which in general is to find some way to bring the morally relevant facts before common human reason. The first step, of course, is to listen to what others are saying. Reason will only lead us to the truth if we listen to what others are saying. But we are not repeating this fact made familiar by every defender of freedom of expression. Listening to others with different viewpoints, different emotions and attitudes, and consequently different blind spots is a beginning, but it is not enough. The confident and complacent do not listen sympathetically to those they feel to be their inferiors, even when they invite these inferiors to speak. Somehow we must design institutions that will help us to listen to others sympathetically. Morally relevant facts that are obscure to us may be vivid to others, and if we listen to them sympathetically, these facts may become vivid to us too. Rousseau believed that institutions that reduced inequalities and dependencies would help us to listen to others sympathetically. We believe he was right, but that is not the point we want to press now. Our point is that only by rational reflection, togeher with adequate understanding of the social and psychological roots of racism can we design the institutions that will help us to listen to others sympathetically and consequently to know what is in conformity with duty.

This paper was written while we were Fellows at the Centre for Social Philosophy and Policy at the Bowling Green University. We thank John Ladd for his encouragement and expertise; Robert Louden for allowing us to read sections on race in his *Kant's Impure Ethics* (New York: Oxford University Press, 2000); and Günter Zöller for providing us with translations of Kant's three essays on race, 'On the Different Races of Human Beings', 'Determination of the Concept of a Human Race', and 'On the Use of Teleological Principles in Philosophy', forthcoming in the Cambridge edition of *The Works of Immanuel Kant, vol.7: Anthropology, History and Education*, edited by G. Zöller, translated by M. Gregor, R. Louden, H. Wilson, and G. Zöller (Cambridge: Cambridge University Press).

NOTES ON THE CONTRIBUTORS

ANTHONY KWAME APPIAH is Professor of Afro-American Studies and Philosophy at Harvard University, and the author of *In My Father's House: Africa in the Philosophy of Culture* (1993), among other works.

PIERRE L. VAN DEN BERGHE is Professor of Sociology Emeritus at the University of Washington. He is the author of over twenty scholarly books including *Race and Racism: A Comparative Perspective* (1967), *Man in Society: A Biosocial View* (1975), and *The Ethnic Phenomenon* (1981).

NED BLOCK is Professor in the Department of Philosophy at NYU and has a joint appointment in Psychology at the Center for Neural Science. Two volumes of his collected papers are due from MIT Press.

BERNARD BOXILL is Professor of Philosophy at the University of North Carolina at Chapel Hill, and the author of *Blacks and Social Justice* (1984, 1992).

RONALD DWORKIN is Sommer Professor of Law and Philosophy at NYU and Quain Professor of Jurisprudence at University College London. His latest book is *Sovereign Virtue* (2000).

MARILYN FRYE is Professor of Philosophy at Michigan State University, and the author of *The Politics of Reality: Essays in Feminist Theory* (1983), and *Willful Virgin: Essays in Feminism 1976–1992* (1992).

J. L. A. GARCIA is Professor of Philosophy at Boston College and is working on a collection of papers to be titled *Heart of Racism*.

ROBERT GOODING-WILLIAMS is Professor of Philosophy and Jean Grimble Lane Professor of the Humanities at Northwestern University. He is the editor of *Reading Rodney King, Reading Urban Uprising* (1993) and the co-editor of the Bedford Books edition of W. E. B. DuBois's *The Souls of Black Folk*. His book, *Zarathustra's Dionysian Modernism* is publishing in Summer 2001.

THOMAS E. HILL JR. is Kenan Professor of Philosophy at the University of North Carolina at Chapel Hill. He is the author of *Autonomy and Self-Respect* (1991), *Dignity and Practical Reason in Kant's Moral Theory* (1992), and *Respect, Pluralism, Justice: Kantian Perspectives* (2000).

MICHAEL LEVIN is Professor of Philosophy at the City College of New York and the Graduate Center, City University of New York. His books include *Metaphysics and the Mind-Body Problem* (1979), *Feminism and Freedom* (1988), and *Why Race Matters* (1997).

TARIQ MODOOD is Professor of Sociology, Politics, and Public Policy, and Director of the Centre for the Study of Ethnicity and Citizenship at the University of Bristol. He is co-author of *Ethnic Minorities in Britain* (1997), and is editor of *Church, State and Religious Minorities* (1997), *Debating Cultural Hybridity* (with Pnina Werbner, 1997) and *The Politics of Multiculturalism in the New Europe* (with Pnina Werbner, 1990).

LUCIUS OUTLAW has recently moved to Vanderbilt University after many years as Professor of Philosophy at Haverford. He is the author of numerous articles on race and racism and related issues.

ADRIAN M. S. PIPER, a well known artist, is Professor of Philosophy at Wellesley College, and the author of numerous articles in philosophy journals. She is currently at work on a book on Kant.

LAURENCE THOMAS is Professor of Philosophy at Syracuse University and the author of numerous articles in philosophical journals. His latest book is *Vessels of Evil* (1993).

RICHARD A. WASSERSTROM is Professor Emeritus of Philosophy at the University of California at Santa Cruz, and the author of numerous works on social and legal philosophy.

IRIS MARION YOUNG is Professor of Political Science at the University of Chicago. Her most recent book is *Inclusion and Democracy* (2000). She has authored several other books, including *Justice and the Politics of Difference* (1990), *Intersecting Voices: Dilemmas of Gender, Political Philosophy and Policy* (1997), and co-edited with Alison Jaggar *A Companion to Feminist Philosophy* (1997).

NAOMI ZACK is Professor of Philosophy at the University of Albany and the author of *Race and Mixed Race* (1994), *Bachelors of Science: Seventeenth Century Identity: Then and Now* (1996), and *Thinking About Race* (1997). Her most recent book is *Women of Color and Philosophy* (2000). She is currently working on two new books, *The Philosophy of Science and Race*, and *Descartes' Dreaming*.

FURTHER READING

I. ANTHOLOGIES

Babbitt, S. E., and Campbell, S. (eds.), *Racism and Philosophy* (Ithaca: Cornell University Press, 1999).

Bell, B., Grosholz, E. R., and Stewart, J. B., *W. E. B. Du Bois on Race and Culture* (New York: Routledge, 1996).

Bernasoni, R., and Iolt, T. L. (eds.), *The Idea of Race* (Indianapolis: Hacket Publishing Company, 2000).

Eze, E. C., *Race and the Enlightenment* (Oxford: Blackwell Publishers, 1997).

Goldberg, D. T. (ed.), *Anatomy of Racism* (Minneapolis: University of Minnesota Press, 1990).

Harris, L. (ed.), *Racism* (Amherst: Humanity Books, 1999).

Pittman, J. P., *African American Perspectives and Philosophical Traditions* (New York: Routledge, 1970).

Zack, N. (eds.), *American Mixed Race* (Lanham: Rowman and Littlefield, 1995).

Zack, N. (ed.), *Race/Sex* (New York: Routledge, 1997).

II. COLLECTIONS

Lott, T. L., *The Invention of Race* (Oxford: Blackwell Publishers, 1999).

Mills, C. W., *Blackness Visible* (Ithaca: Cornell University Press, 1998).

McGary, H., *Race and Social Justice* (Oxford: Blackwell Publishers, 1999).

Outlaw, L. T., *On Race and Philosophy* (New York: Routledge, 1996).

III. HISTORIES OF THE IDEA OF RACE

D'Souza, D. 'Is Racism a Western Idea?', *The American Scholar*, Autumn 1995, 517–39.

Gossett, T. F., *Race* (New York: Oxford University Press, 1963).

Hannaford, I., *Race* (Baltimore: Johns Hopkins University Press, 1996).

Jordan, W. D., *White Over Black* (Williamsburg, Virginia: University of North Carolina Press, 1968).

Lewis, B., 'The Historical Roots of Racism', *The American Scholar*, Winter 1998, 17–25.

Lewis, B., *Race and Slavery in the Middle East* (New York: Oxford University Press, 1990).

Snowden, F., *Blacks in Antiquity: Ethiopians in the Greco-Roman Experience* (Cambridge, MA, 1970).

Snowden, F., *Before Color Prejudice: The Ancient View of Blacks* (Cambridge, MA, 1983).

IV. RACE

Allen, T., *The Invention of the White Race: Volume One: Racial Oppression and Social Control* (London: Verso, 1994).

Appiah, K. A., *In My Father's House* (New York: Oxford University Press, 1992).

Appiah, K. A., 'But Would that Still be Me?', *Journal of Philosophy* 77, No. 10 (October 1990), 493–9.

Appiah, K. A., and Gutmann, A., *Color Conscious* (Princeton: Princeton University Press, 1996).

Davis, D. B., 'Constructing Race: A Reflection', *The William and Mary Quarterly*, 3rd Series, Vol. LIV, No. 1, January 1997, 7–18.

Davis, M., 'Race as Merit', *Mind* (1983) Vol. XCII, 347–67.

Gould, S. J., *The Mismeasure of Man* (New York: W. W. Norton and Company, 1981).

Haslanger, S., 'Gender and Race: (What) Are They? (What) Do We Want Them To Be?', *Nous*, Vol. 34, No. 1, 2000, 31–55.

Hoffman P. (ed.), *Discover*, Special Issue: The Science of Race, November 1994, Vol. 15, No. 11.

Ignatiev, N., *How the Irish Became White* (New York: Routledge, 1995).

Jacobson, M. F., *Whiteness of a Different Color* (Cambridge University Press, 1998).

Kennedy, R., 'My Race Problem—and Ours', *The Atlantic Monthly*, May 1997, 55–66.

Levin, M., 'Race, Biology and Justice', *Public Affairs Quarterly*, Vol. 8, No. 3, July 1994, 267–85.

Levin, M., *Why Race Matters* (Westport Connecticut: Praeger, 1997).

Omi, M., and Winent, H., *Racial Formation in the United States* (New York: Routledge, 1994).

Roediger, D., *The Wages of Whiteness: Race and the Making of the American Working Class* (London: Verso, 1991).

Stubblefield, A., 'Race Identity and Non-Essentialism About Race', *Social Theory and Practice*, Vol. 21, No. 3 (Fall 1995) 341–68.

Zack, N., *Race and Mixed Race* (Philadelphia: Temple University Press, 1993).

Zack, N., *Thinking About Race* (Belmont CA: Wadsworth Publishing Company, 1998).

V. RACISM

Appiah, K. A., 'Racisms', in Goldberg, D. T. in *Analysing Racism* (Minneapolis: University of Minnesota Press, 1990), 3–17.

Card, C., 'On Race, Racism, and Ethnicity', in Bell, L. A., and Blumenfeld, D. (eds.), *Overcoming Racism and Sexism* (Lanham, Maryland: Rowman and Littlefield, 1995), 141–52.

Corlett, J. A., 'Analysing Racism', *Public Affairs Quarterly*, Vol. 12, No. 1, January 1998, 23–50.

Flew, A. G. N., 'Three Concepts of Racism', *Encounter*, 73, September, 63–6.

Garcia, J. L. A., 'Current Conceptions of Racism: A Critical Examination of Some Recent Social Philosophy', *Journal of Social Philosophy*, Vol. XXVIII, No. 2, Fall 1997, 5–42.

Goldberg, D. T., *Racist Culture* (Oxford: Blackwell Publishers, 1993).

Goldberg, D. T., 'Racism and Rationality: The Need for a New Critique', *Philosophy of the Social Sciences*, Vol. 20, No. 3 (September 1990), 317–48.

Gordon, L. R., *Bad Faith and Antiblack Racism* (Atlantic Highlands N.J.: Humanities Press International, 1995).

Gordon, L. R., *Existentia Africana* (New York and London: Routledge, 2000).

Ladd, J., 'Philosophical Reflections of Race and Racism', *American Behavioral Scientist*, Vol. 41, No. 2, October 1997, 212–22.

Mills, C. W., *The Racial Contract* (Ithaca: Cornell University Press, 1998).

Schmid, W. T., 'The Definition of Racism', *Journal of Applied Philosophy*, Vol. 13, No. 1, 1996, 31–40.

Singer, M. G., 'Some Thoughts on Race and Racism', *Philosophia*, Vol. 8, Nos. 2–3, 1978, 153–83.

Singer, P., 'Is Racial Discrimination Arbitrary?', *Philosophia* Vol. 8, Nos. 2–3, 1978, 185–203.

Skillen, A., 'Racism: Flew's Three Concepts of Racism', *Journal of Applied Philosophy*, Vol. 10, No. 1, 1993, 73–89.

West, C., *Race Matters* (Boston: Beacon Press, 1993).

VI. PHILOSOPHERS AND RACE

Bracken, H. M., 'Essence, accident and race', *Hermathena*, No. CXVI Winter 1973, 81–95.

Bracken, H. M., 'Philosophy and Racism', *Philosophia*, Vol. 8, Nos. 2–3, November 1978, 241–60.

Eze, E. C., 'The Color of Reason: The Idea of "Race" in Kant's Anthropology', in Eze, E. C., *Post Colonial African Philosophy* (Oxford: Blackwell Publishers, 1997), 103–40.

Immerwahr, J., 'Hume's Revised Racism', *Journal of the History of Ideas*, Vol. 53, No. 3, 1992, 481–6.

Louden, R., *Kant's Impure Ethics* (New York: Oxford University Press 2000), 95–106.

Palter, R., 'Hume and Prejudice', *Hume Studies*, Vol. XXI, No. 1, April 1995, 3–23.

Popkin, R. H., 'The Philosophical Basis of Eighteenth Century Racism', *Studies in Eighteenth Century Culture*, Vol. 3, *Racism in the Eighteenth Century* (Cleveland and London: Case Western Reserve University Press, 1973), 245–62.

Popkin, R. H., 'Hume's Racism', Watson R. A., and Force, J. E. (eds.), *The High Road to Pyrrhonism* (San Diego: Austin Hill Press, 1980), 251–66. Popkin, R. H. 'Hume's Racism Reconsidered', *The Third Force in Seventeenth Century Thought* (Leiden: E. J. Brill, 1992), 64–75. Squadrito, K., 'Locke's View of Essence and Its Relation to Racism: A Reply to Professor Bracken', *The Locke Newsletter*, No. 6, Summer 1975, 41–54.

Squadrito, K., 'Racism and Empiricism', *Behaviorism*, Vol. 7, No. 1, Spring 1979, 105–15.

VII. RACE AND INTELLIGENCE

Block, N. J., and Dworkin, G., *The IQ Controversy* (New York: Pantheon, 1976).

Flynn, J. R., 'Massive I.Q. Gains in 14 Nations: What I.Q. Tests Really Measure', *Psychological Bulletin*, Vol. 101, No. 2 (1987) 171–91.

Flynn, J. R., 'Race and IQ: Jensen's Case Refuted', in Modgil, S., and Modgil, C. (eds.), *Arthur Jensen: Consensus and Controversy* (London: Falmer International, 1987), 221–32.

Fraser, S., *The Bell Curve Wars* (New York: Basic Books, 1995).

Herrnstein, R. J., and Murray, C., *The Bell Curve* (New York: Simon and Schuster, 1994).

Jacoby, R., and Glauberman, N., *The Bell Curve Debate* (New York: Random House, 1995).

Jensen, A. R., 'How Much Can We Boost IQ and Scholastic Achievement?', *Harvard Educational Review*, Vol. 39, Winter 1969, 1–123.

Sowell, T., 'Race and I.Q. Reconsidered', in *Essays and Data on American Ethnic Groups*, Sowell, T., and Collins. L. D. (eds.) (Washington DC: The Urban Institute, 1978).

INDEX

Achebe, C. 371, 375–7
Adorno, T. 71, 73n.
Aigner, D. 148n.
Airey, C. and Brook, L. 249
Alexander, D. 405
Alexander, R. D. 102n.
Allen, R. 75n.
Allport, G. W. 101n.
Altman, D. 388
Amin, K. and Richardson, R. 246
Anthias, F. and Yuval-Davis, N. 252
Anzaldúra, G. 86n.
Appiah, K. A. 49n., 54, 259–60, 268–9,
    271n., 371–82, 423, 424n., 426n.,
    428, 431n., 433–4, 436n., 442n.
Aquinas, St. Thomas 44
Aristotle 5–6, 14–15, 44, 64, 151, 162,
    195, 354n.
Arthur, J. 25
Arvey, R. 127n.
Asante, M. 43n., 423, 433–6, 438, 439n.,
    442
Asimov, I. 217, 222
Audi, R. 279n.
Ayers, M. 45n., 46n., 55
Azikiwe, N. 377

Back, L. 244
Bakke, A. 268, 297, 299–300, 302, 304–6
Baldwin, J. 313n.
Balibar, E. 93n., 238–9, 252
Balibar, E. and Wallerstein, I. 93n.
Ballard, R. 239
Balzac, H. de 217, 222
Banton, M. 101n., 250, 258n., 435n.
Banton, M. and Harwood, J. 63n., 64–5,
    66n., 69
Barash, D. 102n.
Barber, B. R. 251

Barker, M. 238
Barth, F. 101n.
Bastian, A. 408
Bayes, J. H. 386
Beatty, R. W. and Beatty, J. R. 405
Beitz, C. 415
Bell, D. 415
Benedict, R. 257
Benhabib, S. 438n., 440n.
Benn, S. I. and Peters, R. S. 182n.
Berger, J. 145n.
Berger, P. L. and Luckman, T. 60n.
Berman, P. 357n.
Bernal, M. 44n.
Bernard, J. 315n.
Bettelheim, B. 165
Betzig, L. L. 102n.
Biggs, C. 79
Bittner, R. 209n.
Blalock, H. M. 101n.
Blauner, R. 240
Blight, D. W. and Gooding-Williams
    429n.
Block, N. 114–42, 167n.
Block, N. and Dworkin, G. 132, 139n.,
    167n., 329n.
Blum, L. 260, 269n., 282n., 348n., 445n.
Blumenbach, J. F., *Generis humani
    varietate nativa liber* 64
Boggs, J. 75n.
Bohman, J. and Rehg, W. 440n.
Bonnett, A. 245–7
Bourdieu, P. 380
Boxill, B. 396, 442n., 444n.
Boyd, R. and Richerson, P. J. 102n.
Brandon, R. N and Burrah, R. M. 47n.
Brandt, R. B. 186n.
Breines, P. 75n.
Briggs, C. 79

Brotz, H. 446n.
Bulkin, E., Pratt, M. B., and Smith, B. 88n.
Burt, Sir C. 26
Bush, G. 59
Butler, J. 431n.

Calhoun, J. C. 437
Canter, N. V. 408
Cantor, M. 380n.
Carby, H. 445n.
Carmichael, S. and Hamilton, C. 313n., 386
Carson, C. 75n.
Carter, S. 272n.
Cashmore, E. E. 104n.
Castoriadis, C. 262n.
Caute, D. 78n.
Cavalli-Sforza, L. L. 103n.
Cavalli-Sforza, L. L. and Bodmer, W. F. 223n.
Césaire, A. 78n.
Chagnon, N. and Irons, W. 102n.
Chamberlain, H. S. 25, 36
Chomsky, N. 120n., 142n.
Cleaver, E. 240
Cliff, M. 393
Cohen, J. 440n.
Cohen, M., Nagel, T., Scanlon, T. 163n.
Cohen, P. 244–5
Collins, S. 416
Colvin, R. H. 302, 304
Connolly, W. E. 433n.
Coopersmith, S. 351n.
Copi, I. M. 46n.
Cornell, S. 387, 409
Cottingham, J. 264, 277
Cox, A. 299–302
Cox, O. 75n.
Crenshaw, K. W. 438
Cronon, E. D. 347n.
Cruse, H. 75n., 76, 387
Cunningham, F. 390
Cuvier, G. 64

Daly, M. and Wilson, M. 102n., 104n., 105n.
Daniel, W. W. 249–50
Darwin, C. 65–6, 105
davenport, doris 96
Davis, D. B. 1–2, 9, 12, 13, 21
  Slavery and Human Progress 9, 13–14
Davis, F. J. 49n., 223n., 427n.
Davis, L. 168n.
Davis, M., Marable, M., Pfeil, F., and Sprinkler, M. 60n.
Dawkins, R. 102n., 104n.
de Gobineau, Comte J. A. 25, 36, 65n.
  Essay on the Inequality of Human Races 64
Delaney, M. 444
Deloria, V. and Lytle, C. 387, 410
D'Emilio, J. 388
Dent, N. J. H. 227
Dewey, J. 267n.
Diawara, M. 436n.
Dikötter, F. 248
Dolan, F. M. and Dumm, T. L. 439n.
Dominguez, V. R. 223n.
Donald, J. and Rattansi, A. 431n.
Donnellan, K. 55, 56n.
Douglas, Justice 311n.
Douglass, F. 37
Dretske, F. 148n.
D'Souza, D. 110n.
Du Bois, W. E. B. 12, 32–4, 59, 62n., 375, 396, 423, 445
  Black Reconstruction 379
  'Conservation of Races, The' 30
  Souls of Black Folk 22, 313n., 429–30, 446–7
  'White World, The' 30, 32–3
Dubinin, N. P. 44n.
Dumm, T. L., letter to Anderson, L. 439n.
Dunbar, W. 63
Dunn, L. C. 47n.
Dunn, L. C. and Dobzhansky, T. 47n.
Dworkin, G. 167n.
Dworkin, R. 176n., 177n., 297–306

Edelman, G. M. 196n.
Edley, C. 395
Edmonson, Professor M. S. 223n.
Edwards, M. 93n.
Ellis, L. and Nyborg, H. 170n.
Ellison, R. 313n., 437, 442
Ely, J. H. 319n.
Emerson, R. W. 444–5
Epstein, S. 388, 400
Eysenck, H. J. 26
Eze, E. C. 450, 452–9
Ezorsky, G. 282

Fabian, J. 377, 378n.
Fackenheim, E. 364
Fanon, F. 99
Farley, J. E. 104n.
Feldman, M. and Lewontin, R. 140
Feller, W. 148n.
Finley, M. I. 44n.
Fischer, C. 391
Flew, A. 258n., 285–91
Flowerman, S. H. 73n.
Flynn, J. R. 121, 128, 130
Fodor, J. 119n.
Foster, L. and Herzog, P. 441n., 445n.
Francis, E. K. 101n.
Franklin, J. 313n.
Fredrickson, G. M. 101n.
Freeman, Jo. and Garskof, M. 352n.
Freeman, W. H. 223n., 351n.
French, M. 317n.
Freud, S. 71–2, 74, 308
Fromm, E. 71–2
Frye, M. 83–100
Fullinwide, R. K. 436n., 437n.

Garcia, J. L. A. 257–93, 265n., 267n.,
    276n., 291n.
Garvey, M. 347n.
Gates, H. L. Jr. 99, 128, 287, 374n.,
    422n.
Gelman, D. 346n.
Genovese, E. D. 345n., 350n.
Geschwender, J. A. 80n.

Gewaltney, J. L. 88n.
Gillborn, D. 245
Gilligan, C. 170n.
Gilroy, P. 243–5, 253, 437n.
Glaser, N. 110n.
Glass, B. and Li, C. C. 223n.
Glass, R. 245
Glazer, N. 110n.
Gödel, K. 140
Goldberg, D. T. 58n., 93n., 99n., 239,
    424n.
Goldsby, R. 424n.
Gomberg, P. 271n.
Gooding-William, R. 422–47
Goosens, W. K. 54n.
Gordon, D. M., Edwards, R., and Reich,
    M. 380n.
Gordon, P. and Klug, F. 238, 241, 245,
    253
Gossett, T. F. 1, 62n.
Gould, C. C. and Cohen, R. S. 440n.
Gould, S. J. 114, 116
    The Mismeasure of Man 14, 57n.
Graglia, L. 175n.
Gramsci, A. 60n.
Griffin, C., Black Like Me 40
Griffin, J. H. 311n.
Grossman, H. 71
Guillory, J. 423n.
Guinier, L. 28
Gurr, T. R. and Harff, B. 101n.
Gutmann, A. 411, 424n., 436n., 438n.,
    439n., 440n., 446n.
Gutmann, A. and Thompson, D. 440n.

Habermas, J. 71, 80n., 82n.
Hacker, A. 270n.
Hacking, I. 429
    "Making Up People" 428
Hall, S. 253, 431n.
Hannaford, I. 1
Haraway, D. 399
Harding, V. 76n.
Harman 148
Harms, R. 372n.

Harries, K. 435, 436n.
Harris, L. 57, 60n.
Hart, H. L. A. 331n.
Harwood, S. 174n.
Haywood, H. 75n., 79
Hegel, G. W. F. 71, 74
Held, D. 71n., 75n.
Heller, T. C., Sosna, M., and Wellbery, D. 428n.
Helmreich, W. 165n.
Herbert, R. 115
Herrnstein, R. J. 124, 145n.
Herrnstein, R. J. and Murray, C. 110n., 115–16, 120–2, 125–6, 127n., 128, 130, 135, 138–9, 142
    The Bell Curve 25, 114, 116, 118–19, 121, 123–4, 126n., 128
Hill, T. E., Jr. 461n.
    and Boxill, B. 448–71
Hindelang, M. J. 145n.
Hoare, Q. and Smith, G. N. 60n.
Hobbes, T. 153–4
Hochschild, A. R. 317n.
Hocutt, M. and Graham, G. 160
Hofer, M., critique of Herrnstein and Murray 124
Hoffman, P. 41
Hollinger, D. 427n., 433n.
Hollis, P. 353n.
Holt, J. 116
Honig, B. 439n.
hooks, bell 85n., 88n.
Horkheimer, M. 71, 73
Hountondji, P. 433
Houston, Charles H. 319n.
Hursthouse, R. 278n.

Irigary, L. 397

Jackson, A. 37
Jackson, Jesse 416
Jackson, M. F. 25n.
Jackson, Michael 40
Jaggar, A. 322n., 325n.
Jameson, F. 380n.

Jay, M. 71n., 75n.
Jefferson, T. 22–3, 28, 36
Jencks, C. 131, 133, 138n., 270
Jenkins, R. 245
Jensen, A. 27, 125–7, 136
    'How Much can we boost I. Q. and Scholastic Achievement?' 25
Johnson, C. 436
Johnson, J. W., The Autobiography of an Ex-Coloured man 429–30
Johnson, President Lyndon 228
Jordan, W., White over Black 3, 8–9
Joselit, J. W. 169n.

Kahane, M. 262n.
Kamin, L. 130n.
Kant, I. 8, 13, 18–19, 37, 71, 159, 201, 203–5, 208, 211, 269–70, 448–51
    deliberative reason and visceral racism 464–71
    Eze and 452–9
    rationalism thesis 194–8
    Tahitians and the ideal of reason 459–64
    works
        Critique of Pure Reason 448
        Metaphysics of Morals 448, 455, 466–7
        Observations of the Feeling of the Beautiful and Sublime 455
        Perpetual Peace 456
        Religion 466
Karenga, M. R. 79n.
Karst, K. 386, 402
Kavka, G. 153n.
Kelley, R. D. G. 443
Kennedy, R. 287
Kennedy, T. H. and Leary, T. E. 75n., 79n.
Kevles, D. J. 53n.
King, Martin Luther 363
King, M. L., Jr. 240
Kipling, R. 275
Kirk, M. and Madsen, H. 262, 263n.
Kitcher, P. 120, 142, 275n.

Kleven, T. 408
Knobler, P. 346n.
Knopf, A. A. 313n.
Knox, R. *Races of Man, The* 64
Kolakowski, L. 72n.
Kripke, S. 52
Kuhn, T. 198n.
Kuklick, B. *The Rise of American Philosophy* 359–60
Kuper, L. 57n.

Laclau, E. and Mouffe, C. 390
Lader, L. 386
Laitin, D. 377–8
Landes, D. 21n.
Larsen, R. L. and Marx, M. L. 148n.
Lasch, C. 349n.
Laslett, P. 6
Laslett, P. and Runeiman, W. G. 187n.
Leo, J. 116
Leonardo, Micaela di 445n.
Lerna, G. 349n.
Levi-Strauss, C. 308
Levin, M. 40–1, 145–79
Levinson, D. 73
Lewis, B. 165n.
Lewis, S. 311n., 313n.
Lewontin, R. 125–6, 128, 141, 142n.
Lichtenberg, J. 264, 273n., 280–2
Lieberman, E. 116, 137
Linn, R. 178n.
Linnaeus, C. 64n., 454
Littleton, C. 399, 403–5
Livingstone, D. 372
Livingstone, F. B. 66
Locke, A. 57
Locke, J. 6, 17, 153–4
    nominalism 45–7, 50
Loehlin, J. and DeFries, J. 134
Lopreato, J. 102n.
Lott, T. 33–4
Loury, G. 270n. 283
Lovejoy, A. 19
Lowell, L. 360
Lukács, G. 71

Lumsden, C. J. and Wilson, E. O. 102n.
Lynn, R. 26, 128
Lyotard, J.-F. 383

Mabbott, J. B., *The State and the Citizen* 180–1
Mac an Ghail, M. 245
McCarthy, Senator J. 76
McClurg, A. C. 313n.
McGary, H. 395
McGary, H. and Lawson, Bill E. 444n.
MacIntyre, A. 283n.
Macoby, E. and Nogy, C. 330n.
Maja-Pearce, A. 250
Malcolm X 240
Mansbridge, J. 411
Marable, M. 75n., 79n., 80, 263
Marcuse, H. 71, 74
    One Dimensional Man 75
Marine, G. 346n.
Marshall, Mr. Justice 312
Marx, K. 72n., 74–5, 78n., 308
Marx, K. and Engels, F. 60n
Mayr, E. 424n.
Mead, M. 329n.
Mehta, U. S. 28
Mencke, J. C. 44n.
Mendel, G. J. 65–6
Michaels, W. B. 422–6, 428
Miles, A. 389
Miles, R. 251–2, 257n., 258, 259n., 260n., 262n., 270n., 282n., 427n.
Mill, J. S. 131
    Considerations on Representative Government 28
Millett, K. 314n., 315n., 317n., 331n.
Mills, C. 451
Minow, M. 396, 398, 408
Mitchell, J. 310n.
Modood, M. S. 241, 247
Modood, T. 238–54
Moore, R. B. 79
Moraga, C. 96
Moraga, C. and Anzaldúa, G. 88n., 96n.

Morgan, M. 345n.
Morris, C. 153n.
Morrison, Toni, *Playing in the Dark* 444–5
Morton, S. G. 64
Mosley, A. 24
Motley, Judge 321
Mouffe, C. 438n.
Murphy, D. 250
Murray, A. 436–7
Murray, C. 114, 123–4
Myrdal, G. 101n., 438

Nagel, T. 338n.
Nathanson, S. 263, 264, 271n.
Nickel, J. 390, 409
Nidditch, P. H. 45n.
Nietzsche, F. W. 210
Nisbett, R. 115n.
Norton, A. 439n.
Norton, W. W. 348n.
Nott, J. C. and Giddon, G. R., *Types of Mankind* 64
Nozick, R. 158n., 159, 170n.

Ogbu, J. 128–9
Olson, J. S. 380n.
Omi, M. and Winant, H. 59n., 61n., 62–3, 80–1, 386, 424, 427n.
Ortiz, R. D. 387, 407, 410
Outlaw, L. 58–82

Pappas, G. 267n.
Parekh, B. 253
Park, R. E. 101n.
Patrik, L. 350n.
Patterson, O. 37, 101n.
Pedersen, N. L. 123
Penock, J. R. 153n.
Pevar, S. L. 410
Phipps, Susie 424, 433
Pinkney, A. 79n.
Piper A. M. S. 48n., 193–237, 261, 424–6, 428
Pitkin, H. 413

Plato 64
  Meno 467
  Republic 14–15
Plomin, R. 123, 134, 136–7, 142
Plomin, R. and Bergeman, C. 119, 121
Plomin, R. and Daniels, D. 121
Plomin, R., DeFries, J., and McClearn, G. 127
Poe, E. A. 445
Post, C. H. 348n.
Powell, E. 238, 245, 253
Pratt, M. B. 88
Prichard, J. C., *Generis humani varietate* 64
Putnam, H. 52, 54n.

Quine, W. V. O. 52, 54

Rawls, J. 345n., 354n.
Reagan, R. 59
Reed, T. E. 169, 223n.
Reiter, R. R. 94n., 308
Rex, J. 104n.
Rex, J. and Mason, D. 101n., 104n.
Reynolds, T. 48n.
Rivers, E. 349n.
Roberts, R. C. 136–7
Robinson, C. J. 75n., 78n., 79n., 379n., 380n.
Roediger, D. 444n.
Root, M. P. P. 50n.
Rorty, A. O. and Flanagan, O. 215n.
Rorty, A. O. and McLoughlin, B. 198n.
Rosenkrantz, R. 150n.
Ross, J. 391
Rothschild, J. 391
Rousseau, J.-J. 5, 456–8, 467–8, 471
Rubin, G. 94, 308
Ruchwarger, G. 418
Rushton, J. P. 145n., 168n.

Sacks, O. 196n.
Said, E. 397
Salmon, M. H. 47n.
Sánchez-Eppler, K. 445n.

Sartre, J.-P. 99, 165, 400, 431, 432n.
Savanandan, A. 258
Sayers, D. L. 347n., 355n.
Scales, A. 403
Scarr, S. and McCartney, K. 119, 123n., 135–6
Schaefer, R. 257
Schermerhorn, R. A. 101n.
Schlesinger, A. M., Jr. 433, 438–9, 441–2
  The Disuniting of America 423, 437
Schmitt, E. 406
Schrag, P. 270n.
Schroyer, T. 59n.
Schutz, A. and Luckman, T. 58n., 60n.
Schwartz, S. P. 45n., 46n., 54n., 56n.
Scott, J. 399
Scott, J. W. 443n.
Sears, D. O. and Huddy, L. 408
Sedgwick, E. 436n.
Shafer, C. 95n.
Shepher, J. 102n.
Sher, G. 174n.
Sherman, J. A. 330n., 331n.
Shibutani, R. and Kwan, K. M. 101n.
Shuey, A. 170n.
Sickles, R. J. 44n.
Silberman, C. 356n.
  A Certain People 359
Simon, T. 273n.
Simpson, L. 440, 441n.
Singleton, C. J. 86n.
Sivanandan, A. 258
Skillen, A. 285–6, 288–90
Slote, M. 165n., 265n., 291n.
Smith, A. D. 101n.
Smith C. H., *Natural History of the Human Species, The* 64
Smith, J. F. 441n.
Sober, E. 123n., 141n.
Soble, A. 344n.
Socrates 467
Soyinka, W. 375
Spencer, H. and Gumplowicz, L. 65
Spivak, G. 374n.
Strawson, P. F. 195n., 226n.

Stubblefield, A. 423, 428
Stuckey, S. 79n.
Suedfeld, P. 147n.
Sunstein, C. R. 413
Sweet, J. 3–4

Taguieff, P. A. 239
Takaki, R. 447
Tannen, D. 202n.
Taub, N. and Williams, W. 393, 403
Taylor, C. 445n., 446
Thalberg, I. 319n.
Thomas, C. C. 330n.
Thomas, L. 275n., 344–56, 357–70
  Vessels of Evil 369
Thompson, J. 380
Tiger, L. 308
Todorov, T. 373, 374n.
Tooby, J. and Cosmides, L. 133
Trebilcot, J. 335n.
Treiman, D. J. and Hartman, H. I. 405
Twain, M. 445

Van DeBurge, W. L. 436n.
Van Den Berghe, P. L. 101–11
Vernon, P. 139
Vlastos, G. 187n., 188, 189n., 192n.
  "Justice and Equality" 185–6
Vogel, L. 403

Wacker, R. F. 50n.
Waldron, J. 437n.
Wallace, G. 353
Walzer, M. 431n., 438, 439n.
Wasserstrom, R. 177n., 180–92, 307–43, 352n., 390, 393
  "On Racism and Sexism" 385
Weber, B. 175
Weber, M. 314n.
Webster, M. 257n.
Wechsler, Professor 319n.
Weldon, F. 247
Well, I. E. and Marwell, G. 351n.
Wenzel, H. 83n.
Wertheimer, R. 163n.

West, C. 288
White, Mr. Justice 302
White, R. W. 351n.
Wiggins, D. and McDowell, J. 260n.
Williams, B. 187n., 189n., 190n.
Williams, E., *Capitalism and Slavery* 4, 10
Williams, P. J. 55n.
Williams, W. 403, 409
Williamson, J. 47n., 223n.
Willis, P. 245
Wilson 101n., 104n.
Wilson, J. Q. and Herrnstein, R. J. 145n.
Wilson, T. P. 50n.
Wilson, W. J. 168n., 387
Wilson, W. J. and Bonacich, E. 80
Winston, H. 75n.
Wistrich, R. 261, 262n.

Wittgenstein, L. 156, 265, 427n.
Wolf, S. 446–7
Wolff, K. H. and Moore, B. 75
Wolff, R. P. 195n.
Wolfgang, M. E. 145n.
Wood, A. 461n.
Wood, B. 3, 4, 11
Workman, P. L., Blumberg, B. S., and Cooper, A. J. 223n.
Wright, R. 123

Young, I. M. 243, 269n., 383–421, 389, 440n.
Young, K. 249
Young-Bruehl, E. 263n., 284n., 285n., 288

Zack, N. 3, 11, 13–14, 43–57